THE LEAVEN OF DEMOCRACY

The Growth of the Democratic Spirit
in the Time of Jackson

By Clement Eaton

Freedom of Thought in the Old South

A History of the Old South

A History of the Southern Confederacy

Henry Clay and the Art of American Politics

The Growth of Southern Civilization

Green Mount: A Virginia Plantation Family During the Civil War: Being the Journal of Benjamin Robert Fleet and Letters of his Family (Edited with Betsy Fleet)

THE LEAVEN OF DEMOCRACY

The Growth of the Democratic
Spirit in the Time of Jackson

SELECTED AND EDITED WITH INTRODUCTION
AND NOTES BY

Clement Eaton

GEORGE BRAZILLER

NEW YORK 1963

Preface

Andrew Jackson gave his name to the era between the 1820's and 1850's in part because he dominated it, but even more because he was its prime symbol. Born on the frontier of Scotch-Irish parentage, Jackson became the most famous of the first generation that made its fortunes across the Appalachians. He was a gentleman-planter, entrepreneur, military hero, and above all, political leader. Yet he was the product more than the molder of the national dynamisms that came to the forefront in Jacksonian America.

Small wonder that European visitors in increasing numbers came to tour the adolescent United States, this display case of democracy, taking in all of its sights from Niagara Falls to the old General in the White House, and returning home to write books in which they might gibe at the country's crudities or exclaim with awe at its natural phenomena and institutional achievements. Whatever their reactions, favorable or unfavorable, they were impressed with the scale and activity of life in America. It was a nation of ambitious people, a nation on the march, and a nation which, as it rapidly filled in the great Mississippi Valley, was developing many of the distinct characteristics that have marked it ever since.

It was the age of the common man, or at least of the recognition that he should enjoy equality of opportunity. It was the generation, therefore, in which an energetic few advanced rapidly to wealth and power. This was the heyday of the skilled artisan and the small entrepreneur, but it was also seedtime for the industrial system, with all its blessings and flaws. This was the agrarian era, when most Americans were still engaged in the tilling of family farms, yet the agrarians who exerted most influence were a handful of slave-owning southern planters.

These were democratic years when modern parties and political techniques were receiving their testing, but politics locally was often dominated by machines, and national parties held themselves together most often by obscuring issues rather than elucidating them. These were the years of star-spangled nationalism, when orators proclaimed the manifest destiny of the United States to fill in a continent. But it was also a time of festering sectionalism so soon to lead to fratricidal war.

Such are some of the issues and ironies that Clement Eaton explores in this volume. Eaton, long distinguished for his studies of the antebellum South and the Confederacy, catches in the vivid writings of numerous contemporaries the lights and shadows of the American people in one of their most vital epochs. Through his selections and introductions he recreates and gives meaning to Jacksonian America.

FRANK FREIDEL

Contents

meet with on their way, with a few slices of bacon. Their wardrobe consists of a single shirt, which is worn till it falls to pieces. It cannot, therefore, be matter of astonishment if agues and bilious fevers spread over the country, and even in this case a quart of corn brandy is their prescription.

THE LEAVEN OF DEMOCRACY

The Growth of the Democratic Spirit in the Time of Jackson

Introduction

Clement Eaton

Andrew Jackson was such a dominating leader of the American people from 1820 to 1845 that this period deserves to be described as the Jacksonian Era. No one would think of calling these years "the Age of McGuffey," author of the famous *Eclectic Readers,* or of Horace Mann, who made such a great contribution to American education, or of Emerson, who by his lyceum lectures and Transcendentalist philosophy elevated the moral nature of the nation; no, only a masterful political figure could fulfill the role of a symbol of his age, and Jackson became the symbol of democracy—the rise of the common man.

William Gilmore Simms, the southern novelist, made an acute observation concerning the need of the masses for a political symbol. Writing to Congressman William Porcher Miles on July 15, 1860, he said, "no party, no confederacy can be held together by abstract principles simply. The great body of politicians & people require some symbols which they couple with principles, and which they finally receive as a substitute for it. These symbols are our candidates for office."[1]

The "Gin'ral," as his southern friends continued to call President Jackson, was a complex person. A man of violent hates and loyalties, who seemed always to be in the midst of controversy and battles, he was also a deeply sentimental person, who was extremely kind to children and whose romantic love for Rachel, his wife, was equal to any love affair described in the romantic novels that were so popular in his time. In this tall, slender figure of rude weather-beaten exterior and of turbulent spirit lived the soul of chivalry, certainly as applied to women, if hardly as applied to men.

A Presbyterian minister, Rev. William S. Potts, who visited Jackson at the *Hermitage* in April, 1828, was impressed by his democratic manners. "The Gen.," he wrote, "was out walking when we arrived, but soon came in. He received us in a very friendly, cordial manner. He is above the midling [*sic*] height, has a commanding, dignified, and at the same time benevolent countenance. In conversation the Gen. is very pleasant and interesting. He does not descend to joking, but often shows much pleasantry in the remarks and inferences drawn from observations made. I soon forgot that I was in the presence of a man who was candidate for the highest office in the nation, and only seemed to be conversing with a frank, plain, but intelligent and judicious southern planter. His dress is very plain, indeed it might be thought by persons more nice than wise, too much so. All subjects of general interest were canvassed, with the utmost freedom."[2]

After hearing of his terrible temper and of his relentless punishment of military delinquents, visitors to the Capitol were suprised to find the mildness and gentleness, the courtly manners, and the dignity of the President.

But this outward mien could be highly deceptive. Jackson contained a mighty ocean of feeling, at times serene but often raging with fury. Harriet Martineau, an English visitor, described what happened when a mad assassin tried to kill the President as he was attending the funeral of a congressman on January 30, 1835. Instead of treating this incident calmly, he became enraged and accused one of his deadly enemies, Senator George Poindexter of Alabama, of instigating the attempt on his life.[3]

Jackson was, indeed, a strange mixture of littleness and greatness. He could be exceedingly stern with men who opposed him, and at the same time remarkably indulgent with his adopted son, Andrew Jackson, Jr., who was always in financial difficulties, from which the old soldier would rescue him.[4] His enemies and the Whig Party emphasized his weaknesses —his lack of a formal education, his temper, his limited knowledge of economics. Henry Barnard, the New England schoolteacher who later became famous in the free public school movement, attended a reception at the White House in 1833, concerning which he wrote that the President was extremely penurious—he did not provide his company with coffee, wine, or music—"nothing but his own hard dry features."[5]

Jackson's policies have been variously judged by historians, as Charles G. Sellers, Jr. has demonstrated in a critical essay in the *Mississippi Valley Historical Review* (March, 1958).[6] The historians under Whig influence, an influence that continued until the rise of a new scholarship stimulated by the Progressive Movement, on the whole condemned Jackson's policies, particularly his attitude toward the Second Bank of the United States and the spoils system, but praised him for his nationalistic stand against nullification. This generally unfavorable judgment was revised by Frederick Jackson Turner in the first quarter of the nineteenth century with his frontier interpretation of American history.[7] Arthur M. Schlesinger, Jr., in his brilliant book, *The Age of Jackson*, published during the Administration of Franklin D. Roosevelt, rejected the dominant role of the frontier in Jacksonian democracy and emphasized, probably over-emphasized, the importance of the eastern workingmen.[8]

Today Jackson is perhaps more esteemed as a strong and useful president than at any time since his death. In a poll of historians conducted by Professor Arthur M. Schlesinger, Sr., of Harvard in 1962, Jackson was rated sixth among the notable presidents of the United States, ranking just after Jefferson.[9] In an era when nationalism is running strong in the nation and when the American people, faced by formidable enemies, demand strong leadership, Jackson's prestige stands high, for he greatly strengthened the power of the presidency, not merely by his vigorous exercise of the veto, his clever use of the press, and his shrewd party leadership, but by his ardent patriotism and his ability to dramatize the fact that he was the leader of the masses and not merely of the elite.

His name is rightly associated with the wave of democracy—"Jacksonian democracy"—of the 1820's and 1830's. Some scholars have questioned whether he deserves much credit for the rise of the realistic type of democracy that bears his name.[10] Undoubtedly, the movement had begun in the states before he assumed active leadership of it, but he threw the weight of his tremendous prestige, arising largely from his military fame as hero of the battle of New Orleans, behind the democratic surge after he became a presidential candidate in 1824. He had a Jeffersonian faith in the judgment of the people, partly because they always supported him. Though his political program was negligible, because of his enormous popularity as a person and as a military hero he was unbeatable at the polls.

Jackson had a simple and practical political faith; he thought of himself as carrying out, or rather reviving, Jeffersonian principles in the federal government.[11] He was not an innovator, a man of ideas, but a restorer. He believed in a *laissez faire* type of government, a strict construction of the Constitution, careful economy (one of his strongest ambitions was to pay off the national debt, which he succeeded in doing in 1835), and an administration of the government that would reward his friends— the Spoils System—which he rationalized into the principle of rotation of office. He showed little if any interest in the humanitarian and reform spirit that was arising in America. He was definitely hostile to the abolitionist movement, and in general to the various "isms" of the North. Although letters to his son are strongly opposed to the practice of drinking whiskey, or even touching the dangerous stuff, he does not seem to have participated in any organized movement or crusade for temperance or teetotalism. Nor does he appear to have been interested in the organization of labor or the trade-union movement, although the workingmen in the East, it is the contention of Arthur M. Schlesinger, Jr., gave him their support.[12]

Jackson's financial policies are also the subject of great controversy today. His destruction of the Second United States Bank, his policy of using pet state banks as government depositories, and his hard-money policy have been severely criticized by students.[13] His policy toward this great financial institution, though it appears to have been economically unwise, must be balanced in the scales of democracy. From this point of view the separation of the federal government from a powerful financial institution with great potential political power (although the Bank had shown commendable restraint in the exercise of its power) was an important victory for democracy. The feeling of the country, which was reflected in the resounding re-election of Jackson in 1832, demanded the destruction of monopolies such as the Bank so that small business and all men should have free play to enjoy equal economic opportunities. Jackson's attack on the Second National Bank has appeared to some scholars a precursor to the struggle in the twentieth century of the federal government to regulate huge trusts and monopolies and preserve free competition. In this light the struggle of the Jacksonians against the Bank was an early effort to assert the superiority of the public interest over the vested interests.

The outstanding characteristics of Jackson—the qualities that gave him greatness despite his weaknesses and wrong-headedness at times— were his active and unquenchable patriotism and his masterful will.[14] His was not simply the fighting patriotism of a soldier, although undoubtedly his military experiences as a youth in the American Revolution and his later leadership in the War of 1812 nurtured his love of country. His correspondence, his every act, shows that he placed the preservation and defense of the Union above every earthly duty. He will be remembered best for his suppression of the nullification movement and his strong assertion of the supremacy of the nation over party and sectional interests. His conception of patriotism also included a determination staunchly to uphold the national honor and interests, even at the risk of war. This he demonstrated in his forthright and undiplomatic warning to France over the American spoliation claims. Also he was a moderate expansionist, seeking to acquire Texas for the United States, although for the sake of political expediency he was cautious in regard to recognizing the independence of Texas until after the election of Van Buren to the presidency in the autumn of 1836.

Jackson was only the most prominent of the politicians of Washington who expertly guided national politics from the 1820's to 1850. He was, nevertheless, the "symbol of his age." Professor John William Ward has analyzed that symbol: the American people, hungry for a hero, built up a conception of Jackson as the victorious general who conquered, almost as if by a miracle, a mighty British army at New Orleans; as the representative of the frontiersman with his natural virtues, contrasted with the artificiality and decadence of Europe; as the instrument of Providence; and finally as the man of iron will, leading the common people to their rightful place in government against the "moneyed aristocracy."[15]

One theory of Jackson's success as president attributes it to the clever manipulators who surrounded him—the so-called Kitchen Cabinet, consisting of the wily Martin Van Buren of New York, Secretary of State; Major William B. Lewis of Tennessee, who lived in the White House; Senator John H. Eaton, also of Tennessee; Isaac Hill of New Hampshire; Francis P. Blair of Kentucky, whose name Jackson pronounced "Bla-ar," editor of the Washington Globe, the Administration's organ; and Amos Kendall, a Connecticut Yankee who had been tutor to Clay's children at Ashland.

Harriet Martineau described this last politically powerful individual as thin and frail in health, with cadaverous face, and though only in middle age, with perfectly white hair, who rarely appeared in public and seemed like a ghost. There was a universal belief in Washington, she reported, that Kendall's influence over the Administration was so great, "his was the concealed eye and hand behind the machinery of government, by which everything could be foreseen, and the hardest deeds done."[16] Indeed, Jackson gathered around him men who worked in indirect ways both upon the President's credulous mind and easily inflamed emotions as well as upon the opinions of the masses.

The master politician, the practical psychologist of the group, was Martin Van Buren. Van Buren's humble origin in the village of Kinderhook, New York, was concealed behind a facade of great urbanity, charming and ingratiating manners, and unruffled self-possession. He fitted the definition of a gentleman who is at home in all walks of life, and his politician-son so successfully carried on his father's tradition of polished manners and handsome mien that he was called "Prince John." Contemporaries and historians have been greatly prejudiced against Van Buren because he, like Buchanan, used the political arts with finesse. The poll of historians, referred to above, rated him number seventeen among the presidents, in the middle of the "average" group, below Taft, but above Monroe.

His Administration was ruined by the financial trouble that came upon the country through no fault of his own. He had the misfortune, too, of following after a masterful president and his conception of the office of the chief executive, like that of Buchanan, inhibited him from strong action, for he was a believer in a laissez faire type of government. He was also a sincere democrat, whose proposals of government action were, in general, sound. In his Administration the abolition question became a virulent source of dissension, agitated in Congress especially by John Quincy Adams, and Henry A. Wise of Virginia. Van Buren was an anti-slavery man at heart, but he was a strong believer in states rights and regarded slavery as the concern of the states involved. At the same time he opposed the extension of slavery into the federal territories and in 1848 became the Free Soil Party candidate for president. He was sympathetic to the interests of labor and in his Administration the ten-hour day was adopted on all government projects.

The other inheritor of the Jacksonian tradition was James Knox Polk, whose fame was long obscured by Whiggish historians.[17] He was ranked by the poll of historians as belonging to the "near-great" presidents, just below Theodore Roosevelt; it is doubtful, however, if so high a rank will be accorded him by another generation of historians. His present fame is based primarily on his tenacity in acquiring territory for the United States in disregard of the international ethics of his day and despite the ill will that his ruthless actions won for the United States in all of South America; also on his stout re-assertion of the Monroe Doctrine, and his resistance to Calhoun and those who would weaken nationalism by forming a southern bloc in Congress in 1849 and issuing an ultimatum to the nation on the exclusion of slavery from the federal territories.

Jackson was the tutor of Polk, and the Jacksonian era clearly extended through Polk's Administration. Indeed, this quiet, hard-working, but un-dramatic Tennessean was called "Young Hickory." Polk was elected governor of Tennessee in 1839 but was defeated for re-election in 1841 and again in 1843 by "Lean Jimmy" (James C.) Jones, a comical politician who entertained the voters and obscured the issues by his humor and folksy manners. Polk worked long and faithfully for Jackson's policies both in Tennessee and in Congress, where he was elected Speaker of the House in 1835 and in 1837. He was ardently supported in his campaigns by the "Old Gin'ral" in the *Hermitage*, who tried to secure for him the Democratic nomination for Vice-President in 1840 and again in 1844.

Jackson, Thomas Hart Benton, and Polk were men of the Southwest who were responsive to the desires of their neighbors, relatives, and friends to acquire Texas and seize the whole Southwest. They were not afraid of war with Mexico, as Clay and Van Buren were; they sensed the pulse of the people for westward expansion and national glory. (See Frederick Mark, *Manifest Destiny and Mission in American History*, New York, 1963.) And north of the Ohio River Senator Edward Hannegan and others were willing to risk war with England to acquire Oregon, where freemen only could emigrate.

Polk, though he had hewn his political career with the blessing of

Jackson, was a man of great independence. He gathered about him a new group of politicians whom Glyndon Van Deusen has called "The New Jacksonians."[18] In this alignment the crown prince of the Jacksonian Administration, Martin Van Buren, and also his Barnburner faction of the party in New York were pushed aside; Frank Blair, editor of the *Globe* was discarded in favor of a new spokesman for the Administration, Thomas Ritchie, editor of the Washington *Union*. Among the New Jacksonians was Robert J. Walker of Mississippi, a former New Yorker, who as Secretary of the Treasury was the most powerful man in the Cabinet, which included the historian George Bancroft, Secretary of the Navy William L. Marcy—leader of the "Hunker" faction of New York politics— and two other southerners, John Y. Mason of Virginia and Cave Johnson of Tennessee.

The "New Democracy" that Polk led was much more responsive to southern interests than were the old Jacksonians—a trend which continued until the election of Lincoln. This orientation toward the South was seen particularly in the Walker Tariff of 1846, in Polk's vetoes of internal-improvement bills, and in the ardent expansionist views of the President and his cabinet. Nevertheless, some of the most vital elements of the Old Jacksonianism were retained, especially a strong nationalism and the cherishing of the interests of the common people over the interests of the "moneyed aristocracy."

If the growth of democracy, both in national politics and on the local level, was the central theme of those years, it was a matter of uneven growth and of a strong admixture of violent partisanship, demagoguery, and intrastate factionalism, of fighting over patronage and local advantage. Progress was made, ideals realized, by politicians primarily interested in their own careers—in getting elected. Besides the major actors in the drama of politics there were thousands of small, self-seeking men, such as "Lean Jimmy" Jones or the inimitable demagogue, Congressman W. R. W. Cobb of Alabama, whose antics are described by Mrs. Clement C. Clay, Jr. in one of the selections of this volume. On the other hand, there were some individuals in public life such as Silas Wright, lieutenant of Van Buren, governor of New York, and Jacksonian leader in the Senate until his death in 1847, who worked in the interest of the common man. He was the patriot-statesman, the Cato of the Senate, who refused political honors, and sacrificed his own interests for the welfare of his country. Politicians, much more ambitious than he, such as Clay, Calhoun, and Webster, have been judged by some modern students as opportunists, but they could be more aptly described as men who thought they were fighting for great principles at the same time that they were seeking election to the presidency.

Leonard White in his admirable book, *The Jacksonians,* has noted an apparent decline in the quality and power of Congress during this period. This appearance of an undignified and ineffective Congress was perhaps due fundamentally to the fact that during the Jacksonian era the people for the first time were actively voting in large numbers. In the presidential election of 1824 less than a quarter of the adult white males voted; in 1828, the number rose spectacularly to 56 percent; in the Coonskin-and-hard-cider campaign of 1840 it increased to 78 percent. The free public school movement, which had gotten under way in the 1830's, had not had time to give the masses much education. In the southern states, especially, the farmers were informed on politics, less by the printed word than by the practice of "stump speaking," which was not conducive to the election of well-qualified men. Moreover, the practice of giving legislative instruction to members of Congress, while appearing to be very democratic in theory, often deprived senators and congressmen of the opportunity of using their judgment and of practicing statesmanship; it was greatly abused for partisan political advantage.[19] Also Congress was weakened as an effective legislative body by the seniority system, by the excessive power of the speaker, by the lobby, and by violent sectional wrangles.

Though Congress presented on the whole a rather sorry picture of a functioning democratic body, it contained some of the great orators of American history. The galaxy of orators did not lead to efficient government. John Randolph of Roanoke was an extreme case, but in Van Buren's autobiography this Virginia aristocrat appears as only one of numerous senators who wasted the time of the Senate in speaking for hours on subjects involving personality and on matters that had nothing to do with the real business of making good laws for the country.[20] There was also a vast amount of speaking "for Buncombe County." The great duels between Clay, Calhoun, and Webster, although they often thrilled the gallery, were usually oratorical displays having little practical consequence. It is doubtful whether their eloquence changed many minds or affected the way congressmen voted. James Fenimore Cooper, after listening to a debate in the Senate between Clay and Calhoun, wrote to his wife on March 11, 1837, that the debate was "an intellectual duello—one of those pitiful personal wranglings, in which a day was lost humoring the vanity and self-consequence of two men."

But if we turn from the sparring of the politicians in Washington to observe the people, the Age of Jackson appears to have been characterized by a high degree of patriotism—the patriotism of a provincial people who were virtually untouched by the internationalism of our own day and who as a whole lived close to nature and therefore perhaps had a child's love for the homeland.

The Italian Count Francesco Arese, who traveled in the United States in 1837-8, described this invigorating spirit of patriotism, which he witnessed during a Fourth-of-July celebration in Lexington, Virginia. After the usual fireworks, marching of the militia, and playing by the band of "Hail, Columbia" and "Yankee Doodle," the townspeople sat down to an elaborate banquet. "There were 160 odd people," the Count relates in his journal, "and though Americans are accused of being not too sober, I am forced to say that not a soul got drunk. After the dinner, which didn't last over ½ hour, several toasts were drunk. The first was to "the 4th of July, 1776," the next to General George Washington, the third to General Lafayette; and many others followed. Among the banqueters were two old veterans that had served under Washington, one of whom was a negro who had gone everywhere with the brave general, and for that reason, a half-century later, he was allowed the honor once every year of sitting down to table with white men! There was nothing, absolutely nothing in this celebration that suggested in the remotest degree that trumped-up joy, that official gaiety they gratify us with in Europe, quite contrary to our desire. Here the joy, the enthusiasm, were real, natural, heartfelt. Each individual was rightly proud to feel himself an American. Each one believed himself to share the glory of Washington, Jefferson, Marshall and the other illustrious men whom not only America but the whole world has the right to be proud of. Oh, God, when shall my own beautiful and wretched country be able to celebrate a day like that?"

The image that the Americans had of themselves during the Jacksonian period was a naive belief that they were a chosen people—unshackled from the traditions that bound Europe, virile, energetic, embued with the ideals of democracy—in other words, a virtuous people as contrasted with the corruption and decadence of Europe. This belief is strikingly exhibited in the penal code that Edward Livingston, an ardent Jacksonian, drew up in collaboration with some Creole jurists for the state of Louisiana. In it he omitted any mention of the crime of homosexuality, and his reasons for so doing—which he explains in his introduction to the code—exhibit his conception of America as a land of great virtue and pudency, or as he called it, "pudicity," in contrast with Europe's loose morals and shamelessness.

This sense of the innocence of the youthful nation has an ironic aspect, particularly in respect to Louisiana, the land where the Creole Sunday shocked pious visitors and where the quadroon balls and the system of quadroon concubinage violated the mores of the rest of America. Yet there were many things that were highly paradoxical in Livingston's code, for example, an assembly to witness a boxing match was declared an unlawful assembly, but not to watch a cock fight. Dueling also was sternly prohibited by law but the prohibition was largely ignored in practice.

The democratic revolution in the Jacksonian period made Americans proud of their free political institutions and gave them another reason for feeling superior to other peoples. The westward expansion contributed greatly to the development of nationalism and a spirit of boastfulness, to the feeling of Americans that theirs was a young vigorous nation, with an almost limitless area of land for exploitation. Frederick Jackson Turner has maintained that the rise of the New West with its frontier experience increased the resourcefulness, the individuality, the nationalism, the sense of democracy, and the optimism of the American people. The easy victory over Mexico in 1846-48 tended to make Americans feel even more cocky and confident in the great future of their country.

The westward expansion of the United States had harmful as well as beneficial consequences. While the population of the Mississippi Valley was growing by leaps and bounds, the older Atlantic seaboard states, particularly those that did not recoup their losses of population through immigration—notably the South Atlantic states—suffered both materially and spiritually. To restrain emigration their local politicians talked of the necessity for internal improvements, for the development of public schools, the encouragement of manufacturing enterprises, and the establishment of direct trade with Europe. But this agitation resulted mainly in the fervid orations of politicians and the appeals of editors, particularly J. D. B. De Bow in *De Bow's Review* of New Orleans. Southern Commercial Conventions, held from 1837 to 1860, sought by resolutions and speeches to arouse the southern people from their apathy and addiction to traditional ways. But national politics absorbed the energies of the politicians to the neglect of state, local, and regional improvements. Moreover, the *laissez faire* view of government that prevailed and the great aversion to levying taxes, owing partly to a chronic want of cash of most southern farmers, contributed to a do-nothing policy. It took the great decline in the prices of the agricultural staples, especially the sharp fall in the price of cotton in 1839, to stir up the South during the 1840's to the development of textile mills and other manufactures. With the return of agricultural prosperity in the 1850's, the South lost some of its interest in diversifying its economy.

In the North, there was a spectacular growth of cities and of industry. Most of the large cities of the Northeast more than doubled their population betwen 1840 and 1860. In the Middle West St. Louis increased its population from 10,000 in the 1830's to 160,000 in 1860 and Chicago's growth in the same period was almost miraculous, from 3,000 to 109,000 people. Immigration from Europe, particularly of the Irish and the Germans, is partly the explanation for such growth; it was also the transportation revolution which occurred with the building of railroads, canals, and toll roads, and the enormous expansion of steamboat traffic, that made possible the rapid urbanization of the North.

The enterpreneurial spirit was liberated from old restraints both by the destruction of the Second Bank of the United States and by the decision of the Supreme Court headed by a Jackson appointee, Chief Justice Roger B. Taney, in the Charles River Bridge Case of 1837. The contrast in economic development between the North and the South was indicated by the fact that in 1860 the southern states produced only 15 per cent (according to another computation, based on a different definition of "the South," only 10 per cent) of the manufactured goods made in the United States. These developments contributed to differentiate the patterns of social life and thought in the North from those of the South and to encourage the growth of nationalism and stimulate reform movements above the Mason-Dixon line.

The organization of labor in the Jacksonian period made some gains but not nearly to the extent that capitalism progressed. President Van Buren, as previously noted, issued an executive order establishing the ten-hour labor day on government works. But for the great majority of factory workers this practice was not followed, and child labor flourished in industry. Although Chief Justice Lemuel Shaw of the Supreme Court of Massachusetts rendered an epoch-making decision on the legal right of workers to strike, the mass of workingmen were too individualistic to develop effective labor organizations. Depressions in industry such as those following the panics of 1837 and 1857 weakened the labor movement, and public opinion remained hostile to the exercise of the right to strike. President Polk was probably expressing only a widespread attitude in the country when he was unsympathetic to the application of thirty painters working on the Capitol that they be paid for days lost because of wet weather. He attributed their demands to Whig incitation.[22] And when a group of bricklayers working on an extension of the Capitol in 1853 demanded a closed-shop rule, the Secretary of War, Jefferson Davis, was extremely hostile, giving an order to dismiss them and hire other mechanics if they persisted in their demand.[23]

Despite this denial of what we today regard as a basic right of labor, the Jacksonian period was deeply affected by a broad humanitarian movement. Was this movement owing primarily to the leaven of democracy, a desire to make the Declaration of Independence a reality, or was it inspired by reform movements in Europe, particularly the British anti-slavery agitation, or by a strong religious impulse? It seems probable that all three forces contributed to a period of reform in the North, which Alice Felt Tyler has called "freedom's ferment."[24]

At first the northern people were slow to respond to the greatest reform movement of the period, the abolition crusade. In the 1830's the masses in the North appeared almost as hostile to the radical proposals of the abolitionists as were the southerners whose property and perhaps safety were involved. In truth, the northern people as a whole continued to hold a strong prejudice of color throughout the period; they were finally aroused to support the abolitionists' cause at the end of the Jacksonian period and in the decade of the 1850's. Relatively few people in the North, it is probable, read the lurid and exaggerated propaganda of the abolitionist agitators. But many thousands felt a deep sense of outrage at the violation by Congress of the freedom of petition in passing "gag rules" (which were in force from 1836 to 1844) against the flood of petitions sent to Congress by "the petition strategy" of the abolitionists. Many thousands also were strongly moved by reading a highly sentimental novel, *Uncle Tom's Cabin*, published in book form in 1852. The anti-slavery movement made its strongest appeal through religion—by convincing great numbers of people that slavery was a grave sin and that the North had a responsibility to try to eradicate it. Whether the abolition leaders, especially such extremists as William Lloyd Garrison, did the cause of abolishing slavery more harm than good is a debatable question. But society needs agitators for reform, and the early abolitionists performed this useful function.

Abolition of slavery was only the most prominent and violent of the manifestations of the reform movement in the North. Transcendentalism in New England was a noble reform movement which exalted human dignity; its outstanding exponents and prophets were not interested greatly in organizations; indeed, they rather scorned them, but sought through literature, the pulpit, personal example, and lectures in a new agency, the American lyceum, to effect a more idealistic attitude toward life. Even the Transcendentalists, in the 1840's, organized themselves into a society at Brook Farm in Massachusetts; for the organization of a society was the typical way, as De Tocqueville observed, for Americans to accomplish a reform; indeed, thus early the Americans had become a nation of "joiners." The temperance movement, for example, made considerable progress during this period through the organization of societies such as the Sons of Temperance, and by propagandizing for the adoption of the teetotal pledge. Other notable reforms accomplished were the more humane treatment of the mentally ill, a cause which Dorothea Dix of Massachusetts championed, the improvement of penal codes and prisons, and especially the progress of the woman's rights movement. The latter was led by the Scottish radical Frances Wright; Lucretia Mott, a Quakeress of Philadelphia; Elizabeth Cady Stanton; Lucy Stone; and the Grimké sisters, Sarah and Angelina, who left their native city of Charleston, South Carolina, for Philadelphia, where they became active in both the anti-slavery and woman's rights causes.

Reform was frequently a romantic enthusiasm that appealed to the middle classes. The romantic movement that flourished in America between the years 1820 and 1860 affected both the North and the South, though in different ways. It was in part a reaction against the rationalism of the eighteenth-century Enlightenment. The romantic spirit had a large role in making the Jacksonian and post-Jacksonian periods a time of great literary creativity—a golden age of American literature. Since it was a period of expanding nationalism and of optimism, American literary men strove to free themselves from subservience to European models. Irving and Longfellow, and James Fenimore Cooper (to a degree), followed European models, but the greatest writers of the period—Emerson, Thoreau, Hawthorne, Melville, and Whitman—struck out in new paths. Transcendentalism strongly influenced the New England school, making its writers sensitive to the beauty of nature because they thought of the landscape as infused with the Over-Soul. Only Hawthorne, Melville, and Edgar Allan Poe (who held a most un-Puritan view of art and who is credited with inventing the detective story) portrayed the dark sides of human nature, the evil in the world. In contrast to a modern trend, American writers of this generation had a healthy optimism and did not probe deeply into the complexities of human nature; in general, they wrote for a democratic audience.

The South did not flower in literature during this period as did New England and New York. In William Gilmore Simms of Charleston, however, it produced a novelist who ranked close to Cooper. But southern writers were greatly handicapped by the lack of a large reading public, the want of publishing houses, an excessively romantic taste, and above all by the influence of the institution of slavery, which led to the suppression of free thought and speech. In the 1830's, led by John Pendleton Kennedy with his novel *Swallow Barn,* southern writers sought to glamorize the plantation, but these defenders of the South were not appreciated by their own people. Southerners admired oratory more than literature; they gave to the nation some of its most famous orators, though none as great as Daniel Webster. One of the most admired political orators of the South, Sergeant Prentiss, had emigrated to Mississippi from Maine.

The romantic spirit's greatest expression in the North was the Transcendental movement; in the South the romantic vogue was manifested in an appealing code of manners, the exaltation of women, a tremendous taste for reading Scott's novels, and the concept of honor. From this latter concept flourished the practice of dueling, which had largely disappeared from the North after the tragic duel between Burr and Hamilton in 1804. Southern newspaper editors of this period were frequently forced to fight duels because of their criticisms of individuals in their columns. Though antidueling societies were formed and many legislatures passed laws disqualifying anyone who sent or accepted a challenge to a duel from holding any office in the state, public opinion supported the practice so strongly where honor was involved that it continued. Benjamin F. Perry, editor of the Greenville (S.C.) *Mountaineer,* after he had killed a rival editor in a duel, wrote in his journal (Aug. 23, 1832): "This has been to me the most painful event of my life, but I could not avoid it without sacrificing character and usefulness in life. Public opinion which sanctions duelling is to blame, and it must continue until there is a change in the opinion of the public." In his Autobiography, written over forty years later, he said, "Good results from evil very often. When a man knows that he is to be held accountable for his want of courtesy, he is not so apt to indulge in abuse. In this way duelling produces a greater courtesy in society and higher refinement."[25]

If dueling was a striking example of the romantic spirit in personal relations, the concept of regional honor played an influential role in politics. Toward the close of the Jacksonian period—in fact the year after Jackson died—the Wilmot Proviso was introduced in Congress. The southern people took the position that their honor as a section was at stake in the passage of this bill. If such a law should pass it would place a stigma upon the honor of the South, and its adoption would almost certainly have resulted in a secession of the southern states. One of the noblest of southerners, Jabez Lamar M. Curry, a native of Georgia, who studied law at Harvard and became a Representative in Congress from Alabama, 1857-61, a member of the Confederate Senate, and after the war a great education leader, commented in a letter to James H. Joiner (July 19, 1847): "The discrimination, recognized and adopted in the 'Wilmot proviso' is degrading to the South and all persons must feel that 'death is preferable to acknowledged inferiority.'"[26] Although the extension of slavery into an area manifestly unsuited to its establishment may seem to us an abstraction that realistic common sense should have recognized as such, men often fight for abstractions and live to some degree by myths.

The difference between the North and South over the question of slavery during the Jacksonian years was the greatest single cause for the emergence of the idea of a polarity of cultures existing between the two sections. When Alexis de Tocqueville was traveling in the United States in 1831-32, he asked a prominent lawyer of Baltimore, John L. B. Latrobe, what were the principal traits that distinguished the North from the South. Latrobe replied that the manners of the southerner were frank and open and that he was "very ticklish on the point of honour," in contrast to the New Englander, who was cold, calculating, and patient. "As long as you are staying with a Southerner," Latrobe said, "you are made welcome, and he shares all the pleasures of his house with you. The Northerner when he has received you begins to think whether he can do business with you."[27] The essential distinction between the two sections, he believed, was that the North exhibited the spirit of enterprise, the South the spirit of chivalry. De Tocqueville predicted: "The civilization of the North appears to be the common standard to which the whole nation will one day be assimilated."[28] His prediction seems to be taking shape in our own time, resulting in a gradual homogenizing of the national life.

In 1831-32 De Tocqueville had found little essential difference between the North and the South in respect to tolerance. He observed that whether he traveled in the northern or the southern states, the voice of the majority exercised a remarkable dictatorship over the minds of American citizens, especially oppressing those who held unorthodox religious opinions. Such a tyranny of public opinion, operating completely outside of the realm of law, he noted, contrasted with the free political institutions of the Americans.[28] By the 1850's the northern states seem to have attained a freer intellectual climate with regard to religion and social reforms; the South, in the meanwhile, had regressed in the matter of intellectual freedom.

Latrobe's society of chivalry, honour, and lack of enterprise still existed in 1850, when the Jacksonian period came to an end. But the southern mind had lost its saving grace of nationalism and its relaxed poise; southern society had become more intolerant than in the days of Latrobe and Jackson because it was a very insecure society, violently attacked from the outside by the northern abolitionists, and resolved to stand alone against world opinion. In their concern over the preservation of slavery against external attacks southerners had reached the point virtually of prohibiting free speech on this sensitive subject. Maunsel White, the great Louisiana merchant and sugar planter, writing to Senator Pierre Soulé in 1850, observed, "Anyone even here [he was in New Orleans, which had many Yankees in its population] who permits himself to speak like a Northern man is looked upon as a traitor."[29]

Yet the North had its intolerances also. In its cities where free Negroes had congregated and in the Middle West, there existed, as Professor Leon Litwack's recent study has shown, a bitter intolerance toward the Negro and widespread discrimination against him.[30] Moreover, although the North had a small minority of outspoken religious liberals—which the South did not have—the masses were probably as orthodox as were the southerners. And still another blemish was appearing on the face of northern society. The Austrian traveler Francis J. Grund in his book *Aristocracy in America* (1839) pointed out the growth of an aristocracy based on recently acquired wealth, an aggressive society which did not have the charm or the spirit of *noblesse oblige* that distinguished the southern gentry.[31]

As we look back upon the Jacksonian period today, we see the mysterious interplay of strong leaders with onrushing social forces which were far too powerful for any individual to control. Jackson and Polk undoubtedly left their imprint on American politics, but they themselves were carried forward by the wave of democracy that swept over American life; nor did they have much to do with the resistless folk movement of the American people that settled the Mississippi Valley and Texas. Certainly the romantic movement that permeated literature, social practices, and the reform movements of the time owed virtually nothing to the political leaders. Nor did the different ways of life of South, North, and West that developed during the period—the expansion of southern slavery, the industrialization of the North, the flood of immigration, the growth of a conservative religion, the suppression of free speech and thought in the South—arise in any significant degree from the action of government. Yet it is impossible to think of this epoch of American history, in which the leaven of democracy was working so strongly to modify the national life, without the masterful presence of Old Hickory in the center of the stage.

NOTES

1. Mary C. Simms *et al* (eds)., *The Letters of William Gilmore Simms* (Columbia, S.C., 1952), IV, 232.

2. Joseph G. Smoot (ed.), "A Presbyterian Minister Calls on Presidential Candidate Andrew Jackson," *Tennessee Historical Quarterly* XXI (Sept., 1962), p. 228.

3. Harriet Martineau, *Retrospect of Western Travel* (London, 1838), I, pp. 161-163.

4. John Spencer Bassett (ed.), *Correspondence of Andrew Jackson* (Washington, 1928) V, 248, 262.

5. Bernard C. Steiner (ed.), "The South Atlantic States in 1833, as Seen by a New Englander," *Maryland Historical Magazine*, XIII (Dec., 1918), p. 301.

6. Charles G. Sellers, Jr., "Andrew Jackson versus the Historians," *Mississippi Valley Historical Review*, XLIV (March, 1958), pp. 615-634.

7. Frederick Jackson Turner, *The Rise of the New West, 1819-1829* (New York, 1906).

8. Arthur M. Schlesinger, Jr., *The Age of Jackson* (Boston, 1945); for opposing points of view see Joseph Dorfman, "The Jackson Wage-Earner Thesis" in *American Historical Review*, LIV (January, 1949), pp. 296-306; and William A. Sullivan, "Did Labor Support Jackson?", *Political Science Quarterly*, LXII (December, 1947), pp. 569-580; see also Walter Hugins, *Jacksonian*

Democracy and the Working Class, A Study of the New York Workingman's Movement 1829-1837 (Stanford, 1960).

9. Arthur M. Schlesinger, Sr., "Our Presidents: A Rating by 75 Historians," *New York Times Magazine* (July, 1962), pp. 12 and 40-43.

10. Professor Thomas P. Abernethy, "Andrew Jackson and the Rise of Southwestern Democracy," *American Historical Review*, XXXIII (Oct., 1927), p. 76, and *From Frontier to Plantation in Tennessee: A Study in Frontier Democracy* (Chapel Hill, 1932), pp. 238-49; for an opposing view see Charles G. Sellers Jr., "Banking and Politics in Jackson's Tennessee, 1817-1827," *Mississippi Valley Historical Review*, XLI (June, 1954), pp. 61-84.

11. See Marvin Meyers, *The Jacksonian Persuasion* (Chicago, 1957).

12. Richard B. Morris, "Andrew Jackson, Strike Breaker," *American Historical Review*, LV (Oct., 1949), pp. 54-68.

13. See Bray Hammond, *Banks and Politics in America from the Revolution to the Civil War* (Princeton, 1957) and Thomas P. Govan, *Nicholas Biddle, Nationalist and Public Banker, 1786-1844* (Chicago, 1959).

14. For good character studies of Jackson, see James Parton, *Life of Andrew Jackson* (3 vols., New York, 1861); John Spencer Bassett, *The Life of Andrew Jackson* (2 vols., Garden City, 1911); Marquis James, *The Life of Andrew Jackson* (2 vols., Indianapolis, 1938); Harold C. Syrett, *Andrew Jackson: His Contribution to the American Tradition* (Indianapolis, 1954).

15. John William Ward, *Andrew Jackson, Symbol for an Age* (New York, 1955).

16. Martineau, *Retrospect of Western Travel*, I, p. 156.

17. Two good biographies of Polk are Eugene I. McCormac, *James K. Polk: a Political Biography* (Berkeley, 1922), and Charles G. Sellers, *James K. Polk, Jacksonian, 1795-1843* (Princeton, 1957).

18. Glyndon G. Van Deusen, *The Jacksonian Era, 1828-1848* (New York, 1959), Chapter X.

19. See Clement Eaton, "Southern Senators and the Right of Instruction, 1789-1860," *Journal of Southern History*, XVIII (Aug., 1952), pp. 303-319.

20. J. C. Fitzpatrick (ed.), Autobiography of Martin Van Buren, *American Historical Association Report for 1918*, Vol. II.

21. Count Francesco Arese, *A Trip to the Prairies and in the Interior of North America*, translated by Andrew Evans (New York, 1934), pp. 26-28.

22. M. M. Quaife (ed.), *The Diary of James K. Polk during his Presidency, 1845-1849* (4 vols., Chicago, 1910), IV, pp. 172-174, Oct. 30, 1848.

23. Leonard White, *The Jacksonians, A Study in Administrative History, 1829-1861* (New York, 1954), p. 409.

24. Alice Felt Tyler, *Freedom's Ferment: Phases of American Social History to 1860* (Minneapolis, 1944).

25. Lillian A. Kibler, *Benjamin F. Perry, South Carolina Unionist* (Durham, 1946), p. 135.

26. J. L. M. Curry to James H. Joiner, July 19, 1847. J. L. M. Curry Papers, Ms. in Library of Congress.

27. Alexis de Tocqueville, *Journey to America*, edited by J. P. Mayer (London, 1959), p. 75.

28. Alexis de Tocqueville, *Democracy in America,* translated by Henry Reeve (New York, 1900).

29. Maunsel White to Pierre Soule, 1850, Maunsel White Papers, Southern Collection, University of North Carolina.

30. Leon F. Litwack, *North of Slavery: the Negro in the Free States, 1790-1860* (Chicago, 1961).

31. Francis J. Grund, *Aristocracy in America* (London, 1839).

PART I

A NEW ERA IN POLITICS

Politics in the United States underwent a great change during the 1820's and 1830's—a democratic upheaval. The old generation of dignified statesmen appeared for the last time on the public stage at the Virginia Constitutional Convention of 1829-30, but by this time they had grown conservative and out of touch with the political realities of the new age. In this year Robert Scott, a young Kentuckian who had just finished his law apprenticeship, set out on horseback from Frankfort to see the larger world and the political celebrities. In his journal he described in vivid detail the elder statesmen whom he saw at the Virginia Constitutional Convention. The retiring of another elder statesman, Nathaniel Macon, from the Senate of the United States in 1828 (which Thomas Hart Benton wrote of in his Thirty Years' View) removed from politics one of the most admirable of this vanishing breed, devoted to the ideals of Republican simplicity, Jeffersonian principles, and scorn of demagoguery.

After men such as Macon retired from politics a new generation arose which had to operate under different social and economic conditions. Its members seem less admirable than the leaders of a more aristocratic period, represented by Jefferson, Madison, and Macon. The outstanding political leaders of the new era were Jackson, Van Buren, and Polk, who were much closer to the common man in their thinking than were the Virginia statesmen.

"Old Hickory" occupied an ambivalent position in this dramatic change. On the one hand, he seemed to hold to the older ideal of politics that the office should seek the man, and he personally did not resort to the low arts of the demagogue, which indeed he despised. From his correspondence as edited by John Spencer Bassett and from his public papers I have selected statements he made which sincerely represented, I believe, his political views, and even today they remain admirable principles. But Jackson was surrounded by younger and lesser men who were responsive to the new trends in politics—Van Buren, Blair, Kendall, Eaton, some of whom were wire-pullers, politicians primarily interested in the spoils of victory, men who promoted sectional interests rather than the welfare of the nation. Though Jackson was a masterful individual, he could not control these selfish forces of the new era. His highly partisan nature made him their easy victim.

23

Eminently a man of action, he used direct methods and blunt speech to conduct the federal government. A striking example of these qualities was displayed in the shirt-sleeve diplomacy by which he forced France in 1834 to pay outstanding American claims. A young Frenchman traveling in the country at the time, Michel Chevalier, has given a remarkably candid report of this affair. In general, Chevalier extolled the virtues of the American people and government, but on this occasion he thought Jackson had unwisely endangered the friendship between the two countries.

Chevalier recognized that in the United States the government officials were controlled by the people, who were often poorly informed and highly nationalistic. Wherever the frontier influence remained strong (and in the 1830's a greater percentage of the people were influenced by living under semifrontier conditions than perhaps at any time since the United States became a nation), politics was likely to be highly personal, dramatic, and emotional. Indeed, it was in the state governments and in the local communities that realistic democracy, with its seamy side, appeared most revolutionary. Here the professional politician flourished, party spirit was rampant, and the crudeness of Jacksonian democracy showed most clearly. The representatives elected to the legislatures were usually small-town lawyers, petty tradesmen, and farmers, with, in the southern states, a sprinkling of aristocratic planters.

Mrs. Basil Hall, wife of a captain in the British Navy who traveled in America in 1827 and 1828, saw these legislators as crude and often comical characters but she was highly prejudiced by her Tory views and fastidious nature. Her husband wrote a separate account of their journey that was fairer and more objective. He was much impressed with the party spirit that entered into social relations, religion, and business, as well as politics. Also critical of realistic democracy in America was George Combe (see Part II), a British lecturer on phrenology who came to the United States to lecture on this pseudo-science, which was then a great fad. He observed the power of the lobby in American politics, a factor which militated against the practice of responsible democracy.

Among the intelligent foreign observers of the American scene, Sir Charles Lyell, the famous British geologist, was best disposed. He made two visits to the United States, in 1841-42 and in 1845, primarily to study American geology, but he also wrote travel accounts that are quite valuable. Lyell, on his first journey, witnessed and described in his journal some of the reverberations of the Dorr Rebellion in Rhode Island, which was an outgrowth of the development of Jacksonian democracy. It was a revolution against the aristocratic elements in the state's first constitution, based on the colonial charter of 1663, a constitution that disfranchised over half of the adult males. The revolutionary party in 1842 set up a new state government in defiance of the legal government and elected Thomas R. Dorr governor. The Dorr rebellion was quickly suppressed, but in the following year, after Dorr had been overthrown and imprisoned, the suffrage was liberalized.

Lyell did not, however, have the understanding of American local politics possessed by an intelligent native, such as George D. Prentice or Henry Benjamin Whipple, who realistically described the working of democracy in the southern states. George Prentice had just come to Kentucky from his native Connecticut for the purpose of doing a campaign biography of Henry Clay when he wrote his account of the Kentucky election. After completing the Clay biography the young journalist remained in the state for the rest of his life, becoming the powerful editor of the Whig organ, the Louisville Journal.

In the Jacksonian period many politicians, unrestrained by the older practices, shamelessly courted the electorate with various types of demagoguery. The aristocratic Mrs. Clement C. Clay, Jr., describes in a passage from her charming reminiscences, A Belle of the Fifties, *the tactics of a resourceful southern politician in her state, Alabama; but she herself did not scruple to practice demagoguery to secure the election of her husband to a seat in the United States Senate.*

The Elder Statesmen

Robert Scott

Richmond, Virginia, October 26, 1829. 10 o'clock visited the Hon James
Madison, a member of the [Virginia Constitutional] Convention, residing
with his family with the Hon A. R. Stevenson. As I approached the house
I saw Mrs Madison upstairs standing before a mirror adjusting her cap
and hair: rung the bell, was invited to the drawing room, asked for Mr M.,
sat a few moments when Mrs Madison entered & politely apollogised for
Mr M.'s delay, said he was writing, but would soon finish & come down;
she alluded to my name, seeming to know me. I told her who I was &
what my object, she then commenced a familiar and agreeable conversation on common place topics & after a few moments retired. She is a
fine looking old lady carrying her age remarkably well, having a fair skin
& pleasant countenance; her person large much exceeding the common
size; her dress was rich tasteful & comely but evincing more care & regard
to fashion than is common with ladies of her age. Mr Madison soon entered. I addressed him politely & delivered him my letters, he seated
himself in a large cushioned arm chair, read them & expressed a pleasure
in being acquainted, he enquired for Mr Bryce & Col Johnson the authors
of the letters & then of my family & ancestors, with whom he said he was
well & intimately acquainted: conversed easily & agreeably on various
subjects; his enunciation was clear & distinct though his voice was coarse
& seemed to be much impaired, his manners were easy & dignified & he
was polite to condescention; having proffered his attention and kind
offices I retired.

The Hon Jas Madison is in the 85 year of his age, in tolerably good
health, thin of flesh, rather under the common size, wears a black broad
brimmed hat, black broad cloth dress coat, with pockets under the flaps
behind, black cloth vest & black cloth pantaloons extending only to the
knees with long black stockings, knee buckles & shoes, a white cravat &

Robert Scott, *Memorandum of My Visit to the East in 1829-30.* Ms. owned by Mrs.
S. I. M. Major, Versailles, Ky. Microfilm in University of Kentucky Library.

ruffled shirt with the collar under the cravat, his form erect, his step firm but somewhat slow, walks without a staff, his visage pale & abounding in small wrinkles, his features well proportioned but not striking, his head bald on the top, but excessively powdered, showing a point in front and circular recesses at the sides of the forehead, his hair, behind also much powdered & tied in a que [sic] which is worn under the coat collar, his forehead of common size, his eye brow grey, heavy & projecting, his eyes small & faded, his nose of ordinary size & straight, his mouth rather small, his lips well proportioned, his ears obscured by his whiskers & hair, his sight & hearing both somewhat impaired. . . .

Visited the Hon John Marshall, now a member of the Convention, Chief Justice of the U.S., resident of Richmond, in the 74th year of his age, about 6 feet two inches high, remarkably active and fond of walking in a firm and brisk gait; wears a black broad brim hat, dress coat of black cloth with pockets under the flaps behind, black cloth vest & short black cloth pantaloons, with long grey yarn stockings, knee buckles and shoes, plain shirt, with the collar worn under his white cravat which is tied before, his hair is entire, equally mixed of black & grey, wears it combed down before & trimmed short around his forehead, long behind, plaited & tied in a que [sic] with a black ribbon, wears a pair of short whiskers & has a thick black beard, his complexion dark, his face full, round and much wrinkled, his countenance mild pleasant & intelligent, forehead full, eyebrows greyish, heavy & projecting, his eye dark (but little faded) & sprightly, nose a little turned up at the end, mouth & chin of ordinary size & appearance, his whole appearance venerable & imposing, his motions easy & graceful, in his manners polite, affable, and agreeable, his voice low, coarse & feeble.

Hon James Monroe, now a member of the convention and citizen of Loudon County, in the 73 year of his age, health rather delicate, about 5 feet 8 inches high & well proportioned, his dress neat & genteel consisting of a black cloth dress coat with pockets under the flaps behind, black cloth vest & short black cloth pantaloons & long black stockings, plain shirt collar concealed under his white cravat which is tied behind, a broad brim black hat & shoes, his hair is somewhat grey & thin on the crown of his head, he wears it combed back, showing large recesses on the sides of his forehead, which is of good size, receding & much wrinkled, his eyebrows projecting, eyes faded, sunken & flighty, nose straight & rather large, his mouth & lips of common size & well proportioned, his chin dimpled, he walks without a staff, his step being somewhat feeble & sluggish, his head is inclined a little forward. His conduct & manners evince strong marks of bodily & mental debility and decay, his gestures ungraceful, undignified & often improper, stands in the chair with his hands closed before him & is constantly rubbing his fingers one with another, his voice is coarse & feeble, his enunciation thick & often speaking unintended words.

Hon John Randolph, now a member of the convention, about 58 years of age in delicate health, spare & of middling stature, his person indifferent & unprepossessing, being a little hump shouldered & having a very short neck, his head considerably inclined forward, wears a common black hat, a complete suit of black cloth, white cotton socks & large coarse shoes resembling overshoes, walks with a plain hickory stick with the bark on it & a knot on the handle end, his hair is entire, a little grey, is parted on the top of the head & combed down the sides, is tolerably short & is worn without a que [sic]; his face is rather too small & is unprepossessing; his forehead rather narrow & low somewhat obscured by his hair, his eyebrows thin & smooth, his eyes, small, dark, & sparkling & intelligent, nose straight & of ordinary size, his mouth small, chin somewhat obscured by his shirt collar & cravat, which is a blue & white fancy handkerchief exactly like his pocket handkerchief, he sometimes wears plain spectacles with black frames; his beard is of a light colour & remarkably thin, his voice clear, shrill, & spectoral, his left leg is a little shorter than his right which causes him to limp & in addition to his short neck & stoop shoulders, renders his mien uneasy & ungraceful, his head is rather flat & his face much shrivelled, wears coarse buckskin gloves, a watch with large gold seals.

Rev Alexander Campbell a Baptist minister [born in Ireland of Scottish parents, founder of the Disciples of Christ, or the Campbellite Church], now a member of the Va Convention, in the prime of life, having a robust & well-formed person, his countenance lively, animated & intelligent, his manners, easy, graceful & by no means grave, his features pleasant & expressive, his hair light & somewhat grey, worn naturally of common length, his forehead of good size & a little receding, his eyes blue, his nose a little aquiline, his mouth of common size, his chin a little dimpled, has a thick light-coloured beard, wears short whiskers, his pronunciation imperfect, his dialect not purely English, his voice strong & shrill.

The Last of the Romans

Thomas H. Benton

Philosophic in his temperament and wise in his conduct, governed in all his actions by reason and judgment, and deeply imbued with Bible images, this virtuous and patriotic man (whom Mr. Jefferson called "the last of the Romans") had long fixed the term of his political existence at the age which the Psalmist assigns for the limit of manly life: "The days of our years are threescore years and ten; and if by reason of strength they be fourscore years; yet is their strength labor and sorrow, for it is soon cut off, and we fly away." He [Nathaniel Macon] touched that age in 1828; and, true to all his purposes, he was true to his resolve in this, and executed it with the quietude and indifference of an ordinary transaction. He was in the middle of a third senatorial term, and in the full possession of all his faculties of mind and body; but his time for retirement had come—the time fixed by himself; but fixed upon conviction and for well-considered reasons, and inexorable to him as if fixed by fate. To the friends who urged him to remain to the end of his term, and who insisted that his mind was as good as ever, he would answer, that it was good enough yet to let him know that he ought to quit office before his mind quit him, and that he did not mean to risk the fate of the Archbishop of Grenada. He resigned his senatorial honors as he had worn them—meekly, unostentatiously, in a letter of thanks and gratitude to the General Assembly of his State;—and gave to repose at home that interval of thought and quietude which every wise man would wish to place between the turmoil of life and the stillness of eternity. He had nine years of this tranquil enjoyment, and died without pain or suffering June 29th 1837,— characteristic in death as in life. It was eight o'clock in the morning when he felt that the supreme hour had come, had himself full-dressed with his habitual neatness, walked in the room and lay upon the bed, by turns conversing kindly with those who were about him, and showing by his

Thomas H. Benton, *Thirty Years' View—from 1820 to 1850* (New York, 1875), I, pp. 114-118.

conduct that he was ready and waiting, but hurrying nothing. It was the death of Socrates, all but the hemlock, and in that full faith of which the Grecian sage had only a glimmering. He directed his own grave on the point of a sterile ridge (where nobody would wish to plough), and covered with a pile of rough flintstone, (which nobody would wish to build with), deeming this sterility and that uselessness of this rock the best security for the undisturbed repose of the bones which is still desirable to those who are indifferent to monuments.

In almost all strongly-marked characters there is usually some incident or sign, in early life, which shows that character, and reveals to the close observer the type of the future man. So it was with Mr. Macon. His firmness, his patriotism, his self-denial, his devotion to duty and disregard of office and emolument; his modesty, integrity, self-control, and subjection of conduct to the convictions of reason and the dictates of virtue, all so steadily exemplified in a long life, were all shown from the early age of eighteen, in the miniature representation of individual action, and only confirmed in the subsequent public exhibitions of a long, beautiful, and exalted career.

He was of that age, and a student at Princeton College, at the time of the Declaration of American Independence. A small volunteer corps was then on the Delaware. He quit his books, joined it, served a term, returned to Princeton, and resumed his studies. In the year 1778 the Southern States had become a battle-field, big with their own fate, and possibly involving the issue of the war. British fleets and armies appeared there, strongly supported by the friends of the British cause; and the conquest of the South was fully counted upon. Help was needed in these States; and Mr. Macon, quitting college, returned to his native county in North Carolina, joined a militia company as a private, and marched to South Carolina—then the theatre of the enemy's operations. He had his share in all the hardships and disasters of that trying time; was at the fall of Fort Moultrie, surrender of Charleston, defeat at Camden; and in the rapid winter retreat across the upper part of North Carolina. He was in the camp on the left bank of the Yadkin when the sudden flooding of that river, in the brief interval between the crossing of the Americans and the coming up of the British, arrested the pursuit of Cornwallis, and enabled Greene to allow some rest to his wearied and exhausted men. In this camp, destitute of every thing and with gloomy prospects ahead, a summons came to Mr. Macon from the Governor of North Carolina, requiring him to attend a meeting of the General Assembly, of which he had been elected a member, without his knowledge, by the people of his county. He refused to go; and the incident being talked of through the camp, came to the knowledge of the general. Greene was a *man* himself, and able to know a *man*. He felt at once that, if this report was true, this young soldier was no common character; and determined to verify the fact. He sent for the young man, inquired of him, heard the truth, and then asked for the reason of this unexpected conduct—this preference for a suffering camp over a comfortable seat in the General Assembly? Mr. Macon answered him, in his quaint and sententious way, that he had seen the *faces* of the British many times, but had never seen their *backs*, and meant to stay in the army till he did. Greene instantly saw the material the young man was made of and the handle by which he was to be worked. That material was patriotism; that handle a sense of duty; and laying hold of this handle, he quickly worked the young soldier into a different conclusion from the one that he had arrived at. He told him he could do more good as a member of the General Assembly than as a soldier; that in the army he was but one man, and in the General Assembly he might obtain many, with the supplies they needed, by showing the destitution and suffering which he had seen in the camp; and that it was his duty to go. This view of duty and usefulness was decisive. Mr. Macon obeyed the Governor's summons; and by his representations contributed to obtain the supplies which enabled Greene to turn back and face Cornwallis,—fight him, cripple him, drive him further back than he had advanced (for Wilmington is South of Camden), disable him from remaining in the South (of which, up to the battle of Guilford, he believed himself to be master); and sending him to Yorktown, where he was captured and the war ended. . . .

The military life of Mr. Macon finished with his departure from the camp on the Yadkin, and his civil public life commenced on his arrival at the General Assembly, to which he had been summoned—that civil public life in which he was continued above forty years by free elections —representative in Congress under Washington, Adams, Jefferson, and Madison, and long the Speaker of the House; senator in Congress under Madison, Monroe, and John Quincy Adams; and often elected President of the Senate, and until voluntarily declining; twice refusing to be Postmaster General under Jefferson; never taking any office but that to which he was elected; and resigning his last senatorial term when it was only half run. But a characteristic trait remains to be told of his military life —one that has neither precedent nor imitation (the example of Washington being out of the line of comparison): he refused to receive pay, or to accept promotion, and served three years as a private through mere devotion to his country. And all the long length of his life was conformable to this patriotic and disinterested beginning: and thus the patriotic principles of the future senator were all revealed in early life, and in the obscurity of an unknown situation. Conformably to this beginning, he refused to take any thing under the modern acts of Congress for the benefit of the surviving officers and soldiers of the Revolution, and voted against them all, saying they had suffered alike (citizens and military), and all been rewarded together in the establishment of independence; that the debt to the army had been settled by pay, by pensions to the wounded, by half-pay and land to the officers; that no military claim could be founded on depreciated continental paper money, from the civil functionaries who performed service, and the farmers who furnished supplies, suffered as much as any. On this principle he voted against the bill for Lafayette, against all the modern revolutionary pensions and land bounty acts, and refused to take any thing under them (for many were applicable to himself).

His political principles were deep-rooted, innate, subject to no change and to no machinery of party. He was democratic in the broad sense of the word, as signifying a capacity in the people for self-government; and in its party sense, as in favor of a plain and economical administration of the federal government, and against latitudinarian constructions of the constitution. He was a party man, not in the hackneyed sense of the word, but only where principle was concerned; and was independent of party in all his social relations, and in all the proceedings which he disapproved. Of this he gave a strong instance in the case of General Hamilton, whom he deemed honorable and patriotic; and utterly refused to be concerned in a movement proposed to affect him personally, though politically opposed to him. He venerated Washington, admired the varied abilities and high qualities of Hamilton; and esteemed and respected the eminent federal gentlemen of his time. He had affectionate regard for Madison and Monroe; but Mr. Jefferson was to him the full and perfect exemplification of the republican statesman. His almost fifty years of personal and political friendship and association with Mr. Randolph is historical, and indissolubly connects their names and memories in the recollection of their friends, and in history, if it does them justice. He was the early friend of General Jackson, and intimate with him when he was a senator in Congress under the administration of the elder Mr. Adams; and was able to tell Congress and the world who he was when he began to astonish Europe and America by his victories. He was the kind observer of the conduct of young men, encouraging them by judicious commendation when he saw them making efforts to become useful and respectable, and never noting their faults. He was just in all things, judging political opponents,—to whom he would do no wrong, not merely in word or act, but in thought. He spoke frequently in Congress, always to the point, and briefly and wisely; and was one of those speakers which Mr. Jefferson described Dr. Franklin to have been—a speaker of no pretension and great performance,—who spoke more good sense while he was getting up out of his chair, and getting back into it, than many others did in long discourses; and he suffered no reporter to dress up a speech for him.

He was above the pursuit of wealth, but also above dependence and idleness; and, like an old Roman of the elder Cato's time, worked in the fields at the head of his slaves in the intervals of public duty; and did not cease this labor until advancing age rendered him unable to stand the hot sun of summer—the only season of the year when senatorial duties left him at liberty to follow the plough, or handle the hoe. I think it was the summer of 1817,—that was the last time (he told me) he tried it, and found the sun too hot for him—then sixty years of age, a senator, and the refuser of all office. How often I think of him, when I see at Washington robustious men going through a scene of supplication, tribulation, and degradation, to obtain office, which the salvation of the soul does not impose upon the vilest sinner! His fields, his flocks, and his herds yielded an ample supply of domestic productions. A small crop of tobacco—three hogs-heads when the season was good, two when bad—purchased the exotics which comfort and necessity required, and which the farm did not produce. He was not rich, but rich enough to dispense hospitality and charity, to receive all guests in his house, from the President to the day laborer—no other title being necessary to enter his house but that of an honest man; rich enough to bring up his family (two daughters) as accomplished ladies, and marry them to accomplished gentlemen—one to William Martin, Esq., the other to William Eaton, Esq., of Roanoke, my early school-fellow and friend for more than half a century; and, above all, he was rich enough to pay as he went, and never to owe a dollar to any man.

He was steadfast in his friendships, and would stake himself for a friend, but would violate no point of public duty to please or oblige him. Of this his relations with Mr. Randolph gave a signal instance. He drew a knife to defend him in the theatre at Philadelphia, when menaced by some naval and military officers for words spoken in debate, and deemed offensive to their professions; yet, when speaker of the House of Representatives, he displaced Mr. Randolph from the head of the committee of ways and means, because the chairman of that committee should be on terms of political friendship with the administration,—which Mr. Randolph had then ceased to be with Mr. Jefferson's. He was above executive office, even the highest the President could give; but not above the lowest the people could give, taking that of justice of the peace in his county, and refusing that of Postmaster General at Washington. He was opposed to nepotism, and to all quartering of his connections on the government; and in the course of his forty-years' service, with the absolute friendship of many administrations and the perfect respect of all, he never had office or contract for any of his blood. He refused to be a candidate for the vice-presidency, but took the place of elector of the Van Buren ticket in 1836. He was against paper money and the paper system, and was accustomed to present the strong argument against both in the simple phrase, that this was a hard-money government, made by hard-money men, who had seen the evil of paper-money, and meant to save their posterity from it. He was opposed to securityships, and held that no man ought to be entangled in the affairs of another, and that the interested parties alone—those who expected to find their profit in the transaction—should bear the bad consequences, as well as enjoy the good ones, of their own dealings. He never called any one "friend" without being so; and never expressed faith in the honor and integrity of a man without acting up to the declaration when the occasion required it. Thus, in constituting his friend Weldon N. Edwards, Esq., his testamentary and sole executor, with large discretionary powers, he left all to his honor, and forbid him to account to any court or power for the manner in which he should execute that trust. . . .

. . . He had his peculiarities—idiosyncracies, if any one pleases—but they were born with him, suited to him, constituting a part of his character, and necessary to its completeness. He never subscribed to charities, but gave, and freely, according to his means—the left hand not knowing what the right hand did. He never subscribed for new books, giving as a reason to the soliciting agent, that nobody purchased his tobacco until it was inspected; and he could buy no book until he had examined it. He would not attend the Congress Presidential Caucus of 1824, although it was sure to nominate his own choice (Mr. Crawford); and, when a reason was wanted, he gave it in the brief answer that he attended one once and they cheated him, and he had said that he would never attend another. He always wore the same dress—that is to say, a suit of the same material, cut, and color, superfine navy blue—the whole suit from the same piece, and in the fashion of the time of the Revolution; and always replaced by a new one before it showed age. He was neat in his person, always wore fine linen, a fine cambric stock, a fine fur hat with a brim to it, fair topboots—the boot outside of the pantaloons, on the principle that leather was stronger than cloth. He would wear no man's honors, and when complimented on the report on the Panama mission, which, as chairman of the committee on foreign relations, he had presented to the Senate, he would answer, "Yes; it is a good report; Tazewell wrote it." Left to himself, he was ready to take the last place, and the lowest seat any where; but in his representative capacity he would suffer no derogation of a constitutional or of a popular right. Thus, when Speaker of the House, and a place behind the President's Secretaries had been assigned him in some ceremony; he disregarded the programme; and, as the elect of the elect of all the people, took his place next after those whom the national vote had elected. And in 1803, on the question to change the form of voting for President and Vice-President, and the vote wanting one of the constitutional number of two thirds, he resisted the rule of the House which restricted the speaker's vote to tie, or to a vote which would make a tie,—claimed his constitutional right to vote as a member, obtained it, gave the vote, made the two thirds, and carried the amendment. And, what may well be deemed idiosyncratic in these days, he was punctual in the performance of all his minor duties to the Senate, attending its sittings to the moment, attending all the committees to which he was appointed, attending all the funerals of the members and officers of the Houses, always in time at every place where duty required him; and refusing double mileage for one travelling, when elected from the House of Representatives to the Senate, or summoned to an extra session. He was an habitual reader and student of the Bible, a pious and religious man, and of the *"Baptist persuasion,"* as he was accustomed to express it.

I have a pleasure in recalling the recollections of this wise, just, and good man, and in writing them down, not without profit, I hope, to rising generations, and at least as extending the knowledge of the kind of men to whom we are indebted for our independence, and for the form of government which they established for us. Mr. Macon was the real Cincinnatus of America, the pride and ornament of my native State, my hereditary friend through four generations, my mentor in the first seven years of my senatorial, and the last seven of his senatorial life; and a feeling of gratitude and of filial affection mingles itself with this discharge of historical duty to his memory.

Andrew Jackson's Political Philosophy

TO ANDREW J. DONALDSON, WASHINGTON, APRIL 11, 1824

If I am elected to fill the Presidential chair it must be by the people; and I will be the President of the nation, and not of a party.[1]

TO MRS. ANDREW JACKSON, WASHINGTON, APRIL 12, 1824

We have done nothing yet. I regret to see no national feeling in the majority of congress. Every one appears solely to be ingrossed with the interest alone of his own section of the country—so long as this feeling predominates, it will be unfortunate for the nation. We ought as Legislators to meet with national feelings, and our Legislation ought to be for the general good; and as far as practicable equity and Justice to all sections of our country.[2]

TO L. H. COLEMAN, WASHINGTON, APRIL 26, 1824

I am one of those who do not believe that a national debt is a national blessing, but rather a curse to a republic; inasmuch as it is calculated to raise around the administration a moneyed aristocracy dangerous to the liberties of the country.[3]

TO BRIGADIER-GENERAL JOHN COFFEE, HERMITAGE, JULY 23, 1825

My political creed is neither to seek or decline office, and it might be considered a departure from this my Republican creed even to visit [the Harrodsburgh, Ky.] springs . . . [to which he had received pressing invitations from politicians].[4]

[1] John S. Bassett (ed.), *Correspondence of Andrew Jackson* (Washington, 1928), III, p. 247.
[2] *Ibid.*, III, p. 247.
[3] *Ibid.*, III, p. 250.
[4] *Ibid.*, III, p. 288.

TO VICE-PRESIDENT JOHN C. CALHOUN, HERMITAGE, JULY 26, 1826

You may still confide in the support of the people; they may be led away for a moment by designing demagogues, and the influence of men who in the pursuit of office will sacrifice the greatest good of the country to procure it, but their reason is soon enlightened by truth and rallying round their true interests, they will throw aside the instruments of corruption, and accept those of good and faithful service.

I trust that my name will always be found on the side of the people, and as their confidence in your talents and virtue has placed you in the second office of the government, that we shall march hand in hand in their cause.[5]

TO A COMMITTEE OF THE DAVIDSON CO. BIBLE SOCIETY,
HERMITAGE, SEPT. 30, 1826

I must be excused [from speaking to you]—having lost many of my teeth it is with great difficulty I can articulate, and not being in the habit of public speaking of late, it is very unpleasant for me to appear in that character— There is still a stronger reason for my declining—it is this— Under existing circumstances, was such an address to go forth to the world, I might be charged by my political enemies with having come forth hypocritically under the sacred garb of religion thus to electioneer—never having worn this mask I cannot permit myself to appear in an attitude which might justify my enemies in raising imputations so unpleasant.[6]

FIRST ANNUAL MESSAGE, DEC. 8, 1829

The duties of all public officers are, or at least admit of being made, so plain and simple that men of intelligence may readily qualify themselves for their performance; and I can not but believe that more is lost by the long continuance of men in office than is generally to be gained by their experience. . . .

In a country where offices are created solely for the benefit of the people no one man has any more intrinsic right to official station than another. Offices were not established to give support to particular men at the public expense. No individual wrong is, therefore, done by removal, since neither appointment to nor continuance in office is a matter of right. The incumbent became an officer with a view to public benefits, and when these require his removal they are not to be sacrificed to private interests. It is the people, and they alone, who have a

[5] *Ibid.*, III, p. 308.
[6] *Ibid.*, III, p. 315.

right to complain when a bad officer is substituted for a good one. He who is removed has the same means of obtaining a living that are enjoyed by the millions who never held office. The proposed limitation [of a tenure of four years] would destroy the idea of property now so generally connected with official station, and although individual distress may be sometimes produced, it would, by promoting that rotation which constitutes a leading principle in the republican creed, give healthful action to the system.[7]

VETO OF THE BANK RECHARTER BILL, JULY 10, 1832

It is to be regretted that the rich and powerful too often bend the acts of government to their selfish purposes. Distinctions in society will always exist under every just government. Equality of talents, of education, or of wealth can not be produced by human institutions. In the full enjoyment of the gifts of Heaven and the fruits of superior industry, economy, and virtue, every man is equally entitled to protection by law; but when the laws undertake to add to these natural and just advantages artificial distinctions, to grant titles, gratuities, and exclusive privileges, to make the rich richer and the potent more powerful, the humble members of society—the farmers, mechanics, and laborers—who have neither the time nor the means of securing like favors to themselves, have a right to complain of the injustice of their Government. There are no necessary evils in government. Its evils exist only in its abuses. If it would confine itself to equal protection, and, as Heaven does its rains, shower its favors alike on the high and the low, the rich and the poor, it would be an unqualified blessing. In the act before me there seems to be a wide and unnecessary departure from these just principles.

Nor is our Government to be maintained or our Union preserved by invasions of the rights and powers of the several States. In thus attempting to make our General Government strong we make it weak. Its true strength consists in leaving individuals and States as much as possible to themselves—in making itself felt, not in its power, but in its beneficence; not in its control, but in its protection; not in binding the States more closely to the center, but leaving each to move unobstructed in its proper orbit.[8]

PROCLAMATION TO THE PEOPLE OF SOUTH CAROLINA, DEC. 10, 1832

If the doctrine of a State veto upon the laws of the Union carries with it internal evidence of its impracticable absurdity, our constitutional history will also afford abundant proof that it would have been repudi-

  [7] James D. Richardson, A Compilation of the Messages and Papers of the Presidents, 1789-1897 (Washington, 1901), II, p. 449.
  [8] Ibid., II, pp. 590-591.

ated with indignation had it been proposed to form a feature in our Government.

Our present constitution was formed . . . in vain if this fatal doctrine prevails. It was formed for important objects that are announced in the preamble, made in the name and by the authority of the people of the United States, whose delegates framed and whose conventions approved it. The most important among these objects—that which is placed first in rank, on which all the others rest—is *"to form a more perfect union."* Now, is it possible that even if there were no express provision giving supremacy to the Constitution and laws of the United States over those of the States, can it be conceived that an instrument made for the purpose of *"forming a more* perfect union" than that of the Confederation could be so constructed by the assembled wisdom of our country as to substitute for that Confederation a form of government dependent for its existence on the local interest, the party spirit, of a State, or of a prevailing faction in a State? Every man of plain, unsophisticated understanding who hears the question will give such an answer as will preserve the Union. Metaphysical subtlety, in pursuit of an impracticable theory, could alone have devised one that is calculated to destroy it.

I consider, then, the power to annul a law of the United States, assumed by one State, *uncompatible with the existence of the Union, contradicted expressly by the letter of the Constitution, unauthorized by its spirit, inconsistent with every principle on which it was founded, and destructive of the great object for which it was formed.*[9]

TO THE SYNOD OF THE REFORMED CHURCH, JUNE 12, 1832,
REFUSING TO APPOINT A DAY OF FASTING, HUMILIATION AND PRAYER

I could not do otherwise without transcending those limits which are prescribed by the Constitution for the President and without feeling that I might in some degree disturb the security which religion now enjoys in this country in its complete separation from the political concerns of the General Government.[10]

TO MAUNSEL WHITE, JULY 12, 1837

We must have a metallic currency to cover the labour of our country and as a standard value of property. . . ."[11]

TO MRS. MARY EASTIN POLK IN TENNESSEE, WASHINGTON,
MARCH 14, 1836

I am looking forward with great anxiety to the 4th of next March when

[9] *Ibid.*, II, p. 640 ff.
[10] Bassett, *Correspondence of Andrew Jackson*, IV, p. 497.
[11] Bassett, *Correspondence of Andrew Jackson*, V, pp. 498-499.

I will be once more freed from the shackles of slavery of office. I am indeed tired of the scenes of corruption and treachery with which I have been surrounded ever since I have been here. When I see men who has [sic] professed republican principles, opposing the corrupting influence of great monied corporations & by this course obtaining the confidence of the people all at once aband[on]ing all those principles, *for office sake* and personal agrandisement [sic], I begin to loath [sic] the corruption of the times, and debas[e]ment of the human character that prevades [sic] our country at the present day and am anxious for retirement to the pleasant shades of my Hermitage, where my deary Mary, I will always be happy to see you, your dear children, with your dear husband; altho I am informed that he has become one of the modern Whiggs—say to him he is in bad company—those modern Whiggs are the political Arnolds of the day, and differ from those gallant Washingtonian Whiggs of the revolution to which his revered father belonged. They could not be bought by the Bank as sheep in the shambles, as the modern Whiggs have been & are—or for the sake of personal agrandisement [sic], sell their principles & party, and enlist under the hypocritical garb of the no party, party, which is as much as to say we offer ourselves to that party or any party that will offer us the best offices— I am sure your dear husband does not know these hypocrites as well as I do, or he never would be one of the no party, party, for he will adhere to principles & if he does, he must abandon them.

Your affectionate
UNCLE, ANDREW JACKSON[12]

---

[12] George Polk Papers, Mss. in Southern Collection, University of North Carolina.

Jackson's Inaugural Reception

Margaret Bayard Smith

The *Majesty of the People* had disappeared, and a rabble, a mob, of boys, negros, women, children, scrambling fighting, romping. What a pity what a pity! No arrangements had been made, no police officers placed on duty and the whole house had been inundated by the rabble mob. We came too late. The President, after having been *literally* nearly pressed to death and almost suffocated and torn to pieces by the people in their eagerness to shake hands with Old Hickory, had retreated through the back way or south front and had escaped to his lodgings at Gadsby's. Cut glass and china to the amount of several thousand dollars had been broken in the struggle to get the refreshments, punch and other articles had been carried out in tubs and buckets, but had it been in hogsheads it would have been insufficient, ice-creams, and cake and lemonade, for 20,000 people, for it is said that number were there, tho' I think the estimate exaggerated. Ladies fainted, men were seen with bloody noses and such a scene of confusion took place as is impossible to describe,—those who got in could not get out by the door again, but had to scramble out of windows.

Margaret Bayard Smith, *The First Forty Years of Washington Society*, family letters of Mrs. Samuel Harrison Smith, edited by Gaillard Hunt (Scribner's, London, 1906), pp. 295-296.

Old Hickory in Action

Michel Chevalier

Louisville [Kentucky], December 15, 1834. You must have been astonished in France at the President's message on the French debts. Here the sharp and reckless tone of some of the press had prepared the public mind for some energetic demonstration; but the message has exceeded the hopes of those who wished to assume an attitude of defiance in regard to France and the fears of those who dreaded some imprudent step. Had such a paper come from any former President—from Washington to John Quincy Adams—it would have been looked upon as an expression of the sentiments of a majority of the American people. Neither of them would have been willing so to commit the United States without being sure that the national will really required it. Their rule of action would have been to let themselves be pushed on by the nation, rather than to draw it after them or to go beyond it; and this, in fact, is more conformable to notions of self-government. They would have had the question profoundly discussed by the cabinet, not only orally, but in writing, as Washington did at the time of the establishment of the first bank in 1791. They would have personally consulted some of the leading statesmen of the country of all parties and all interests. They would have listened patiently to the representations of those upon whom the heavy burden of war would have fallen most directly, the merchants of Boston, New York, Philadelphia, Baltimore, Charleston, New Orleans, and other large ports; and finally, after having weighed all objections, measured all difficulties, if they had been convinced that the interest and honor of their country absolutely required the appeal to the last argument, they would have reluctantly addressed the challenge to their oldest ally and friend, to the firmest stay of liberty and improvement in the Old World.

General Jackson has changed all this; the rules of conduct and the

Michel Chevalier, *Society, Manners, and Politics in the United States* (Boston, 1839), pp. 176-182.

policy of his Administration are no longer those established by the wisdom of his predecessors. Some may maintain that this change is for the better; on this point, the future, and no distant future, will decide. But the fact of a change is undeniable. General Jackson possesses in the highest degree the qualities necessary for conducting partisan warfare. Bold, indefatigable, always alert, quick-sighted, with an iron will and a frame of adamant, devoted to his friends, harsh and terrible to his enemies, making light of obstacles, passionately fond of danger, his campaigns against the Creeks and Seminoles were marked by the most brilliant success and his resistance to the English army under Pakenham at New Orleans was heroic. By these exploits and the enthusiasm which military services excite in all countries, General Jackson found himself the most popular man in the Union when the founders of national independence disappeared and he naturally became the candidate for the presidential seat. Objections were made to his unbending temper, the impatience of contradiction which he had shown throughout his whole career, his obstinacy in following his own impulses despite the law, and his disposition to use the sword of Alexander rather than to conform himself to the delays of constitutional forms. His natural propensities, strengthened by the habits of military command and by the peculiarities of that kind of warfare in which he had been engaged, must, it was urged, have become ungovernable; and it would be impossible for him to acquire that moderation which is necessary in the exercise of civil authority. It was predicted that in politics, as in war, he would be zealous for his friends, implacable toward his adversaries, violent against whoever should attempt to check his course; that, instead of being above party quarrels, he would come down into the arena in person. His arrest of a judge in New Orleans, the execution of the militiamen, and of the two Englishmen, Arbuthnot and Ambrister, his invasion and conquest of Florida in time of peace, his anger and threats when Congress was deliberating upon charges founded on these summary acts, were all dwelt upon.

But his chivalric character, his lofty integrity, and his ardent patriotism seemed sufficient guarantees for his conduct. For reasons of domestic policy which it would take too much time to explain, many enlightened men who had at first treated the idea of supporting him for the presidency with ridicule gave in to the plan, trusting that they should be able to exercise a salutary influence over him. His fiery temper seemed in fact to be calmed by his elevation; the recollection of his oath of office which, at the moment it was made, was made in good faith, was yet fresh. He had conscientiously resolved to observe the principles consecrated by Washington, Jefferson, and the other patriarchs of America to keep himself scrupulously within the narrow limits of prerogative, as he had traced them or allowed them to be traced out for him; to follow the current of public opinion, without seeking to bar its course or divert it from its regular channels; to be moderate, patient, and calm. During his first term, he continued pretty faithful to his resolution, to his professed principles, and to the advice of those who raised him to his seat. But this state of constraint was insupportable to him; it is too late to reform at the age of sixty years.

Besides, not all temperaments, or, I should say, the distinctive qualities of all men, can adapt themselves to that high sphere of serenity in which he who governs others should move. Such a conformity was even more difficult for General Jackson than for any other man; the turbulence and impetuosity of youth had not been tempered in him either by age or by the fatigues of war. And in a country where universal suffrage prevails, political disputes are of a character to exhaust the patience of an angel. Step by step, then, the stormy propensities of the Tennessee planter were seen returning. The character of the bold, daring, restless, obstinate, fiery, indomitable partisan chief, of the conqueror of the Creeks, and Seminoles, gradually broke through the veil of reserve, caution, gravity, and universal good will which had covered it and tore in pieces the constitutional mantle in which his friends had taken so much pains to wrap him.

At length, in 1832, South Carolina furnished a natural occasion for giving the rein to his warlike propensities, which had been curbed for four years. That State had, on its own authority, declared the Tariff Act of Congress null and void and had armed its militia to sustain its Nullification Ordinance. The President immediately began preparations for war, retaining however the language of moderation, and obtained an act of Congress (the Force Bill) authorizing him to employ all means to maintain the laws of the United States. When this storm was laid, General Jackson was proclaimed the savior of the Constitution; and perhaps sufficient care was not taken to prevent a very natural mistake by an old soldier and to make him sensible that the congratulations of a grateful people were addressed less to his warlike attitude than to the pacific measures taken under his auspices. In the heat of debate and the shout of acclamation that followed the restoration of order, the old military leaven began to ferment in the President's heart and without a pause he rushed into a vigorous campaign against the Bank. This was a war almost without provocation, certainly without a just cause, and for some time it appeared that the General would be worsted. But he held his own and neither bent nor broke. In this affair he was the same Old Hickory that the Indians had found always and everywhere on their trail, whom they could neithor tire nor surprise and upon whom they could get no hold, either by force or fraud. The last congressional election assures him victory, and the Bank is condemned to the fate of the Creeks and Seminoles, of Mr. Clay and Mr. Calhoun, of the Spanish government of Florida, and of the English General Pakenham.

The intoxication of success seems to have restored all the fire of his youth and, at an age when other men look only toward repose, he requires new perils and new trials. Last winter, Mr. Clay declared in the Senate that if phrenology were a true science President Jackson must certainly have the bump of combativeness, for his life had been nothing but the perpetual exercise of that passion; at fourteen years of age against the English; then against his neighbors, the first settlers of Tennessee, not a very tractable race, who handled the knife, the sword, the pistol, and the rifle with as much promptness as himself; next against the Indians, the English, the Indians again, and the inoffensive Spaniards; then against Mr. Clay, Mr. Calhoun, and South Carolina; and finally, for want of other adversaries, he was engaged in a bout with the Bank. The General seems, in fact, to be possessed with the demon of war; for no sooner had he put his foot on the throat of the Bank than he required a new enemy, and finding in America none but vanquished adversaries, or objects unworthy of his anger, he flings down the glove to France. Thus far the defiance thrown out to France is merely the expression of General Jackson's humor. But, unluckily, this act of an individual emanates from a man who is President of the United States until the fourth of March, 1837, and who is even more pertinacious in his enmities than in his friendships. Unluckily too, the defiance has been inserted in a solemn document which is looked upon in Europe as a true indication of the sentiments of the American people. And finally, the man who has put the United States in this posture has just made an experiment which shows the degree to which he can lead the people to espouse his personal quarrels.

His tactics in politics, as well as in war, is to throw himself forward with the cry of, *Comrades, follow me!* This method succeeded admirably in the case of the Bank. If he had recommended to Congress to withdraw the public deposits from that institution, he would certainly have failed; Congress would have declared against it. He therefore boldly took the first step himself and ordered the removal, in opposition to the advice of the majority of his cabinet, two months before the meeting of Congress, without the slightest possible pretense of the urgency of the measure. "I will take the responsibility," he said. The Secretary of the Treasury refused to execute the order because he considered it a fatal abuse of power, and he was dismissed. The majority of the House of Representatives and, in the last elections, of the people, have sanctioned these dictatorial acts. General Jackson has, indeed, lost most of his friends in the enlightened classes and among the business community, but he cares little for individuals, however distinguished; by virtue of universal suffrage, it is numbers that rule here.

Will the bold policy by which he carried the multitude against the Bank be as successful now that he attempts to excite against France? It may be compared to one of those feats of strength in which one may succeed the first and even the second time, but will break the third. General Jackson may possess that sort of popularity which is irresistible for a short time, but the duration and solidity of which are in the inverse ratio to its intensity and brilliance. This, however, is mere conjecture. One thing is certain, that the General has the majority in the House of Representatives, and from what is known of the composition of the next Congress there is every appearance that he will keep it during the term of his Presidency; while the Opposition, which now has the majority in the Senate, may lose it after the present session. Besides, it is not plain to me that the Opposition will be unanimous in censuring the measures of General Jackson in regard to France. The opponents of General Jackson, as well as his friends, are obliged to court their common sovereign, the people. Now in all countries the multitude are very far from being cosmopolites; their patriotism is more lively and warm, but it is also more brutal, more unjust, and more arrogant than that of the higher classes. In France, they cry with enthusiasm, *Our Country before all things!* Here the word is, *Our country, right or wrong!* which is the perfection of national selfishness.

Van Buren: Advocate of *Laissez Faire* Government

All communities are apt to look to government for too much. Even in our own country, where its powers and duties are so strictly limited, we are prone to do so, especially at periods of sudden embarrassment and distress. But this ought not to be. The framers of our excellent Constitution and the people who approved it with calm and sagacious deliberation acted at the time on a sounder principle. They wisely judged that the less government interferes with private pursuits the better for the general prosperity. It is not its legitimate object to make men rich or to repair by direct grants of money or legislation in favor of particular pursuits losses not incurred in the public service. This would be substantially to use the property of some for the benefit of others. But its real duty—that duty the performance of which makes a good government the most precious of human blessings—is to enact and enforce a system of general laws commensurate with, but not exceeding, the objects of its establishment, and to leave every citizen and every interest to reap under its benign protection the rewards of virtue, industry, and prudence.[1]

It is believed, however, that the great purposes for the attainment of which the Federal Government was instituted have not been lost sight of. Intrusted only with certain limited powers, cautiously enumerated, distinctly specified, and defined with a precision and clearness which would seem to defy misconstruction, it has been my constant aim to confine myself within the limits so clearly marked out and so carefully guarded. Having always been of opinion that the best preservative of the union of the States is to be found in a total abstinence from the exercise of all doubtful powers on the part of the Federal Government rather than in attempts to assume them by a loose construction of the Constitution or an ingenious perversion of its words, I have endeavored to avoid recom-

[1] Special Message to Congress, Sept. 4, 1837—Richardson, *Messages and Papers,* III, p. 344.

mending any measure which I had reason to apprehend would, in the opinion even of a considerable minority of my fellow-citizens, be regarded as trenching on the rights of the States or the provisions of the hallowed instrument of our Union. Viewing the aggregate powers of the Federal Government as a voluntary concession of the States, it seemed to me that such only should be exercised as were at the time intended to be given.[2]

[2] Fourth Annual Message, Dec. 5, 1840—Richardson, *op. cit.*, III, p. 614.

May the Best Man Win

Basil Hall

During our stay at Albany, we went frequently into company, especially to dinners and to evening parties, both large and small, which afforded us the most agreeable opportunities of seeing and judging of the state of domestic society; one feature of which ought to be mentioned, as it meets a stranger's observation in every quarter of that wide country. I mean the spirit of party—not to call it politics—or rather, to define it more correctly, the spirit of electioneering, which seems to enter as an essential ingredient into the composition of every thing.

The most striking peculiarity of this spirit, in contradistinction to what we see in England, is that its efforts are directed more exclusively to the means, than to any useful end. The Americans, as it appears to me, are infinitely more occupied about bringing in a given candidate, than they are about the advancement of those measures of which he is conceived to be the supporter. They do occasionally advert to these prospective measures, in their canvassing arguments in defence of their own friends, or in attacks upon the other party; but always, as far as I could see, more as rhetorical flourishes, or as motives to excite the furious acrimony of party spirit, than as distinct or sound anticipations of the line of policy which their candidate, or his antagonist, was likely to follow. The intrigues, the canvassings for votes, all the machinery of newspaper abuse and praise, the speeches and manœuvres in the Legislature, at the bar, by the fireside, and in every hole and corner of the country from end to end, without intermission, form integral parts of the business— apparently far more important than the candidate's wishes—his promises—or even than his character and fitness for the office.

All these things, generally speaking, it would seem, are subordinate considerations; so completely are men's minds swallowed up in the technical details of the election. They discuss the chances of this or that

Basil Hall, *Travels in North America in the Years 1827-28* (Edinburgh, 1829), II, pp. 59-62.

State, town, or parish, or district, going with or against their friend. They overwhelm one another with that most disagreeable of all forms of argument—authorities. They analyze every sentence uttered by any man, dead or alive, who possesses, or ever did possess, influence; not, it must be observed, to come at any better knowledge of the candidate's pretensions as a public man, but merely to discover how far the weight of such testimony is likely to be thrown into their own scale, or that of the opposite party.

The election of the President, being one affecting the whole country, the respective candidates for that office were made the butts at which all political shafts were aimed, and to which every other election was rendered subservient, not indirectly, but by straight and obvious means. It was of no importance, apparently, whether the choice to be made, at any given election, were that of a governor, a member to Congress, or to the Legislature of the State—or whether it were that of a constable of the obscure ward of an obscure town—it was all the same. The candidates seldom, if ever, that I could see, even professed to take their chief ground as the fittest men for the vacant office—this was often hardly thought of—as they stood forward simply as Adams men or Jackson men —these being the names, it is right to mention, of the two gentlemen aiming at the Presidency. Although the party principles of these candidates for any office, on the subject of the Presidential election, could not—nine cases in ten—afford any index to their capacity for filling the station to which they aspired, their chance of success was frequently made to hinge upon that matter exclusively. Thus the man who could bring most votes to that side of this grand, all-absorbing Presidential question, which happened to have the ascendency for the time being, was sure to gain the day, whether he were or were not the best suited to fill the particular vacancy.

More or less this interference of Presidential politics in all the concerns of life, obtained in every part of America which I visited. There were exceptions, it is true, but these were so rare, that the tone I have been describing was assuredly the predominant one every where. The consequence was, that the candidates for office, instead of being the principals, were generally mere puppets—men of straw—abstract beings, serving the purpose of rallying points to the voters from whence they might carry on their main attack in the pursuit of an ulterior object, which, after all, was equally immaterial in itself, but which served, for the time being, to engross the attention of the people as completely as if it were of real consequence to them. In these respects, therefore, the Presidential contests in America resemble those field sports in which the capture of the game is entirely subordinate to the pleasures of its pursuit.

A State Legislature in 1827

Margaret Hall

September 16 [Albany, N.Y.]—I went yesterday morning first to the House of Assembly and then to the Senate. Perhaps you do not know that each State in the Union has its own Legislature independent of the general Congress or Government. The laws of each State are made by its Legislature but must not interfere with the general laws of the Constitution. The House of Assembly of this State consists of one hundred and twenty-eight members who are selected annually and chosen by universal suffrage, at least every male citizen of the age of twenty-one years and who has been an inhabitant in the State for a year preceding the election and six months a resident in the town or country where he wishes to offer his vote, has a right to do so. There are thirty-two members in the Senate. The State is divided into eight districts, each of which chooses four senators. In the House of Assembly I heard the continuation of a debate they had had the day before. I am not much qualified to judge of public speaking as I have rarely heard any, but I should imagine that what I heard yesterday was very bad. The speakers wandered strangely from their subjects, and less elegance either of language or action I cannot imagine. The favourite attitude of the principal speaker was his left hand in his breeches pocket whilst with his right he clutched a pencil and sawed the air in a like manner that showed him much in want of Hamlet's advice to the Players. Now and then he shifted his left hand from the favourite pocket back further than it would be quite delicate to particularise. In the Senate they occupied a complete hour in discussing whether or not there was a sufficient number present for the transaction of business, and then there was so long a paper read that we came away before they got through it. I believe that the members of the House of Commons in England are not very particular either as to their dress or manners, but I do not suppose they

Margaret (Mrs. Basil) Hall, *The Aristocratic Journey*, edited by Una Pope-Hennessy (courtesy of Putnam & Co., Ltd., London, 1931), pp. 64-68.

hoist their legs across the table nearest to them nor spit all over the floor, both of which inelegancies were practised by the Senators I saw yesterday. The spitting is really more abominable than I can find words to express. Some bad practices one gets, if not reconciled to, at least less annoyed by them with the habit of seeing them daily, but the spitting makes me more sick every time that I am condemned to see it.

Democratic Turbulence

Sir Charles Lyell

1. ELECTION DAY IN TRENTON, NEW JERSEY

October 11, [1841]—Reaching Trenton, the capital of New Jersey, late in the evening, we found the town in all the bustle of a general election. A new governor and representatives for the State legislature were to be chosen. As parties are nearly balanced, and the suffrage universal, the good order maintained was highly creditable. Processions, called "parades," were perambulating the streets headed by bands of music, and carrying transparencies with lights in them, in which the names of different counties, and mottoes, such as Union, Liberty, and Equality, were conspicuously inscribed. Occasionally a man called out with a stentorian voice, "The ticket, the whole ticket, and nothing but the ticket," which was followed by a loud English hurra, while at intervals a single blow was struck on a great drum, as if to imitate the firing of a gun. On their tickets were printed the names of the governor, officers, and members of whom the committee of each party had determined to vote.

The next day on our return to Philadelphia, we found that city also in the ferment of an election, bands of music placed in open carriages, each drawn by four horses, and each horse decorated with a flag, attached to its shoulder, which had a gay effect. All day a great bell tolls at the State house, to remind the electors of their duties. It sounded like a funeral; and on my inquiring of a bystander what it meant, one of the democratic party answered, "It is the knell of the whigs." In their popular addresses, some candidates ask the people whether they will vote for the whigs who will lay on new taxes. As it is well known, that such taxes must be imposed, if the dividends on the State bonds are to be paid, these popular appeals are ominous. The rapid fall in the value of State securities shows that the public generally have no confidence that the majority of the electors will be proof against the insidious arts of these demagogues.

Sir Charles Lyell, *Travels in North America in the Years 1841-42* (New York, 1845), I, pp. 83-84.

2. THE DORR REBELLION

[April 17, 1842]—I was struck with the lively interest he [William Ellery Channing, Unitarian minister, of Boston] took in the political affairs of Rhode Island,—a neighbouring State, containing about 110,000 inhabitants, and now convulsed by a revolutionary movement in favor of an extension of the suffrage. The sympathies of Dr. Channing appeared to lean strongly to the popular party, which, in his opinion, had grievances to complain of, however much, by their violent proceedings, they had put themselves in the wrong.

As some alarmists assured me that the railway to Providence, by which I intended to pass southwards in a few days, "was commanded by the cannon of the insurgents," my curiosity was awakened to inquire into this affair, the details of which were not uninstructive, as giving a curious insight into the character of the New England people, and showing their respect for law and order, even when their passions are highly excited. I found that Rhode Island was still, in the year 1842, governed according to a charter granted by Charles II. in the year 1663, no alteration having been made in the qualifications of voters at the period when the sovereignty was transferred from the crown of Great Britain to the freeholders of Rhode Island. Although the State has been flourishing, and is entirely free from debt, a large majority of the people have, for the last forty years, called loudly on the privileged landholders to give up their exclusive right to voting, and to extend the suffrage to all the adult males, in accordance with the system established in all the neighboring States. The dispute turned mainly on a question of a very abstract nature for the comprehension of the multitude, though in reality one of great constitutional importance; namely, whether the change should be made according to the forms prescribed in charter of 1663, or might be effected by the people in its capacity of sovereign, without regard to any established forms. The latter method was advocated by the democratic leaders as most flattering to the people, and with such success that they organized a formidable association in opposition to the government. Their demands did not differ very materially from those which the legislature was willing to concede, except that the democrats claimed the suffrage, not only for every American-born citizen, but also for the new-comers, or the settlers of a few years' standing. Both parties agreed to exclude the free blacks. At length, as their wishes were not complied with, the "Suffrage Convention" resolved to intimidate their opponents by a military enrollment and drilling, and were soon joined by several companies of militia.

The governor of Rhode Island was so much alarmed as to call on the

Lyell, *Travels in North America*, II, pp. 2-4.

President of the United States to afford him aid, which was declined on the ground that no overt act of violence had been committed. The insurgents then elected a separate senate and house of representatives and one [Thomas W.] Dorr as governor of the State, who proceeded to Washington, and had an interview with the President of the United States and with several members of congress. Meanwhile military preparations were making on both sides. A second appeal was made in vain by the State of Rhode Island for aid from the federal government at Washington. Meetings of sympathizers were held at New York to co-operate with the popular party, who had now obtained some pieces of cannon, and attempted to get possession of the arsenal at Providence. On this occasion, however, the State government called out the militia, who mustered in great force, and, after a bloodless affray, the popular party, which had already dwindled down to a few hundreds, deserted their leader, Dorr. This champion made his escape, but was soon after taken, tried for high treason, and condemned to imprisonment. Before the conclusion of this affair the government at Washington signified their readiness to furnish the required troops, but their offer of aid came late, and the assistance was no longer needed.

The firmness of the Rhode Island legislature under the threats of the armed populace at home, and, what was more formidable, of the sympathizers from without, and the respect shown to constitutional forms by the mass of the people in the midst of this excitement, are circumstances highly creditable to the majority of the citizens. It remains to be seen whether an extension of the suffrage, which was afterwards granted, will promote or impede the cause of freedom and good government in this small State.

A Kentucky Election
George D. Prentice

I have just witnessed a strange thing—a Kentucky election—and am disposed to give you an account of it. An election in Kentucky lasts three
days, and during that period whisky and apple toddy flow through our
cities and villages like the Euphrates through ancient Babylon. I must
do Lexington the justice to say that matters were conducted here with
tolerable propriety; but in Frankfort, a place which I had the curiosity to
visit on the last day of the election, Jacksonism and drunkenness stalked
triumphant—"an unclean pair of lubberly giants." A number of runners,
each with a whisky bottle poking its long neck from his pocket, were
busily employed bribing voters, and each party kept half a dozen bullies
under pay, genuine specimens of Kentucky alligatorism, to flog every
poor fellow who should attempt to vote illegally. A half a hundred of
mortar would scarcely fill up the chinks of the skulls that were broken
on that occasion. I barely escaped myself. One of the runners came up
to me, and slapping me on the shoulder with his right hand, and a whisky
bottle with his left, asked me if I was a voter. "No," said I. "Ah, never
mind," quoth the fellow, pulling a corn cob out of the neck of the bottle,
and shaking it up to the best advantage, "jest take a swig at the cretur
and toss in a vote for old Hickory's boys—I'll fight for you, damme!"
Here was a temptation, to be sure; but after looking alternately at the
bottle and the bullies who were standing ready with their sledge-hammer
fists to knock down all interlopers, my fears prevailed and I lost my
whisky. Shortly after this I witnessed a fight that would have done honor
to Mendoza and Big Ben. A great ruffian-looking scoundrel, with arms
like a pair of cables knotted at the ends, and a round black head that
looked like a forty-pound cannon shot, swaggered up to the polls and
threw in his bit of paper, and was walking off in triumph. "Stop, friend,"
exclaimed one of the Salt River Roarers, stepping deliberately up to him,

Letter from George D. Prentice to a New England paper in 1830, reprinted in
W. H. Perrin, *The Pioneer Newspaper Press of Kentucky* (Louisville, 1888), pp. 77-79.

"are you a voter?" "Yes, by———," replied he of the Bullet Head. "That's a lie," rejoined the Roarer, "and you must just prepare yourself to go home an old man, for I'll be damned if I don't knock you into the middle of your ninety-ninth year." "Ay, ay," replied the other, "come on, then; I'll ride you to hell, whipped up with the sea sarpint!" They had now reached an open space, and the Salt River bully, shaking his fist a moment by way of a feint, dropped his chin suddenly upon his bosom and pitched headforemost toward the stomach of his antagonist with the whole force of his gigantic frame. Bullet Head, however, was on his guard, and, dodging aside with the quickness of lightning to avoid the shock, gave the assailant a blow that sent him staggering against a whisky table, where he fell to the ground amid the crash of bottles, mugs, and tumblers. Nothing daunted by this temporary discomfiture, the bully gathered himself up, and with a single muttered curse renewed his place in front of his foe. Several blows were now given on both sides with tremendous effect, and in a few moments the Salt River boy, watching his opportunity, repeated the maneuver in which he had first been foiled. This time he was successful. His head was planted directly in his antagonist's stomach, who fell backward with such force that I had no expectation of his ever rising again. "Is the scoundrel done for?" inquired the temporary victor, walking up and looking down on his prostrate foe. Bullet Head spoke not, but with the bound of a wildcat leaped to his feet and grappled with his enemy. It was a trial of strength, and the combatants tugged and strained and foamed at the mouth, and twined like serpents around each other's bodies, till at length the strength of the Bullet Head prevailed and his opponent lay struggling beneath him. "Gouge him!" "Gouge him!" exclaimed a dozen voices, and the topmost combatant seized his victim by the hair and was preparing to follow the advice that was thus shouted in his ear, when the prostrate man, roused by desperation and exerting a strength that seemed superhuman, caught his assailant by the throat with a grasp like that of fate. For a few moments the struggle seemed to cease, and then the face of the throttled man turned black, his tongue fell out of his mouth, and he rolled to the ground as senseless as a dead man. I turned away a confirmed believer in the doctrine of total depravity.

A Southern Demagogue
Virginia Clay

Nor should I omit to name the most conspicuous man on that memorable north-bound train, Congressman W. R. W. Cobb, who called himself the "maker of Senators," and whom people called the most successful vote-poller in the State of Alabama. Mr. Cobb resorted to all sorts of tricks to catch the popular votes, such as the rattling of tinware and crockery—he had introduced bills to secure indigent whites from a seizure for debt that would engulf all their possessions, and in them had minutely defined all articles that were to be thus exempt, not scorning to enumerate the smallest items of the kitchen—, and he delighted in the singing of homely songs composed for stump purposes. One of these which he was wont to introduce at the end of a speech, and which always seemed to be especially his own, was called "The Homestead Bill." Of this remarkable composition there were a score of verses, at least, that covered every possible possession which the heart of the poor man might crave, ranging from land and mules to household furniture. The Song began, "Uncle Sam is rich enough to give us all a farm!" and Mr. Cobb would sing it in stentorian tones, winking, as he did so, to first one and then another of his admiring listeners, and punctuating his phrases by chewing, with great gusto, a piece of onion and the coarsest of corn "pone." These evidences of his democracy gave huge delight to the masses, though it aroused in me, a young wife, great indignation, that, in the exigencies of a public career my husband should be compelled to enter a contest with such a man. To me it was the meeting of a Damascus blade and a meat-axe, and in my soul I resented it.

In 1849 this stump-favourite had defeated the brilliant Jere Clemens, then a candidate for Congress, but immediately thereafter Mr. Clemens was named for the higher office of U. S. Senator and elected. In 1853 an exactly similar conjunction of circumstances resulted in the election

Virginia Clay-Clopton, *A Belle of the Fifties*, edited by Ada Sterling (New York, 1905), pp. 21-22.

of Mr. Clay [her husband, Clement C. Clay, Jr.]. I accompanied my
husband during the canvass in which he [Cobb] was defeated, and
thereby became, though altogether innocently, the one obstacle to Mr.
Cobb's usually unanimous election.

It happened that during the campaign Mr. Clay and I stopped at a
little hostelry, that lay in the very centre of one of Mr. Cobb's strongest
counties. It was little more than a flower-embowered cottage, kept by
"Aunt Hannah," a kindly soul, whose greatest treasure was a fresh-faced,
pretty daughter, then entering her "teens." I returned to our room after
a short absence, just in time to see this village beauty before my mirror,
arrayed in all the glory of a beautiful and picturesque hat which I had
left upon the bed during my absence. It was a lovely thing of the period,
which I had but recently brought back from the North, having purchased it while *en route* for Doctor Wesslhoeft's Hydropathic Institute
in Brattleboro, Vermont.

The little rustic girl of Alabama looked very winsome and blossomy
in the pretty gew-gaw, and I asked her impulsively if she liked it. Her
confusion was sufficient answer, and I promptly presented it to her, on
condition that she would give me her sunbonnet in return.

The exchange was quickly made, and when Mr. Clay and I departed
I wore a pea-green cambric bonnet, lined with pink and stiffened with
pasteboard slats. I little dreamed that this exchange of millinery, so
unpremeditated, and certainly uncalculating, was a political master-
stroke; but, so it proved. It undermined Mr. Cobb's Gibraltar; for at
the election that followed, the vote in that county was practically solid
for Mr. Clay, where formerly Mr. Cobb had swept it clean.

PART II

THE POLITICIANS IN WASHINGTON

Jackson's powerful and partisan personality tended to polarize American national politics. One group of political leaders supported him on the "whole hog" principle, while the opposition, a heterogeneous group which after 1834 was called the Whigs, did not have a single leader but rather three masterful factional leaders—Clay, Calhoun, and Webster. The setting of their partisan struggles—their debates and orations— was far from heroic. A Methodist minister of Illinois, William H. Milburn, who was elected chaplain of Congress in the 1840's, has described in his reminiscences the informality of the Senate Chamber—the undignified conduct of legislators and the seamy side of Congress. The British phrenologist, George Combe, attempted to read the character of some of the senators by observing the configuration of their skulls. A great advocate of proper ventilation, he was shocked by the disregard of this health measure by the senators as well as disgusted by the widespread habit of tobacco chewing. Mrs. Basil Hall expressed a similar disgust for the filthy American habit and, besides, she thought American society was very crude in its social diversions.

The leading politicians of Washington are portrayed here by a young Virginian, Lucian Minor, who stopped by Washington on his way to New England and in his journal left an account of the political leaders he observed. A cultivated young southerner, he was very fair-minded in his judgments; later he became a professor of law at William and Mary College. The personalities of the government in Washington are sketched with refreshing piquancy by Harriet Martineau, an English intellectual who visited America in 1834-36 and wrote an intelligent and entertaining account of her experiences. She was highly prejudiced against slavery, and her portrait of Calhoun seems to have been strongly colored accordingly by this prejudice. Handicapped by partial deafness, she used a large ear trumpet with which she carried on her interviews, nevertheless, she was very observant and had a keen intelligence that gives value to her report on America and its people.

Francis J. Grund's account of the Washington politicians represents the view of a very well-educated Austrian, who liked Americans—but was surprised to see arising in the United States an aristocracy based on

63

wealth to challenge the egalitarian ideas of American society. His view of Calhoun was almost diametrically opposed to that of Miss Martineau. Van Buren also stands out very favorably in his pages as a sincere democrat, and not a supple intriguer.

The greatest debate that has occurred, perhaps, in the United States Senate between two individual senators was the Webster-Hayne debate of 1830. It was really a debate between sections, a precursor of the great debate that resulted in the Compromise of 1850. It is noticeable in Robert Scott's account of this debate that Hayne is one of the earliest southern leaders to maintain in Congress that slavery was morally and politically justified, that Scott, a Kentuckian, regarded himself as a westerner, and not a southerner, that he continually referred to the North as "the East," and that his sympathies in this debate were with Webster and not Hayne, the spokesman of the South.

A Squeezy Party

Margaret Hall

January 25 [1828, Washington]—Well, a great dinner is a very long business at any time, and to-day I have assisted, as the French say, at one of the very biggest, a great reunion of all the *Corps Diplomatique* at the President's. Thirty persons at least, O dear, I should dislike much to be obliged to give such huge dinners. I tire so much sitting so long. I had my former luck of the deaf Baron de Krudener [the Russian Ambassador]; however, I tried speaking low and found that I succeeded admirably. On the other side I had Chevalier Huygens, the Dutch Minister, who is a very intelligent person. All the foreigners were in their dress coats, and you cannot imagine how gay the assemblage looked to eyes that have been accustomed for so many months to the blackness and badness and slovenliness of American dress.

We went to a particularly squeezy party at Mr. Southard's, the Secretary of the Navy. Those heads of departments are obliged to ask all the rag-tag and bob-tail, so that their parties are really anything but agreeable, more especially as their houses, generally speaking, are so low-roofed, and then the spitting! O the spitting! It seems to increase daily. One night lately as I was walking upstairs to valse my partner began clearing his throat. This I thought ominous. However, I said to myself, "Surely he will turn his head to the other side." The gentleman, however, had no such thought but deliberately shot across me. I had not courage to examine whether or not the result landed in the flounce of my dress.

Margaret (Mrs. Basil) Hall, *The Aristocratic Journey*, pp. 64-68.

The Informality of Congress
William Henry Milburn

The first effect of life in Washington for a young enthusiast is that of disenchantment; and he must become familiarized with the routine of business and inured to the commonplaces and platitudes of speeches for "Buncombe," before he is thoroughly prepared to enjoy the gladiatorship of the Capitol. It was mortifying enough to see an honorable representative or senator speaking to "a beggarly account of empty boxes," while even such of his colleagues as were present seemed to treat him and his discourse with utter contempt, engaged as they were in writing, reading newspapers, chatting jovially, or even lunching. Few speeches in Congress have any effect upon Congress itself; nevertheless, there is scarcely one delivered which is not productive of good results. A nation that has assumed the awful responsibility of self-government needs abundant instruction. The abstract doctrines of political science can have little interest or weight with the masses of the people. They have neither the education nor the powers of reflection to appreciate or apply them.

They must be addressed on their own level, and while their plane should be an ever ascending one, the politicians must meet them on the common ground of their capacities. If the majority of the nation are fitly represented by the inhabitants of Buncombe County, North Carolina, of necessity the greater part of our political eloquence must be of the Buncombe order. I fancy that the reason why our public speaking has assumed a lower range of discussion, and a less finished style, is that the audience in the Republic has become wider and less select. In the days of Hamilton, Jay, and Jefferson, public opinion was created by a few men, and Congress represented an oligarchy. But now the multitude claims its rights.

William Henry Milburn, *Ten Years of Preacher-Life* (New York, 1860), pp. 124-125.

A Phrenologist's View of the Senators

George Combe

Feb. 20. Ther. 29°. This morning we proceeded to the Capitol. In approaching it, I could not help feeling ashamed of the barbarism of my countrymen, who in the war of 1814 consigned it to the flames. The external walls have been painted white to obliterate the smoky traces of that unworthy deed. The grand vestibule is under the dome, and has no opening upwards to allow of the escape of air. The consequence is, that the effluvia of human bodies and of tobacco-juice greet the nostrils and afflict the lungs the moment it is entered. We found also that the senate chamber and House of Representatives are, in this weather, hermetically sealed; except at the doors and chimneys. Although these may provide some change of air for the members, who are all accommodated on the floor, the unhappy visiters in the galleries receive all the vitiated air from below, render it worse by their own breathing, and are nearly doomed to suffocation. The ladies are accommodated with the front seat, and occasionally faint from the impurity of the atmosphere. I sat three hours in the gallery of the senate chamber to-day, and afterwards experienced those debilitating, irritable, and unpleasant sensations which are generated by imperfectly decarbonised blood.

Mr. Calhoun of South Carolina spoke two or three times. He seemed to be about sixty, tall and slender, and of a highly bilious and nervous temperament. The lower ridge of his forehead projects much, indicating great powers of observation, but the superior ridge devoted to reflection, is much smaller. Although the latter region looks narrow and retreating, yet there is enough of brain to give average power to his reflecting faculties. He has very large Self-Esteem and Firmness. The head indicates much self-will and determination: great powers of perseverance; a capacity for details, but little profound judgment.

I saw also Mr. Clay, but he did not speak. He is nearly bald. The

George Combe, *Notes on the United States of America during a Phrenological Visit in 1839-40* (New York, 1842), I, pp. 271-272.

anterior lobe of his brain is long and high, the middle perpendicular portion predominating. He seems to have large Acquisitiveness and considerable Ideality. In him also Self-Esteem and Firmness are large. The coronal region rises moderately high above Cautiousness and Causality, and the head altogether is high and long, rather than broad. It is of ample size. His temperament is nervous-sanguine, with a little bilious. He is tall and slender; and apparently between 60 and 70. This combination indicates great natural vivacity, readiness of apprehension, facility of illustration, with force of character; but there are two defects in the brain which will prevent such an individual from rising to the first class of minds. Causality and the moral organs do not present the highest degree of development. Men thus constituted do not sufficiently appreciate the influence of the moral sentiments as a natural *power*, nor do they trace the causes with which they deal, to their first elements, nor follow them to their remote consequences. Mr. Clay's head, however, bespeaks a man greatly above an average in point of mental power, and also practical in his tendencies; and therefore well adapted to the general American mind of the present day.

Here, also, sits Daniel Webster, looking like an intellectual giant among the senators. His enormous anterior lobe, and generally large head, reinforced by large lungs, mark him as a natural leader; but his reflective organs are too much developed in proportion to his Individuality to render his eloquence equally popular with that of Henry Clay. Mr. Webster needs a great subject, involving a profound principle and important consequences, before his strength can be called forth. Give him these, and he will rise to the highest eminence as a pleader and a statesman; but his intellect is too profound and comprehensive to be fully appreciated by the people. On seeing the man, therefore, I am not surprised at a circumstance which I have remarked, that, while Mr. Webster is regarded by a few as *the* great political character of the United States, Mr. Clay has at least a hundred devoted followers for each one of Mr. Webster's admirers. Webster, however, like Burke, will be quoted for the depth of principle and wisdom involved in his speeches, when the more fascinating but less profound orations of Mr. Clay have sunk into oblivion.

I heard Mr. Cuthbert, senator for Georgia, make a long speech on a bill for preventing the officers of government from interfering in elections. He is a slow and forcible, but not a refined speaker.

The appearance of the members of the senate is favorable. With few exceptions, their brains, and especially the organs of the intellectual faculties, are large, while there is a good average development of the organs of the moral sentiments. Collectively, they seemed to me to be a highly respectable and gifted body of men.

A Kentucky Lawyer Hears the Webster-Hayne Debate

Robert Scott

Jan. 26, 1830. Attended the Senate to hear Mr Webster reply to Mr Hayne of S. Carolina who had spoken on the day previous & then concluded a long & animated speech, commenced a few days previous and being a part of a debate arising out of a Resolution introduced by Mr Foot of Connecticut to enquire into the expediency of suspending the surveys of public land & abolishing a land office, it being suspected that the final effect of the Resolution might be to discourage emigration to the West, it was warmly opposed by Mr Benton . . . accusing the East of entertaining feelings hostile to the prosperity of the West. Mr Hayne soon after made a speech on the same side in which he lost sight of the resolution, the drift of his speech being to show that the East had been hostile while the South had been favourable, referring to many acts of the Eastern legislatures & of their representations in congress & also many acts of the Southern Legislature & Southern Reps. in Congress to prove his position. The question thus having become whether the South or East was most partial to Western interest, Mr Webster rose in vindication of N England particularly of Massachusetts, showing by argument that Southern policy opposes the Western interest while that of N. England fostered, he, like Mr Hayne, speaking highly in praise of the western states, from which a stranger might have supposed that the west was in market & was to be bought by extravagant compliments, the East & South being the bidders. This speech of Mr Webster was extempore & of about an hours length, was followed in a short speech by Mr Benton, he rising arrogantly & presumptuously as the champion of the West, disclaiming the alleged partiality & rejecting the profered kindness of the East. By this time the question again began to change, the propriety of negro slavery, the policy of the tariff & constitutionality of congress making roads & now coming before the views of the speakers,

Robert Scott, *Memorandum of My Journey to the East in 1829-30.* Ms. owned by Mrs. S. I. M. Major, Versailles, Ky. Microfilm in University of Kentucky Library.

Mr Hayne again replied to Mr Webster in a speech two days long &
saturday and sunday intervening between the first & second parts of it
giving time to prepare & me an opportunity of describing his person,
manners, etc.

Robert Y. Hayne Senator of South Carolina looks to be about 38 or
40 years of age, in fact much older, about 6 feet high & well proportioned person, neither delicate or corpulent, he is genteel in dress &
personal appearance, his complexion rather dark, his countenance open
and youthful, rather prepossessing yet showing no marks of superior
greatness, his head of good proportion, his hair black entire, a little grey,
worn with considerable care & attention, combed toward his face &
forehead in front, combed up over the forehead & turned over to the
right with much care, his forehead is high & broad, his eye brows dark
and smooth, his eye round tolerably full & hazle, his nose of good
size & straight, his cheeks of proper fullness & without whiskers, having
little beard, his mouth & chin of common size & appearance, the latter
a little dimpled & having but little beard, his whole face is rather long
than broad & rather handsome than great or intelligent. He is married
& has several children. In speaking his tones are loud & animated his
voice being full & strong, his chief gesture is with his right hand, the
elbow being lifted higher than the shoulders or hand in an ungraceful
manner; his emphasis & modulation are generally good except at the
close of sentences when they are whining & disagreeable and though
studied are unnatural, his language is chaste & grammatical, on the
whole he may be truly called a good speaker. In the last speech he justified southern men & measures vindicated african slavery in the south
as morally & politically justified, censured the Tariff as obnoxious & unconstitutional, assailed the East as wanting patriotism in [the] last war
in refusing loans to [the] government, spoke of the treaty concerning the
navigation of the Mississippi, the embargo, the Hartford Convention &
the "Coalition of 1825" charging the East as wanting to sever the Union
at one time & to "consolidate" it at another, vindicating his own political
course & consistency & assailing that of Mr Webster with some acrimony
& personality. The debate in the mean time turning upon the consistency
of the litigating parties & the sections & states which they represented
& the policy they advocate, & their loyalty to the Union & desire for the
general welfare, debate all the time rising in importance & becoming
more animated & personal. He concluded his remarks yesterday & this
morning a dense crowd of the most respectable gentlemen & ladies assembled as on yesterday, crowded the floor & galleries, the ladies oust-
ing the senators & besieging the speakers chair. They listened for two
hours & a half to Mr Webster in the grandest & most interesting specimen of parliamentary eloquence which it has ever been my good

fortune to hear. Like Hayne, Benton, & others, he spoke from notes previously prepared: while taking them yesterday the unusual redness of his face evinced excitement, but this morning he appeared calm, & rising proceeded in a temperate & calm yet firm & dignified manner to defend himself & his country & to assail his antagonist with the most ingenious satire & penetrating & cutting sarcasm, refuting his facts & attacking & subverting his arguments; his manner & countenance now sickening as from disgust & contempt, now smiling in ridicule, now fired by his subject, his countenance brightened while his attitude & voice rose with eloquence the most impassioned & convicting. After replying to some personal remarks in which he said that the Bow of the hon. member was too weak to send an arrow to his breast, he alluded to the wide range which he had taken, having said something about every thing else but the subject under consideration, referred to the Resolution & then proceeded to vindicate his course during the debate, then the policy & acts of his state, showing that the tariff policy originated in the South & that Mr Hayne once supported it, etc.

Jan. 27. Mr Webster concluded his speech in the most convincing argument & forcible eloquence. His remarks chiefly related to the nature of our government, & were intended to show the impropriety & unconstitutionality of a State resisting the Gen. Govt. & closed in appropriate & eloquent terms invoking Union, happiness & glory upon our common country.

Mr Hayne made a short & forcible reply, the debate all the time assuming a more amicable cast. Mr Webster again spoke a few moments & the Senate adjourned.

The Politicians as Seen by a Young Virginian

Lucian Minor

Wednesday, June 18, 1834. From the wharf at Washington, an omnibus, capable of 24, carried 15 of us into the city—me to Gadsby's Hotel—the rest elsewhere.—It was nearly 6 p. m. yet flags on the Capitol showed both Houses to be still sitting. So strolled thither. Met the Senators coming out. But in the H. of R. was a debate, in which a Mr. Beaty of Ky. and Bailie Peyton of Tennessee spoke: Beaty a speech poorly written, badly spoken, and worse listened to;—Peyton, plain good sense, in a homely, but forcible style, which gained him 10 times the hearers.— Saw my late representative, Patton. At the hotel, found Mr. Calhoun in the bar-room. Shook hands with him, in virtue of an acquaintance formed here last winter. He seemed not to recollect me quite; but carried it smoothly, as if he did. Asked about public sentiment in my part of Virginia; and only gave a slight, sardonic laugh, when told that the late course of Administration had produced few or no changes against Jackson. Last winter, I had brought him (he then said) the first news of any portion of Virginia's approving the removal of the Deposites. He and his clique had then appeared civilly skeptical of my report. It was but a few weeks after, that it was confirmed by unquestionable demonstrations from nearly all parts of the Commonwealth. The sneer now seems less of incredulity than of scorn for the man-worshipping subserviency of our people. He tells me the Senate will to-morrow take up the subject of indemnity to our citizens for French spoliations—those committed before 1800—not the subject of Mr. Rives' right able and successful, tho' well nigh frustrate negotiation.

Thursday, June 19. Dressed early, for a walk: and in the bar-room met Mr. Calhoun again, who had just called in from *his* morning's walk. Introduced me to a major—(I could not catch the name) with whom he

Lucian Minor, "A Virginian in New England Thirty-five Years Ago," edited by James Russell Lowell, *Atlantic Monthly*, XXVI (Sept., 1870), pp. 336-339.

was conversing; and I left them. Went to Fuller's Hotel, in hopes of breakfasting with my lady fellow-passengers of yesterday—and of seeing Mr. Gurley, champion and secretary of the Colonization Society, who lived there at my last visit. But he had removed thence. Saw Mr. Bowman. The ladies were not there, though the guestbook said they were. Called at the Colon. Office, neither Mr. Gurley nor Mr. Fendall there. After breakfast, saw Miss ——— and her companion, Miss ——— in the stage, bound for Baltimore. Hardly time for 'good morning,' before off it went.

To Senate chamber at 11. Admission to the Lobby, on the Senate floor, through Mr. Clay's means. At 12, Mr. Van Buren as Vice-President, took the chair—calling to order by raps with an ivory something upon his table. Mr. Hatch, the spruce chaplain, said a prayer shorter than some graces before meat; and business began. A Report from the Secretary of the Senate, reckoning up the number of memorialists about the Bank and the Deposite question, gave rise to some happy cutting and thrusting between Messrs. Clay and Forsyth. Mr. Webster, Mr. Leigh, Mr. Chambers, and Mr. Poindexter were all up for a few moments. Mr. Forsyth has for some time had to stand foremost here, almost alone, as defender of the Administration; and has done so with singular success, considering the overwhelming reputations and abilities arrayed against him. With a smile perpetually on his lips, they launch forth sarcasms of unmatched keenness, and ofttimes arguments of hardly matched power. Poindexter's colleague, Black,—very youthful in look: and, if I rightly 'read the mind's construction in the face,' no more senatorial in wisdom than in years: one of the many bubbles borne onward, aloft, by the billowy tide of Party-excitement. Sprague of Maine, a right intellectual looking, spare man, who too much affects the tragical, in his oratory. His gesture is palpably, and awkwardly, copied from the introduction and plates to Scott's Lessons, or Enfield's Speaker. For the life of him, he cannot hold his hand or bend his arm naturally or gracefully. Tyler—Old Virginia forever! He has no great measure, or force, of intellect: but for a bland, persuasive manner,—I speak of tone, head-and-hand gesture, turn of period, and winningness of words and thought—Gov. T. has not his superior in the Senate. Clayton of Delaware—how fallacious a guide physiognomy is! If nature has written *nihil* on any front here, it is upon his, when he is not roused by any mental spur. Yet he is a second-rate, at least, in a body where to be 4th rate is no mean praise—and at the head of the Delaware Bar.

Mr. Calhoun was up for five or ten minutes, upon his own motion to postpone the French-spoliation Bill until the next session. His grounds were, its vast importance,—the questions, not only of individual claims against our government, but of international right, which it involved—

the immense sum (probably $5,000,000) of which it contemplated the expenditure—the diversified and momentous bearings of those questions and that expenditure, upon the yet smouldering fires of the scarcely adjusted Tariff controversy—and the extreme temerity, not to say madness, of taking up a subject of such varied and awful import just at the close of a session, when the detailed examination and discussion it would require were absolutely impossible.—I never heard him in public before —never had a precise idea of his peculiar sort of power. He is one of the purest of originals. Nothing can be more unique than his style, of diction and delivery. Heedless of words, he yet pours out the most apt and forcible in a torrent. Not one superfluous—his sentences are pared of every redundancy. So rapid seem his conceptions, that his tongue (though of extraordinary volubility) cannot mould them into language fast enough —they crowd and choak the vent, like water poured from a narrow-necked bottle. Hence perhaps a vicious habit, of clipping his words. The torrent is not a smooth, continuous one. Ever and anon there was a dead pause; evidently not for lack of matter, but at once to breathe himself amid the intensity of his mental exercitation, and to give his hearers time to ponder what he had uttered. Very little gesture—his hands generally stretched at arms' length down his sides, only now and then raised and put forward, to strengthen the emphasis upon some burning thought, or some flooring argument. I have somewhere seen—it is in Combe's Phrenology—a masterly delineation of a powerful debater's mind, whose 'words fall, like minute-guns, upon the ear'; his faculties acting, at first, 'slowly, but deeply, like the first heave of a mountain-wave.' But Mr. Calhoun's first onset is the storm itself: at once deep, strong, impetuous, overwhelming. Instead of minute guns, a running broadside would best typify the rapidity of his utterance: gun succeeding gun, as fast as thought, till one side is discharged; and then after a moment's pause, the other side brought to bear with equally fatal effect. Each word—at least each sentence—is a twenty-four pounder, and each paragraph a broadside. He looked mostly, not at the presiding officer, whom Order requires him to address,—but at Mr. Webster, whose arguments he was answering. His lofty port, his mind-quelling eye, his self-assured look of conscious truth and conscious power, and his resistless argumentation, held him forth incontestably the master-spirit of the assembly.—Van! little Van!—he is not to be named in the same day—I am ashamed of bringing him into the same page—with Calhoun. Yet there is no denying that he bids fair to reach the highest place first. Animals that crawl as well as those which fly, attain, the loftiest elevations: and it may well happen, if the eagle's wing be crippled, or if unworthy obstacles retard him, that he may be outstript by the caterpillar.

Isaac Hill is diminutive in person, as in morals; and limps in his gait, from some accident, or natural deformity. He has always been writing, when I have seen him in the Senate; commonly, letters—in a large, engrossing hand—so large, that I have read several words of one, from the gallery over his head. To-day, he was correcting the proof of a newspaper. Wonder if it was the N. H. Patriot, or a speech of his own, or one of his editorials in the Globe?—Isaac has a strongly marked physiognomy,—a large and not ill formed forehead, black eyes, and an expression of countenance intelligent enough, but ominous of nothing good.

The colossal bronze statue, meant for Mr. Jefferson, brought by Lt. Levy from Paris, and given to Congress, stands in the great Rotunda of the Capitol. Not a good likeness, by any means. Too broad-shouldered, and too stout every way. The color, nearly black, conveys unpleasing associations. Some Southerner the other day swore, that it ought to be tossed out of the Capitol; for, said he, "by G .. it makes old Tom a negro!"

Some pictures were exhibiting in the Rotunda: said to be master-pieces, of eminent artists. I could not understand the plots, or discern the merits, of most.—Col. Crockett and some ladies were looking at them, and at the statue. The Col. played the tame bear very quietly, for the ladies; and seemed to be a pet. I was disappointed at finding him so tame. He should always appear in character—i. e. with hunting shirt and tomahawk—moccasins and leggings of deerskin with the hair on. As it is, he looks like any Christian: you would never suppose him to be the man what can wade the Mississippi, tote a steamboat, whip his weight in wild-cats, grin the bark off an oak-knot,—swim further, dive deeper, and come out drier, than any other man in the Western District.

In the H. of R. a debate of no consequence was going forward, in which C. Fenton Mercer, and Mr. Marshall of Kentucky, spoke. The latter is a young man—fluent and bold, as what Kentuckian is not? The former—oh, what a falling off, since I heard him in the Va. Convention, 1829! It is impossible now not to be struck with the slight attention paid him. His silver voice and pretty oratory, once so admired, could not command a quorum of listeners, tho' the House was full. His voice, formerly all music, verges upon a cracked treble. But his weight of character has chiefly gone, from his being reputed a visionary.—The yeas and nays chancing to be called, the clerk, Franklin, ran them over with such incredible speed, that I could not catch more than one in three—though reasonably familiar with them. How the owners could recognize each his own, when thus rattled off, is hard to say.

Adjourned before the House. On the way home, saw several beggars— would not give them 'a single sous.' Called on Mr. Moncure Robinson (Engineer) at Brown's Hotel. We walked out: and on returning, whom should we meet at the Hotel door but Mr. W. Pope of Powhatan—Uncle Billy! he 'of infinite jest'—whose gibes, whose gambols, whose 'songs, whose flashes of merriment' so 'wont to set the table in a roar,' I have so often roared at with the rest!—But this evening he seems lifeless.

Have removed to Mrs. McDaniel's boarding house, where Messrs. Patton and Gordon stay, and where the latter had arranged for my lodging, before I came. Miss G., and the Miss McD.'s—the latter, Catholics. Gov. Tyler, Moore of Rockbridge, and Col. Davenport of Pittsylvania, are also of the mess. Had a two hours' confab with Patton. Verily, he seems to me the most rational and independent man in Washington.— He thinks that Mr. Clay's friends give plain tokens of a design to cease maintaining the constitutionality of Internal Improvements. And now I bethink me, something like it was manifested by Mr. Marshall, in his speech to-day. Whether principle or policy be the motive, the change will be a good one for state-rights.

To bed at 12.

Friday, June 20. Up at 5.—On my walk along Pennsa. Avenue, met Mr. Calhoun. Gen. G. was with me. While we were talking, Campbell P. White came up—the Irish representative from the city of N. Y. He is a merchant—said to be an adept in the mysteries of commerce, exchange, Banking, &c. Next to Cambreleng, he is the foremost administration-member from the city. Stoutly built, with a broad, English face, but Irish mouth and accent.

At ½ past 8, off for Baltimore. Mr. Calvert's estate, 4 or 5 miles from Washington: mansion house, and porter's lodges at outer gate—All symptomatic of great wealth. Descendant of Calvert, Ld. Baltimore. Remarkable, that so much hereditary wealth should have descended to the 3d or 4th generation. Primogeniture abolished in Md. 1786.

Bladensburg—miserable, decayed village, on the Eastern Branch. The Battle ground is much flatter than I had supposed. The driver—I sit outside always, when it is practicable—shewed me where our militia valiantly awaited the enemy, till they came within little more than a quarter of a mile; and then—the Bladensburg races began. The Bridge, defended by Barney and his marines, does not look like an advantageous post. There seem several far more defensible, within a mile, than either that, or the militia station.—Country onward from Bladensburg to Baltimore, old Virginia over again. Gullies, red hillsides, bare of soil— broom-sedge—persimmon, sassafras, and stunted oak—rickety, ineffectual worm-fences—blue-birds, bee-martins, and red-headed woodpeckers— gave me a vivid reminiscence of my poor, good old commonwealth.

The Politicians as Seen by an English Bluestocking

Harriet Martineau

We arrived at Washington on the 13th of January, 1835, the year of the short session of Congress which closes on the 4th of March, so that we continued to see the proceedings of Congress at its busiest and most interesting time.

It is in Washington that varieties of manners are conspicuous. There the Southerners appear to the most advantage, and the New-Englanders to the least; the ease and frank courtesy of the gentry of the South (with an occasional touch of arrogance, however) contrasting favourably with the cautious, somewhat *gauche,* and too deferential air of the members from the North. One fancies one can tell a New-England member in the open air by his deprecatory walk. He seems to bear in mind perpetually that he cannot fight a duel, while other people can. The odd mortals that wander in from the western border cannot be described as a class, for no one is like anybody else. One has a neck like a crane, making an interval of inches between stock and chin. Another wears no cravat, apparently because there is no room for one. A third has his lank black hair parted accurately down the middle, and disposed in bands in front, so that he is taken for a woman when only the head is seen in a crowd. A fourth puts an arm round the neck of a neighbour on either side as he stands, seeming afraid of his tall wirehung frame dropping to pieces if he tries to stand alone; a fifth makes something between a bow and a courtesy to everybody who comes near, and proses with a knowing air: all having shrewd faces, and being probably very fit for the business they come upon.

Our pleasantest evenings were some spent at home in a society of the highest order. Ladies, literary, fashionable, or domestic, would spend an hour with us on their way from a dinner or to a ball. Members of Congress would repose themselves by our fireside. Mr. Clay, sitting upright on the sofa, with his snuffbox ever in his hand, would discourse for

Harriet Martineau, *Retrospect of Western Travel* (London, 1838), I, pp. 143-182.

many an hour in his even, soft, deliberate tone, on any one of the great subjects of American policy which we might happen to start, always amazing us with the moderation of estimate and speech which so impetuous a nature has been able to attain. Mr. Webster, leaning back at his ease, telling stories, cracking jokes, shaking the sofa with burst after burst of laughter, or smoothly discoursing to the perfect felicity of the logical part of one's constitution, would illuminate an evening now and then. Mr. Calhoun, the cast-iron man, who looks as if he had never been born and never could be extinguished, would come in sometimes to keep our understandings upon a painful stretch for a short while, and leave us to take to pieces his close, rapid, theoretical, illustrated talk, and see what we could make of it. We found it usually more worth retaining as a curiosity than as either very just or useful. His speech abounds in figures, truly illustrative, if that which they illustrate were but true also. But his theories of government (almost the only subject on which his thoughts are employed), the squarest and compactest that ever were made, are composed out of limited elements, and are not, therefore, likely to stand service very well. It is at first extremely interesting to hear Mr. Calhoun talk; and there is a never-failing evidence of power in all he says and does which commands intellectual reverence; but the admiration is too soon turned into regret, into absolute melancholy. It is impossible to resist the conviction that all this force can be at best but useless, and is but too likely to be very mischievous. His mind has long lost all power of communicating with any other. I know of no man who lives in such utter intellectual solitude. He meets men, and harangues them by the fireside as in the Senate; he is wrought like a piece of machinery, set a going vehemently by a weight, and stops while you answer; he either passes by what you say, or twists it into a suitability with what is in his head, and begins to lecture again. Of course, a mind like this can have little influence in the Senate, except by virtue, perpetually wearing out, of what it did in its less eccentric days; but its influence at home is to be dreaded. There is no hope that an intellect so cast in narrow theories will accommodate itself to varying circumstances; and there is every danger that it will break up all that it can, in order to remould the materials in its own way. Mr. Calhoun is as full as ever of his nullification doctrines; and those who know the force that is in him, and his utter incapacity of modification by other minds (after having gone through as remarkable a revolution of political opinion as perhaps any man ever experienced), will no more expect repose and self-retention from him than from a volcano in full force. Relaxation is no longer in the power of his will. I never saw any one who so completely gave me the idea of possession. Half an hour's conversation with him is enough to make a necessarian of anybody. Accordingly, he is more complained of than blamed by his enemies. His moments of softness in his family, and when recurring to old college days, are hailed by all as a relief to the vehement working of the intellectual machine; a relief equally to himself and others. Those moments are as touching to the observer as tears on the face of a soldier.

One incident befell during my stay which moved everybody. A representative from South Carolina was ill, a friend of Mr. Calhoun's; and Mr. Calhoun parted from us one day, on leaving the Capitol, to visit this sick gentleman. The physician told Mr. Calhoun on his entrance that his friend was dying, and could not live more than a very few hours. A visiter, not knowing this, asked the sick man how he was. "To judge by my own feelings," said he, "much better; but by the countenances of my friends, not." And he begged to be told the truth. On hearing it, he instantly beckoned Mr. Calhoun to him, and said, "I hear they are giving you rough treatment in the Senate. Let a dying friend implore you to guard your looks and words so as that no undue warmth may make you appear unworthy of your principles." "This was friendship, strong friendship," said Mr. Calhoun to me and to many others; and it had its due effect upon him. A few days after, Colonel Benton, a fantastic senator from Missouri, interrupted Mr. Calhoun in a speech, for the purpose of making an attack upon him, which would have been insufferable if it had not been too absurdly worded to be easily made anything of. He was called to order; this was objected to; the Senate divided upon the point of order, being dissatisfied with the decision of the chair; in short, Mr. Calhoun sat for two full hours hearing his veracity talked about before his speech could proceed. He sat in stern patience, scarcely moving a muscle the whole time; and, when it was all settled in his favour, merely observed that his friends need not fear his being disturbed by an attack of this nature from such a quarter, and resumed his speech at the precise point where his argument had been broken off. It was great, and would have satisfied the "strong friendship" of his departed comrade if he could have been there to see it.

Our active-minded, genial friend, Judge Story, found time to visit us frequently, though he is one of the busiest men in the world; writing half a dozen great law-books every year; having his full share of the business of the Supreme Court upon his hands; his professorship to attend to; the District Courts at home in Massachusetts, and a correspondence which spreads half over the world. His talk would gush out for hours, and there was never too much of it for us; it is so heartfelt, so lively, so various; and his face all the while, notwithstanding his gray hair, showing all the mobility and ingenuousness of a child's. There is no tolerable portrait of Judge Story, and there never will be. I should like to bring him face to face with a person who entertains the common English idea of how an American looks and behaves. I should like to see what such a one would make of the quick smiles, the glistening eye, the gleeful tone, with passing touches of sentiment; the innocent self-complacency, the confiding, devoted affections of the great American lawyer. The preconception would be totally at fault.

With Judge Story sometimes came the man to whom he looked up with feelings little short of adoration—the aged Chief-justice Marshall. There was almost too much mutual respect in our first meeting; we knew something of his individual merits and services; and he maintained through life, and carried to his grave, a reverence for woman as rare in its kind as in its degree. It had all the theoretical fervour and magnificence of Uncle Toby's, with the advantage of being grounded upon an extensive knowledge of the sex. He was the father and the grandfather of women; and out of this experience he brought, not only the love and pity which their offices and position command, and the awe of purity which they excite in the minds of the pure, but a steady conviction of their intellectual equality with men; and, with this, a deep sense of their social injuries. Throughout life he so invariably sustained their cause, that no indulgent libertine dared to flatter and humour; no skeptic, secure in the possession of power, dared to scoff at the claims of woman in the presence of Marshall, who, made clearsighted by his purity, knew the sex far better than either.

How delighted we were to see Judge Story bring in the tall, majestic, brighteyed old man! old by chronology, by the lines on his composed face, and by his services to the republic; but so dignified, so fresh, so present to the time, that no feeling of compassionate consideration for age dared to mix with the contemplation of him. The first evening he asked me much about English politics, and especially whether the people were not fast ripening for the abolition of our religious establishment; an institution which, after a long study of it, he considered so monstrous in principle, and so injurious to true religion in practice, that he could not imagine that it could be upheld for anything but political purposes. There was no prejudice here on account of American modes being different; for he observed that the clergy were there, as elsewhere, far from being in the van of society, and lamented the existence of much fanaticism in the United States; but he saw the evils of an establishment the more clearly, not the less, from being aware of the faults in the administration of religion at home. The most animated moment of our conversation was when I told him I was going to visit Mr. Madison on leaving Washington. He instantly sat upright in his chair, and with beaming eyes began to praise Mr. Madison. Madison received the mention of Marshall's name in just the same manner; yet these men were strongly opposed in politics, and their magnanimous appreciation of each other underwent no slight or brief trial.

Judge Porter sometimes came, a hearty friend, and much like a fellow-countryman, though he was a senator of the United States, and had previously been, for fourteen years, Judge of the Supreme Court of Louisiana. He was Irish by birth. His father was vindictively executed, with cruel haste, under martial law, in the Irish rebellion; and the sons were sent by their noble-minded mother to America, where Alexander, the eldest, has thus raised himself into a station of high honour. Judge Porter's warmth, sincerity, generosity, knowledge, and wit are the pride of his constituents, and very ornamental to the Senate. What their charm is by the fireside may be imagined.

Such are only a few among a multitude whose conversation filled up the few evenings we spent at home. Among the pleasantest visits we paid were dinners at the president's, at the houses of heads of departments, at the British legation, and at the Southern members' congressional mess. We highly enjoyed our dinings at the British legation, where we felt ourselves at home among our countrymen. Once, indeed, we were invited to help to do the honours as English ladies to the seven Judges of the Supreme Court, and seven great lawyers besides, when we had the merriest day that could well be. Mr. Webster fell chiefly to my share, and there is no merrier man than he; and Judge Story would enliven a dinner-table at Pekin. One laughable peculiarity at the British legation was the confusion of tongues among the servants, who ask you to take fish, flesh, and fowl in Spanish, Italian, German, Dutch, Irish, or French. The foreign ambassadors are terribly plagued about servants. No American will wear livery, and there is no reason why any American should. But the British ambassador must have livery servants. He makes what compromise he can, allowing his people to appear without livery out of doors except on state occasions; but yet he is obliged to pick up his domestics from among foreigners who are in want of a subsistence for a short time, and are sure to go away as soon as they can find any employment in which the wearing a livery is not requisite. The woes of this state of things, however, were the portion of the host, not of his guests; and the hearty hospitality with which we were ever greeted by the minister and his attachés, combined with the attractions of the society they brought together, made our visits to them some of the pleasantest hours we passed in Washington.

Slight incidents were perpetually showing, in an amusing way, the village-like character of some of the arrangements at Washington. I remember that some of our party went one day to dine at Mr. Secretary Cass's, and the rest of us at Mr. Secretary Woodbury's. The next morning a lady of the Cass party asked me whether we had candied oranges at the Woodburys'. "No." "Then," said she, "they had candied oranges at the attorney-general's." "How do you know?" "Oh, as we were on the way, I saw a dish carried; and as we had none at the Cass's, I knew they must either be for the Woodburys or the attorney-general." There were candied oranges at the attorney-general's.

When we became intimate some time afterward with some Southern friends, with whom we now dined at their congressional mess, they gave us an amusing account of the preparations for our dinner. They boarded (from a really self-denying kindness) at a house where the arrangements were of a very inferior kind. Two sessions previous to our being there they had invited a large party of eminent persons to dinner, and had committed the ordering of the arrangements to a gentleman of their mess, advising him to engage a French cook in order to ensure a good dinner. The gentleman engaged a Frenchman, concluding he must be a cook, which, however, he was not; and the dinner turned out so unfortunately, that the mess determined to ask no more dinner-company while they remained in that house. When we arrived, however, it was thought necessary to ask us to dinner. There was little hope that all would go rightly; and the two senators of the mess were laughingly requested, in case of any blunder, to talk nullification as fast as possible to us ladies. This was done so efficaciously, that, when dinner was over, I could not have told a single dish that was on the table, except that a ham stood before me, which we were too full of nullification to attack. Our hosts informed us, long afterward, that it was a bad dinner badly served; but it was no matter.

At the president's I met a very large party, among whom there was more stiffness than I saw in any other society in America. It was not the fault of the president or his family, but of the way in which the company was unavoidably brought together. With the exception of my party, the name of everybody present began with J, K, or L; that is to say, it consisted of members of Congress, who are invited alphabetically, to ensure none being left out. This principle of selection is not, perhaps, the best for the promotion of ease and sociability; and well as I liked the day, I doubt whether many others could say they enjoyed it. When we went in the president was standing in the middle of the room to receive his guests. After speaking a few words with me, he gave me into the charge of Major Donelson, his secretary, who seated me, and brought up for introduction each guest as he passed from before the president. A congressional friend of mine (whose name began with a J) stationed himself behind my chair, and gave me an account of each gentleman who was introduced to me; where he came from, what his politics were, and how, if at all, he had distinguished himself. All this was highly amusing. At dinner the president was quite disposed for conversation. Indeed, he did nothing but talk. His health is poor, and his diet of the sparest. We both talked freely of the governments of England and France; I, novice in American politics as I was, entirely forgetting that the great French question was pending, and that the president and the King of the French were then bandying very hard words. I was most struck and surprised with the president's complaints of the American Senate, in which there was at that time a small majority against the administration. He told me that I must not judge of the body by what I saw it then, and that after the 4th of March I should behold a Senate more worthy of the country. After the 4th of March there was, if I remember rightly, a majority of two in favour of the government. The ground of his complaint was, that the senators had sacrificed their dignity by disregarding the wishes of their constituents. The other side of the question is, that the dignity of the Senate is best consulted by its members following their own convictions, declining instructions for the term for which they are elected. It is a serious difficulty, originating in the very construction of the body, and not to be settled by dispute.

The president offered me bonbons for a child belonging to our party at home, and told me how many children (of his nephew's and his adopted son's) he had about him, with a mildness and kindliness which contrasted well with his tone upon some public occasions. He did the honours of his house with gentleness and politeness to myself, and, as far as I saw, to every one else. About an hour after dinner he rose, and we led the way into the drawing-room, where the whole company, gentlemen as well as ladies, followed to take coffee; after which every one departed, some homeward, some to make evening calls, and others, among whom were ourselves, to a splendid ball at the other extremity of the city.

General Jackson is extremely tall and thin, with a slight stoop, betokening more weakness than naturally belongs to his years. He has a profusion of stiff gray hair, which gives to his appearance whatever there is of formidable in it. His countenance bears commonly an expression of melancholy gravity; though, when roused, the fire of passion flashes from his eyes, and his whole person looks then formidable enough. His mode of speech is slow and quiet, and his phraseology sufficiently betokens that his time has not been passed among books. When I was at Washington albums were the fashion and the plague of the day. I scarcely ever came home but I found an album on my table or requests for autographs; but some ladies went much further than petitioning a foreigner who might be supposed to have leisure. I have actually seen them stand at the door of the Senate Chamber, and send the doorkeeper with an album, and a request to write in it, to Mr. Webster and other eminent members. I have seen them do worse; stand at the door of the Supreme Court, and send in their albums to Chief-justice Marshall while he was on the bench hearing pleadings. The poor president was terribly persecuted; and to him it was a real nuisance, as he had no poetical resource but Watts's hymns. I have seen verses and stanzas of a most ominous purport from Watts, in the president's very conspicuous handwriting, standing in the midst of the crowquill compliments and translucent charades which are the staple of albums. Nothing was done to repress this atrocious impertinence of the ladies. I always declined writing more than name and date; but senators, judges, and statesmen submitted to write gallant nonsense at the request of any woman who would stoop to desire it. . . .

[On a visit to the Supreme Court] I was kindly offered the reporter's chair, in a snug corner, under the judges, and facing the counsel; and there I was able to hear much of the pleadings and to see the remarkable countenances of the attorney-general, Clay, Webster, Porter, and others, in the fullest light that could be had in this dim chamber.

At some moments this court presents a singular spectacle. I have watched the assemblage while the chief-justice was delivering a judgment; the three judges on either hand gazing at him more like learners than associates; Webster standing firm as a rock, his large, deep-set eyes wide awake, his lips compressed, and his whole countenance in that intent stillness which easily fixes the eye of the stranger; Clay leaning against the desk in an attitude whose grace contrasts strangely with the slovenly make of his dress, his snuffbox for the moment unopened in his hand, his small gray eye and placid half-smile conveying an expression of pleasure which redeems his face from its usual unaccountable commonness; the attorney-general, his fingers playing among his papers, his quick black eye, and thin tremulous lips for once fixed, his small face, pale with thought, contrasting remarkably with the other two; these men, absorbed in what they are listening to, thinking neither of themselves nor of each other, while they are watched by the groups of idlers and listeners around them; the newspaper corps, the dark Cherokee chiefs, the stragglers from the Far West, the gay ladies in their waving plumes, and the members of either house that have stepped in to listen; all these I have seen at one moment constitute one silent assemblage, while the mild voice of the aged chief-justice sounded through the court.

Every one is aware that the wigs and gowns of counsel are not to be seen in the United States. There was no knowing, when Webster sauntered in, threw himself down, and leaned back against the table, his dreamy eyes seeming to see nothing about him, whether he would by-and-by take up his hat and go away, or whether he would rouse himself suddenly, and stand up to address the judges. For the generality there

was no knowing; and to us, who were forewarned, it was amusing to see
how the court would fill after the entrance of Webster, and empty when
he had gone back to the Senate Chamber. The chief interest to me in
Webster's pleading, and also in his speaking in the Senate, was from
seeing one so dreamy and *nonchalant* roused into strong excitement. It
seemed like having a curtain lifted up through which it was impossible
to pry; like hearing autobiographical secrets. Webster is a lover of ease
and pleasure, and has an air of the most unaffected indolence and careless self-sufficiency. It is something to see him moved with anxiety and
the toil of intellectual conflict; to see his lips tremble, his nostrils expand,
the perspiration start upon his brow; to hear his voice vary with emotion,
and to watch the expression of laborious thought while he pauses, for
minutes together, to consider his notes, and decide upon the arrangement of his argument. These are the moments when it becomes clear
that this pleasure-loving man works for his honours and his gains. He
seems to have the desire which other remarkable men have shown, to
conceal the extent of his toils, and his wish has been favoured by some
accidents; some sudden, unexpected call upon him for a display of
knowledge and power which has electrified the beholders. But on such
occasions he has been able to bring into use acquisitions and exercises
intended for other occasions, on which they may or may not have been
wanted. . . .

Mr. Webster owes his rise to the institutions under which he lives;
institutions which open the race to the swift and the battle to the
strong; but there is little in him that is congenial with them. He is
aristocratic in his tastes and habits, and but little republican simplicity
is to be recognized in him. Neither his private conversation nor his public
transactions usually convey an impression that he is in earnest. When
he is so, his power is majestic, irresistible; but his ambition for office,
and for the good opinion of those who surround him, is seen too often
in alternation with his love of ease and luxury to allow of his being confided in as he is admired. If it had been otherwise, if his moral had
equalled his intellectual supremacy, if his aims had been as single as
his reason is unclouded, he would long ago have carried all before him,
and been the virtual monarch of the United States. . . .

Mr. Webster speaks seldom in the Senate. When he does, it is generally on some constitutional question, where his reasoning powers and
knowledge are brought into play, and where his authority is considered
so high, that he has the glorious satisfaction of knowing that he is
listened to as an oracle by an assemblage of the first men in the country.
Previous to such an exercise he may be seen leaning back in his chair,

not, as usual, biting the top of his pen, or twirling his thumbs, or bursting into sudden and transient laughter at Colonel Benton's oratorical absurdities, but absent and thoughtful, making notes, and seeing nothing that is before his eyes. When he rises, his voice is moderate and his manner quiet, with the slightest possible mixture of embarrassment; his right hand rests upon his desk, and the left hangs by his side. Before his first head is finished, however, his voice has risen so as to fill the chamber and ring again, and he has fallen into his favourite attitude, with his left hand under his coat-tail, and the right in full action. At this moment the eye rests upon him as upon one under the true inspiration of seeing the invisible and grasping the impalpable. When the vision has passed away, the change is astonishing. He sits at his desk, writing letters or dreaming, so that he does not always discover when the Senate is going to a division. Some one of his party has not seldom to jog his elbow, and tell him that his vote is wanted.

There can scarcely be a stronger contrast than between the eloquence of Webster and that of Clay. Mr. Clay is now my personal friend; but I have a distinct recollection of my impression of his speaking while he was yet merely an acquaintance. His appearance is plain in the extreme, being that of a mere west-country farmer. He is tall and thin, with a weather-beaten complexion, small gray eyes, which convey an idea of something more than his well-known sagacity, even of slyness. It is only after much intercourse that Mr. Clay's personal appearance can be discovered to do him any justice at all. All attempts to take his likeness have been in vain, though upward of thirty portraits of him, by different artists, were in existence when I was in America. No one has succeeded in catching the subtile expression of placid kindness, mingled with astuteness, which becomes visible to the eyes of those who are in daily intercourse with him. His mode of talking, deliberate and somewhat formal, including sometimes a grave humour and sometimes a gentle sentiment, very touching from the lips of a sagacious man of ambition, has but one fault, its obvious adaptation to the supposed state of mind of the person to whom it is addressed. Mr. Clay is a man of an irritable and impetuous nature, over which he has obtained a truly noble mastery. His moderation is now his most striking characteristic; obtained, no doubt, at the cost of prodigious self-denial on his own part, and on that of his friends of some of the ease, naturalness, and self-forgetfulness of his manners and discourse. But his conversation is rich in information, and full charged with the spirit of justice and kindliness, rising, on occasion, to a moving magnanimity.

The finest speech I heard from Mr. Clay in the Senate was on the sad subject of the injuries of the [Cherokee] Indians. . . .

It was known that Mr. Clay would probably bring forward his great topic that day. Some of the foreign ambassadors might be seen leaning against the pillars behind the chair, and many members of the other house appeared behind and in the passages; and one sat on the steps of the platform, his hands clasped, and his eyes fixed on Mr. Clay, as if life hung upon his words. As many as could crowd into the gallery leaned over the balustrade; and the lower circle was thronged with ladies and gentlemen, in the centre of whom stood a group of Cherokee chiefs, listening immoveably. I never saw so deep a moral impression produced by a speech. The best testimony to this was the disgust excited by the empty and abusive reply of the senator from Georgia, who, by-the-way, might be judged from his accent to have been about three months from the Green Island. This gentleman's speech, however, showed us one good thing, that Mr. Clay is as excellent in reply as in proposition; prompt, earnest, temperate, and graceful. The chief characteristic of his eloquence is its earnestness. Every tone of his voice, every fibre of his frame bears testimony to this. His attitudes are, from the beginning to the close, very graceful. His first sentences are homely, and given with a little hesitation and repetition, and with an agitation shown by a frequent putting on and taking off of the spectacles, and a trembling of the hands among the documents on the desk. Then, as the speaker becomes possessed with his subject, the agitation changes its character, but does not subside. His utterance is still deliberate, but his voice becomes deliciously winning. Its higher tones disappointed me at first; but the lower ones, trembling with emotion, swelling and falling with the earnestness of the speaker, are very moving, and his whole manner becomes irresistibly persuasive. I saw tears, of which I am sure he was wholly unconscious, falling on his papers as he vividly described the woes and injuries of the aborigines. I saw Webster draw his hand across his eyes; I saw every one deeply moved except two persons, the vice-president, who yawned somewhat ostentatiously, and the Georgian senator, who was busy brewing his storm. I was amazed at the daring of this gentleman; at the audacity which could break up such a moral impression as this Cherokee tale, so told, had produced, by accusing Mr. Clay of securing an interest in opposition to Georgia "by stage starts and theatric gesticulations." The audience were visibly displeased at having their feelings thus treated, in the presence even of the Cherokee chiefs; but Mr. Clay's replies both to argument and abuse were so happy, and the Georgian's rejoinder was so outrageous, that the business ended with a general burst of laughter. The propositions were to lie over till the next day; and, as I soon after left Washington, I never learned their ultimate fate.

The American Senate is a most imposing assemblage. When I first entered it I thought I never saw a finer set of heads than the forty-six before my eyes: two only being absent, and the Union then consisting of twenty-four states. Mr. Calhoun's countenance first fixed my attention; the splendid eye, the straight forehead, surmounted by a load of stiff, upright, dark hair; the stern brow; the inflexible mouth; it is one of the most remarkable heads in the country. Next him sat his colleague, Mr. Preston, in singular contrast; stout in person, with a round, ruddy, good-humoured face, large blue eyes, and a wig, orange to-day, brown yester-day, and golden to-morrow. Near them sat Colonel Benton, a temporary people's man, remarkable chiefly for his pomposity. He sat swelling amid his piles of papers and books, looking like a being designed by nature to be a good-humoured barber or innkeeper, but forced by fate to make himself into a mock-heroic senator. Opposite sat the transcendant Webster, with his square forehead and cavernous eyes; and behind him the homely Clay, with the face and figure of a farmer, but something of the air of a divine, from his hair being combed straight back from his temples. Near them sat Southard and Porter; the former astute and rapid in countenance and gesture; the latter strangely mingling a boyish fun and lightness of manner and glance with the sobriety suitable to the judge and the senator. His keen eye takes in everything that passes; his extraordinary mouth, with its overhanging upper lip, has but to unfold into a smile to win laughter from the sourest official or demagogue. Then there was the bright *bonhommie* of Ewing of Ohio, the most primitive-looking of senators; and the benign, religious gravity of Frelinghuysen; the gentlemanly air of Buchanan; the shrewdness of Poindexter; the somewhat melancholy simplicity of Silsbee; all these and many others were striking, and for nothing more than for their total unlikeness to each other. No English person who has not travelled over half the world can form an idea of such differences among men forming one assembly for the same purposes, and speaking the same language. Some were descended from Dutch farmers, some from French Huguenots, some from Scotch Puritans, some from English cavaliers, some from Irish chieftains. They were brought together out of law-courts, sugar-fields, merchants' stores, mountain farms, forests, and prairies. The stamp of originality was impressed upon every one, and inspired a deep, involuntary respect. I have seen no assembly of chosen men, and no company of the highborn, invested with the antique dignities of an antique realm, half so imposing to the imagination as this collection of stout-souled, full-grown, original men, brought together on the ground of their supposed sufficiency, to work out the will of their diverse constituencies.

In this splendid chamber, thus splendidly inhabited, we spent many hours of many weeks. Here I was able to gain no little knowledge of the state, political and other, of various parts of the country, from my large acquaintance among the members of the Senate. When dull official reports were read, and uninteresting local matters were discussed, or when the one interminable speaker, Benton, was on his legs, one member or another of the body would come and talk with us. I have heard certain of the members, stalking from their seats towards those of the ladies, compared to cranes in search of fish. The comparison is not a bad one.

I wished every day that the ladies would conduct themselves in a more dignified manner than they did in the Senate. They came in with waving plumes, and glittering in all the colours of the rainbow, causing no little bustle in the place, no little annoyance to the gentlemen spectators, and rarely sat still for any length of time. I know that these ladies are no fair specimen of the women who would attend parliamentary proceedings in any other metropolis. I know that they were the wives, daughters, and sisters of legislators, women thronging to Washington for purposes of convenience or pleasure, leaving their usual employments behind them, and seeking to pass away the time. I knew this, and made allowance accordingly; but I still wished that they could understand the gravity of such an assembly, and show so much respect to it as to repay the privilege of admission by striving to excite as little attention as possible, and by having the patience to sit still when they happened not to be amused, till some interruption gave them opportunity to depart quietly. If they had done this, Judge Porter would not have moved that they should be appointed seats in the gallery instead of below; and they would have been guiltless of furnishing a plea for the exclusion of women, who would probably make a better use of the privilege, from the galleries of other houses of parliament.

I was glad of an opportunity of hearing both the South Carolina senators soon after my arrival in Washington. They are listened to with close attention, and every indication of their state of feeling is watched with the interest which has survived the nullification struggle. Mr. Calhoun on this occasion let us a little into his mind; Mr. Preston kept more closely to the question before the body. The question was whether a vote of censure of the president, recorded in the minutes of the proceedings of the Senate the preceding session, should be expunged. The motion for the expunging was made by Colonel Benton, and rejected, as it had been before, and has been since; though it was finally carried, to the agony of the opposition, at the end of last session (February, 1837).

Mr. Preston was out of health, and unable to throw his accustomed force into his speaking; but his effort showed us how beautiful his eloquence is in its way. It is not solid. His speeches, if taken to pieces, will be found to consist of analogies and declamation; but his figures are sometimes very striking, and his manner is as graceful as anything so artificial can be. I never before understood the eloquence of action. The action of public speakers in England, as far as I have observed (and perhaps I may be allowed to hint that deaf persons are peculiarly qualified to judge of the nature of such action), is of two kinds; the involuntary gesture which is resorted to for the relief of the nerves, which may or may not be expressive of meaning, and the action which is wholly the result of study; arbitrary, and not the birth of the sentiment; and, therefore, though pleasing, perhaps, to the eye, perplexing to the mind of the listener. Mr. Preston's manner unites the advantages of these two methods, and avoids most of their evils. It is easy to see that he could not speak without an abundant use of action, and that he has therefore done wisely in making it a study. To an unaccustomed eye it appears somewhat exuberant; but it is exquisitely graceful, and far more than commonly appropriate. His voice is not good, but his person is tall, stout, and commanding, and his countenance animated.

Mr. Calhoun followed, and impressed me very strongly. While he kept to the question, what he said was close, good, and moderate, though delivered in rapid speech, and with a voice not sufficiently modulated. But when he began to reply to a taunt of Colonel Benton's, that he wanted to be president, the force of his speaking became painful. He made protestations which it seemed to strangers had better have been spared, that he would not turn on his heel to be president; and that he had given up all for his own brave, magnanimous little State of South Carolina. While thus protesting, his eyes flashed, his brow seemed charged with thunder, his voice became almost a bark, and his sentences were abrupt, intense, producing in the auditory that sort of laugh which is squeezed out of people by the application of a very sudden mental force. I believe he knew little what a revelation he made in a few sentences. They were to us strangers the key, not only to all that was said and done by the South Carolina party during the remainder of the session, but to many things at Charleston and Columbia which would otherwise have passed unobserved or unexplained.

The Politicians as Seen by an Austrian Traveler

Francis J. Grund

From the secretary of the Treasury I drove to the lodgings of Mr. Henry Clay, the celebrated senator from Kentucky. I found this extraordinary man, who was then already a little past his prime, the very type of what passes in Europe, ever since the clever caricatures of Mrs. Trollope, as "an American character." Mr. Clay stands upwards of six feet; has a semi-Indian, half-human, half-savage countenance, in which, however, the intellectual strongly preponderates over the animal. His manners, at first sight, appear to be extremely vulgar; and yet he is graceful, and even dignified, in his intercourse with strangers. He chews tobacco, drinks whisky punch, gambles, puts his legs on the table or the chimney, and spits, as an American would say, "like a regular Kentucky hog-driver"; and yet he is all gentleness, politeness, and cordiality in the society of ladies. Add to this that his organs of speech are the most melodious; and that, with great imagination and humour, he combines manly eloquence, and the power of sarcasm in the most extraordinary degree; and it will easily be conceived why he should have been able to captivate high and low,—*l'homme du salon*, and the "squatter" in the Western wilderness.

Much as Mr. Clay is esteemed in America, I do not think the people have as yet done justice to his talents. These, to be sure, are, owing to his advanced age, on the decline; but even the *remnants* of a mind like Clay's are great, and entitle him to be ranked among the greatest living statesmen. He was for a long time the advocate of the system of internal improvements, combated with so much success by General Jackson. He advocated successively the establishment of national roads and canals, the continuance of a United States' bank, the tariff, and, in short, every measure conducive to centralization. That this system, while it strength-

Francis J. Grund, *Aristocracy in America* (London, 1839), II, pp. 212-220; 316-323.

ens the government, and introduces order and uniformity into the administration of the country, diminishes, at the same time, the liberties
of the individual States, and, in general, ill agrees with the principles of
a pure democracy, such as are laid down in the American constitution,
no one, who is not himself interested in the question, can reasonably
deny; but it would be equally absurd to suppose every man who is an
advocate of a central measure, to be at once an enemy to republican
institutions, and a traitor to his country.

Mr. Clay advocated every measure he proposed, not as a mere partisan, but as a statesman who clearly saw its first and ultimate bearings
on national politics. His is a mind of vast conceptions, which, if it had
not at one time speculated too much in elections,—I allude to the trick
he played at the election of Mr. John Quincy Adams,—might have long
ago enabled him to fill the station to which his unfortunate ambition a
little too early aspired.

From Mr. Clay I called upon Mr. Thomas H. Benton, the democratic
senator from Missouri. This gentleman is altogether in a false position;
for he is, in my opinion, as much over-rated by his friends as he is under-
rated by his enemies. I was the bearer of a letter to him by one of his
most intimate friends, and a person of high standing and much influence in
the country; and yet the reception I met with was cold and ceremonious,
—his manners forced, and almost ludicrously dignified. The truth is, Mr.
Benton behaves on most occasions like a man who has not yet found his
level in society; being continually on his guard lest he might not be
done justice to, and afraid lest his unrestrained familiar manners might
derogate from the estimation in which he is held by the public. The
first impression that he makes upon a stranger I should judge to be
decidedly unfavourable, though he greatly improves upon acquaintance,
and, as he drops his dignity, shows his truly estimable points of character. As Mr. Benton's democracy is probably proof against the seduc-
tions of Europe,—a thing I would not assert of one American out of ten,
—I would recommend to him a trip to Paris,—not to London,—in order
that he might learn to carry himself with a little more ease. It would
vastly improve his manners and general appearance, and perhaps make
him find favour even with *female* philosophers.

Mr. Benton is perhaps the most unfortunate speaker in the Senate;
not, indeed, as regards the substance of his discourses, most of which
are clever and full of information; but with regard to his disjointed,
broken, sometimes loud, and again sometimes scarcely audible, delivery.
This is undoubtedly the reason why his speeches are so much under-
rated, though they contain more solid matter of statistics and history
than can be found in the perhaps more eloquent efforts of his colleagues.
Mr. Benton is a most uncommonly laborious man, and is constantly col-

lecting facts, not only in America but also in Europe, in support of his political doctrines; though his partiality for France, and his eternal and irksome comparisons between the republic under the consulate of Bonaparte and the confederation of the United States, rather injure than establish his theories with a considerable portion of the American public. Another fault with which Mr. Benton has been reproached consists in his indelicate allusions to his personal prowess. Every one knows that Mr. Benton is as brave as Caesar; but it is not necessary that he himself should refer to it. An appeal to arms in a deliberative assembly is always vulgar, if not absolutely savage; and ought to be avoided in the most studious manner, not only by every man of religion and principle, but also by every gentleman of good taste. There is, as yet, too much bullyism in the legislative assemblies of America; many worthy representatives forgetting that it is easier to fight for, than to establish by argument, the correctness of a political principle. On the whole, Mr. Benton is a clever politician, an industrious collector of statistics, and, with the exception of his delivery, a most skilful debater in Congress. He has, during a certain period, been almost the only and valiant defender of General Jackson's policy in the Senate; and has, by his perseverance, honesty, and good faith, become universally popular among the labouring classes, whose interests he has during his whole life constantly and successfully advocated.

My next visit was to Mr. Salis [Silas] Wright, senator from the State of New York, the avowed democratic champion of the State, and indeed a man of the most extraordinary talents. He is one of those men whose urbanity and frankness the Americans indicate by saying, "he has not a bit of starch in him." Mr. Wright is a statesman, not a mere politician; and will if his talents be properly placed before the public, play an important part in the history of his country. He and Mr. Calhoun are almost the only two senators free from the "Congressional" sin of making everlasting speeches. He is always concise, rigorously logical, and, what is very rare in an American politician, singularly free from personal abuse. His mind is of the rigid composition which does not allow him to depart, for one instant, from the point under consideration; and hence, instead of indulging himself in irrelevant rhapsodies, sneers, and side-thrusts at the character of his antagonists, he confines himself strictly to his argument; a method which, if it were imitated by every senator, would enable them to transact the same business in about the one-seventh part of the time now needed, saving annually a sum of not less than a million of dollars.

Mr. Wright's delivery is rapid, but distinct; proving that every thought is digested and arranged, and flowing from a well-stored mind. In his private life he is not a fashionable, but a plain, unassuming, modest gentleman; who, notwithstanding his own brevity, possesses that most extraordinary talent of powerful minds—of listening patiently to the tedious prosings of others. I saw him, in his own room, listen to an endless recital of an Indian campaign given by an officer in the army, without even once heaving a sigh, though the thermometer ranged at 96°; his room being one of the closest in the whole city of Washington. At last, having listened to the hero for more than an hour, he told him patiently that he found his story exceedingly entertaining; but, having a few words to say to one of his friends waiting in the parlour, he should be obliged to leave him for a few moments, in order to afterwards hear the conclusion of so interesting a narrative. I must yet observe that Mr. Wright is seldom seen at the crack parties in Washington, and is, therefore, not in the way of being much noticed by foreign tourists.

My next call was on my old acquaintance, Mr. Buchanan, senator from Pennsylvania. This is a gentleman of plain common sense, agreeable and dignified manners, and the most resolved, unchangeable disposition. As a speaker, he does not attempt to soar on the wings of genius; but his arguments being always founded on experience and practical good sense, and his unimpeachable honesty being proverbial, he is always sure of producing effect. Mr. Buchanan never had the character of an office-seeker, though he has always been one of the most strenuous defenders of General Jackson's policy; and is even now rarely seen at the White-house or the levees of the cabinet ministers. And yet in his externals he is the most courtier-like senator in Congress; his dress and manners being always what a master of ceremonies at any European court could wish them to be in order to usher him into the presence of his royal master. In addition to this, Mr. Buchanan is a bachelor, and not yet past the age at which bachelors cease to be interesting; which accounts sufficiently for his being universally beloved, even by those who are opposed to him in politics. Indeed, I heard it positively asserted, more than four years ago, that he was "too much of a gentleman," and "had remained too long in the Senate," to continue much longer an advocate of democracy. This was evidently among the *on dits*, which, as far as regards the conclusion, had not the least foundation in it. Mr. Buchanan is, at this moment, as sound a democrat as ever. . . .

We drove from the White-house towards Georgetown; stopping at one of the houses, called "The Seven Buildings." This was the dwelling of the Vice-President. My friend gave both our names, and in a moment after we were admitted into the presence of Mr. Van Buren. He received us in the same manner as General Jackson, only with less solemnity. His conversation was rapid, but concise and logical; his voice calm and steady, and his manners those of a perfect courtier. Understanding that

I was a German, he introduced the subject of travelling, which gave him an opportunity of comparing the scenery of the Rhine with that of the Hudson, and pointing out the distinct beauties of each; which he did with more taste and less affectation than I had yet heard from an American when speaking of foreign countries. He gave the preference to his native river, and supported his opinion with such forcible arguments that he converted me to his doctrine. He then drew a parallel between the state of Europe and that of the United States; pointing to the advantages of the latter, to their government, the manners and customs of the people, and to their happiness. All this he did with so much gentleness, with such an entire absence of conceit, and such admirable management of terms, that it was impossible either to resist his eloquence or to be offended with his conclusions.

Our visit was interrupted by the arrival of several Western members, who, being alarmed at General Jackson's message in relation to the differences with France, desired to know whether it was the Vice-President's opinion that France would pay "without having a tug for it." Mr. Van Buren, without being for one moment embarrassed by this abrupt question, instead of an answer, took up a British periodical, the name of which I do not now recollect, but which treated the French-American question in a very sensible manner. From this he read to the members several passages, which expressed themselves favourably to General Jackson's policy; and at last the conclusion, which ran thus, "Jonathan has claimed the money, and Jonathan will have it." The members were delighted; and the conversation then passed to other topics. I mention this as an instance of Mr. Van Buren's tact, a quality full as indispensable to a statesman as a sound knowledge of politics.

"Well, and what do you think of our Vice-President?" asked my friend, as we were driving towards the lodgings of Mr. John C. Calhoun.

"I have certainly left him with the highest respect for his mind and character."

"And yet, sir! there are those who call him an *intrigant,* a 'little magician,' a 'non-committal man,' &c. though there is not one man in the country whose attachment to the democratic cause is better known or understood. The firmness of a man's political principles is, in this country at least, always commensurate with the degree of abuse heaped upon him by the opposite party. Our people, I mean 'the higher and better informed classes,' are seldom inexorable with regard to a politician holding out some chances of conversion; but let a man's character be established, and there is no end to their vituperation. This has happened to Mr. Van Buren, and ought to be considered by every democrat as a pledge of his fidelity.

"What act of Mr. Van Buren has ever had any other than democratic tendency? What principle did he ever advocate that was not strictly conformable to that doctrine? If he be a non-committal man, it must be that he never committed himself *to his enemies.*

"The reason why in America, more than in every other country, political controversies are personal, is, that the opposition, which in consequence of universal suffrage can only triumph by popular majorities, is obliged to apparently uphold the principles maintained by the democracy; so that, while it cannot make war upon the general doctrines of the administration, it is concentrating all its venom in its attacks on particular measures, and the men who support them. Let any Whig, either in or out of Congress, deny the correctness of this proposition and, I say, he either does not understand our institutions, or he is wilfully disguising the truth. There is no other real distinction of parties in the United States, except that one really does or means to do what it says; while the other is saying one thing, and preparing or hoping to be able to do another. There is more political hypocrisy in this country than perhaps anywhere else,—not among the people, but among 'the upper classes'; owing to the basis of our society being purely democratic, and the superstructure a lamentable imitation of the usages of Europe.

"I know," continued he after a pause, "that no administration or set of men is without its political misconceptions and mistakes; but have the opposition calculated how many of these are to be charged to their own account? Into how many errors they force the administration by their reckless and indiscriminate resistance against all measures emanating from the executive? And do they not thus force the government to avail itself continually of 'the party' in carrying measures which ought to originate in calm reflection and sound statesmanship, and be applied in a generous spirit to all classes of society? The spirit of party is, indeed, at the basis of our institutions; an opposition we *must* have, and the peculiar nature of our government requires a powerful one; but most unfortunately our demagogues—Whigs and Democrats—oppose men, not principles. If there be a man in the country capable of acting as mediator between the two hostile parties,—appeasing the one without sacrificing the principles of the other,—that man is Mr. Van Buren; and future events will prove it."

We now halted before a small house in Pennsylvania Avenue, situated not far from the Capitol. This was the temporary residence of Mr. John C. Calhoun, senator from South Carolina. If the South, in general, have a right to be proud of the great number of eminent statesmen and orators who represent its interests in Congress, South Carolina in particular may glory in Mr. Calhoun. He is a statesman, not a lawyer; and perhaps the only senator in Congress whose course of reading was strictly adapted to the high functions he was to assume. When my friend and I entered the room, he was stretched on a couch, from which he rose to offer us a warm Southern welcome. He almost immediately introduced the subject of politics, in which his superiority over my friend soon reduced the latter to the situation of a mere listener.

As he was explaining his views and theories, which, contrary to the usual American practice, he did in the most concise manner, and with a degree of rapidity which required our utmost attention to follow him, his face assumed an almost supernatural expression; his dark brows were knit together, his eyes shot fire, his black hair stood on end, while on his quivering lips there hung an almost Mephisthophelean scorn at the absurdity of the opposite doctrine. Then, at once, he became again all calmness, gentleness, and good-nature, laughing at the blunders of his friends and foes, and commencing a highly comical review of their absurdities.

Mr. Calhoun is, without contradiction, the greatest genius in Congress, and secretly acknowledged as such even by his most declared political enemies. His speeches are the shortest, his political views the most elevated, his delivery the most impressive of any one of his colleagues; and he adds to all these qualities the most unsparing irony. He was Vice-President at the commencement of General Jackson's administration; but subsequently joined the Whigs in order to oppose the tariff, *nullified* by his native State. Without this step, which destroyed his popularity in the North, he would, with very little opposition, have become General Jackson's successor in office. This alone proves the absurdity of the charge of unlawful ambition repeatedly brought against him. The Presidential chair of *the United States,* once within his reach, was assuredly a higher mark than the Presidency of "the *Southern* Union," the *bête noire* of the enlightened opposition. Mr. Calhoun has lately again joined the administration in its endeavour to separate itself from the banks. . . .

PART III

THE NORTH:
LAND OF ENTERPRISE

In Jackson's time the "North" was a vague geographical term for three regions: New England, the Middle (Eastern) States, and the Middle West. After the slavery question became a divisive force in American life, southerners tended to think of all northerners as having similar characteristics, the "Yankees"—the New Englanders—being the symbol of the northern qualities that they disliked.

New England is represented in this volume by a selection from Lucy Larcom's nostalgic reminiscences, entitled A New England Girlhood. Born in 1824, Miss Larcom worked as a girl in the Lowell, Massachusetts, cotton mills, where her mother was the matron of a girls' boarding house. She educated herself largely by reading, and became a teacher, poet, and editor of a much admired juvenile magazine. Miss Larcom saw New England with the eyes of a native, while Lucian Minor, who made a tour of New England in 1834 and kept a journal, presents the way that New England looked to a liberal young southerner.

During her tour of New England the same year Harriet Martineau (see Part II) visited Harvard College, and in her travel account gave a very unfavorable report of this first American college, which appeared to be in a state of decline. Another British traveler, Alexander Mackay, a barrister of the Middle Temple of London, who landed in Boston in 1846, drew an attractive picture of the Puritan city, just as the Irish immigrants were beginning to inundate it. Nevertheless, the city retained enough of the Old Puritan characteristics to levy fines against persons who smoked cigars on the streets.

The Middle States were also strongly affected by a flood of immigrants. Because of their commercial contacts with the South, the business class of this section was favorably disposed to southerners and less inclined to condemn slavery than were the New Englanders. Very representative of the merchants of New York was Philip Hone, who kept a remarkable diary from 1828 until his death in 1851. Hone was mayor of New York in 1825; he acquired a fortune from his auction house and merchant-commission business, retired from active business when he was forty-one years old, and spent the remainder of his life as a public-spirited citizen, active in many enterprises. An ardent Whig, he strongly

101

adhered to the conservative views of the business community of the North of his day, including a strong dislike of the abolitionists.

The Erie Canal, completed in 1825, contributed enormously to the growth of New York. Captain Basil Hall traveled along this famous highway to the West in 1827. To British eyes the girdling of trees, which he describes, was a unique phenomenon and he also closely observed other characteristics of the vanishing frontier in America. His wife Margaret observed the Americans in a restless state of hurry, particularly their hasty dispatch of their food at dinner, and their want of romance. National characteristics change over relatively short periods of time, as Boyd Shafer has pointed out in an article in the American Historical Review *(1952) entitled "Men Are More Alike." Certainly Mrs. Hall's observations that Americans (northerners) were lacking in warm feeling as contrasted with her own people is a reversal of the stereotype in many Americans' minds of the British as a highly self-controlled and unemotional people.*

Philadelphia was quite different from the polyglot New York, largely because of its history rather than because of its economic development. Its founding by Quakers, the versatile contributions of Benjamin Franklin to civic affairs, and its role as the capital of the young republic until 1801 left an imprint of strong patriotic pride and self-assurance. Its nearness to the South resulted in its becoming a haven for a large number of free Negroes, as well as the resort of southern merchants seeking to buy stock for their stores, and of medical students from the slave states who came to study at the University of Pennsylvania and the Jefferson Medical College. Alexander Mackay's description of Philadelphia in 1846 caught much of the unique, conservative character of that city.

Old New England

Lucy Larcom

When I first opened my eyes upon my native town, [b. 1824, Beverly, Mass.] it was already nearly two hundred years old, counting from the time when it was part of the original Salem settlement,—old enough to have gained a character and an individuality of its own, as it certainly had. We children felt at once that we belonged to the town, as we did to our father or our mother.

The sea was its nearest neighbor, and penetrated to every fireside, claiming close intimacy with every home and heart. The farmers up and down the shore were as much fishermen as farmers; they were as familiar with the Grand Banks of Newfoundland as they were with their own potato-fields. Every third man you met in the street, you might safely hail as "Shipmate," or "Skipper," or "Captain." My father's early seafaring experience gave him the latter title to the end of his life.

It was hard to keep the boys from going off to sea before they were grown. No inland occupation attracted them. "Land-lubber" was one of the most contemptuous epithets heard from boyish lips. The spirit of adventure developed in them a rough, breezy type of manliness, now almost extinct.

Men talked about a voyage to Calcutta, or Hong-Kong, or "up the Straits"—meaning Gibraltar and the Mediterranean—as if it were not much more than going to the next village. It seemed as if our nearest neighbors lived over there across the water; we breathed the air of foreign countries, curiously interblended with our own.

The women of well-to-do families had Canton crape shawls and Smyrna silks and Turk satins, for Sabbath-day wear, which somebody had brought home for them. Mantel-pieces were adorned with nautilus and conch-shells, and with branches and fans of coral; and children had foreign curiosities and treasures of the sea for playthings. There was

Lucy Larcom, A New England Girlhood (Boston, 1889), pp. 93-117.

one imported shell that we did not value much, it was so abundant—the freckled univalve they called a "prop." Yet it had a mysterious interest for us little ones. We held it to our ears, and listened for the sound of the waves, which we were told that it still kept, and always would keep. I remember the time when I thought that the ocean was really imprisoned somewhere within that narrow aperture.

We were accustomed to seeing barrels full of cocao-nuts rolled about; and there were jars of preserved tropical fruits, tamarinds, ginger-root, and other spicy appetizers, almost as common as barberries and cranberries, in the cupboards of most housekeepers.

I wonder what has become of those many, many little red "guinea-peas" we had to play with! It never seemed as if they really belonged to the vegetable world, notwithstanding their name.

We had foreign coins mixed in with our large copper cents,—all kinds, from the Russian "kopeck" to the "half-penny token" of Great Britain. Those were the days when we had half cents in circulation to make change with. For part of our currency was the old-fashioned "nine-pence,"—twelve and a half cents, and the "four pence ha'penny,"—six cents and a quarter. There was a good deal of Old England about us still.

And we had also many living reminders of strange lands across the sea. Green parrots went scolding and laughing down the thimbleberry hedges that bordered the cornfields, as much at home out of doors as within. Java sparrows and canaries and other tropical songbirds poured their music out of sunny windows into the street, delighting the ears of passing school children long before the robins came. Now and then somebody's pet monkey would escape along the stone walls and shed-roofs, and try to hide from his boy-persecutors by dodging behind a chimney, or by slipping through an open scuttle, to the terror and delight of juveniles whose premises he invaded.

And there were wanderers from foreign countries domesticated in many families, whose swarthy complexions and un-Caucasian features became familiar in our streets,—Mongolians, Africans, and waifs from the Pacific islands, who always were known to us by distinguished names,—Hector and Scipio, and Julius Caesar and Christopher Columbus. Families of black people were scattered about the place, relics of a time when even New England had not freed her slaves. Some of them had belonged in my great-grandfather's family, and they hung about the old homestead at "The Farms" long after they were at liberty to go anywhere they pleased. There was a "Rose" and a "Phillis" among them, who came often to our house to bring luscious high blackberries from the Farms woods, or to do the household washing. They seemed pathetically out of place, although they lived among us on equal terms, respectable and respected.

The pathos of the sea haunted the town, made audible to every ear when a coming northeaster brought the rote of the waves in from the islands across the harbor-bar, with a moaning like that we heard when we listened for it in the shell. Almost every house had its sea-tragedy. Somebody belonging to it had been shipwrecked, or had sailed away one day, and never returned.

Our own part of the bay was so sheltered by its islands that there were seldom any disasters heard of near home, although the names of the two nearest—Great and Little Misery—are said to have originated with a shipwreck so far back in the history of the region that it was never recorded.

But one such calamity happened in my infancy, spoken of always by those who knew its victims in subdued tones;—the wreck of the "Persia." The vessel was returning from the Mediterranean, and in a blinding snow-storm on a wild March night her captain probably mistook one of the Cape Ann light-houses for that on Baker's Island, and steered straight upon the rocks in a lonely cove just outside the cape. In the morning the bodies of her dead crew were found tossing about with her cargo of paper-manufacturers' rags, among the breakers. Her captain and mate were Beverly men, and their funeral from the meeting-house the next Sabbath was an event which long left its solemnity hanging over the town.

We were rather a young nation at this time. The History of the United States could only tell the story of the American Revolution, of the War of 1812, and of the administration of about half a dozen presidents.

Our republicanism was fresh and wide-awake. The edge of George Washington's little hatchet had not yet been worn down to its latter-day dullness; it flashed keenly on our young eyes and ears in the reading books, and through Fourth of July speeches. The Father of his Country had been dead only a little more than a quarter of a century, and General Lafayette was still alive; he had, indeed, passed through our town but a few years before, and had been publicly welcomed under our own elms and lindens. Even babies echoed the names of our two heroes in their prattle.

We had great "training-days," when drum and fife took our ears by storm; when the militia and the Light Infantry mustered and marched through the streets to the Common, with boys and girls at their heels,—such girls as could get their mother's consent, or the courage to run off without it. We never could. But we always managed to get a good look at the show in one way or another.

"Old Election," "'Lection Day" we called it, a lost holiday now, was a general training day, and it came at our most delightful season, the last of May. Lilacs and tulips were in bloom, then; and it was a picturesque fashion of the time for little girls whose parents had no flower-gardens to go around begging a bunch of lilacs, or a tulip or two. My mother always made "Lection cake" for us on that day. It was nothing but a kind of sweetened bread with a shine of egg-and-molasses on top; but we thought it delicious.

The Fourth of July and Thanksgiving Day were the only other holidays that we made much account of, and the former was a far more well-behaved festival than it is in modern times. The bells rang without stint, and at morning and noon cannon were fired off. But torpedoes and fire-crackers did not make the highways dangerous;—perhaps they were thought too expensive an amusement. Somebody delivered an oration; there was a good deal said about "this universal Yankee nation"; some rockets went up from Salem in the evening; we watched them from the hill, and then went to bed, feeling that we had been good patriots.

There was always a Fast Day, which I am afraid most of us younger ones regarded merely as a day when we were to eat unlimited quantities of molasses-gingerbread, instead of sitting down to our regular meals.

When I read about Christmas in the English story-books, I wished we could have that beautiful holiday. But our Puritan fathers shook their heads at Christmas.

Our Sabbath-school library books were nearly all English reprints, and many of the story-books were very interesting. I think that most of my favorites were by Mrs. Sherwood. Some of them were about life in India,—"Little Henry and his Bearer," and "Ayah and Lady." Then there were "The Hedge of Thorns," "Theophilus and Sophia," "Anna Ross," and a whole series of little English books that I took great delight in.

I had begun to be rather introspective and somewhat unhealthily self-critical, contrasting myself meanwhile with my sister Lida, just a little older, who was my usual playmate, and whom I admired very much for what I could not help seeing,—her unusual sweetness of disposition. I read Mrs. Sherwood's "Infant's Progress," and I made a personal application of it, picturing myself as the naughty, willful "Playful," and my sister Lida as the saintly little "Peace." . . .

The book that I loved first and best, and lived upon in my childhood, was "Pilgrim's Progress." It was as a story that I cared for it, although I knew that it meant something more,—something that was already going on in my own heart and life. Oh, how I used to wish that I too could start off on a pilgrimage! It would be so much easier than the continual, discouraging struggle to be good!

The lot I most envied was that of the contented Shepherd Boy in the Valley of Humiliation, singing his cheerful songs, and wearing "the herb called *Heart's Ease* in his bosom"; but all the glorious ups and downs of the "Progress" I would gladly have shared with Christiana and her children, never desiring to turn aside into any "By-Path Meadow" while Mr. Great-Heart led the way, and the Shining Ones came down to meet us along the road. It was one of the necessities of my nature, as a child, to have some one being, real or ideal, man or woman, before whom I inwardly bowed down and worshiped. Mr. Great-Heart was the perfect hero of my imagination. Nobody, in books or out of them, compared with him. I wondered if there were really any Mr. Great-Hearts to be met with among living men. . . .

That, indeed, was one peculiar attraction of the town itself; it was old, and it seemed old, much older than it does now. There was only one main street, said to have been the first settlers' cowpath to Wenham, which might account for its zigzag picturesqueness. All the rest were courts or lanes.

The town used to wear a delightful air of drowsiness, as if she had stretched herself out for an afternoon nap, with her head towards her old mother, Salem, and her whole length reclining towards the sea, till she felt at her feet, through her green robes, the dip of the deep water at the Farms. All her elder children recognized in her quiet steady-going ways a maternal unity and strength of character, as of a town that understood her own plans, and had settled down to peaceful, permanent habits.

Her spirit was that of most of our Massachusetts coast-towns. They were transplanted shoots of Old England. And it was the voice of a mother-country more ancient than their own, that little children heard crooning across the sea in their cradle-hymns and nursery-songs.

A Virginian Likes New England

Lucian Minor

On landing there, [New Haven, 1834], we were put into stage coaches, which carried us into the city. Slender opportunity of viewing it was afforded. Some fine churches, more fine trees, and not a few handsome dwelling houses, with the Yale college buildings and *their* trees and square—were all that I could see of the far famed beauties of New Haven. And these certainly are not to be contemned.

I had resolved, in N. York, to attend Miss S. to Northampton, Massachusetts, where her friends reside. We are bound to Hartford, 24 miles further, tonight. The managers of affairs have put us into the mail coach, which goes by Middletown. We drove on, without alighting at the stage house in N. Haven. Passed a *salt-marsh:* i. e. a meadow, daily inundated by the tide, and producing a coarse grass, which is much impregnated with salt. This makes it very toothsome to cattle: and the hay thus made is much valued.

And now I am in Connecticut! not only in Yankee land, but in the very land of steady habits, itself!—I could hardly realize it to myself. Driving on, we were, in a stage very like those in Virginia; drawn by horses not materially different from ours; along a road, sometimes muddy, sometimes sandy, sometimes rocky; bordered by fences, and farms, and trees, shrubs, weeds, grass, and flowers, not strikingly dissimilar to those of my native land. Ox-eyed daisies, in plenty. No worm fences—chiefly post-and-rail—(chestnut rails), sometimes staked fences, straight,—and sometimes stone. The houses, too, upon a plan rather different; oftener painted than ours, and more snug. The farms are certainly smaller than with us; and not so superior in neatness, as I expected.

Towards night, we met groups of school children going home. They

Lucian Minor, "A Virginian in New England Thirty-five Years Ago," edited by James Russell Lowell, *Atlantic Monthly*, XXVI (Sept., 1870), pp. 333-335; (Oct., 1870), pp. 490-492; (Dec., 1870), pp. 740-746.

curtsied and bowed to us in the most mannerly way. This, Miss S. told me, was what N. England children are carefully taught to do.

From near N. Haven, two very high peaks—mountains, in fact—appear on either hand, called East Rock, and West Rock. The former towers most naked and pointed; almost an entire mass of dark, *trap* rock. It is 800 feet high, I believe.—The fields shewed little wheat; much more rye, and most hay. Some Indian corn, which is very small, not averaging above 6 or 8 inches in height. Rye bread, I am told is much used; commonly mixed with flour, or corn meal. What flour they have, is mostly gotten from N. York, and the South.

Our fellow passengers are a civil young student of Yale, and his sister Louisa M., a very pretty girl of 15 or 16 going home from a boarding school in Fairfield; a man from Rochester, N. Y., with a deformed, limping wife, and a coarse, Irish servant girl. In my greenness, I helped the servant girl into the stage, and offered her some other civility, as if she had been a *lady;* being accustomed to do so to all white women. Something in the looks of my fellow passengers, and the girl's own drawing back, shewed me the blunder. The student says, Yale college has about 500 students; viz. 350 academical, and 150 professional (Law, physic, and divinity). Temperance flourishing there—majority of them, members of Total Abstinence Society, even from wine. He and his sister stopped before we reached Middletown,—near their father's house. "I shall not soon forget that sweet girl," said another passenger. Indeed her looks, manners, and discourse with her brother (whom she met that afternoon the first time for several months), all excited interest. I did not learn what the *M.* stood for,—upon her trunk.

Our Rochester companions helped to beguile the time, while Miss S., veiled, was reading. The man is concerned in one of the immense wheat mills there. One of them manufactures into flour, 700,000 bushels of wheat, a year. His wife is a genius; and made some amusing efforts at literary conversation. Among other things, she had read Calebs, and admired Miss More; only thought her books "difficult to read."—Passing a village grave yard, enclosed with stone, entirely outside of the village, I asked why it was placed so? The lady said it was "for the convenience of those who live at a distance."—As clear as mud.

Entered Middletown, a town of 3 or 4000 inhabitants, near sunset; coming to the western Bank of Connecticut River just below. Took tea there; and drove on, having still 9 or 10 miles to go. Just above Middletown, on the opposite side of the River, is the village of Chatham, where a large quarry of dark brown rock, soft, and much prized for building, is wrought, out of the high river bank. The grave yard being found to rest over the seam of rock, the quarriers are about to make a stir among the dry bones—i. e. remove them to some other resting place.—Cultivation in some places is carried close to the highwater mark. The river banks are planted with willows, to prevent abrasion by the water.

At Rocky Hill, and Wethersfield (famous for its onion fields) we parted with our remaining companions; and arrived in Hartford about 9, at night. Our hostelrie, the City Hotel, kept by a Mr. Morgan. Hartford and New Haven are regularly incorporated as *cities*, by the Legislature of Connecticut: having, each, 12 or 13000 people. The legislature meets in them, alternately.

Hartford! how could I sleep here, for thinking of the horrible convention, of 1814? Yet sleep I did, and soundly, for 5 or 6 hours.

Wednesday, July 2. Rose before 4. White waiters. They make me feel awkward. Left the city at 5—several persons in stage besides Miss S. and me. In driving out, saw an elegant church, built of the brown stone dug at Chatham quarry. Several other churches, and other public buildings, of uncommon beauty to the transient eye. A tall pole, nearly as high as a church steeple, presented itself upon a sort of public square. It was a Liberty Pole, such as is described in McFingal! Nothing yet, in N. England, has so excited me.

> ' When sudden met his angry eye,
> A pole ascending through the sky,' &c.

Let nobody fail to read the passage—and the poem.

Our road lay chiefly along the Connecticut River—its W. bank—great diversity of cliff, woods, field, low ground, and ravine—much pretty country visible, mainly on t'other side. Hemlock trees, exactly what we in Louisa have called juniper, on river hills. Plenty of a kind of fern, or *brake*. The country people here call it *farn;* and an old Scotchwoman with us called it *bracken,* and said it was common in the mountains of Scotland. So we set it down as the very sort of plant which hid Roderic Dhu's men on the mountain side, near Coilantogle Ford. Beyond the river, amidst much agricultural richness and beauty, lay the village of East Windsor. A church steeple there had a clock, the hands of which were so large, that I could easily see the hour and minute they told— 6 or 800 yards off. Two or 3 miles higher, on one side of the river, was Windsor (proper), at the junction of Windsor river with the Connecticut.

Breakfast at a Tavern 12 miles from Hartford; at the locks belonging to the Five-mile canal, which leads round the Rapids of C. river. The waiter at breakfast was a right handsome—young lady, I should call her; a blooming rose-and-lily lassie, of 18 or 20; quite as genteel-looking as any among ⅘ of the real young ladies that I have met with. Tho' brisk in her motions around the table, she had an air of *nonchalance* withal; and at every interval in her services, she sat, half reclining, upon a settee.

Her look and manner said that she asked no odds, either of us passengers, or of her employers.

In the morning's drive, patches of tobacco, growing on the river lowlands, repeatedly presented themselves. To my wondering inquiry touching this phenomenon, a facetious old gentleman of Springfield said, it was to make Havana cigars. The villages of Warehouse Point, and Enfield in Connecticut, Long Meadow and Springfield in Massachusetts, appeared on the opposite shore; Suffield in Conn., and West Springfield in Mass., on the Western side.—Crossed the River on a covered Bridge, into Springfield; and after a few minutes' stay, drove back again, and resumed our road to Northampton, now 18 miles distant.

Striking landscapes and objects thickened upon us. The River was more unruly—oftener cramped and turned by bluffs and rocks. Mountains rose, both far and near. Mount Tom and Mount Holyoke, especially prominent, engaged the eye—Holyoke, a single, sharp peak; Mount Tom, more rounded, and giving its name to a whole range. From several points, church steeples and spires lent their beautifying power to the prospect—and beautifiers they truly are; speaking even more eloquently to the mind than to the eye.

In exchange for some of our companions, at Springfield, we took in a lady passenger, evidently single, and of no particular age; sour-faced, and sour-tempered; yet at times displaying kind feelings. Very communicative.

Before one, we reached Northampton.

They gave me dinner at the Hotel, about one. A female, white waiter, again. She was troublesomely assiduous. We had apple-pie, and rhubarb-pie, or tart. This was new to me: and it was with difficulty I could understand her question, if I would take some of the r'barrb? expending all the sound upon the last syllable.—After a brief visit to Miss S. at her brother's—where only her mother was,—he being yet in N. York—I sauntered over the town. The Court House, neat and commodious. Several good churches, many handsome private houses, all of wood, painted white. A well filled bookstore. The afternoon was rainy. Invitation to breakfast with Mrs. and Miss S. tomorrow. Agreed. Tea with them today.

A good deal of drinking about the public houses.

A gentleman of the town encourages my design of walking among the country people, by telling me of the kind usage to be expected, and that they will not refuse pay for what they afford me. New Englandisms begin to multiply upon my ear. This gentleman says Worcester is "considerable of a place," &c., &c.

My landlord is a sulky scrub: and though I complained of his dining room maid's officiousness, there is in general a plentiful lack of proper attentions to a guest at his house.

After an early and loathed dinner, having directed that my trunk be sent by tomorrow's stage to Hartford, I set out on foot, westward, into the country; with no baggage but an umbrella. Crossed the canal. Poor lands—pine and hemlock hills. Hay growing, or "being mowed," in three fourths of the fields. Roads ridged up in the middle, like turnpikes. Met two young ladies, driving unattended in a chaise, going to N. Hampton. Called in at a right large but shabby looking farm house, for a draught of water. The owner looked intemperate: yet he asked if strong drink was not the cause of the late riot and murder among the Irish on the Rl. Road near Baltimore.—A school house, where a good-looking young woman taught. Longed to go in, and see how it was managed: but could not frame an excuse, or muster boldness enough. Westhampton meeting-house, 9 miles from N. Hampton. There I meant to stay all night; and asked quarters of a decent man, who kept a sort of store near the meeting-house—his wife, to whom I first applied, referring me to him— Mr. Jordan, or Mr. Judd,—uncertain which. After saying there was a tavern but a mile off, and being told by me that I was tired, and wanted to see the ways of private houses, he consented to my stay. I asked him to sell me a sheet of paper. He offered to *give* it. Wrote a letter for the mail; and then my host and I ascended the church steeple to see the prospect. It was sunset; and he had but a dim spy glass. However, the view was extensive, and fine if not compared with that at Round Hill. It reached to East, and South-hampton—six or 8 miles off. Just above the church rose a mountain, offering a far wider prospect. Before writing my letter, I had joined them in their evening meal; taken, in the sensible New England manner, at six o'clock, instead of near bedtime. It consisted of tea, with brown sugar, currant tart, and warm rolls, leavened with salæratus. The master prefaced it with a grace, which showed him evangelical. Another, giving thanks, when we had done.

He has much to esteem. Was a student at Williams College, among the mountains of Berkshire, in the extreme N. W. of Massachusetts. There, Dr. Justin Edwards, the great Temperance champion, was also a student—used to walk thither from his home near this place where he was born—and back again.

After our descent from the steeple, my host went out to milk the cow for his wife. He filled one pail brimming, and called for another—18 quarts a day!—Rich butter.

Temperance and Colonization, he says, flourish hereabouts. When he attended me up stairs to bed, (intending to set out very early in the morning,) I offered him the usual compensation, for my entertainment. He would not touch a doit. "He had always heard much of Virginia hospitality; and if he should ever visit Va., perhaps I might show him some of it."—After I got into bed, I heard him at family prayers.

Friday, July 4. It was not 4 o'clock when I rose, dressed, and left the house—no one else being awake, that I could perceive.

Took the road to Southhampton. At Sunrise, heard cannon, at North-hampton or Springfield, welcoming the FOURTH.—Country hilly, and wooded—barren. Much of the fern, which I saw the day before yester-day. Hemlock too, and white pine. Approaching a cabin, where an old man and his family were at breakfast, I plucked a sprig of fern, and asked him what it was? "Why, that's sweet *farn*," said he, rather testily. No invitation to breakfast, or to come in.—Hay fields; and cattle grazing.

Reached S. hampton (6 miles) at 7 o'clock; and asked for breakfast at the Tavern. It was soon ready,—a good breakfast. Price, 17 cents! Tipplers there. Landlady.

Off towards Springfield—eastwardly. Come again to yesterday's canal. At it, met an erect old man, of 75; 6½ feet high, and very well propor-tioned; who with alacrity entered into conversation, though he had seemed in a hurry, driving some oxen. He "was out agin Burgyne," in '77. Inveighed against the canal, and its Company. It was useless, and an imposition. For lands taken to dig it, the damages assessed were paid in *canal-stock!* Can it be so?

Presently a man overtook me, who was in a Jersey wagon, collecting rags to make paper. He invited me to ride with him. Accepted, of course. He was chatty to a degree! and quite intelligent—the very man I needed. The tall, fine looking malcontent I had just parted with was old Squire Judd. My new Palinurus and Automedon (both in one) ex-plained to me a simple and admirable system of mutual insurance against fire, which is concurred in by almost every householder hereabouts. Example—On a valuation of $1000, the insured pays a premium of $12 for 7 years, and gives bond for $25 more, to answer quotas, should losses require them. Thus, for $37 at the utmost, he is insured 7 years to the amount of $1000.—Cost of painting a house 40 feet by 30, $60. Renewed every 5 or 6 years.—Passed a natural mole, or mound, dividing the 2 Springfield Ponds. They are a mile long; ¼ wide.—Here my new friend and I parted.

Passed through W. Springfield, along the stage road of day before yesterday. Got a man to ferry me over Connecticut River in a canoe. It was 80 rods (440 yards) wide, and swollen with rain; yet he asked only 6¼ cents. A by-path carried me through fields into a public road. Some fine oxen grazing.—Stood half an hour to see a man cutting shingles out of white-pine blocks, with a circular saw. It made I forget how many hundred, or thousand, revolutions in a minute. The machinery was turned by the water of Chickopee River; and just beyond was a cotton factory, in the Lower Chickopee Village. The factory was not at work, as it was the 4 of July.

Being informed that the famous Paper-Mills, nominally of Springfield, were at the Upper Chickopee Village, 2 or 3 miles up the River, I proceeded thence, guided a little way by a strapping fellow in a round jacket, and of the surliest manners that I had yet encountered. He strode on so far before, regardless of my briefer stride and jaded limbs, that I let him go his ways, with a muttered curse upon his rudeness; and trusted to my own sharpness in finding the road,—which was quite plain.

The Paper Mills were shown me thoroughly by an obliging man who belonged to them. Luckily, they were not stopped, in honor of the day: and all stages of the curious and interesting process were for the first time presented to my view. Perhaps the greatest curiosity was a newly invented cylinder (hollow, and filled with steam) for drying the paper which passed under it.—'T was near 2, p. m. I was then 4 miles from Springfield. The sun had been, all day, and still continued, absolutely torrid: feet sore, and somewhat blistered. Signs of drinking, rife as I walked. Between Lower and Upper Chickopee, a man staggered on before me, and after many diverting tacks and gyrations in his course, losing his hat by the way, he tripped and tumbled into a ditch by the roadside. I "left him alone in his glory." Rum is here the popular drink; not whiskey.

Proceeded to Springfield, along a fine turnpike road, thickly planted with sorry-looking refectories, or grog shops, and now and then, sumptuous dwelling houses. Bought a bottle of spruce beer, and drank it. Approaching Springfield, heard cannon. Presently, saw a group, who were firing it. Went to them. Close by was an extempore enclosure, boarded over at top, whence waved a flag. In it, I was told, a dinner was "being eaten" by a large company, in honor of the Fourth. The toasts began. A man near the flag waved it when a toast was announced; and immediately the cannon was fired. Then followed loud cheers from within. This was the Jacksonian celebration, and was near the U. S. barracks, and arsenal, where a body of troops are stationed. The cannon had its name, "La Perilleuse," stamped upon it—a brass 6 or 9 pounder. A bystander said, it was one of those taken from Burgoyne. I stood by, till 18 or 20 discharges had been made; a silent spectator and listener: then went on into the town—but not the thickest, or genteelest part of it. Entered a 3d. or 4th. rate tavern, where people (rustics, evidently) were crowded to get refreshments. Ate a poor dinner, and then sat, to rest, and hear, and talk, in the portico.

The glass, manifestly, had circulated and was yet circulating very freely. The buzz of voices was incessant; equal to what I am used to on a Louisa Court day.—Specimens of Yankee speech abounded; *guessings* were numberless.—A decent young man (perhaps of my own age, or older—i. e. 32), in blue broad-cloth, with metal buttons—reminding me of the South—and with head perhaps half as gray as mine, entered into conversation with me. He was communicative and right sensible, though no scholar. His reverent demeanor towards me, whether for my gray-hairs, or for my being a stranger, was marked, and amusing. "Legis's-la-túre," was his pronunciation of that word; with a strong accent upon the 2d. syllable. He says that *breeds* of horses are not much thought of. The serviceable ones are sought.—Racing almost unknown.—Not a race-course in Massachusetts, or (as he supposes) in New England. Does not know whether colonization is popular or not.

Two orations were delivered in town today; one to the Jackson party, by Mr. Eldridge, editor of the Hampden *Whig;* one to the National Republicans, by Wm. B. Calhoun, speaker of the Mass. H. of Representatives. The latter seems to fill a large space here, in the public eye.

At 4 or 5, p. m., I walked down the hill, towards the dense part of the town—a mile from my first hostelrie. A company of volunteers, in uniform, enlivened the walk by their music, and marching with me. The arsenal was closed, so that its interior could not be seen.—Entered, and explored an extensive Brewery, and drank a glass of the porter made there—pretty good. It makes 1700 barrels a year, each containing 144 bottle-fuls, i. e. a gross. Worth $23 a gross, including bottles. Barley sells for 90 to 100 cents a bushel. It is *malted,* then dried, then cracked, between rollers. After malting, it is sweet, because the saccharine principle is retained, while others pass off.

Chose for mine inn a Temperance Tavern, kept, as the sign said, by B. Fuller Jr. very churlish, and unaccommodating—Either every body is put out of mood by the festivities of the Fourth, or this is a house whose doors ought never to be darkened by another traveller. However, my beard was long, and I must have looked very shabby.

Heard conversation about Temperance, between Mr. Fuller and Mr. Morris, a lawyer, who said he had been out into the country today, to make a Temperance address.

Paid my bill before going to bed. For supper and lodging, it is only 42 cents!—Distances today,—to Southampton 6 miles, to Lower Chickopee 10, to Upper do. 2, to Springfield 4—Total 22, of which 4 were performed in the carryall of my friend the paper-mill agent.

Sunday, July 5. Up at 4. Legs and feet very sore, and aching. Off at ¼ past 4. Nobody up, as I walked the street, except a man 2 or 3 hundred yards before me. —Met an old woman going to market, and asked her which was the road to Enfield. "Well, you keep straight ahead, and you'll come to it in time. Ah, you slept too late this morning!"—What or whom could she take me for?—Not far out of town, along the bank of the Connecticut, met sundry laughing lads and lasses, in curricles; returning, probably, from some place of pleasure, where they had spent "Independence," as the 4th. is called here. From a curve in the river and its bank, 2 miles below Springfield, is a view of the town &c. which would that I could spread upon canvas. The graceful bend of the stream— its glassy smoothness, reflecting houses, trees, church, and spire, clouds and blue sky—the adjacent hills, with some shagginess of woods and rocks—made the whole scene, soon after sunrise, one of rare beauty. —Two or 3 miles yet lower down was the State line, between Mass. and Conn. On the boundary stone I sat 20 or 30 minutes, writing the notes from which this paragraph is penned. "Long-Meadow," a neat village, is not far above—several handsome houses.

Having walked 8 miles,—the heat waxing tropical, again—my lower limbs began to feel much worried. The Enfield Hotel, said to be near the meeting house, which of course was near the centre of that village, was to be my breakfasting place. Asking a rough fellow in a carter's frock, how far to Enfield? in my civilest manner,—he replied, in a tone of curdling surliness, and without looking at me, "Little more 'n a mile to th' meetin' house"—not stopping—his voice coarse and ill-natured in the extreme.

Enfield (Conn.)—Meachum's Hotel, at 7—shaved—breakfasted—and walked on. The village extends 5 or 6 miles, at least, along the road. Handsome and populous. While my breakfast was getting ready, I took a short nap on a bench in the bar room. Landlord's razor passing dull, and all his appointments for shaving no better than would be met with at a country tavern in Va.

In ten or 15 minutes after leaving the Hotel, reached the village Meeting house. Large—with a cupola, and spire of immense height. —Presently, not far to my right, and down upon the River Bank, appeared *Thompsonville,* a manufacturing village,—tho' I did not hear of any but a carpet-factory. The shuttles are thrown by hand, without steam, or water power. *Warehouse point* was another village. Canal. *Windsor,* township and village.

Saw a bluff, fat, and extremely stupid old man at his own door, churning cream with a paddle, in an earthen pot. I could not, by any cross-examination, extract from him an intelligible account of how the churches are built here. From his house-door, on a beautifully swelling knoll, was a prospect more extensive and hardly less beautiful than that of the early morning, just below Springfield. It commanded E. and W. Suffield, 7 or 8 miles up the river, Warehouse point, and Windsor,—with a large extent of farm-land, meadows, hills, woods, and water, agreeably diversified. —The low grounds near Warehouse Point contained much tobacco; 100 acres of it, in one body. A long shed there for curing it. It looks nearly or quite as well as ours usually does at this season. The corn very thickly planted, and luxuriant—knee high, and more.

Just before reaching the stupid old man's house, I lay down for an hour under a walnut-tree, on some deliciously soft grass; napping, part of the time. While there, heard the church-clock at Warehouse Pt., nearly a mile off, strike 10 and 11.

Stept into a tinner's shop by the road side. Process of wiring tin pans. Saw much of the ware making, which in childhood used so to dazzle me, when displayed by the pedlers. —East Windsor—West Windsor.

Two carryalls drove by me. No invitation to ride. But one seemed in a prodigious hurry; and 't other carried a fat man, of 250, at least, with a horse poor and small.

Many good rye and hay crops—fed away on the farm, or sold in Hartford, or at some neighboring tavern.

About 3 miles from Hartford, overtook a low, weather beaten, badly dressed man, walking with apparent difficulty, in darned and ragged socks and no shoes, with an especially shabby old Leghorn hat, half brimless, and no coat. He greeted me with much frankness, and proposed having my company to H. —We were forthwith *hail fellow* &c. to each other. He presently told me that he was an English seaman, just 2 months from Plymouth, in the brig of war Falcon, of 18 guns, commanded by Capt. Auplin, a great tyrant, from whom he had deserted at Halifax. Had walked all the way from Bath, Maine; was moneyless, shoeless—feet blistered and sore—now suffering under a fever and ague. Evidently (as he self-complacently said he was) a right well informed man. Spoke far better English than many of our gentry—said he knew something of navig^n, could write a good hand, &c. Had begged his way, —and never asked for food or lodging in vain, among these Yankees. Going to Elizabeth Town, N. J., where he has an uncle. His name, Robt. Johnson. —Was once given to drink; and is now, if appearances do not deceive me. On being paid off once, he had £123, 5, 6— It was all gone in 3 weeks!—Expressed great surprise at my asking for a glass of water, by the wayside: a gentleman of my appearance, he said. He thought I should have called for wine, ale, or cider. No Temperance reform in the British Navy, that he ever heard of. The grog-ration (half a pint daily) still drawn, and drunk. Is quite sure that sailors never can be cured of drinking. A good deal staggered at hearing of the reform in our service. —Said he had been at the Battle of Navarino, and received 2 wounds. Sir E. Codrington was promoted only from the Asia, a 2 decker, to the Caledonia, a 3 decker [quære?]. Thought, or pretended to think, that I was beyond all doubt a naval officer,—from some of my phrases and demeanor.—

As he said a Doctor had prescribed flannel for him, I took him to a clothing store in the suburbs of Hartford, near the river, and gave him a flannel shirt and drawers, a new hat, jacket, &c. He begged earnestly to know my name, but I childishly refused—and we parted. He said he should embark in a small steamboat, which goes hence to New York.

Bought a summer frock-coat, (of faded green bombazette), pantaloons, and waistcoat as a walking suit for myself: directing the bundle to be sent to the City Hotel.

On my way thither, called at the storehouse and counting room of Mr. Charles Sigourney, husband of the poetess, and delivered to him a letter of introduction from Mr. Cresson to her. —He will do himself the pleasure to wait on me at the Hotel in the morning; and engages me to call and see Mrs. S. tomorrow afternoon.

Found my trunk at the Hotel; brought by the stage from N. hampton. Peeped into Miss Sedgwick's Hope Leslie, lent me by Miss H. S.

I have walked 26 miles today. The Thermometer has been at 91 or '2. —I am overdoing the matter. Such fatigue takes away much of the pleasure, and profit, of travel. —To bed at 9½.

Mem. The factory at Thompsonville, Enfield, makes 800 yards of carpeting a day. 200 hands employed. The fly shuttle not used, because it cannot be changed readily enough, for the different colors. The highest priced made there, $1.75 per yard.

Hartford, Sunday, July 6. Rose at half past 5—stiff, sore, and feverish— with a headache. Lounged in the Barroom, conversing with several gentlemen; especially a young Mr. Horace Barber, a native of Connecticut, who seems to have lived in Louisville, Kentucky—a lawyer, I take him to be—intelligent, clever, accessible. He confirms that N. England contains not a race ground; nor any race horses, proper.

Judges in Conn. chosen by Legislature: judges of county courts, for one year; of Sup^r courts, during good behavior, or till 70 years of age, when they are disqualified by the Constitution. This provision sometimes deprives the state of matured and most valuable minds; but perhaps oftener, saves the Bench from being incumbered by dotage or its cousin german. Clerks, appointed by the respective courts.

After 10, Mr. Sigourney called to take me with him to Church (Episcopal). A grand, solemnly elegant structure. Nothing could better suit its reverend nature and imposing ceremonials, than the dark, yellowish brown sandstone of which it is built, from the Chatham quarry, 14 miles down the river. The material has an appropriate gravity, which, connected with the great height and bulk of the building, is absolutely awe-striking. The steeple is not a "taper spire," but has a tower-like top. It surpasses in beauty and grandeur any church that I have ever seen. Cost $70,000! —We sat in Mr. Sigourney's pew—Mrs. S. not being there this morning. The organ seemed to me the best-sounding I had ever heard. Mr. S. read the Bible passages of the Service in a copy of the Greek, Septuagint Bible, and a Greek Testament of 1592, "Coloniæ"— Cologne. (?) I read with him—never having seen the Septuagint before. The chapter we read (in Exodus) was very easy. I marked some strange freedoms which either the Greek version, or the common English one read by the preacher, had taken with the original: for they differed from each other in a startling manner. The New Testament chapter (Acts) was in the contracted letter, hardly decipherable to me. Short, and indifferent sermon: a preparation for the Lord's Supper—finished soon after 12. Mr. S. invites me again to his pew in the afternoon, and then to his house, to see Mrs. S. —Agreed.

P. M. To Church again at 3. Took my seat in Mr. S.'s pew, alone. Survey of the church, inside. Four very large, Gothic arched windows, on each side—sashes divided into small panes of the *rhombus,* or diamond form—catercornered squares—about 6 or 7 inches long and wide. Galleries and pews, painted of a sort of jalap color—rest of the interior, white —some gilding about the orchestra and pulpit. Presently, Mrs. and Mr. Sigourney entered the pew. A bow, as courteous as might beseem the Synagogue,—an appearance of conjectural recognition,—met me from Mrs. S.—I sat by her during the service and sermon—she putting her own prayer book into my heathenish hand, and pointing out the several places to be read. The heat was still oppressive: and she lent me her fan. She looked not over 40, if so much. Her cheeks bloom like 18. With bonnet on, countenance very pleasing. Mr. S. seems 55 or 60.

Sermon by the morning preacher—Mr. Wheaton, of Rh. Island— rather better. His cousin (a Mr. Wheaton too) is pastor of this church, and read the services, hymns, &c. The latter is of decided ability. He announced a Colonization Meeting for next Saturday, and his own design to enter at length then into the Abolition question,—which, he said, he regarded as a most delicate one; doing, or threatening, great mischief to the community. His few words betokened power; and a justness of thinking on that topic, highly grateful to me.

Mrs. Sigourney accepted my arm—her husband politely affording me the opportunity: and we chatted all the way to their house, a beautiful retreat, 100 rods or more (5 or 600 yards) from church, and just out of town. Among her inquiries, was "Do you enjoy many religious *privileges* in Virginia?" My answer, blundering out something about our Act of Religious Freedom, and the perfect unrestraint upon conscience which we enjoy (for I was dunce enough not to see at first, that she used the word *privileges,* evangelically) plainly showed her what a pagan I was.

Common-schools, and the fund ($2,000,000) in a great degree useless, because people did not pay out of their own pockets for their schools. A plan like that of Massachusetts is talked of; where the State gives a sum towards a school in a district, only upon condition that its people raise an equal sum. This makes them feel an interest in the school; and send their children punctually, to get the worth of their money. Female Academy. Female education much attended to in Connecticut. Girls not seldom taught the learned languages. Infant schools discontinued in Hartford, because the Doctor said they injured the brains, and nervous systems of children, by over-excitement. The mental effect not good, either learn like parrots, by sound, by rote, alone—without exercise of thought. Domestic education now preferred, for young children. Infant schools perhaps still useful, for children of very poor parents, who else would have to leave them at home alone, at working hours. . . .

Back to town. With my new friend Mr. Barber, who seems to think he cannot do enough for my entertainment,—visited two of the belles of Hartford—Miss Woodbridges. One of them handsome—both tall, clever, and agreeable. No dancing parties in Hartford—no ball for the last 6 years. No theatrical amusements in N. England, except in Boston.

2

Northampton, Mass., 1834. And you will positively excommunicate me, if I do not send you "some First Impressions" of Yankee land? Have at you, then: though, really, my time has been so filled with seeing and hearing, that hardly a scrap remains to write down a hundredth part of the curious or striking things that meet my eyes and ears.

Unusual opportunity has been afforded me, for using various lights and shades of Yankee character. In stage, steamboat, and railway-car,— in jersey wagon and on foot, on highways and by-ways, in farm-houses and city palaces, I have seen and chatted with all sorts of people, from the * * * of the * * * to the tavern porter and the country laborer. Five days I have spent in a pedestrian stroll, calling often at the country houses to get a draught of water, rest myself, and talk with the farmer or his wife. These gossipings, you may well suppose, commonly produced amusement, and frequently solid information; or at least solid materials for reflection. And, considering that it is only a few weeks since my first entry into New England, methinks I have a pretty exact measure of Jonathan's foot. —Yet, for all this preface, do not expect any very astounding revelations. From the thousand incidents that unitedly make my tour exceedingly interesting to myself, it is not certain that any one, or any dozen, can be selected, which will very much interest another person. Though sore at times from long walks, and sorer still, once or twice, from rude manners and uncivil answers to civil questions, I have experienced kindnesses and pleasure preponderating a thousand fold over all.

In the visible face of Massachusetts and Connecticut, the features which by their novelty or beauty most strike a Virginian eye, are the small farms, usually of from fifty to two hundred acres; the fields, disproportionally small, there being sometimes fifteen or twenty on one farm; the stone fences, often rendered necessary and numerous by scarcity of timber, and by the troublesome superabundance of stones which can be best got rid of by piling them in fences; the universality of hay-crops, on hills as well as in low land; the almost entire absence of wheat —for the prevalent grain-crops are oats, rye, and indian corn; the clustering of habitations in villages, instead of dispersing them at intervals of a mile over the country; the white-painted village churches, all with stately spires, visible for miles around, having gilt vanes, and clocks with hands so large and stroke so loud, that I have repeatedly seen and heard the hour half a mile off. The country is more hilly, or *rolling*, as our farmers would say, than the lower half of Virginia; and the hills have a smaller base, and a more gracefully swelling, dome-like top, than our hills. These rotundities, with their attendant hollows, traversed by numberless stone fences, with here and there patches of woodland, and detached white farm-houses half embosomed in elms and fruit-trees,— while perhaps two or three villages with steeples piercing the sky are at once within view,—exhibit countless landscapes of a beauty unknown to Eastern or to Western Virginia.

Here is not apparent a hundredth part of the abject squalid poverty that our State presents. I have not seen a log house in New England; nor a dwelling-house without one or more glass windows. And nine tenths of the common farm-houses are painted. Indeed, paint for the outside of a house is here considered an indispensable piece of economy; and is applied to many humble dwellings, of one story, and one, or two, or three rooms. Brick and stone buildings are not common, except in the cities. This village, the loveliest in all the North, and Worcester, (take care to call it *Wooster*)—having, respectively, 4,000 and 5 or 6,000 inhabitants—contain, both together, hardly more than a hundred and fifty brick and stone houses.

But the *morale* of New England—the character of her people—their tones of thought and feeling on some important subjects—their social and political institutions and usages—their modes of promoting comfort and convenience in their houses, and in all departments of life—have interested me far more than her physical lineaments.

Would that I had time and space to unfold the Road, Pauper, and School systems of Massachusetts and Connecticut,—the only Yankee States except Rhode Island that I have visited. But that would require too much detail. Their happy organization may be inferred from their effects.

The common roads are nearly all *ridged up*, turnpike fashion; and are as good as our turnpikes. I do not mean such as a certain one leading from F* * * * * to * * * * * *, which the traveller knows to be a turnpike only by the tolls and the jolts; but those in the great Valley, and near Richmond. For mending roads, two instruments are used here, which many road-overseers in Virginia have long been vainly urged to employ: the plow and the scraper. A two-horse plow is said by those who have tried it fairly to be equal to six men with hoes; and a scraper, to sixteen. The latter implement may be bought for five, or even three dollars. The making and repair of roads here is wholly a concern of the township,— or *town* as the provincial dialect hath it. If any one is damaged by a road's being out of order, he can sue the township for it. Several instances have been told me of such damages recovered: $7,000 against the town of Lowell, by a man and girl who, driving a gig along the road, plunged over a precipice made by a deep cut of a new railroad, crippled themselves, killed their horse, and crushed the gig.

There is probably not a beggar by trade in New England—except solicitors for pious charities, and for subscriptions. The needy are sent to a poor-house, having a farm attached to it, on which they work for *their* parish, the township; or are *let* to the lowest bidder for their maintenance; as the people of the township choose. In different townships the number of paupers greatly varies. I have heard of five, ten, and thirty or more upon the lists: and as a county contains many "towns," perhaps the number of such pensioners here equals ours. But (mark!) the expense here is next to nothing; sometimes absolutely nothing; nay, some "towns" derive a revenue from the labors of their parish poor. Salem has thus gained several thousand dollars in a year. All the paupers who are able to render a fair equivalent, and some render more, for the relief they receive. The problem so puzzling to England, Virginia, and other countries these Yankees have solved by a union of tact, shrewdness, and vigilance—the problem, how to make poor-houses not attractive enough to tempt and foster laziness, yet not repulsive enough to frighten away real misery from asking relief. The secret is the simple one, of furnishing plain, clean, and comfortable houses, lodgings, and diet; with *labor as the inexorable condition of their enjoyment,* if the pauper can labor. Two things mitigate the hardship of living at the township poor-house: first, that it is in the poor's own neighborhood, within reach of relations or friends, and not involving a rough transportation of ten or twenty miles, like our county poor-houses; and secondly, that a COMMON-SCHOOL, open and free alike to rich and poor, is always near. The comfort of this, to such paupers as have children, need not be descanted on.

This is the general usage: but near this village there happens to be, at the poor-house, a school purely for its juvenile inmates. I walked out to it—a mile or two—one day. It (the poor-house) is managed by a superintendent, who keeps the sufficiently able-bodied inmates at work. I went by invitation, into his house: entered also the schoolroom. The teacher is an elderly man, himself a pauper. There were two black scholars, sitting rather apart from the whites. In nearly all the approaches between white and black in New England, there is a manifest shrinking back in the former; a *noli me tangere* air, which seems to snuff contamination in the slightest fellowship with Cuffee. These dark-skinned school children are evidently in bad odor in more senses than one.

The Brighton Cattle Fair

Nathaniel Hawthorne

Sept. 27, 1841. A Ride to Brighton yesterday morning, it being the day of the weekly cattle fair. William Allen and myself went in a wagon, carrying a calf, to be sold at the fair. The calf had not had his breakfast, as his mother had preceded him to Brighton; and he kept expressing his hunger and discomfort by loud, sonorous baa-s, especially when we passed any cattle in the fields or on the road. The cows, grazing within hearing expressed great interest, and some of them came galloping to the roadside to behold the calf. Little children, also, on their way to school, stopt to laugh and point at poor little Bossie. He was a prettily behaved urchin, and kept thrusting his hairy muzzle between William and myself, apparently wishing to be stroked and patted. It was an ugly thought, that his confidence in human nature, and Nature in general, was to be so ill rewarded as by cutting his throat, and selling him in quarters. This, I suppose, has been his fate before now.

It was a beautiful morning, clear as chrystal [*sic*], with an invigorating, but not disagreeable coolness. The general aspect of the country was as green as summer;—greener indeed than mid or latter summer—and there were occasional interminglings of the brilliant hues of Autumn, which made the scenery more beautiful, both visibly and in sentiment. We saw no absolutely mean or poor-looking abodes along the road. There were warm and comfortable farm-houses, ancient, with the porch, the sloping roof, the antique peak, the clustered chimneys, of old times; and modern cottages, smart and tasteful; and villas, with terraces before them, and dense shade, and wooden urns on pillars, and other such tokens of gentility. Pleasant groves of oak and walnut, also, there were, sometimes stretching along vallies [*sic*], sometimes ascending a hill and cloathing [*sic*] it all round, so as to make it a great clump of verdure.

Nathaniel Hawthorne, *The American Notebooks*, edited by Randall Stewart (New Haven, 1932, courtesy of Ohio State University Press), pp. 76-78.

Frequently, we passed people with cows, oxen, sheep or pigs, for Brighton fair.

On arriving at Brighton, we found the village thronged with people, horses, and vehicles. Probably there is no place in New England where the character of our agricultural population may be so well studied. Almost all the farmers, within a reasonable distance, make it a point, I suppose, to attend Brighton fair pretty frequently, if not on business, yet as amateurs. Then there are all the cattle-people and butchers who supply the Boston market, and dealers from far and near; and every man who has a cow or yoke of oxen, whether to sell or buy, goes to Brighton on Monday. There were a thousand or two of cattle in the extensive pens, belonging to the tavern keeper, besides many standing about. You could hardly stir a step without running upon the horns of one dilemma or the other, in the shape of ox, cow, bull, or ram. The yeomen appeared to be more in their element than I ever saw them anywhere else, except, indeed, at labor—more than at musterings and such gatherings of amusement. And yet this was a sort of festal day, too, as well as a day of business, Most of the people were of a bulky make, with much bone and muscle, and some good store of fat, like people who lived on flesh-diet—with mottled faces, too, hard and red, as if they adhered to the old fashion of spirit-drinking;—great round-paunched country squires were there too, sitting under the porch of the tavern, or waddling about, whip in hand, discussing the points of the cattle. There, also, were gentlemen farmers, neatly, trimly, and fashionably dressed, in handsome surtouts, and pantaloons strapt under their boots. Yeomen, too, in their black or blue sunday suits, cut by country tailors, and awkwardly worn. Others (like myself) had on the blue stuff frocks which they wear in the fields—the most comfortable garment that ever man invented. Country loafers, too, were among the throng—men who looked wistfully at the liquors in the bar, and waited for some friend to invite them to drink—poor shabby, out at elbowed devils. Also, dandies from the city, stayed and buckramed, who had come to see the humors of Brighton fair. All these, and other varieties of mankind, either thronged the spacious bar-room of the hotel, drinking, smoking, talking, bargaining; or walked about among the cattle-pens, looking with knowing eyes at the horned people. The owners of the cattle stood near at hand, waiting for offers; there was something indescribable in their aspect that showed them to be the owners, though they intermixed among the crowd. The cattle, brought from a hundred separate farms, or rather a thousand, seemed to agree very well together, not quarreling in the least. They almost all had a history, no doubt, if they could but have told it—the cows had each given their milk to support families— had roamed the pastures, and come home to the barn-yard—had been looked upon as a sort of member of the domestic circle, and was known by a name, as Brindle or Cherry. The oxen, with their necks bent by the heavy yoke, had toiled in the plough-field and in haying time, for many years, and knew their master's stall as well as the master himself did his own table. Even the young steers, and the little calves, had something of domestic sacredness about them; for children had watched their growth, and petted them, and played with them. And here they all were, old and young, gathered from their thousand homes to Brighton fair; whence the great chance was that they would go to the slaughter-house, and thence be transmitted, in sirloins, joints, and such pieces, to the tables of the Boston people.

William Allen had come to buy four little pigs, to take the places of our four, who have now grown large, and are to be fatted and killed within a few weeks. There were several hundreds, in pens appropriated to their use, grunting discordantly, and apparently in no very good humor with their companions or the world at large. Most, or many, of these pigs had been imported from the state of New York. The drovers set out with a large number, and peddle them along the road, till they arrive at Brighton with the remainder. William selected four, and bought them at five cents per pound. These poor little porkers were forthwith seized by the tails, their legs tied, and then thrown into our wagon, where they kept up a continual grunt and squeal, till we got home. Two of them were yellowish, or light gold colored; the other two black and white speckled; and all four of very piggish aspect and deportment. One of them snapt at William's finger most spitefully, and bit it to the bone.

All the scene of the fair was very characteristic and peculiar—cheerful and lively, too, in the bright, warm sun. I must see it again; for it ought to be studied.

The Capitol of New England

Alexander Mackay

As seen from the bay, there is no city in the Union which has a more imposing appearance than Boston. It seems to envelope, from its apex to its base, a conical hill, which rises from the water with a slight acclivity; the successive terraces in which it mounts to the summit, being crowned by the spacious dome of the "State House," the seat of the legislature of Massachusetts. In addition to being thus ornamental to the city, this prominent object is highly useful to the mariner, the gilded cone at its top being discernible at sea long before any surrounding object becomes visible. At its base the town appears girdled with a frame-work of masts, sustaining a network of rigging. To give life to the scene, steamers are plying constantly to and fro, connecting the city with its different suburbs. That great shapeless mass, just seen a little to the right in the distance, looming up over every thing in its vicinity, is the obelisk erected on Bunker's Hill to commemorate a battle, which if not exactly won by the Americans, was the first irretrievable step taken by them in a long, eventful, and ultimately successful struggle. Hundreds of the "tall chimneys" in our manufacturing districts have quite as imposing an appearance as has Bunker's Hill monument. The small villages which are scattered about in every direction, glistening in the morning sunlight, are so many suburbs of the city, with which it is connected by long wooden bridges, with the exception of the insular suburb of East Boston, where we land, and with which, being separated from the town by a branch of the harbour, the communication is maintained by steam ferry-boats.

Landed at length—and if the reader will accompany me, we will take a stroll together through the town.

It is early, but the custom-house officers are at their posts. They do

Alexander Mackay, *The Western World; or Travels in the United States in 1846-47* (London, 1849), I, pp. 18-28.

not look very promising, but we pass without difficulty or delay; the examination being more nominal than otherwise. I afterwards found that civility and courtesy were uniformly extended by the federal officers, both to strangers and natives landing in the country—a pleasing contrast to the wanton and unmannerly conduct which is sometimes pursued in our own ports, particularly in Liverpool, where custom-house officials too frequently conduct themselves as if vulgarity and insolence constituted the chief qualifications for office.

Carriages now convey us, baggage and all, to the ferry-boat; which, in its turn, conveys us, carriages, baggage and all, in less than five minutes, to the city. Our first object is to search for an hotel, and refresh ourselves with a thorough ablution and a comfortable meal on land. Passing the Tremont House, which is full, we draw up at the United States Hotel, an enormous pile of red brick, perforated by, I am afraid to say, how many rows of windows having a large wing on one side called Texas, and one in process of completion, on the other, to be called Oregon. The next addition made will, doubtless, be California. We are ushered up a marble staircase into a spacious hall, the floor of which looks like a gigantic chequer-board, being composed of alternate squares of black and white marble, looking exceedingly elegant, but, during this season of the year, being both very cold and very slippery. We apply for rooms at the bar, which, in the usual sense of the term, is no bar, but the counting-house of the establishment, in which a clerk, elaborately caparisoned, sits enthroned, at a considerable elevation, before a desk, which in point of cost and construction would be a piece of extravagance in the Bank parlour. The walls around him are literally covered with bells, each having beneath it the number of the room to which it corresponds, and they count by hundreds. My flesh creeps at the bare contemplation of the possibility of their being all rung at once. . . .

Although Boston is almost entirely surrounded by water, you perceive that the real harbour is not very extensive. Some of the wharves are built of wood, others are securely faced with stone, the latter presenting a very substantial appearance. The depth of the water enables vessels of all sizes, devices, and rigging to commingle, as it were, with the houses and warehouses that line the shore, some of the slips running short distances into the land, and being flanked by piles of massive and durable buildings, exclusively set apart for commercial purposes. Here is a slip devoted apparently to the exclusive use and occupation of European packets; large placards, attached to the shrouds, announcing their destinations and times of sailing. Here we are now in front of the coasting craft; and an extraordinary medley do they present. What a variety of rig and build; and how unfit some of the smaller ones appear for the

dangerous navigation of the American coast! Having grown a little familiar with them, you can almost tell, from their appearance, between what
points they trade. That substantial looking schooner which you see scud-
ding before a gentle land breeze, will be off Cape Cod to-night, in her
intricate and circuitous voyage to New York. That prim looking brig,
with her masts so tall and tapering, her spars so trim, her rigging so
regular, her sham port-holes so very white, and her hull of so shiny
a black, will, as soon as she clears—and she is already loaded—be off for
the Delaware, and be moored, in a few days, in front of the Quaker city.
The cluster of less elegant looking craft, which lie a little beyond her,
are, as their placards inform us, "direct for Charleston," for "Mobile,"
or for "New Orleans"; that is to say, as direct as baffling winds and
the gulf stream will admit of. But what have we here? A whole slip
full of small fry, packed as closely together as herring boats at a fishing
station, and their slender masts standing as thick as bulrushes in a
swamp. There can be no mistake about them, their rig and rakish con-
tour bespeaking them for the Chesapeake. They are, in fact, the far-
famed Baltimore clippers; and "For Baltimore direct" say most of them.
You may well stare, but that extraordinary naval abortion, which you
are now contemplating, is a veritable steamer. True, it seems to be built
of Bristol board; but, in these matters, such is the taste here. It is
for Newport, Rhode Island, and has to ply along one of the stormiest
of coasts. The huge upper deck, stretched, from end to end, on such
slender posts, looks as if it would flutter before the slightest breeze,
like the canvass spread over a peripatetic menagerie. It seems, in fact, to
be neither more nor less than a huge compound of scantlings and white
paint, with a touch of black at some of the seams. Put a match to it, and
off goes the inflammable monster like gun-cotton. Its engines are good
as compared with those on the Mississippi, though they would cut but
a sorry figure on a stormy night off the Isle of Man. As the steam hisses
through the escape-pipe, the whole mass tumbles like a very jelly. Yet,
notwithstanding all this, you have before you one of the strongest class
of American steamers. You have to witness those constructed for the
navigation of the inland waters. But let me not anticipate your surprise.

    Along the wharves there is every appearance of great activity; and,
thickly strewn around you, are all the insignia of an extensive commerce.
Raw cotton in countless bales; piles of manufactured goods for the South
American and Chinese markets; whole acres covered with parallel rows
of clean white barrels, some of them well-nigh bursting with flour, others
full of salt; hogsheads of sugar, and others of leaking molasses; stacks of
leather, and pyramids of marble blocks; bags of coffee, chests of tea, and
bulging orange boxes, are discernible on every hand. By each pile is a
clerk, busily noting all that may be added to, or subtracted from it;

dealers, wholesale and retail, masters and men, consignors and consignees, and light and heavy porters, are bustling about; the apparent confusion being heightened by the drays, some of which are rattling empty, and others crawling heavily laden, over the hard granite.

Leaving the water-side, you enter some short crooked streets of warehouses, almost as dark and dingy as Tooley-street, or Thames-street. Most of them are fireproof, and seem to be mailed in iron shutters. Passing them, we come to the Irish quarter, which, as usual, having no attractions, but the reverse, we may as well retrace our steps a little, and make for the heart of the town.

You are surprised to find, in a country like this, with so much spare land, and so many symmetrical towns built upon it, the streets of one of its finest capitals so straitened and devious. But this is easily accounted for. In the first place the foundations of Boston were laid ere the old irregular system of building had been departed from; and in the next, although there is land enough around it, the precise ground which the city occupies is of rather limited dimensions. It consists of an irregular peninsula, with a very uneven surface, the strip of ground called "the neck," joining it to the main land. This peninsula, to which the city proper is confined, is covered with houses, and the city now relieves itself from the pressure of population by means of the many small towns and villages, which are scattered like so many colonies over the mainland and islands around it. . . .

As might be expected, as you recede from the water-side, the business of the town assumes more of a retail character. As you advance towards the centre, you come in contact with its different markets and with its banking, civic, and other public establishments. Fanneuil Market is inferior in size, but superior in architecture and internal arrangements, to that of Liverpool. Immediately beyond is the very focus of the retail business of the town. The shops are large, having, in general, a wider frontage than with us. They are gorged with goods, so much so as literally to ooze out at doors and windows; and what a gaudy flaunting show they make! Piled in tempting masses on the hard brick pavement, you are ready to stumble over goods at every step you take, whilst from the upper windows stream whole pieces of flaring calicos and gaudy ribbons; the whole impressing one with the idea that business was making a holiday of it, and had donned, for the occasion, its most showy habiliments. A winding and irregular street now leads us up a rather steep ascent, in climbing which, we find ourselves in front of old Fanneuil Hall. There is no building in America held in such reverence as this. It is held sacred from the Atlantic to the Pacific, from the Lakes to the Gulf, as the "cradle of liberty," and the place in which the tocsin of the revolution was first sounded. It is large, but, in an architectural point of view, unworthy of notice, its historic associations constituting its chief attraction. We now advance up State-street, a fine business street, but neither so spacious nor imposing as Tremont Row into which it leads. Passing the Tremont House, we emerge upon "the Common," a large open space, about seventy acres in extent, in the upper part of the town. For this miniature park the Bostonians are indebted to the munificence of a private individual, who devised it to the corporation, on condition of its being left perpetually open for the health and recreation of the citizens. On a commanding site on one side of this common, and over-looking the whole town, the circumjacent suburbs, and a vast stretch of sea and land beyond, stands the State House, with its classic colonnade, surmounted by the dome already alluded to. In the large hall, as you enter it, is a statue of Washington, from the chisel of Chantrey, the chief features of the interior being the two chambers of the legislature. The House of Representatives is a large square room, capable of accommodating about 400 persons, scantily ornate, and looking as cold and comfortless as a country meeting-house. The Senate Chamber is a smaller apartment, and somewhat more attractive in its appearance. Its chief ornament, and placed over the door opposite the speaker's chair, is an old drum, captured in one of the earlier battles of the Revolution. It is placed there as an incitement to American youth, and as a terror to all British drummers. It is not beaten, that I am aware of, in the senate, but it by no means follows therefrom that hollow sounds are alien to that body.

In the more immediate vicinity of the Common is the fashionable quarter of Boston. The terraces, which line it on either side, consist of spacious mansions built in the main of brick and granite: the hall doors being approached by granite or marble steps, and the window-sills and capping being frequently composed of marble. Almost every house is garnished by Venetian blinds outside the windows, the green colour of which contrasts pleasingly with the red brick, sometimes painted of a deeper red, with white pencillings at the joinings, which impart to the whole a light, airy, and elegant appearance. Everything about these comfortable-looking dwellings is scrupulously clean; indeed, generally speaking, the credit of great cleanness is due to Boston as a whole, being admirably situated with respect to drainage, and its opportunities, in this respect, not having been neglected. But having glanced at their town, it is now time to take a passing peep at the Bostonians themselves. Let us then to Washington-street—the Regent-street of Boston—as it is now the hour for promenade. You had better, however, put up your cigar case, for smoking is not allowed in the streets. You may chew until you expectorate yourself away, and may poison your dwelling with smoke to your heart's content, but a whiff in the open air is a luxury not to be enjoyed in Boston under a penalty of five dollars.

This is Washington-street, as varying in width, and as irregular in its architecture, as the Strand. The shops on either side make a goodly display of rich, tempting, and ornamental wares; the pavement is spacious, and covered with pedestrians, who pass on, without looking to the right or to the left, or linger, as their fancy may dictate, by the "Dry Goods Store," the "Hardware Store," the "Book Store," the "Grocery Store," the "Hat Store," or the "Shoe Store,"—for they are all "Stores," without a single *shop* amongst them. Let no Englishman insinuate to any American that he keeps a shop—that would be a grade too low for a free and enlightened citizen to stoop to. In all this flitting crowd, you can scarcely point to a single individual who is not well dressed. The Americans cannot afford to be niggard of broad-cloth, for there is no nation on earth in which the coat goes so far to make the man. Fustian (not moral) is little known in America. Canvass-back ducks they have in abundance, but no canvass-backed people. The countenances of those we pass bespeak a very general diffusion of intelligence, an intellectuality of expression being, as I afterwards discovered, more common to the Bostonians than to the inhabitants of any other city in the Union. The ladies form a very fair proportion of the throng. They are generally of the middle height, well rounded, of a good carriage, with features as pleasing as their complexions are florid. The bracing air of the seaboard, however, is fatal to many of them, groups of consumptive patients having annually to fly from New England into the interior. They are not shy, and yet, at the same time, are not bold; discarding in their promenades the affected prudery with which they are so generally charged, and acting, as they pass, as if they saw no reason why a daughter of Adam should not look upon a son of Eve.

Our Good City of New York

Philip Hone

Tuesday, March 21, 1843 [Whig Ball].—Gen. Harrison was sung into the Presidency, and if Mr. Clay should succeed it will be effected in some degree by dancing. . . . Clay balls are quite in vogue. They answer a good purpose; for while they assist by a little surplus of funds to furnish the ways and means of electioneering, they enlist the women on our side, and wives and daughters are famous auxiliaries in a righteous cause, and good supporters of a tottering conscience.

I went last evening by invitation to one of those political jollifications, given by the Clay Club of the third ward at Washington hall. The large ballroom was handsomely decorated and well filled. There was a fair collection of ladies, some of whom were fair, dressed generally without much pretension and of modest deportment; but the male division of the dancing part of the company would hardly have passed muster in former days at the Bath assemblies, when Beau Nash was the *arbiter elegantiarum,* or at present in the courtly saloons of Almack's. Colored handkerchiefs and unpolished boots declared the determination of their wearers not to be laid neck and heel by the mandates of fashion; and O Terpsichore! how they did dance! Their independent ears scorned to be controlled by the arbitrary measures of the music, and their pliant legs described every letter in the alphabet from A to Z. But it went off very well. The elderly ladies were pleased with their children, the young ones with their beaux, and the beaux with themselves. The Whig common councilmen and other politicians gave their august countenance with solemn jocularity to the affair as a piece of political machinery, and the third ward gets $250 towards the charter election.

January 29, 1847 [Rich and Poor].—Our good city of New York has already arrived at the state of society to be found in the large cities of

The Diary of Philip Hone, 1828-1851, edited by Bayard Tuckerman (New York, 1889), II, pp. 77-78, 293-295, 359-361.

Europe; overburdened with population, and where the two extremes of costly luxury in living, expensive establishments, and improvident waste are presented in daily and hourly contrast with squalid misery and hopeless destitution. This state of things has been hastened in our case by the constant stream of European paupers arriving upon the shores of this land of promise. Alas! how often does it prove to the deluded emigrant a land of broken promise and blasted hope! If we had none but our own poor to take care of, we should get along tolerably well; we could find employment for them, and individual charity, aiding the public institutions, might save us from the sights of woe with which we are assailed in the streets, and the pressing applications which beset us in the retirement of our own houses. Nineteen out of twenty of these mendicants are foreigners cast upon our shores, indigent and helpless, having expended the last shilling in paying their passage-money, deceived by the misrepresentations of unscrupulous agents, and left to starve amongst strangers, who, finding it impossible to extend relief to all, are deterred from assisting any. These reflections upon the extremes of lavish expenditure and absolute destitution are forced upon me by my own recent experience. I partook yesterday of a most expensive dinner, where every article of costly food which the market affords was spread before the guests, and fine wines drunk in abundance, some of which might command eight or ten dollars a bottle; and from this scene of expensive hospitality I was conveyed to another more splendid and expensive entertainment, where the sparkling of diamonds, the reflection of splendid mirrors, the luster of silks and satins, the rich gilding of tasteful furniture were flashed, by the aid of innumerable lights, upon the dazzled eyes of a thousand guests. Now this is all right enough; in both these cases our entertainers could well afford the expense which attended the display of their hospitality, nor is it within the scope of the most remote probability that the money of any others than themselves can be involved in the outlay of their entertainments.

It may be painful to reflect how far the cost of a single bottle of Mr. Spofford's wine or one of Mr. Ray's *pâtés de foie gras* might contribute to alleviate the distress of those miserable objects who stretch out the attenuated arms of wasted poverty, or display the haggard countenance of infantile deprivation, or the tattered habiliments incapable of resisting the inclemency of the winter's cold. These gentlemen are liberal and charitable, and no doubt do their part in almsgiving; but they have other duties to perform.

May 8, 1849.—Mr. MaCready commenced an engagement last evening at the Opera-House, Astor place, and was to have performed the part of

"Macbeth," whilst his rival, Mr. Forrest, appeared in the same part at the Broadway theatre. A violent animosity has existed on the part of the latter theatrical hero against his rival, growing out of some differences in England; but with no cause, that I can discover, except that one is a gentleman, and the other is a vulgar, arrogant loafer, with a pack of kindred rowdies at his heels. Of these retainers a regularly organized force was employed to raise a riot at the Opera-House and drive Mr. MaCready off the stage, in which, to the disgrace of the city, the ruffians succeeded. On the appearance of the "Thane of Cawdor," he was saluted with a shower of missiles, rotten eggs, and other unsavory objects, with shouts and yells of the most abusive epithets. In the midst of this disgraceful riot the performance was suspended, the respectable part of the audience dispersed, and the vile band of *Forresters* were left in possession of the house. This cannot end here; the respectable part of our citizens will never consent to be put down by a mob raised to serve the purpose of such a fellow as Forrest. Recriminations will be resorted to, and a series of riots will have possession of the theaters of the opposing parties.

May 10.—The riot at the Opera-House on Monday night was children's play compared with the disgraceful scenes which were enacted in our part of this devoted city this evening, and the melancholy loss of life to which the outrageous proceedings of the mob naturally led.

An appeal to Mr. MaCready had been made by many highly respectable citizens, and published in the papers, inviting him to finish his engagement at the Opera-House, with an implied pledge that they would stand by him against the ferocious mob of Mr. Forrest's friends, who had determined that MaCready should not be allowed to play, whilst at the same time their oracle was strutting, unmolested, his "hour upon the stage" of the Broadway theater. This announcement served as a firebrand in the mass of combustibles left smoldering from the riot of the former occasion. The *Forresters* perceived that their previous triumph was incomplete, and a new conspiracy was formed to accomplish effectually their nefarious designs. Inflammatory notices were posted in the upper ward, meetings were regularly organized, and bands of ruffians, gratuitously supplied with tickets by richer rascals, were sent to take possession of the theater. The police, however, were beforehand with them, and a large body of their force was posted in different parts of the house.

When Mr. MaCready appeared he was assailed in the same manner as on the former occasion; but he continued on the stage and performed his part with firmness, amidst the yells and hisses of the mob. The strength of the police, and their good conduct, as well as that of the Mayor, Recorder, and other public functionaries, succeeded in preventing any serious injury to the property within doors, and many arrests were made; but the war raged with frightful violence in the adjacent streets. The mob—a dreadful one in numbers and ferocity—assailed the extension of the building, broke in the windows, and demolished some of the doors. I walked up to the corner of Astor Place, but was glad to make my escape. On my way down, opposite the New York Hotel, I met a detachment of troops, consisting of about sixty cavalry and three hundred infantry, fine-looking fellows, well armed, who marched steadily to the field of action. Another detachment went by the way of Lafayette Place. On their arrival they were assailed by the mob, pelted with stones and brickbats, and several were carried off severely wounded.

Under this provocation, with the sanction of the civil authorities, orders were given to fire. Three or four volleys were discharged; about twenty persons were killed and a large number wounded. It is to be lamented that in the number were several innocent persons, as is always the case in such affairs. A large proportion of the mob being lookers-on, who, putting no faith in the declaration of the magistrates that the fatal order was about to be given, refused to retire, and shared the fate of the rioters. What is to be the issue of this unhappy affair cannot be surmised; the end is not yet.

May 30, 1850.—If they do not pull down the houses in the annual renovation of Broadway, they fall of their own accord. The large three-story house, corner of Broadway and Fourth Street, occupied for several years by Mrs. Seton as a boarding-house, fell to-day at two o'clock with a crash so astounding that the girls, with whom I was sitting in the library, imagined for a moment that it was caused by an earthquake. Fortunately, the workmen had notice to make their escape. No lives were lost, and no personal injury was sustained. The mania for converting Broadway into a street of shops is greater than ever. There is scarcely a block in the whole extent of this fine street of which some part is not in a state of transmutation. The City Hotel has given place to a row of splendid stores; Stewart is extending his stores to take in the whole front from Chambers to Reade Street; this is already the most magnificent dry-goods establishment in the world. I certainly do not remember anything to equal it in London or Paris; with the addition now in progress this edifice will be one of the "wonders" of the Western World. Three or four good brick houses on the corner of Broadway and Spring Street have been leveled, I know not for what purpose,—shops, no doubt. The houses—fine, costly edifices, opposite to me, extending from Driggs's corner down to a point opposite to Bond Street—are to make way for a grand concert and exhibition establishment. All this is very well; men have a right to improve their property as they please; but it really would be well if more precautions were used in pulling down an underpropping. Lives enough have been sacrificed; but the inquisitive people require something to gratify their curiosity, and some went away from the ruins to-day a little disappointed that no lives were lost. It was nothing to the accident in Hague Street.

Albany Manners

Margaret Hall

September 20, 1827:—I dare say many of our acquaintances here are extremely surprised to see us so long in one place, indeed the daily enquiries that are made of when we go and the numerous hopes expressed that we do not mean to go to-morrow and to-morrow are sufficiently indicative of their surprise at finding us so long stationary without the tie of business, which is the only thing that fixes Americans for any length of time in one place. Here, at this moment, many of the most intelligent men belonging to the State are so tied by their seat either in the House of Assembly or the Senate and the opportunity of making acquaintance with them is not to be lost, and as we are in no hurry we stay very quietly where we are, leaving our friends to wonder, whilst we wonder in our turn of the flying about which they choose to term traveling, for whether in the pursuit of wealth or pleasure, the rapidity of their movements is the same. The same quickness runs through their eating as I have already frequently mentioned, and how is it possible that in this way they are to become a polished nation? But there is a sort of inconsistency, too, along with all this rapidity of motion. One would imagine that such activity implied an equal liveliness of manner, but this is far from the case; they are the gravest people I ever associated with, and when seated in groups under the verandah of an inn they look so listless and idle that you would think they would never set to work. We are told by those who are in the habit of employing Americans and Europeans indiscriminately as labourers that, altho' an American will do a great deal occasionally for a spurt, they are not really equal in the daily routine of work. In the higher classes there is a great want of—I would call it romance, if I were not afraid that you would laugh at me, but even under that name I think you must understand what I mean; it is the charm of conversation and feeling which arises from more

Margaret (Mrs. Basil) Hall, *The Aristocratic Journey*, pp. 68-69.

or less familiarity with the fine arts and acquaintance with the elegancies of life, mixed up certainly with tenderness of feeling. I really feel quite at a loss to explain myself, but I feel convinced that before you were six weeks in the country anyone of you would feel it and very likely give expressions more easily to the feeling. There is no want of talking, too, about sensibility and romantic scenery and being passionately fond of this thing and having a passion for that; a great deal more than would be considered either good sense or good taste in England, but it is all "words, words, words," and there is plainly a want of the sentiment, a want of enthusiasm, which is another of those bad things to talk of but admirable to have.

We dined yesterday at Governor Clinton's. Mrs. Clinton invited us to a family dinner, and so it strictly was, for the party consisted entirely of members of the family, namely the Governor and Mrs. Clinton, her mother Mrs. Jones, the two Miss Clintons, daughters of the Governor by a former marriage, and Mrs. Clinton's niece, Miss Allen. Perhaps you would like to know what is considered a family dinner in the first style at Albany, which you know is the capital of the State and the seat of government, so I took a more particular survey of the table than I am apt to do, and on the other page you will find a bill of fare. I must first premise that we had beautiful china and cut glass an inch thick. [A sketch made by Captain Hall of Mrs. Clinton's dinner table is inserted in the letter.]

Tarts, fruit, and cheese are always put on the table at the same time in this country, except at quite dress parties, when the fruit is a separate concern, but the ice is always along with the second course. The party was really very agreeable. Mr. Clinton is a very superior man, and Mrs. Clinton, tho' by no means elegant, is extremely good-natured and animated and amuses me very much by her strong aristocratic feelings, of which I believe she is quite unconscious. She has a little niece living with her, a child five months older than Eliza, who I was requested to take along with us yesterday. The little girl is a delicate little bit of a thing, by no means a match for my tomboy, which Miss Eliza soon found out, and when she discovers that any child is afraid of her, from that moment she tyrannises over her without mercy. So it was yesterday, and the poor little Livingstone was thoroughly frightened by Eliza's rough ways. We owe at least half our popularity in this country to Eliza; she is so perfectly at home with everyone, so ready to laugh and talk in her own fashion to those who will laugh and talk with her, that her good humour is quite irresistible, and altho' she is not what can strictly be called a pretty child there is something in her long, flowing hair, white skin, merry blue eyes, and broad shoulders that attracts the attention of all strangers.

We went from the Governor's to a party at General Solomon van Rennselaer's the Post Master. It was very much of the same kind as the night before, not so numerous, but the eatables, were of the same quality and quantity. The attendance was not so good and was a very tolerable specimen of how ill that branch of polite society or at least of its accomplishment is understood. The first in the train was a black man in white trousers, next followed a lass in a black stuff dress and white apron with not a few holes, and last of all came a little girlie not more than ten or twelve years old. One of my correspondents remarked that the ladies in America must be very stupid not to arrange their domestic concerns and their tables better, but it must be remembered that such a luxury as a good servant is not to be had, nothing but the very riff-raff of the Irish, and the ease of getting another place or doing for themselves in some way in case of dismissal, is so great that if you venture to find fault with your housemaid or butler they will tell you that you may suit yourself elsewhere. Exactly the same thing happens in Canada and from the same reasons so that the inconvenience need not be set down as the result of Republican principles, tho' they too may have their share. You may remember that the beauty of the ladies struck us very much in New York the beauty did not appear at all conspicuous, nor did we find it so on returning here. Philadelphia and Boston are both much famed for handsome women, and indeed for everything that is delightful, Boston too is reckoned quite the emporium of learning. We shall probably be there shortly and shall have an opportunity of judging for ourselves.

We went this afternoon to the English Church and heard a tolerable sermon from a young Irishman. We thought of paying some of our visits after Church, but upon questioning Mr. de Witt Bloodgood as to whether it was a proper time he advised us to wait till to-morrow, as here there is no visiting upon Sunday except amongst intimate friends.

Along the Erie Canal

Basil Hall

On the 19th of June we reached the village of Syracuse, through the very centre of which the Erie Canal passes. During the drive we had opportunities of seeing the land in various stages of its progress, from the dense, black, tangled, native forest—up to the highest stages of cultivation, with wheat and barley waving over it: or from that melancholy and very hopeless-looking state of things, when the trees are laid prostrate upon the earth, one upon top of another, and a miserable log-hut is the only symptom of man's residence,—to such gay and thriving places as Syracuse; with fine broad streets, large and commodious houses, gay shops, and stage-coaches, waggons, and gigs flying past, all in a bustle. In the centre of the village, we could see from our windows the canal thickly covered with freight boats and packets, glancing silently past, and shooting like arrows through the bridges, some of which were of stone, and some of painted wood. The canal at this place has been made of double its ordinary width, and being bent into an agreeable degree of curvature, to suit the turn of the streets, the formality is removed, as well as the ditch-like appearance which generally belongs to canals. The water, also, is made to rise almost level with the towing path, which improves the effect. I was amused by seeing, amongst the throng of loaded boats, a gaily-painted vessel lying in state, with the words CLEO-PATRA'S BARGE painted in large characters on her broadside.

In the course of 50 miles' travelling, we came repeatedly in sight of almost every successive period of agricultural advancement through which America has run, or is actually running. At one place we found ourselves amongst the Oneyda tribe of Indians, living on a strip of land called a reservation, from being appropriated exclusively to these poor remains of the former absolute masters of the territory—the native burghers of the forest! They were dressed in blankets, with leggings of skin

Basil Hall, *Travels in North America*, III, pp. 126-127.

laced not very tightly, and reaching to the hide moccasins on their feet. Their painted faces, and lank, black, oily hair, made them look as like savages as any lion-hunting travellers could have desired.

In merely passing along the road, it was of course difficult to form any conjecture as to how much of the country was cleared; especially as new settlers naturally cling to canals, roads, and lakes, and it was such settlers only that we saw. Sometimes our track lay through a thick forest for a mile or two; though, generally speaking, the country for some distance on both sides of the road was thickly strewed with houses. Every now and then we came to villages, consisting of several hundred houses; and in the middle I observed there were always several churches surmounted by spires, painted with some showy colour, and giving a certain degree of liveliness or finish to scenes in other respects rude enough. In general, however, it must be owned, there prevailed a most uncomfortable appearance of bleakness or rawness, and a total absence of picturesque beauty in these villages; whose dreary aspect was much heightened by the black sort of gigantic wall formed of the abrupt edge of the forest, choked up with underwood, now for the first time exposed to the light of the sun.

The cleared spaces, however, as they are called, looked to our eyes not less desolate, being studded over with innumerable great black stumps; or, which was more deplorable still, with tall scorched, branchless stems of trees, which had undergone the barbarous operation known by the name of girdling. An American settler can hardly conceive the horror with which a foreigner beholds such numbers of magnificent trees standing round him with their throats cut, the very Banquos of the murdered forest! The process of girdling is this: a circular cut or ring, two or three inches deep, is made with an axe quite round the tree at about five feet from the ground. This, of course, puts an end to vegetable life; and the destruction of the tree being accelerated by the action of fire, these wretched trunks in a year or two present the most miserable objects of decrepitude that can be conceived. The purpose, however, of the farmer is gained, and that is all he can be expected to look to. His corn crop is no longer overshadowed by the leaves of these unhappy trees, which, in process of time, are cut down and split into railings, or sawed into billets of firewood,—and their misery is at an end.

Even in the cultivated fields, the tops of the stumps were seen poking their black snouts above the young grain, like a shoal of seals. Not a single hedge or wall was to be seen in those places, all the enclosures being made of split logs, built one upon the top of another in a zig-zag fashion, like what the ladies call a Vandyke border. These are named snake fences, and are certainly the most ungraceful-looking things I ever saw.

Most of the houses are built of rough unbarked logs, nicked at the ends so as to fit closely and firmly; and roofed with planks. The better sort of dwellings, however, are made of squared timbers framed together neatly enough, and boarded over, at the sides and ends; and then roofed with shingles, which are a sort of oblong wooden slates. The houses are generally left unpainted, and being scattered about without order, look more like a collection of great packing boxes, than the human residences which the eye is accustomed to see in old countries. In the more cleared and longer settled parts of the country, we saw many detached houses, which might almost be called villas, very neatly got up, with rows of wooden columns in front, shaded by trees and tall shrubs running round and across the garden, which was prettily fenced in, and embellished with a profusion of flowers.

Sometimes a whole village, such as that of Whitesborough, was composed entirely of these detached villas; and as most of the houses were half hid in the thick foliage of the elm-trees round them, they looked cool and comfortable when compared with the new and half-burnt, and in many places burning country, only a few miles off.

The village of Utica stands a step higher in this progressive scale of civilisation; for it has several church spires rising over it, and at no great distance an institution, called Hamilton College, intended, I was told, for the higher branches of science. We also visited Syracuse, a village with extensive salt-works close to it; and had numerous opportunities of examining the Erie canal, and the great high-road to Buffalo;—so that what with towns and cities, Indians, forests, cleared and cultivated lands, girdled trees, log-houses, painted churches, villas, canals, and manufactories, and hundreds of thousands of human beings, starting into life, all within the ken of one day's rapid journey, there was plenty of stuff for the imagination to work upon.

It has been the fashion of travellers in America, I am told—for I have read no travels in that country—to ridicule the practice of giving to unknown and inconsiderable villages, the names of places long hallowed by classical recollections. I was disposed, however, at one time to think, that there was nothing absurd in the matter. I did not deny that, on first looking at the map, and more particularly on hearing stage-drivers and stage-passengers, talking of Troy, Ithaca, and Rome, and still more when I heard them speaking of the towns of Cicero, Homer, or Manlius, an involuntary smile found its way to the lips, followed often by a good hearty laugh. The oddity and incongruity of the thing were much heightened by the admixture of such modern appellations as Truxton, Sullivan, and Tompkins, jumbled up with the Indian names of Onondaga, Oneida, and Chitteningo.

A little longer personal acquaintance with the subject, however, led me to a different conclusion. All those uncourteous, and at first irrepressible, feelings of ridicule, were, I hoped, quite eradicated; and I tried to fancy that there was something very interesting, almost amiable, in any circumstances, no matter how trivial, which contributed to show, even indirectly, that these descendants of ours were still willing to keep up the old and generous recollections of their youth; and although they had broken the cords of national union, that they were still disposed to bind themselves to us, by the ties of classical sentiment at least. For these reasons, then, I was inclined to approve, in theory, of the taste which had appropriated the ancient names alluded to. I had also a sort of hope, that the mere use of the words would insensibly blend with their present occupations, and so keep alive some traces of the old spirit, described to me as fast melting away.

By the same train of friendly reasoning, I was led to imagine it possible, that the adoption of such names as Auburn,—"loveliest village of the plain,"—Port Byron, and the innumerable Londons, Dublins, Edinburghs, and so on, were indicative of a latent or lingering kindliness towards the old country. The notion, that it was degrading to the venerable Roman names to fix them upon these mushroom towns in the wilderness, I combated, I flattered myself, somewhat adroitly, on the principle that, so far from memory of Ithaca or Syracuse, or any such place, being degraded by the appropriation, the honour rather lay with the ancients, who, it is the fashion to take for granted, enjoyed a less amount of freedom and intelligence than their modern namesakes.

"Let us," I said one day, to a friend who was impugning these doctrines, "let us take Syracuse for example, which in the year 1820 consisted of one house, one mill, and one tavern: now, in 1827, it holds fifteen hundred inhabitants, has two large churches, innumerable wealthy shops filled with goods, brought there by water-carriage from every corner of the globe; two large and splendid hotels; many dozens of grocery stores or whiskyshops; several busy printing presses, from one of which issues a weekly newspaper; a daily post from the east, the south, and the west; has a broad canal running through its bosom;—in short, it is a great and free city. Where is this to be matched," I exclaimed, "in ancient Italy or Greece?"

A British Traveler in Philadelphia

Alexander Mackay

On landing, I found all as still as if we had entered the precincts of a churchyard. The ferry-boat slip was deserted, not a soul appearing to welcome us, or give us succour. On inquiry of the captain, as to the means of getting my luggage transported to Jones's Hotel, to which I was recommended by a friend in New York, that functionary informed me that outside were plenty of porters to execute our orders. "Outside" had reference to a high and close wooden paling, which railed off the slip from the adjacent street, in which paling was a door, which, in due course of time, was thrown open. The gush which follows the displacing of the plug from a water cask, is not more spontaneous or impetuous than was then the crush of the grinning, jabbering, and officious negroes, who sprung upon us from their ambuscade, and overpowered us before we had time to recover from our surprise. I found myself in a moment between two of them, who leered at me most hideously, their white teeth, and the whites of their eyes, shining ghastlily in the feeble light of the solitary lamp, which did its best to illuminate the slip.

"Porter, Sa," said one of them, thrusting, at the same time, into my hand a card, with 23 upon it, in large characters, as black as himself.

"I'm in de cheap line, massa," said the other,—"no 'nop'ly's my word."

"Cheap!—neber mind him, Sa; he's only a nigga from Baltimore, just come to Philadelphy," retorted the first speaker, regarding his competitor with scowling eyes and pouting lips. He then continued: "I'se born here, Sa, and know de town like a book. Dat ere nigga not seen good society yet—knows nuffin—habn't got de polish on.—Git out, nigga, and clean you self"; and he turned upon his heel, and laughed heartily—yhaw—yhaw—yhaw.

It was not his familiar contact with good society, or any superior

Alexander Mackay, *The Western World; or Travels in the United States in 1846-47* (London, 1849), pp. 130-144.

grace which I perceived in him, but the circumstance of his nativity, which induced me to give the preference to 23, judging myself safer in the hands of a native citizen, who had a reputation to sustain, than in those of a mere bird of passage. I accordingly commissioned him to carry my luggage to Jones's.

"De best house in Philadelphy, Sa," said he, as he transferred my portmanteau to his truck.

"Is it far off?" I inquired.

"Good bit from de water," he said, "but not fur when you get dere."

Having delivered himself of this incontrovertible proposition, he disappeared in the crowd, from which he soon emerged, bearing upon his shoulders a huge leather trunk, formidably studded with what appeared to be the heads of large brass bolts.

"Where to, Sa?" he demanded of the owner, as he suffered it to drop heavily beside my portmanteau.

"Congress Hall," was the reply.

"De best house in town, Sa," he added, in a tone which displayed an utter unconsciousness of having contradicted himself.

"You told me Jones's was the best," I remarked.

"Well, so I did," he replied, coolly; "some say one de best, some toder, —I tink both best,—dat's all."

There was no rebutting this view of the case, so off we started.

Philadelphia goes early to bed, and the streets were lonely and silent, but much better lighted than the portion of the town abutting upon the Delaware. Our course lay up Chestnut-street, the lofty and regular terraces of which frowned gloomily, at that hour, over the narrow thoroughfare.

"Holloa, 23, where are you going?" asked I, as he turned his truck into a street, which led to the right.

"Only up dis turnin' a bit, to Congress Hall," said that sable numeral: "but you needn't wait—dis child follow with de luggage—he knows de way to Jones's by husself, by dis time, I s'pose."

"Yes, but I don't know the way," added I.

"Straight ahead, Sa, and that's Jones's," said he; and he left me to act as I pleased. I made the best use I could of this very definite direction, and discovered the hotel, some distance further up Chestnut-street. It was fully half an hour, however, ere Blackey made his appearance; and, on my remonstrating with him for his delay, he assured me that it was all right, as he had only stopped to converse in the street with a "coloured gen'leman, a friend of his, in the shaving line," who was a "great genias," and "knowed all about de foreign relations." I asked him how he would like to wait half an hour for his pay, to which he replied that he had "no objections, if I would pay de discount for de use of de money."

The city of Philadelphia, perhaps more than any other upon the continent, is marked by characteristics peculiarly American. A European, suddenly transferred to Boston, might mistake his whereabouts, from its crowded, crooked, and intricate appearance. New York, too, is distinguished by but a partial regularity, which is the case with all the growing towns of the Old World. But everywhere in Philadelphia are discernible the same symmetry of outline and regularity of plan. Long, straight streets, each of which is the counterpart of all the rest, and intersecting each other at right angles, with a few small and well wooded squares, will enable the reader to form a tolerably accurate estimate of the town. There is but one short cut that I could discover in all Philadelphia, and that is in the neighbourhood of the Exchange. So unlooked-for an oddity in such a place put me on inquiry; but nobody could tell me how it got there. It is found so useful, however, that many wish it multiplied to an indefinite extent. Distances within the town are measured by blocks,—a block being the square space enclosed between four streets. The same flaring red brick, which enters into the composition of New York, stares you everywhere in the face, relieved here and there by a marble building, or a terrace, stuccoed and painted to resemble marble. Most of the streets are lined on either side with trees, the boughs of which frequently intermingle above the thoroughfare, and, in the summer time, conceal, by the luxuriance of their foliage, as you look along the vista of the streets, the houses on both sides from your view. This is chiefly confined to the private streets, although some of the busiest thoroughfares are marked by the same arborescent feature. At every intersection of two streets, the country is visible in four different directions, seen as through the diminishing end of a telescope. In one respect it differs from most other American towns; for, with plenty of room to spread in, the streets are equally narrow. With the exception of Market-street, which is very wide, the other streets of Philadelphia scarcely exceed the width of Ludgate-hill. In nothing did the prudent Penn show his foresight more than in this. To make a street wider than is absolutely necessary is a great mistake,—a very wide street, whilst the expense of keeping it in repair is great, being but ill adapted for business purposes,—a fact, in discovering which, Penn seems to have been a couple of centuries in advance of his countrymen. Besides, whether deservedly or not, Philadelphia enjoys the reputation of being the hottest city in the Union, the feature in question greatly contributing, during summer, to the comfort of its inhabitants, the streets lying in one direction, being constantly in shade, which, with the exception of a short period, at noon, may also be said of those intersecting them. The value of this may be appreciated, when it is understood that, in summer the thermometer sometimes rises to above 100° of Fahrenheit in the shade. It rose to 104° one Sunday that I afterwards spent there, when, if a breath of air swept by, it gave little relief, feeling more like a hot blast than otherwise. On the following day the thermometer ranged at about the same point, when nearly thirty deaths occurred in Philadelphia from strokes of the sun, almost all the victims being labourers, and such as were exposed to its fierce mid-day heat. Horses too, everywhere, dropped dead in the streets; a similar mortality, though to less extent, visiting on the same day the cities of Boston, New York, and Baltimore. It is as a resource against this intense heat that the windows of all the private residences are flanked outside by Venetian blinds, and many of them by solid shutters. Curious enough is the spectacle which a fashionable street in Philadelphia presents from about ten in the morning till five in the evening of a broiling summer's day. It looks quite deserted, the shutters being all closed, so as not only to exclude every particle of light, but also every breath of air; the families melting, in the meantime, in some secluded back room in the more sheltered part of their respective habitations. About the latter mentioned hour, they begin to migrate to the front, when the street presents a new aspect, shutters, windows, doors, and all being now thrown open to catch every breath of the cool evening air. Without this strategy against sun and heat, there would be no living in Philadelphia during the months of July and August. Such of the residents as can add to this the luxury of summer furniture, exchanging the carpet for a light grass matting, and substituting slim cane-bottomed chairs for those of a heavier calibre, manage, during the period referred to, to eke out a tolerable existence. The same plan, as far as the means of parties will permit, is adopted during the hotter months, throughout the Union; the only mode of keeping a house then comfortable being to close it up for the day, and to open it at night.

Philadelphia abounds in public buildings, some of which, architecturally speaking, are of considerable pretensions. The most striking within the precincts of the town, both as regards appearance, and the associations connected with it, is the old United States Bank. It assumes the form of a Greek temple, with a fine massive portico turned upon Chestnut-street. The whole edifice, which is large, is constructed of marble, and is approached in front by a broad and magnificent flight of marble steps, by which you ascend to the lofty platform, on which it appears to be elevated from the street. It has now a deserted and gloomy look, as if ashamed of the transactions of which it was formerly the scene. The marble steps, once so crowded with busy and scheming multitudes, now echo but to the occasional footsteps of the stranger who is curious enough to ascend them. The carcass is still there, in all its pristine beauty, but the restless, scheming, and unscrupulous soul which once animated it, has fled. I looked upon it and thought of Sidney Smith; and then crowded to my mind recollections of the misery which had been wrought, both in Europe and America, by the injudicious transactions and criminal speculation of the fallen monster. The vaunted "regulator," which was so beneficially to influence the financial movements of a continent, could not properly control its own; and the institution which was to consolidate business by moderating speculation, became itself the most audacious and the most unfortunate speculator of the time. The Exchange, in which is included the post-office, is a showy building, but merits no very particular attention.

To me the most interesting building of all was the "State House." It is a long pile of red brick, having stone facings, with an open archway through the centre, passing into a small square behind, and surmounted by a quaint-looking cupola, which rises to a considerable elevation. It is situated in Chestnut-street, a little back from the line of the street, having a broad, open, brick pavement in front. Its architectural pretensions are of a very slender order, but its historic recollections are stirring and suggestive. It is one of the few remnants now left in Philadelphia of colonial times. And to what events in the history of humanity did it give birth! Within its walls took place the earliest meetings of the Continental Congress; and, in a small room on the ground floor on your left, as you enter the centre archway, was discussed and adopted the declaration of American independence—the great deed of separation between the mother-country and her tributary continent—a document which, in view of the influence, whether for weal or for woe, which it is yet destined to wield over the fortunes of the human race, is entitled to be regarded as the most remarkable ever penned. It is painful to contrast with the noble race of men which the trying circumstances of their country then called forth, the many degenerate successors who have since represented them at Washington. The pile which witnessed their steady resolution and anxious deliberations is already more a monument of the past than a thing of present utility, the transference of the state government to Harrisburg having deprived it of its legislative character. But it is not for what it is, but for what it has been, that the Philadelphians justly prize their old "State House."

The principal edifice in the outskirts of the town, and indeed the finest in the whole city, is Girard College, a marble structure, built after the fashion, and of about the same dimensions, as the Madelina in Paris.

It is the result of a magnificent bequest made by a wealthy banker of the city, whose name it bears, for the education of poor orphan children, the trustees being strictly enjoined by the will, to erect a plain edifice, and thus economise the funds for the principal object in view; and to prohibit the entrance into the institution, in an official capacity, of any clergyman of any denomination. I believe that in the latter particular they have been faithful to their trust, although as to the former, they contrived to overstep the terms of the will, and, in building a marble palace, have so crippled their resources, that the chief purpose of the testator has been well nigh frustrated. The city and its neighbourhood abound in charitable institutions, some of them established on the most extensive scale, one of which forms, as it were, a small town by itself, on the right bank of the Schuylkill, on the road from Philadelphia to Baltimore.

The street architecture of Philadelphia is of a high order, being much more regular and pleasing in its effect than that of either Boston or New York. The private residences in the fashionable quarters are large and exceedingly commodious; but such is the sameness in their internal arrangements, that when you have seen one, you have virtually seen all.

For most purposes connected with a great city, the situation of Philadelphia was admirably chosen. Occupying a site more than a hundred miles above the mouth of the Delaware, but yet not beyond the reach of tide-water, and being accessible to ships of the deepest draught and the largest burden, the real capital of Pennsylvania combines all the advantages of a seaport with the safety of an interior town. About four miles below the city, the Schuylkill, after running parallel with it for several miles of its course, turns suddenly to the left, and empties itself into the Delaware. Where the city stands, the distance between the main stream and its tributary is about two miles. One set of streets runs parallel to each other, from stream to stream; the others intersecting them at regular distances, and running parallel to the rivers which flank them. The spot chosen was such as almost necessarily to have suggested this arrangement for the future city. Its greatest length is now in the direction from river to river, the space between them being almost entirely filled up; the town, at the same time, resting on a broad basis on the Delaware, where it is most densely built and its chief business is carried on. Front-street, which looks upon the river, with a broad quay before it, has, in some places, a rather dilapidated look; but in it, as in the two streets immediately behind it, is conducted the chief wholesale business of the town. The streets parallel to the river are named, 1st, 2nd, 3rd, and so on; whilst those which stretch from stream to stream are called after the different kinds of trees abounding in the neighbourhood, such as Chestnut, Pine, Walnut, &c. and by other names, to distinguish them from the numbered streets. In receding from the Delaware, Third-street seems to be the dividing line between the whole-sale and the retail business of the town; partaking itself largely of both, and with the exception of Market-street, which is the great retail mart, being the most bustling of any in the city, comprising, as it does, the Exchange, some of the banks, and many of the newspaper offices.

It is to the Schuylkill that Philadelphia is indebted for that super-abundant supply of fresh water which ministers so much to the comfort of its inhabitants. Close to the town, a dam is thrown across the river, and by the power thus attained, the Schuylkill is made to pump itself into an enormous reservoir, constructed on the top of a contiguous mound, which goes by the name of Fairmount. It is from this elevation, perhaps, that the best bird's-eye view of Philadelphia is obtained, lying, as it does on a hot July day, like a great flat overbaked brick-field below you. The supply of water, distributed from this reservoir, is inexhaustible; at least, the Philadelphians use it as if it were so. You meet it everywhere, lavished on every purpose, municipal, domestic, and personal. Philadel-phia seems to begin each day with a general ablution. On arriving one morning early from the south, I found the streets deluged with water, some recondite plug seeming to have been extracted in front of every house, and the water so squirting and gushing about in all directions, that it was no easy matter to avoid it. Not only were windows, doors, and doorsteps being cleaned, but the brick pavements themselves came in for their share of scrubbing; and, shortly afterwards, when the sun had dried them, they looked as clean and fresh as if they had just been laid down. In winter, of course, the general bath is less frequently repeated. Nowhere is the utility of this superfluity so perceptible as in the market, so widely and justly celebrated for its cleanliness. And no thanks to it. St. Giles's would itself be clean, if subjected to such an ordeal. The market consists of a long succession of narrow sheds, run-ning down the centre of Market-street, which sheds, at the close of each day's operations, are, one and all of them, copiously visited by the purifying influences of Fairmount.

Nowhere does Philadelphia present the same impetuous activity as New York. It has an orderly and decorous look about it, very much at variance with the turbulent scenes of which it has recently been the witness. It is nevertheless a lively town in its external aspect, and, under a prim surface, conceals a good deal of gaiety. But of society in Phila-delphia I shall have occasion hereafter to speak. A mannerism pervades the streets different from any thing witnessed elsewhere. In Chestnut-street, the principal promenade, there is far less jauntiness than in Broadway. Philadelphians, both in dress and manner, are subdued, as compared with their more showy neighbours. But their manner combines grace with quietness; their dress, elegance with simplicity. Catch your Philadelphia belle dress in anything but the richest stuff, but yet she wears it as if the severer attire of her ancestors was constantly before her eyes. They do not discard the fashions, but then they do not worship them with the devotion characteristic of their sisters on the Hudson. . . .

With this exception, external life in Philadelphia is pretty much what life in New York is. Indeed, so constant and regular is the intercourse now between the two, that it could not be otherwise. Amusements are as varied in the former as in the latter, but the passion for them is not so great. The number of theatres is small in proportion to the population, and it is seldom that they are all open together. The Philadelphians are fond of music, and when a good operatic company make their appearance, they receive them well. They do not dislike the ballet, but they have no enthusiasm for its extravagances. The city abounds with libraries and literary institutions, and to the credit of its inhabitants, most of them are well sustained. There are also many pleasant excursions in the neighbourhood, to which they resort in the summer time. Steam ferry-boats connect the city every ten minutes with the New Jersey shore of the Delaware. On a summer afternoon, hundreds crowd these boats on their way to the gardens in Camden, a small but scattered town on the other side, and which may be, in fact, regarded as one of the suburbs of the city. Many of those whose business is in Philadelphia reside here, escaping in New Jersey the heavy taxation of overburdened Pennsylvania. In the tea gardens there is a touch of Parisian life; crowds regaling themselves in the open air, beneath the trees, with the multiform drink of the country. . . .

The city is seen to great advantage, when viewed from Camden, on a bright summer day. And with such a view I shall take leave of it for the present. The river is about a mile in width, and the town seems to rise from the water on its opposite shore as abruptly as a sea-wall. Its outline is almost unbroken by a single spire or turret. Down the river its limit seems to be marked by the navy yard, the sheds of which loom over every object in the level district which surrounds them. Out of these sheds have issued some of the largest ships in the world, and some of the finest in the American service. The district contiguous to them is Southwark, chiefly inhabited by working people. Carrying your eye over the body of the city, you have to your right, some distance up the river, the suburban district of Kensington, of which it is enough to say that it is the Irish quarter of Philadelphia. Farther up still, and terminating the city in that direction, is the port of Richmond, called into existence by the rapid increase of the coal trade. It is easy to distinguish it by the cluster of coasters which are constantly at its wharves. The city too, is in front well lined with shipping, which come close to the shore, as at New York; but as compared with which, Philadelphia as a sea-port is insignificant. It is destined to be more of a manufacturing than a maritime town.

PART IV

THE OLD SOUTH:
LAND OF CHIVALRY

Two of the most striking developments in the southern states during the Jacksonian period were the expansion of the Cotton Kingdom and the economic recovery of the old states of the upper South. The fine plantation, Shirley, on the James River, had, for example, long before Henry Barnard visited it in 1833, shifted from its colonial staple of tobacco to raising wheat, thus achieving a new prosperity. Shirley, then owned by Hill Carter, a descendant of the famous "King Carter" of colonial days, was a model of the paternal type of plantation as contrasted with the many commercialized slave plantations of the Southwest. Barnard was a Connecticut schoolteacher, a graduate of Yale College, who later became famous as one of the most prominent leaders in the movement to establish free public schools in the United States.

The work of Edmund Ruffin in introducing the use of marl in the 1830's to restore the fertility of worn, old fields and the importation later of guano as a fertilizer worked wonders on old colonial estates, such as Sabine Hall on the Potomac River, which Solon Robinson, an agricultural editor from Indiana, visited in 1850.

In Richmond, which Alexander Mackay describes, the rapid growth of tobacco factories, operated by slave labor, gave a new prosperity to the city. The English traveler found that its people were different from those in Philadelphia and New York; they had a higher sense of honor, a chivalric spirit. "In Virginia," he noted, "convention is, perhaps, more than anywhere else subjugated by the heart."

A fresh view of the life of the planters and of slavery is revealed in the letters of Sarah Williams, a New York girl from an abolitionist family who married a turpentine planter of eastern North Carolina. As a young bride coming to live on a slave plantation in 1852, she had a hard time adjusting to strange southern ways. But adjust she did, gave up her abolitionist views, and worked hard, as did most other planters' wives, in the manifold tasks required of the mistress of a slave plantation. Indeed, her vivacious account of southern women living on plantations and farms, instead of in cities such as Charleston or Natchez, does much to destroy the stereotype of southern women as living idle lives of ease and freedom from domestic work.

157

British travelers who visited the South in this period viewed its society often from radically different backgrounds. One of the most interesting accounts of southern society was given by William Thomson, a Scottish wool carder and spinner, in A Tradesman's Travels in the United States and Canada. He observed American society from the point of view of a skilled laborer seeking employment. The majority of British travelers, however, were from the upper classes. Such was George Featherstonhaugh, an English geologist, with a very aristocratic, conservative outlook, whose travel account, An Excursion through the Slave States, has a delightful ironic quality. Some, notably Sir Charles Lyell, carried letters of introduction that opened to them the doors of aristocratic planters' homes. His two travel books, accordingly, present a very favorable view of the way the planters lived.

He apparently did not see very much of the life of the yeoman farmers or other members of the middle class as did Frederick Law Olmsted, the northern traveler. Olmsted traveled in the South in 1853-54, his expenses paid by the New York Times. He wrote his descriptions of southern life in three valuable books: A Journey in the Seaboard Slave States, A Journey in the Back Country, and A Journey Through Texas, from all of which a compilation was made in 1861 entitled The Cotton Kingdom. He had had some experience as a northern farmer, which enabled him to observe more accurately than most travelers the southern agrarian economy. Although he held a strong abolitionist prejudice, that fact did not prevent him from reporting honestly and realistically conditions as he saw them. A characteristic of his writing that makes his travel accounts very valuable is his technique of recording significant details of southern life that he observed as well as conversations with overseers, yeoman farmers, poor whites, slaves, and planters.

The abolitionists propagated a stereotype of a three-class society, consisting of haughty aristocratic planters, degraded poor whites, and oppressed slaves. Daniel R. Hundley [see Part VIII], a native of Alabama educated at Harvard College and the University of Virginia, combated this distorted image of the South in his pioneer sociological work entitled Social Relations in Our Southern States. Here he described the existence of an important middle class and a large body of yeoman farmers. His view has been substantiated in modern times by the researches of Professor Frank L. Owsley and his graduate students at Vanderbilt University, who by the study of the manuscript reports of the censuses of 1850 and 1860, showed the great importance of the middle class.

Although the Old South was overwhelmingly an agrarian region, it began to develop industry to diversify its economy, especially during the agricultural depression of the 1840's. A leader in the movement to promote cotton mills in the region was William Gregg of South Carolina, *who not only propagandized for the use of poor white labor in textile mills but established a successful pilot mill at Graniteville, S.C. The account of this pioneer industrialist given in this section appeared in De Bow's* Review *of New Orleans, the leading commercial magazine of the Old South.*

In the 1830's, partly as a result of the attack of the abolitionists, southerners became more conscious of their identity and a movement arose to encourage the growth of a native literature. William Gilmore Simms of South Carolina was an outstanding leader in this movement, not only in publishing novels that glamorized southern society but in founding magazines. In this latter project he encountered a discouraging apathy on the part of the southern people, a tendency which he condemned in a letter to the editor of the Magnolia.

The institution of slavery was the most important influence in shaping the mind of the Old South. In the 1820's, before the abolitionist movement had arisen, prominent men in South Carolina were maintaining that slavery was not an evil to be apologized for, but was a positive good. This doctrine repudiated the liberal views held by the great generation of Virginians and Marylanders and reflected the growing profitableness of slavery in the new Cotton Kingdom. In 1831 the southern states were shocked by the Nat Turner Insurrection in Southampton County, Virginia, which caused the Virginia legislature to engage in a great debate on emancipation. Shortly thereafter Professor Thomas Roderick Dew of William and Mary College published an influential defense of slavery. The ablest politician to espouse the cause of slavery was John C. Calhoun, an excerpt from whose speech in the Senate in 1837 is included in this section. Calhoun relied scarcely at all upon the Biblical texts in defending slavery, an argument which to southerners in general was most persuasive and conclusive, but instead, boldly based his defense on the idea of a Greek democracy. The defense of slavery against the condemnation of world opinion made southern society one of the most conservative societies in the world and led to the suppression of freedom of thought and speech below the Potomac River.

A New England Visitor in the Old South

Henry Barnard

Petersberg, March 14, 1833

From this family [John W. Campbell, book dealer and historian] thus described I received the most kind attention and am indebted for one of the pleasantest and most profitable weeks I ever spent. I expected to leave Petersburgh the next morning, but Mrs. Campbell sent down for my trunk and lodged [me] immediately in her best chamber. She gave me an invitation to accompany her and Elizabeth to Shirley, where she was just agoing, and I assure you I accepted the proposal without hesitation. Shirley and the neighboring plantations on James river, are the richest and oldest estates in Va. So we started off the next morning, for Shirley about 15 miles from Petersburgh and 25 from Richmond. The Old house, large and commodious was built nearly 2 centuries since, by the progenitors of the present proprietor, Mr. Carter. It consists of about 900 acres improved land of the first quality and 100 slaves and yields an income of nearly 10,000 dollars. He has this year *a field of wheat, of only 320 acres,* and raises for market about 300 barrels of corn. He keeps 20 horses. With such an income you may imagine his splendid hospitality. His service is all of silver, and you drink your porter out of silver goblets. The table at dinner is always furnished with the finest Virginia ham, and saddle of mutton—Turkey, then canvas back duck—beef—oysters etc, etc, etc,—the finest cellery—then comes the sparkling champagne—after that the desert—plum pudding—tarts—ice cream—peaches preserved in Brandy etc. etc—then the table is cleared, and on comes the figs, almonds and raisins, and the richest Madeira, the best Port and the softest Malmsey wine I ever tasted. . . .

While at Shirley, I visited, by invitation the ancient seat of Westover

Bernard C. Steiner (ed.), "The South Atlantic States in 1833 as seen by a New Englander" (*Maryland Historical Magazine*, Dec., 1918), XIII, pp. 317-328.

and Berkley, which with one or two exceptions, are the richest plantations in Virginia.

This excursion of a week gave me more insight into the manners and
customs of the higher classes of this State, than I could have derived
from any other source. We returned to Petersberg this evening. In crossing the James which is two miles wide, opposite Shirley to City Point,
we had a tempestuous sea, and the Ladies were excessively frightened,
and to tell the truth there was danger of being overset.

I have had as yet no time to visit or become much acquainted in this
city—but I believe I shall leave here tomorrow unless it rains very hard
for Raleigh—spend several days there, as I have been furnished with
letters of introduction to the first families there—and then go on to
Salisbury. I do think without exaggeration that this trip will be of more
advantage to me than any two years I spent in college. . . .

Petersberg, March 15th 1833

My Dear Betty

I think you would delight to visit this region, merely to observe the
difference of manners and habits, from what you have been accustomed
to, aye and to experience the princely hospitality of the *gentle* born families. For the last week I have had a succession of feasts. I accompanied
Mrs. Campbell who is one of the most devoted mothers and well educated women I ever met with, and her daughter Miss Betty, a beautiful
sprightly accomplished girl, to Shirley, the seat of the Carter family. Mrs.
Carter, is of a high and wealthy family, and is one of the plainest most unassuming women, you will meet with any where. Now, that you may
understand how we lived there, and how one of these large establishments
are carried on. I will describe a single day there—I will suppose also
that it is a day upon which company is expected etc, etc.

When you wake in the morning, you are surprised to find that a servant has been in, and without disturbing you, built up a large fire—
taken out your clothes and brushed them, and done the same with your
boots—brought in hot water to shave, and indeed stands ready to do
your bidding—as soon as you are dressed, you walk down into the dining
room— At eight o'clock you take your seat at the breakfast table of rich
mahogany—each plate standing separate on its own little cloth—Mr.
Carter will sit at one end of the table and Mrs. Carter at the other—Mrs.
C. will send you by two little black boys, as fine a cup of coffee as you
ever tasted, or a cup of tea—it is fashionable here to drink a cup of tea
after coffee—Mr. Carter has a fine cold ham before him of the real Virginia flavor—this is all the meat you will get in the morning, but the
servant will bring you hot muffins and corn batter cakes every 2 minutes

—you will find on the table also, loaf wheat bread, hot and cold—corn bread—

After breakfast visitors consult their pleasure—if they wish to ride, horses are ready at their command—read, there are books enough in the Library,—write, fire, and writing materials are ready in his room— The Master and Mistress of the House are not expected to entertain visitors till an hour or two before dinner, which is usually at 3. If company has been invited to the dinner they will begin to come about 1—Ladies in carriage and gentlemen horseback— After making their toilet, the company amuse themselves in the parlor—about a half hour before dinner, the gentlemen are invited out to take grog. When dinner is ready (and by the way Mrs. Carter has nothing to do with setting the table, an old family servant, who for 50 years has superintended that matter, does all that) Mr. Carter politely takes a Lady by the hand and leads the way into the dining room, and is followed by the rest, each Lady lead by a gentleman. Mrs. C. is at one end of the table with a large dish of rich soup, and Mr. C. at the other, with a saddle of fine mutton, scattered round the table, you may choose for yourself, ham—beef—turkey—ducks —eggs with greens—etc—etc—for vegetables, potatoes, beets—hominy— This last you will find always at dinner, it is made of their white corn and beans and is a very fine dish—after you have dined, there circulates a bottle of sparkling champagne. After that off passes the things, and the *upper* table cloth, and upon that is placed the desert, consisting of fine plum pudding, tarts, etc, etc,—after this comes ice cream, West India preserves—peaches preserved in brandy, etc,— When you have eaten this, off goes the second table cloth, and then upon the bare mahogany table is set, the figs, raisins, and almonds, and before Mr. Carter is set 2 or 3 bottles of wine—Madeira, Port, and a sweet wine for the Ladies— he fills his glass, and pushes them on, after the glasses are all filled, the gentlemen pledge their services to the Ladies, and down goes the wine, after the first and second glass the ladies retire, and the gentlemen begin to circulate the bottle pretty briskly. You are at liberty however to follow the Ladies as soon as you please, who after music and a little chit chat prepare for their ride home.

Raleigh, Wednesday March 20th
. . . I reached this seat of the University of N. Carolina [Chapel Hill] in the evening of Friday, a distance of 30 miles. The country is not interesting, except that it is more broken than that on the other side of Raleigh. After supper I delivered my letters to Dr. Caldwell, the venerable President of this college, of which he was pleased to take such *kind* notice as to send for my baggage and beg of me to consider his house as my home during my stay in Chapel Hill; and so I have done,

and here I am now hurrying over this sheet in his office and in his venerable looking chair. This reconciles me more to the delay. I expected to have left yesterday evening for Salisbury, but the stage was very much crowded, and the night was dark and stormy and the roads excessively bad, and so I concluded to remain till the next stage—till tomorrow night.

Dr. C, is a very distinguished man—has travelled in Europe, and by his energy and perseverence, built up and sustained this institution for 30 years. There are 3 buildings for students, and recitation rooms etc, and a small chapel and observatory. It numbers about 100 students— 8000 vols. in all the Library and a very respectable chemical and philo-[sophical], apparatus. It was for a long time doubted at the North whether any thing like college discipline could be maintained at the South, but I did not observe any difference between the habits of students here and at Yale—except that in this boasted land of refinement their manners are more rough and their dress, even vulgarly plain.

The germs are beginning to exhibit their tender green now. Indeed the peach and plum trees are in full blossom and the early flowers are to be seen in the gardens. I wish you to recur to the date of this letter with you. Here I am writing with the door and windows open—with rich and yet delicate blossom of the peach before my eyes and the fragrance of the early flowers upon the warm air. . . .

I shall pass over to Hillsboro tomorrow morning, if I can get a conveyance. It is but 12 miles, and is one of the most flourishing places in the State. Saving accidents, I shall reach Salisbury on Friday morning, where I hope to receive letters from my friends.

Chapel Hill March 25th 1833

My dear Brother—

How long before I reach Salisbury is a matter of some doubt. I expected to have left here in the stage last evening but it was full, and the night dark and stormy, and the roads excessively bad, so I concluded to go by another stage, which will come on tomorrow am therefore still enjoying the hospitality of Dr. Caldwell the president of the College at this place.

While at Raleigh I enjoyed the kindness and hospitality of several wealthy and intelligent families, indeed a stranger is very well treated through this whole section of country Especially if he bring letters along with him.

I left Raleigh on Friday noon, and reached this place about 7 in the evening, a distance of 30 miles. I immediately delivered my letters to Dr. Caldwell, who sent for my baggage and wished me to consider his home as my home during my stay. Now this is a very convenient way of travelling indeed, and makes one better contented with delays than he would otherwise be. There are 5 professors and two tutors. There are 3 college buildings, and a chapel and observatory. The college is situated on a hill, amid a thick and extensive grove of native oaks, which must present a fine appearance when in full foliage. The village is small, not consisting of more than 20 houses and owes its importance if not existence to the University.

The inhabitants, like most southerners are indolent, and like very much to lounge about and let the slaves do the work. The enterprising men are mostly from the North— They generally grow rich here, and are looked upon with suspicion.

Took tea this evening at Prof. Mitchell—felt myself back again into Con.—Mrs. M. is a daughter of Dr. North of N. London, and a younger sister of hers is now visiting her. Prof. M. is a good man and a patient thorough scholar with eccentric manners— He gave very distinct ideas of men and things as far as they have fallen under his observation—after tea, Mr. [Peter] Norwood came in, told me about Bunker, and to illustrate the manners of the Western part of this [State] mentioned an anecdote that was told of the wife of one of their former Governors—that she would not remove to Raleigh, because she would be obliged to wear stockings and shoes. Several students came in, a more raw set of fellows you don't see often collected.

Prof. M. thought N. C. must always remain poor—no large cities and could be none—no prospect of establishing any gen'l system of education.

[March 26]

Rose about 7—Walked over the garden—examined a sundial on a stone pillar—peach trees in full bloom—looked over Webster's speech—spoke at breakfast of what I had seen and heard at Washington—Dr. C. spoke pretty strongly against Nullification and the authors of it—with great discouragement of the enterprise of this State—the almost utter impossibility of rousing the people to a sense of the improvements of the age—entertained some of the students with an account of what I had seen at W—was invited by several to visit the Libraries—did so—the dialectic is one of the finest I have ever seen—I noticed mostly all very fine standard works—English works—English editions and in English binding—several portraits of members who have become distinguished—visited the Philanthropic Library—about the same no. of vols.—but less splendidly bound and many new books—walked out to the observatory and the burying ground—stones erected by the Societies—great rivalry between them—walked over the village—saw a great many while at one of the Stores—visited the University Library—rather small—the old building quite dilapidated—the State not liberal toward—rather jealous —no ladies here—good deal of music—after dinner was introduced to

Prof. Hooper called on Prof. Mitchell, who had gone out to a Saw Mill with some Ladies—so out we went—and a very agreeable time we had of it too, conversed with the professor about rocks, stones and fossil shells —and the Ladies about appropriate matters. This institution has been built up by the perseverance and energy of Dr. Caldwell—Took tea with Prof. Hooper, a very good and intelligent man—complained about the want of gusto in the pursuit on the part of the Students—Dr. Caldwell gave me a very interesting account of his travels in Europe. Slept over breakfast Bell—walked out to Prospect Point—and then to the Observatory. Heard Mr. Mitchell preach—after dinner conversed with the Dr. and wrote letters—Doubt the propriety of locating [a college] in a village.—

Hillsborough, March 27th 1833

My dear Brother—

I wrote you a few lines from Chapel Hill on Monday afternoon. I spent the evening at Prof. Mitchell's, one of the ablest men of the faculty. He is a graduate of Yale, and a native of Con., and married his wife in N. London, a daughter of Dr. North. A younger Sister of his is spending some time with her. I should not have known from anything I saw at his table, or the manners of his family, that I was out of Connecticut. I didn't see two or three black servants standing at your elbows to execute your slightest wish, even to pushing the salt cellar a little nearer, if it is a foot from you. He gave me a good deal of information about the habits of these people, and the nature of the country I should travel through. He told me of an incident which frequently occurs at the camp meetings of the Methodists. The preacher in the midst of a fervent prayer, will all of a sudden burst out into a loud boisterous laugh— as though his soul was rejoiced at the conversion of sinners around him. The most godly of his brethren join with him. This is called the "Holy Laugh."

A Colonial Estate Restored

Solon Robinson

[May, 1851] Thou shalt not covet, is a commandment which we should not break; yet, if any one can visit Sabine Hall, and not disobey that injunction, he is a more perfect Christian than I can pretend to be. It is one of those noble old mansions which are to be found scattered all over the tidewater region of Virginia, marking an age of wealth and refinement, that in some measure has faded away. For the ancient families have forsaken the old halls, and in many cases, house and household are known no longer in the land that was once graced by their presence.

Sabine Hall still retains its pristine grandeur, and is owned and occupied by as true a nobleman as ever welcomed a guest beneath the hospitable roof of a Virginia gentleman of the good old time. Let the traveller who happens to enjoy the pleasure of Captain Mayer's company upon the steamer Mary Washington, from Baltimore to Fredericksburg, (a very pleasant route it is too, and good boat and very accommodating officers), ask him to point out this prominent landmark, a couple of miles below Rappahannock, on the opposite side of the river. It stands upon an elevated site, some two miles from the shore, overlooking a broad tract of rich bottom land, upon which great fields of wheat and corn are spread out in bounteous profusion. Covering the slope of the hill, immediately in front, is a terraced garden of fruits and flowers, and grassy banks; and a little lower down, a full supply of esculents for the table. Here the fig ripens its luscious sweetness, and the peach gives its subacid goodness in great perfection. The carriage approach is from the rear, or rather the landward front, through a park of noble old trees, green grass, and hedges. There is one thing about this entrance which I wonder is not more common. A neat lodge stands by the outer gate, the residence of one of the house servants, and some of the chil-

Herbert A. Kellar (ed.), Solon Robinson, Pioneer and Agriculturist, Selected Writings (Indianapolis, 1936, courtesy of Indiana Historical Bureau), II, pp. 493-495.

dren are always on hand to open and close it when passed by resident or stranger. The house itself is not extraordinary in its dimensions, nor grandeur of appearance; but it is sufficiently roomy, and is one of that class of old-time dwellings whose walls are as substantial as the hospitality which welcomes the stranger within.

Through the centre, runs a broad hall, big enough to parade a militia company; upon the right, are two parlors large enough to entertain another; upon the left, a dining room and sitting room, and between them a heavy wain-scotted and balustered, deep-worn staircase, and a passage out upon the gallery of the wing, leading to the store rooms and kitchen. Of course, there is a gallery, or colonnade, upon the river front, for what finished southern house ever lacked this ornamental appendage?

The present proprietor, Colonel Robert W. Carter, is a descendant of one of the oldest and most wealthy families in the state, and almost the only one upon the northern neck of Virginia, where the name was once great among the great names of that region.

Like many other countries which depend upon a single staple crop, this sunk into a state of unproductiveness, after its staple, tobacco, failed to remunerate the cultivator. Lands which once gave forth golden harvests, returned to a state of wooded wildness. A hundred years works wondrous changes. Old walls of extensive mansions, seen through avenues of old trees; fine old churches, dilapidated, though yet strong in their old age, speak of what this region was, ere Washington was born, for here was his birthplace. Till within a few years, but a little of the country besides the alluvial bottoms of the Potomac or Rappahannock, such as those of Colonel Carter, were considered worth cultivating. Now, a new era is dawning upon this long-neglected, poverty-stricken portion of Virginia. Guano, lime, plaster, bone dust, and other fertilisers have been imported; better plows, and other implements used; and if ever that adage was applicable to any country, it is to this, for truly, the wilderness has been made to blossom like the rose. Not only the desert places in the forest have been renovated, but such lands as those at Sabine Hall have been made to double their products.

Taking all things into consideration, there are few more desirable sections of our great country than this one, so long neglected and almost despised on account of its poverty. Certainly, there are few places that have more of the characteristics desirable to make a comfortable home, than can be found upon the fine plantation and noble old hall of the place I have endeavored to draw such a picture of as would interest my readers.

The People of Richmond

Alexander Mackay

... The site of Richmond was selected chiefly with a view to the water power which is afforded it by the rapids of the James. These commence a considerable distance above the city, and terminate immediately in front of it. The fall which thus gradually takes place in the channel of the river, is altogether about eighty feet, the formation of the banks on either side being such as to render the great power thus afforded perfectly available. It has, as yet, been but partially taken advantage of. Opposite the city, on the southern bank, is the small village of Manchester, aspiring, I suppose, to that name, from the fact of its comprising two cotton factories, which, indeed, with their adjuncts, form its sum total. It is approached from Richmond by means of bridges thrown across the rapids from the mainland on either side, to the islands; but the chief industry of the spot is centred in the city itself, which derives its water power from the basin of the James River, and Kanawha canal, designed to unite the Virginian sea-board with the great valley of the West. The canal is here fed from the upper level of the river, and as it approaches the town, the difference of level between it and the falling stream becomes greater and greater, until at length a fall of eighty feet is obtained from the canal basin to the river. Here the water may be easily used three times over in changing its level; a little further up it can only be used twice, and still further up again, only once. As yet fully three-fourths of the power thus available is unemployed. The manufactures of Richmond are various, comprising woollen and cotton goods, tobacco factories, and some very large iron and steel works; but its chief feature in this respect is the manufacture of flour, the largest flour-mills in the United States being found here, one of which, when in full play, can turn out from 750 to 1,000 barrels of flour per day. It is from Richmond that the South American market is chiefly supplied with

Alexander Mackay, *The Western World*, pp. 72-86.

this necessary of life; the wheat of Virginia, when ground, being better adapted for tropical voyages than the produce of any other part of the country, including Ohio and Genesee wheat.

Richmond is also one of the first tobacco markets of the country, the produce of the State being concentrated upon it both for export and manufacture. The tobacco, after having been dried, as it now is, chiefly in the fields, is closely packed into hogsheads, in which state it is forwarded to Richmond, where such portion of it (the greater) as cannot be disposed of by private sale is stored in public warehouses, to await the auction sales, which take place within certain hours of the day. When a hogshead is to be put up, it is unhooped, and the compact mass, as yet but raw material, exposed to view. One of the inspectors on duty, then, by means of a crow-bar, forcibly separates it in three different places, from which a few leaves are taken to form the sample of the bulk, which is then sold according to its quality as thus ascertained. The staves are then put together again, the hogshead receives the purchaser's mark, and it is left in store until he chooses to take it away. The quantity of tobacco which is thus sometimes accumulated upon Richmond, is only exceeded by that which is generally to be found in bond at the London Docks.

Much of the tobacco thus disposed of is purchased for local manufacture, Richmond containing several large establishments for the conversion of the crude tobacco into a form fit for chewing. Over the most extensive of these I was kindly piloted by one of the owners, where I witnessed all the processes which the weed underwent in its passage from dry leaves to the marketable shape of Cavendish tobacco, in which form it was packed in small cakes, in oblong boxes, labelled with the seductive name of "Honeydew." In all the departments of the factory the labour was performed by slaves, superintended by white overseers. They appeared to be very contented at their work, although the utmost silence was observed amongst them, except within certain hours of the day, when they were permitted to relieve their toil by singing, performing a succession of solos, duets, glees, &c. &c. in a way that was truly surprising, considering that they were entirely self-taught. Having heard them sing, I was permitted to see them eat; their noon-day meal consisting of cornbread and beef; the males and females occupying different apartments, and each appearing to have as much to eat as he or she could possibly enjoy. The factory was so complete as to be provided even with its own tailor, who was engaged, whilst I was there, in cutting out the summer suits of the workmen, from thick cotton cloth, tolerably well bleached, and of a close and by no means very coarse texture.

In a street contiguous to the public warehouses, I encountered piles of boxes filled with a very coarse liquorice, and which were being disposed of in lots by auction. The liquorice was purchased that it might be mixed with a portion of the tobacco, in the process of its manufacture, the poison being thus sweetened, to render it palatable to the uninitiated.

The neighbourhood of Richmond is rich in mineral resources. The coal strata are not only abundant, but in some places approach so near the surface as to be worked at but little cost. The largest coal company is that called the English company; the coal, when raised, being carried from its pits, by means of a private railway, to the port of Richmond, a few miles below the city, whence it is shipped to the different markets of the Union. There is also a good deal of iron in the vicinity; but either from the difficulty of mining it, or from the hold which English and Pennsylvania iron has got of the market, it is as yet but little worked.

The people of Richmond are a peculiar people. They are proud and sensitive to a degree. They are proud, in the first place, of their State, and in the next, of its capital; in addition to which, they are not a little satisfied with the moral superiorities to which they lay claim. Their code of honour is so exceedingly strict that it requires the greatest circumspection to escape its violation. An offence which elsewhere would be regarded as of homeopathic proportions, is very apt to assume in Richmond the gravity of colossal dimensions; even a coolness between parties is dangerous, as having a fatal tendency speedily to ripen into a deadly feud. Once arrived at this point, a personal encounter is inevitable, unless, to avoid it, one party or the other is induced to quit the city. It is curious enough to witness the cool and matter-of-course way in which even the ladies will speculate upon the necessities for, and the probabilities of, a hostile meeting between such and such parties, and in which, when they hear of a duel, they will tell you that they long foresaw it, and that it could not be avoided. After all, this state of things, although it may indicate less of a healthy habit than of a morbid sensibility, gives to Richmond society a chivalrous and romantic cast, which is rarely to be met with in matter-of-fact America. It is seldom, indeed, that they imitate, in their personal warfare, the savage brutalities of the south-western States; their quarrels, generally speaking, taking some time to mature, and the parties, when the day of reckoning at length comes, fighting like gentlemen instead of like tigers or hyenas.

The society of Richmond adds the warmth and fervour of the south to that frank and ready hospitality which is characteristic of American society in general. It is rarely that the stranger, in his social contact with the Americans, has to encounter the frigid influences of formalism. In Virginia, convention is, perhaps, more than anywhere else subjugated by the heart. It is astonishing how soon each party in an assembly appears in his or her real character. Entering a drawing-room at Richmond is like entering a theatre with the curtain up, when there is no ugly, green-baize screen between you, the scenery, and the performers. In no other place has it ever appeared to me that life was so little disfigured by masquerade. The thoughts are accorded a freedom of utterance, which is never abused, and dislikes and partialities come equally to the surface; the one not being smothered, the other not concealed. He must look into himself for the cause, who does not feel himself at once at home with his frank and hospitable friends. The ladies of Richmond partake of that easy grace, the causes of which, as a characteristic of Virginian society, I shall presently trace.

At an evening party, which I had the pleasure of attending, it was my good fortune to meet with Mr. W. C. Rives, for many years one of the representatives of Virginia in the Senate of the United States, and for some time American Minister at Paris. I found him to be a man of liberal views and varied information. As a politician, however, he is now regarded as somewhat *passé*, having differed with his own party without receiving any cordial welcome from the Whigs. When I met him, he was gradually yielding to the seductive influences of Mr. Abbott Lawrence, the prince of manufacturers and protectionists in America, who had recently addressed to him several letters, in favour of a high tariff, through the columns of the newspapers, with a view, if possible, to enlisting the sympathies of Virginia in favour of protection. Mr. Lawrence was, at that very time, in Richmond, which, as the chief seat of Virginian manufacture, he was striving to convert to the prohibitory doctrines of New England.

As already intimated, American society has a peculiar development in Virginia. The social system is there beset with influences which in most parts of the country are unknown, and some of which are but partially experienced in others. Not that the manifestation of society which obtains in Virginia is exclusively confined to that State, for most of its social characteristics are common to some of the adjacent States, particularly to Maryland and South Carolina. In its peculiarities therefore, in this respect, Virginia is not to be regarded as the sole exception to the general tenor of American society. It is at once the type and the most striking specimen of the social development peculiar to the slave-holding States of the Atlantic sea-board; and it is only as illustrative of such that I have here particularly alluded to the more distinctive features of Virginian society.

The division of property in Virginia is totally different from that which prevails in the northern and north-western States. In the latter it is very rarely that one meets with great accumulations of landed property in the hands of a single individual or family. The system of land tenures is adverse to such accumulations; as it is indeed in Virginia, so far as statutory enactments are concerned; but these enactments are controlled by other circumstances, which go far to counteract their operation. In the north and north-west, large landed estates are the rare exception; in Virginia they are the rule. Both in the one case and in the other, the same general principle may be recognised as prevailing—that no one should occupy more land than he can cultivate; but, from the diversity of social and political institutions, this principle does not, in the two instances, lead to the same results. Throughout the whole north and north-west, where the frame is hardy, where the climate invites to work, where the competition is great and the people are inured to toil, where slavery does not exist and labour is not considered as dishonourable, the land is divided into small holdings, few possessing more than they can occupy and cultivate. But in Virginia and the adjacent States the case is very different; the land being there parcelled off into large estates, called plantations, consisting, in many cases, of tens of thousands of acres. In the real property system of these States, the Revolution has, practically, wrought but very little change. The estate of a Virginian landlord is, in some of its features, very closely assimilated to an English manor. The transatlantic proprietor has certainly none of the political or judicial prerogatives of his English prototype; but, in all other respects, he exercises the same control over his property as the lord exercises, or was wont to exercise, over the demesne lands of the manor. In the most convenient part of the estate is generally to be found the manor-house, and, with the exception of his family and his guests, all who live upon it are the vassals or slaves of the proprietor. Each estate, too, has its appropriate name, as is the case in England; but this is very different from the principle which obtains in the north, where each man's property is known as such and such a lot, in such and such a division, of such and such a township. In short, the real property system of Virginia is the closest approximation to that which, until a very recent period, was so generally prevalent in England, of any that is to be found in the United States.

The influence which this exercises upon society is great and strikingly perceptible. It is almost impossible, in civilized life, to find two states of being more in contrast with each other than those of the landed proprietors of the north and south. It is rarely that the former is not found personally occupied in the cultivation of his own lot or piece of ground. The latter is wholly unaccustomed to labour, and, not unfrequently, delegates to others the business even of superintending the affairs of his estate. These conditions will suggest to the English reader the different positions of the country gentleman and the small farmer in this country. Not only is the American farmer generally the chief labourer on his own land, but the different members of his family—his wife, his daughters, and sons, unless ambition prompt the last-mentioned to seek the towns for the purpose of engaging in mercantile or professional pursuits, take their respective and appropriate shares in the management of the farm. This daily habit of cheerful toil, if not very favourable to the growth of the amenities of life, keeps the energies from becoming dormant, begets self-reliance, and gives rise to a sturdy feeling of independence. Very different is it with the luxurious planter of the south. To him labour would be disgrace. Vegetating, as it were, upon his estate, and surrounded by hundreds of slaves ready to obey his nod, he frequently disencumbers himself even of the management of his property, which he entrusts to the care of overseers, giving himself up to recreation and amusement, and, in many cases, to study, to which he is invited by the beauteous repose and the glorious serenity of nature, which mark his enervating climate. And so with his family. Strangers to toil, and dependent for almost every comfort upon the labour of others, they have time and opportunity to cultivate that indescribable ease and grace which are typical of the more polished circles in older communities. It is thus that one much more frequently meets with the conventional lady and gentleman in the slave, than in the free States; the latter being not only more polished in manner than his northern countryman, but also presenting a higher standard of intellectual cultivation; and the former only finding her parallel, as a general rule, in the more accomplished circles of the northern cities.

Domestic slavery predominates, perhaps, to a greater extent in Virginia than in any of the adjoining States, where it is more generally to be met with in its predial and harsher aspect. The slaves about the household are usually divided amongst the different members of the family, as is the case in Russia; and it is singular to witness the attachment which sometimes springs up between the master and the slave. Frequently, too, when there are guests in the house, to each is assigned a slave or slaves, whose duty it is to wait upon him or her during the visit.

An incident in Virginia, which will be recognised as analogous to some of the habits of English, country life, is to be found in the visiting parties, which, during a portion of the year, take place throughout the State. A planter and his family will then have their friends in the neighbourhood, and frequently some of those at a distance, under their roof for weeks together, the whole time being spent in one continued round of gaiety and amusement. For this their mansions are well adapted, being constructed on a large and commodious scale, as compared with the rural dwellings to be found in the free and grain-growing States; and many of them presenting to the eye large piles of irregular architecture, quite in contrast with the prim and formal style of the north, and consisting generally of a colonial nucleus, to which a variety of wings have been appended since the epoch of the Revolution. I was

startled the first time I saw quaint old turrets and projecting and multi-
tudinous gable ends, embowered amid the foliage of the New World.
It seemed to me that such things were more in keeping when in juxta-
position with the spreading oak and the beech, than with the hickory,
the black walnut and the acacia. What I would have looked for on the
Severn and the Dee, surprised me, at first, when met with on the Roanoke and the Shenandoah.

During the continuance of these visits, the guests sometimes meet
each other at, and at other times not till after, breakfast. When a general
excursion is proposed, they set off immediately, before the heat of the
day comes on. When nothing of the kind is contemplated, a portion of
the morning is spent in walking about the grounds, or in making some
preliminary preparations for the amusements of the evening. About
eleven o'clock they all disappear, to avoid the heat of the day; the
ladies retiring to their rooms, the gentlemen, with the exception of such
as go hunting or fishing, to theirs. The chambers are partially darkened,
to avoid the heat and fierce glare of mid-day; and the burning hours
are thus passed either in reading or in yielding to their somnolent influences. In the afternoon, when parties dare to face the sun, they emerge
from their hiding places, and all is life again; attention being occupied
by a variety of amusements till dinner-time. The evening is generally
devoted to dancing, which, when the heat is too oppressive to admit
of its continuance within, is sometimes transferred to the lawn; and a
pretty sight it is, in the broad moonlight, and when the dew has forgotten to fall, to see a whole party thus engaged—the ringing laugh
accompanying, every now and then, the evolutions of the dance; whilst
hard by may be seen a dusky crowd of both sexes, jabbering and grinning
in innocent mirth, and apparently, in being permitted to witness it, enjoying the scene as much as their masters, who are mixing in it.

The English reader has already, through a variety of channels, been
made familiar with the appearance presented by an American table. I can
scarcely avoid, however, here briefly referring to the prominent part borne
by Indian corn in southern, and particularly in Virginia, dietary. With
us the term "corn" is applied preeminently to wheat—in America it is
exclusively used to designate the Indian grain, which is consumed in
enormous quantities by man and beast, not only in the States, but also
in the Canadas and the other British provinces. The extent to which
it is used over the entire continent, is only equalled by the variety of
modes in which it is prepared. Whilst it is yet green in the ear, it becomes, by boiling, a delicious vegetable for the table; and when ripe,
is capable, before it is ground, of being prepared for food in a great
variety of ways. To describe the multifarious uses to which it is applied
in the shape of flour is almost impossible; making its appearance in every

form, from the crude condition of gruel and stirabout, through the stages of pancakes, to bread in twenty different shapes, and compounds of the richest and most luscious description. In Virginia, corn-bread has almost entirely banished every other species of bread from common use, and this not only with the poorest, but also with the wealthiest classes. It is customary when Virginians have guests in their houses, to put wheaten bread upon the table; but when the family is left to itself, wheaten bread may not make its appearance, at any meal, for weeks at a time. I once saw Indian flour in seven different forms of preparation upon a private breakfast-table. It is thus universally used, because it is universally preferred to wheat in any form, although the very best wheat raised in the country is the produce of Virginia. I mention these facts to remove, as far as possible, the prejudice which, from two causes, exists in this country against Indian corn. The first is, that it is looked upon as an inferior diet, to which those who use it are driven by a species of necessity; and that it is deficient in nutritious qualities. The fact that it is not only extensively used by all classes throughout America, whilst in the south its use is almost exclusive in the shape of bread, not only in the hut of the slave, but in the mansion of his master, and that those who undergo the greatest toil, in many parts of the country, seldom consume any other grain, is sufficient to demonstrate the groundlessness of this supposition. The second cause of the prejudice is the unpalatable shape in which it has generally been presented to the people of this country. In no form in which it is used in America is it ever taken cold. When wanted in the shape of bread, no more is baked than is necessary for the time being. It is never baked, as it has been here, in large quantities, and in the shape of loaves, as ordinary flour is baked into bread; nor is it mixed with any other species of flour or meal. Indian corn is always best when used by itself, with the exception of such ingredients as eggs, butter, milk, sugar, &c., which are frequently superadded in its preparation to give it additional richness and flavour. To my palate it was never so sweet as when prepared in the very simplest manner. In preparing it for their own use, the negro women generally mix it simply with water and a little salt; the dough, which is thus formed, being made up into a roll about the size and shape of a soda-water bottle, without the neck. This is enveloped in the hot ashes of a wood fire, which is the simple process by which it is baked. When ready it is taken to the pump, and whilst yet hot the ashes are washed off it. When they wish to be a little particular, they protect it, by enveloping it in leaves before covering it with the ashes. Simple though this preparation be, the bread produced by it is, whilst warm, exceedingly sweet. The "hoe cake" is the product of a similar ceremony, with the exception of its being toasted by the fire, instead of being baked in the ashes.

In no other part of the country, perhaps, is the pride of ancestry so greatly cherished as in Virginia. Indeed, I found throughout the Republic that, when an American was positive that he had a grandfather, he was quite as partial to his memory as grandchildren are wont to be in more aristocratic communities. It is not without considerable satisfaction that descent is thus traced back to the Colonial era, which is of course proportionably enhanced when the Atlantic can be crossed, and the Propositus John Stiles of the genealogical diagram can be traced to some English locality. There are many Virginian families who greatly pride themselves on their direct and demonstrable English connexion, more demonstrable here, perhaps, than elsewhere, because the property of Virginia has changed hands, since the Revolution, to a less extent than in any other State of the Union. A Virginian was once dilating to me upon this weakness, as he termed it, in the character of his countrymen, but about five minutes afterwards he confidentially informed me that he could trace a very direct family connexion between himself and William the Conqueror. He must have read in my look that I regarded this as rather a strange commentary upon his previous criticism on Virginian character, for he immediately added, that it was his delight to curb the pride of a maiden aunt of his, who was very fond of referring to the circumstance, by reminding her that on the female side they were descended from a poor Irish girl, who had been transported, and purchased for a hogshead of tobacco on the banks of the James.

A Yankee Bride in North Carolina

Sarah Williams

Clifton Grove, [N. C.] Oct. 10, 1853
Monday

My dear Parents:

I arrived safely at my new home on Friday last, but have had no time to write until now. . . . You may imagine I have seen many strange things. As for my opinions, in so short a time, it would not be fair to give them. I have seen no unkind treatment of servants. Indeed, I think they are treated with more familiarity than many Northern servants. They are in the parlor, in your room and all over. The first of the nights we spent in the Slave Holding States, we slept in a room without a lock. Twice before we were up a waiting girl came into the room, and while I was dressing, in she came to look at me. She seemed perfectly at home, took up the locket with your miniatures in it and wanted to know if it was a watch. I showed it to her. "Well," she said, "I should think your mother and father are mighty old folks." Just before we arrived home, one old Negro caught a glimpse of us and came tearing out of the pine woods to touch his hat to us. All along the road we met them and their salutation of "Howdy (meaning How do you) Massa Ben," and they seemed so glad to see him, that I felt assured that they were well treated. As we came to the house, I found Mother Williams ready to extend a mother's welcome. Mary and Harriett were both here and delighted to see me. I felt at home. At dinner we had everything very nice. It is customary when the waiting girl is not passing things at table, to keep a large broom of peacock feathers in motion over our heads to keep off flies,

J. C. Bonner (ed.), "Plantation Experiences of a New York Woman," *North Carolina Historical Review*, XXXIII, pp. 389-400, 532-533.

etc. I feel confused. Everything is so different that I do not know which way to stir for fear of making a blunder. I have determined to keep still and look on for a while, at any rate. Yesterday I went to Church in a very handsome carriage, servants before and behind. I began to realize yesterday how much I had lost in the way of religious privileges. We went six miles to church, as they have preaching at Snow Hill only every one or two Sabbaths. On arriving I found a rough framed building in the midst of woods, with a large congregation, consisting of about equal numbers of white and black. These meetings are held about one a month and then addressed by two or three exhorters, who are uneducated, and each speaks long enough for any common sermon. The singing is horrible. Prize your religious privileges. They are great and you would realize it by attending Church here once. I shall miss these much. Things that Northerners consider essential are of no importance here. The house and furniture is of little consequence. To all these differences I expect to become accustomed, in time. My husband is all kindness and loves me more than I am worthy. With him I could be happy anywhere. I have seen enough to convince me that the ill-treatment of the Slaves is exaggerated at the North but I have not seen enough to make me like the institution. I am quite the talk of the day, not only in the whole County, but on the plantation. Yesterday I was out in the yard and an old Negro woman came up to me, "Howdy, Miss Sara, are you the Lady that won my young Master. Well, I raised him." Her name was Chaney and she was the family nurse. Between you and me, my husband is better off than I ever dreamed of. I am glad I didn't know it before we were married. He owns 2000 acres of land in this vicinity, but you must bear in mind that land here is not as valuable as with you. But I'll leave these things to talk of when I see you, which I hope may be before many months. I will write you more fully when I have the time. Some of our friends leave this morning and I must go and see them. Write soon, very soon. Ben sends love. Love to all. Ever your

SARA

I wish you could see the cotton fields. The bolls are just opening. I cannot compare their appearance to anything but fields of white roses. As to the cotton picking, I should think it very light and pleasant work. Our house is very unassuming. Not larger than Mary's. I shall feel unsettled until my furniture comes and after our return from Charleston next month. Then I hope to settle down and be quiet for a while. The house has been full of relatives ever since we came and more friends are expected tomorrow. . . .

Clifton Grove, Oct. 22, 1853
Saturday Morning

My dear Parents:

Your letter enclosing others has been received and ere this you have received one from me informing you of our safe arrival here. It would be wrong, perhaps, for me to form or express an opinion in regard to the manners and customs of the people, after only two weeks tarry among them. I shall not speak for or against, but will state things as I have seen them and you may form your own opinions. The woods present a beautiful appearance now, the rainbow hues of autumn contrasting beautifully with the deep dark green of the pines. Many of the trees are hung with vines of the honeysuckle, woodbine and others. Now to mingle the bitter with the sweet, in those woods are snakes of various sizes, both harmless and poisonous, among the latter are large adders and occasionally a rattlesnake. Scorpions, too, they tell me, are plentiful. There is one thing I miss sadly, and that is our beautiful grass. The soil is sandy and the grass is of a different character entirely, being coarse and full of weeds. But when the ground is planted and cultivated with the different products of the country, it presents a fine appearance. The cotton fields are beautiful, the corn will range from ten to twelve feet in height, and the sweet potatoes and yams look fine. Ambition is satisfied here by numbering its thousands of dollars, acres of land and hundreds of negroes. Houses, furniture, dress are nothing. For instance, the Dr.'s brother, a very wealthy man, lives in a brown wood house without lathing or plastering. To be sure, he has a handsome sofa, sideboard and chairs in his parlor, which contrast strangely with the unfinished state of the house. However, he purposes building soon. This, I might say, is the common style of house, and ours, which is finished, the exception. As to household arrangements, I have discovered no system. Wash, bake or iron, just as the fit takes. . . . Baking is all done in bake kettles and cooking at a fire place. Chimneys are all built on the outside of the houses. The Negroes are certainly not overtasked on this plantation. One house girl at the North will accomplish more than two here. But I think the great fault lies in the want of system. Mother Williams works harder than any Northern farmer's wife, I know. She sees to everything. The Dr. has another place, seven miles from here, mostly pine land. That with his other business demands a good share of his time. He has gone with his brother to Greenville to engage his turpentine, which is selling for $4.00 per barrel. I don't expect him back until Monday. As to the treatment of servants, the overseer that Ben employed while he was away, struck one of the Negroes, and his mother would not speak to him afterwards, and had him discharged. They are not diffident, either. One of the field hands asked me to fix a dress for her the other day. Another servant wanted to know if Massa Ben and I couldn't ride over to Snow Hill and get her a new dress. They have plots of ground they cultivate and have what they make from them. They can go to Church (Preaching, as they say) on the Sabbath. Indeed, a majority of the congregation is colored. On Sundays they dress up and many of them look very nice. They leave off work at sundown during the week. You will not wonder, finding everything here so entirely different, if I should feel like a stranger in a strange land. It must take time for me to become accustomed to such an utter change, but with a husband who has proved so devoted, I could not be unhappy anywhere. I think I can appreciate Miss Ophelia's feelings for I have not approached any of the little negroes very closely yet, like her I should wish a good application of soap and water, comb & clean clothes. I have just received a letter from Malvina full of good kindly feelings. In it she said "I meant to write to your mother ere this." Will you tell her that a rush of engagements has prevented me. Give her my very best love and tell her that I very often think of the family alone in the dear pleasant homestead. "Mother sends her regards with many thanks for the liberal supply of wedding cake she received." By the way, the cake that John brought, came safely and we have had it on the table twice. The house was full for a week after we came with relatives. We had a very pleasant time & we felt rather lonely after they all left. I expect my furniture is in New Bern, but we cannot get it until the river rises. Ben, I expect, will go away next week to Beaufort, where he is talking of purchasing a lot and perhaps of building a residence at some future time. My paper is full and I have just room to say to both Write often to your

Sara

Dr. sends love. Please send me a good receipt for soda biscuit. Love to all. I hope our neighbors have buried their unkind feelings ere this. I can assure you I cherish no hard feelings toward them. I still think their course mistaken for my Bible tells me that "Charity suffereth long & is kind." And even our Saviour could eat with publicans and sinners.

Clifton Grove, Nov. 7, 1853
Monday Morning

My dear Parents:

. . . Before this you have received another letter from me, but as I have forgotten now what I wrote, I shall answer your questions in order.
. . . Our travelling South was entirely by railroad. We passed through Richmond and Petersburg, stopping only long enough to get dinner and tea. We came by cars to Wilson, twenty miles from here, where the Dr. expected his carriage to meet us, but was disappointed and so hired

a carriage and came to within seven miles by plank road. The rest of the way is good common road. In the whole of that twenty miles I don't think we passed over a half dozen houses. The road on both sides was bounded by woods, mostly pine, and the trees are much taller and larger than ours. Well, Mother, you like quiet. If you come and see me I'll promise you a plenty of it. Ben was gone eight days with Richard to Beaufort on business and there were just three persons in the house, besides Mrs. Williams, myself and the servants. These were John, a nephew and a niece of the Dr.'s. For a week after we came we had company a plenty in the house. Mary and her husband, Dr. Blount, Richard, John and Joseph and their sister, Harriet, and her husband and child and nurse, and their mother, also Brother James and wife, with one or two children almost every day. But since the first week, we have been very quiet. I ride horseback very often and enjoy it much. Have been twice to the Dr.'s brother's and stayed all night once. Have also called twice at Mr. Dowell's in Snow Hill, the teacher in the Academy. I find my wardrobe quite too extravagant, I assure you, but Experience is a good teacher and I don't intend to cry over what can't be helped. You have no idea how entirely different everything here is. If you call Long Island behind the times, I don't know what you would call North Carolina. It has been rightly termed Rip Van Winkle. I am a regular curiosity. You can imagine how thickly the country is settled when I tell you that in the whole of Greene County there are only about as many inhabitants as there are in the town of New Hartford, and more than half of these colored. There are only two hundred voters in the county. If you want to know about the country and people you must come and see for I cannot give you a description. The servants are treated better in most respects than I expected. We have one that can read. I asked who taught her "My young mistress, before I came here." She told me that she had had four and they were all kind to her. As for religious privileges, they enjoy all that their masters do. I should say more, for all the preaching I have heard has been more suited to the illiterate than to the educated.

Clifton Grove, Nov. 18, 1853

My dear Parents:

You have before this received mine mailed at Wilmington. We had a very pleasant time there. Harriett and quite a large number of her friends met us and we returned with them to Sampson County & from there to Duplin County, to visit her mother. We returned home on Tuesday & found her husband (Dr. Blount) here. They remained two days with us. Our furniture arrived during our absence, all but one bureau & I feel most tired out putting things to order. There is but one closet in our house, so you can imagine that I find some difficulty in knowing where to put things. And Mother William's ways are so entirely different from anything I have ever been used to that I sometimes feel disheartened and discouraged. She is very kind to me & I intend making my will bend to hers in every respect, but I assure you I miss the order and neatness which pervades a Northern home. I can but feel that it would have been much better for us to have gone to housekeeping at once, even if we had deferred our marriage a year. I do not pretend to know much of housekeeping, but I know I could improve on some things here in the way of order. The weather today is summerlike. I have windows up all through the house and doors open. The Dr. and I sat on the piazza for a long time this morning and our roses are still blossoming in the yard. The Synod was in session in Wilmington & we attended several of its meetings. You may imagine I appreciated the opportunity once more of attending an orderly religious service. In the gallery were the colored (I should say slave population, for some are quite too light-colored to be Negroes) people & quite a large proportion of them found their places in the hymn books & joined the singing. So, it seems, that some at least can read. I think I told you in my last, of one (a house servant) in our family who reads and asked me for a Testament. I gave her one, and a tract. But the print of the former is too fine and I intend getting her a larger one. I told my husband and he approved my course. . . . I have been helping to make pumpkin pies, a new dish here, and they promise to be good. We made some a short time since and they were very good. Write soon to your affectionate daughter

SARA

I had forgotten to tell you that servants here have some means for self support. Dr. has one man who will probably lay by fifty or sixty dollars this year. He attended the pine trees and Ben gave him a certain share & he told me the other day he would make that sum.

Clifton Grove, Dec. 10th, 1853

My dear Parents:

Your last was received Tuesday evening. Some of the Dr.'s friends at Snow Hill sent us word that there was to be preaching there that evening & we were well paid for going. We heard an excellent sermon from Mr. Miner, an agent for the Baptist State Convention and in addition received your letter and papers. Mr. Miner is from New York state & also his wife. He is talking of coming to Snow Hill to live. Ben has offered to give him an acre of land if he will build on it and another to Mr. McDowell, the teacher of the Academy. The latter accepts the gift and conditions. Whether Mr. Miner does, we have not yet heard. Mr.

McDowell has a pleasant wife. She was from Alexandria in Virginia. I have become quite well acquainted with them. We expected them here last night to spend the day with us, but a severe storm has prevented. You ask if I am allowed to do anything. I attend to the part of the house I am in. Keep it in order. However, in it Mrs. Williams has furniture and a right, though she seldom enters it. At present there is sewing a plenty on hands for the servants. At this season the women have each a thick dress, chemise, shoes, & a blanket given them. The men pantaloons & jacket, shirt, blanket & shoes, besides caps & bonnets. The children, too, are clothed in the same materials. Now, many keep a seamstress to do this, but Mother Williams has always done it herself with the assistance of her daughters when they were home. Of course, I choose to do my part. One week we made seven dresses & a few jackets and pantaloons we sent to a poor white woman. I have made two pairs of pantaloons and we are now to work on the underclothes. The servants have three suits of clothes a year and as much more in clothes and money as they choose to earn. But as a whole, they are naturally filthy & it is discouraging to make for them, for it is soon in dirt & rags. There are exceptions, of course. You wish a description of my house—the part I stay in. On the lower floor is the parlor and my room. . . . I have not yet quite regulated upstairs & can't until my things come. I feel the need of good closets, I assure you, but the houses here are built with only a small one under the stairs. On my bed I have the dark quilt you gave me. I assure you I shall be very glad of the petticoat you spoke of giving me. I am sorry I did not bring the cotton one. We need quite as thick clothing as you do. The houses are not as tightly built as with us, and they use fireplaces altogether, and there is a chill in the air. I have been very sorry I did not bring my woolen sack. Then, too, the people most always sit with open doors, even though they sit over the fire shivering. Last week I went with the Dr. to visit his sister Mary, stayed two nights and a day & had a very pleasant visit. We are now expecting her here to spend some time at Christmas. Hattie, we found living very quietly in a beautiful oak grove. They are living in what is to be their kitchen. Mr. Faison will build this year a very large and commodious house. Ben has gone on to Sandy Run to see how they are getting along with his turpentine. He intends returning by Snow Hill & I am hoping for letters and papers in yesterday's mail. Richard and John may return with him. We made them a short visit in their bachelor home the other day. Everything was neat and tidy & they always seem in first rate spirits. John is going to take his servants in February and going on to another plantation to reside. Tell Em I can't help wishing she was going there, too. I almost forgot to tell you of my baking. I have made pumpkin pies, or helped, twice & the last, which are best, I made all alone, crust & all.

They never had had them before & Ben particularly liked them. So, of course, my success pleased me. Soda biscuits, I have made twice with good success and measure cake. Not until you come here can you imagine how entirely different is their mode of living from the North. They live more heartily. There must always be two or three different kinds of meats on Mrs. Williams' table for breakfast & dinner. Red pepper is much used to flavor meat with the famous "barbecue" of the South & which I believe they esteem above all dishes is roasted pig dressed with red pepper & vinegar. Their bread is corn bread, just meal wet with water & without yeast or saleratus, & biscuit with shortening and without anything to make them light and beaten like crackers. The bread and biscuit are always brought to the table hot. Now, I want you to send me a receipt for bread with yeast and your corn bread. Is there any way of making yeast without hops or Irish potatoes? I wish we could send you some of our beautiful sweet potatoes & yams. The Dr. spoke of it, but it is now too late & cold as they would spoil before we could get them to you. Perhaps another year we will be more fortunate. They tell me they have beautiful peaches and apples, but we were too late for the peaches and the apple orchard is young & they say the Negroes got more than their share. You don't know how I have longed for some of those in the cellar at home & for a slice of Peggy's good bread and butter. In season we have fine grapes. . . .

Clifton Grove, March 3rd, 1854

My dear Mother:

Our windows are open today, there is a soft balmy air, the peach & plum trees are in blossom. One of our servants is very sick with dropsy. The Dr. thinks she will never be any better. I did not answer some questions which you asked. The Northern Branch of the Neuse River runs between us and Snow Hill, viz. Contentnia Creek. It bounds this plantation on the southern side for about five miles. There are about 750 acres, worth from 12 to 15 dollars per acre. The pine land averages from 3 to 6 dollars per acre. Of that land there are 1400 acres. Besides these there are 73 acres at Snow Hill, of which we don't know the value. If that town should wake up it would be quite valuable. But all these things we will talk over, I hope, next month. I wish you could spend the summer with me, somehow, I can't help dreading it. If I have left anything at home, which you think I may need, & you can bring it and do not wish them, I wish them, I wish you would. Will you get me some tapioca & sago & isinglass & I will pay you. Mrs. Shays uses a kind of yeast I wish you would inquire about. Maybe it would do for me. We have ordered a stove. With love to Pa, I am still your affectionate daughter. Ben sends love.

Clifton Grove, March 17, 1853 [1854]
Friday

My dear Parents:

Yours was received on Wednesday & I hasten to reply. You may imagine that the very thought of seeing you filled me with joy, but there are circumstance which surround us, & which I feel due to you as well as to us to explain, some things that we feel must be changed before you come in order to make a visit pleasant. We ordered a stove some time since from New York, hoping to receive it & be installed at our own house keeping (a proposition of Mother Williams) by this time, but we hear nothing from Luther or the stove. I do feel that I want to see you very much. I want your council particularly, but under the circumstances, I do not feel at liberty to make friends of mine guests at Mother's. I feel quite sensitive enough at being here myself. . . . There is one thing that to me throws light on the whole matter, although Ben is hardly willing to allow it. A Southern lady generally receives a number of servants as her marriage dower. I have no doubt that Mother had looked forward to her son marrying such an one & thus adding to the rather small number of hands (Sister Mary having removed about twenty last spring, they being her portion) & leaving about the same number here, which are not sufficient to work so large a farm. Then, too, I can look back and see wherein I have erred. Had my wardrobe been plainer I would have pleased her better. But I do not imagine that she is wholly destitute of kindness to me. I have received favors from her, but Ben's marrying seems to have turned her against him. She proposes for him to attend the business this year, divide profits next fall, then each attend to their own. 250 acres are his now, the rest not until she is through with it. . . . Ben talks some of moving to Snow Hill in the fall to a house in which he owns an interest and renting his land here. He does not like to remove any of his hands from his turpentine land, the income from that being much larger than from the plantation & he would have to in order to farm to any advantage. His most valuable farm hand is now sick with dropsy & will probably never be any better. In attending to her I find that I can be useful, also in sewing. . . .

Burnt Fort, Ga., April 12th, 1859

My dear Parents:

I am going to attempt a letter, but whether it will ever be finished, will be known in the sequel. We are now planting & as usual in such times, everything else must give in—washing, ironing, scouring, &c. The consequence is everything and everybody looks dirty and cross and sour. The Dr. has gone to Ware County much against his inclination. I look for him tomorrow. In the meantime it's "Miss Sarah here" and "Miss Sarah there" & then little children must run to Mama and the little black images will be around. I lie down at night tired enough to sleep like a rock & yet cannot tell what I have done but trot after the children, trot after the Negroes, trot after the chickens, eggs, & hens & turkeys & trot, trot, trot, all day. Then too, I have not the satisfaction of using my hands as I would like to do. This waiting other peoples motion is not my will, but it is the Lord's will & I know I ought to be more submissive and more patient. Today rafts have come down the river with one white and four black men aboard, all to have dinner here. So, you may think in addition to a family of eighteen or twenty, if there is any more house work than the way you live. . . . I have not been out of sight of the chimney nor inside a neighbor's house since I entered this last October. The other day Miss Guerard called & on her return we crossed the river. That is the farthest I have been gone. You would have thought her sufficiently dressed for Broadway. She was very pleasant and expressed a wish to be more sociable. . . .

A Dinner and Ball in Columbia, S.C.

Margaret Hall

The people here are very hospitable, which is indeed the character of all the Southern States. The Coopers wished us to make their house our home and Chancellor de Saussure sent his carriage to me this morning to make what use I pleased of it the whole day. After sitting an hour with Dr. and Mrs. Cooper, they took us to see the College and the Lunatic Asylum, which is just finished, but is yet untenanted. Several gentlemen joined us whilst we were there and we staid a long while talking to them. We were asked to dine at the Governor's, Mr. Taylor's, to a military ball by some officers, and to a party at Judge de Saussure's. All this we were resolved to accomplish as well as we could. To the dinner we went at half past four [Feb. 22, 1828], and I must say that in spite of all my experience of the strange arrangements of American dinners I confess this style did astonish me, and what any of you who have never seen such would have thought I cannot say. There was a huge party invited to meet us, all gentlemen with the exception of four ladies belonging to the house. I ought to premise that I had before been informed that both Mr. and Mrs. Taylor belonged to the old stock families in South Carolina, families who pique themselves on their ancient standing, quite the old aristocracy, in short, and possessing immense wealth. There was the same fuss before of calling the mistress of the house out of the room and so on, and finally she and another elderly, female relation disappeared altogether and we found them standing ready placed at the upper end of the table, and then with one consent the gentlemen fell to carving the dishes nearest to them with a degree of dispatch and eagerness that I never saw equalled anywhere out of a steamboat. The top dish was a ham which Mrs. Taylor herself showed her power of carving upon by beginning to cut it in pieces from the knuckle upwards. The rest of the entertainment consisted of

Margaret (Mrs. Basil) Hall, *The Aristocratic Journey*, pp. 208-210.

turkeys, roast and boiled, chickens, roast ducks, corned beef, and fish, together with various dishes of sweet potatoes, Irish potatoes, cabbage, rice, and beetroot, to demolish which we were furnished with two pronged forks, and if you were troublesome enough to call for a second knife you were furnished with one merely half wiped. For second course we had *eight pies* down the side of the table, six dishes of glasses of syllabub and as many of jelly, besides one or two "floating islands," as they denominate what we call whipped cream, and odd corners filled up by ginger and other preserves. I was fortunately well placed next an exceedingly agreeable old man, Judge De Saussure, a most gentlemanlike person. On the other side I had one of the young ladies of the house, for ladies in America have a vile custom of crowding all together at dinner tables and leave the gentlemen likewise to herd by themselves. We had neither tea nor coffee after dinner and at seven o'clock went off to the ball, but if the dinner was queer, what was the ball! Thank goodness no one was with me that I am intimate with except Basil, and you know he has no great genius for quizzing, but even his gravity could scarcely stand it. However, I did not laugh, for which I take the greater merit to myself than for anything I ever did or left undone in my life. It is quite out of my power to describe it to you. The day was Washington's birthday, and I suppose that the ball was in honour of the occasion. The Military, that is to say the Militia, Yeomanry, and Volunteers, were all in uniform, which made the *gaucherie* of the individuals all the more conspicuous. Then the ladies I can compare to nothing I ever saw except girls at the circus or strolling players at the Dundee Theatre, dressed in my cast-off finery fitted up according to their own taste. Such heads, such fabrications of silver muslin and tinsel, such feathers and such flowers it would require the pen of a poet or the pencil of a painter to do justice to. I was asked by the Captain of the Troop to dance, but the honour I declined, fortunately, for I should have been strangely thrown out by what they imagine to be quadrilles but which a Frenchman, I think, would have scarce recognised. An hour of this was, you will believe, enough, and we were glad to exchange the ball for a party at Judge De Saussure's, where I had as tough an argument regarding slavery with some ladies as ever Basil had on any subject with gentlemen, and by ten o'clock we were at home.

All the best society of Columbia, with a very few exceptions, is at present at Charleston where the races which are to take place next week have attracted great crowds, so that the ball must have consisted of very second rate company. We crossed the Congaree River this evening on leaving Columbia by a covered bridge which is not yet finished overhead.

In Defense of Slavery

John C. Calhoun

I hold that in the present state of civilization, where two races of different origin, and distinguished by color, and other physical differences, as well as intellectual, are brought together, the relation now existing in the slaveholding States between the two, is, instead of an evil, a good—a positive good. I feel myself called upon to speak freely upon the subject where the honor and interests of those I represent are involved. I hold then, that there never has yet existed a wealthy and civilized society in which one portion of the community did not, in point of fact, live on the labor of the other. Broad and general as is this assertion, it is fully borne out by history. This is not the proper occasion, but if it were, it would not be difficult to trace the various devices by which the wealth of all civilized communities has been so unequally divided, and to show by what means so small a share has been allotted to those by whose labor it was produced, and so large a share given to the non-producing classes. The devices are almost innumerable, from the brute force and gross superstition of ancient times, to the subtle and artful fiscal contrivances of modern. I might well challenge a comparison between them and the more direct, simple, and patriarchal mode by which the labor of the African race is, among us, commanded by the European. I may say with truth, that in few countries so much is left to the share of the laborer, and so little exacted from him, or where there is more kind attention paid to him in sickness or infirmities of age.

Speech on the Reception of Abolition Petitions in the Senate, Feb. 6, 1837, in Richard K. Crallé (ed.), *The Works of John C. Calhoun,* (New York, 1853), II, p. 631.

Slavery on a Rice Plantation

Frederick Law Olmsted

. . . After a ride of several miles through the woods, in the rear of the plantations, we came to [Mr. X.'s] largest negro-settlement. There was a street, or common, two hundred feet wide, on which the cabins of the negroes fronted. Each cabin was a frame building, the walls boarded and whitewashed on the outside, lathed and plastered within, the roof shingled; forty-two feet long, twenty-one feet wide, divided into two family tenements, each twenty-one by twenty-one; each tenement divided into three rooms—one, the common household apartment, twenty-one by ten; each of the others (bedrooms), ten by ten. There was a brick fire-place in the middle of the long side of each living room, the chimneys rising in one, in the middle of the roof. Besides these rooms, each tenement had a cock-loft, entered by steps from the household room. Each tenement is occupied, on an average, by five persons. There were in them closets, with locks and keys, and a varying quantity of rude furniture. Each cabin stood two hundred feet from the next, and the street in front of them being two hundred feet wide, they were just that distance apart each way. The people were nearly all absent at work, and had locked their outer doors, taking the keys with them. Each cabin has a front and back door, and each room a window, closed by a wooden shutter, swinging outward, on hinges. Between each tenement and the next house, is a small piece of ground, inclosed with palings, in which are coops of fowl, with chickens, hovels for nests, and for sows with pig. There were a great many fowls in the street. The negroes' swine are allowed to run in the woods, each owner having his own distinguished by a peculiar mark. In the rear of the yards were gardens—a half-acre to each family. Internally the cabins appeared dirty and disordered, which was rather a pleasant indication that their home-life was

Frederick Law Olmsted, *A Journey in the Seaboard Slave States* (New York, 1856), pp. 421-425, 431-440.

not much interfered with, though I found certain police regulations were enforced. . . .

. . . I occupied myself in making a sketch of the nursery and the street of the settlement in my note-book. On the verandah and the steps of the nursery, there were twenty-seven children, most of them infants, that had been left there by their mothers, while they were working their tasks in the fields. They probably make a visit to them once or twice during the day, to nurse them, and receive them to take to their cabins, or where they like, when they have finished their tasks—generally in the middle of the afternoon. The older children were fed with porridge, by the general nurse. A number of girls, eight or ten years old, were occupied in holding and tending the youngest infants. Those a little older—the crawlers—were in the pen, and those big enough to toddle were playing on the steps, or before the house. Some of these, with two or three bigger ones, were singing and dancing about a fire that they had made on the ground. They were not at all disturbed or interrupted in their amusement by the presence of their owner and myself. At twelve years of age, the children are first put to regular field-work; until then no labor is required of them, except, perhaps, occasionally, they are charged with some light kind of duty, such as frightening birds from corn. When first sent to the field, one-quarter of an able-bodied hand's day's work is ordinarily allotted to them, as their task.

But very few of the babies were in arms; such as were not, generally lay on the floor, rolling about, or sat still, sucking their thumbs. The nurse was a kind-looking old negro woman, with, no doubt, philoprogenitiveness well developed; but she paid very little attention to them, only sometimes chiding the older ones for laughing or singing too loud. I watched for half an hour, and in all that time not a baby of them began to cry; nor have I ever heard one, at two or three other plantation-nurseries which I have visited. I remember, in Amsterdam, to have seen two or three similar collections of children, voluntarily deposited by their mothers, who went out from home to work. These seemed to be looked out for by two or three poor women, who probably received a small fee for their trouble, from the parent thus relieved. Not being able to converse in Dutch, I could get no particular information about it; but I especially noticed, in each case, that there was no crying or fretting. On the contrary, they appeared to be peculiarly well-disposed and jolly, as if they were already on the straight road to the right place, and were fully satisfied with the vehicles they had got to drive through the world. They had, in short, thus early learned that it did not do any good to cry —for the nurse could n't, if she would, feed, or cuddle, or play with one every time she was wanted to. I make a note of it, as indicating how young the little twig is bent, how early the formation of habits commences, and that, even in babyhood, the "product of happiness is to be found, not so much in increasing your numerator, as in lessening your denominator." . . .

In the next field, twenty men, or boys, for none of them looked as if they were full-grown, were ploughing, each with a single mule, and a light, New-York-made plough. The soil was very friable, the ploughing easy, and the mules proceeded at a smart pace; the furrows were straight, regular, and well turned. Their task was nominally an acre and a quarter a day; somewhat less actually, as the measure includes the space occupied by the ditches, which are two to three feet wide, running around each quarter of an acre. The ploughing gang was superintended by a driver who was provided with a watch; and while we were looking at them he called out that it was twelve o'clock. The mules were immediately taken from the ploughs, and the ploughboys mounting them, leaped the ditches, and cantered off to the stables, to feed them. One or two were ordered to take their ploughs to the blacksmith, for repairs.

The ploughmen got their dinner at this time: those not using horses do not usually dine till they have finished their tasks; but this, I believe, is optional with them. They commence work at sunrise, and at about eight o'clock have breakfast brought to them in the field, each hand having left a bucket with the cook for that purpose. All who are working in connection leave their work together, and gather in a social company about a fire, where they generally spend about half an hour, at breakfast time. The provisions furnished them consist mainly of meal, rice, and vegetables, with salt and molasses, and occasionally bacon, fish, and coffee. The allowance is a peck of meal, or an equivalent quantity of rice per week, to each working hand, old or young, besides small stores. Mr. X. says that he has lately given a less amount of meat than is now usual on plantations, having observed that the general health of the negroes is not as good as formerly, when no meat at all was customarily given them. The general impression among planters is, that the negroes work much better for being supplied with three or four pounds of bacon a week.

Leaving the rice-land, we went next to some of the upland fields, where we found several other gangs of negroes at work; one entirely of men engaged in ditching; another of women, and another of boys and girls, "listing" an old corn-field with hoes. All of them were working by tasks, and were overlooked by negro drivers. They all labored with greater rapidity and cheerfulness than any slaves I have before seen; and the women struck their hoes as if they were strong, and well able to engage in muscular labor. The expression of their faces was generally repulsive, and their *tout ensemble* anything but agreeable to the eye. The dress of most of them was uncouth and cumbrous, dirty and ragged; reefed up, as I have once before described, at the hips, so as to show their heavy legs, wrapped round with a piece of old blanket, in lieu of leggings or stockings. Most of them worked with bare arms, but wore strong shoes on their feet, and handkerchiefs on their heads; some of them were smoking, and each gang had a fire burning on the ground, near where they were at work, to light their pipes and warm their breakfast by. Mr. X. said this was always their custom, even in summer. To each gang a boy or girl was also attached, whose business it was to bring water for them to drink, and to go for anything required by the driver. The drivers would frequently call back a hand to go over again some piece of his or her task that had not been worked to his satisfaction, and were constantly calling to one or another, with a harsh and peremptory voice, to strike harder or hoe deeper, and otherwise taking care that the work was well done. Mr. X. asked if Little Sam ("Tom's Sue's Sam") worked yet with the "three-quarter" hands, and learning that he did, ordered him to be put with the full hands, observing that though rather short, he was strong and stout, and, being twenty years old, well able to do a man's work.

The field-hands are all divided into four classes, according to their physical capacities; the children beginning as "quarter-hands," advancing to "half-hands," and then to "three-quarter hands"; and, finally, when mature, and able-bodied, healthy and strong, to "full hands." As they decline in strength, from age, sickness, or other cause, they retrograde in the scale, and proportionately less labor is required of them. Many, of naturally weak frame, never are put among the full hands. Finally, the aged are left out at the annual classification, and no more regular field-work is required of them, although they are generally provided with some light, sedentary occupation. I saw one old woman picking "tailings" of rice out of a heap of chaff, an occupation at which she was literally not earning her salt. Mr. X. told me she was a native African, having been brought when a girl from the Guinea coast. She spoke almost unintelligibly; but after some other conversation, in which I had not been able to understand a word she said, he jokingly proposed to send her back to Africa. She expressed her preference to remain where she was, very emphatically. "Why?" She did not answer readily, but being pressed, threw up her palsied hands, and said furiously, "I lubs 'ou mas'r, oh, I lubs 'ou. I don't want go 'way from 'ou."

The field-hands are nearly always worked in gangs, the strength of a gang varying according to the work that engages it; usually it numbers twenty or more, and is directed by a driver. As on most large plantations, whether of rice or cotton, in Eastern Georgia and South Carolina, nearly all ordinary and regular work is performed by *tasks:* that is to say, each hand has his labor for the day marked out before him, and can take his own time to do it in. . . .

These tasks certainly would not be considered excessively hard, by a Northern laborer; and, in point of fact, the more industrious and active hands finish them often by two o'clock. I saw one or two leaving the field soon after one o'clock, several about two; and between three and four, I met a dozen women and several men coming home to their cabins, having finished their day's work.

Under this "Organization of Labor," most of the slaves work rapidly and well. In nearly all ordinary work, custom has settled the extent of the task, and it is difficult to increase it. The driver who marks it out, has to remain on the ground until it is finished, and has no interest in over-measuring it; and if it should be systematically increased very much, there is danger of a general stampede to the "swamp"—a danger the slave can always hold before his master's cupidity. In fact, it is looked upon in this region as a proscriptive right of the negroes to have this incitement to diligence offered them; and the man who denied it, or who attempted to lessen it, would, it is said, suffer in his reputation, as well as experience much annoyance from the obstinate "rascality" of his negroes. Notwithstanding this, I have heard a man assert, boastingly, that he made his negroes habitually perform double the customary tasks. Thus we get a glimpse again of the black side. If he is allowed the power to do this, what may not a man do?

It is the driver's duty to make the tasked hands do their work well. If, in their haste to finish it, they neglect to do it properly, he "sets them back," so that carelessness will hinder more than it will hasten the completion of their tasks.

In the selection of drivers, regard seems to be had to size and strength —at least, nearly all the drivers I have seen are tall and strong men—but a great deal of judgment, requiring greater capacity of mind than the ordinary slave is often supposed to be possessed of, is certainly needed in them. A good driver is very valuable and usually holds office for life. His authority is not limited to the direction of labor in the field, but extends to the general deportment of the negroes. He is made to do the duties of policeman, and even of police magistrate. It is his duty, for instance, on Mr. X.'s estate, to keep order in the settlement; and, if two persons, men or women, are fighting, it is his duty to immediately separate them, and then to "whip them both." . . .

Having generally had long experience on the plantation, the advice of the drivers is commonly taken in nearly all the administration, and frequently they are, *de facto*, the managers. Orders on important points of the plantation economy, I have heard given by the proprietor directly to them, without the overseer's being consulted or informed of them; and it is often left with them to decide when and how long to flow the rice-grounds—the proprietor and overseer deferring to their more experienced judgment. Where the drivers are discreet, experienced, and trusty, the overseer is frequently employed merely as a matter of form, to comply with the laws requiring the superintendence or presence of a white man among every body of slaves; and his duty is rather to inspect and report, than to govern. Mr. X. considers his overseer an uncommonly efficient and faithful one, but he would not employ him, even during the summer, when he is absent for several months, if the law did not require it. He has sometimes left his plantation in care of one of the drivers for a considerable length of time, after having discharged an overseer; and he thinks it has then been quite as well conducted as ever. His overseer consults the drivers on all important points, and is governed by their advice.

Mr. X. said, that though overseers sometimes punish the negroes severely, and otherwise ill-treat them, it is their more common fault to indulge them foolishly in their disposition to idleness, or in other ways to curry favor with them, so they may not inform the proprietor of their own misconduct or neglect. He has his overseer bound to certain rules, by written contract; and it is stipulated that he can discharge him at any moment, without remuneration for his loss of time and inconvenience, if he should at any time be dissatisfied with him. One of the rules is, that he shall never punish a negro with his own hands, and that corporal punishment, when necessary, shall be inflicted by the drivers. The advantage of this is, that it secures time for deliberation, and prevents punishment being made in sudden passion. His drivers are not allowed to carry their whips with them in the field; so that if the overseer wishes a hand punished, it is necessary to call a driver; and the driver has then to go to his cabin, which is, perhaps, a mile or two distant, to get his whip, before it can be applied.

I asked how often the necessity of punishment occurred.

"Sometimes, perhaps, not once for two or three weeks; then it will seem as if the devil had got into them all, and there is a good deal of it."

As the negroes finish the labor required of them by Mr. X., at three or four o'clock in the afternoon, they can employ the remainder of the day in laboring for themselves, if they choose. Each family has a half-acre of land allotted to it, for a garden; besides which, there is a large vegetable garden, cultivated by a gardener for the plantation, from which they are supplied, to a greater or less extent. They are at liberty to sell whatever they choose from the products of their own garden, and to make what they can by keeping swine and fowls. Mr. X.'s family have no other supply of poultry and eggs than what is obtained by purchase from his own negroes; they frequently, also, purchase game from them. The only restriction upon their traffic is a "liquor law." They are not allowed to buy or sell ardent spirits. This prohibition, like liquor laws elsewhere, unfortunately, cannot be enforced; and, of late years, grog-shops, at which stolen goods are bought from the slaves, and poisonous liquors—chiefly the worst whisky, much watered and made stupefying by an infusion of tobacco—are clandestinely sold to them, have become an established evil, and the planters find themselves almost powerless to cope with it. They have, here, lately organized an association for this purpose, and have brought several offenders to trial; but, as it is a penitentiary offence, the culprit spares no pains or expense to avoid conviction—and it is almost impossible, in a community of which so large a proportion are poor and degraded, to have a jury sufficiently honest and intelligent to permit the law to be executed.

The President of a Southern University

George W. Featherstonhaugh

Columbia, the capital of South Carolina, is pleasantly situated, and in some of its airy streets there are genteel-looking houses, which at once indicate a respectable state of society; but I was very much surprised to find the capital of the State built on a piece of ground so barren, that even grass will scarcely grow upon it. Having walked through the streets to see what the town looked like, I rambled in the afternoon about two or three miles off to call upon Dr. Cooper, whom I had met before in New York. This gentleman, always conspicuous, had made himself particularly so of late, in the agitation of the *Nullification* question, which the Tariff law had given birth to, and which had so nearly brought the State of South Carolina into hostile collision with the power of the federal government under the administration of President Jackson. Although the excitement—which at one time threatened such fatal consequences—had been calmed by the judicious conduct of Mr. Clay and Mr. Calhoun in agreeing to the Compromise Act, yet the same question is of such vital consequence to South Carolina, and so important to the Northern manufacturers, that it is always liable to be agitated again. The leading planters of South Carolina are generally men who, having inherited large estates with numerous slaves born upon them, and received liberal educations, consider themselves, not without some reason, *the gentlemen of America;* looking down upon the trading communities in the Northern States, where slavery does not exist, with that habitual sense of superiority which men born to command—and above all others slaveholders—always cherish when they are placed in competition with men engaged in mercantile pursuits, whom they consider to be, by the nature of their avocations, incapable of rising to their level: to this feeling, the seeds

George Featherstonhaugh, *Excursion Through the Slave States* (New York, 1844), pp. 155-157.

of which are planted in infancy, is added a distrust sometimes amounting to hatred.

The planter, although his crops of cotton and rice often produce him an annual income far exceeding that of the cultivator of the North, and tempt him to live in a style corresponding to the rank he believes himself to hold in society, yet is frequently less independent than the opulent merchant or farmer he undervalues, his annual expenditures being large and certain, whilst his returns are somewhat precarious. He has perhaps to feed and clothe several hundred slaves, and it is not convenient for him to reduce his style of living: so that not unfrequently the merchant at the north, who is his agent, and to whom he consigns his productions for sale, sends him an account current, where, instead of small charges being deducted from large returns, he finds the advances made to him in money, the bills for feeding and clothing his slaves, his wines and luxuries, and other charges, swelled to an amount far exceeding the sum-total that his crops have sold for; perceiving himself therefore the debtor and quasi slave of the man he despises, his pride, his interest, and his passions, all combine to rouse his indignation: at such moments the agitated planter is easily led to follow in the wake of any politicians who flatter him with the prospect of redress.

When the politicians and manufacturers of the Northern States combined to enact the tariff of 1828, "for the *protection* of home manufactures," alleging that the productions of the Southern States were admitted without competition into the ports of England, a general feeling of resistance arose in the State of South Carolina: the duties now to be levied upon those articles of British manufacture which the planter was compelled to purchase for the use of his slaves, must necessarily greatly augment his expenditures, and to this was added the apprehension of another evil of still greater magnitude, viz. that Great Britain might lay retaliatory duties upon his exports, and gradually look to other countries to be supplied with them. Politics and interests therefore combined in South Carolina to rouse the people into a resistance to that law, and the government of the State taking the lead, finished by declaring that when the United States government manifestly exceeded its powers—of which fact they held that the suffering State must be the best judge—every single State had a natural and constitutional right to "nullify its acts."

Armies now were raised, and everything was prepared for resistance, as much as if a foreign invader was about to enter their territory. Such was the indomitable spirit that appeared to prevail, and the determination not to permit the revenue laws of the United States to be executed in South Carolina, that if President Jackson, as it was believed he was disposed to do, had attempted to execute them by force, there is no doubt that a furious civil war would have raged in the State, of which the consequences—let the questionable result have been either one way or the other—must have been signally fatal; for no one can predict the ultimate consequences of giving military habits to a numerous slave population, which must upon so fatal a contingency have unavoidably taken place. Happily for the country, the wise compromise which took place, the effect of which was to provide for the gradual reduction of those oppressive tariff duties to an amount limited by the wants of the public revenue, and not by the demands for *protection,* averted this great danger. Mr. Clay, whom the protection-party claimed as their leader, and Mr. Calhoun, the avowed leader of the Nullifying party, patriotically concurred in making sacrifices in favour of peace, by carrying the measure called the Compromise Act through the national legislature.

No man had taken a more energetic and animated part in this dangerous agitation than the veteran Dr. Cooper, now approaching his eightieth year, and one of the most remarkable men that have emigrated from England—his native country—to the United States. Cooper was a philosophical *élève* of the famous Dr. Priestley, and finding that everything in England was too long or too short for him, he passed over to the "asylum of oppressed humanity," with the intention of making it his home for life. He was a man of singular versatility of talent, of unceasing activity, and great natural benevolence. His attainments were various; there was nothing in law, physic, divinity, chemistry, or general science that he had entirely overlooked; and although some of his screws were uncommonly loose, particularly his religious ones, he was capable of being a very useful member of society, and was always—as such a man with so much experience must be—a most agreeable and instructive companion. But that which above all things made the Doctor happy, and which wherever he went seemed to be his study to provide a quantum sufficit of, was persecution, and this he was fortunate enough to find even in America. On his arrival his talents procured him an official appointment of some distinction in Pennsylvania, but he soon contrived to be driven from it, and to be fined heavily into the bargain. At length he took refuge in South Carolina, was well received by the leading planters there, and placed in the honourable and lucrative situation of President of the College in the town of Columbia.

Here the Doctor might have flourished in renown, and have pursued a career of usefulness, but the current was too gentle for him, and preferring troubled waters, he began to insinuate that it was unworthy of free men to be educated in religious prejudices, and ended by openly denouncing the Christian religion. If there were a few persons in the State to whom this was agreeable, there were a great many to whom it was very offensive. The friends of the college had hoped that in placing an amiable person with such various attainments at its head, he would have possessed sufficient judgment to have looked to the interests of the institution, and would have endeavoured to support that which supported him. The sons of persons entertaining different opinions both in religion and politics were to be educated here, and it was expected by all that though theology was not to be a principal branch of study, yet a reverence for religion would be inculcated; it was soon made evident, however, that anything but this was instilled into the young minds entrusted to his care, and parents immediately began to withdraw their children from an institution where the Christian religion was openly derided. The Doctor having succeeded in driving away all those who were not disposed to imbibe his irreligious opinions, proceeded to practise the same tactics with those who would not agree with him in defying the government of the country, as established by law, in regard to Nullification; so that his students became at length very few in numbers, and not long before I reached Columbia, the friends of the college, to save it from total ruin, caused the Doctor to be removed from his situation. In doing this they acted with great delicacy and generosity, creating for him a sort of sinecure office, under which, unless he again oscillates out of his orbit, he may enjoy a very competent salary for the rest of his life.

I found Doctor Cooper in a pleasant little villa, which the ladies of his family had furnished with a great many comforts. He received me very cordially, and although about eighty years old, began to talk with wonderful energy and vivacity upon a variety of subjects. The Compromise Act, however, was uppermost in the Doctor's mind, and I soon saw that he did not like it at all, for it had extinguished all the eloquence, patriotism, and achievement which Nullification might have brought forth at a future day. Upon my congratulating him upon that measure, and the happy consequences which would flow from it, he rose from his easy chair, and although almost bent double like a hook, he seized the hearth-brush, and with his eyes full of fire, and wielding the brush as if it were a broadsword, denounced the Compromise Act as an ignoble measure which he never could approve of; declared that the Nullifiers were quite in the wrong to make peace with the Union men (their opponents in South Carolina), and that it would have been a much better course for them to have taken the field against General Jackson, and have fought all the power he could have brought against them. "We have lost a fine opportunity, sir, of carrying this State to the highest renown," said this little crooked octogenarian; and then giving General Jackson a desperate cut with the hearth-brush, he went back to his easy chair again.

I was perfectly delighted with the vivacity of the old gentleman, and never passed a pleasanter evening. At tea we were joined by some very well-bred neighbours, amongst whom were several ladies, to whom the Doctor, constantly paddling about amongst them, paid his lively compliments, and then returned to his chair to laugh and dispute about chemistry, geology, law, and, above all, religion and politics. Whatever side of the question he took he maintained it with wonderful energy, and always with pertinacity when he could not do it with reason, as if it was too late in life for him to be convinced about such matters.

The next morning I visited the college, which had the appearance of being very much neglected; there was a collection of minerals, but it was in wretched disorder; indeed everything seemed to be out of place. On my return I learnt that some gentlemen, with whom I had been previously acquainted, had called upon me, and I willingly accepted an invitation to dine with one of them. Our party consisted of some gentlemen of the place, Dr. Cooper, and a few professors belonging to the college. Some of them were very intelligent men, and hearty in their manners. What particularly struck me at this dinner was the total want of caution and reserve in the ultra opinions they expressed about religion and politics; on these topics their conversation was not at all addressed to me, but seemed to be a resumption of the opinions they were accustomed to express whenever they met, and upon all occasions. A stranger dropped in amongst them from the clouds would hardly have supposed himself amongst Americans, the language they used and the opinions they expressed were so diametrically opposed to the self-laudatory strain they too generally indulge in when speaking of their country or themselves. It was quite new to me to hear men of the better class express themselves openly against a republican government, and to listen to discussions of great ability, the object of which was to show that there never can be a good government if it is not administered by gentlemen. Not having shared in the conversation, I ventured at one time to name Mr. Madison, at whose house I was in the habit of making autumnal visits, as a person that would have ranked as a gentleman in any country; but I was immediately stopped by a declaration that he was a false hypocritical dissembler, that he was one of the favourites of the Sovereign People, and one of the worst men the country had produced. At a period of less excitement such a sentiment would not have been tolerated, and I could not but attribute their present pique against this eminent statesman to the inflexible opposition he had given to Nullification, which went to destroy the efficacy of the constitution he had been one of the principal framers of. A short time after, something very extravagant having been said, I could not help asking, in a good-natured way, if they called themselves Americans yet; the gentleman who had interrupted me before, said, "If you ask *me* if I am an American, my answer is, No, sir, I am a South Carolinian." If the children of these Nullifiers are brought up in the same opinions, which they are very likely to be, here are fine elements for future disunion; for, imbibing from their infancy the notion that they are born to command, it will be intolerable to them to submit to be, in their own estimation, the drudges of the northern manufacturers, whom they despise as an inferior race of men. Even now there is nothing that a southern man resents so much as to be called a *Yankee,* a term which in the Southern States is applied exclusively to the New England people, and in quite as sarcastic a sense as it is sometimes applied in Europe to all citizens of the United States.

Having secured seats in the mail for the north on the 22nd of January, we were standing near the stage-coach at the door of the tavern waiting the arrival of the mail from Charleston, when it drove up with a negro male slave, about thirty years old, *chained flat on the roof,* the poor devil having been overtaken by his master after an ineffectual attempt to run away.

A Scottish Weaver Describes the Planters of Georgia

William Thomson

I will now describe a planter's house in the State of Georgia, about eight miles from Augusta, who owned a manufacturing establishment, to whom I went in search of employment. It was a handsome, but not large frame house, with everything in good taste about it. I went up to the front door, and asked if Judge Sley was at home: a lady answered "No, that he was on his circuit (he was a district judge), and that it would be some days before he returned." She shewed me into an elegantly-furnished room; I then told the lady, who was the judge's wife, my name, and that I was a wool-carder and spinner, wanting employment. A lady in her circumstances in this country (Scotland), would very quickly have changed her manners on such a piece of information; but such was not the case here. I was treated with the greatest consideration and unobtrusive politeness, and desired to make myself at home, and remain with them till the judge returned, which he did in a few days. His reception, after a fortnight's absence, is worthy of notice. The old lady caught hold of him first, and kissed him; the daughters, handsome grown-up ladies, put their arms about his neck and hugged him, the younger ones scrambling to get at him; and, what struck me as most remarkable, two of the house-servants, negroes, black as Erebus, made a bold push at the old gentleman, holding out their hands, which he shook heartily, with kind words of inquiry after their health. I was pleased, too, with my reception, and could not help drawing a comparison between his manner to me, and the hauteur and indifference I have experienced when asking for employment from gentlemen in similar circumstances in this country. In speaking, he treated me with perfect equality, called me "Mr. Thomson," said "Yes, Sir," or "No, Sir,"

William Thomson, *A Tradesman's Travels in the United States and Canada in the Years 1840, 41 & 42* (Edinburgh, 1842), pp. 16-21.

just as I would do, in speaking to a gentleman I held in high estimation. I sat at the same table. The young ladies played on the piano, and sung Scotch songs. The old gentleman, too sung "Scots wha hae" with great spirit. And all this, not to please, and make comfortable, a gentleman who could repay them in kind, but to a stranger seeking employment, not fashionably dressed, but clean and decent. I have travelled and wrought in the principal manufacturing districts of England and Scotland, but never had a tithe of the kindness and consideration shown me that I had here. And this was not a solitary instance: on another occasion, in the State of South Carolina, I applied to Colonel Beausket, who has a cotton and woollen-manufactory at Vacluce (Vaucluse), about 100 miles from Charleston. On calling on him at his house, near Charleston, I received the same consideration and politeness. It was in the evening when I called, and he was at home, in the midst of his family. Under such circumstances in this country, I would have been told to call again. Here I was immediately shown into the parlour, and seated in the family circle. He told me he could not employ me, but that as I wished to go up the country, I might stop at his place, and see the establishment, which I will take notice of when I come to speak of the manufactories of America. It was something new to me to be treated with such attention by those from whom I was seeking work. This gentleman being about to return that evening to the city, asked me to ride down with him in his carriage; and as it was now dark, I gladly accepted his offer. I may here mention, that a few days after I went up the country to the manufactory, where I remained a week, and received the same hospitality from the manager.

While endeavouring to illustrate the manners of the people of this section of the country, by stating these facts, I will here notice what generally applies to the whole community, viz., the kindly manner of parents to their children, and the affectionate and respectful conduct of children to their parents. In this country there is not a shadow of the distant and reserved manner of the poorer and middle classes of Scotland to their children. I have sometimes envied the kisses that were imprintd on old wrinkled brows by sweet young girls, as they said "Good night, pa." "Good night, my daughter," replies the old man.

The character of the southern states, for hospitality, stands high, and it is not overrated. They are quite a distinct race from the "Yankees." They have a high sense of honour; treating every white man as a gentleman, but rigidly exacting the same respect in return; and although many young men carry bowie-knives, sword-canes, or pistols, after I knew them I felt myself as safe from injury or outrage as in my own house. In short, the society in this part of the country was the most agreeable I ever associated with. In passing along the streets or crowded thoroughfares of the cities, it would be a rare circumstance if any one should jostle or accidentally come against you without making an apology. Ladies are treated on all occasions with great deference and respect. Amidst many instances that came under my observation, I will mention one: I was inquiring if there were any letters for me at the post-office in Augusta. At the same time that I went up to the opening at which the clerk was standing, a woman came up, but rather after than before me: however, I spoke first, and I was civilly desired to wait till the lady was attended to; and I am sure it was neither her dress nor her youth and beauty that gave her precedence, for she was not rich in any of these.

Master and Slaves on a Georgia Plantation

Sir Charles Lyell

Dec. 31 [1845]—At the end of a long day's sail, our steamer landed us safely at the village of Darien [Georgia]—on the sandy banks of the river Altamaha (which is pronounced [with] the a's broad). The sky was clear, and the air mild, but refreshing, and we were told that we must walk to the inn, not far off. Five negroes were very officious in offering their services, and four of them at length adjusted all our packages on their backs. The other, having nothing else to do, assumed the command of the party, having first said to me, "If you not ready, we will hesitate for half an hour." We passed under some of the noblest evergreen oaks I had yet seen, their large picturesque roots spreading on all sides, half out of the loose, sandy soil, and their boughs hung with unusually long weepers of Spanish moss. When I had paid our four porters, the one who had gone first, assuming an air of great importance, "hoped I would remember the pilot." As the inn was almost in sight from the landing, and our course a direct one in a bright moonlight night, and all the men quite familiar with every step of the way, we were not a little diverted at the notion of paying for a guide, but the good-humored countenance of the pilot made his appeal irresistible. The bed at our humble inn was clean, but next morning we were annoyed by having to sit down to breakfast with a poor white family, to whom the same compliment could not be paid—a man and his wife and four children, belonging to the class called "crackers" in Georgia. The etymology of this word is rather uncertain, some deriving it from the long whips used by the wagoners. They are a class of small proprietors, who seem to acquire slovenly habits from dependence on slaves, of whom they can maintain but few.

Sir Charles Lyell, *A Second Visit to the United States of North America* (New York, 1849), pp. 243-249, 261-273.

The next morning, while we were standing on the river's bank, we were joined by Mr. Hamilton Couper, with whom I had corresponded on geological matters, and whom I have already mentioned as the donor of a splendid collection of fossil remains to the museum at Washington, and, I may add, of other like treasures to that of Philadelphia. He came down the river to meet us in a long canoe, hollowed out of the trunk of a single cypress, and rowed by six negroes, who were singing loudly, and keeping time to the stroke of their oars. He brought us a packet of letters from England, which had been sent to his house, a welcome New Year's gift; and when we had glanced over their contents, we entered the boat and began to ascend the Altamaha.

The river was fringed on both sides with tall canes and with the cypress (*Cupressus disticha*), and many other trees, still leafless, which, being hung with gray moss, gave a sombre tone to the scenery at this season, in spite of the green leaves of several species of laurel, myrtle, and magnolia. But wherever there was a break in the fringe of trees, which flourishd luxuriantly in the swamps bordering the river, a forest of evergreen pines was seen in the back ground. For many a mile we saw no habitations, and the solitude was profound; but our black oarsmen made the woods echo to their song. One of them taking the lead, first improvised a verse, paying compliments to his master's family, and to a celebrated black beauty of the neighborhood, who was compared to the "red bird." The other five then joined in chorus, always repeating the same words. Occasionally they struck up a hymn, taught them by the Methodists, in which the most sacred subjects were handled with strange familiarity, and which, though nothing irreverent was meant, sounded oddly to our ears, and, when following a love ditty, almost profane.

Darien is on the left or northern bank of the Altamaha. About fifteen miles above it, on the opposite bank, we came to Hopeton, the residence of Mr. H. Couper, having first passed from the river into a canal, which traversed the low rice fields. Here we put up prodigious flights of the marsh blackbird (*Ajelaius phœniceus*), sometimes called the red-winged starling, because the male has some scarlet feathers in the upper part of his wing. When several thousands of them are in rapid motion at once, they darken the air like a cloud, and then, when the whole of them suddenly turn their wings edgeways, the cloud vanishes, to reappear as instantaneously the next moment. Mr. Couper encourages these birds, as they eat up all the loose grains of rice scattered over the field after the harvest has been gathered in. If these seeds are left, they spring up the year following, producing what is called volunteer rice, always of inferior quality to that which is regularly sown. From the rice grounds we walked up a bank to a level table land, composed of sand, a few yards above the river, and covered with pines and a mixture of scrub oak. Here, in this genial climate, there are some wild flowers in bloom every day of the year. On this higher level, near the slope which faces the rice fields and the river, stands the house of Hopeton, where we spent our time very agreeably for a fortnight. Much has been said in praise of the hospitality of the southern planter, but they alone who have traveled in the southern states, can appreciate the perfect ease and politeness with which a stranger is made to feel himself at home. Horses, carriages, boats, servants, are all at his disposal. Even his little comforts are thought of, and every thing is done as heartily and naturally as if no obligation were conferred. When northerners who are not very rich receive guests in the country, where domestic servants are few and expensive, they are often compelled, if they would insure the comfort of their visitors, to perform menial offices themselves. The sacrifices, therefore, made by the planter, are comparatively small, since he has a well-trained establishment of servants, and his habitual style of living is so free and liberal, that the expense of a few additional inmates in the family is scarcely felt. Still there is a warm and generous openness of character in the southerners, which mere wealth and a retinue of servants cannot give; and they have often a dignity of manner, without stiffness, which is most agreeable.

The landed proprietors here visit each other in the style of English country gentlemen, sometimes dining out with their families and returning at night, or, if the distance be great, remaining to sleep and coming home the next morning. A considerable part of their food is derived from the produce of the land; but, as their houses are usually distant from large towns, they keep large stores of groceries and of clothing, as is the custom in country houses in some parts of Scotland.

A few days after our arrival (January 4, 1846), Mr. Couper took us in a canoe down the river from Hopeton to one of the sea-islands, called St. Simon's, fifteen miles distant, to visit his summer residence, and to give me an opportunity of exploring the geology of the coast and adjoining low country. We saw, on the banks of the river, the *Magnolia glauca*, attaining a height of thirty feet, instead of being only ten feet high, as in the swamps of New England. The gum tree (*Nyssa aquatica*), out of leaf at this season, was conspicuous, from the manner in which the smooth trunk swells out at the base, being partially hollow in the interior, so that it is often used by the negroes for bee-hives. Jays and blue-birds were very abundant, and there were several large hawks' nests on the tops of tall dead trees. . . .

On our way we landed on Butler's Island, where the banks of the river, as is usual in deltas, are higher than the ground immediately behind them. They are here adorned with orange trees, loaded with golden fruit, and very ornamental. We saw ricks of rice raised on props five feet high, to protect them from the sea, which, during hurricanes, has been known to rise five or six feet. The negro houses were neat, and whitewashed, all floored with wood, each with an apartment called the hall, two sleeping-rooms, and a loft for the children; but it is evident that on these rice farms, where the negroes associate with scarcely any whites, except the overseer and his family, and have but little intercourse with the slaves of other estates, they must remain far more stationary than where, as in a large part of Georgia, they are about equal in number to the whites, or even form a minority. The negroes, moreover, in the interior, are healthier than those in rice plantations, and multiply faster, although the rice grounds are salubrious to the negroes as compared to the whites. In this lower region the increase of the slaves is rapid, for they are well fed, fitted for a southern climate, and free from care, partly, no doubt, because of their low mental development, and partly because they and their children are secured from want. Such advantages, however, would be of no avail, in rendering them prolific, if they were overworked and harshly treated.

During a fortnight's stay at Hopeton, we had an opportunity of seeing how the planters live in the south, and the condition and prospects of the negroes on a well-managed estate. The relation of the slaves to their owners resembles nothing in the northern states. There is an hereditary regard and often attachment on both sides, more like that formerly existing between lords and their retainers in the old feudal times of Europe, than to any thing now to be found in America. The slaves identify themselves with the master, and their sense of their own importance rises with his success in life. But the responsibility of the owners is felt to be great, and to manage a plantation with profit is no easy task; so much judgment is required, and such a mixture of firmness, forbearance, and kindness. The evils of the system of slavery are said to be exhibited in their worst light when new settlers come from the free states; northern men, who are full of activity, and who strive to make a rapid fortune, willing to risk their own lives in an unhealthy climate, and who can not make allowance for the repugnance to continuous labor of the negro race, or the diminished motive for exertion of the slave. To one who arrives in Georgia direct from Europe, with a vivid impression on his mind of the state of the peasantry there in many populous regions, their ignorance, intemperance, and improvidence, the difficulty of obtaining subsistence, and the small chance they have of bettering their lot, the condition of the black laborers on such a property as Hopeton, will afford but small ground for lamentation or despondency. I had many opportunities, while here, of talking with the slaves alone, or seeing them at work. I may be told that this was a favorable specimen of a well-managed estate; if so,

I may at least affirm that mere chance led me to pay this visit, that is to say, scientific objects wholly unconnected with the "domestic institutions" of the south, or the character of the owner in relation to his slaves; and I may say the same in regard to every other locality or proprietor visited by me in the course of this tour. I can but relate what passed under my own eyes, or what I learnt from good authority, concealing nothing.

There are 500 negroes on the Hopeton estate, a great many of whom are children, and some old and superannuated. The latter class, who would be supported in a poor-house in England, enjoy here, to the end of their days, the society of their neighbors and kinsfolk, and live at large in separate houses assigned to them. The children have no regular work to do till they are ten or twelve years old. We see that some of them, at this season, are set to pick up dead leaves from the paths, others to attend the babies. When the mothers are at work, the young children are looked after by an old negress, called Mom Diana. Although very ugly as babies, they have such bright, happy faces when three or four years old, and from that age to ten or twelve have such frank and confiding manners, as to be very engaging. Whenever we met them, they held out their hands to us to shake, and when my wife caressed them, she was often asked by some of the ladies, whether she would not like to bring up one of the girls to love her, and wait upon her. The parents indulge their own fancies in naming their children, and display a singular taste; for one is called January, another April, a third Monday, and a fourth Hard Times. The fisherman on the estate rejoices in the appellation of "Old Bacchus." Quash is the name of the favorite preacher, and Bulally the African name of another negro.

The out-door laborers have separate houses provided for them; even the domestic servants, except a few who are nurses to the white children, live apart from the great house—an arrangement not always convenient for the masters, as there is no one to answer a bell after a certain hour. But if we place ourselves in the condition of the majority of the population, that of servants, we see at once how many advantages we should enjoy over the white race in the same rank of life in Europe. In the first place, all can marry; and if a mistress should lay on any young woman here the injunction so common in English newspaper advertisements for a maid of all work, "no followers allowed," it would be considered an extraordinary act of tyranny. The laborers begin work at six o'clock in the morning, have an hour's rest at nine for breakfast, and many have finished their assigned task by two o'clock, all of them by three o'clock. In summer they divide their work differently, going to bed in the middle of the day, then rising to finish their task, and afterward spending a great part of the night in chatting, merry-making, preaching, and psalm-singing. At Christmas they claim a week's holidays, when they hold a kind of Saturnalia, and the owners can get no work done. Although there is scarcely any drinking, the master rejoices when this season is well over without mischief. The negro houses are as neat as the greater part of the cottages in Scotland (no flattering compliment it must be confessed), are provided always with a back door, and a hall, as they call it, in which is a chest, a table, two or three chairs, and a few shelves for crockery. On the door of the sleeping apartment they keep a large wooden padlock, to guard their valuables from their neighbors when they are at work in the field, for there is much pilfering among them. A little yard is often attached, in which are seen their chickens, and usually a yelping cur, kept for their amusement.

The winter, when the whites enjoy the best health, is the trying season for the negroes, who are rarely ill in the rice-grounds in summer, which are so fatal to the whites, that when the planters who have retreated to the sea-islands revisit their estates once a fortnight, they dare not sleep at home. Such is the indifference of the negroes to heat, that they are often found sleeping with their faces upward in a broiling sun, instead of lying under the shade of a tree hard by. We visited the hospital at Hopeton, which consists of three separate wards, all perfectly clean and well-ventilated. One is for men, another for women, and a third for lying-in women. The latter are always allowed a month's rest after their confinement, an advantage rarely enjoyed by hard-working English peasants. Although they are better looked after and kept more quiet, on these occasions, in the hospital, the planters are usually baffled; for the women prefer their own houses, where they can gossip with their friends without restraint, and they usually contrive to be taken by surprise at home.

The negro mothers are often so ignorant or indolent, that they can not be trusted to keep awake and administer medicine to their own children; so that the mistress has often to sit up all night with a sick negro child. In submitting to this, they are actuated by mixed motives—a feeling of kindness, and a fear of losing the services of the slave; but these attentions greatly attach the negroes to their owners. In general, they refuse to take medicine from any other hands but those of their master or mistress. The laborers are allowed Indian meal, rice, and milk, and occasionally pork and soup. As their rations are more than they can eat, they either return part of it to the overseer, who makes them an allowance of money for it at the end of the week, or they keep it to feed their fowls, which they usually sell, as well as their eggs, for cash, to buy molasses, tobacco, and other luxuries. When disposed to exert themselves, they get through the day's task in five hours, and then amuse themselves in fishing, and sell the fish they take; or some of them employ their spare time in making canoes out of large cypress trees, leave being readily granted them to remove such timber, as it aids the landowner to clear the swamps. They sell the canoes for about four dollars, for their own profit.

If the mistress pays a visit to Savannah, the nearest town, she is overwhelmed with commissions, so many of the slaves wishing to lay out their small gains in various indulgences, especially articles of dress, of which they are passionately fond. The stuff must be of the finest quality, and many instructions are given as to the precise color or fashionable shade. White muslin, with figured patterns, is the rage just now.

One day, when walking alone, I came upon a "gang" of negroes, who were digging a trench. They were superintended by a black "driver," who held a whip in his hand. Some of the laborers were using spades, others cutting away the roots and stumps of trees which they had encountered in the line of the ditch. Their mode of proceeding in their task was somewhat leisurely, and eight hours a day of this work are exacted, though they can accomplish the same in five hours, if they undertake it by the task. The digging of a given number of feet in length, breadth, and depth is, in this case, assigned to each ditcher, and a deduction made when they fall in with a stump or root. The names of gangs and drivers are odious, and the sight of the whip was painful to me as a mark of degradation, reminding me that the lower orders of slaves are kept to their work by mere bodily fear, and that their treatment must depend on the individual character of the owner or overseer. That the whip is rarely used, and often held for weeks over them, merely *in terrorem*, is, I have no doubt, true on all well governed estates; and it is not that formidable weapon which I have seen exhibited as formerly in use in the West Indies. It is a thong of leather, half an inch wide and a quarter of an inch thick. No ordinary driver is allowed to give more than six lashes for any offense, the head driver twelve, and the overseer twenty-four. When an estate is under superior management, the system is remarkably effective in preventing crime. The most severe punishment required in the last forty years, for a body of 500 negroes at Hopeton, was for the theft of one negro from another. In that period there has been no criminal act of the highest grade, for which a delinquent could be committed to the penitentiary in Georgia, and there have been only six cases of assault and battery. As a race, the negroes are mild and forgiving, and by no means so prone to indulge in drinking as the white man or the Indian. There were more serious quarrels, and more broken heads, among the Irish in a few years, when they came to dig the Brunswick Canal, than had been known among the negroes in all the surrounding plantations for half a century. The murder of a husband by a black woman, whom he had beat violently, is the greatest crime remembered in this part of Georgia for a great length of time.

Under the white overseer, the principal charge here is given to "Old Tom," the head driver, a man of superior intelligence and higher cast of feature. He was the son of a prince of the Foulah tribe, and was taken prisoner, at the age of fourteen, near Timbuctoo. The accounts he gave of what he remembered of the plants and geography of Africa, have been taken down in writing by Mr. Couper, and confirm many of the narratives of modern travelers. He has remained a strict Mahometan, but his numerous progeny of jet-black children and grandchildren, all of them marked by countenances of a more European cast than those of ordinary negroes, have exchanged the Koran for the Bible.

During the last war, when Admiral Cockburn was off this coast with his fleet, he made an offer of freedom to all the slaves belonging to the father of my present host, and a safe convoy to Canada. Nearly all would have gone, had not African Tom, to whom they looked up with great respect, declined the proposal. He told them he had first known what slavery was in the West Indies, and had made up his mind that the English were worse masters than the Americans. About half of them, therefore, determined to stay in St. Simon's Island, and not a few of the others who accepted the offer and emigrated, had their lives shortened by the severity of the climate in Canada.

The slave trade ceased in 1796, and but few negroes were afterward smuggled into Georgia from foreign countries, except indirectly for a short time through Florida before its annexation; yet one fourth of the population of this lower country is said to have come direct from Africa, and it is a good sign of the progress made in civilization by the native-born colored race, that they speak of these "Africanians" with much of the contempt with which Europeans talk of negroes.

I was agreeably surprised to see the rank held here by the black mechanics. One day I observed a set of carpenters putting up sluices, and a lock in a canal of a kind unknown in this part of the world. The black foreman was carrying into execution a plan laid down for him on paper by Mr. Couper, who had observed it himself many years ago in Holland. I also saw a steam-engine, of fifteen horse power, made in England by Bolton and Watt, and used in a mill for threshing rice, which had been managed by a negro for more than twelve years without an accident. When these mechanics come to consult Mr. Couper on business, their manner of speaking to him is quite as independent as that of English artisans to their employers. Their aptitude for the practice of such mechanical arts may encourage every philanthropist who has had misgivings in regard to the progressive powers of the race, although much time will be required to improve the whole body of negroes, and the movement must be general. One planter can do little by himself, so long as education is forbidden by law. I am told that the old colonial statutes against teaching the slaves to read were almost in abeyance, and had become a dead letter, until revived by the reaction against the Abolition agitation, since which they have been rigorously enforced and made more stringent. Nevertheless, the negroes are often taught to read, and they learn much in Sunday schools, and for the most part are desirous of instruction.

In the hope of elevating the character of some of his negroes, and giving them more self-dependence, Mr. Couper, by way of experiment, set apart a field for the benefit of twenty-five picked men, and gave up to them half their Saturday's labor to till it. In order that they might know its value, they were compelled to work on it for the first year, and the product, amounting to 1500 dollars, was divided equally among them. But when, at length, they were left to themselves, they did nothing, and at the end of two years the field was uncultivated. But there appears to me nothing disheartening in this failure, which may have been chiefly owing to their holding the property in common, a scheme which was found not to answer even with the Pilgrim Fathers when they first colonized Plymouth—men whom certainly none will accuse of indolence or a disposition to shrink from continuous labor. The "dolce far niente" is doubtless the negro's paradise, and I once heard one of them singing with much spirit at Williamsburg an appropriate song:—

"Old Virginia never tire,
Eat hog and hominy, and lie by the fire";

and it is quite enough that a small minority should be of this mind, to make all the others idle and unwilling to toil hard for the benefit of the sluggards.

When conversing with different planters here, in regard to the capabilities and future progress of the black population, I find them to agree very generally in the opinion that in this part of Georgia they appear under a great disadvantage. In St. Simon's island it is admitted, that the negroes on the smaller estates are more civilized than on the larger properties, because they associate with a greater proportion of whites. In Glynn County, where we are now residing, there are no less than 4000 negroes to 700 whites; whereas in Georgia generally there are only 281,000 slaves in a population of 691,000, or more whites than colored people. Throughout the upper country there is a large preponderance of Anglo-Saxons, and a little reflection will satisfy the reader how much the education of a race which starts originally from so low a stage of intellectual, social, moral, and spiritual development, as the African negro, must depend not on learning to read and write, but on the amount of familiar intercourse which they enjoy with individuals of a more advanced race. So long as they herd together in large gangs, and rarely come into contact with any whites save their owner and overseer, they can profit little by their imitative faculty, and can not even make much progress in mastering the English language, that powerful instrument of thought and of the communication of ideas, which they are gaining in exchange for the limited vocabulary of their native tribes. Yet, even in this part of Georgia, the negroes are very far from stationary, and each generation is acquiring habits of greater cleanliness and propriety of behavior, while some are learning mechanical arts, and every year many of them becoming converts to Christianity.

Although the Baptist and Methodist missionaries have been the most active in this important work, the Episcopalians have not been idle, especially since Dr. Elliott became Bishop of Georgia, and brought his talents, zeal, and energy to the task. As he found that the negroes in general had no faith in the efficacy of baptism except by complete immersion, he performed the ceremony as they desired. Indeed, according to the old English rubric, all persons were required to be immersed in baptism, except when they were sick, so that to lose converts by not complying with this popular notion of the slaves, would hardly have been justifiable. It may be true that the poor negroes cherish a superstitious belief that the washing out of every taint of sin depends mainly on the particular manner of performing the rite, and the principal charm to the black women in the ceremony of total immersion consists in decking themselves out in white robes, like brides, and having their shoes trimmed with silver. They well know that the waters of the Altamaha are chilly, and that they and the officiating minister run no small risk of catching cold, but to this penance they most cheerfully submit.

Of dancing and music the negroes are passionately fond. On the Hopeton plantation above twenty violins have been silenced by the Methodist missionaries, yet it is notorious that the slaves were not given to drink or intemperance in their merry-makings. At the Methodist prayer-meetings, they are permitted to move round rapidly in a ring, joining hands in token of brotherly love, presenting first the right hand and then the left, in which manœuver, I am told, they sometimes contrive to take enough exercise to serve as a substitute for the dance, it being, in fact, a kind of spiritual *boulanger,* while the singing of psalms, in and out of chapel, compensates in no small degree for the songs they have been required to renounce.

However much we may feel inclined to smile at some of these outward tokens of conversion, and however crude may be the notions of the Deity which the poor African at first exchanges for his belief in the evil eye and other superstitious fears, it is nevertheless an immense step in his progress toward civilization that he should join some Christian sect. Before he has time to acquire high conceptions of his Creator, or to comprehend his own probationary state on earth, and his moral and religious duties, it is no small gain that he should simply become a member of the same church with his master, and should be taught that the white and colored man are equal before God, a doctrine calculated to raise him in his own opinion, and in that of the dominant race.

Until lately the humblest slave who joined the Methodist or Baptist denomination could feel that he was one of a powerful association of Christians, which numbered hundreds of thousands of brethren in the northern as well as in the southern states. He could claim many schools and colleges of high repute in New England as belonging to his own sect, and feel proud of many celebrated writers whom they have educated. Unfortunately, a recent separation, commonly called "the north and south split," has severed these bonds of fellowship and fraternity, and for the sake of renouncing brotherhood with slave-owners, the northern churches have repudiated all communion with the great body of their negro fellow Christians. What effect can such estrangement have on the mind, whether of master or slave, favorable to the cause of emancipation? The slight thrown on the aristocracy of planters has no tendency to conciliate them, or lead them to assimilate their sentiments to those of their brethren in the faith, with whom formerly, throughout the northern and free states, they had so intimate a connection; and as for the slaves, it is to them a positive loss to be thus rejected and disowned. The rank and position of the negro preachers in the south, whether Baptist or Methodist, some of them freemen, and of good abilities, is decidedly lowered by the severance of the northern churches, which is therefore adverse to the gradual advancement of the African race, which can alone fit them for manumission.

Some of the planters in Glynn County have of late permitted the distribution of Bibles among their slaves, and it was curious to remark that they who were unable to read were as anxious to possess them as those who could. Besides Christianizing the blacks, the clergy of all sects are doing them incalculable service, by preaching continually to both races that the matrimonial tie should be held sacred, without respect to color. To the dominant race one of the most serious evils of slavery is its tendency to blight domestic happiness; and the anxiety of parents for their sons, and a constant fear of their licentious intercourse with slaves, is painfully great. We know but too much of this evil in free countries, wherever there is a vast distance between the rich and poor, giving a power to wealth which insures a frightful amount of prostitution. Here it is accompanied with a publicity which is keenly felt as a disgrace by the more refined of the white women. The female slave is proud of her connection with a white man, and thinks it an honor to have a mulatto child, hoping that it will be better provided for than a black child. Yet the mixed offspring is not very numerous. The mulattoes alone represent nearly all the illicit intercourse between the white man and negro of the living generation. I am told that they do not constitute more than two and a half per cent. of the whole population. If the statistics of the illegitimate children of the whites born here could be compared with those in Great Britain, it might lead to conclusions by no means favorable to the free country. Here there is no possibility of concealment, the color of the child stamps upon him the mark of bastardy, and transmits it to great-grand-children born in lawful wedlock; whereas if, in Europe, there was some mark or indelible stain betraying all the delinquencies and frailties, not only of parents, but of ancestors for three or four generations back, what unexpected disclosures should we not witness!

There are scarcely any instances of mulattoes born of a black father and a white mother. The colored women who become the mistresses of the white men are neither rendered miserable nor degraded, as are the white women who are seduced in Europe, and who are usually abandoned in the end, and left to be the victims of want and disease. In the northern states of America there is so little profligacy of this kind, that their philanthropists may perhaps be usefully occupied in considering how the mischief may be alleviated south of the Potomac; but in Great Britain there is so much need of reform at home, that the whole thoughts and energies of the rich ought to be concentrated in such schemes of improvement as may enable us to set an example of a higher moral standard to the slave-owning aristocracy of the Union.

On one of the estates in this part of Georgia, there is a mulatto mother who has nine children by a full black, and the difference of shade between them and herself is scarcely perceptible. If the white blood usually predominates in this way in the second generation, as I am told is the case, amalgamation would proceed very rapidly, if marriages between the races were once legalized; for we see in England that black men can persuade very respectable white women to marry them, when all idea of the illegality and degradation of such unions is foreign to their thoughts.

Among the obstacles which the Christian missionaries encounter here when they teach the virtue of chastity, I must not omit to mention the loose code of morality which the Africans have inherited from their parents. My wife made the acquaintance of a lady in Alabama, who had brought up with great care a colored girl, who grew up modest and well-behaved, till at length she became the mother of a mulatto child. The mistress reproached her very severely for her misconduct, and the girl at first took the rebuke much to heart; but having gone home one day to visit her mother, a native African, she returned, saying, that her parent had assured her she had done nothing wrong, and had no reason to feel ashamed. When we are estimating, therefore, the amount of progress made by the American negroes since they left their native country, we ought always to bear in mind from how low a condition, both morally and intellectually considered, they have had to mount up.

William Gregg, Pioneer Southern Industrialist

There is a natural propensity in mankind to feel a greater degree of interest in the biography of illustrious statesmen and heroes, who by their political knowledge or heroism have contributed largely to their country's glory, than that of individuals who, with humbler pretensions, have pointed out to their countrymen those means by which labor can be honorably and profitably employed, and those sources of industry and enterprise by which the humble can find the means of profitable employment, by which capital may be safely invested, and the resources of a country at the same time greatly augmented.

We propose to give a brief sketch of the incidents in the life of an individual who, although not the earliest manufacturer of cotton cloth in Carolina, was the first in our estimation who, by his sound judgment and knowledge of machinery, demonstrated, to the conviction of the inhabitants, that our southern states were as well adapted to the manufacture of cotton as the most favored countries either in Europe or America.

WILLIAM GREGG was born in Monongala county, in Virginia, in February, 1800. His ancestors were Quakers, residing at Wilmington, in Delaware. His father, during the Revolutionary War, took up arms in behalf of his native country, and was among the troops who fought in defence of Charleston. Here he was taken prisoner by the British, at the surrender of the city. Whilst on the road to Ninety-Six, with other prisoners, he managed to make his escape in one of our swamps, and found his way back to his native state. There he married, and returned to South Carolina, and settled in Newberry District. He subsequently removed to Monongala, in Virginia, where the subject of our present memoir was born. At the age of four years, his mother died, which caused the separation of the family. He was now placed with an uncle, Jacob Gregg, who resided at Alexandria, D. C. He was a watchmaker by trade, by

De Bow's Review, X (1851), pp. 348-352.

which means he had accumulated a large fortune. He also engaged largely in the manufacture of spinning machinery. In 1810, Jacob Gregg removed to Georgia, taking his nephew with him. Here he erected one of the first cotton factories in the South. It was located on Little River, (Whatley's Mills,) midway between Monticello and Madison. The machinery was principally of his own manufacture. During the continuance of the war, the enterprise was successful, and the return of peace brought with it such a flood of foreign goods into the country, that nearly all the establishments of this kind were prostrated. The depreciation of property invested in manufacturing establishments, ruined the fortune of Jacob Gregg, and he placed his nephew William with one of his old friends in Lexington, Kentucky, to learn the trade of a watchmaker.

William Gregg remained in Kentucky until 1821, when he went to Petersburg, to perfect himself in his profession. In 1824, he established himself in business in Columbia, S. C. By faithfulness and punctuality in his profession, he gained the confidence of the community, and prospered in his business. Much of a man's success in life, as well as the peace and happiness of his home, depends on his choice of a companion in life, to cheer him in solitude, to strengthen his good resolutions, and render his home the seat of hospitality, of innocence and bliss. In this selection Mr. Gregg was eminently fortunate, having in 1829 married Miss Marina Jones, of Edgefield District, a lady whose intelligence, and the general excellency of her character, render her an ornament to her sex and a blessing to her family.

Mr. Gregg commenced business in Columbia with a limited capital, which had been accumulated by untiring industry, economy, and an assiduous attention to the duties of his profession. Not wanting in enterprise, he gradually enlarged his business. This was soon extended to an extensive European correspondence and direct trade. To effect this, he visited England and France in 1834 for the purpose of forming the necessary connections.

Having amassed a moderate fortune, and being in delicate health, he retired from business, believing that he possessed the means of providing his children with a good education, yet, at the same time, not such a superabundance as would lead them to believe that they were raised above dependence or self-exertion, which in so many instances proves the ruin of the sons of the wealthy.

When a man has accumulated a certain amount of wealth, the farther acquisition is comparatively easy; Mr. Gregg, however, did not possess that love of money that would induce him to avail himself of these advantages. Instead of becoming a broker, or a money-changer, he invested his means in commerce and manufactures.

In 1837 he purchased a large interest in the Vaucluse Manufacturing

Company, in Edgefield, intending to enter extensively into the manufacturing of cotton, but ill-health prevented him from purchasing that establishment when the Company sold out.

In 1838, Mr. Gregg removed to Charleston, where he resumed his former business in the firm of Hayden, Gregg & Company, successors to the old house of Eyland, Hayden & Co. It is now the house of Gregg, Hayden & Co., known in the South as extensive importing merchants; the terms of copartnership being such as to afford the senior partner of the house entire leisure from the active labors of business. Naturally possessed of an active temperament, with a mind to which knowledge of every kind is easily accessible, his time and advantages have not been suffered to pass unimproved. He is, in every sense of the word, a self-made man. He sought for information from all quarters, and intuitively applied it to practical purposes, and in this way has laid up a fund of useful knowledge, which he has, from time to time, communicated to the public. His essays on domestic industry, originally published in Charleston, were re-published in nearly all the papers of Georgia, Alabama, and other southern states. They are believed to have been the origin of the extensive manufacturing operations at Augusta, the Charleston factory, the abandonment of the restrictions on steam in Charleston, the erection of the Graniteville factory, and numerous others in Georgia, and other states farther to the south.

Preparatory to writing these essays, Mr. Gregg visited the manufacturing districts of the Northern States. His notes were made whilst sojourning among the cotton spinners of the North. There is a vein of practical good sense running through these essays that cannot fail to carry conviction to every unprejudiced mind.

In his preface he says,

"We all know what the manufacturing of cotton has done for Great Britain. It has given her an influence which makes all other states tributary to her. We also know, that this branch of manufactures was the foundation on which that vast and continually increasing structure has been reared in New-England, which has given an impetus to all other species of manufactures, infusing a spirit of enterprise, health, and vigor, into every department of industrial pursuits. I have always been a close observer of things, but when I visited the mountainous districts of Connecticut, Massachusetts, Vermont, and New-Hampshire, (for it is pushing itself to the very summits of the mountains,) I could not but notice, with surprise, the effect which this branch of manufactures had produced. Wherever it finds its way, all other branches of industry follow. It brings into requisition every element around it, gives value to every species of property, and causes each and every individual to cling to his little domain as the future home of his children, and resting place for his bones; and though it be but a barren rock, he places a value on it scarcely to be estimated. Every water-fall is brought into use; every forest tree is measured, even to its topmost branches, (for nothing is lost in that country) after the trunk has been worked into boards and shingles, the tops are cut into laths. Compare this state of things with that of our state, in which a man hesitates about building a comfortable dwelling-house, lest the spirit of emigration deprive him of its use, in which the cream of its virgin soil is hardly exhausted, before the owner is ready to abandon it, in search of a country affording new and better lands,—in which our forest lumber cutters fell, with ruthless hand, the finest timber trees on the face of the globe, selecting those portions which are the most easily turned into merchantable lumber, and leaving the balance to rot on the ground where it was cut, in which so soon as the best timber is exhausted, a water-fall, which would be worth thousands of dollars in any other country, is abandoned as wholly worthless, and in which men possessing the capital of the country, complain that it will not yield them three per cent."

"When I saw bags of our cotton arrive in those mountainous districts, which had been packed in the interior of South Carolina, and wagoned over miserable bad roads (in some instances one hundred miles) to Hamburg or Columbia; thence transported one hundred and thirty-six miles by rail-road to Charleston, where it is sold, after being submitted to the charges of drayage, wharfage, commissions, and perhaps storage; thence re-shipped to New-York to undergo similar charges, where it is purchased by one of these manufacturers and again re-shipped to Hartford, and from the last-named place, making a dangerous and difficult passage up the Connecticut River, is landed, and again hauled in wagons, some thirty or forty miles, over mountainous roads; and having now reached its final destination, (at double its original cost,) is manufactured into coarse cloth. Going over the same ground again, it reaches New-York, where it is re-shipped to Charleston, and finds its way back again into the interior of our state. I repeat, when I saw these things, and knowing, as I do, the rich resources of South Carolina, and the facility with which this cotton could be turned into cloth, by the labor around us, which might be applied to it without detriment to other pursuits—could it be expected, that I would write without using strong terms?"

We re-published in our volumes last year, the major portion of the valuable essays of Mr. Gregg, upon cotton manufacture at the South, and have since received his able address before the South Carolina Institute for the promotion of arts, mechanical ingenuity and industry, which we hope to publish before long. Meanwhile we quote the closing paragraph, in which Mr. Gregg looks into the future of Carolina.

"And her prosperity will be in full tide when we shall hear of large factories putting up at the East to be filled with thousands of power looms to weave up our Southern yarn. When the live stock and hemp bagging which we receive from Kentucky will be brought on rail-road cars, to return laden with our cotton domestics. When we shall see a large portion of the swamps of the Santee, Pee Dee, Wateree, Congaree, Edisto, Savannah, and other swamps, brought into cultivation, the Ashly and Edisto connected by canal, the stock of the Santee Canal restored to its original value by the transit of boats loaded with grain and hay, supplying our low country with that which we are importing from other States. When our hills shall be covered with green pastures and grazing flocks of sheep, and we shall have rail-roads and turnpikes leading to every portion of the state. When our lumber cutters shall be found to be engaged in producing materials for the construction of towns and villages in our own state,—then will the tide of our prosperity be in full flood; we will then be no longer under the necessity of looking for relief through limited production; we will have ceased to be under the influence of the fluctuations of the Liverpool market; we will have rid ourselves of that position which has made us of recent days a foot ball to be kicked about by the Manchester Spinners and Liverpool Cotton Brokers. Our tub will stand on its own bottom."

In 1845, application was made to the Legislature of South Carolina, for a charter of incorporation of the Graniteville Company. As incorporations were at that time unpopular in the state, it was doubtful whether such a charter could be obtained as would be acceptable to the stockholders; these doubts enlisted his anxious efforts, and caused him to publish the pamphlet entitled "An inquiry into the expediency of granting charters of incorporation for manufacturing purposes in South Carolina," signed, "one of the people." A copy of this pamphlet was placed into the hands of each member of the Legislature, and we have no doubt, that it was finally instrumental in producing the great change in public sentiment which has since taken place. The Graniteville charter, which is a very liberal one, was passed by a large majority of both houses. The same pamphlet was re-published in Georgia, and was laid before the Legislature of that state, and no doubt had its effect in producing a favorable view of this subject in that state.

Immediately after obtaining a charter, the Graniteville establishment was commenced with a capital of $300,000. Mr. Gregg took the entire supervision of the work, and devoted three years of laborious and assiduous attention to its erection without any charge to the company for his very efficient services. The work is now completed, and has been for some time in successful operation. There are 9,000 spindles, 300 looms, producing 12,000 yards per day of drillings, sheetings, and shirtings from 14 yarn. The establishment giving support to 900 people, who formerly enjoyed but scanty means of procuring food and clothing, and less for educating their children, but have now comfortable homes—the means of making an honest livelihood—of educating their children free of expense, and of worshiping God in the churches of their choice.

We regard the establishment at Graniteville as a model factory, where ornament and taste are combined, where the labors of the operatives are rewarded, whilst due attention is paid to their comforts, education, and morals, reflecting credit on the institution, and above all, on its enterprising, intelligent, and benevolent founder.

Having published in our previous volumes very full and minute accounts of the practical operation and improvements at Graniteville, we cannot better conclude this hurried sketch than by presenting to our readers a view of one of the most thriving manufacturing villages in the Union, and unquestionably the first in all the South.

The Literature of the Old South

William Gilmore Simms

Woodlands, (S.C.) Dec. 1, 1840

To P. C. Pendleton, Esq.

Dear Sir:—

When, something like a year ago, you drew my attention, by letter, to the Literary project which you had in view, and solicited my aid in its behalf, it was with a degree of indifference, which you must have seen in my reply, and which almost amounted to coldness, that I yielded to your wishes, and in a promise of compliance, to a certain, but very limited extent. It was not that I was unfriendly to your purpose. That was noble, and I could admire its aim, however much I might question its policy. But I had no faith in the project then; and, you will pardon me if I confess, I have very little more faith in it now. I have had so much experience, either as an editor or as a contributor, in the making of Southern Magazines, and know so thoroughly their history, and the inevitable event, that my conviction of the almost certain fate which awaits them, inspires me with a feeling, very like disgust, when I am told of any new experiment of this kind in contemplation. I know, and can predict, the usual story of confident hope and bold assurance with which they commonly begin. The editor feels his strength and his friends willingly promise theirs. His neighbors pledge their subscriptions, and the beginning of the work is made with considerable energy and eclat. But the progress of a few months soon undeceives the confiding, and blunts the energy of the most sanguine. The editor discovers that he has overtasked himself. His contributors,—men, generally, in our country, devoted to other professions,—can only write for him at moments of leisure, which good nature and an amicable desire to oblige, prompts them to employ in this manner. He is necessarily compelled to

Mary C. Simms Oliphant, Alfred Taylor Odell, T. C. Duncan Eaves (eds.), *The Letters of William Gilmore Simms* (courtesy of University of South Carolina Press, Columbia, S. C., 1952), pp. 196-208.

225

wait upon them for their articles, which, good, bad or indifferent, he is compelled to publish. The constant drain upon himself, enfeebles his imagination and exhausts his intellect. He has little time for thought, and no opportunity for the exercise of taste and fancy; and the station which he has self-assumed, so far from being a chair of state, from which he may dispense judgment, and exercise a dignified authority over the world of letters, becomes one of pain, disquiet and the most unintermitted mental drudgery. To these are added other evils. The collections are to be made over an extensive tract of interior country, from a community scattered "broad-cast" over thousands of miles, and are realized too slowly for the current expenses of his journal. The printer, who is seldom a capitalist, clamors for his monthly dues, and the subscriber recedes from the subscription list, the moment that he is called upon for his. Under the pressure of pecuniary difficulties, the publication of the work becomes irregular—it is finally sent forth on villainous paper, "but half made up," and then, chiefly, of such material as is tecknically called "Balaam" among the journalists;—by which is meant that inoffensive sort of commonplace, which is usually furnished by young Misses from their school exercises, and young Masters when they first begin to feel the startling sensations of the tender passion. The subscribers, under these circumstances, naturally reject the work which fails to reward them for perusal; and the general dissatisfaction of all the parties concerned,—the editor being among the first—soon leads to the early abandonment of an attempt in which nothing has been realized but discredit, annoyance, and expense.

This, I know to have been the usual history heretofore; and the results promise to the inevitable, and the same, in consequence of certain causes which control the subject, and which, in the future pages of this examination, I shall endeavour to develop. You, however, if I am to judge from the tenor of your late communications to myself, entertain better hopes of the future of your bantling. You may be right in your opinions, and your anticipations may be justly founded. For your sake—to say nothing of the public,—I sincerely trust that they are. Yet,—may I ask,—on what do you build? What are the peculiar circumstances, which, in your case, are to operate results, so very different from those which have marked the fate of all your predecessors? Are your contributors better able to win the regards, and beguile from the reluctant pockets of the Southern people, that support which the Southern Review could not secure? I speak not now of the numerous miscellaneous works of less pretension which have betrayed equally the various talent and the unhappy apathy of the people to whom they were addressed—which have begun in hope, and closed their brief time of life and light, in a feeble, flickering struggle, through months of unsustained continuance.

The name of the Southern Review, calls up some mournful associations, which warningly tell us of what the South has lost, of her literary men, her pride, strength and glory, in the course of a few short seasons. The gentle and persuasive [Stephen] ELLIOTT, whose pure seductive style was itself a delight to the ear, apart from the sterling truth, clear argument and varied knowledge which it conveyed:—the argumentative and philosophic [Dr. Thomas] COOPER, whose vast resources and ready judgment, prepared him to be a teacher in so many of the most difficult departments of human speculation and inquiry:—the amiable and witty [Prof. Henry Junius] NOTT, whose clear and copious humour, prompt utterance, and singular felicity of expression, enabled him to adorn with grace, and commend, with a charm almost entirely his own, those topics of grave research, which in ordinary hands, vex the taste and make the mind to weary of its toils:—the earnest and impassioned [Robert Y.] HAYNE,—the keen and scrutinizing [Robert G.] TURNBULL,—all gone down to the grave, and severed forever from any resumption of those noble labors,—of the earth, not earthy—which we have never so thoroughly or justly esteemed, as when it ceased to be in our power to command them. They have not left their superiors behind them,—and for their equals,—with a few splendid exceptions, it would be an equal wrong to the living and the dead, were we to name them in this category. But these writers, with LEGARE, HARPER, DRAYTON, DICKSON, WILLIAM ELLIOTT, and a few others—less shining, perhaps, but well deserving names,—formed the chief resource of the Southern Review in its palmiest days of honor. Half of this glorious constellation—the burning and the shining lights—as we have seen, are withdrawn; and it would not be an easy task to persuade the rest to resume their ministry at the shrine of letters. There is something mournfully repressive of the mental energies in the contemplation of a favorite altar overthrown; and even were this feeling wanting, it is difficult, with the approach of years, to reawaken the imagination to new efforts in fields which it has long abandoned. *The habit of literary composition is an essential element to all successful periodical writing.* You are requested to keep this sentence in memory. The fact which it conveys is of no small import to the discussion of this subject.

The names that I have given in the preceding paragraph may safely challenge comparison with any, not merely in the South, but throughout the nation. I utter this with no design of boast, but simply with the view to correct argument. I know that our kindred States of the South and Southwest are abundantly supplied with talent of the most promising description; but it may safely be assumed that none of this will ever achieve more thoroughly and nobly, than those who have gone before. The hope of success for your periodical must be built upon something more than an array of formidable names. Is it upon the increasing intellectual appetite among our people? I wish I could believe it. If this could be shown, my confidence would be as strong as your own, for it is this very appetite upon which all depends—which is first necessary to any calculation of success. But, I cannot help but doubt;— and when I sit down to write for a Southern periodical—which I do only as a professional duty—I do so under the enfeebling conviction that my labors and those of the editor are taken in vain;—that the work will be little read, seldom paid for, and will finally, and after no very long period of spasmodic struggle, sink into that gloomy receptacle of the "lost and abused things of earth," which, I suspect, by this time possesses its very sufficient share of Southern periodical literature. In the introductory paper of your first number, (for January last) which now lies before me, you have a reference to this invariable fate of your predecessors. You admit that, with one exception, "Signal failure has been the doom of every literary enterprise of a similar character which has originated in the South." I am only surprised that you should have contented yourself with a simple reference to this humiliating fact. To repeat a truism which is so shamefully obvious without seeking to ascertain the sources of the evil, and to provide a remedy in future, seems to me a very doubtful policy;—the timidity of which, will scarcely serve—as it should be served,—the cause you have undertaken, and will certainly avail but little in the prosecution of your own purposes. Chronic disorders are not to be treated after this fashion. The disease should be laid bare to examination, and then—and not until then—may we have some hope of a perfect or a partial cure. . . .

But, let me not be drawn aside from my object. An examination into the history of our periodical literature may be made at other stages in our progress. The constant influx into our country of foreign books and men, which, under any circumstances, might be supposed to have a disparaging effect upon our national character, and must inevitably contribute towards baffling us in its formation; is materially assisted in producing this effect, by the instability of our own people and their wandering habits. They are constantly in motion. The unwise measures of our statesmen, by which the public lands have been thrown into the market at almost nominal prices, and long before they were necessary to the growing wants of our people, were calculated to fix this injurious habit upon them. It led to the profligate and wasteful abuse of the lands already in cultivation, and, in the end, to their subsequent abandonment. The vast temptations to cupidity, and mercenary enterprise, held out by the immense, and but partially opened, tracts of plain and prairie in the west, produced a sleepless discontent with their existing condition, which is natural enough to a people, poor at first, successful only by the singular bounty of Providence, and deficient in that moral prudence which would have kept them so. This is more particularly the characteristic of the Southern people,—who are themselves so thoroughly aware of their own tending in this respect, that they prepare, negatively, for removal from their homesteads, long before they have actually resolved upon the measure. They expend only so much labor and money upon their plantations as is absolutely essential to the making of a crop. They build houses which scarcely shelter them from the inclemency of the weather—cultivate no luxuries; avoid all improvements; and neither seek to beautify, nor make of permanent value, those habitations, which they think it likely they will soon be persuaded to abandon. In this way, they deny themselves those thousand little additaments of comfort and indulgence, the possession of which, might produce in their bosoms a natural feeling of regret and reluctance at their loss; a reluctance which, if it could only be felt in sufficient force, would very soon provoke those efforts of energy and industry which would most assuredly enable them to remain and prosper. The literature of a nation is, in plain terms, the picture of its national character—the distinct embodiment of its moral aims; its political achievements; the taste which it loves to indulge, and the amusements which it enjoys. It is noble or base, according to the moral standards which graduate these exercises. The national character, it need scarcely be said, is the representation of its permanent and inflexible social and political condition. The literature of a nation which is without these distinctive characteristics, will be purely imitative; and the mind of a nation, the habits of which are unsettled, will, in degree, be as liable to the constant influence of foreign causes, as that of our North American Indians. The constant disruption of the bonds of society, which is produced by the wandering habits of its members, results invariably in moral loss to the whole. Principles become impaired in value, and standards of judgment fluctuate, with increasing insecurity, at each additional remove. —There is an utter surrender of all the moral drapery —the grace, the taste, and the elegances of social life. The Arts cannot bear travelling and shrink, in terror, from the uncleared, untrodden forests. Poetry must have, "audience fit though few," and Painting has only effected her achievements, at periods, and in places, where the domestic Gods have had their "pure rites undisturbed" through unbroken ages. All these must the habitual wanderer forfeit; all these moral sweets, and sacred influences; when, unsolicited by taste, undriven by necessity, he leaves the hearth stones of his fathers, for a lodge in the vast wilderness. But it is not these merely that he surrenders. He cuts off the inheritance and the hope of the future, in the most vital of all respects. His children are doomed to a condition of barbarian ignorance;—and, deprived of the customary attrition of equal and rival minds,—removed from the sleepless vigilance of those watchful laws of courtesy which society always imposes upon its members—the heads of families, thus wandering, yield themselves up to low indulgencies and follow false Gods into the wilderness:—too fortunate, if the new Deities be not quite as bestial as they are false!

PART V

THE EMIGRANTS AND MANIFEST DESTINY

The Jacksonian period was a time of great social and economic change; in this development the westward movement of population played a most important role. Captain Basil Hall describes the restless spirit, at times romantic and irrational, that motivated many of the emigrants. Charles Fenno Hoffman rode on a ship carrying emigrants from Cleveland to Detroit in 1834 and his description of this voyage shows the variegated human materials that composed the westward movement.

Among the emigrants to the Southwest was a Connecticut Yankee, Henry Watson, Jr., who joined the southwestward flow of population in 1830 to secure a job as a teacher. After teaching in Alabama he returned to New England and prepared to be a lawyer. He then came back to Alabama in 1834 and in letters to his father and friends in Connecticut he described the acquisitive but hospitable society of planters among whom he had settled. The letters published in this volume are from a rather extensive collection of manuscripts in the Duke University Library. In later letters, not published here, he described a popular hysteria of fear that he witnessed among the people of Alabama over a reported slave insurrection, and he strongly condemned the abolitionists for endangering the safety of the southern people.

Watson's letters are supplemented by the delightful, witty account by Joseph G. Baldwin of the speculative and expansive spirit of the Black Belt of Alabama during the 1830's when cotton planting and land speculation resulted in a great land boom that collapsed after the issuance of Jackson's Specie Circular of 1836 and the panic of 1837. Baldwin was a young Virginia lawyer who emigrated in 1836 first to Mississippi and then to Alabama, where he practiced law and engaged in politics as a member of the Whig Party, until the western fever seized him again in 1854 and he emigrated to California. He had a fine sense of humor and a good faculty of expression which he used in portraying the hectic spirit of speculation that he observed during the flush days of the 1830's in the Southwest.

The roads leading to the Southwest were often the scenes of slave gangs moving from the declining plantations of the tobacco country to the rich cotton lands of the Gulf area. Many of these emigrating Negroes were taken by their masters to start new plantations and these servants

233

seemed to have been relatively relaxed and happy. But there was, on the other hand, a large migration of unwilling slaves to the slave markets of Natchez and New Orleans who usually appeared sad and dejected or sullen and apathetic. One of these coffles is described by George Featherstonhaugh, whom we have previously met.

During the great emigration to the Southwest the aristocrats, men with money and slaves, were the exception; the poor people formed the great majority. Good examples of the well-to-do planter emigrating to the Southwest were Thomas Dabney of Elmington in Virginia, who established a flourishing cotton plantation in Mississippi, and the Lide family of Society Hill, South Carolina, who abandoned their old plantation to start afresh in the rich black belt of Alabama. An idyllic picture of a southern planter is portrayed in the reminiscences of Susan Dabney Smedes, Thomas Dabney's daughter, in Memorials of a Southern Planter (1887). A more realistic account of the hardships and the enterprising spirit of emigrant planters is found in the letters of the Lide family, as edited by Fletcher Green.

In the letters and travel accounts of the period are found vignettes of a few of the wealthy and of the numerous poor emigrants to the West. The letters of Mrs. Horace Holley, for example, give a view of the upper class of Texas and of the land speculators, for she came from a distinguished family, being the wife of the brilliant president of Transylvania University and the cousin of Stephen F. Austin, who gave her a league of land in Texas. She made five trips to Texas between 1831 and her death in 1846 and published a book on this new country. Frederick Law Olmsted, on the other hand, saw the crude side of Texan life in the 1850's especially in his picture of a pathetic group of emigrants, something like the Joads of Steinbeck's Grapes of Wrath, going to settle in the Land of Promise. Despite modern criticism of Frederick Jackson Turner's "safety-valve" thesis of the frontier, there is much evidence to show that the frontier did serve as a haven for many poor people, enabling them to escape the pressures of the older societies of the East—not so much for the workingmen in towns and cities, but for the yeoman farmers and their landless sons.

This folk movement to the West was a part of the insatiable demand of Americans for more territory in which to expand. Out of it arose the doctrine of Manifest Destiny—that it was the destiny of the United States to reach the Pacific, even to occupy the continent. The greatest expansionist president of the United States, with the possible exception of Jefferson, was James Knox Polk, a quiet man, not showy at all, but able, and determined to carry the American flag to the Pacific coast. In his frank and straightforward diary, he tells of the events and decisions that led to the war against Mexico and the acquisition of a vast

western territory. The most prominent orator of the expansionist move-
ment was Senator Edward Hannegan of Indiana, "a tall man of gladi-
atorial port . . . of courtly grace, passionate in his friendships and hates."
His vigorous and flamboyant personality is described by Lew Wallace,
author of the novel Ben Hur, *who was befriended by Hannegan as he*
struggled to establish a law practice in the little town of Covington,
Indiana, where Hannegan lived. Wallace is kind to his benefactor in
passing over Hannegan's great weakness, his addiction to strong drink,
which ruined his career. This masterful man stood at the forefront of
the politicians who spoke for the doctrine of Manifest Destiny, as his
speech on Oregon, here included, shows.

Bound for Detroit

Charles Fenno Hoffman

Detroit, Michigan, Nov. 25. I had just left the reading-room of the
Franklin Hotel, in Cleaveland, and was making myself at home for
the rest of the evening in my own neat chamber, when the sound of a
steamboat bell, about nine o'clock, gave note that one of these vessels,
which at this stormy season cannot navigate the lake with any regularity,
had touched at Cleaveland on her way to this place. No time was to be
lost; and huddling my clothes, &c. into my trunk as quickly as possible, I
jumped into a vehicle waiting at the tavern door, and in a few minutes
was upon the quay. Here I witnessed a scene of indescribable confusion.
The night was dark and somewhat gusty; and the boat and the wharf
were both crowded with boxes, bales, and the effects of emigrants, who
were screaming to each other in half as many languages as were spoken
at Babel. Lanterns were flashing to and fro along the docks, and hoarse
orders and countermands mingled with the harsh hissing of the steam
on every side. At length we pushed from the shore, and escaping in a
moment from the head of the mole, stood fairly out into the lake; while
the bright beacon of the Cleaveland lighthouse soon waned in the distance, and was at last lost entirely. I found myself, upon looking around,
on board of the fine steamboat New-York, captain Fisher, to whose
politeness I was much indebted for showing me about the boat before
turning in for the night. Taking a lantern in his hand, and tucking my
arm under his, he groped about among his motley ship's company like
Diogenes looking for an honest man.

Our course first led us through a group of emigrants collected around
a stove midships, where an English mother nursing her infant, a child
lying asleep upon a mastiff, and a long-bearded German smoking his
meerchaum on the top of a pile of candle-boxes, were the only complete

Charles Fenno Hoffman, *A Winter in the West* (New York, 1835), I, pp. 103-113.

figures I could make out from an indefinite number of heads, arms, and legs, lying about in the most whimsical confusion. Passing farther on, we came to two tolerable cabins on either side of the boat just forward of the wheels, both pretty well filled with emigrants, who were here more comfortably bestowed. We next passed the forward bar-room (there being another abaft for cabin passengers), and finally came to the bow, of which a horse and several dogs had already been the occupants for so many days—the New-York having been twice driven into port and delayed by stress of weather—that it might have been mistaken for either stable or kennel. A noble English blood-hound, the second dog only of that rare breed that I have ever seen, here attracted my attention, and delayed me until I made his acquaintance; which was but a moment, however, for every dog of a generous strain can tell instinctively when a friend of his kind approaches him.

Among others of the canine crew, too, there was a fine spaniel, whose deplorable fate subsequently I may as well mention here as elsewhere. The master of poor Dash, it seems, went ashore during the night at Huron, where the boat put in to land way-passengers; and the animal, springing eagerly along a plank at his call, was kicked from his narrow foothold by some brute of a fellow into the lake. The night was dark, and the shadow of the high wharf shut out the few lights on shore from the view of the poor animal, while those on board of the boat led him away from the land. He swam after us, yelling most piteously, until his suffocating cries were lost in the freshening sea; which probably the next morning tossed him a carrion on the shore. Had I witnessed the act of throwing him overboard, I could scarcely have restrained myself from pitching the dastardly perpetrator of the cruelty after the victim of his brutality; for if there be one trait in men which awakens in me indignation amounting almost to loathing of my kind, it is to see human beings treating those parts of the animal creation beneath them as if this earth was meant for none of God's creatures but man.

But to return to our travels through this floating castle. We next ascended a steep stairway to the upper deck of all, and I here spent some moments rather amusingly in surveying the furniture of the emigrants with which it was crowded. They differed according to the origin of their owner. The effects of the Yankee were generally limited to a Dearborn wagon, a feather bed, a saddle and bridle, and some knick-knack in the way of a machine for shelling corn, hatchelling flax, or, for aught I know, manufacturing wooden nutmegs for family use. Those of the Englishman are far more numerous; for John Bull, when he wanders from home, would not only, like the roving Trojan, carry his household goods with him into strange lands, but even the fast anchored isle itself, could he but cut it from its moorings. Whenever, therefore, you see an antique-fashioned looking-glass, a decrepit bureau, and some tenderly-preserved old china, you will probably, upon looking further, have the whole housekeeping array of an honest Briton exposed to your view.

But still farther do the Swiss and Germans carry their love of family relics. Mark that quaint looking wagon which lumbers up a dozen square feet of the deck: you may see a portrait of it among the illuminated letters of a vellum-bound edition of Virgil's Bucolics. It was taken from an Helvetian ancestor that transported Cæsar's baggage into winter quarters. It might be worth something in a museum, but it has cost five times its value in freight to transport it over the Atlantic. What an indignity it is to overwhelm the triumphal chariot with the beds and ploughs, shovels, saddles, and sideboards, chairs, clocks, and carpets that fill its interior, and to hang those rusty pots and kettles, bakepans, fryingpans, and saucepans, iron candlesticks, old horse-shoes, and broken tobacco-pipes, like trophies of conquest over Time, along its racked and wheezing sides. That short man yonder, with square shoulders and a crooked pipe in his mouth, is the owner: he with the woollen cap, that is just raising his blue cotton frock to thrust his hand into the fob of his sherrivalleys. That man had probably not the slightest idea of the kind of country he was coming to: his eyes are but now just opening to his new condition; nor will he sacrifice a particle of his useless and expensive trumpery until they are completely open. That man has not yet a thought in common with the people of his new abode around him. He looks, indeed, as if he came from another planet. Visit him on his thriving farm ten years hence, and, except in the single point of language, you will find him (unless perchance he has settled among a nest of his countrymen) at home among his neighbours, and happily conforming to their usages; while that clean looking Englishman next to him will still be a stranger in the land.

I subsequently looked into the different cabins and compartments of the boat not yet visited, and had reason to be gratified with the appearance of all; though the steamboat Michigan, which I have since visited at the docks here, puts me completely out of conceit of every part of the New-York, except her captain. The Michigan, machinery and all, was built at Detroit; and, without entering into a minute description of it, I may say that, fine as our Atlantic boats are, I do not recollect any on the Atlantic waters, for strength and beauty united, equal to this. A great mistake, however, I think, exists here in building the boats for these waters with cabins on deck, like the river boats. In consequence of such a large part of the hull being above water, they are rendered dangerous during the tremendous gales which sweep Lake Erie, and are often compelled to make a port of safety several times during a passage. The English steamers which ply between Dover and Calais are built like other sea vessels; and having their machinery below, can consequently keep on their course in a sea where one of ours would live but a few minutes. I was fortunate, considering the stormy season of the year, in having a tolerably smooth passage across the lake; there being but few persons seasick on board of the boat, and I happily not included in the number. But it must be very unpleasant, during a heavy blow, to be tossed on the short cobble sea which the light fresh water of these lakes always break into beneath the wind. . . .

It was during a shower, shortly after noon, when some low wooded islands on the American side of the lake, with a tall flag-staff peering above the haze from the little town of Amherstburg on the British shore, indicated that we had entered the mouth of the Detroit River. The wind, which was now beginning to rise into a threatening tempest, compelled us to hug the Canadian shore so closely, that the red coated sentinel pacing along the barracks above Fort Malden was plainly seen from the boat. The river soon after narrows sufficiently for one to mark with ease the general appearance of its banks, and the different settlements upon their course. Their appearance must be pretty in summer, when fields and woods show to the most advantage; but now, though slightly undulating, with a sudden rise from the river of some fifty or sixty feet, the adjacent country is too low to be strikingly beautiful. Those, however, who admire the Delaware below Trenton, if they can dispense with the handsome seats which ornament its not very clear waters, may find a charm in the gentle banks and transparent tide of the Detroit River.

The City of Detroit itself stands upon an elevated piece of table land, extending probably for some twenty miles back from the river, and being perfectly unbroken for at least two miles along its margin. Beneath the bluff—for the plain is so high as almost to deserve the name—is a narrow bustling street of about half a mile in length, with the wharfs just beyond it; and fifty yards inboard runs a spacious street called Jefferson Avenue, parallel with the lower street and the river; the chief part of the town extends for a mile or two along the latter. The dwelling houses are generally of wood; but there are a great many stores now building, or already erected, of brick, with stone basements. The brick is generally of an indifferent quality; but the stone, which is brought from Cleaveland, Ohio, is a remarkably fine material for building purposes. It is a kind of yellow freestone, which is easily worked when first taken from the quarry, and hardens subsequently upon exposure to the air. There are at this moment many four-story stores erecting, as well as other substantial buildings, which speak for the flourishing condition of the place.

The want of mechanics is so great, however, that it is difficult as yet to carry on these operations upon the scale common in our Atlantic cities; although the demand for houses in Detroit, it is said, would fully warrant similar outlays of capital. The public buildings are the territorial council-house, situated upon an open piece of ground, designated on an engraved plan of the city as The Campus Martius; a court-house, academy, and two banks. There are also five churches,—a Catholic, an Episcopal, a Presbyterian, Baptist, and Methodist. The Catholic congregation is the largest; their stone church, after remaining several years in an unfinished state, is soon, it is said, to be completed with funds derived from Rome; it will make an imposing appearance when finished. The population of Detroit is, I believe, between three and four thousand; it increases so rapidly, however, that it is difficult to form an estimate. The historical associations, the safety and commodiousness of the harbour, with its extensive inland commercial advantages, must ever constitute this one of the most interesting and important points in the Union, although other causes may combine to make newer places in the territory equally as flourishing as Detroit.

The appearance of the place is anything but what you would expect from a town founded in the same year with Philadelphia. The ancient houses, which formerly stood upon streets hardly ten feet wide, were all swept away in the great fire twenty years since; and the new white dwellings, standing upon broad avenues of twenty-five yards, make the town look like a place of yesterday.

On the Way to Florida

Basil Hall

... During the morning's drive, we overtook several bodies of migrants—if there be such a word—farmers errant, proceeding with all their worldly goods, according to the usual tide of these matters in this country, from East to West, or rather, to be quite correct, from North-east to South-west—from Virginia and Maryland to Florida, Georgia, and Alabama.

The first party consisted of a planter and his wife, accompanied by his brother-in-law and family, a whole troop of their children—and some forty or fifty slaves of all ages and sizes. The wanderers were encamped near a creek, as it is called in America, or what we should term a brook, or burn, on the grassy banks of which they were scattered, over a space of several hundred yards, on both sides of the road, under the shade of a grove of sycamore-trees. Their travelling equipage consisted of three waggons, and one open carriage, under the lee of which some of the party were busy cooking the dinner when we came up.

We stopped, of course, and conversed for some time with the principal person, who was on his way, he said, to Florida with his whole establishment. He had left a good property, he told us, farther to the north, near Cheraw, on the banks of the Great Pedee River in South Carolina; but though he had no distinct idea where he should settle, he seemed quite sure that he could not possibly go wrong in so fertile and unoccupied a country. Our new acquaintance was a tall, stout, cheerful-looking man, with a cast of enterprise and determination about him, which I daresay have enabled him, long ere this time, to convert a considerable portion of the useless forest into rich and cultivated ground.

While we were talking with this hardy pioneer of the wilderness—as these frontier settlers are well called in America—our little girl and her maid were fully occupied in their own way at the opposite window of

Basil Hall, *Travels in North America in the Years 1827-28* (Edinburgh, 1829), pp. 126-133.

the carriage. We had drawn up just abreast of a group of slaves, consisting of two or three women with six or eight little children playing about them, none of whom—I mean the infantry—were much encumbered with clothing, but who did not on that account excite less of the child's admiration. She literally screamed with delight, but would not be satisfied till she got hold of a large sponge-cake we had brought with us, as part of our stores, from Fayetteville. Having broken it into bits, she distributed the cake amongst the shining little blackies, to the unspeakable satisfaction of the mothers, who sat on the bank smiling with as much freedom of soul as if they had been resting by the side of some far away African stream, the home of their ancestors, which—according to their simple belief—will still be their residence, when death shall step in to restore the long-lost liberty of their race.

The second party of emigrants, who had already taken their dinner, were on the march. It was smaller than the other, and did not consist of above thirty persons in all, of whom five-and-twenty at least were slaves. The women and children were stowed away in waggons, moving slowly up a steep sandy hill; but the curtains being let down, we could see nothing of them, except an occasional glance of an eye, or a row of teeth as white as snow. In the rear of all came a light, covered vehicle, with the master and mistress of the party. Along the roadside, scattered at intervals, we observed the male slaves trudging in front. At the top of all, against the sky line, two men walked together, apparently hand in hand, pacing along very sociably. There was something, however, in their attitude, which seemed unusual and constrained. When we came nearer, accordingly, we discovered that this couple were bolted together by a strong, short chain or bar, riveted to broad iron clasps, secured in like manner, round the wrists.

"What have you been doing, my boys," said our coachman, in passing, "to entitle you to these ruffles?"

"Oh, sir," cried one of them, quite gaily, "they are the best things in the world to travel with."

The other man said nothing. I stopped the carriage, and asked one of the slave drivers why these men were chained, and how they came to take the matter so differently. The answer explained the mystery. One of the men, it appeared, was married, but his wife belonged to a neighbouring planter, not to his master. When the general move was made, the proprietor of the female not choosing to part with her, she was necessarily left behind. The wretched husband was therefore shackled to a young unmarried man, who, having no such tie to draw him back, might be more safely trusted on the journey.

We arrived in the evening at Columbia, the seat of the government of South Carolina. In the course of next morning, while we were sitting

in the public parlour, at the hotel, a party came in, which we soon recognised as belonging to one of the groups of wanderers we had overtaken the day before. While I was hesitating whether or not I might take
the liberty of introducing myself,—for I was curious to know their history,—the door opened, and a gentleman came forward who claimed the
chief of the party for his brother. After shaking hands very cordially,
the visitor, who was evidently a resident of the city, stepped back, took
a seat a little way off, as if to command a better view of the whole party,
looked his relative in the face, and nodding his head slowly for some
time, broke out thus—"Well! this is the strangest resolution for a man
of your years to take into his head! Why, where are you going?"

"I am going to Florida, to be sure."

"To Florida!" cried the other; "what on earth takes you there?"

"Oh," said the migrant, "it is the finest country in the world—a delightful climate—rich soil—plenty of room."

"Have you been there?" asked his brother.

"No, not yet," said the wanderer; "but I know all about it."

"Know all about it! why, you'll be drowned in some creek before you
get there."

"No, I shan't, though," retorted the traveller, taking the words in their
literal sense; "there is no fear of that, as all the water-courses are bridged."

"Well, well," cried the brother, laughing, "you must have your own
way, I suppose. But, pray tell me, what have you done with your estate
in Maryland, on which you were fixed when I last got tidings of you—
about four years ago, I think it was?"

"I've sold that property."

"What, all?"

"Yes, all, every inch of it, and I have brought away every movable
thing with me. Here we are, you see—my wife, my son there, and my
daughter—all my slaves, too, my furniture, horses, and so forth."

"And now, pray, answer me this question—were you not well off where
you were located before—had you not plenty of good land?"

"Oh yes, plenty."

"Did you, in fact," continued his cross-questioner,—"did you want for
any thing under the sun?"

"I can't say I did."

"What, then, possesses you to go seeking for a fresh place in such a
country as Florida, where you must be content to take up your quarters
amongst tadpoles and mosquitoes?"

While the hardy rover was puzzling himself in search of a reasonable
answer, his wife took up the discourse, and, half in joke, half in earnest,
said, "It is all for the mere love of moving. We have been doing so all
our lives—just moving from place to place—never resting—as soon as

ever we get comfortably settled, then it is time to be off to something new."

"Yes, I know my brother's rambling disposition well; but why don't you prevent him, madam?"

"Ah, my dear sir," sighed the lady, "you don't know what it is to be married to a gadding husband."

At this moment I caught my own wife's eye, and the lady who had spoken seeing us smile, fancied we were agreeing with her, and being well pleased with our sympathy, said no more.

But the inexorable interrogator went on in these words,—"Well, well, after all, you understand your own matters best, I suppose; but I should like to know what sort of a scrape you will be in, if you find Florida sickly, and bad in other respects?"

"Oh, no," cried the pioneer of the wilderness, "not a bit of a scrape."

"What will you do, then?"

"Why, move along westward, to be sure;—and if I don't find any thing to suit me by the way, in the State of Georgia or Alabama, I can easily put my whole establishment, wife and children, furniture, slaves, and other articles, on board of a steam-boat, and proceed up the Mississippi."

"And where will you land?"

"Indeed, I do not know, and, for that matter, I don't much care. It is a wide, empty country, with a soil that yields such noble crops, that any man is sure to succeed, go where he will."

"Ay! ay! I see it's no use talking. —However, you must come with me, you and all your family, and pass some time with me at my house— for we shall never meet again, I see that,—and we have many things to talk over, upon which, I trust, we shall agree better than upon these points."

But the wanderer said he could not stop; a night's delay would lose him a hundred dollars, besides the time, neither of which he could spare. So they separated as they had met.

A New England Lawyer in Alabama

Henry Watson, Jr.

Greensborough, Ala., Feb. 10, 1834

Dear Father [at East Windsor, Conn.],

. . . This whole state seems to be in a ferment. Jackson is becoming rapidly unpopular here and his partizans are going over to Clay. The people are loud in their clamors against his usurpation of power in the case of the removal of the deposits, and base their whole opposition nominally upon this ground. I have no doubt it goes a great way for they are strongly imbued with thorough-going democratic notions but I strongly suspect that the evil lies mainly in the purse. Cotton bore a high price at the early part of the season, most of the merchants made advances to a greater or less extent and as it has now fallen nearly one half they feel the loss. The planters in anticipation of high prices have run greatly in debt for negroes and lands and they too feel it in their purses. In this distress they all, both high and low, run to the Banks. The Banks thus flooded with applications can only discount to the accomodation of a few. The remainder go home growling and scolding at the General for the removal of the deposits, firmly believing this to be the origin of their distress and a sufficient cause for their disappointment at Bank and for all their suffering. Those who know & feel nothing of the matter join in with the general voice. I have not seen a man that has spoken of the subject that has not come out against the president and professedly for his late conduct. I only know from hearsay that they at the same time become supporters of Mr. Clay. —The General will lose this state. It still has no reference to the question of nullification or the Creek Controversy, at least they will not admit that it has. That matter is all forgotten. —The state is almost unanimously for the Union. Many however are secretly with the Governor [Gayle] who would come

Henry Watson, Jr., Papers. Mss. in the Duke University Library.

out were they certain of a majority. In *this* neighborhood those who avow their sentiments are all either lately from S. Carolina or are the Randolph's & Bolling's connexion of Lieut. Randolph of Virginia, who are excited by family feelings. —The next question of importance here is that regarding the public lands. The people cannot be satisfied till they get them for nothing or what is next to nothing. They did not succeed in getting a Penitentiary at the last session of the Legislature, but the question is referred to the people who will vote upon it in August next. With the exception of the Penal Law, their system here is an excellent one, even preferable to our own which might be improved by adopting some of its provisions. I bought the statutes and the Reports of the [?] at Tuscaloosa and am now busying myself upon the first. I was struck with a clause that I came across today. Before Physicians can be allowed to practice in the state it is necessary that they should be examined and licensed by a Board appointed for the purpose by the Legislature; at the end of the whole it is provided that this act should not be construed to extend to those practicing after the Thompsonian or Botanical System; to which is appended a still further proviso that if one of these practisers shall bleed or blister of spanish flies or administer calomel or any [mercurial] preparation, antimony, arsenic, tartar emetic, opium or laudanum they shall be liable to its penalties, this making these articles the criterion as if they of course were rank poisons while vegetably may be tampered with at pleasure with impunity."

Greensborough, Ala., Feb. 12, 1834

Dear Julius [A. Reed at New Haven, Conn.],

. . . The villages from which I was to choose [to locate as a lawyer], unless I saw good reason to change my destination, were Tuscaloosa, Erie, Greensboro, Clinton, Springfield or Demopolis. On my arrival I at once concluded upon either Clinton or Greensborough and such were the inducements held out by both that I was in some hesitation—Some friends wished me to go to Clinton, that is take the fork [between the two rivers], for this is its main village and there is no lawyer in that whole section of the country. There was but one thing to prevent my fixing upon that as a place of residence, which was that it is too much in the woods. Clinton itself has but three stores, two taverns, a saw mill, blacksmith's and druggist's shop, though the Fork itself polls about 950 votes, a little over half of the whole county—but they are all of the lowest cast, much below the common population, and scattered through the woods. In *this* village things wear a different aspect. The village itself polls 400 votes, and its population embraces many well informed, talented and highly respectable men. The merchants are very respectable. The country about is now settled by emigrants from Virginia and the

Carolinas who have come out with large bodies of negroes and bought lands of the original settlers at an advanced price, these old settlers having gone to the fork or to the new country in the Choctaw Nation. They are some of the nobility of the old states. There are many of the Randolph Family, the Meades, the Taylors, the Bollings, etc., etc. The county is thus filled with much more intelligence than you would have expected. The lands are rich and comparatively thicky settled. A Rail Road is about to be made to Erie on the Warrior [River] and another to Prairie Bluff on the Alabama river which will tend much to the growth of the village and of the whole country—Greensboro is a place of a great deal of Business; though the buildings are poor for a place of its size, the streets have all the appearance of those of a city. I went to Tuscaloosa and was examined in the Supreme Court and got a license to practice, so that I am now a regular *Alabama* lawyer also. I find it as yet impossible to get board in a private family and so am obliged again to eat at a tavern. As for getting a private room in a house it was impossible and I spent one most uncomfortable week sleeping in the loft of the tavern, and such places as these lofts are you can easily imagine. The public houses (three in number) are all of logs—. There had been but two lawyers in the place and one died before I got here—

Greensborough, March 23, 1834

Dear Brother [Theodore Watson],

. . . I wish you to ask Pa to subscribe for the Times to be sent to the "Green County Sentinel"—Mr. Frederick Peck, of this place, of whom I think I have before spoken, a fine, good hearted man, has gone to N. Y. and has taken a daughter with him. He will leave her at school. Three other merchants of this place will soon start for N. York. . . .

You know our N. England way of clearing land. I will now endeavor to give you some idea of the way it is done here. If prairie, ploughing only is necessary [in the black belt]. If wooded, they go over the field in February, cutting down all the small trees and saplings, cut oaks and cedars enough to make rails to fence the field & then girdle all the large trees. The rails are split up for Virginia fences. After the field is thus all girdled & cut, the *negroes of the neighborhood* collect & in a body proceed to rol the logs & buts which were cut or had fallen and put them into piles at convenient distances. This is called "log rolling," a term so common in politics. They are then burnt up with the brush. The field is then ready for ploughing & the corn or cotton is planted at once. The [standing] trees generally put out their leaves, but die soon after, so that they give little or no shade. In about two years nothing is left of them but the strait trunk & they some of them stand as long as seven years. The trees of the ridges are the white oak, pine, gum tree—of the prairies, the white & black oak, the gum tree, the poplar, the cedar, but no pine. There is also the chesnut, the butternut or Black Walnut, and the Hickory; also the Pecan in great abundance. —There is a great demand for grass here, and nothing but wire grass can be found to survive the summers. The game is wild turkies, deer, quails & squirrels. Some few bear, wolves, foxes, and catamounts are sometimes found. Almost the only way of getting about is upon horseback, upon a trotting horse. I have learnt to ride this gait, going about four miles an hour. Nobody goes faster. The horses are generally poor and they depend wholly upon Tennessee for them and raise none. There is no course in the neighborhood & no attention is paid to their racing qualities. —We have another *rarity*, clock and Book pedlars, who ransack the whole country. Wooden clocks, costing about five dollars sell for 35 or 40. Pa asks some questions about Tuscaloosa. Land is falling very fast, which can be no evidence of its prosperity. It is a pleasant place, but has not grown since my former visit. Dr. [Alva] Woods [of Conneticut] at the College [University of Alabama, founded 1831] is unpopular and unless he manages with more discretion can never succeed; it is rather at a low ebb. At the last session of the legislature, he spent all his time in town electioneering with the members. The legislature was not in session when I was there. They are a strange set of beings I expect, but not worse than our Con. Members.

Greensborough, July 23, 1834

Dear Julius,

Your letter was received last week and I am much obliged to you for the information upon the subject of the Cholera. I believe it to be the only treatment in the case which can be of any avail. Yet the physicians say they should not much fear it, taken in season the cases are easily managed. "And how would you treat them?" "Oh give large doses of calomel immediately and frequently, and don't spare the calomel" is the reply. This is their mode of treatment. But we have had none of it yet. Though it rages in New Orleans, it is very doubtful whether it has been in Mobile. You ask if I expect Slavery to be perpetuated. I answer that I do not. The slave population increases so fast that this is impossible, and I wish some way might be devised which would free us from them. But I can imagine no feasible one.

Politics are running high here. The candidates are about the county electioneering. The election is close at hand. There are seven candidates, and we are entitled to three representatives. They are endeavoring to make it Jacksonianism or Nullification. And the advocates of both will allow of no neutrality but claim as Jackson whatever is not for nullification, and so on the other side. This causes a total confusion and the

Union opposition men hardly know what to do, or where to find themselves. The election will not therefore give a true showing of the state of parties; many an opposition man will vote for Jackson in preference to Nullification, while many, holding that nullification has *now* no existence, except in the Brains of a few demagogues, and not likely to be again soon applied to practice, while the usurpations of the Executive are *sensibly* felt will take the opposite course. It seems strange to me that so numerous a class as the Union opposition men should have allowed matters to be placed as they now stand. I feel somewhat interested, but remain a mere "looker on in Venice." After going to meetings and barbecues all over the country, they finally met (in a body, as usual) at this place on Monday and made stump speeches, in regular, and, in irregular order, making known their own sentiments, and endeavoring to show to a disadvantage the sentiments and conduct of their opponents. A pretty scene to exhibit to the people in a land where all claim to be sages & politicians. One thing pleases me, that with the whole of it, the open & the underhand attempts to gain votes, no one of the candidates *treats*, and this too without concert on their part. The fashion is getting out of date. The contest among them is warm and is getting to be personal, which they *say* has never been the case before in the country— But these "say so's" are not entitled to much credit, perhaps in any community, and least of all in a lying one. Every one of the candidates is making great calculations from the *promises* which have been made to them. But the people, in a state where *universal* suffrage is allowed, are proverbially fickle. In Con. they are fickle *enough*.

Flush Times in Alabama and Mississippi

Joseph G. Baldwin

This country was just settling up. Marvellous accounts had gone forth of the fertility of its virgin lands; and the productions of the soil were commanding a price remunerating to slave labor as it had never been remunerated before. Emigrants came flocking in from all quarters of the Union, especially from the slaveholding States. The new country seemed to be a reservoir, and every road leading to it a vagrant stream of enterprise and adventure. Money, or what passed for money, was the only cheap thing to be had. Every cross-road and every avocation presented an opening,—through which a fortune was seen by the adventurer in near perspective. Credit was a thing of course. To refuse it—if the thing was ever done—were an insult for which a bowie-knife were not a too summary or exemplary a means of redress. The State banks were issuing their bills by the sheet, like a patent steam printing-press *its* issues; and no other showing was asked of the applicant for the loan than an authentication of his great distress for money. Finance, even in its most exclusive quarter, had thus already got, in this wonderful revolution, to work upon the principles of the charity hospital. If an overseer grew tired of supervising a plantation and felt a call to the mercantile life, even if he omitted the compendious method of buying out a merchant wholesale, stock, house and good will, and laying down, at once, his bull-whip for the yard-stick—all he had to do was to go on to New-York, and present himself in Pearl-street with a letter avouching his citizenship, and a clean shirt, and he was regularly given a through ticket to speedy bankruptcy.

Under this stimulating process prices rose like smoke. Lots in obscure villages were held at city prices; lands, bought at the minimum cost of

Joseph G. Baldwin, *The Flush Times in Alabama and Mississippi* (San Francisco, 1853), pp. 82-93.

government, were sold at from thirty to forty dollars per acre, and considered dirt cheap at that. In short, the country had got to be a full ante-type of California, in all except the gold. Society was wholly unorganized: there was no restraining public opinion: the law was well-nigh powerless—and religion scarcely was heard of except as furnishing the oaths and *technics* of profanity. The world saw a fair experiment of what it would have been, if the fiat had never been pronounced which decreed subsistence as the price of labor.

Money, got without work, by those unaccustomed to it, turned the heads of its possessors, and they spent it with a recklessness like that with which they gained it. The pursuits of industry neglected, riot and coarse debauchery filled up the vacant hours. "Where the carcass is, there will the eagles be gathered together"; and the eagles that flocked to the Southwest, were of the same sort as the *black eagles* the Duke of Saxe-Weimar saw on his celebrated journey to the Natural Bridge. "The cankers of a long peace and a calm world"—there were no Mexican wars and filibuster expeditions in those days—gathered in the villages and cities by scores.

Even the little boys caught the taint of the general infection of morals; and I knew one of them—Jim Ellett by name—to give a man ten dollars to hold him up to bet at the table of a faro-bank. James was a fast youth; and I sincerely hope he may not fulfil his early promise, and some day be *assisted up still higher*.

The groceries—*vulgice*—doggeries, were in full blast in those days, no village having less than a half-dozen all busy all the time: gaming and horse-racing were polite and well patronized amusements. I knew a Judge to adjourn two courts (or court twice) to attend a horse-race, at which he officiated judicially and ministerially, and with more appropriateness than in the judicial chair. Occasionally the scene was diversified by a murder or two, which though perpetrated from behind a corner, or behind the back of the deceased, whenever the accused *chose* to stand his trial, was always found to have been committed in self-defence, securing the homicide an honorable acquittal *at the hands of his peers*.

The old rules of business and the calculations of prudence were alike disregarded, and profligacy, in all the departments of the *crimen falsi*, held riotous carnival. Larceny grew not only respectable, but genteel, and ruffled it in all the pomp of purple and fine linen. Swindling was raised to the dignity of the fine arts. Felony came forth from its covert, put on more seemly habiliments, and took its seat with unabashed front in the upper places of the synagogue. Before the first circles of the patrons of this brilliant and dashing villainy, Blunt Honesty felt as abashed as poor Halbert Glendinning by the courtly refinement and supercilious airs of Sir Percie Shafton.

Public office represented, by its incumbents, the state of public morals with some approach to accuracy. Out of sixty-six receivers of public money in the new States, sixty-two were discovered to be defaulters; and the agent, sent to look into the affairs of a peccant office-holder in the South-West, reported him *minus* some tens of thousands, but advised the government to retain him, for a reason one of Æsop's fables illustrates: the agent ingeniously surmising that the appointee succeeding would do his stealing without any regard to the proficiency already made by his predecessor; while the present incumbent would probably consider, in mercy to the treasury, that he *had* done *something* of the pious duty of providing for his household.

There was no petit larceny: there was all the difference between stealing by the small and the "operations" manipulated, that there is between a single assassination and an hundred thousand men killed in an opium war. The placeman robbed with the gorgeous magnificence of a Governor-General of Bengal.

The man of straw, not worth the buttons on his shirt, with a sublime audacity, bought lands and negroes, and provided times and terms of payment which a Wall-street capitalist would have to re-cast his arrangements to meet.

Oh, Paul Clifford and Augustus Tomlinson, philosophers of the road, practical and theoretical! if ye had lived to see those times, how great an improvement on your ruder scheme of distribution would these gentle arts have seemed; arts whereby, without risk, or loss of character, or the vulgar barbarism of personal violence, the same beneficial results flowed with no greater injury to the superstitions of moral education!

With the change of times and the imagination of wealth easily acquired came a change in the thoughts and habits of the people. "Old times were changed—old manners gone." Visions of affluence, such as crowded Dr. Samuel Johnson's mind, when advertising a sale of Thrale's Brewery, and casting a soft sheep's eye towards Thrale's widow, thronged upon the popular fancy. Avarice and hope joined partnership. It was strange how the reptile arts of humanity, as at a faro table, warmed into life beneath their heat. The *cacoethes accrescendi* became epidemic. It seized upon the universal community. The pulpits even were not safe from its insidious invasion. What men anxiously desire they willingly believe; and all believed a good time was coming—nay, had come.

"Commerce was king"—and Rags, Tag and Bobtail his cabinet council. Rags was treasurer. Banks, chartered on a specie basis, did a very flourishing business on the promissory notes of the individual stockholders ingeniously substituted in lieu of cash. They issued ten for one, the *one* being fictitious. They generously loaned all the directors could not use themselves, and were not choice whether Bardolph was the endorser for

Falstaff, or Falstaff borrowed on his own proper credit, or the funds advanced him by Shallow. The stampede towards the golden temple became general: the delusion prevailed far and wide that this thing was not a burlesque on commerce and finance. Even the directors of the banks began to have their doubts whether the intended swindle was not a failure. Like Lord Clive, when reproached for extortion to the extent of some millions in Bengal, they exclaimed, after the bubble burst, "When they thought of what they had got, and what they might have got, they were astounded at their own moderation."

The old capitalists for a while stood out. With the Tory conservatism of cash in hand, worked for, they couldn't reconcile their old notions to the new regime. They looked for the thing's ending, and *then* their time. But the stampede still kept on. Paper fortunes still multiplied—houses and lands changed hands—real estate see-sawed up as morals went down on the other end of the plank—men of straw, corpulent with bank bills, strutted past them on 'Change. They began, too, to think there might be something in this new thing. Peeping cautiously, like hedge-hogs out of their holes, they saw the stream of wealth and adventurers passing by—then, looking carefully around, they inched themselves half way out—then, sallying forth and snatching up a morsel, ran back, until, at last, grown more bold, *they* ran out too with their hoarded store, in full chase with the other unclean beasts of adventure. They never got back again. Jonah's gourd withered one night, and next morning the vermin that had nestled under its broad shade were left unprotected, a prey to the swift retribution that came upon them. They were left naked, or only clothed themselves with cursing (the Specie Circular on the United States Bank) as with a garment. To drop the figure: Shylock himself couldn't live in those times, so reversed was every thing. Shaving paper and loaning money at a usury of fifty per cent, was for the first time since the Jews left Jerusalem, a breaking business to the operator.

The condition of society may be imagined:—vulgarity—ignorance— fussy and arrogant pretension—unmitigated rowdyism—bullying inso- lence, if they did not rule the house *seemed* to wield unchecked domin- ion. The workings of these choice spirits were patent upon the face of society; and the modest, unobtrusive, retiring men of worth and charac- ter (for there were many, perhaps a large majority of such) were almost lost sight of in the hurly-burly of those strange and shifting scenes.

Even in the professions were the same characteristics visible. Men dropped down into their places as from the clouds. Nobody knew who or what they were, except as they claimed, or as a surface view of their characters indicated. Instead of taking to the highway and magnani- mously calling upon the wayfarer to stand and deliver, or to the fashion- able larceny of credit without prospect or design of paying, some unscrupulous horse-doctor would set up his sign as "Physician and Surgeon," and draw his lancet on you, or fire at random a box of his pills into your bowels, with a vague chance of hitting some disease unknown to him, but with a better prospect of killing the patient, whom or whose administrator he charged some ten dollars a trial for his marksmanship.

A superannuated justice or constable in one of the old States was metamorphosed into a lawyer; and though he knew not the distinction between a *fee tail* and a *female*, would undertake to construe, off-hand, a will involving all the subtleties of *uses and trusts*.

But this state of things could not last for ever: society cannot always stand on its head with its heels in the air.

The Jupiter Tonans of the White House saw the monster of a free credit prowling about like a beast of apocalyptic vision, and marked him for his prey. Gathering all his bolts in his sinewy grasp, and standing back on his heels, and waving his wiry arm, he let them all fly, hard and swift upon all the hydra's heads. Then came a crash, as "if the ribs of nature broke," and a scattering, like the bursting of a thousand magazines, and a smell of brimstone, as if Pandemonium had opened a window next to earth for ventilation,—and all was silent. The beast never stirred in his tracks. To get down from the clouds to level ground, the Specie Circular was issued without warning, and the splendid lie of a false credit burst into fragments. It came in the midst of the dance and the frolic—as Tam O'Shanter came to disturb the infernal glee of the warlocks, and to disperse the rioters. Its effect was like that of a general creditor's bill in the chancery court, and a marshalling of all the assets of the trades-people. Gen. Jackson was no fairy; but he did some very pretty fairy work, in converting the bank bills back again into rags and oak-leaves. Men worth a million were insolvent for two millions: promising young cities marched back again into the wilderness. The ambitious town plat was re-annexed to the plantation, like a country girl taken home from the city. The frolic was ended, and what headaches, and feverish limbs the next morning! The retreat from Moscow was performed over again, and "Devil take the hindmost" was the tune to which the soldiers of fortune marched. The only question was as to the means of escape, and the nearest and best route to Texas. The sheriff was as busy as a militia adjutant on review day; and the lawyers were mere wreckers, earning salvage. Where are ye now my ruffling gallants? Where now the braw cloths and watch chains and rings and fine horses? Alas! for ye—they are glimmering among the things that were—the wonder of an hour! They live only in memory, as unsubstantial as the promissory notes ye gave for them. When it came to be tested, the whole matter was found to be hollow and fallacious. Like a sum ciphered out through a long column, the first figure an error, the whole, and all the parts were wrong, throughout the entire calculation.

Such is a charcoal sketch of the interesting region—now inferior to none in resources, and the character of its population—during the FLUSH TIMES; a period constituting an episode in the commercial history of the world—the reign of humbug, and wholesale insanity, just overthrown in time to save the whole country from ruin. But while it lasted, many of our countrymen came into the South-West in time to get "a benefit." The *auri sacra fames* is a catching disease. Many Virginians had lived too fast for their fortunes, and naturally desired to recuperate: many others, with a competency, longed for wealth; and others again, with wealth, yearned—the common frailty—for still more. Perhaps some friend or relative, who had come out, wrote back flattering accounts of the El Dorado, and fired with dissatisfaction those who were doing well enough at home, by the report of his real or imagined success; for who that ever moved off, was not "doing well" in the new country, himself or friends being chroniclers?

Superior to many of the settlers in elegance of manners and general intelligence, it was the weakness of the Virginian to imagine he was superior too in the essential art of being able to hold his hand and make his way in a new country, and especially *such* a country, and at *such* a time. What a mistake that was! The times were out of joint. It was hard to say whether it were more dangerous to stand still or to move. If the emigrant stood still, he was consumed, by no slow degrees, by expenses: if he moved, ten to one he went off in a galloping consumption, by a ruinous investment. Expenses then—necessary articles about three times as high, and extra articles still more extra-priced—were a different thing in the new country from what they were in the old. In the old country, a jolly Virginian, starting the business of free living on a capital of a plantation, and fifty or sixty negroes, might reasonably calculate, if no ill luck befell him, by the aid of a usurer, and the occasional sale of a negro or two, to hold out without declared insolvency, until a green old age. His estate melted like an estate in chancery, under the gradual thaw of expenses; but in this fast country, it went by the sheer cost of living—some *poker* losses included—like the fortune of the confectioner in California, who failed for one hundred thousand dollars in the six months keeping of a candy-shop. But all the habits of his life, his taste, his associations, his education—every thing—the trustingness of his disposition—his want of business qualifications—his sanguine temper—all that was Virginian in him, made him the prey, if not of imposture, at least of unfortunate speculations. . . .

Slave Gangs on the Move to the Lower South

George W. Featherstonhaugh

Just as we reached New River, in the early grey of the morning, we came up with a singular spectacle, the most striking one of the kind I have ever witnessed. It was a camp of negro slave-drivers, just packing up to start; they had about three hundred slaves with them, who had bivouacked the preceding night *in chains* in the woods; these they were conducting to Natchez, upon the Mississippi River, to work upon the sugar plantations in Louisiana. It resembled one of those coffles of slaves spoken of by Mungo Park, except that they had a caravan of nine waggons and single-horse carriages, for the purpose of conducting the white people, and any of the blacks that should fall lame, to which they were now putting the horses to pursue their march. The female slaves were, some of them, sitting on logs of wood, whilst others were standing, and a great many little black children were warming themselves at the fires of the bivouac. In front of them all, and prepared for the march, stood, in double files, about two hundred male slaves, *manacled and chained to each other*. I had never seen so revolting a sight before! Black men in fetters, torn from the lands where they were born, from the ties they had formed, and from the comparatively easy condition which agricultural labour affords, and driven by white men, with liberty and equality in their mouths, to a distant and unhealthy country, to perish in the sugar-mills of Louisiana, where the duration of life for a sugar-mill slave does not exceed seven years! To make this spectacle still more disgusting and hideous, some of the principal slave-drivers, who were tolerably well dressed, and had broad-brimmed white hats on, *with black crape round them,* were standing near, laughing and smoking cigars.

Whether these sentimental speculators were, or were not—in accord-

George W. Featherstonhaugh, *Excursion Through the Slave States* (New York, 1844), pp. 37, 45-47.

ance with the language of the American Declaration of Independence—in mourning "from a decent respect for the opinions of mankind," or for their own callous inhuman lives, I could not but be struck with the monstrous absurdity of such fellows putting on any symbol of sorrow whilst engaged in the exercise of such a horrid trade; so wishing them in my heart all manner of evil to endure, as long as there was a bit of crape to be obtained, we drove on, and having forded the river in a flat-bottomed boat, drew up on the road, where I persuaded the driver to wait until we had witnessed the crossing of the river by the "gang," as it was called.

It was an interesting, but a melancholy spectacle, to see them effect the passage of the river: first, a man on horseback selected a shallow place in the ford for the males slaves; then followed a waggon and four horses, attended by another man on horseback. The other waggons contained the children and some that were lame, whilst the scows, or flat-boats, crossed the women and some of the people belonging to the caravan. There was much method and vigilance observed, for this was one of the situations where the gangs—always watchful to obtain their liberty—often show a disposition to mutiny, knowing that if one or two of them could wrench their manacles off, they could soon free the rest, and either disperse themselves or overpower and slay their sordid keepers, and fly to the Free States. The slave-drivers, aware of this disposition in the unfortunate negroes, endeavour to mitigate their discontent by feeding them well on the march, and by encouraging them to sing "Old Virginia never tire," to the banjo.

The poor negro slave is naturally a cheerful, laughing animal, and even when driven through the wilderness in chains, if he is well fed and kindly treated, is seldom melancholy; for his thoughts have not been taught to stray to the future, and his condition is so degraded, that if the food and warmth his desires are limited to are secured to him, he is singularly docile. It is only when he is ill-treated and roused to desperation, that his vindictive and savage nature breaks out. But these gangs are accompanied by other negroes trained by the slave-dealers to drive the rest, whom they amuse by lively stories, boasting of the fine warm climate they are going to, and of the oranges and sugar which are there to be had for nothing: in proportion as they recede from the Free States, the danger of revolt diminishes, for in the Southern Slave-States all men have an interest in protecting this infernal trade of slave-driving, which, to the negro, is a greater curse than slavery itself, since it too often dissevers for ever those affecting natural ties which even a slave can form, by tearing, without an instant's notice, the husband from the wife, and the children from their parents; sending the one to the sugar plantations of Louisiana, another to the cotton-lands of Arkansas, and the rest to Texas. . . .

About noon we reached Knoxville, a poor, neglected-looking place, which notwithstanding makes a great figure on the map. I saw some tolerable dwelling-houses, and called upon a gentleman of the name of Campbell, to whom I had a letter, and who was very polite to me; but we only stayed an hour, just long enough to let the passengers dine at the tavern. I also called upon a very worthy and well-known gentleman with whom I had the pleasure of being acquainted, Judge Hugh White, a senator of the United States, who resides here; but he was from home. There is a steam-boat navigation from Knoxville down the Holston and Tennessee into the Mississippi when the water is high enough; but, to judge from the inactivity of the place, there is very little commerce going on. Fourteen miles farther we came to Campbell's Station, a place where the white settlers used to assemble, after they had first penetrated into these remote parts, to chastise the Indians. As we drove up to the door of the tavern, I saw General Jackson, the venerable President of the United States, seated at a window smoking his long pipe, and went to pay my respects to him, apologising for my dirty appearance, which I told him I had very honestly come by in hammering the rocks of his own State. He laughed and shook hands cordially with me; and learning that my son was with me, requested me to bring him in and present him. My son, who had been scampering about the country all the time we were in Knoxville, was in a worse pickle than myself, and felt quite ashamed to be presented to so eminent a person; but the old General very kindly took him by the hand, and said, "My young friend, don't be ashamed of this: if you were a politician, you would have dirty work upon your hands you could not so easily get rid of." We had a very agreeable chat with the old gentleman; he was in fine spirits; and we left his cheerful conversation with great reluctance, amidst the kindest expression of his wishes for our welfare, and an injunction to call upon him at Washington as soon as we returned. The President was then on his way to the seat of government.

. . . On resuming our places in the stage-coach, our companion in black pronounced a most decided eulogium upon *General* Jackson, but in such language as was quite inimitable. With a strange solemnity of tone and manner, he said, "The old Gineral is the most greatest and most completest idear of a man what had ever lived. I don't mean to say nothing agin Washington—he was a man too; but Jackson *is* a man, I tell *you*: and when I see'd him in his old white hat, with the mourning crape on it, it made me feel a kind of particular curious." This mysterious sympathy betwixt the two white hats in mourning opened a vein of sentiment in our companion that presently took a very sublimated form, and he commenced thinking aloud as it were, keeping his right hand pressed on the thigh of the Tuscaloosan. He now attempted to cover a farrago of bad grammar with an affected pronunciation of his words; and at last got into such a strain of talking fine, that my son and myself had great difficulty in suppressing our laughter. He spoke of a niece that he had, and said, in quite a staccato style, "She-is-a-most-complete-" and there he rather equivocally left the matter, adding, however, that he had given her "a most beautiful barouche," and that he expected to overtake her that night. By and by, he said he expected to overtake another barouche which belonged to him; and then told us what the two barouches had cost him. In short, he so thoroughly mystified us, that we could not make out what stratum in society he belonged to. If it had not been for these barouches, we might have conjectured, but they threw us out. We knew we had no barouches on the road, and were disposed to respect any one who had, for a barouche is a barouche always; and what must a man be who had two on the road, and "a complete" in one of them?

A vague idea had once or twice crossed my mind that I had seen this man before, but where I could not imagine. On coming, however, to a long hill, where I got out to walk, I took occasion to ask the driver if he knew who the passenger was who had two barouches on before. "Why," said the man, "don't you know it's Armfield, the negur-driver?" "Negur-driver!" thought I, and immediately the mystery was cleared up. I remembered the white hat, the crape, the black, short-cut, round hair, and the barouches. It was one of the identical slave-dealers I had seen on the 6th of September, crossing his gang of chained slaves over New River. On re-entering the vehicle I looked steadily at the fellow, and recollecting him, found no longer any difficulty in accounting for such a compound of everything vulgar and revolting, and totally without education. I had now a key both to his manners and the expression of his countenance, both of them formed in those dens of oppression and despair, the negro prisons, and both of them indicating his abominable vocation.

As he had endeavoured to impose himself upon us for a respectable man, I was determined to let him know before we parted that I had found him out; but being desirous first of discovering what was the source of that sympathy which united his hat with that of General Jackson, I asked him plump who he was in mourning for. Upon this, drawing his physiognomy down to the length of a moderate horse's face, "Marcus Layfeeyate" (Marquis Lafayette) was his answer. "Do you mean General Lafayette?" I inquired. "I reckon that's what I mean," said he. "Why, General Lafayette," I replied, "gloried in making all men free, without respect of colour; and what are you, who I understand are a negro-driver, in mourning for him for? Such men as you ought to go into mourning only when the price of black men falls. I remember seeing you cross your gang in chains at New River; and I shouldn't be at all surprised if Lafayette's ghost was to set every one of your negroes free one of these nights."

The fellow did not expect this, and was silent, but my son burst into a violent fit of laughter; and, to add to our amusement, the negur-driver's black man—who had been vastly tickled with the idea of the ghost coming to help the negurs—boiled over into a most stentorious horse-laugh of the African kind. His enraged master now broke out, "What onder arth is the matter with you, I reckon? If you think I'll stand my waiter's sniggering at me arter that fashion, I reckon you'll come to a nonplush to-night." These awful words, which Pompey knew imported very serious consequences, brought him immediately into a graver mood, and he very contritely said, "Master, I warn't a larfing at you, by no manner of means; I was just a larfing at what dat ar gemmelman said about de ghose." Soon after this the fellow pretended he was taken ill, and determined to stop at a tavern on the road, a few miles from Bean's Station. He accordingly told Pompey to go on with the stage-coach until he overtook the gang, and then to return for him with one of the barouches.

Here we left him to digest our contempt as well as he could. Pompey now told us a great many things that served to confirm my abhorrence of this brutal land-traffic in slaves. As to his master, he said he really thought he was ill: "Master's mighty fond of ingeons," said he, "and de doctors in Alexandria tells him not to each sich lots of ingeons; but when he sees 'em he can't stand it, and den he eats 'em and dey makes him sick, and den he carries on jist like a house a fire; and den he drinks brandy upon 'em and dat makes him better; and den he eats ingeons agin, and so he keeps a carrying on." From which it would appear that the sum total of enjoyment of a negro-driver, purchased at such a profligate expense of humanity, is an unlimited indulgence in onions and brandy.

Before we stopped for the night, but long after sunset, we came to a place where numerous fires were gleaming through the forest: it was the bivouac of the gang. Having prevailed upon the driver to wait half an hour, I went with Pompey—who was to take leave of us here—into the woods, where they were all encamped. There were a great many blazing fires around, at which the female slaves were warming themselves; the children were asleep in some tents; and the males, in chains, were lying on the ground, in groups of about a dozen each. The white men, who were the partners of Pompey's master, were standing about with whips in their hands; and "the complete" was, I suppose, in her tent; for I judged, from the attendants being busy in packing the utensils away, that they had taken their evening's repast. It was a fearful and irritating spectacle, and I could not bear long to look at it.

Letters from Alabama and the Southwest, 1835-1854

The Lide Family

SARAH L. FOUNTAIN TO HANNAH L. COKER, SOCIETY HILL, S. C.

Carlowville, Dalas County, Ala., Dec. 27, 1835

My Very Dear Sister: We have at length arrived at our place of destination after 5 weeks and 2 days travel we reached this place last evening and took up camp and expect to remain here until we can get a house we are about 3 miles from the place where Mr. Rowel [the overseer] and the Negroes stay, they soon heard of our arrival and came up very quick and such rejoicing and ado I never heard, they all look quite fat and hearty. We are very near Mr. Crumpton's himself and family came immediately to see us and insisted on as many of us as could to go and stay with them until we could get better fixed but we prefered staying at our tents; he is building and said he had been making an effort to get his house done that he might accomodate us but was disappointed. Brother has the prospect of a house but Pa has none the house that he calculated on getting is otherwise disposed of. O my sister I can't describe to you my feelings here in this strange country without house or home so far seperated from my dear friends, and as yet I see nothing enticing in the place but I do not wish to condemn it unless I knew more about it.

I feel that we have been most signally blessed in our journey though we have been long on the road we have all reached here safely and in usual health, there has however been considerable sickness among the negroes but they are pretty well at present. Pa sold 3 yoke of his oxen on the way 1 he sold for $16. the other 2 he gave for a little poney for Joseph and Brother put 2 of his saddle horses in the waggon. One of my oxen gave out entirely so that we had to leave him a gentleman was so

Fletcher Green (ed.), *The Lides Go South and West* (University of South Carolina Press, Columbia, S. C., 1952), pp. 9-14, 16-17, 26-27, 35-36.

good as to let him go in his field about 20 miles from this place, but I never expect to hear of him again. My little waggon broke down with me about the middle of the indian nation we had to travel with it so until we got to mount meggs which was 50 miles but it was with much difficulty, we got to mount meggs about 2 o'clock last tuesday spent the night with Cousin Mary Temples found them all well, cousin Mary had a babe about ten days old which is her tenth child, we passed by old Mrs. AcAll's the next day the old Lady looks badly says she had a very sick family this summer.

I felt much safer passing through the Indian nation than I expected saw but few indians and they appeared quite friendly, we entered the nation about 11 O'clock thursday and got out of it about 12 O'clock the tuesday after the road through the nation was better than we expected from what we had heard but it was very rough and hilly generally. . . .

SARAH L. FOUNTAIN TO HANNAH L. COKER, SOCIETY HILL, S. C.

Carlowville, Ala., Feb. 10, 1836

. . . . Mr. Wm. Kervin arrived here yesterday and spent the night with us, he has gone out to procure houses for his family by the time they arrive he left them saturday morning about mount meggs, in company with cousin Robert Lide he thinks they will be certain to be here to-day. Mr. John Coker was in company also, they have made much better progress than we did notwithstanding the road and weather have been so much worse they have been only four weeks on the road, but they traveled every Sabbath. It is cheering indeed to see so many of our friends and relatives coming to this country, but there is still a breach and ever will be unless yours our dear brothers and uncles families were here.

We have been living at this place (pa's new purchase) about three weeks the house is far from being comfortable but is much more so than the one we left over the creek, it is a double house with a narrow passage between; the rooms are small and very open, there are cracks where the joists go in almost large enough for a dog to go through but they answer for windows as we have no others, the loft is nothing but some loosse boards laid down and no way to get up but to climb up the logs but we can put a good deal of trumpery up there, we have two beds in one room and three in the other, consequently we have to set our door (for we have no table) in the passage which is very uncomfortable in cold rainy weather and we have had a good deal of both since we have been here. Pa and Samuel have made us four teaster bedsteads out of little saplins, since we have put our curtains up we find it much more comfortable. We have pretty good out-buildings except negroe-houses and Pa is making preparations to build them, the negroes are still in their tents, we are surrounded by very tall oaks and chestnuts and some pines. Pa and brother are trying very hard to get situations on nubbin-ridge, they are afraid it will be sickly here as it has been for two years past, they are out on that business today: we have well-water and when it rains much we can almost dip the water out, but it is very clear and not well tasted. Pa is very busy clearing land and splitting rails, he has not near enough open for his hands to cultivate and he dreads the idea of giving four or five dollars per acre rent, Ma has [hired?] out all her girls but sophy and [Peggy?]. Cousin Evan Pugh has spent two nights with us since we have been [here] he was quite well and very lively, he has hired Nancy and is to give $50 for her. Pa has sold one of my horses and both waggons, the horse for $75 the large waggon $120 and the small one $75. My expenses out here were a little more than $100. Pa got his clock here safe and it is running as well as ever.

Will you not be astonished when I tell you that we have not been to preaching since we have been here? Pa and brother went out last Sabbath to look for [a church?] but it was in vain they found none. There is no school in reach [but?] I hope there will be by the spring. I am trying to teach the children a little at home but find it very difficult. Lizzy begs me every few days to let her write to you but I tell her she must learn to write on the slate first. . . .

MARIA LIDE TO HANNAH L. COKER, SOCIETY HILL, S. C.

Chesnut Grove, Ala., Mar. 7, 1836

My Dear Sister: It is with pleasure that I now write I propose telling you something of this place but I hope you will not consider it a description for you know I have no turn to discribe. We live in a very public place a road passes right close by and a great many waggons pass. Some one is passing nearly all the time. We are surrounded by very tall trees mostly oaks and chestnuts a few pines. It is a right pretty place I think I like it better than any place I have seen. In front of the dwelling are the negro houses and their patches. The front yard is very flat and when it rains holds a great deal of water. In the yard in front is a potatoe house in the back yard is a kitchen and smokehouse and a very small dairy but it is a great deal better than none near the garden is a pen made of rails for the fowl house. Pa has just had the garden enlarged it looks like a field now to what it was but it is not near large enough yet. The cotton field joins the garden next to that is the peach orchard at the end of that is potatoe patch.

. . . We have no table yet still take the door down to eat off of. We eat in the passage all this rainy and cold weather but we have curtains now which makes it a little more pleasant. The house has no window at all which makes it very dark it is almost impossible to see to sew when it is cloudy the floor is very open indeed.

There are a great many persons moving away from this place and going to the Chocktaw purchase and great many coming in which keeps the number pretty much the same. Several families from the neighbour-hood of Charlestown have just arived I dont know but they are some of your acquaintances any how they are very ugly looking things to make the best of them. Ma says they look more like animals than human beings they have very large whiskers which covers nearly all of their face one of them doesn't shave his upper lip which you know must look very strange. Pa expects to move out on nubbin ridge this summer and I am very sorry for it I dont like the looks of it at all and then we will have another moveing and packing up frolick but I had rather go than risk being sick. We have got acquainted with no person at all except those new comers the Charlestown folks they have called on us but business drew them but I must stop and go to dinner. Pa has had some wild strawberys planted in the garden a good large square. Strawberys grow wild here so you may know what a rich country it is. . . .

ELI H. LIDE TO CALEB COKER, SOCIETY HILL, S. C.

Carlowville, Ala., March 24, 1836

. . . I have been all this while holding up to your view the dark side of the subject. I will now let you take peep at what I call the bright side, we live in a delightful neighborhood a kind of village place something like Society Hill not quite so dense a population but far more numerous which in point of intelligence is inferiour to none. As to health from all the information which I can gather it must be equal to the hills of Ches-terfield the people here say equal to any in the world, of this however I prefer to be no judge but can see no local cause for sickness. Here is natural scenery which is grand and sublime, entirely superior to any thing I saw on the Blue Ridge, as to the *soil* it would do your very heart good to look at it.

I am often very much diverted to see Father, he is indeed the most busy man you ever saw, and he lets nothing keep him from his farm he is all the time among his negroes in the field and seems to be as active about his business as he could be at eighteen, he seems to have forgotten that he is old. He has a valuable tract of land and he can get double (as I was told to-day) what it cost him. Some days ago I was walking with him over some of his beautiful hammocks and he said it appeared to him that land could not be any better than that was. He also says he has better prospects before him *now*, than he ever had and that a man might live here clear and aboveboard, he is fully as well pleased with the country as I am.

I have between 1800 and two thousand acres of land here which is too much for me. I some times think of selling 480 acres but am afraid to offer it for fear some one will want to purchase it. I put out a negro boy to learn the Blacks[mith] trade for whom I get $150 dollars a year hire. Corn is worth from 75/100 to 1.00 per bushel and scarce at that price. . . .

SARAH L. FOUNTAIN TO HANNAH L. COKER, SOCIETY HILL, S.C.

Nubbin Ridge, Ala., Nov. 11, 1836

My Dear Sister: . . . . We went to the Presbyterian church last Sunday with the expectation of hearing a baptist preach, (a Mr. Tolbert who is said to be quite a smart preacher) but were disappointed, we however heard a very good sermon by a Methodist (a Mr. Freeman) who frequently preaches at the church, he is very wealthy said to be worth half a million of dollars, he lives within a few miles of this place. Mr. Martin a presbyterian preacher who has attended this church regularly twice a month is to preach his farewell sermon next Sunday. I understand he has an idea of going to the Mississippi Valley where I suppose good preachers are greatly needed as the Roman Catholics are trying to get possession of it. O what horrid beings they are, and how much to be dreaded.

When I wrote you last I told you my children were going to school, they did not go another day after that, the teacher got into a scrape and stabbed a man, but fortunately his arm received the wound which was very severe. Dunn was immediately taken prisoner, but by some means made his escape that night. I have not heard of him since, nor am I sorry for it. I hope the people will be more cautious hereafter how they employ strangers . . . .

MARY E. LIDE TO HANNAH L. COKER, SOCIETY HILL, S.C.

Carlowville, Ala., Sept. 20, 1838

My Dear Sister: . . . . I suppose you have heard all the particulars of our meeting, and it will be useless for me to say any thing about it. Oh it was very interesting indeed no very great excitement at any time, but a great solemnity. I think on Sunday while Mr. Crofford was preaching the falling of a pin might have been distinctly heard, and the congregation was very large too, the largest congregation I have seen in this state. I believe the people were faithfully warned and that the preachers cleaned their skirts of the blood of souls. We had eight or nine preachers, and the most of them very good. Mr. Crofford was very sublime and forceful, he described eternity to us on Sunday. . . . 14 joined our church at the meeting and two of them were my sunday school schollars, and another of my schollars was a constant mourner she was one of the first that went up to be prayed, and continued to go up until the meeting closed but had no hope at that time, her family are Methodist she had been from home ever since the meeting. Oh we had a real Methodist meeting one night a parcel of the Methodist girls went up to be prayed for and their Mothers collected a round them crying, shouting, and groaning, one girl obtained a hope (a sister to the one I have just mentioned) and she shouted and ran through the congregation shaking hands with her brothers and sisters they became so noisy that several of our members left. I should have done so, if I could have got my company off, but they would not go and I thought it would not to do to leave them. Peter was baptised at the meeting, Betty and Mary . . . . the sunday after. . . .

MARIA LIDE TO CALEB COKER, SOCIETY HILL, S.C.

Carlowville, Ala., Sept. 16, 1844

My Dear Brother: . . . . I am glad to hear you are getting along so finely with your house I wish I could go and help occupy it. I assure you nothing would afford me more pleasure, but it is a privilege I never expect to enjoy again. I expect to spend the remainder of my days in moving about from place to place. I have made up my mind that we will leave this place, and that before a great while Pa is quite in the notion of moving somewhere; he is urging brother Samuel to sell his land, and take the hands and go off and buy land in the cane break or somewhere else; he has a very fine prospect this year thinks he will make 70 bales of cotton if he can gather it, he already has 20 out, his having such a good crop seems to make him more anxious to move. I dont know why it is but none of them are satisfied here. I have no idea that we will stop short of red river; brother has seen that place and was so perfectly delighted with it that he can find no place equal to it. I have been trying my best to get brother in the notion of going to California; because I think he would be obliged to stop then for he could go no farther, and I think he would be far enough away from society to be satisfied to settle himself permanently. You have no idea how tired I am of hearing about moving; it is the subject of conversation every time pa and brother meet and that is very often. . . .

The Gentry of Texas

Mary Austin Holley

Decr 30 1837

. . . The beauty of the scenery decreases as you recede from the lovely Bay, San Jacinto, at whose head meet the waters of rivers Jacinto & Buffalo Bayou—forming the most delightful sites for residences you can imagine. The Bayou shuts in & narrows till you see nothing but trees above & around, & it needs much attention to preserve the chimneys & wheels of the boat. Smaller boats will be necessary, as the *Comanchee,* boasts 30 feet, nearly touches on both sides, though there is good depth of water & no obstruction by snags. The Bayou is like a deep canal—the trees forming an arch above, & touching the water below—like a bower of evergreens. There are large pines among the timber—making it verdant even in winter—sometimes without undergrowth—beautiful openings inviting the settler. At Houston the Bayou is but 60 feet wide. The steamboat could not turn round were it not for a creek just opposite the landing. The main street of this city of a year extends from the landing into the prairie—a beautiful plain of some six miles wide, & extending, with points & islands of timber, quite to the Brazos. On this main street are two large hotels, 2 stories, with galleries (crowded to overflowing) several stores 2 stories— painted white—one block of eleven stores (rent $500 each) after—some 2 story dwelling houses—& then the capitol—70 feet front—140 rear— painted peach blossom, about ¼ mile from the landing. Other streets, parallel, & at right angles, are built on here & there, but chiefly designated by stakes. One story dwellings are scattered in the edge of the timber which forms an amphitheatre round the prairie, according to the bend of the Bayou, which, being wider, would render this a most eligible town site. As it is, it is too inconvenient, besides being unhealthy, & a removal of the government is talked of.

Congress had adjourned when we arrived—remaining members called on us, with many other persons, whom we received in the cabin. We kept

Letters from Mary Austin Holley to her daughter and son-in-law, Mr. and Mrs. William Brand, of Lexington, Ky.

our lodging in the boat, at the reasonable rate of $2 per day, there being no place in the city so comfortable. The President returned from a visit to the country next day & came immediately to pay us his respects. He afterwards dined with us 2 days one of which was sunday, & gallanted us to the Capitol, in one wing of which is a gallery of portraits of distinguished characters of the last campaign. Also the room of a portrait-miniature painter. You see the arts flourish in this new land already. . . .

[On the way to Brazoria] Staid first night at a house better than the common run of Kentucky houses, any between Lexington & Louisville. Weather charming—summer heat—no need of shawls—clothes oppressive —birds—beautiful tufted red birds—& we singing all the way. arrived 2nd night after dark.

Egg-nog not plenty at Christmas—eggs worth 50^{cts} each $6 per doz in Houston. Heard of one doz: sold for $13. Sperm candles 50^{cts} each. Sugar—none.

We are now (Dec: 30) domesticated at Mrs Andrews' in Brazoria. Expect brother every minute. Hear he has fitted up his house & stocked it with provisions. You will observe, in a Telegraph [the local newspaper] I sent, his advertisement of Bolivar lots. Mr Andrews says will go well. Has been offered $25,000 for the whole & can get it now—So hope to get what cash I want. Towns are all the go. . . .

People are busy, as in Houston, with meetings, Etc, to prepare for the enemy [an expected Mexican attack]. . . . We have been out this morning firing at a mark with a rifle, under Capt Dolrocha of the army—ourselves, Mrs Franklin & Mrs Andrews—We did not exactly hit the mark—but my first fire cut a line—a clothes line in the way. Henrietta bore the Texan Star as ensign. This grew out of a boast of a gentleman from Matagorda, of a young lady there who was a superior *marksman*. We propose to form a corps of *rifle men*—as an army of reserve—were treated with champagne, 2 bottles & cakes, by Mrs Blandine, where we were. . . .

Peach Point Plantation, Feb 21, 1838

. . . There is to be a great Ball at Velasco tomorrow (22nd) night—being the period of the races. All the world, who can move, *wind & weather permitting* are to be there. It rains to day, however. We are going, the girls & Miss Perry (Mr Perry's neice), the two young Bryans & myself—in a small covered wagon (without spring seats) which I have persuaded them is a good thing to ride about here in. We shall be attended by a valet & femme de chambre—en cheval—with a sack of corn for our horses—in primitive style we shall go to Quintana—on this side of the river—& stop, *with our bandboxes,* at Mrs McKenneys. Every thing available for dresses in Texas has been bought up for the occasion. Confectionary & ornaments &c &c are to be brought by the *Columbia* from N Orleans. The gentlemen dress remarkably well—The clothes being all brought from N York ready made & of the newest fashions. I expect it will be a great occasion, one at least I have never seen. The steamboat plying constantly on the Brazos, will fetch & carry the people. They have only to ride to some convenient landing to embark. I shall use the occasion, besides seeing the world, to select my lot in Quintana which Mrs Perry has given me. It will be a valuable property, whether I occupy it or not. They import houses there ready to be put up, & if I can (as I expect) get a person to put one on my lot, to be forfeited in case of non-payment, I shall do so. Such property is increasing rapidly in value. . . .

Mrs Sayres, Texas, March 21, 1838

Dear Harriette & *Spouse,*
 . . . There seems to be an incubus on all things here, in consequence of embarrassments in the United States. Every body has land for sale, but they keep up their prices, & purchasers—the few who have money (& there is no use in selling on credit) are waiting for a fall. The greatest part of the emigration consists of small farmers who come in by land & settle above, where land is cheaper, & they get small tracts, in healthy situations. The capitalists come by sea, travel every where & remain undecided—not knowing where to choose—& as I said, waiting until the still greater embarrassments of the proprietors shall compel them to sacrifice their estates. Most of those who come by sea go first to Houston, being the seat of government. That place by its sudden growth, & the influx of foreigners, without comforts, or even a lodging place for half who arrive there, presents to the new comer a scene of vice greater, I suppose, than can be found elsewhere in the same compass. There is not room even for villainy to hide itself. Hence, many of the better sort, without reflection, & less philosophy, go off in disgust, in the same vessel that brought them. *Much do they know of Texas*—or its people. Houston is a great disadvantage to the country in one respect, while it is a benefit in another. If it keeps off some honest folks who lack enterprise & perseverance to penetrate to the good of the land, it concentrates the rascals, with the government and its hangers-on, & leaves the rest of the people in peace. . . .

Emigrants to Texas

Frederick Law Olmsted

We overtook, several times in the course of each day, the slow emigrant trains, for which this road, though less frequented than years ago, is still a chief thoroughfare. Inexorable destiny it seems that drags or drives on, always Westward, these toil-worn people. Several families were frequently moving together, coming from the same district, or chance met and joined, for company, on the long road from Alabama, Georgia, or the Carolinas. Before you come upon them you hear, ringing through the woods, the fierce cries and blows with which they urge on their jaded cattle. Then the stragglers appear, lean dogs or fainting negroes, ragged and spiritless. An old granny, holding on, by the hand, a weak boy—too old to ride and too young to keep up. An old man, heavily loaded, with a rifle. Then the white covers of the wagons, jerking up and down as they mount over a root or plunge into a rut, disappearing, one after another, where the road descends. Then the active and cheery prime negroes, not yet exhausted, with a joke and a suggestion about tobacco. Then the black pickininnies, staring, in a confused heap, out at the back of the wagon, more and more of their eyes to be made out among the table legs and bedding as you get near; behind them, further in, the old people and young mothers, whose turn it is to ride. As you get by, the white mother and babies, and the tall, frequently ill-humored master, on horseback, or walking with his gun, urging up the black driver and his oxen. As a scout ahead is a brother, or an intelligent slave, with the best gun, on the look-out for a deer or a turkey. We passed in the day perhaps one hundred persons attached to these trains, probably an unusual number; but the immigration this year had been retarded and condensed by the fear of yellow fever, the last case of which, at Natchitoches, had indeed begun only the night before our arrival. Our chances

Frederick Law Olmsted, A Journey Through Texas (New York, 1857), pp. 55-57.

of danger were considered small, however, as the hard frosts had already come. One of these trains was made up of three large wagons, loaded with furniture, babies, and invalids, two or three light wagons, and a gang of twenty able field hands. They travel ten or fifteen miles a day, stopping wherever night overtakes them. The masters are plainly dressed, often in home-spun, keeping their eyes about them, noticing the soil, sometimes making a remark on the crops by the roadside; but, generally, dogged, surly, and silent. The women are silent, too, frequently walking, to relieve the teams, and weary, haggard, mud-bedraggled, forlorn, and disconsolate, yet hopeful and careful. The negroes, mud-incrusted, wrapped in old blankets or gunny-bags, suffering from cold, plod on, aimless, hopeless, thoughtless, more indifferent than the oxen to all about them.

The Declaration of War Against Mexico

James K. Polk

Saturday, 9th May, 1846.—The Cabinet held a regular meeting to-day; all the members present. I brought up the Mexican question, and the question of what was the duty of the administration in the present state of our relations with that country. The subject was very fully discussed. All agreed that if the Mexican forces at Matamoras committed any act of hostility on Gen'l Taylor's forces I should immediately send a message to Congress recommending an immediate declaration of War. I stated to the Cabinet that up to this time, as they knew, we had heard of no open act of aggression by the Mexican army, but that the danger was imminent that such acts would be committed. I said that in my opinion we had ample cause of war, and that it was impossible that we could stand in *status quo,* or that I could remain silent much longer; that I thought it was my duty to send a message to Congress very soon & recommend definitive measures. I told them that I thought I ought to make such a message by tuesday next, that the country was excited and impatient on the subject, and if I failed to do so I would not be doing my duty. I then propounded the distinct question to the Cabinet and took their opinions individually, whether I should make a message to Congress on tuesday, and whether in that message I should recommend a declaration of War against Mexico. All except the Secretary of the Navy gave their advice in the affirmative. Mr. Bancroft dissented but said if any act of hostility should be committed by the Mexican forces he was then in favour of immediate war. Mr. Buchanan said he would feel better satisfied in his course if the Mexican forces had or should commit any act of hostility, but that as matters stood we had ample cause of war against Mexico, & he gave his assent to the measure. It was agreed that the message should be prepared and submitted to the Cabinet in their meeting on tuesday. A

M. M. Quaife (ed.), *The Diary of James K. Polk* (Chicago, 1910), I, pp. 384-394.

history of our causes of complaint against Mexico had been at my request previously drawn up by Mr. Buchanan. I stated that what was said in my annual message in December gave that history as succinctly and satisfactorily as Mr. Buchanan's statement, that in truth it was the same history in both, expressed in different language, and that if I repeated that history in [a] message to Congress now I had better employ the precise language used in my message of December last. Without deciding this point the Cabinet passed to the consideration of some other subjects of minor importance. The Cabinet adjourned about 2 O'clock P.M. Before they separated I directed the Secretary of State to have all the correspondence of Mr. Slidell with the Mexican Government, & such portions of his correspondence with the Department of State as it was proper to communicate copied; and in like manner I directed the Secretary of War to have all his orders to Gen'l Taylor commanding the army in Texas copied, so as to have these documents ready to be communicated to Congress with my message.

About 6 o'clock P.M. Gen'l R. Jones, the Adjutant General of the army, called and handed to me despatches received from Gen'l Taylor by the Southern mail which had just arrived, giving information that a part of [the] Mexican army had crossed to the Del Norte, [crossed the Rio Grande] and attacked and killed and captured two companies of dragoons of Gen'l Taylor's army consisting of 63 officers & men. The despatch also stated that he had on that day (26th April) made a requisition on the Governors of Texas & Louisiana for four Regiments each, to be sent to his relief at the earliest practicable period. Before I had finished reading the despatch, the Secretary of War called. I immediately summoned the Cabinet to meet at 7½ O'Clock this evening. The Cabinet accordingly assembled at that hour; all the members present. The subject of the despatch received this evening from Gen'l Taylor, as well as the state of our relations with Mexico, were fully considered. The Cabinet were unanimously of opinion, and it was so agreed, that a message should be sent to Congress on Monday laying all the information in my possession before them and recommending vigorous & prompt measure[s] to enable the Executive to prosecute the War. The Secretary of War & Secretary of State agreed to put their clerks to work to copy the correspondence between Mr. Slidell & the Mexican Government & Secretary of State and the correspondence between the War Department & Gen'l Taylor, to the end that these documents should be transmitted to Congress with my message on Monday. The other members of the Cabinet tendered the services of their clerks to aid in preparing these copies.

Mr. Senator Houston, Hon. Barkley Martin, & several other members of Congress called in the course of the evening, & were greatly excited at the news brought by the Southern mail from the army. They all approved the steps which had been taken by the administration, and were all of opinion that war with Mexico should now be prosecuted with vigor.

The Cabinet adjourned about 10 O'Clock, & I commenced my message; Mr. Bancroft and Mr. Buchanan, the latter of whom had prepared a history of our causes of complaint against Mexico, agreed to assist me in preparing the message.

Sunday, 10th May, 1846.—As the public excitement in and out of Congress was very naturally very great, and as there was a great public necessity to have the prompt action of Congress on the Mexican question, and therefore an absolute necessity for sending my message to Congress on tomorrow, I resumed this morning the preparation of my message. About 9½ O'Clock Mr. Bancroft called, and with his assistance I was engaged in preparing it until 11 O'Clock, at which time I suspended my labours in order to attend church. I left the part of the message which had been written to be copied by my Private Secretary, and accompanied Mrs. Polk, my niece, Miss Rucker, & my nephew, Marshall T. Polk, to church. As we were leaving for church the Hon. Mr. Haralson & the Hon. Mr. Baker, members of the Committee of Military affairs, called to see me on the subject of the legislative action proper to be had to provide for the vigorous prosecution of the war with Mexico. I told them I would see them at 5 O'Clock this afternoon.

On my return from church about 1 O'Clock P.M. I resumed the preparation of my message. In the course of half an hour Mr. Bancroft and Mr. Buchanan called and the part of the message which had been written was examined & approved. At 2 O'Clock my family dinner was announced. I invited Mr. Buchanan and Mr. Bancroft to dine with me. Mr. Buchanan declined and Mr. Bancroft dined with me. After dinner Mr. Bancroft and myself returned to the preparation of the message. Two confidential Clerks, *viz.*, H. C. Williams from the War Department and ——— ———, from the Navy Department were engaged in assisting my Private Secretary in making two copies of my message, one for the Senate and one for the House.

At 5 O'Clock Mr. Haralson & Mr. Baker called according to the appointment made this morning. They informed me that deeming the present a great emergency they had called the Committee on Military affairs of the Ho. Repts. together this morning and that they had unanimously agreed to support a Bill appropriating ten million of Dollars, and authorizing the President to raise fifty thousand dollars [men] to prosecute the war with Mexico. They showed to me a copy of the Bill which they proposed to pass. I pointed out some defects in it & advised them to consult with the Secretary and officers connected with the War Department, including Gen'l Scott and Adj't Gen'l Jones. They said they would do so. I discovered in the course of the conversation that both Mr. Haralson and Mr. Baker desired to be appointed to high commands in the army of Volunteers which their Bill proposed to raise. I talked civilly to them but made no promises.

After night and whilst the clerks were still copying my message in my Private Secretary's office, the Secretaries of State, of the Treasury, of the Navy, the P.M. Gen'l, and [the] Atto. Gen'l called, but were not all present at any one time. The Secretary of War was indisposed as I learned, and did not call during the day. Senator Houston & Bartley [sic] Martin & Ch. J. Ingersoll called to consult me on the Mexican question, and to learn what I intended to recommend in my message. The two former had retired before Mr. Ingersoll called. I addressed notes to Senator Allen, Ch. of the Comm. of Foreign Affairs of the Senate, & Mr. McKay of N.C., Ch. of the Com. of Ways and Means of the Ho. Repts. requesting them to call at my office to-night. In the course of half an hour they called, and the message being copied, I read it to them and Mr. Ingersoll in presence of some of the members of [the] Cabinet who had remained. They all approved it.

At 10½ O'Clock the company left and I retired to rest. It was a day of great anxiety to me, and I regretted the necessity which had existed to make it necessary for me to spend the Sabbath in the manner I have.

Monday, 11th May, 1846.—I refused to see company generally this morning. I carefully revised my message on the Mexican question, but had no time to read the copies of the correspondence furnished by the War & State Departments which was to accompany it. I had read the original correspondence and presume the copies are correct.

I addressed [notes] to Senators Cass and Benton this morning requesting them to call. Gen'l Cass called first. The message was read to him and he highly approved it. Col. Benton called before Gen'l Cass left, and I gave him the copy of the message and he retired to an adjoining room and read it. After he had read it I had a conversation with him alone. I found he did not approve it in all its parts. He was willing to vote men and money for defence of our territory, but was not prepared to make aggressive war on Mexico. He disapproved the marching of the army from Corpus Christi to the left Bank of the Del Norte, but said he had never said so to the public. I had a full conversation with him, and he left without satisfying me that I could rely upon his support of the measures recommended by the message, further than the mere defence of our territory. I inferred, too, from his conversation that he did not think the territory of the U. S. extended West of the Nueces River.

At 12 O'Clock I sent my message to Congress. It was a day of great anxiety with me. Between 5 & 6 O'Clock P.M. Mr. Slidell, U.S. Minister to Mexico, called and informed me that the Ho. Repts. had passed a Bill carrying out all the recommendations of the message by a vote of 173 ayes to 14 noes, and that the Senate had adjourned after a debate without coming to any decision.

My Private Secretary brought me a note from Col. Benton desiring information as to the number of men and amount of money required to defend the country. There was nothing in his note to commit him to any course of policy beyond what he had intimated in his conversation this morning. My Private Secretary informed me that Col. Benton would call for an answer at 8 O'Clock this evening. I immediately sent his note to the Secretary of War and requested him to call at that hour. The Secretaries of War and State called a few minutes before 8 O'Clock but before I had consulted him [the former] in relation to Col. Benton's note, Col. Benton came in. I told Col. B. that the Secretary of War had just come in & that I had no opportunity to consult him on the subject of his note. I told him that my own opinion was that it was at present impossible to say what number of troops would be wanted, and that until Congress acted I could not tell what authority would be given to the Executive; but that if the Bill which had passed the House to-day should also pass the Senate, no more men would be called out and no more money expended than would be absolutely necessary to bring the present state of hostilities to an end. I told him if the war [was] recognized by Congress, that with a large force on land and sea I thought it could be speedily terminated. Col. B. said that the Ho. Repts. had passed a Bill to-day declaring war in two hours, and that one and [a] half hours of that time had been occupied in reading the documents which accompanied my message, and that in his opinion in the 19th Century war should not be declared without full discussion and much more consideration than had been given to it in the Ho. Repts. Mr. Buchanan then remarked that War already existed by the act of Mexico herself & therefore it did not require much deliberation to satisfy all that we ought promptly and vigorously to meet [it]. Mr. Marcy and Mr. Buchanan discussed the subject for some time with Mr. Benton, but without any change of the opinions which he had expressed to me in conversation this morning. I saw it was useless to debate the subject further with him & therefore I abstained from engaging further in the conversation. After remaining near an hour Col. Benton left. Mr. Buchanan, Mr. Marcy, and myself were perfectly satisfied that he would oppose the Bill which had passed the House to-day, and that if the Whigs on party grounds acted with him the Bill might be defeated.

Gov. Yell of Arkansas, Senator Houston, & other members of Congress called in in the course of the evening, and were highly gratified at the action of the House in passing the Bill by so overwhelming a majority.

The part taken by Mr. Calhoun in the Senate to-day satisfies me that he too will oppose the Bill passed by the House to-day if he thinks he can do so safely in reference to public opinion. The Whigs in the Senate will oppose it on party grounds probably, if they can get Mr. Calhoun, Mr. Benton, and two or three other Senators professing to belong to the Democratic party to join them, so as to make a majority against the Bill. Should the Bill be defeated by such a combination, the professed Democratic members who by their votes aid in rejecting it will owe a heavy responsibility not only to their party but to the country. I am fully satisfied that all that can save the Bill in the Senate is the fear of the people by the few Democratic Senators who wish it defeated.

Tuesday, 12th May, 1846.—The Cabinet held a regular meeting to-day; all the members present except the P.M. Gen'l, who was understood to be engaged in his office in examining the bids for mail contracts at the late letting in the Western & S. Western States.

The Mexican question was the subject of conversation, and all had doubts whether the Bill which passed the House on yesterday would pass the Senate to-day. Should it pass, the course of operations was considered. Mr. Bancroft at my request brought from his office all the orders and letters of instruction to our squadrons in the Pacific & Gulf of Mexico, and they were read. This was done 1st, because I desired to refresh my memory of what they were, & 2nd, because they may be called for by Congress.

Some other business of minor importance was considered; & the Cabinet adjourned about 2 O'Clock P.M.

At 7 O'Clock P.M. my Private Secretary returned from the Capitol and announced to me that the Bill which passed the Ho. Repts. on yesterday, making a formal declaration of War against Mexico, had passed the Senate by a vote of 42 ayes to 2 noes, with some immaterial amendment in its details. He represented to me that the debate in the Senate to-day was most animating and thrilling, and that Mr. Calhoun, who spoke in opposition to the Bill, but finally did not vote, had suffered much in the discussion. Mr. Crittenden and other Whigs, he informed me, had made speeches against portions of the Bill & made indirect opposition to it, [but had] finally voted for it. He represented the whole debate as a great triumph for the administration. The Senate, he informed me, adjourned as soon as the Bill was passed. The Ho. of Repts. he informed me, had adjourned to meet this evening at 7½ O'Clock with a view to receive the Bill from the Senate, if that body should act upon it to-day. At 8½ o'clock P.M. I learned that the House had concurred in the amendments of the Senate to the Bill, so that when the Bill is signed by the President War will be declared against Mexico.

Edward Hannegan, Orator of Manifest Destiny

Lew Wallace

I have heard three men whose faces in animated speech suffused with glow suggestive of trans-figuration—S.S. Prentiss, Edward A. Hannegan, and David Wallace. . . .

Edward A. Hannegan was the great man of the town, and he ruled it baronially. As United States senator of democratic persuasion, he had distinguished himself in the debate on the boundary-line between our possessions on the Pacific coast and those of the British. The famous utterance "54—40, or fight," had been his. Could his policy have been resolutely carried out, the tremendous fortification on the northern shore of Vancouver's Island known as the Esquimalt would not now be dominating the inlet to Puget Sound. More recently he had returned from a residence in Berlin as minister. I have spoken of him as orator. It may be added that he was a man of courtly grace, passionate in his friendships and his hates. To a faculty of attraction, he had the opposite faculty of repulsion, both in larger degree than I have ever seen them in the same person. He and my father had been warm friends in despite of politics. I was much surprised one morning by a visit from him at my office. Besides giving me encouragement, he invited me to make myself free at his house and study. Returning the call, I was astonished at his library, so completely did it cover the world of miscellaneous literature. The privilege of that study was much more than a sounding compliment.

I recall Senator Hannegan as attorney defending a man indicted for murder. In the examination of a witness an objection was offered to one of his questions. The case turned upon the point involved. If the objection were sustained, the conviction of his client was inevitable. He met the opposition with an eloquence so passionate that for years after the speech continued one of the legends of the court. The ruling was in his favor, followed by a verdict of acquittal. His reputation was that of an impromptu speaker. In this instance, however, the argument was so perfect, the sentence so finished, that I smelled the oil of the lamp in it. . . .

Lew Wallace, *An Autobiography* (New York, 1906), pp. 215-216.

Speech on Acquiring Oregon
Edward A. Hannegan

The argument of the Senator from Massachusetts [Rufus Choate] involves this strange position: that the entire region of country known as
the Territory of Oregon, extending from the parallel of 42° to 52°40′
north latitude, belonged to the United States by a clear and indefeasible
title; but that it would not do for us to adopt this resolution, lest, by
doing so, we offend Great Britain. That, notwithstanding the unquestionable right by which we hold the country, we must refrain from even
giving the notice contemplated here, of our intention to bring to a close
the joint occupancy. Instead of doing so, we must meekly and patiently
await the pleasure of this formidable and haughty power in everything
connected with the question.

The senator from Massachusetts is apparently overcome with alarm,
and endeavors to infuse that alarm into the Senate and the country at
the proposition before us. He inquired, in terms and with a manner
indicative of deep anxiety, where we would be—where we should stand,
if the resolution passed and the required notice was given? Need I tell
that senator we will be doing nothing more in this, than complying with
the provisions of the convention which created this joint occupation,
and which requires such notice as the means of determining the joint
occupancy. If this resolution passes, and the notice is given, this government will stand precisely where it stood before the convention, which
gave England admission into Oregon; just where we stood before our
own imprudence gave her a foothold on our western borders. Strange,
indeed, does it seem, that compliance with a provision, inserted in the
treaty expressly to avoid difficulty, and to prevent hostility, should be
construed here into matter of offence. The very means which the two
parties selected for the preservation of peace, the honorable gentleman
deprecates as a measure of hostility, leading to war. Adopt the resolution,
give the notice it requires, and he tells us that "our claim and that of

Appendix to the Congressional Globe, 28th Congress, 1st Session, Senate, pp.
243-245 Feb. 23, 1844.

England will at once stand front to front"—in plain words, we will immediately find her in the attitude of hostility. Singular inconsistency! If I understood the gentleman correctly, he declared our title to the country to be good, and that England has no intention of asserting a claim of right to any portion of it; yet immediately afterwards, he would deter the Senate from the proposed action, because it will bring our claim and that of England front to front. Where is the claim with which England is to confront us? In what does it consist? Will the gentleman be good enough to inform the Senate of that claim which he has told us is without foundation, and which, baseless as it is, he deems sufficient to awe us into silence?

The senator from Massachusetts saw proper occasionally to indulge a tone of sarcasm towards this measure and its friends, which, in my opinion, ill became the occasion, or the character of this chamber, on a subject like the present. From some information in his possession, (the source of which I did not understand,) he informed us that Doctor McLaughlin, and some 1,000 or 1,200 hunters of musk-rats, constituted the entire British force in Oregon, and that their only fortification was a log fort. With mock seriousness, he asked if it could be possible that I understood the senator aright? Sir, upon a grave and momentous question like the present, I did not expect such attempts at ridicule from the honorable gentleman. I was not prepared for such ironical attacks from him, before the American Senate, and before the world, upon a large portion of his countrymen, whose feelings he well knows are deeply enlisted in this question. . . .

Is it, as he would create the impression, that ten or twelve hundred trappers constitute the whole force with which we can be brought in contention for Oregon? or is it the power of England? Need I tell that gentleman that it is the latter, when we have his own authority for it that we will have England on us if we move even so far as to adopt the present resolution? Terrified at these thousand trappers! No, sir; the word, in the sense he uses it, has no place in our vocabulary. England, with all her power—her armies and her navies—has not the power to strike terror to our hearts. Come when and how she will, she will find us at least undismayed. . . .

I am well aware that the senator used the language as he states; but I cannot see that this, in any manner, changes its meaning. If Great Britain does not intend to persist in her claim to the soil; if she makes none; if she acquiesces in our settlement of the country, and thereby acknowledges our claim, then every reason he has urged against this resolution falls to the ground. They are certainly no longer entitled to consideration, and the resolution must be adopted as a matter of course, and the notice given, without resistance from any quarter.

I must confess that I feel far more cause for terror in some of the sentiments advanced by that senator, than England, with all her armament by sea and land, can ever inspire. Sir, I allude especially to the appeal which he made to the worst, the sordid passions of the human heart—his address to the representatives of the woollen manufacturers and the ironmongers, whether they would be willing to place the country in an attitude of hostility with England, without first counting the cost; and this, too, accompanied by a significant allusion of a reference to the Committee of Ways and Means, to ascertain, in the first place, what that cost would be. And what then? What did all this mean? There can be but one meaning to it. If the cost, in their opinion, should be too great —if too much money is required—then the Oregon is to be abandoned. England, without title and without right, is to possess herself of that fair land, equal, in extent, to the thirteen original States. And this is not all—not half; but national honor, national character, weighed in the scale against gold, shall kick the beam. The heart sickens at the thought that such things can be possible; that such a sacrifice can be meditated; a sacrifice forbidden by every principle dear and holy in an American heart.

Mr. President, I represent a people on this floor who, without distinction of party or creed, no matter under what name their political preferences may be expressed, are as one man, with one heart, one sentiment, attached, with idolatrous devotion, to the integrity and the perpetuity of the Union. They are ready to preserve it, in the hour of need, with their blood. But, as their representative, I here avow—and I am willing to stake my future fortunes on that avowal—that, sooner than see the honor and character of the nation prostrated before the altars of filthy Mammon—sooner than see national glory bartered for gold, I would embrace with delight the Utopia of the senator from South Carolina:— ay, three distinct, separate, independent republics, rather than one government, which would stoop to such deep and damning degradations.

But suppose that by such means we preserve peace—by surrendering to Great Britain a portion of the country, and placing the question in the broadest possible light—suppose she gives us what gentlemen may term an equivalent for it: under existing circumstances, what would it be but a bargain made under the mouths of her cannon—a *purchased peace?* And what, let me ask, is the value of a purchased peace? What has been the fate of nations preceding us who have resorted to such infamous expedients? History warns us that their existence thereafter is brief; their days are thenceforth numbered; their march is on the road, the inevitable road, to swift destruction. If we purchase peace once, we must do it again, and again, and again, until all means of purchase are exhausted. Then shall it follow with us as it has followed with others—

nothing remains but to fasten the easy yoke upon the effeminate and degenerate people who have bartered character for peace, honor for ease. How widely do such principles contrast with the glorious sentiment of our own heroic countrymen, indelibly graven on every true American heart—"Millions for defence, but not one cent for tribute!"

Before leaving this matter of cost, I cannot refrain from an expression which occurred to me in the course of remarks of the senator from Massachusetts. Whenever the pecuniary interests of his section of the Union are at stake, or likely to be affected, (no matter how slightly,) this Capitol resounds with loud and impassioned appeals against any policy which may thus affect them. But, in reply to my friend from Missouri, [Mr. Atchison,] who described to us the declination and final destruction of the fur trade in the hands of Americans, effected solely by the British fur company in Oregon, he did not extend one word of sympathy, or deign a passing notice of a fact which ought certainly to inspire some consideration, even with those who reside on the Atlantic.

I shall now endeavor briefly to review the real question before us; but, as the question of title is conceded—the gentleman from Massachusetts himself, as strongly as any one else, having expressed his convictions of the perfect nature of our title, and the total want of it in Great Britain—it is unnecessary for me to review the sources of our claim.

In the debate on this subject which occurred in this chamber at the last session, all, I believe, concurred in relation to our title. No gentleman entertained or expressed a doubt of its entire soundness against all others. No one, I believe, pretended that England had even a colorable title to the country. The question is, consequently, narrowed down; it is shrouded in no mystery; it requires no ingenuity to unriddle it. The whole matter is resolved into this: For certain purposes, and at a time when the exclusive occupancy was not necessary to us, we granted to Great Britain certain privileges within the territory concurrent with our own—the right being mutually reserved to annul the joint occupancy by which these privileges exist, on giving the notice provided for by the resolution under consideration. This is the whole case. And with what propriety can it be affirmed that the action now proposed is, in effect, an act of hostility? Upon what principle can it be regarded as belligerent? So far from it, that it is impossible for me to regard it as unfriendly, or even unkind.

The country is ours—I hesitate not at the assertion; I defy contradiction—by a title as strong as that by which we hold any other part of the American republic. The only rights which Great Britain has in the premises, are permissive, derived from us, and subject to termination at our will. With this view of the subject, (and it is the only view I can take of it, after the most mature reflection,) it only remains to inquire into the motives which, on every side, should impel us to prompt and decided steps in the matter. The voice and the interest of the West, and of the Union, demand the occupation of that land by its true and proper owners. The claim of England, however unsupported by rights or justice, will lose nothing by an extension of time. Every day that transpires serves to increase the strength of her pretensions, because hesitancy on our part implies doubt and distrust of our own demands, or, at best, of our capacity to maintain them. Her preparations in that quarter imply a determination to rivet her claim by any means that necessity may ultimately require. She has extended her laws, civil and criminal, over the whole territory. As shown to us on yesterday by the senator from Missouri, [Mr. Atchison,]—and the authority cannot be doubted, for he read from a volume of the laws of the British Parliament—she has extended the jurisdiction and the force of her laws across the Rocky mountains to the very confines of Missouri and Iowa. She is disposing, through her fur company, of the best lands, in perpetuity—bestowing them in parcels on the retired servants of this company. While we have been looking idly on, she has been silently advancing with measures that give both speciousness and power to her claim. And this condition of things is progressive. She still advances whilst we hesitate. Is this right? is it proper? Every other consideration aside, does not the national character demand something more? But to add to the necessity of action here, whilst the government has faltered, the enterprising spirit of our people is aroused by the prospect of this new and fertile region, which limits at last the hitherto boundless West. The emigrants, and those who desire to become so, are every day increasing in number. They are pressing forward with an alacrity which nothing can subdue, whilst their neighbors and associates are regarding things with an interest as intense as was ever felt on any subject. I ask senators if they are not willing to extend at least the protection of the American laws over their own fellow-citizens within American limits? As the matter now stands, these emigrants may at any moment come in collision with the British subjects resident in Oregon; and the result is their immediate subjection to British laws, administered by British tribunals, for alledged offences within the territorial limits of the United States. The senator from Massachusetts told us that entire amity existed between the two classes in Oregon—the Englishmen and the Americans there. I do not know from whence his authority for this statement is derived; but certainly we have very different information from this, contained in a petition now lying on our tables, and signed by a number of American emigrants in that territory, complaining of various grievances at the hands of the English authorities there, and asking the interposition of this government to protect them. Some of these petitioners are personally known to both the senators from Missouri, who vouch for them as men of worth and probity. . . .

The increasing emigration of our people to Oregon presents the strongest possible argument for unequivocal measures on the part of this government.

As our population there increases, so are their possessions increasing in value and importance; their villages will be springing up, their farms extending, their flocks and herds covering hill and valley. If England intends to persist in a claim to the country, the longer we delay the greater will be the injury inflicted on us there when the blow does come; for every growing village, every additional farm-house, adds to English cupidity, increases her desire to hold on, and increases for our people there the horrors of war.

It is true, I have seen lately, in some of the leading papers of the adjoining cities, denunciations of this course of emigration. These denunciations, I presume, may very properly be traced to the speech of the honorable and distinguished senator from South Carolina, [Mr. McDuffie,] delivered in this chamber at the last session—a gentleman, let me say, for whom I have ever cherished the highest admiration, and the most profound respect. On that occasion, the senator, in substance, characterized this system of emigration as the mere spirit of wanton adventure, injurious to the best interests of the country. Differing entirely with this opinion, let me ask why the spirit should be checked, or why encouraged by the government? If it is merely the spirit of wanton adventure, without any laudable aim, it should be checked, and checked promptly. But, sir, I say for those with whom I am acquainted, who are desirous of emigrating to Oregon, as will every senator here who knows anything of this class of our people, that they have other and higher motives in view than the mere gratification of a roving inclination. Mingle and talk with them, sir; hear from their own lips their feelings and their views; and, my life upon it, the humblest man among them will tell you, in the warm language of the heart, his anticipations of the future glory and the growing grandeur of his country—of its increasing power, of the day not distant, when he hopes to see the American ensign swing from a thousand masts on the waters of the Columbia. It would ill become this government to rebuke such a spirit in her people, when (as here) it is lawfully directed. To this identical spirit do we mainly owe our existence as a nation. What else was it that brought Sir Walter Raleigh, and Captain Smith, and their brave comrades, to these shores? And notwithstanding all their regard for religious freedom, but for this same spirit our pilgrim fathers never would have sought a new home in the inhospitable North, nor the persecuted Huguenot a resting place in the savannahs of the South. To the influence of this spirit alone, the republic owes the brightest jewel in her diadem—the

West—the giant—the all-glorious West. Fifty years ago, an almost un-trodden wilderness; to-day, her teeming millions speak through upwards of twenty senators on this floor, and nearly one hundred representatives in the opposite wing of the Capitol. Rebuke it? Never! It is the spirit that founds and sustains empires.

The senator from Massachusetts implores us to pause, to delay yet a little longer—but six months more—before we proceed to action, by the adoption of a measure like this, or anything else, I suppose, that would advance us a foot from our present position. Why should we pause longer? So far as I have read or heard, no man in America admits a doubt of our title to the country. But the senator says that England does not want the country for agricultural purposes; that the fur trade fur-nishes the only value she attaches to it; that beyond this it has no other importance in her eyes; and, as she does not want it for the purposes of agriculture, if we will but let her finish her hunting there, she will be up and away to the Russian dominions north of us. The purposes of agriculture are the least amongst the views which England has in ex-tending her dominions. Would the gentleman have us to believe that, because England does not want it for agriculture, she attaches no value to it? would hazard no struggle for it? What is her history on this score? She did not want the tops of the mountains of Maine for agriculture, and yet she would have gone to war for them. She did not require the rock of Gibraltar as a garden—no; it was because it commanded the pass from the Atlantic to the Mediterranean; and to preserve it she maintained an armed front towards Europe. It is not for the sake of agriculture that she desired the island of Malta, with earth some eight or ten inches in depth; yet sooner than restore it, she refused to let the torch of war be quenched which held all Europe in a blaze. It was not for advancement in agriculture that she has just before our own eyes deluged the plains of Affghanistan with blood. No, sir, no; it is power—power—the power which position gives that she seeks. Give her the mouth of the Columbia, and she commands the Pacific. . . .

Wait a little longer, says the senator from Massachusetts. What, I ask, have we to hope, what to dread, from immediate action? What that may not be anticipated from any decisive action in future? Is it likely that Great Britain will withdraw her claim? that she will relent of her unjust pretensions to this territory? When, in the history of the last eight cen-turies, from William the Norman to this hour, has she relented—even paused in her career of conquest and domination?

"The uttermost parts of the earth are our inheritance," is the sentiment which animates the British warrior; it governs the British council; it is the avowed language of her writers, and its home is to be found in every true Englishman's bosom.

Before this tremendous spirit, sustained equally by her policy and her arms, the mighty monarchies of Europe have successively dwindled, until in all the old world but one power remains, equal and undaunted to confront her. When gentlemen are talking about negotiating with England for a territory like Oregon, involving such great interests as I have shown she attaches to it, they will allow us, who feel an equal interest in it, to remind them that her present condition of unparalleled power is as much the fruit of her diplomacy as of her arms; that to such men as her Walsinghams and her Walpoles, her Pitts and her Castle-reaghs, she owes as much as to her Marlboroughs, her Rodneys, her Nelsons, or her Wellingtons. With the last she is and ever has been ready, without scruple, to second the designs of the first. And with the one or the other, she has thus far carried those designs, as well as I can recol-lect, except in the single instance of the two wars with this country. Retract! No, sir; judging her by the past, if she deals with us as she has dealt with others, she never will retract in peace from such a stake as this. Her foot is on the Columbia; and when she lifts it we will not owe it to diplomacy. We must win it if we wear it.

Is it asked why we should pass this measure at once? Because, in plain truth, it is time that the present condition of things should be brought to a close. It is time for us to know where we stand. Soon or late we must move; she never will; she has no cause to stir; the country is in her possession, occupied by her arms, and governed by her laws, to all intents and purposes a portion of her dominions. It is not necessary for her to commence; our people in the territory can cause her no dis-turbance, as they are at all times subject to her laws, and her laws alone, without the interference or protection of ours. In this state of things it is plain she must repose. What have we to gain by delay? Nothing; nothing on earth that I can see or imagine. We are in the position of a man whose house has been entered in his absence, and who, on his return, finds the intruder at the door forbidding his entrance. Shall the lawful owner desert his family and property through dread of the man of violence, and in the hope that, after a time, he will be allowed to enter his home in peace? Shall we delay a manly assertion of our rights?—rights in the eye of God, and all mankind, because a mighty nation, in the insolence of her bloated power, dares to cast on us an angry or a threatening glance? Or shall we, after the example of our ancestors, assert the right, and leave the consequence to God—let that consequence be peace, or let it be war?

The honorable senator from Massachusetts, on yesterday, asserted that those who would advocate a war in preference to a treaty that would give us this territory, or an equivalent for so much as we might lose of it, "were fitter for hell than for earth."

Sir, if by this it is implied that those who advocate an appeal to arms, rather than be forced to treat, are "fitter for hell than for earth," I am one of them. I utter it. I proclaim the sentiment, fitter though the gentleman may think it "for hell than for earth." Sooner than dispose of one foot under restraint, let the last alternative come. It will not find us unprepared. The senator speaks of an equivalent. What equivalent would he take? Shall we be compelled to take money for it, when we have no wish to sell, and no motive to prompt us, but the will—the iron will of haughty England? Countless millions would be no equivalent. Its very touch would blister the patriot's hand.

Whenever a question involving anything connected with Oregon—no matter in what shape—has been before us; when, upon a resolution by the senator from Ohio, a few weeks since; or at the commencement of this week, when some book question agitated the matter,—we are assailed with complaints that anything like action at present is premature; that negotiation will soon settle the whole matter for us. Why is this plea of expected negotiation constantly interposed? Will gentlemen be good enough to inform us what there is to negotiate about? To afford ground for negotiation, there must be conflicting, or, at any rate, separate and independent rights involved.

Where the rights of a question are all on one side—plain, well-defined, and understood, and that question is one simply of title, as here—what is there for negotiators to act upon? Suppose that Great Britain should assert a claim to the unoccupied country east of the Rocky Mountains, or to the Territory of Iowa, or to the State of Louisiana; would you negotiate about it? Who is here that for an instant would harbor the thought? And yet, to my mind, there is as much propriety in the one case as in the other. Our title to the one is as clear and strong as to the other.

That Great Britain is sincerely desirous of retaining this territory, no one can doubt, that observes the current of affairs with ordinary attention. She sees and fully appreciates the vast advantages to be derived from its possession. The wealth which lies dormant in the extensive and fertile valley of the Columbia and its tributaries, and the mineral wealth of the mountains which encompass that valley—the admirable position which the mouth of that river is described to be, by all who know it for a great commercial city—the facilities which it will furnish for a direct and safe intercourse and trade with the islands of the Pacific, with China, and with India—advantages which as yet cannot be computed, but which all concede must be immense;—and last, and indeed the highest immediate consideration, is the power which it would give her to operate upon the numerous Indian tribes; now congregated in that direction, on the whole line of our western frontier. With them, her intercourse must be continued and unchecked, if she is permitted to retain this or any other portion of this territory.

In selecting a permanent home for the Indian tribes, one great and leading object with this government was to remove them from the neighborhood of any foreign power; but especially, and above all other, from the vicinity of the British dominions. Sir, this proximity will not do. This facility of access and communication will not answer. Who can tell the fearful extent of the consequences, if, through the active and artful emissaries of England, these tribes should be confederated and stirred up? In a single hour, ere the alarm could be sounded, the knives of fifty thousand Indian warriors might consign the vast frontier of the West to the fell genius of desolation. Along the whole line one protracted scene of fire and blood—the blood of the generous, brave and simple-hearted pioneers, their helpless wives, and innocent children. When gentlemen remind us of their commerce and their seaboard, let them remember that their brethren in the West have causes of both interest and alarm not less weighty. I appeal to the Senate, shall England be left in possession of this terrific check? Remove every other motive; is it not sufficient to determine us? Considerations like these, sir, it seems to me, must outweigh all questions of intrinsic value, if, indeed, the question of intrinsic value can attract us, for a moment, from other and paramount considerations. By paramount considerations—for, in the noble language of the distinguished senator from Missouri, [Mr. Benton,] on Monday last—this is not a question of dollars and cents. No, sir; it is a question of national honor or national shame. In the attitude which the controversy now holds, I would not weigh the mere value of the country as a feather. I would not stop to ask if it be rich or poor, fruitful or barren. It is enough for me to know that, without the shadow of a title, and conscious of the wrong she meditates, Great Britain attempts to wrest from us that which is our own—our own. If the whole face of the earth there were volcanic—if no blade of grass ever grew, from the snowy mountains to the 54th degree of latitude, sooner than yield it to her, I would take the hazards of a war which should end only in the destruction of the one or the other. Yes, regardless of the appeal made to our nerves by the senator from Massachusetts, notwithstanding the bold figure with which he would frighten our fancies—yes, fearless of that "eagle," if thwarted, as he described England, ready to stoop, beak, talons, and all, on Oregon. If declaring our own to be our own, brings England, beak, talons, and all, on Oregon, let her come. Sir, I little expected to hear such appeals from one whose home is fast by the early and glorious battle-fields of the revolution. Surely he did not learn to dread England when standing on the consecrated field of Bunker's Hill. Let England dare to stoop from her lofty poise on Oregon; if she does, she will never, never, resume that poise again. Her flight hence will be slow and unsteady, with her wings clipped, and her talons harmless.

PART VI

THE MISSISSIPPI
VALLEY

In the time of Jackson the Mississippi Valley was more distinctively "American" in its characteristics than the eastern states, for here the imprint of the frontier was very strong. The Mississippi River with its vast down-river traffic tied the northern and southern parts of the valley together by powerful economic bonds. Not until the 1850's with the building of railroads connecting the Northwest with the Northeast and the rise of antislavery sentiment in the free states of the Ohio Valley did the northern section draw away in sentiment from the lower one. The role of the great river in the life of the people of the valley is vividly portrayed by Samuel L. Clemens (Mark Twain) in his reminiscences of his boyhood in Hannibal, Missouri, when the ambition of every boy in the river towns was to become a pilot.

Three major zones of culture could be distinguished in the Mississippi Valley, based partly on climate and geography, and partly on the different types of settlers. In the upper zone settlers from the Northeast, who came usually along the Erie Canal and the National Road in Pennsylvania, and foreign immigrants established rapidly growing communities in the prairie lands. Running through Ohio, Indiana, and Illinois was the terminal moraine line left by the last retreating glacier, marking the southern boundary of the flat black lands. South of this line is a hilly, hardwoods region, to which many of the settlers had emigrated from the Piedmont area of the South, and they gave a strong southern flavoring to the civilization of this area. The rapid settlement of the northern part of the valley, especially of Indiana and Illinois, is described by Karl Postel, a German-American who wrote under the pseudonym of "Charles Sealsfield" an account of his travels in 1827 in this region. Edward Eggleston in A Hoosier Schoolmaster and his brother George Cary Eggleston in his recollections caught the unique quality of this region. So did Charles Fenno Hoffman, a New York writer and editor who spent a winter in the West in 1834, and William H. Milburn, a Methodist preacher who grew up in Jacksonville, Illinois, and recreated in his reminiscences the rural atmosphere of the midwestern towns.

Below the Ohio and the Missouri rivers was a second zone of culture. Here, except in favored regions such as the Bluegrass region of Kentucky, the Nashville basin, and the alluvial lands in the Mississippi Valley, where plantations arose, the typical inhabitant was a small farmer whose principal crop was corn supplemented by small patches of cotton. Some of them were newly arrived rough settlers such as those delineated by the English geologist George Featherstonhaugh during his travels through Arkansas, or hospitable but poor farmers such as Frederick Law Olmsted described in his A Journey in the Back Country, *or drowsy villagers like those whom Charles Fenno Hoffman met in the little hill town of Tazewell, Tennessee.*

The lower Mississippi Valley was semitropical, quite different from the middle zone, for here were the great plantations, the gangs of slave field hands, and the Creole influence. Solon Robinson made several trips into this region, seeking out planters who were experimenting and making improvements, such as Bishop Leonidas Polk. His highly realistic letters present the good side of slavery, for he became convinced by his observations that slavery as it existed in the South was the best condition for the welfare of both races. Both a cruel side and some of the favorable aspects of slavery are presented in the diary of Bennet H. Barrow, who lived in West Feliciana Parish (one of the so-called Florida parishes) of southeastern Louisiana. He was a stern disciplinarian of his slaves, but he also gave them incentives for good work, holidays, presents, and feasts, and they developed a pride in their skill at picking cotton. Consequently he was very successful and increased the land that he owned from the fourteen hundred arpents which he had inherited to the 5,000 arpents that he held at the time of his death in 1854. A more appealing picture of the planters of the lower Mississippi Valley is presented in the account given by De-Puy Van Buren, a young man from Michigan, who came to Mississippi toward the close of the antebellum period to teach. He formed a cordial attachment to and admiration for the warm-hearted, hospitable planters of the Yazoo Valley.

The picture of life in the lower Mississippi Valley is completed by the description which Henry Benjamin Whipple gave in his diary of the busy levee at New Orleans, the mixed population, and the French atmosphere of Mobile and New Orleans, the great cotton ports of the South. Whipple was a young northerner, a native of New York, who came south in 1843 for his health. During his stay (1843–44) he kept a diary that was on the whole very favorable to the South. When he came there he was, as he described himself, "a rational abolitionist," but first-hand observation of southern conditions tempered his original opinion on the subject of slavery.

The New States of Illinois and Indiana, 1834

"*Charles Sealsfield*"

The accommodations in Trinity [Cairo, Illinois] are comfortable, and the tables are well furnished, but the prices exorbitant. It cannot, however, be expected to be otherwise, owing to the new settlers, whose anxiety never permits them to neglect an opportunity of improving their means on their first outset. We found this to be the case on all occasions. Whenever some of our passengers made purchases of trifles, such as cigars, &c., they had to pay five times as much as in Louisville. It is therefore advisable to provide oneself with every thing, when travelling in these backwoods; the generality of the settlers on these banks being needy adventurers, partly foreigners, partly Kentuckians, who, with a capital of not quite 100 dollars, with which they purchase some goods in New Orleans, begin their commercial career, and may be seen with both hands in their pockets, their legs on the table or chimney-piece, and cigars in their mouths, selling their goods for five hundred per cent. above prime cost. Towards the north on the banks of the Mississippi, the settlers are generally Frenchmen, who now assume by degrees the American manners and language. Many of them are wealthy store-keepers, merchants, and farmers; but for the most part, however, a light-footed kind of people, who, from their fathers, have inherited frivolity, and from their mothers, Indian women, uncleanliness. The towns of Kaskaskia, Cahokia, &c., as well as several villages up the Mississippi to the Prairie des Chiens, owe their origin to them. The solid class of inhabitants live on the big and little Wabash, and between these two rivers and the Illinois. This is, no doubt, the finest part of the state, and one of the most delightful countries on the face of the earth. It is mostly inhabited by Americans and Englishmen. Agriculture, the breeding of cattle, and improvements of every kind, are making rapid progress. The settlements in Bond, Crawford, Edward's, Franklin, and

"Charles Sealsfield," *The Americans as They Are* (London, 1828), pp. 84-89.

White Counties, are to be considered as forming the main substance of the state. A number of elegant towns have arisen in the space of a few years: among others, Vandalia, the capital, and for these three years past the seat of government, with a state house and a projected university, for which 36,000 acres of land have been assigned. An excellent spirit is acknowledged to prevail among the inhabitants of this district. Still, however, the style of architecture—if the laying of logs or of bricks upon each other deserves this name—the manners, the attempted improvements, every thing announces a new land, which has only a few years since started into political existence, and the settlers of which do not yet evince any anxiety for the comforts of life. Illinois has now 80,000 inhabitants, 1500 of whom are people of colour; the rest are Americans, English, French, and a German settlement about Vandalia. The state was received into the Union in the year 1818. The constitution, with a governor and a secretary at its head, resembles that of the state of Ohio. In the year 1824, the question was again brought forward concerning the possession of slaves: it was, however, negatived, and we hope it will never be pressed upon the people. The state is much indebted in every point to the late Mr. Birkbeck, who died too soon for the welfare of his adopted country. He was considered as the father of the state, and whenever he could gain over a useful citizen, he spared no expense, and sacrificed a considerable part of his property in this manner. The people of Illinois, in acknowledgment of his services, had chosen him for secretary of the state, in which character he died in 1825. He was generally known under the name of Emperor of the Prairies, from the vast extent of natural meadows belonging to his lands. It is to be regretted, however, that Mr. Birkbeck was not acquainted with the country about Trinity. His large capital and the number of hands who joined him, would no doubt succeed in establishing a settlement here. This will sooner or later take place, and will eventually render it one of the finest towns in the United States, as the advantages of its situation are incalculable. Illinois is, in point of commerce, more advantageously situated than any of the Ohio states; being bounded on the west by the river Mississippi, which forms the line between this state and that of Missouri, to the east by the big Wabash, and to the south by the Ohio, the river Illinois running through it with some smaller rivers; thus affording it an open navigation to the north-west, the west, the south, and the east. Towards the north the banks of the Upper Mississippi form a range of hills which join the Illinois mountains to the east, and lowering by degrees lose themselves in the plains of lakes Huron and Michigan. The country is, on the whole, less elevated than Indiana, and forms the last slope of the northern valley of the Mississippi, the hills being intersected by a number of valleys, plains, prairies, and marshes. The fertility of this state is extraordinary, surpassing that of Indiana and Ohio. In

beauty, variety of scenery, and fertility, it may vie with the most celebrated countries. Wheat thrives only on high land, the soil of the valleys
being too rich. Corn gives for every bushel a hundred. Tobacco planted in
Illinois, if well managed, is found to be superior to that of Kentucky and
Virginia. Rice and indigo grow wild, their cultivation being neglected for
want of hands. Pecans, a product of the West Indies, grow in abundance
in the native forests. This state having a temperate climate, possesses
many of the southern products. The timber is of colossal magnitude. Syca-
mores and cotton trees of an immense height, walnut, pecan trees, honey-
locusts and maples, cover the surface of this country, and are the surest
indications of an exceedingly rich soil. The most fertile parts of the state
are the bottom lands along the Mississippi, Illinois, and the big and little
Wabash. The country is complained of as being sickly. There is no doubt
that a state which abounds in rivers, marshes, and ponds, must be subject
to epidemic diseases, but the climate being temperate the fault lies very
much with the settlers and the inhabitants themselves. The settler who
chooses for his dwelling-house a spot on an eminence, and far from the
marshes, taking at the same time the necessary precautions in point of
dress, cleanliness, and the choice of victuals and beverage, may live without fear in these countries. All agree in this opinion, and I have myself
experienced the correctness of it. The greatest part, however, of the new
comers and inhabitants live upon milk or stagnant water taken from the
first pond they meet with on their way, with a few slices of bacon. Their
wardrobe consists of a single shirt, which is worn till it falls to pieces. It
cannot, therefore, be matter of astonishment if agues and bilious fevers
spread over the country, and even in this case a quart of corn brandy is
their prescription. This being the general mode of living, and we may add
of dying, among the lower classes, disease must necessarily spread its
ravages with more rapidity.

A Cocktail on the Kalamazoo Prairie

Charles Fenno Hoffman

Prairie Ronde, Kalamazoo Co., M. T., Dec. 26. "Stranger, will you take a cocktail with us?" called out a tall athletic fellow to me as I was making my way through a group of wild looking characters assembled an hour since around the fire by which I am now writing. There was a long-haired "hoosier" from Indiana, a couple of smart looking "suckers" [so called after the fish of that name, from his going up the river to the mines, and returning at the season when the sucker makes its migrations] from the southern part of Illinois, a keen-eyed leather-belted "badger" from the mines of Ouisconsin, and a sturdy yeoman-like fellow, whose white capot, Indian moccasins, and red sash, proclaimed, while he boasted a three year's residence, the genuine *wolverine,* or naturalized Michiganian. Could one refuse to drink with such a company? The spokesman was evidently a "red-horse" from Kentucky, and nothing was wanting but a "buck-eye" from Ohio to render the assemblage as complete as it was select. I was in the midst of the first real prairie I had ever seen—on an island of timber, whose lee, while making slow headway for the last two hours, with a biting breeze on my beam, it had been my whole object, aim, and ambition to get—a comfortable bar-room, a smoking "cocktail," a worshipful assemblage (Goldsmith's Club was a fool to it,) had never entered my dreams! Could I refuse to drink with such a company? The warm glass is in my frozen fingers. The most devout temperance man could see no harm in that! It is touched smartly by the rim of the red-horse,—it is brushed by the hoosier,—it rings against the badger,—comes in companionable contact with the wolverine,—"My respects to you, gentlemen, and luck to all of us!"

Here was a capital commencement with just the sort of salad of society I have been long wishing to meet with, having as yet only tasted its com-

Charles Fenno Hoffman, *A Winter in the West* (New York, 1835), I, pp. 210-211.

ponent parts in detail. But, auspicious as was the beginning, I nearly got into a difficulty with my new acquaintances a few moments afterwards, by handing the landlord a share of the reckoning; and I took back the coin forced upon me, with many apologies upon my part for having presumed to pay part of a "general treat," while labouring under the disqualifications of being a stranger. Room was then civilly made for me by the fireplace, and, accepting a pipe proffered by one of the company, a few whiffs made me sufficiently sick and at home to lay it by without further ceremony. "There's *a smart chance of cigars* there in the bar, stranger, if you'd try some of them," said one of the hooshiers. "Yes," echoed the other; "and they are a heap better than those pipes." "I allow," rejoined another of the company; "but I wish that fellow would shut the door; he must think that we were all raised in a saw-mill, and then he looks so *peert* whenever he comes in." "Poor fellow!" ejaculated one who had not yet spoken, "he is considerably troubled with youngness."

"From the eastern side, stranger?" said another to me; "I'm told it's tolerable frog pasture. Now, here the soil's so deep one can't raise any long sarce—they all get pulled through the other side. We can winter our cows, however, on wooden clocks, there's so many Yankees among us," &c.

A scattering conversation was kept up in similar quaint expressions for some time; but I will not tire you with enumerating more of those which fell under my observation. These unique terms, indeed, were poured out so copiously, that it was impossible for one's memory, though elastic as a pair of saddle-bags, to retain them. At last a *train* [a rough kind of sled] and a couple of carioles drove up to the door; and I discovered, upon their bundling merrily into these vehicles, that the whole company were bound for a wedding. "Jim," cried one driver to another, snapping his whip, "let our horses run near the silk." *Jim* cracked his snapper, and the light carioles taking the lead, the more humble train skimmed rapidly after them: their dark shadows were soon lost upon the moonlit prairie, and the sound of their bells died away in the distance by the time I had regained my now solitary seat by the fire.

An Illinois Town on Market Day

William Henry Milburn

In the centre of the town [Jacksonville, Ill.] was the public square. From this proceeded the four principal streets, which in their continuation kept us in correspondence with the four quarters of the globe; and many a time have I looked upon stages running their several ways and fancied them monster shuttles weaving us into the world's web, and laying our life threads side by side with our fellows in the vast fabric of humanity. The sides of the square were lined with the shanties in which was transacted the business of the place. The occupants of these lowly shops, in which was sold all manner of merchandise—from the ribbon that trimmed the bonnet of the rustic belle, to the plough which broke up her father's acres—were styled merchants, and the occupation of bartering molasses and calico, for beeswax, butter and eggs, was denominated the mercantile. At frequent intervals were located "groceries," most commonly called "doggeries," where "spirits" were sold by "the small" i.e. the glass. In the centre of the square stood the court and market houses, the one brick, the other frame. The market was two stories high, the lower story devoted to the sale of meats, and the upper to a newspaper and lawyers' offices, the gallery at the side serving as a rostrum for stump orators. Saturday was a great day, when from many miles around the old and young, male and female, came with every product of the land, by every means of conveyance, to trade. Homespun dames and damsels, making the circuit of the square inquiring at every door: "D'ye buy eggs and butter yer?" and sometimes responding indignantly, as I heard a maiden once when told that eggs were bringing only three cents a dozen: "What, do ye s'pose our hens are gwine to strain theirselves a laying eggs at three cents a dozen? Lay 'em yourself, and see how you'd like the price."

It was a lively scene on a market day; with its crowds of prairie wagons, long, low uncovered boxes placed on wheels, in which the articles sold and bought, to which the generic name of plunder was applied, were

William Henry Milburn, *Ten Years of Preacher-Life* (New York, 1860), pp. 24-30.

conveyed to and from the town; while groups of saddled horses, pawing the earth and neighing their neighborly recognitions to each other, stood fastened at the posts. Here you might descry a piratical cow, boarding a wagon by adroitly raising her fore legs into it, smelling around, while the trading owner was absent, for fruits and vegetables, or even devouring his purchased stock of sugar; and there sweeping along at full gallop, some half drunken jockey, showing off the points of his steed, and with stentorian voice offering to bet any man ten dollars that it was the best piece of horse flesh on the ground. Groups are gathered in front of all the "doggeries," at the street corners, and at the doors of the court-house, discussing politics, or other urgent questions of the time; differences of opinion, stimulated by bald-face whisky, often bringing these conferences to a pugilistic termination. Meanwhile the older ladies, arrayed in dark linsey-woolsey dresses—the lower front adorned by blue check aprons— their heads covered with sun-bonnets, and their feet with yarn stockings and brogan shoes or moccasins, having brought the interesting and complicated operations of trading to a close, stand idly about with folded arms, regaling themselves with fumes of tobacco, inhaled from a corncob or sweet potato pipe. The exercises of the day were usually varied by political speeches, a sheriff's sale, a half dozen free fights, and thrice as many horse swaps. Just before sundown the traders departed, and the town was left to its inhabitants.

The principal denominations of Christians had houses of worship in the village, and the society of the place made up of representatives from all sections of the Union, had a higher intellectual, moral and religious tone than is usual in a new country.

Besides the President and Professors of Illinois College, there was quite a number of men, distinguished in the State by their positions at the bar and in politics; and from all sides the new comers, who deserved it, received cordial welcome and hospitable courtesy. . . .

My father raised a small capital, and taking heart of grace, ventured once more into the uncertainties of business, and I was installed as my mother's assistant in housekeeping, and as my father's in merchandising. In that free and independent country, such things as servants were not— not even help or hired girls—so that the women of the household had their own work to do, their husbands and sons aiding them by attending to the "chores." Therefore this saying passed into a proverb—"It is a good country for men and horses, but it is death on women and oxen."

It devolved upon me to draw the water and cut the wood; but I cannot boast that, with my best endeavors, I ever acquired much facility in milking a cow. Early rising was the habit of the land, and our family was not second to the foremost; but whether from constitutional indisposition or excess of the discipline, or a failure in it, I cannot tell, yet I fear much that the practice then submitted to from necessity has implanted in me an unconquerable repugnance to Dr. Franklin's adage, and in spite of my better judgment, I feel the tip of my nose suddenly aspiring whenever I hear that wise counsel preached—

"Early to bed, and early to rise,
Makes a man healthy, wealthy, and wise."

In winter-time we always breakfasted by candlelight; and, by the way, although I do not believe I should ever have acquired eminence as a tallow-chandler, it is fair to state that I did acquire some skill in the manufacture of "dips and moulds," and also of "soft soap," the kind chiefly in use—I mean the literal, not the metaphorical. It fell to my lot to prepare the early repast. After kindling the fire and putting on the kettle, I ground and made the coffee, laid the table, and then hurried to the store, where another fire was to be lighted, and the premises swept and dusted. Returning, I was in time for the meal, and at its close, my father went to the counter, while I staid to play domestic. These duties ended, I entered upon those of clerk and bookkeeper, making small entries, measuring what the natives call—not, I suppose, with the cognizance of Lindley Murray—"them molasses," or weighing out coffee, tea, and sugar.

The Glamour of the Mississippi

Samuel L. Clemens

When I was a boy, there was but one permanent ambition among my comrades in our village [Hannibal, Missouri] on the west bank of the Mississippi River. That was, to be a steamboatman. We had transient ambitions of other sorts, but they were only transient. When a circus came and went, it left us all burning to become clowns; the first negro minstrel show that ever came to our section left us all suffering to try that kind of life; now and then we had a hope that, if we lived and were good, God would permit us to be pirates. These ambitions faded out, each in its turn; but the ambition to be a steamboatman always remained.

Once a day a cheap, gaudy packet arrived upward from St. Louis, and another downward from Keokuk. Before these events, the day was glorious with expectancy; after them, the day was a dead and empty thing. Not only the boys, but the whole village, felt this. After all these years I can picture that old time to myself now, just as it was then: the white town drowsing in the sunshine of a summer's morning; the streets empty, or pretty nearly so; one or two clerks sitting in front of the Water Street stores, with their splint-bottomed chairs tilted back against the walls, chins on breasts, hats slouched over their faces, asleep—with shingle-shavings enough around to show what broke them down; a sow and a litter of pigs loafing along the sidewalk, doing a good business in water-melon rinds and seeds; two or three lonely little freight piles scattered about the "levee"; a pile of "skids" on the slope of the stone-paved wharf, and the fragrant town drunkard asleep in the shadow of them; two or three wood flats at the head of the wharf, but nobody to listen to the peaceful lapping of the wavelets against them; the great Mississippi, the majestic, the magnificent Mississippi, rolling its mile-wide tide along, shining in the sun; the dense forest away on the other side; the "point" above the town, and the "point" below, bounding the river-glimpse and turning it into a sort of sea, and withal a very still and brilliant and lonely

Samuel L. Clemens, *Life on the Mississippi* (Boston, 1883), Chap. IV, pp. 62-69.

one. Presently a film of dark smoke appears above one of those remote
"points"; instantly a negro drayman, famous for his quick eye and prodigious voice, lifts up the cry, "S-t-e-a-m-boat a-comin'!" and the scene
changes! The town drunkard stirs, the clerks wake up, a furious clatter
of drays follows, every house and store pours out a human contribution,
and all in a twinkling the dead town is alive and moving. Drays, carts,
men, boys, all go hurrying from many quarters to a common center, the
wharf. Assembled there, the people fasten their eyes upon the coming
boat as upon a wonder they are seeing for the first time. And the boat *is*
rather a handsome sight, too. She is long and sharp and trim and pretty;
she has two tall, fancy-topped chimneys, with a gilded device of some
kind swung between them; a fanciful pilot-house, all glass and "ginger-
bread," perched on top of the "texas" deck behind them; the paddle-boxes
are gorgeous with a picture or with gilded rays above the boat's name;
the boiler-deck, the hurricane-deck, and the texas deck are fenced and
ornamented with clean white railings; there is a flag gallantly flying from
the jack-staff; the furnace doors are open and the fires glaring bravely;
the upper decks are black with passengers; the captain stands by the
big bell, calm, imposing, the envy of all; great volumes of the blackest
smoke are rolling and tumbling out of the chimneys—a husbanded grandeur created with a bit of pitch-pine just before arriving at a town; the
crew are grouped on the forecastle; the broad stage is run far out over
the port bow, and an envied deck-hand stands picturesquely on the end
of it with a coil of rope in his hand; the pent steam is screaming through
the gauge-cocks; the captain lifts his hand, a bell rings, the wheels stop;
then they turn back, churning the water to foam, and the steamer is at
rest. Then such a scramble as there is to get aboard, and to get ashore,
and to take in freight and to discharge freight, all at one and the same
time; and such a yelling and cursing as the mates facilitate it all with!
Ten minutes later the steamer is under way again, with no flag on the
jack-staff and no black smoke issuing from the chimneys. After ten more
minutes the town is dead again, and the town drunkard asleep by the
skids once more.

   My father was a justice of the peace, and I supposed he possessed the
power of life and death over all men, and could hang anybody that
offended him. This was distinction enough for me as a general thing; but
the desire to be a steamboatman kept intruding, nevertheless. I first
wanted to be a cabin-boy, so that I could come out with a white apron
on and shake a tablecloth over the side, where all my old comrades could
see me; later I thought I would rather be the deck-hand who stood on
the end of the stage-plank with the coil of rope in his hand, because he
was particularly conspicuous. But these were only day-dreams—they were
too heavenly to be contemplated as real possibilities. By and by one of

our boys went away. He was not heard of for a long time. At last he turned up as apprentice engineer or "striker" on a steamboat. This thing shook the bottom out of all my Sunday-school teachings. That boy had been notoriously worldly, and I just the reverse; yet he was exalted to this eminence, and I left in obscurity and misery. There was nothing generous about this fellow in his greatness. He would always manage to have a rusty bolt to scrub while his boat tarried at our town, and he would sit on the inside guard and scrub it, where we all could see him and envy him and loathe him. And whenever his boat was laid up he would come home and swell around the town in his blackest and greasiest clothes, so that nobody could help remembering that he was a steamboatman; and he used all sorts of steamboat technicalities in his talk, as if he were so used to them that he forgot common people could not understand them. He would speak of the "labboard" side of a horse in an easy, natural way that would make one wish he was dead. And he was always talking about "St. Looy" like an old citizen; he would refer casually to occasions when he was "coming down Fourth Street," or when he was "passing by the Planter's House," or when there was a fire and he took a turn on the brakes of "the old Big Missouri"; and then he would go on and lie about how many towns the size of ours were burned down there that day. Two or three of the boys had long been persons of consideration among us because they had been to St. Louis once and had a vague general knowledge of its wonders, but the day of their glory was over now. They lapsed into a humble silence, and learned to disappear when the ruthless "cub"-engineer approached. This fellow had money, too, and hair-oil. Also an ignorant silver watch and a showy brass watch-chain. He wore a leather belt and used no suspenders. If ever a youth was cordially admired and hated by his comrades, this one was. No girl could withstand his charms. He "cut out" every boy in the village. When his boat blew up at last, it diffused a tranquil contentment among us such as we had not known for months. But when he came home the next week, alive, renowned, and appeared in church all battered up and bandaged, a shining hero, stared at and wondered over by everybody, it seemed to us that the partiality of Providence for an undeserving reptile had reached a point where it was open to criticism.

This creature's career could produce but one result, and it speedily followed. Boy after boy managed to get on the river. The minister's son became an engineer. The doctor's and the postmaster's sons became "mud clerks"; the wholesale liquor dealer's son became a barkeeper on a boat; four sons of the chief merchant, and two sons of the county judge, became pilots. Pilot was the grandest position of all. The pilot, even in those days of trivial wages, had a princely salary—from a hundred and fifty to two hundred and fifty dollars a month, and no board to pay. Two months of his wages would pay a preacher's salary for a year. Now some of us were left disconsolate. We could not get on the river—at least our parents would not let us.

So, by and by, I ran away. I said I would never come home again till I was a pilot and could come in glory. But somehow I could not manage it. I went meekly aboard a few of the boats that lay packed together like sardines at the long St. Louis wharf, and humbly inquired for the pilots, but got only a cold shoulder and short words from mates and clerks. I had to make the best of this sort of treatment for the time being, but I had comforting day-dreams of a future when I should be a great and honored pilot, with plenty of money, and could kill some of these mates and clerks and pay for them.

A Tennessee Hill Town

Charles Fenno Hoffman

Tazewell, Tennessee, April 21, 1834. I write to you from a small county town in Tennessee. It is composed of about a hundred wooden houses, scattered along a broad street, which traverses the side of a high hill or mountain slope, and which, though partly shut in by wooded elevations, still commands a wide view of cultivated country. This is the first day of court-week, and the village, which presents rather a desolate appearance, from the want of shrubbery or ornamental enclosures of any kind around the houses, is somewhat enlivened by the troops of country people moving to and fro. There is a group of the white beaver and hunting shirt gentry collected at this moment around a blood-horse, whose points a groom is showing off opposite to my window; and farther up the street, round the steps of the little unpainted wooden court-house, is a collection of old women, in scarlet cloaks or plaid wrappers, gossipping together.

I entered Tazewell about sunset, a day or two since. My horse had fallen lame within ten miles of the place; and taking the bridle in my hand, I trudged leisurely along, till I gained the inn, where I have established myself. The afternoon was perfectly still, and a herd of cows, which a mounted negro was urging homeward, were the only objects stirring in the town. I could discern, however, that it was inhabited, from seeing the village tailor and other dignitaries of the place lounging upon rush-bottom chairs in front of their dwellings, while the lazy vapour that curled from their pipes, in the evening air, bespoke a sort of indolent repose, such as whilom reigned in the drowsy region of Sleepy Hollow. I looked from my window in the morning, and there, at ten o'clock, sat the same set of luxurious worthies, a low chuckle or a short laugh, as some acknowledged wag doled out his good things, being the only sound of animation that met my ears. I looked when the heat of the noonday sun had made their position no longer tenable, and the industrious Taze-

Charles Fenno Hoffman, *A Winter in the West*, II, pp. 183-189.

wellites had retired within doors to their various avocations. Evening, with its shadows, brought them again, also; and, maugre the example of my attentive and stirring little landlord, I found that I had imbibed a portion of the indolence prevailing around me. I sauntered across the way, and lighted my cigar by the most accessible looking of the company; and dropping into an unoccupied chair, balanced it on two legs, with an air that at once made good my claim to a share in their gossip.

I had just got comfortably embarked with one of the seniors in a quiet dish of local politics, when an outcry, a few yards off, attracted our attention. Stepping up to the group of persons from which it arose, I saw a queer-looking little bantam figure, in an old straw hat and coarse shrunk-up hunting-shirt, who appeared to be in the highest paroxysm of rage. At one moment, he would vent his fury in a torrent of outrageous epithets, and then, gripping the shrunken skirt of his hunting-shirt with one hand, while the other was shaken angrily at the crowd, he would leap a yard in the air, turning round on his heel as he came down, and crowing like a game cock. In performing this evolution, I caught a sight of his face by the moonlight, and discovered that he had undergone a very common piece of western waggery, having had his face blacked, while lying asleep in a state of intoxication.

"Who has dared to make a nigger of me?" shouted the unfortunate votary of Bacchus, as I approached him, dilating his little pony-built person with great pomposity; "who dared treat little John like a brute? Let me but get at him, and I'll drink his blood. I'll eat his liver" (gnashing his teeth); "if God has breathed the breath of man into him, let him speak, and I'll knock it out. Little John is not the man to be walked over; little John never insulted anybody, but he knows how to mount them that don't treat him like a gentleman,—wheugh, whoop, whoop!—whe-ug-h!—I'm a real screamer!" And here he bounced up, crowing in the air, as if he had springs in his heels.

"I'm the man, John," cried one of the crowd, throwing off his coat.— "You, you, indeed!" answered the little champion, without stirring from the spot; "Why, Bill, you know you lie! You wouldn't dare to play such a trick on me; but only let me catch the real fellow."—"It's a shame, a shame, to treat John so," cried half a dozen voices around.—"No, no, it's no shame; it's only a shame, that the black villain should hide himself after he did it; thank God, John can take care of himself"—(here he flapped his arms, and crowed defiance). "I'm as good a bit of man's flesh as skin ever covered" (here he crowed again). "I'm the first-born of my mother, and knock under to no white man. 'John,' says she, 'you are a true one,'—and so I am. My mother knows I am as good a little fellow as ever mother brought forth: she said I was a screamer the moment she saw me; 'John,' says she, 'you're a real out-and-outer;' and am I not?" (crowing:) "who says little John was ever afraid of man or beast? Come out here, any ten of you, and I'll mount you one after another."

The rapidity with which these whimsical expressions of wrath, and thrice as many more, were poured upon each other, was perfectly astonishing; and the mad antics with which the valorous little fellow accompanied them were irresistibly ludicrous. At length his rage appeared nearly to have spent itself, and he listened with some composure to the wicked wags who, collecting around him, pretended to sympathize in his wrongs. One of them even undertook to wash his face for him; but smearing it over with oil as his patient bent over the basin, the inky dye became so fixed in the pores that the office of eradicating it must have been no sinecure. It was then proposed to bring him a looking-glass; which I presume was done, for, pausing a moment on the steps, ere I entered my lodgings, in expectation of another explosion, I heard the merrymakers shouting with peals of laughter, while poor little John seemed to have retired, completely done up.

I could not help reflecting, while retiring for the night, that the subject of all this village uproar,—who, in language and manners, was an exact impersonation of the western character, as it is generally portrayed,— was anything but a fair specimen of the western population; for, though you meet with some such extravagant character in almost every hamlet, you might as well form your idea of the New England yeomanry from the Yankee pedlers that prowl through the western states, as conceive that the mass of the population over the mountains are of this "half-horse and half-alligator" species. I had a long conversation this morning with a middle-aged country lawyer, upon western life and character, in which I gave my sentiments with great freedom; and though, like our countrymen in every part of the Union, he was sufficiently exacting of the praise of strangers, he did not seem to take offence at some of my observations, which were not altogether palatable.

"Well, sir," he began, after bidding me good morning, "what do you think of *our country?*"

"It is a rich and beautiful one, sir."

"There's no two ways about that, sir; but aren't you surprised to see such a fine population?"

"You have certainly a fine-looking set of men, with good manners, and a great deal of natural intelligence."

"But their knowledge of things, sir, and the way in which they live— don't you think our plain country people live in a very superior way, sir?"

"Have you ever been in the northern or eastern states, sir?—New York or New England?" I replied. While answering negatively, he gave a look of utter amazement at the idea of comparing those districts with that in which he lived.

I then,—while doing justice to the many attractive points in the character of these mountaineers, their hardihood and frank courtesy to strangers, their easy address, and that terseness of expression and command of language which often strikes and interests you in the conversation of men who actually cannot read,—explained to him the superiority which greater industry and acquired knowledge of useful facts gives the northern man, of the same class, in providing comforts and conveniences for himself and family, and living in a style that approaches that of the independent planter of the West. But, countryman as he was, I could not persuade one who had probably, in western phrase, been "raised on hog and hominy," and kept all his life on "bacon and greens," of the advantages of a thoroughly cultivated garden, a well-kept dairy, and flourishing poultry-yard; much less could I make him understand the charm which lay in neat enclosures, and a sheltered porch or piazza, with shrubbery clustering around it. He only replied, when I commented upon the fields, which I sometimes saw, that had run out from indolence or bad tillage, that "there was land enough to make new ones;" and added, as we placed ourselves at the breakfast-table, "that if the people did not live up to other people's ideas, they lived as well as they wanted to. They didn't want to make slaves of themselves; they were contented with living as their fathers lived before them."

I remember, while passing him an old-fashioned salt-cellar over our frugal table, that he had Horace on his side, and could not but acknowledge that contentment was the all in all.

A Barefoot Tennessee Squire

Frederick Law Olmsted

June 20, 1854. Fortunately I did not have to go much further before I came to the best house I had seen during the day, a large, neat, white house, with negro shanties, and an open log cabin in the front yard. A stout, elderly, fine-looking woman, in a cool white muslin dress sat upon the gallery, fanning herself. Two little negroes had just brought a pail of fresh water, and she was drinking of it with a gourd, as I came to the gate. I asked if it would be convenient for her to accommodate me for the night, doubtingly, for I had learned to distrust the accommodations of the wealthy slaveholders.

"Oh yes, get down, fasten your horse there, and the niggers will take care of him when they come from their work. Come up here and take a seat."

I brought in my saddle-bags.

"Bring them in here, into the parlor," she said, "where they'll be safe."

The interior of the house was furnished with unusual comfort. "The parlor," however, had a bed in it. As we came out she locked the door.

We had not sat long, talking about the weather, (she was suffering much from the heat), when her husband came. He was very hot also, though dressed coolly enough in merely a pair of short-legged, unbleached cotton trowsers, and a shirt with the bosom spread open—no shoes nor stockings. He took his seat before speaking to me, and after telling his wife it was the hottest day he ever saw, squared his chair toward me, threw it back so as to recline against a post, and said gruffly, "Good evening, sir; you going to stay here to-night?"

I replied, and he looked at me a few moments without speaking. He was in fact so hot that he spoke with difficulty. At length he got breath and asked abruptly: "You a mechanic, sir, or a dentist, eh—or what?"

I presently asked what railroad it was that I had crossed about six miles

Frederick Law Olmsted, *A Journey in the Back Country* (New York, 1860), pp. 233-238.

east of Chatanooga. I had not expected to find any railroad in this direction. He answered pompously that it was "the Atlantic and Pacific railroad. It began at Charleston and ended at Chatanooga, but was to be carried across to a place called Francisco in California."

Valuable information, but hardly as interesting as that which the old lady gave me soon afterward. We had been talking of Texas and the emigration. She said "there was a new country they had got annexed to the United States now, and she reckoned people would all be for going to that, now it was annexed. They called it Nebrasky; she didn't know much about it, but she reckoned it must be a powerful fine country, they'd taken so much trouble to get possession of it."

Supper was cooked by two young women, daughters of the master of the house, assisted by the two little negro boys. The cabin in front of the house was the kitchen, and when the bacon was dished up, one of the boys struck an iron triangle at the door. "Come to supper," said the host, and led the way to the kitchen, which was also the supper room, One of the young ladies took the foot of the table, the other seated herself apart by the fire, and actually waited on the table, though the two negro boys stood at the head and foot, nominally waiters, but always anticipated by the Cinderella, when any thing was wanted.

A big lout of a youth who came from the field with the negroes, looked in, but seeing me, retired. His father called, but his mother said, " 't would n't do no good—he was so bashful."

Speaking of the climate of the country, I was informed that a majority of the folks went barefoot all winter, though they had snow much of the time four or five inches deep, and the man said he did n't think most of the men about here had more than one coat, and they never wore any in winter except on holidays. "That was the healthiest way," he reckoned, "just to toughen yourself and not wear no coat; no matter how cold it was, he did n't wear no coat."

The master held a candle for me while I undressed, in a large room above stairs; and gave me my choice of the four beds in it. I found one straw bed (with, as usual, but one sheet), on which I slept comfortably. At midnight I was awakened by some one coming in. I rustled my straw, and a voice said, "Who is there in this room?"

"A stranger passing the night; who are you?"

"All right; I belong here. I've been away and have just come home."

He did not take his clothes off to sleep. He turned out to be an older son who had been fifty miles away, looking after a stray horse. When I went down stairs in the morning, having been wakened early by flies, and the dawn of day through an open window, I saw the master lying on his bed in the "parlor," still asleep in the clothes he wore at supper. His wife was washing herself on the gallery, being already dressed for the day; after drying her face on the family towel, she went into the kitchen, but soon returned, smoking a pipe, to her chair in the doorway.

Yet every thing betokened an opulent and prosperous farmer—rich land, extensive field crops, a number of negroes, and considerable herds of cattle and horses. He also had capital invested in mines and railroads, he told me. His elder son spoke of him as "the squire."

A negro woman assisted in preparing breakfast (she had probably been employed in the field labor the night before), and both the young ladies were at the table. The squire observed to me that he supposed we could buy hands very cheap in New York. I said we could hire them there at moderate wages. He asked if we could n't buy as many as we wanted, by sending to Ireland for them and paying their passage. He had supposed we could buy them and hold them as slaves for a term of years, by paying the freight on them. When I had corrected him, he said, a little hesitatingly, "You do n't have no black slaves in New York?" "No sir." "There's niggers there, ain't there, only they're all free?" "Yes sir." "Well, how do they get along so?" "So far as I know, the most of them live pretty comfortably." (I have changed my standard of comfort lately, and am inclined to believe that the majority of the negroes at the North live more comfortably than the majority of whites at the South.) "I would n't like that," said the old lady. "I would n't like to live where niggers was free, they are bad enough when they are slaves: it's hard enough to get along with them here, they're so bad. I reckon that niggers are the meanest critters on earth; they are so mean and nasty" (she expressed disgust and indignation very strongly in her face). "If they was to think themselves equal to we, I do n't think white folks could abide it—they're such vile saucy things." A negro woman and two boys were in the room as she said this.

At night I was again troubled to find a house at which my horse could be suitably fed, and was finally directed to a place at some distance off my direct road. To reach it, I followed a cart path up a pretty brook in a mountain glen, till I came to an irregular-shaped cattle yard, in the midst of which was a rather picturesque cabin, the roof being secured by logs laid across it and held in place by long upright pins. The interior consisted of one large "living-room," and a "lean-to," used as a kitchen, with a sleeping loft over half the living-room. For furniture, there were two bedsteads, which occupied one-third of the room; a large and small table, on the latter of which lay a big Bible, and other books; several hide-bottomed chairs, two chests, shelves with crockery, and a framed lithographic portrait of Washington on the white horse. Women's dresses hung as a curtain along the foot of one bed; hides, hams, and bunches of candles from the rafters. An old man and his wife, with one hired man, were the occupants; they had come to this place from North Carolina two years before. They were very good, simple people; social and talkative, but at frequent intervals the old man, often in the midst of conversation, interrupting a reply to a question put by himself, would groan aloud and sigh out, "Glory to God!" "Oh my blessed Lord!" "Lord, have mercy on us!" or something of the sort, and the old woman would respond with a groan, and then there would be silence for reflection for a few moments, as if a dead man were in the house, and it had been forgotten for a time. They talked with great geniality and kindness, however, and learning that I was from New York, said that I had reminded them, "by the way I talked," of some New York people who had moved near to where they had lived in North Carolina, and whom they seemed to have much liked. "They was well larned people," the old man said; "though they warn't rich, they was as well larned as any, but they was the most friendly people I ever see. Most of our country folks, when they is well larned, is too proud, they won't hardly speak civil to the common; but these Yorkers was n't so, the least bit; they was the civilest people I ever seed. When I seed the gals coming over to our housen, I nat'rally rejoiced; they always made it so pleasant. I never see no people who could talk so well."

Rough Settlers in Arkansas

George W. Featherstonhaugh

This territory of Arkansas was on the confines of the United States and Mexico, and, as I had long known, was the occasional residence of many timid and nervous persons, against whom the laws of these respective countries had a grudge. *Gentlemen,* who had taken the liberty to imitate signatures of other persons; *bankrupts,* who were not disposed to be plundered by their creditors; *homicides, horse-stealers,* and *gamblers,* all admired Arkansas on account of the very gentle and tolerant state of public opinion which prevailed there in regard to such fundamental points as religion, morals, and property. . . . Such a community I was anxious to see, as well as to observe the form society had taken in it; more especially as a very curious movement was now going on from this very territory in relation to the adjoining province of Texas in Mexico, which, being somewhat in want of an enlightened government, seemed preparing to receive one from those persecuted individuals who had shown so much aversion to become the victims of civilized society.

On entering the breakfast-room I found a very motley set at table, and took my seat opposite to a dignified looking person with a well-grown set of mustachios, a round-about jacket, with other vestments made in the Spanish fashion, and a profusion of showy rings on his fingers. The gravity of his deportment was quite Spanish, and being informed that he was from New Spain, I promised myself a good deal of pleasure in conversing with him in his native tongue about his own country: but after bolting what was before him with an enviable rapidity—a talent I had never before observed in a Spaniard—he left the room ere I had an opportunity of speaking to him. During the day, however, as I was strolling round the place, how great was my surprise at seeing Don Bigotes seated on a shopboard close to a window, and sewing away cross-legged in a most approved sartorial fashion! This led me to make some inquiries about him, and then I learnt that he had arrived in Little Rock not long before from Santa Fe in Mex-

George W. Featherstonhaugh, *Excursion Through the Slave States* . . . pp. 94-99.

ico, on a fine barb horse with a showy Spanish saddle and housings; and finding that wages were very high in Little Rock, he had declared himself to be a tailor by trade, and had engaged for a month as a journeyman. This certainly was an odd character to begin with in Arkansas, but my amusement was infinitely increased afterwards when my son informed me that having had occasion to want the assistance of an artist in that line, he had been to the shop where the Don worked, had had some conversation with him, and that notwithstanding his gravity, his mustachios, and his rings, he was neither more nor less than a Connecticut Yankee of the name of Patterson, who *having occasion* to leave the land of steady habits, had straggled to New Mexico, where he had practised his art successfully, and having made a little speculation in his barb—upon which he set an immense price—had got so far on his way back again to his native country. Such is the plastic nature of Jonathan, his indomitable affection for the almighty dollar, and his enterprise in the pursuit of it, that it is far from being impossible that there are lots of his brethren at this time in the interior of China, with their heads shaved and long pig-tails behind them, peddling cuckoo clocks and selling wooden nutmegs.

Before I left the room one of the *gentlemen* who had slept in our apartment came in, looking rather frouzily; there was a great attempt at finery about his clothes, and a tremendous red beard under his chin: it was impossible not to admire him, and equally so not to see that in his haste to come down before everything was devoured, he had forgotten to wash himself and brush his hair. The voice of this worthy was precisely like that of Colonel Smith of the British army, whose adventures have been narrated; and the exquisite manner in which he drawled out his ungrammatical absurdities left no room for conjecture as to his real character. When I asked the landlord who he was, he told me he was "a sportsman," a designation by which all the bloods who live by faro and rouge et noir are known in Arkansas.

I was obliged to remain two days in this house, all the others being full of adventurers, who were constantly pouring into the place. Decent people, I was told, got into private families; but, although we applied in several places, we could find nobody disposed to receive us: our landlord, Colonel Leech, who perceived that we were only travelling for information, was very kind and obliging, but he could not let us have a private room, and we were, therefore, very uncomfortable, walking about the town and passing, I dare say, in the eyes of every body for adventurers. At length we heard of a *clergyman* who lived on the skirts of the town, and sometimes "took in boarders," so we immediately hied to the *Rev. Mr. Stevenson's*. It was a nice-looking cottage enough, separated from the road by a paling, inside of which was standing a somewhat dried-up looking individual, in a seedy-looking, light-coloured jacket, an old hat with a broken

rim on his head, only one eye in that, and a rifle in his hand. "Pray, sir,"
said I, touching my hat, "can you inform me if this is the Reverend Mr.
Stevenson's?" Upon which he immediately replied, "I *expect* I am the
Reverend Mr. Stevenson!" That being his opinion, it would not have forwarded my purpose at all to have commenced a dispute with him about it,
so we immediately entered upon business. I told him who I was, what my
pursuits were, that we had got mixed up with very bad society, and that I
should be very happy to pay any thing for a private room and board in his
family. Mr. Stevenson turned out to be a much better man than his externals indicated: he entered into my situation, presented us to Mrs. Stevenson—who had *two* remarkably good eyes in her head—and who not
only assigned us a roomy bed-chamber, which we lost no time in taking
possession of, but during the whole time we staid in her house was uniformly obliging to us. Mr. Stevenson had been one of the earliest settlers
in Arkansas, had travelled in every part of it, and had occasionally officiated in the remote parts as a missionary: as he cultivated a piece of land
somewhere near the town, whenever he visited it he was in the habit of
taking his rifle with him, and this accounted for my having seen him
armed.

At the supper-table we first met the rest of his family, which consisted
of several small children, three other boarders, two of whom were tradesmen of the place, and a very intelligent person from Switzerland of the
name of T——. This gentleman's conversation interested me very much,
and when I had become sufficiently acquainted with him to learn his history and adventures, I could not help taking great interest in his welfare.
He was of a good family in Switzerland, had been well educated, and had
been officially employed in one of the bureaux of the national government.
In the revolution that overthrew the aristocratic families, he and others
determined to abandon their country and found a colony in America.
Forming their plans upon little other evidence than what a map furnished
them, they came to the conclusion that the most desirable situations were
to be found betwixt the 34th and 35th degrees of North latitude, and
Mr. T—— and a colleague were sent to explore and report. They had arrived at New Orleans, and proceeded from thence immediately into the
interior of Arkansas, where they had resided for several months; here their
funds became exhausted, and, receiving no remittances nor communications of any sort from their friends at home, they fell into a perfect state of
destitution, and led a most miserable life for a long time in the woods. At
length they separated, each to provide for himself, and Mr. T—— arriving
pennyless at Little Rock, had succeeded in getting some sort of employment in the Land Office, where his talent as a draughtsman made him very
useful. When I met him he was half broken-hearted, longing to return to
his native country, but with no prospect before him of ever getting out of

Little Rock, where the emoluments of his daily labour barely sufficed to keep him alive.

Having thus cast anchor for a few days in a quiet and safe harbour, I began to look about me and collect information. The town of Little Rock receives its name from being built upon the first rock,—a slate which underlies the sandstone and dips S.E. at a great inclination—which juts out into the Arkansa, in coming up the river from its mouth in the Mississippi; it is tolerably well laid out, has a few brick houses, and a greater number of indifferently built wooden ones, generally in straggling situations, which admit of their having a piece of ground attached to them. The population was at this time betwixt 500 and 600 inhabitants, a great proportion of them mechanics; lawyers and doctors without number, and abundance of tradesmen going by the name of merchants. Americans of a certain class, to whatever distant point they go, carry the passion for newspaper reading with them, as if it were the grand end of education. A town in England with a population of 8000 souls will have a few of the lower classes who do not know how to read at all, but those who are not of the educated classes, and who do read, generally apply that noble art, when proper occasions present themselves, to reading the Bible and religious and moral books.

Newspapers are too expensive for the poorer classes in England, and therefore the minds of by far the greater part of them are not distracted, enfeebled, and corrupted by *cheap* newspapers; and although the exceptions are painfully obvious, still it is true that there is not a passion in England for reading low newspapers as there is in America. Now the only newspapers that deserve to be read in England pay a great tax to the government, and are only within the reach of the opulent classes, those who are at ease in their circumstances, and men of business; but these being conducted by men of approved talents and fair character, reflect to the public all the intelligence that the inquiring spirit of a great nation requires, and assist to keep down corruption rather than cherish it. How could a town of 8000 inhabitants in England support a newspaper printed in the place? Where would its useful or instructive matter come from? Why, from those quarters which have already supplied it to those alone *who want it*. If such a town had a newspaper it could not be supported, and therefore it remains without one. But in Little Rock, with a population of 600 people, there are no less than three *cheap* newspapers, which are not read but devoured by everybody; for what pleasure can be equal to that which,—through the blessings of universal suffrage,—those free and enlightened citizens called the "sovereign people" are made partakers of once a day, or at least three times a week, on finding that the political party which has omitted to purchase their support is composed of scoundrels and liars, and men who want to get into power for no other purpose but to ruin their country? It seems impossible that there should be any time or inclination for Bible reading where this kind of cheap poison gets into the hands of human beings; you might as well expect to find a confirmed Chinese opium smoker engaged in the solution of the problems of Euclid. In this part of the country it has struck me as the worst of all signs, that I have never seen a Bible in the hands of any individual, even on a Sunday.

I have not, however, been in every body's house, nor would I infer that every individual in Little Rock is to be included in this irreligious category. What I have said I would apply exclusively to what are called the "sovereign people," that mass which it is the business and interest of political demagogues to mislead and debase, for the purpose of directing it —as they have too successfully done in many parts of the United States— against the virtuous and praiseworthy efforts of good men and their families in every part of this extensive government; men who struggle to bring their country back to the honourable principles that illustrated the period of George Washington, but whose long struggle will be made in vain until the evil consequences of universal suffrage present themselves in such an appalling form, that the people, rendered wise by great suffering and experience, will consent to surrender to the guidance of men of character and property that governing power which is now both cause and effect of their blind passions.

It was my good fortune to become acquainted with a few respectable and agreeable individuals here. Governor Pope, the governor of the territory, is an unaffected, worthy person: he was once a conspicuous politician in Kentucky, and by some accident has lost one of his arms. This gentleman has been of great service here in various ways, especially in the judicious use he has made of the funds entrusted to him by the general government for the erection of a legislative hall, which is a very handsome building, placed in an advantageous situation, on the brink of the river, and one of the neatest public buildings I have seen in North America. The Governor showed it to me with great exultation, and I complimented him sincerely on the taste he had shown.

He lives amongst the inhabitants in an unpretending and plain manner, encouraging them to use no ceremony in talking to him, and appearing to me to carry his affability and familiarity with them quite as far as it was expedient to do. Ceremony and circumlocution seem to have found no resting-place amongst the inhabitants of Little Rock; if they have anything to say to you, they come to the point (*pynt* as they pronounce it) at once, and are not very shy of their expletives. Soon after my arrival I went to call upon his Excellency the Governor, and being told that he lived in a small house in a particular quarter of the town, I went in that direction, and seeing a house which I supposed might be the one I was in search of, I

knocked at the door, upon which an odd-looking man enough came to me.
Not knowing, after my experience of the Reverend Mr. Stevenson, what
might be trumps here, I touched my hat and said, "Will you be so obliging
as tell me whether the Governor is in the house?" I fancy this fellow had
never lived in Belgrave-square, for his answer was, "No, I'm ——— if he
is." He told me, however, very obligingly, where the house was, and at last
I found it, and knocking with my knuckles against the door, a dame came,
who, as I found afterwards, was the Governor's lady. She was a strange-
looking person for one of her rank, and I had been so tickled with the last
answer I got, that I could not help cherishing the hope that she, too would
say something very extraordinary. With the most winning politeness,
therefore, I inquired, "If his Excellency the Governor was at home?" Upon
which, without mincing the matter, she very frankly told me that "he was
gone to the woods to hunt for a sow and pigs belonging to her that were
missing." Now this might very reasonably happen to a territorial governor
in such a practical way of life as he was, and still be, as it really was, creditable to him. Sows and pigs will stroll into the woods, and the wolves will
pick them up if they meet with them. Mrs. Pope had sent one of her
"negurs" to the woods upon a previous occasion, and the fellow had neglected his duty and gone somewhere else; this time, therefore, she sent the
Governor, who, being a man of sense, and knowing how little dependence
was to be placed upon his "negur," and perhaps wanting a walk, had undertaken the task of driving piggies home.

Besides the Governor there were other agreeable persons with whom I
became acquainted; a Colonel A*****, a clever good-tempered lawyer.
Mr. Woodruff, the editor of the principal Gazette of the place, and post-
master, was always obliging, and is one of the most indefatigably industrious men of the territory. At his store we used to call to hear the news of
the day, which were various and exciting enough; for, with some honourable exceptions perhaps there never such another population assembled
—broken tradesmen, refugees from justice, travelling gamblers, and some
young bucks and bloods, who, never having had the advantage of good
examples for imitation, had set up a standard of manners consisting of
everything that was extravagantly and outrageously bad. Quarrelling
seemed to be their principal occupation, and these puppies, without family, education, or refinement of any kind, were continually resorting to
what they called the "Laws of Honour," a part of the code of which, in
Little Rock, is to administer justice with your own hand the first convenient opportunity. A common practice with these fellows was to fire at
each other with a rifle across the street, and then dodge behind a door:
every day groups were to be seen gathered round these wordy bullies,
who were holding knives in their hands, and daring each other to strike,
but cherishing the secret hope that the spectators would interfere. At one

time they were so numerous and overbearing that they would probably have overpowered the town, but for the catastrophe which befel one of their leaders, and checked the rest for awhile.

Mr. Woodruff, like most of the postmasters, kept a store, and thither these desperadoes used to resort; but it became so great a nuisance at last as to be intolerable, and being a firm man he determined to put a stop to it. The young fellow in question dared him to interfere, threatened him more than once, and coming to the store one evening provoked the post-master so much by his insolent violence, that a scuffle ensued, in which the bully got a mortal wound. Mr. Woodruff described the scene to me, and showed me the place where he fell, but said that he got his death by the awkward use of his own weapon. The public opinion sided with the post-master, who was very popular at the period of our visit.

One of the most respectable inhabitants told me, that he did not suppose there were *twelve* inhabitants of the place who ever went into the streets without—from some motive or other—being armed with pistols or large hunting knives about a foot long and an inch and a half broad, originally intended to skin and cut up animals, but which are now made and orna-mented with great care, and kept exceedingly sharp for the purpose of slashing and sticking human beings. These formidable instruments, with their sheaths mounted in silver, are the pride of an Arkansas blood, and got their names of *Bowie* knives from a conspicuous person of this fiery climate.

A large brick building was pointed out to me that had been erected for stores and warehouses, but the owner thinking he could do better by ap-plying it to the uses of a more steady line of business, rented the large store on the ground floor as a drinking shop, commonly called here a "groggery;" here it was the custom of the bloods to convene and discuss the last quarrel, and to tell how such a one "drew his pistol," and then how such a one "whipped out his knife;" adjourning when they had drunk to the warehouse up stairs, which they called "the college," and which was converted into a gambling-room for faro and rouge et noir. I had a descrip-tion given me of some of the scenes that took place here by persons who were present, which would appear incredible to even any gamblers who were not familiar with this den of infamy. To this place it was the practice to inveigle all the young men they could, who had any property or any credit, make them mad with drink (the youth of these climes become frantic, not stupid, with the fiery potations they use), and then ruin them with the most atrocious foul play. Out of this class they recruit their in-famous gang, and teach them how to decoy and ruin others. When they have nobody to fleece, they play amongst themselves—having no idea of any other mode of occupying the time. Many stories were related to me of a trader at the mouth of *White River,* named Montgomery, a finished *sportsman* in every sense, passionately fond of gambling, excessively addicted to whiskey, and who always used to sit down to the faro table with his Bowie knife unsheathed by his side, to insure fair play. This man, with some others, succeeded in effecting the ruin of a promising young officer in the United States service, a Lieutenant ———, who was an acting quartermaster. He had had the weakness to permit himself to become acquainted with some of these wretches, and although he was a married man, and had his wife with him, became at length their familiar companion. Having government drafts in his possession, they contrived to defraud him, when drunk, of them, to the amount of ten thousand dollars. Such was the infatuation of this young man, that finding that he was ruined for ever in his profession, he went off with Montgomery and a party of the sharpers to New Orleans, to get the drafts cashed that he had still left. But it so happened that an active officer, who was acting in the commissariat service, heard of this movement, and pushing across the country, reached the banks of the Mississippi, far to the south of the Arkansa and White River, where the gamblers were to embark. He had scarce been there an hour when a steamer heaving in sight he went on board, and to his great surprise found his brother officer and the whole gang of villains on the deck. They were thus frustrated in their nefarious plans, for on their arrival at New Orleans, he immediately stopped the payment of the drafts, and the party returned to White River, where the unhappy victim of these scoundrels afterwards died of delirium tremens.

So general is the propensity to gambling in this territory, that a very respectable person assured me he had seen the judges of their highest court playing publicly at faro, at some races. The senators and members of the territorial legislature do the same thing; in fact, the greater part of these men get elected to the legislature, not to assist in transacting public business, but to get the wages they are entitled to per diem, and to gratify their passion for gambling. A traveller, whom I met with at Little Rock, told me that he was lodging at an indifferent tavern there, and had been put into a room with four beds in it. There he had slept quietly alone two nights, when on the third, the day before the legislature convened, the house became suddenly filled with senators and members, several of whom, having come up into his room with their saddlebags, got out a table, ordered some whiskey, and produced cards they had brought with them. The most amusing part of the incident was that they asked him to lend them five dollars until they could get some of their legislative "wages." Not liking this proposition very much, he told them that he was as hard up as themselves. They therefore proposed to play on tick, sat up almost the whole night smoking, spitting, drinking, swearing and gambling; and about five in the morning two of them threw off their clothes and came to bed with **him.**

The Sugar Planters

Solon Robinson

[*December 29, 1848*] Having spent a night with Dr. Bingay, at whose house the reader will bear in mind I stopped over to rest. It was here that I saw the coco grass, mentioned in a former letter, as growing out of the top of a sugar-house chimney. The Doctor is a small planter, and has just erected a new horse mill, of which I shall speak more particularly hereafter. He is a practicing physician, and I believe a very well-informed man, full of activity and enterprise. But as I shall have occasion to speak of the Doctor again, let us ride on.

The next place worthy of note, is that of Col. [John S.] Preston, of South Carolina, son-in-law of the late Gen. [Wade] Hampton II. It is a part of the "Houmas Grant," the other part being owned by his brother-in-law Col. [John L.] Manning. Col. P. has about 2,000 arpents, under cultivation, and 350 hands in the field and 750 in all, upon the place, under the management of Capt. Sheafer, a very intelligent and pleasant gentleman. It takes 150 horses and mules to work this place, which is rather under the usual number upon other plantations. The last crop, which he considers "almost a failure," was 1,100 hogsheads of sugar. All the land on the river is measured by *arpents*, which contain, within a small fraction of 18 per cent. less than an acre.

I counted in one "quarter," (the name given to the negro houses,) upwards of 30 double cabins, all neatly whitewashed frame houses, with brick chimneys, built in regular order upon both sides of a wide street, and which is the law, must be kept in a perfect state of cleanliness. Feeding the force on this place is not quite equal to feeding an army, but it takes nine barrels of pork every week, which, at an average of $10, is $4,680, per annum, cash out, for that item alone. The regular allowance of pork to all field hands, is four pounds, clear of bone, per week, with as much corn meal as they can eat, besides molasses, sweet potatoes, vegetables, and occasional extras of fresh beef and mutton. Children's rations,

Herbert Kellar (ed.), *Solon Robinson*, II, pp. 171-177, 201-204, 364-368.

1½ pounds of pork per week, and full supply of other things. This place being in a bend of the river, the front is comparatively very narrow, (34 arpents, or about 28 to a mile,) and "opens out," as the lines run back, like a fan, which is the way that all the lands were originally laid off. On points, on the contrary, the lines run together in the rear, the fan opening the other end foremost. . . .

Mr. Fagot, a very polite French gentleman, whose first inquiry after introducing myself, as is almost always the case at that particular time of day, "have you dined?" has a brick-drying shed, under which he can dry 30,000 at once, upon the "bearing-off-boards," put on slats fastened to posts. By this plan, he can have the shed filled with bricks at odd times through the summer, which may be burnt when ready. Owing to the very frequent showers in this country, brick making is a very "catching business," but by this plan, all that trouble and loss is obviated.

Mr. F's place is a short distance above the "convent," in St. James' parish, which is a very imposing looking structure, or rather structures, neatly formed and where a large school is kept; and where all looks in a healthy, flourishing condition. This was a state-fostered institution, and is said to have cost near half a million of dollars.

Along the road, the small Creole places are thick as "three in a bed,"— all the tracts being 40 arpents deep, and the reluctance of old families to sell out, has caused divisions and subdivisions among heirs until the land is thrown into a shape almost worthless, as I have already mentioned. Fancy a farm three rods wide, and 480 rods deep, and if you like it here is a lot on 'em.

My entertainer at night was a French gentleman by the name of Ferry, where I found a small house well furnished, standing separate from the dwelling, in which to lodge travellers, where all their wants are as well cared for as though it were in a hotel.

Among the beautiful plantations passed, was that of "Golden Grove," belonging to C. M. Shepherd, Esq., for which I would willingly exchange all my interest in the California golden groves, or "placers." The most of the interest of a visit to this splendid plantation, was lost by not meeting the owner, whose character as a planter and as a gentleman of taste and refinement, stands very high. A few miles below, is the plantation of Dr. Loughborough, on the point, which, owing to the shape of the tract, as before mentioned, has no woodland, and where I saw the whole force of the estate at work "catching drift;" a job of no small amount upon a place making 500 hogsheads of sugar, as the alone would consume, at least, 2,000 cords of wood of the usual quality of drift. The process of catching drift is by sending out a skiff, which fastens a rope to a whole tree, perhaps, and a very large one too, sometimes, and towing the prize ashore. One end of a chain cable is made fast to it, and the other to a powerful capstan, turned by horses or mules. I say powerful, for I saw them snap the chain like threads, when getting hold of "an old settler," before they could get it upon the beach far enough to take off a cut, which is done, cut after cut, until they are able to pull out the remainder. This may seem a very precarious way of supplying a large plantation with fuel, and yet it is the only dependence of many. Formerly, it was a tolerably easy method, but of late, there are so many hundreds of persons whose whole income is derived from this source, besides the great amount required by plantations, that the supply is hardly sufficient to meet the demand, and a great deal of very poor stuff is now caught with avidity, that, in those good old times of plenty, would have been despised.

On my way I called on my old friend and acquaintance, David Adams. As is the general custom among the planters in the "rolling season," he eats and sleeps in the sugar house. I am well satisfied that the "Mayor of Pittsburg," who is a brother of Mr. Adams, did not enjoy a more pleasant dinner than was our sugar-house fare that day. Mr. A. says that he made 60 bushels of corn to the arpent upon one piece, this year, of a choice white kind, by manuring and deep plowing, which is three times the usual crop. His molasses cisterns are of cement, plastered directly upon the pit dug in the earth, which he thinks preferable to brick work. As he has had to catch or buy fuel, he has made a part of his crop this season, as an experiment, with Pittsburg coal, and is well satisfied with the result. He mixes a small portion of wood under his kettles with the coal, which he thinks should always be done. Out of the many planters and farmers, whose early life was spent in other pursuits and who afterwards made successful tillers of the soil, although mere *book farmers,* Mr. A. may justly be ranked.

Among other enterprising and improving Creole planters, Mons. Boudousquie, below Mr. Adams', deserves mention, as does Mr. Felix Reine, in whose garden I found a great abundance of very large and most delicious sweet oranges, which are rendered quite unsaleable, even at the low price of 40 cents a hundred, by the alarm of cholera in New Orleans, with the idea that indulgence in fruit is dangerous.

Mr. J. Gasset, from Kentucky, at Bonnet-Carré Bend, with whom I spent a night, lives in the house built by the old Spanish Commandante, 70 years ago, which is still in a sound condition. It is built of red cypress, which is as much more durable than white, as is red cedar more durable than white cedar. Mr. G. has the first draining machine that I have met with. It is a steam engine and wheel which elevates the water five feet, and cost $5,000. He has 600 acres in cultivation, ditched every half arpent (about 100 feet). The machine works on an average about three days a week, at an expense of 300 cords of wood a year, which is worth $2 to $3 a cord, and one hand to tend. . . .

[*February ?, 1849*] Visit to the Plantation of Bishop [Leonidas] Polk.—
This is situated upon the right bank of the bayou Lafourche, about a mile
above Thibodaux, and contains 2,500 arpents, 1,000 or 1,100 of which are
in cultivation, and a portion of the rest cultivable. Of this, 600 arpents
were in cane last year—358 used for sugar, and balance for planting cane,
it being the bishop's intention, this year, to have 800 arpents. Whether he
will succeed in getting that amount in, I cannot say; but I learn that the
terrible ravages of cholera upon his place, which carried off above 70 of his
people, has seriously injured his growing crop. From the 358 arpents last
year, he made 510 hogsheads of sugar, and the usual quantity of molasses.
The year before, he made from 470 arpents, 720 hogsheads. His usual crop
of corn is about 200 arpents.

When I was on the place, Bishop P.'s people numbered 370; but the effective force of field hands was not more than one third of that number,
owing to the fact that the stock is a very old one, and has been in the same
family, (that of Mrs. P.s ancestors, in North Carolina,) ever since the year
1697. Now, he has upwards of 30 entirely superannuated. There are, also,
or were, at that time, upwards of 70 children under ten years of age. What
a host to feed and clothe, and all to be looked after and provided for by
the care of one man! Quite enough to frighten a New-England farmer.

The bishop is an experimenting and improving planter. He believes in
good tillage and manure. He has one of the best fluke plows, made upon
the place, that I have seen anywhere. . . . He tried an experiment, last year,
of stripping the cane of leaves, to give it a better opportunity to mature,
and thinks he found his account in the experiment largely in his favor. At
any rate, he obtained upwards of 21 hogsheads of good sugar from seven
acres, which was a much larger yield than any other acres gave. The stripping was done by children, whose labor was not of much value at that season for any other purpose; and even if it had been valuable, he thinks that
the labor was not lost, because the work of the cane cutters was greatly
facilitated. I forgot to inquire whether he used the leaves for fodder. The
cane experimented upon, was first-year rattoons. It is needless to say that
it was good, independent of the stripping.

The bishop also tried an experiment, last season, to ascertain the quantity of juice obtained. He weighed 2,300 pounds of cane, which gave 163
gallons of juice, weighing 8½ lbs. to the gallon. He then reground the
bagasse, and got 5 gallons more. Another experiment gave 67 lbs. of juice
to 100 lbs. of cane. To do this, the mill must be first rate. . . .

The amount of team required upon this place, besides oxen, is about 75
mules or horses, the latter being preferred. Upon this point, there is great
difference of opinion. Many contend that, as horses only cost about half as
much as mules, will do more work, and live nearly as long, that it is economy to use them.

The annual expenses of this plantation average about $8,000; and yet, they make a full supply of corn and hay, and manufacture almost everything that can be done upon the place. The wool and cotton are purchased in the bale, and cloth is spun and wove by the feeble portion of the people. Carts, wagons, plows, spades, hoes, &c., are all made upon the place. So are the shoes. But there is half a pound of pork for every mouth, every day, to be paid for, which swells the amount; but it is the intention of the bishop to try hard to obviate this by raising his own hogs. This is an experiment I doubt the policy of. The difficulty of curing pork in this climate, is one objection, but the main one is, that the labor bestowed upon cane, instead of corn, will buy more pork than the corn will fatten. Then why try to make it? I also doubt the policy, upon most plantations, of manufacturing cloth; though the bishop says that his is spun and woven by old people, and by mothers, just before and after giving birth to children, and by invalids, or convalescents, who are unable to go to the field. The whole business of manufacturing of the materials and clothing all the people, is in the hands of one negro, who receives a certain number of bales of wool and cotton, and therefrom provides all the clothes required by the people, without ever troubling his master, or overseer, about the matter.

It is worthy of note here, that all labor ceases upon this plantation, even during the rolling season, upon the Sabbath. As the bishop himself is necessarily absent much of the time, he employs a curate, who preaches to his people, every Sunday, and conducts a large Sabbath school, and performs all the marriages and sepulture rites required. About one third of the whole number are members of the church, and are as consistent Christians as are usually found in any community.

The average yield of corn upon this place, is about 26 bushels to the acre, and the amount required for plantation use, about 11,000 bushels.

Mr. Botner, the very intelligent overseer, is of the opinion that green bagasse injures land; but when rotten, is the best manure in the world. . . .

I am not willing to close the sketch of my visit to this place, without bearing testimony to the high character, both as a gentleman, an improving agriculturist, and a kind master to those whom Providence has placed him in charge of, which is universally accorded to Bishop Polk. As to his most excellent wife, she is certainly such a one as a great many planters' ladies might well imitate.

[March ?, 1850] Visit to Jehossee Island, S. C.—Rice Plantation of Ex-Governor William Aikin.—I hope my readers have read with some degree of interest, my account of Col. Carson's rice plantation, in the March number of the Agriculturist. The minuteness of that description will enable me to shorten the present one. I left Charleston on the morning of January 25th. [1850], which was like a mild summer day in autumn with us, and followed the windings of a crooked, narrow channel, through which small steamboats run towards Savannah by the inside channel to Beaufort. We were several times interrupted by meeting large timber rafts that come down the Edisto River, and through this passage to Charleston, and had to wait till they could be separated, to give us a passage through this fit abode of aligators, that are often to be seen "as thick as three in a bed."

Although my point of destination was only thirty miles direct from the city, was twelve hours on the passage. This island contains about 3,300 acres, no part of which is over ten or fifteen feet above tide, and not more than 200 to 300 acres but what was subject to overflow until diked out by an amount of labor almost inconceivable to be performed by individual enterprise, when we also take into account the many miles of navigable canals and smaller ditches. There are 1,500 acres of rice lands, divided into convenient compartments for flooding, by substantial banks, and all laid off in beds between ditches 3 feet deep, only 35 feet apart. Part of the land was tide-water marsh, and part of it timber swamp. Besides this, Gov. A. cultivates 500 acres in corn, oats, and potatoes; the balance is gardens, yards, lawns, and in woods, pasture, and unreclaimed swamp. Wood is becoming scarce on the island, so much so, that he drives the steam engine to thresh the crop, by burning straw, which answers a good purpose, but is of doubtful economy; though he intends carefully to save and apply the ashes, which are very abundant, and note the difference in value, between that application and the manure made from the decomposed straw. It is generally calculated that two thirds of the straw will be sufficient fuel to thresh the crop; but Governor Aikin has not found it so. He says there is no more danger of fire in the use of straw than in any other fuel. The flue is carried off fifty or sixty feet along the ground and there rises in a tall stack that *never emits any sparks.* Sugar planters, and all farmers who use steam, may do well to notice this. I recollect Mr. Burgwayn carries his off from his barn in the same way, with the same effect. . . .

The average annual sales of the place do not vary materially from $25,000, and the average annual expenses not far from $10,000, of which sum $2,000 is paid the overseer, who is the only white man upon the place, besides the owner, who is always absent during the sickly months of summer. All the engineers, millers, smiths, carpenters, and sailors are black. A vessel belonging to this island goes twice a week to Charleston, and carries a cargo of 100 casks. The last crop was 1,500 casks—the year before, 1,800, and all provisions and grain required, made upon the place. Last year, there was not more than half a supply of provisions.

Like nearly all the "lower-country" plantations, the diet of the people is principally vegetable. Those who work "task work" receive as rations, half a bushel of sweet potatoes a-week. As all the tasks are very light, affording them nearly one fourth of the time to raise a crop for themselves, they always have an abundance, and sell a good deal for cash. They also raise pigs and poultry, though seldom for their own eating. They catch a great many fish, oysters, crabs, &c.

The carpenters, millers, &c., who do not have an opportunity of raising a crop for themselves, draw large rations, I think a bushel of corn a week, which gives them a surplus for sale. The children and non-workers are fed on corn bread, homminy, molasses, rice, potatoes, soup, &c.

The number of negroes upon the place is just about 700, occupying 84 double frame houses, each containing two tenements of three rooms to a family, besides the cock loft. Each tenement has its separate door and window and a good brick fireplace, and nearly all have a garden paled in. There are two common hospitals, and a "lying-in hospital," and a very neat, commodious church, which is well filled every Sabbath with an orderly, pious congregation, and service performed by a respectable methodist clergyman who also performs the baptismal, communion, marriage and burial rites.

There is a small stock of cattle, hogs, and sheep kept upon the place for meat, which are only allowed to come upon the field in winter, under charge of keepers, The buildings are all of wood, but generally plain, substantial, and good. There is a pretty good supply of tools, carts, boats, &c., and the land is estimated to be worth

$100 an acre for the rice land, which would be	$150,000
The 500 acres upland, $25 per acre,	12,500
The negroes, at $300 each,	210,000
Stocks, tools, and other property, say	7,500
	$380,000

which will show a rather low rate of interest made from sales of crops, notwithstanding the amount of sales look so large.

Now the owner of all this property lives in a very humble cottage, embowered in dense shrubbery, and making no show, and is in fact, as a dwelling for a gentleman of wealth, far inferior in point of elegance and convenience, to any negro house upon the place, for the use and comfort of that class of people.

He and his family are as plain and unostentatious in their manners as the house they live in; but they possess, in a most eminent degree, that true politeness and hospitality that will win upon your heart and make you feel at home in their humble cot, in such a manner that you will enjoy a visit there better than in a palace.

Nearly all the land has been reclaimed, and the buildings, except the house, erected new within the twenty years that Governor Aikin has owned the island. I fully believe that he is more concerned to make his people comfortable and happy, than he is to make money.

The Diary of a Cotton Planter

Bennet H. Barrow

October 2, 1837. Cloudy picking Gns hauling it Home—great deal of Cotten open—More Whiping to do this Fall than all together in three years owing to my D mean Overseer—never will have another unless I should be compelled to leave—they are a perfect nuisance

10. Clear cool cotten verry much staind Parson Burruss called to see me yesterday—wishes to sell his blood stock mares and colts—*he is the most perfect connoisseiur in the Horse line* I ever met with—excellent judgment &c.

November 12. Cloudy warm—pressing to day picked yesterday—Ateam picked 511 Ben 461—Dave Bartley 511—Lize 310. every day cotten can't be beat—431 each—315 B. out—330 this time last year—the six men picked 2823—An average of 471½ two women not racing 8 in all 3448.- 431 average—Demps picked in 1830 572 lbs L. Dare 543 fair cotten

December 31. Cloudy pleasant. Negros seemed to enjoy Christmas verry much ran two of Uncle Bats negros off last night—for making a disturbance—no pass—broke my sword Cane over one of their skulls

January 14, 1838. . . . . The times are seriously hard—all most impossible to raise one dollars. and that in shin plasters—great Excitement in Congress. Northern States medling with slavery—first they com'ced by petition —now by openly speaking of the sin of Slavery in the southern states—on the floor of congress—must eventually cause a separation of the Union.

April 4. Morning cool went out Turkey hunting before day with Dr. Desmont. and L. Purnell—shot twice Flying missed—hoeing corn first

Edwin Davis (ed.), *Plantation Life in the Florida Parishes of Louisiana, 1836-1846, as Reflected in the Diary of Bennet H. Barrow* (courtesy of editor and Columbia University Press, New York, 1943), *passim.*

time   looks verry badly. running ten ploughs breaking out middles   can't wait for rain any longer

October 12. Clear   verry cold morning—hands picked worse yesterday than they have done this year. Lowest average 157—picked in the morning—in the bottom on L creek—rotten open long time—the same this morning—Whiped near half the hands to day for picking badly & trashy   Tom Beauf came up and put his Basket down at the scales and it is the last I've seen of him—will Whip him more than I ever Whip one, I think he deserves more—the second time he has done so this year— light Frost yesterday and to day

31. Clear   pleasant. Mr. Warfield my Cotten merchant or "Factor" came home with me last night. looking through the Country for business— Com'enced as comm merchant this Fall—as Finley & Co. Verry much pleased with him as well as the sales of my cotten shiped 83 Bales this shipment—229 in all. gain—19 over. making 248 of 400.

May 21, 1839. Clear   verry warm—Finished hilling Cotten—Darcas & Fanny are the greatest shirks of any negroes I have—*laid* up *twicet* a month . . .

August 6.—judge Wades driver was killed by one of his men—in attempting to Whip him—Which proves What I've often said—that it is wrong to allow a driver to use any authority—but to report injustice to him the negro in general—& yourself—negros are not Capable of self government —want of discretion—judgment &c.

January 18, 1840. Clear verry cold. Went to Town—there was considerable party feeling in N. Orleans on the 8th   Genl. Jackson appeared in fine spirits   some one went so far as to take his wife up for old Jackson to kiss   got it   Democracy of the present day, man worship in all its glory —one old French man that was in the Battle of N. Orleans under Jackson became so Elated as to through his arms 'round the Genl neck and gave him a *kiss*

March 6. Foggy morning—spring &c. Finished Ploughing 4 furrows for cotten by . . . *oclock*. breaking out middles "since"—My driver sent for me this morning   Lize & Fanny had a fight last night—gave them three oake switches each—& made them Fight it out—they seemed quit sick of it—after one switch was gone

30. women spinning—men doing little or nothing—several Sunday Gentleman here yesterday to go a Hunting—nothing provokes me more—Sunday being a day of rest to the negros. I like to be about—allowance day—& they frequently want things not convenient to get any other day—& My orders for every negro to come up every Sunday morning cleaned & head combed—&c.

April 16. Cotten improving verry much & corn looks well   half leg high in new ground   10 inches in old Land, My Hands appear determined to make a crop, if work can do it. never saw hands Work as Well, have never said a word to them—feeling an interest, they look a head & see What is to be done—I dowbt if Jacks eaquel can be found to work, at any work you put him at, "rascally" &c. I am well paid for my trouble in teaching my small gang to Hoe, never saw such hoe hands as they are, two year ago took two on a row—now Eaquel to a woman, am directing them to make a slow & sure lick in one place & to cut the full width of the hoe every time—unless reminded of it they would stand & make 4 or 5 licks in one place, tire themselves & do no work, have several grown ones that work harder & do less work than any in the field. had the best colt Foaled this morning I ever had—Nancy Miller & Jos Bell—stoped 5 ploughs to scrape cotten—15 running.

July 4. Clear Beautifull day, Wish the prospects of every one were as bright, as this *memorable* day, preparations for great doings at Douces to day   Barn dance &c.   will not go having been started by a few Loco Focos Who have the impudence to call themselves democrats, such men at the Howells figure Largely, Political Excitement is such that the greater the sycophant the more notice does he get. old Capt Howells breed are a head of any thing in these diggins, Killed more negros by their cruelty, & find them dead in the stocks, and yet A. G. Howell calls himself a big man, Married Dawsons niece. Dawson being a man that never looks for merit When appointing aids &c. Thinks it is not *Democratic,* Democracy of the present day means serve your party   right or wrong your party, they are the zelous supporters of Martin Van Buren, and all under the name of *Democracy,* All this corruption has grown out of the conduct of Genl. Jackson, Federal acts done every day by the V. B. party yet they are Democrats

January 7, 1842. Came on to my House to dinner, sent & collected the neighbours. A. G. Barrow & family   Miss Swifts   Flower & family Miss Mary Barrows   Miss Sophia Johnson   Mrs Collins   12 or 13 gentlemen —danced all night by the Piano & Violin

8. Would not let any Leave—got a violin player from Town "Norman"

Let them rest & knap during the day some times. playing smut—at dark began to dance, at 12 Oclock their consciences made them refuse to dance any Longer, it Being Saturday night, to punish them fastened the doors 'till near two ok some blew the Lights out others tried to get out at the windows, Any thing, but dance they would'ent, retired at 2 OK all nearly broke down, never have seen A collection so sudden and so perfectly free easy & happy for two days & nights, All restraint thrown aside never enjoyed myself as much

June 15. Clear quit cool since last evening. never saw my corn worse burnt than the new ground in places, hoeing lane place new ground splendidly branched & formed bolled &c. Ginney Jerry has not been seen since Monday morning. ran off and for What can't imagine—Came up Sunday for a dose of oil, has been for 8 or 10 days getting timber no one to watch him his old habits returned "of shirking," will shoot to kill him if an opportunity offers—otherwise will sell him, am satisfied will allways run away unless constantly watched—has not been touched this year, nor have I said a word to him, pray for a shot at him

August 23. Damp foggy morning, Hoeing Pressing & getting Logs for a Jail, several negros sick colds, one or two cases of scarlet fever, Bleeding When first taken and Emetics immediately, will cure it in nine cases in one hundred, Most of Physicians object to Bleeding from the fact the pulse is so small, it is certain to rise When you bleed in the 1st stage—they bleed mostly after trying other remedies no doubt will these prove fatal in a majority of Cases—shower at 1 ok picking cotten since dinner, great deal open

September 23. Cloudy morning, Began raining at 1 ok most rain yesterday & to day that has fallen this summer—My Hands have divided themselves in two companys—Atean & D. Bartley the Heads to day at 11 0 only 12 lb. difference—highest picked 275 lbs, but for rain would have done the Bigest days work ever done by them or I ever heard of

January 15, 1843. Clear pleasant day—My Old negro Orange died last night of Old age—Considerable over 100 yrs A more perfect negro never lived, faithfull honest & purely religious, never knew him guilty of a *wrong*

September 9, 1844. Clear cool N. East wind working Causeway to day Wade overseer, picking at Gibson place. The Army worm or Caterpiller has Began in Earnest in few days will be over the Whole place, my crop is now making more than any time since 15th June. would make very

Large crop Barring worms & storm, must cut the cotten crop short   eaquel
to a frost on the 10 of Sept. some parts of the state Began Eating the cotten six weeks ago   Alabama & Mi. allso

October 2. Clear pleasant   dry   North wind   Went to town yesterday
by Turnbulls, all Look improved by their trip to Ky. great excitement in
the Political world. the Democrats have at Last rallied on principles
Droped Martin Van Buren—& Thomas Benton, united on Polk & Dallas
as their candidates for President & Vice President in Opposition to the
Whigs or consolodationist & Abolitionist headed by Henry Clay, & supported by such traitors "to Southern interest & rights" as A. Barrow & his
clique—Begging for office   should Clay be Elected—God grant he may
be defeated, the main question is slavery & anti slavery & Texas

15. Hard rain Last night at Dark, two men from Mississippi came Last
night with pack of negro Dogs to hunt Miss Swifts negros. Caught one
woman this morning & very foolish endeavored to make her direct us to
the Camp & fooled the day off to no purpose, Brought her to my house
tried the cold water on her Ladyship

January 1, 1845. . . . . the Prospects of the cotten planter seems quite gloomy
from the immense amt of cotten made, and still increasing—my own situation is better than for 10 years Back obtained a Loan of $24000 out of the
Louisiana Bank on mortgage 8 pr ct interest   I think will be able to get
out of Debt without being cramped to Death, (Bad Beginning For New
Year)

February 20. Cloudy spring morning—Killed two fine Deer yesterday one
with each Barrel—Very hard rain at 12 ok   Wm H & family expected
down to day

June 4. Cloudy warm—Finshed Ploughing all cotten Above by . . . ok
second time & part the 3d time, Finished hoeing bottom field & planted
5 acres more by 11 ok   Had Quite a Frollic Among the negros Last Sunday   missed several of my young Hogs. found 8 or 10 Guilty, ducked &
gave them a good thrashing, Mr. Ginney Jerry next morning Felt insulted
at his treatment & put out, would give "freely" $100 to get a shot at him

November 11. Raining at day light, Cleared off at 11 ok   Mrs. Haile &
Mrs Flower left for Woodville,   Dr K & sister here last night, the negro
dogs to Mrs Wades Quarter, went through Ruffins beyond & Back. gave
up, Et dinner, concluded he had returned to Wades, Went in his pasture
& 5 minutes had him up & a going, And never in my life did I ever see

as excited beings as R & myself, ran ½ miles & caught him   dogs soon tore him naked, took him Home Before the other negro at dark & made the dogs give him another over hauling, has been drawing a knife & Pistol on persons about Town

January 1, 1846. Raining and Very warm morning, Bad Beginning for New Year,   negros had a dinner yesterday, some danced all night, those that did not will start to work this morning,   But for the Apprehension of War, the prospects for the country are better than for many years, sugar planter all ready reaping immense profits, Cotten will pay a fair profit to those out of Debt, Produce Very high. Pork 15 & 16 Dollars pr Barrel, Flower $6 & 7—corn from 60c to 80 c pr bushel, Horses & Mules reasonable, Horses from 40 to 70 dollars. Mules some What higher, Will try and make 600 Bales of Cotten this year with 68 hands, started all the hands that were not at the dance Last night to work at the Gin House, finding no Cotton to trash sent for the Fiddle and made them Dance from 12 till dark, other from the Quarter soon joined for the frollic & became quite Lively to the close. . . .

Hospitality in the Yazoo Valley

A. De Puy Van Buren

Major Wildie came home soon after my return. He is one of South Carolina's chivalrous sons; a courteous gentleman, of fine intellect, much reading, and good literary taste.

He is six feet high, though not a heavy man, has light brown hair, bluish grey eyes, and, were it not for the browning of this clime, would have a fair complexion.

His plantation, as I before noticed, is in the valley. He has selected this spot among the hills, for his home, some two miles from it, on account of its healthier locality.

From the "sunny memories" of my sojourn in this pleasant land, that cluster about the Ridge House,—my first home in the South—it deserves a description in these Jottings.

It is about mid-way, on the "Big Road" between Vicksburgh and Yazoo City. The house, though it is now being finished inside and out, like a frame building, is built of oak logs hewn square. It is some thirty feet wide by sixty feet long, and a story-and-a-half high, while the roof extending out, like a planter's broad rimmed hat, over its sides, and, resting on posts, forms wide porches, a cool and pleasant shade in the warm summer weather. An open hall connects these two porches.

It is situated on a gentle eminence that slopes down gradually to the road. You approach it, in front, through a carriage gate that opens from the road into a broad lawn of several acres, graced with many a sylvan honor of the forest.

Riding across this lawn, you come to a little gate, in the palings of cypress boards that enclose the inner grounds about the house. To the left of the yard, running to the rear of the house, are three fine rows of locust trees; a tall hickory stands at the right, and a few others are standing in the rear-yard, while in the back-ground, the primeval forest rises up against the sky.

A. De Puy Van Buren, *Jottings of a Year's Sojourn in the South* (Battle Creek, Mich., 1859), pp. 81-93.

Major W. usually orders his horse in the morning, and rides along a fine, high, carriage road, that winds through an interval of beautiful woodland, to his plantation, "down in the valley."

Here, from the porch of the old plantation-house, or riding out over the plantation, he can see how affairs are daily managed, over his whole domain.

Some thirty slaves, under command of his "field-marshal" work his large and beautiful prairie-farm; and the fruit of their labor is an "argosy" of cotton, which is annually shipped to New Orleans.

My first conversation with him, was about the panic among the Northern banks. He discoursed at some length on the banking system. Old JOHN LAW had, years a-gone, founded a bank, for the French people, on the El Dorado treasures of the Mississippi valley. His scheme had since been known as "The Mississippi bubble." This "bubble" burst, and its explosion was more fatal to the French then all the "infernal machines" in BONA-PARTE's time. But they had no more bubbles to burst, their banks were as enduring, as—

"These rich vales that feed the marts of the world."

He spoke of our Congress as if it were a chess-board, and he clearly understood the games that were being and had been played on it, by those men in Congress.

In speaking about their schools to him, he told me that there were good situations for teachers, but I must "bide my time," get better acquainted, and I would not have any trouble in securing a pleasant place. Schools among them, were mostly got up by individual effort. Of this, I had had a little experience.

To-night, the sky was all aglow with a roseate hue. Never did I see the stars shining out from so lovely a setting. Sand-hill cranes were flying South—an indication of cold weather.

The frost, that great chamberlain of old "Dame Earth," is now spreading her carpet throughout the wood-lands, before winter sets in.

But to another theme.

The main road running through Yazoo and Warren counties, is as crooked as an Indian trail, save where it is sometimes straightened, running between plantations, but as soon as it leaves them, off it goes again, as wild and wandering as ever; following the wayward freak of some ridge. A short rain makes the soil, of clay loam, as tenacious as tar to the foot or carriage wheel. But you find no stone, not even the slightest indications of gravel in the country.

A telegraph line, between Vicksburgh and Yazoo city, once followed the windings of this road, the wires being attached to trees, instead of posts. But it was so often broken by the falling of trees across it, that it was soon abandoned.

One meets, in traveling here on the road, throughout the country, the negro, driving fine carriages or costly coaches, with his beautiful *"proteges"* in them—the planter's wife and her daughters; also ladies on their palfreys galloping through the woods; the planter and his sons, ever on horse-back, with a large portmanteau swung across their saddles, for carrying sundries; or, if he is on the hunt, he is equipped for it, followed by his hounds; and, if returning from the chase, the most of them will have a deer swung across their horses, behind the saddle, and negroes mounted, carrying others. Or you may meet this sable cavalier, and his dulcena, riding their favorite steed, the mule; or perhaps you may find the solitary gin-stand agent, or traveler, wending his way, a-horse-back, through the State; or now and then, a German-Jew peddler, seated on his well-filled box, making his transit across the country, attended by his black satellite as a "whip;" and lastly, especially in the ditching season, wandering "Exiles of Erin," straggling along the road.

This is about all the travel you see. The stranger finds no welcome signpost, an index to a "Way-side Inn," where he can pause and refresh himself and his weary beast. Neither does the thirsty traveler hail, near the road-side, by the planter's home, the accustomed well-sweep, so common in the country North, poised like an angler's rod, with its line suspending a bucket ready to dip into the fountain below, and bring up the cooling beverage. The planter seldom digs a well; its waters are too often affected by the mineral impurities of the earth. He uses cistern water.

Neither do you see any barns in the country; the green-cane pasture of the woods, the year round, saves him from stowing away fodder for his cattle, and the mildness of the climate precludes the use of them for shelter.

All the buildings you see, are, the plantation-house, a lonely church, a solitary school-house, standing off from the road-side, telling where some northern teacher has been; the gin-house, where the cotton is separated from the seed; here and there a stray rick for corn, or corn-leaves for fodder; and, occasionally, a roof over an open stall for horses. These are all the buildings one sees in the country, and they are all built of logs, save very rarely a planter's house.

There are no grist-mills, in town or country. All the corn they use is ground by one-horse-power mills, in the gin-house. The saw-mill is more of a *sine qua non;* but still you see but very few of them, the country is too ridgy for water-mills. Neither have I seen any bridges over the rivers —they are all crossed in ferry-boats.

Life is surely rather primitive here. There is more nature and less art than at the North, more forest and uncultivated land, less husbandry and good tillage. Houses are built more from want and convenience, and less from pride and for sale. They are homes for life, and are never placarded with notices "to sell or rent," like Northern farms and farm-houses. Their best houses are not costly. What man does for comfort and convenience costs him but little. But let him build to suit his pride, and his house rivals the "Taj of India."

I have noticed many traits of old English life in the South. The plantation-house, like the old English manor-house, has its broad grounds, but without the carpet of green, between its shady retreat and the road. The beauties of the landscape, about his rural seclusion, have not been violated. The planter also, may be considered a lord in possession of a large estate, and his slaves are his vassals. And, like your English gentleman of landed possessions, he loves the chase, keeps a parliament of hounds, and the requisites for the hunt. His horse is ordered at early dawn, when from his porch you can hear the winding of his horn. . . .

An overseer on one of the plantations, during the fall, had killed fourteen bears. He told many thrilling stories of the "hair-breadth 'scapes" he had made while hunting them.

But, to resume, our subject, there is much provincialism in the habits and customs of the South. And finally, should an Englishman seek the hospitality of the planter's roof, he could repose on a mattress spread on an old English bed-stead, the same lofty and rich posts, and richly ornamented canopy, with curtains, that once graced the royal bed-chamber of "Good Old Queen Bess."

The planter's fare is simple, and the chase supplies his table with much of its meat. I am not only pleased with this simple fare of the planter's board, but with their manner of sitting at table.

Their tables are usually long, and remain stationary in the dining-room. This is sometimes a little log building separate from the house.

The father, at meals, takes seat at one end of the table, his eldest son at his right, then the next younger, and so on, down to the "wee bairn" that can "toddle" to his seat.

The mother is seated at the other end of the table, and her eldest daughter at her right, the sister next in age succeeding, down to the youngest. The guests, if gentlemen, are seated at the planter's left hand; if ladies, at his wife's left. If the father is a member of the church, a blessing is asked. I have known those, who did not profess to be Christians, ask blessings at their tables.

The boiled ham, cooked whole always, and which, on extra occasions, is tricked off with cloves, green leaves, and various-colored dainty bits, in a tasteful manner, is placed before the planter; his wife has the tea, coffee, and the delicacies before her. By the aid of servants every one at table is served.

In no place, not even in the most back-woods part of the country, have I ever heard what one often hears in the country, especially at the North, immediately after being seated at table, "Now take hold and help yourself."

The civilities of life generally "roughen" as you go from city into the country. Whether the South claims it as a part of her chivalry or not, is a matter of indifference to me, but, I certainly have not found the politeness and civilities of her town-life changed to boorishness, among the most back-woods planters of her country.

But again. The planter takes his time in eating—don't "bolt it down," as the Yankees do. Leisure and ease are inmates of his roof. He takes no note of time. Your Yankee will take time by the fore-lock, and push business through. But a Southron, never heard of the "old man with the scythe."

A friend of mine from Dowagiac, Michigan, making a trip to the South, stopped with me a few days; he, being a practical Yankee lawyer, was surprised at the air of indifference with which the planter spoke of time. He was not aware that time here,

"Had lost his glass and was asleep on flowers."

A clock, almanac, and a good fire, are hard things to find in a planter's house. The only chronometer he has, is the cotton-plant, and that "ticks" but once a year. The word, haste, is not in a Southron's vocabulary. He has reversed the old adage, and never does that to-day which can be done to-morrow.

While waiting, a few days, at the Ridge House, for a letter in regard to a school from Dover, ere venturing out again in a new direction, I took a pleasant ride to Satartia. The day was fine, and, in an easy carriage, accompanied by a Southern lady, we rode alternately through beautiful wood-lands, and by fine cotton-plantations.

On coming out of the uplands to the bluffs that wall up a wide border of valley, on both sides of the river, and from which you descend into it, I had one of the most picturesque landscape views, I had yet enjoyed any where in the country.

The long winding strip of valley, that lay spread out below me, looked like a broad strip of variegated green carpet; the village of Satartia, and the planters' houses, five or six in sight, with their little negro villas about them, looked like beautiful raised figures on it; the fences looked like leaden-colored vines traced across it; while the Yazoo river looked like a winding strip of blue water-colored ribbon, running through the middle of it between green fingers.

From the bluffs we descended, by two gradual sweeps in the road, to the valley. A mile or so brought us to the town. In Satartia I saw some of the yeomanry of Mississippi. A knot of them in their dress and general appearance might be mistaken for a group of our wealthy Michigan farmers. But one would notice more than a usual number of riding-whips, or "raw-hides," on their hands, and the same undue proportion of spurs in the heel of the right boot. And in their conversation he would hear nothing of the farm and its products, but of the plantation and cotton. The Southron does not have such a variety of topics about his affairs in his conversation. They are fewer than with the Northerner. Neither do the business, cares, and toils of this life worry and torment his mind.

He talks about the weather as it is pleasant, or disagreeable to his own feelings, not as it affects his crop, or his business. If a "freshet" should have inundated and ruined half his cotton crop, or even the whole of it, he would talk about it with the nonchalance of a TALLEYRAND. One listening to the range, spirit and humor of their conversation could tell them from Northerners.

And furthermore, the peculiar words and phrases—"I reckon," "right smart," "a-heap," and others that they used, would be a sure indication that they were Southrons. But, aside from all this, were I as blind as BARTIMEUS, and ignorant that I was in the South, I could, on riding up to the planter's gate, after having given the halloo, tell where I was, and who was addressing me, from the very words that I heard.

I defy a Northerner—even a Yankee, with all his natural adaptation of character, to address you and invite you in, like a true Southron. He invites you, in a way that no one else does. He answers your halloo, by meeting you at the gate, and in the kindliest manner extends you his hand, with his warm and friendly, "How do you do, sir? Won't you alight, come in, take a seat, and sit a while?"

In the first place, he addresses you in a gentlemanly manner, using the old Norman or knightly "sir." But let us remark here, that many words, phrases, and much of the manner and bearing of a Southron, are true remnants of the days of chivalry. Besides the use of the word "sir," we have mentioned, notice the word, "alight," or the expression, "get down from your horse," both of which they use, and both are words or phrases found, used in like manner, as characteristic of the feudal days. And the next sentence—"come in, take a *seat*, and *sit* awhile," expresses the true hospitality of the gentleman or knight in those hospitable days. Or, it is, with the other two terms mentioned, "part of the loyalty to the honorable and chivalric, which forms the subsoil" of a Southron's nature.

Now, your Yankee would, on hearing the halloo at his gate, eye you a moment, by way of "guessing" who you were, and then answer your salutation with his laconic "how-d'-ye-do." Would he go out to the gate to meet you? What *for*? He would, if he thought "'twould pay," or if he wished to—— ——"*dun you.*" And if he invited you in, it would be, "Won't ye hitch and come in?"

We saw nothing in the streets of Satartia to indicate that it was not a Southern town. The number of horses, saddled and hitched to posts, appeared to tally with the "riding-whips" and "spurs" we have before mentioned.

We saw but a carriage or two in the streets, hence few ladies were in town. But those few did, no doubt, as much trading as five times the number of Northern ladies would have done. A little incident, over which we were much amused, occurred in a town near this place, that will illustrate what we have said about their shopping.

The planter came into the store, where his wife was trading, and inquired about some bills of purchase that several merchants had presented him. He did not know that he owed these men a farthing. His wife glanced over them and smiled as she said, "Why, that bill of eighty-five dollars is the amount of FANNIE's shopping at Mr. F.'s store. The one of one hundred dollars is mine. I could not get here half the articles I wanted, and so I traded a little at Mr. G.'s. And these other bills, (that amounted in all to over one hundred and fifty dollars,) why, you know CARRIE's going off to school, of course she must have her 'outfit,' these are hers."

The planter appeared to be satisfied with this story; paid the amount of the different bills, his wife and daughter stepped into their fine carriage, the negro driver mounted to his seat, and drove off to their plantation-home; and he, mounting his horse, rode on after them, as if he was the mere "attache," or "purser," belonging to this lady and her splendid equipage.

There are but two stores in Satartia, yet each trades to the amount of sixty thousand dollars annually. The one is owned by Mr. H., a gentleman from Germany, who has amassed a fortune here among Southern planters; the other, by Mr. W., who, like very many other Northerners, left his home in search of the "golden fleece" South, and luckily has found it.

A Southern town, or road, never lacks one unmistakable sign of its being in the South. Though it moves along the streets and the road as slow and monotonous as the hour-hand on the dial-plate, yet it just as truly arrives at its point of destination; it is the negro with his prolix mule-team, before his lumbering cotton-wagon. You can follow him anywhere through the woods, by the crack of his long-lashed ox-whip, which he appears to execute, ever and anon, with a flourish about the heads of his mules, for the ostensible purpose of keeping them in motion. It is as good as a bell.

Our ride, both to Satartia and home again, we enjoyed very much. The road was very dry and smooth, and although it was near winter—the very last of November, it seemed to me, so recently from the cold Northern regions, "that the winter was past, the rain over and gone; for the flowers appeared on the earth; the time of the singing of birds was come, and the voice of the turtle was heard in the land."

Arriving at the gate, a servant was called, we alighted from the carriage, and walked into the hospitable mansion of our friend Major W.

And here let me describe the belongings, the moveables—what one would notice about a plantation-house:

Sitting on a board-shelf, resting on pegs driven into the logs, either on the side of the logs within the hall, or in front under the porch, you invariably find a water-pail, with the long handle of a cocoa-nut dipper sticking out of it. Also, in the porch, you see several long pegs driven into the logs, some four or five feet from the floor; these are for hanging the saddles, bridles, and that sort of things upon. But very often you see the vacant pegs, and the saddles and bridles lying on the floor beneath them.

> "And o'er the chimney rests the gun,
> And hang in idle trophy, near,
> The powder-pouch, fishing-rod and spear."

Between the logs, which are seldom "chinked," you will notice newspapers sticking out, and books or various things that have been casually placed there. You also usually find several vacant chairs in the porch, placed just as the last group who were seated in them, left them. Perhaps sprinkles of ashes from their pipes scattered on the floor near each chair, and the pipes themselves, lying between the logs hard by. Or you may catch the party there, seated in their chairs, chatting on the various things incident to such a group, and all smoking the accustomed cane-stemmed, thick, clay pipe with a man's head on it. If one of the group knows you, you are politely introduced to the rest. And whatever luxury they are enjoying, you are offered a share of it. If smoking, a pipe is handed you; or, if chatting, and you have no errand, you are supposed to be a participant in it. You are entitled to, or they seem to consider you as deserving their attention and hospitality. And, what is so common to man, "couchant or levant," in the old or new world, should that

> "Real, old, particular, friendly, punchy feeling"

seize them, you are invited to drink with them, whatever you choose; many of the planters keep the various wines and choice drinks. Or, should dinner be ready, you are invited in to dine with them. You find the planter a most agreeable, courteous and hospitable man; and that his guest is the best entertained man in the world.

This is of a log plantation-house in the uplands, in the valley you find better buildings, everything else the same.

We had forgotten to notice the hounds; they are "belongings," and *"moveables"* that one would be apt to notice, from the fact that they are so much inclined to notice you. They are principally the terrier, and a hound between the blood and the greyhound. You will find them baying at you, at the gate, or lounging about the porch, or under it, or about the grounds, while whole tribes of Shanghaes, troops of Turkeys, convoys of Ducks, and bevies of Guinea Hens, in vast numbers, are about the ground in the rear-yard.

New Orleans in the 1830's

Carl David Arfwedson

New Orleans is built in a semicircle, along the shore of the Mississippi, one hundred and five miles from its mouth at Balize and one thousand from its junction with the River Ohio. The streets follow the curve of the stream, and are crossed by others running from the Mississippi. Only one of them was paved when I visited the city, but I was assured that the others would undergo the same process in the course of a short time: a beginning was already made in one of the principal streets when I left New Orleans. Paving is of the greatest consequence to this town, for after rain it was next to impossible to move without sinking knee-deep in mud: after a long drought again, the dust was intolerable, when spectacles were indispensable requisites to prevent blindness. Mud and dust were the only alternatives.

The city is divided into two parts, the town itself, or the old French town, and the Faubourgs, of which the northern and nearest goes by the name of the American town. The old town is a parallelogram, formed on three sides by wide streets, planted with trees, and on the fourth inclosed by the Mississippi. No stranger can help observing the wide difference there exists in every thing between the French and Creole, and the American part of the town: they appear like two different cities, inhabited by different natives, governed by different principles and laws. In the first are seen a number of wooden houses, only one story high, containing three or four rooms, opening into the street by means of glass-doors. Those that have been built of late years are of brick, and plastered, which gives the town more of a European than American appearance. Creoles, who inhabit the old parts of New Orleans, are generally satisfied with little, and not fond of trouble. This circumstance, the effect of a warm and relaxing climate, operates sensibly on the appearance of this part of the city, which has received very little improvement.

Carl David Arfwedson, *The United States and Canada in 1832, 1833, and 1834* (London, 1834), II, pp. 52-60.

In the American part again, every thing advances, the enterprising Yankees setting no bounds to improvements of every kind. Possessing considerable capital, which they know how to lay out to advantage, their activity in every branch of commerce must insure the success which they anticipate. The extensive and lucrative cotton trade, the principal source of wealth to New Orleans, is drawing gradually towards the American quarter, and now seems to have established itself there for good. Attempts have been made, and are making to divide the trade, by rendering the Southern Faubourg a free port, with commodious warehouses; but I much doubt whether the object can be accomplished in the manner proposed by sanguine speculators.

In the mean time, the American part of the town is flourishing and increasing in a most astonishing degree. Large brick buildings and warehouses spring up, and are finished in a shorter time than Europeans require to lay foundations. Streets are filled with goods, principally bales of cotton; and between these American merchants are seen running in a continual hurry, their minds filled with schemes and speculations. The price of cotton was the topic of conversation from one end of the street to the other; and a fall or rise occupied the dealers so intensely, that their countenances became at last actual barometers, in which a physiognomist could easily discern if the difference in price since the preceding day was one-quarter, one-half, one, or two cents per pound.

The port of New Orleans is called the Levee, a wide unpaved street, always filled with mud or dust, equally annoying to man and beast; on one side a row of stores and dwelling-houses has been erected. The rapidity of the river prevents the building of a pier, so common and convenient in other towns of America, running in a straight line from the shore, and so wide that ships may load and unload with the greatest ease on both sides. Instead of such a structure (unquestionably leaving more space), the ships lie in tiers alongside the harbour, sometimes three or four deep. A visit to the port offers a very interesting spectacle, both on account of the river, majestically washing its shores, and of the many different languages there spoken. One day I remarked individuals of the following nations: Americans, English, French, Scotch, Spaniards, Swedes, Germans, Irish, Italians, Russians, Creoles, Indians, Negroes, Mexicans, and Brazilians.

This mixture of languages, costumes, and manners, rendered the scene one of the most singular that I ever witnessed. The liveliness of the Italians, the proud air of the Spaniards, the elasticity of the French, the composure of the English, the stern countenances of the Indians, the slavish conduct of the Negroes, formed altogether such a striking contrast, that it was not a little extraordinary to find them united in one single point. If there is a place where it is possible to form any thing like a correct idea of the confusion of tongues at the Tower of Babel, it certainly is New Or-

leans. Contemplate this group of polite and volatile Frenchmen, of grinning Creoles—do they not appear as if they passed through life dancing?
Yonder stalk a few Spaniards—does not their gait denote their national
pride? And this group of robust Swedish mariners, encamped on a pile
of bar-iron, brought by them from the Scandinavian Peninsula—what
forms the topic of their interesting conversation but the country that produces this metal? Here the fruiterer exhibits a variety of fruit, and raises
pyramids of oranges, bananas, lemons, pineapples, &c. See with what
voracity these South Americans, stretched on the ground, devour the half-
ripe fruit. There, an Italian is performing on a miserable organ, while two
monkeys are dancing on the top. Yonder, again, an itinerant Yankee
spreads a thousand different articles on the ground, exclaiming that he
sells them at a loss, merely for the sake of ensuring custom. Here, coffee
is sold by Negro women; there, oysters are swallowed; there, Indians are
draining their whisky-bottle, after having given a small quantity to their
wives and children. There, again, is a countryman from Kentucky, who has
just sold his crop, and has his pocket full of money, which he is anxious
either to lose or to double at a gaming-house as soon as evening arrives.
Finally, listen to the noise of the Mulatto, Negro, and Irish women, offering their goods for sale, and the rolling of carts and waggons, sinking
under the weight of produce from all parts of the world. Who will deny
that these afford innumerable subjects for the painter and the poet?

The population of the city amounted, according to the census of 1830,
to forty-eight thousand four hundred and fifty-six souls; during the winter
months, it may probably be very little short of sixty thousand. More than
half are natives of Africa, or their progeny, such as Mulattoes and Quar-
teroons; and the other half consists of Whites, of whom the Creoles form
a greater proportion than settled Americans. I remember having often
heard in Europe the name "Creole" applied indiscriminately to all people
of colour. This is, however, a great mistake; for it means a free native of
the country, and belongs exclusively to white people born in the neighbourhood. In conversation, for instance, it is often said, "a Creole of New
Orleans," "a Creole of St. Croix," "a Creole of Guadaloupe," which implies
a person born in these places. A Creole of New Orleans considers it as
degrading to be taken for a Mulatto or a Quarteroon, as an inhabitant of
the Northern States would, and never fails, both in word and deed, to
show this distinction. Descending from a mixed race of Spaniards and
French, the Creoles have inherited all the characteristics of their forefathers, such as jealousy, and an impetuosity of temper, that often drives
them to the commission of acts which in other parts of the globe would be
severely punished, though they are here passed over unnoticed. At play-
houses it was not unusual to see persons attack each other with drawn
daggers.

I was myself an eye-witness of two scenes in the French Opera House, which left on my mind a strong impression of the passionate and vindictive disposition of the Creoles. On both occasions, a dispute arose between two well-dressed gentlemen on the subject of their seats; a sharp expression led to a retort, and then followed the drawing of dirks, which are carried by every one at New Orleans. One of the combatants received a very severe wound in the shoulder, and the other a dangerous cut in the side, which put his life in jeopardy. As soon as the bleeding heroes had been carried out of the house by their friends, all sensation ceased, and the play was resumed as if nothing had happened. On another occasion, at a public ball, which was attended by the principal people of the city, two gentlemen had a misunderstanding respecting a lady, with whom both wished to have the honour of dancing. They retired immediately from the ball-room to settle their quarrel with balls of a different kind.

The Creoles are in general handsome, with large bright black eyes, fine figure, and an agreeable carriage. They have something of the French *tournure,* and dress tastefully and elegantly. The climate, however, produces a relaxing effect, observable in their movements, which indicate indolence, and in their conversation, tainted with a kind of debility. Few are able to express themselves in English; their French is a kind of *patois,* which annoyed me a little at first, until the ear became more familiarized with the strange sound.

PART VII

THE REFORMERS AND THE PREACHERS

The decades of the 1830's and 1840's were characterized by a fervid spirit of reform in the northern states. This region became a fertile seed-bed of sprouting isms. Among the varied causes of this new attitude was the development of the Unitarian religion, advanced by William Ellery Channing of Boston, which contributed greatly to the breakdown of the old Calvinist philosophy of New England and to the rise of a humanitarian spirit. A seminal reform movement in this region arose with the organized agitation for the abolition of slavery, which was strongly influenced by the British movement that in 1833 culminated in the abolition of slavery in the British West Indies. The abolition movement in New England was led by William Lloyd Garrison, a printer, who on January 1, 1831, founded The Liberator to work for the immediate abolition of slavery. Though Garrison was an effective and vehement agitator, he lacked the practical ability to guide a national movement, and, besides, he scattered his energies in championing at the same time a wide range of other reforms.

In New York the abolition movement was advanced by two merchants, Lewis and Arthur Tappan, the latter being elected the first president of the American Anti-Slavery Society (1833). In the western states Theodore D. Weld of Ohio was the outstanding agitator and organizer of the abolition crusade, an intensely serious, humorless man, who wrote a terrible tract portraying the evils of southern slavery, entitled American Slavery as It Is (1839). The early agitators in the antislavery cause encountered the greatest intolerance in the northern states, resulting in the mobbing of Garrison in Boston, the attack on the house of Lewis Tappan in New York, the burning of Pennsylvania Hall in Philadelphia, where abolition meetings were held, and the murder in 1837 of Elijah Lovejoy at Alton, Illinois. Below the Mason-Dixon line an abolitionist was after 1831 continually in danger of being killed or tarred and feathered.

The deepest force in the abolition movement in the northern states seems to have been the religious impulse. It was this force that motivated Weld, who was powerfully stirred by the New York and Ohio evangelist Charles Grandison Finney. Indeed Weld applied the technique of the religious revival to convince huge audiences in the northern states that slavery was a great sin, and not to be considered in its economic and *political relations. Another effective leader in the antislavery cause who devoted his life to the great cause because of religious considerations was James G. Birney of Kentucky, candidate of the Liberty party for president in 1840 and 1844.*

The woman's rights movement was largely an outgrowth of the antislavery crusade. Women were permitted to join the antislavery societies and soon they asserted the right to speak in public for this great humanitarian cause. The woman's rights movement was led in the North, first by a Scottish woman, Frances Wright, who came to this country in 1825 and shocked Americans by lecturing in public on social reforms, and then by a group of Quaker women, including Lucretia Mott and the Grimké sisters, Sarah and Angelina. Angelina and Sarah were born in Charleston into an aristocratic slave-owning family, but after they were grown women they came to Philadelphia, where they adopted the Quaker religion. In the early 1830's they became ardent abolitionists and Angelina extended her zeal to marrying Theodore D. Weld. In 1838 Sarah published a significant pamphlet in the woman's rights movement entitled Letters on the Equality of the Sexes and the Condition of Woman.

The reform movement of the Jacksonian era expressed itself in numerous causes besides abolition of slavery and woman's rights, but space limitations prevent including in this volume documents illustrative of such reform movements. They embraced the temperance movement, Sabbath observance, founding free public schools, reform of penal codes and prisons, care for the mentally sick, and such fads as the Lucy Stone movement, the Graham reform of diet, the Bloomer fad, and the free-love movement. To many reformers the organization of society on a communistic basis seemed to represent the wave of the future. Brook Farm, established at West Roxbury, Massachusetts, by the Transcendentalists in 1841, was a famous experiment in communal living. Others were the phalansteries inspired by the French reformer Charles Fourier, notably the North American Phalanx at Red Bank, New Jersey, which Miss Fredrika Bremer describes in her vivacious travel book, Homes in the New World (1853). *This Swedish lady was a strong feminist and abolitionist, who despite her antislavery zeal appreciated the good points of American society which she observed during her travels in this country.*

Of the various reform movements that agitated the North during this period, the Transcendentalist movement attracted the greatest minds, particularly in the fields of literature and religion. Emerson's address on the death of Thoreau gives perhaps the most penetrating insight into the nature of the Transcendentalist movement. Although the Transcendentalists were influenced by German and Hindu philosophies, and by Platonism, the strongest influence in the development of their philosophy seems to have been a reaction against Calvinism with its gloomy view of human nature. The Transcendental movement was at bottom a liberal religious movement. (Emerson, its prophet, was a Unitarian minister in his early career.)

Liberalism in religion was largely confined to reformist circles in the North, and perhaps its best expression was Emerson's Harvard Divinity School Address of 1838. But the great masses of the people in America during the Jacksonian era held to a traditional type of religion and they would have been shocked by Emerson's views of a religion that did not rest on the literal word of the Bible. Their religious beliefs were vigorously expressed by Peter Cartwright, who was born in Virginia in 1785, reared in Kentucky, and spent a strenuous life as a Methodist circuit rider in the Ohio Valley states. He was defeated for Congress in 1846 by Abraham Lincoln, but continued to preach and found educational institutions until his death in 1872.

The American people of this era wanted an emotional religion that centered on immortality and escape from the supposed torments of hell. The camp meetings were dominated by this thought, and the preachers at these religious meetings in the woods exhorted their simple audiences against "sin" and sought to "save souls." Many people in the South as well as in the North condemned the excesses, the emotional orgies of the camp meetings, but nevertheless they continued to have a powerful attraction, for they represented much more than a religious service; they provided an emotional outlet for thousands of rural people who lived drab, lonely lives. They constituted the great American entertainment.

Keeping of the Sabbath day as a holy day was one of the great taboos of orthodox Protestant religion, but the Creoles of Louisiana had a different idea, and their worldly observance of the day as one of pleasure and recreation shocked the northern traveler Henry Benjamin Whipple, as it did most southerners who visited New Orleans during this era. Intolerance of hedonistic practices in observing Sunday was only one manifestation of the great intolerance of religious dissent that characterized American religion of this period, which Alexis de Tocqueville observed and described in his Democracy in America.

The Liberator's Principles

William Lloyd Garrison

In the month of August, I issued proposals for publishing, *"The Liberator"* in Washington City; but the enterprise, though hailed in different sections of the country, was palsied by public indifference. Since that time, the removal of the *Genius of Universal Emancipation* to the Seat of Government has rendered less imperious the establishment of a similar periodical in that quarter.

During my recent tour for the purpose of exciting the minds of the people by a series of discourses on the subject of slavery, every place that I visited gave fresh evidence of the fact, that a greater revolution in public sentiment was to be effected in the free states—*and particularly in New England*—than at the south. I found contempt more bitter, opposition more active, detraction more relentless, prejudice more stubborn, and apathy more frozen, than among slave owners themselves. Of course, there were individual exceptions to the contrary. This state of things affected, but did not dishearten me. I determined, at every hazard, to lift up the standard of emancipation in the eyes of the nation, *within sight of Bunker Hill and in the birth place of liberty.* That standard is now unfurled; and long may it float, unhurt by the spoliations of time or the missiles of a desparate foe—yea, till every chain be broken, and every bondman set free! Let Southern oppressors tremble—let their Northern apologists tremble—let all the enemies of the persecuted blacks tremble.

I deem the publication of my original Prospectus unnecessary, as it has obtained a wide circulation. The principles therein inculcated will be steadily pursued in this paper, excepting that I shall not array myself as the political partisan of any man. In defending the great cause of human rights, I wish to derive the assistance of all religions and of all parties.

Assenting to the "self evident truth" maintained in the American Declaration of Independence, "that all men are created equal, and en-

William Lloyd Garrison, 1805-1879: The Story of His Life Told by His Children (New York, 1885-89), I, pp. 277-278.

dowed by their Creator with certain inalienable rights—among which are life, liberty and the pursuit of happiness," I shall strenuously contend for the immediate enfranchisement of our slave population. In Park-Street Church, on the Fourth of July, 1829, in an address on slavery, I unreflectingly assented to the popular but pernicious doctrine of *gradual* abolition. I seize this opportunity to make a full and unequivocal recantation, and thus publicly to ask pardon of my God, of my country, and of my brethren the poor slaves, for having uttered a sentiment so full of timidity, injustice and absurdity. A similar recantation, from my pen, was published in the *Genius of Universal Emancipation* at Baltimore, in September, 1829. My conscience is now satisfied.

I am aware, that many object to the severity of my language; but is there not cause for severity? I *will* be as harsh as truth, and as uncompromising as justice. On this subject, I do not wish to think, or speak, or write, with moderation. No! No! Tell a man whose house is on fire, to give a moderate alarm; tell him to moderately rescue his wife from the hands of the ravisher; tell the mother to gradually extricate her babe from the fire into which it has fallen;—but urge me not to use moderation in a cause like the present. I am in earnest—I will not equivocate—I will not excuse—I will not retreat a single inch—AND I WILL BE HEARD. The apathy of the people is enough to make every statue leap from its pedestal, and to hasten the resurrection of the dead.

It is pretended, that I am retarding the cause of emancipation by the coarseness of my invective, and the precipitancy of my measures. *The charge is not true.* On this question my influence,—humble as it is,—is felt at this moment to a considerable extent, and shall be felt in coming years—not perniciously, but beneficially—not as a curse, but as a blessing; and posterity will bear testimony that I was right. I desire to thank God, that he enables me to disregard "the fear of man which bringeth a snare," and to speak his truth in its simplicity and power. . . .

Abolition—Our Blessed Cause

Theodore D. Weld

Oberlin (Ohio) 17 Nov. 1835

My dear brother Tappan,

I received yours of Oct. 14 some days since at Elyria. I am quite at a loss what to say in reply to that part of your last letter which treats of brother [Rev. Charles Grandison] Finney. That Finney is a coward I cannot believe and for this simple reason: I have seen in him more frequent and more striking exhibitions of courage physical and moral than in any other man living. That brother Finney has been (as you say you fear) "sinning against conviction" I cannot believe. An acquaintance with him of the most *intimate* character for *nine years* forbids me to harbour the suspicion for a moment. Everything in his character and history—all that I have seen of him—(and nobody has seen more of him) goes utterly against it.

Nobody on earth could convince me that *you* were deliberately "sinning against conviction." And if you were to do *just the things* which you allege against brother F. I could account for it on a supposition far more charitable than to suppose that you were sinning against conviction. I have looked over all the facts and details in your letter on this subject and have talked the whole over and over with brother Finney, and I find my mind exactly in this state. 1—I do not believe he has been *"afraid"* of anything except of *doing wrong.* 2—I believe he is an abolitionist in full. 3—That he has given the subject as much prominence in his preaching, and at Communions, etc., *as he conscientiously believed was his duty.* 4—I have no doubt but he had thought, felt, said and done less on the subject than he should have done. I have no doubt but he ought to have given it more prominence in his public prayers and preaching. He would

G. H. Barnes and D. L. Dumond (eds.), *Letters of Theodore Dwight Weld, Angelina Grimké Weld, and Sarah Grimké* (American Historical Association, New York, 1934), I, pp. 242-245.

have encouraged the monthly concert for the abolition of slavery more heartily. This I have told him in full.

The truth is Finney has always been in revivals of religon. It is his great business, aim and *absorbing passion* to promote them. He has never had hardly anything to do with Bible, Tract, missionary, Education, Temperance, moral Reform and anti-slavery societies. The last three he has joined and has decidedly committed himself before the public in favor of their principles, and taken a bold and high stand with reference to them at the Communion table. Finney feels about revivals of religion and the promotion of the church and ministry in doctrines and measures, just as you and I do about anti slavery. Now I feel as tho Finney could take hold of you and me and upbraid us, because we feel so little and pray with so little faith and fervor, and labor with so little of the tireless activity of Paul, in summoning men night and day with tears to repent; and that, too, as far at least as I am concerned with far more reason for the upbraiding than you have for upbraiding him with his coldness and unfaithfulness in the cause of anti slavery. God has called *some* [to be] prophets, *some apostles,* some *teachers.* All the members of the body of Christ have not the same office. Let Delavan drive Temperance, McDowell moral Reform, Finney Revivals, Tappan anti-slavery, etc. Each of these is bound to make his own *peculiar* department his *main* business, and to promote *collaterally* as much as he can the other objects. I have no doubt but Finney has erred in not giving as much *collateral* attention to anti slavery as the present emergent crisis demands. And I am equally certain that I have not done as much collaterally to promote temperance and Revivals while I have been lecturing on slavery as I ought, and I havent a particle of doubt but you can say the same. As to brother F's not praying for the oppressed *in public,* I am clear that he has not done his duty; and that if he had "remembered those in bonds as bo[u]nd with them" he would have done it. I *cant help* praying for them *whenever* I pray in public on *whatever* occasion. But brother F. has been *conscientious* in the omission. He never prays you know for Temperance, moral Reform, or any other moral enterprise in public except at a meeting held expressly to promote that object. His invariable rule is to pray in public only for and about *the things* which are there and then before him. Here I am persuaded he misconceives duty, for the sin of slavery in this country is *omnipresent.* At the present crisis it not only *overshadows* all others, but it involves all others and *absorbs* them into itself; and it is my deliberate conviction that revivals, moral Reform, etc., etc., must and [will] remain nearly stationary until the Temple is cleansed. [Mutilated] . . . the thieves, the man stealers, the whore mongers must be thrus[t out] with headlong haste and in holy horror, that God may come in. Slavery, its exactions, robberies, kindred sunderings, adulteries, bloody baptisms, human burnt offerings and its hellish tramplings on God's image, Jesus' purchase, and the Spirits Temple—all sit enthroned in the sanctuary of God, eat the sacramental bread, are baptised at the font, consecrated to minister at the alter, clad in sacred vestments and ushered into the holy of holies, to make it ring with blasphemies and reek with lust and smoke with the blood of its damnable abominations. . . .

I have been here ten days, lectured every day, occupied the sabbath with the Bible argument, and expect to next sabbath. Our meetings are held in one of the new buildings. It is neither plastered nor lathed and the only seats are rough boards thrown upon blocks; and you may judge something of the interest felt at Oberlin on the subject of abolition when I tell you that from five to six hundred males and females attend every night, and sit shivering on the rough boards without fire these cold nights, without anything to lean back against, and this too until nine o'clock. I meet the five brethren who are going out to lecture on Abolition and spend an hour or two every day in indoctrinating them in the principles, facts, arguments, etc., of the whole subject. I shall probably stay here ten days longer. A letter from (James G.) Birney yesterday. It is doubtful whether he will be able to publish his paper. I am a little doubtful whether he would answer for the situation you propose. In most respects he would do admirably. His tender spirit, interesting address, dignified mien, unflinching firmness, high thorough principle, great practical wisdom, as well as the very high estimation in which he is universally held, would all contribute to make him exactly the man if his business habits and tact and accomplishment had been *sufficiently tested.* You ask for small shot for the Slaves Friend. I could give you a locker full if I could only get time to run them, but am driven to death with lecturing and correspondence. . . .

Do write me at once and direct *here*—Oberlin, Lorain Co. I am distressed about duty—whether to go to Western N. York this winter or stay in the West. The friends of the Cause in this state and Western Pennsylvania remonstrate against my leaving. I have desired[?] to be in Pittsburg, Pa. [by the] middle of December. I have now more applications in the West than I could answer in six months. Forever, my dear brother, most affectionately yours for the perishing.

Abolition and Women's Rights

Angelina Grimké

Brookline (Mass.) 8th Mo. 20 (1837)
To Theodore D. Weld and John Greenleaf Whittier,
Brethren beloved in the Lord.

As your letter came to hand at the same time and both are devoted mainly to the same subject we have concluded to answer them on one sheet and jointly. You seem greatly alarmed at the idea of our advocating the *rights of woman*. Now we will first tell you *how* we came to begin those letters in the Spectator. Whilst we were at Newburyport we received a note from Mary Parker telling us that Wm. S. Porter had requested her to try to obtain some one to write for his paper in order that it might be better sustained. She asked him whether *she* might choose the subject and named the *province of woman:* he said yes, he would be glad to have such pieces to publish. Just at this time the Pastoral Letter came out, and Mary requested us to write something every week about *Woman* for the Spectator. We consulted together and viewed this unexpected opportunity of throwing our views before the public as providential. As I was writing to C. E. B[eecher], S. M. G. undertook it and as this paper was not an abolition paper we could not see any impropriety in embracing this opening. These letters have not been the means of *arousing* the public attention to the subject of Womans rights, it was the Pastoral Letter which did the mischief. The ministers seemed panic struck at once and commenced a most violent attack upon us. I do not say *absurd* for in truth if it can be fairly established that women *can lecture,* then why may they not preach and if *they* can preach, the woe! woe be unto that Clerical Domination which now rules the world under the various names of Gen'l Assemblies, Congregational Associations, etc. *This Letter* then roused the attention of the whole country to enquire what *right* we had to open our mouths for the dumb; the people were continually told "it is a *shame for a woman* to speak in the churches." Paul suffered not a *woman*

Weld-Grimké Letters, I, pp. 427-432.

to *teach* but commanded *her* to be in silence. The pulpit is too *sacred* a *place* for *woman's* foot etc. Now my dear brothers *this invasion of our rights* was just such an attack upon *us*, as that made upon Abolitionists generally when they were told a few years ago that *they had no right* to discuss the subject of Slavery. Did *you* take no notice of this assertion? Why no! With one heart and one voice you said, We will settle *this right before* we go one step further. The *time* to assert a right is *the* time when *that* right is denied. We must establish this right for if we do not, it will be impossible for us to go on with the work of Emancipation. But you will say that nothwithstand[ing] the denial of your right you still had crowded audiences—*curiosity*, it was a new thing under the sun to see a *woman* occupy the place of a lecturer and the people were very anxious to *hear* and *see* for themselves: but you certainly *must* know that the leaven which the ministers are so assiduously working into the minds of the people *must* take effect in process of time, and *will close every church to us*, if we give the community no reason to counteract the sophistry of priests and levites. In this State particularly there is an utter ignorance on the subject. Some few noble minds bursting thro' the trammels of educational prejudice FEEL that woman does stand on the same platform of human rights with man, but even these cannot sustain their ground by argument, and as soon as they open their lips to assert her *rights,* their opponents throw perverted scripture into their faces and call O yea, clamor for *proof*, proof, PROOF! and this *they cannot* give and are beaten off the field in disgrace. Now we are confident that there are scores of such minds panting after light on this subject: "the children *ask* bread and no MAN giveth it unto them." There is an eagerness to understand our views. Now is it wrong to give those views in a series of letters in a paper NOT devoted to Abolition?

And can you not see that women *could* do, and *would* do a hundred times more for the slave if she were not fettered? Why! we are gravely told that we are out of our sphere even when we circulate petitions; out of our "appropriate sphere" when we speak to women only; and out of them when we *sing* in the churches. Silence is *our* province, submission *our* duty. If then we "give *no reason* for the hope that is in us," that we have *equal rights* with our brethren, how can we expect to be permitted *much longer to exercise those rights?* IF I know my own heart, I am NOT actuated by any selfish considerations (but I do sincerely thank our dear brother J. G. W[hittier] for the suggestion) but we are actuated by full conviction that if we are to do any good in the Anti Slavery cause, our *right* to labor in it *must* be firmly established; *not* on the ground of Quakerism, but on the only firm bases of human rights, the Bible. Indeed I contend brethren that *this* is not *Quaker* doctrine, it is no more like *their* doctrine on Women than our Anti Slavery is like their Abolition, just about the same difference I will explain myself. Women are regarded as equal to men on the ground of *spiritual gifts,* not on the broad ground of *humanity.* Woman may *preach;* this is a *gift;* but woman must *not* make the discipline by which *she herself* is to be governed. O that you were here that we might have a good long, *long* talk over matters and things, then I could explain myself far better. And I think we could convince you that *we* cannot push Abolitionism forward with all our might *until* we take up the stumbling block out of the road. We cannot see with brother Weld in this matter. We acknowledge the excellence of his reasons for urging us to labor in this cause of the Slave, our being Southerners, etc., but then we say how can we expect to be able to hold meetings much longer when people are so diligently taught to despise us for thus stepping out of the sphere of woman! Look at this instance: after we had left Groton the *Abolition* minister there, at a Lyceum meeting poured out his sarcasm and ridicule upon our heads and among other things said, he would as soon be caught robbing a hen roost as encouraging a woman to lecture. Now brethren if the leaders of the people thus speak of our labors, *how long* will we be allowed to prosecute them? Answer me this question. You may depend upon it, tho' to meet *this* question *may appear* to be turning out of our road, that *it is not.* IT IS NOT: we *must* meet it, and meet it *now* and meet it like *women* in the fear of the Lord. Why the language of the priests and levites to us women is that of Davids brother to him. "Why camest thou down hither? and with whom hast thou left those few sheep in the wilderness? I know thy pride and the naughtiness of thy heart; for thou art come down that thou mightest see the battle." They utterly deny *our right* to interfere with this or any other moral reform except in the particular way *they* choose to mark out for us to walk in. If we dare to stand upright and do our duty according to the dictates of *our own* consciences, why then we are compared to Fanny Wright and so on. Why, my dear brothers can you not see the deep laid scheme of the clergy against us as lecturers? They know full well that if they can persuade the people it is a *shame* for us to speak in public, and that every time we open our mouths for the dumb we are breaking a divine command, that even if we spoke with the tongues of *men* or of angels, we should have *no hearers.* They are springing a deep mine beneath our feet, and we shall *very* soon be compelled to retreat for we shall have *no* ground to stand on. If we surrender the right to *speak* to the public this year, we must surrender the right to petition next year and the right to *write* the year after and so on. What *then* can *woman* do for the slave when she is herself under the feet of man and shamed into *silence?* Now we entreat *you* to weigh candidly the *whole subject,* and then we are sure you will see, this is no more than an abandonment of our first love than the effort made by Anti Slavery men to establish the *right* of free discussion.

With regard to brother Welds ultraism on the subject of marriage, he is quite mistaken if he fancies he has got far *ahead* of *us* in the human rights reform. We do *not* think his doctrine at all shocking: it is *altogether right*. But I am afraid I am *too proud* ever to exercise the right. The fact is we are living in such an artificial state of society that there are some things about which we dare not speak out, or act out the most natural and best feelings of our hearts. O! *when* shall we be "delivered from the *bondage* of *corruption* into the glorious liberty of the sons of God!" By the bye it will be very important to establish this right, for the men of Mass. stoutly declare that women who hold such sentiments of *equality* can never expect to be courted. They seem to hold out this as a kind of threat to deter us from asserting our rights, not *knowing whereunto this will grow*. But jesting is inconvenient says the Apostle: to business then.

Anti Slavery men are trying very hard to separate what God hath joined together. I fully believe that so far from keeping different moral reformations entirely distinct that no such attempt can ever be successful. They are bound together in a circle like the sciences; they blend with each other like the colors of the rain bow; they are the parts only of our glorious whole and that whole is Christianity, pure *practical* Christianity. The fact is I believe—but dont be alarmed, for it is only I—that Men and Women will have to go out on their own responsibility, just like the people. The whole Church Government must come down, the clergy stand right in the way of reform, and I do not know but this stumbling block too must be removed *before* Slavery can be abolished, for the system is supported by *them;* it could not exist without the Church as it is called. This grand principle must be mooted, discussed and established viz. The Ministers of the Gospel are the successors of the *prophets*, not of the *priests*, the latter were types of the great eternal high priest of his Church; they were struck dumb as soon as the birth of his fore-runner was announced. Zacharias could *not speak unto* the people after he had seen the vision in the temple. The Church is built *not* upon the priests at all but upon the *prophets* and *Apostles*, Jesus Christ being the chief corner stone. This develops three important inferences: 1. True ministers are called like Elisha from the plough and Amos from gathering sycamore fruit, Matthew from the receipt of custom and Peter and John from their fishing nets. 2. As prophets *never were paid*, so ministers ought not to be. 3. As there were *prophetesses* as well as prophets, so there *ought* to be now *female* as well as male ministers. Just let this one principle be established and what will become of the power and sacredness of the pastoral office? Is brother Weld frightened at *my ultraism?* Please write to us soon and let us know what you think after reflecting on this letter. We are now at S. Philbricks and will we expect be there two weeks more lecturing in the neighboring towns. May the Lord bless you my dear brothers is the prayer of your sister in Jesus

A Visit to the North American Phalanstery

Fredrika Bremer

Nov. 12, 1849. We arrived in New Jersey amid rain, and in rain we reached the little town of Redbank. Here a wagon from the Phalanstery met us, which had been sent for the guests, as well as for potatoes, and in it we stowed ourselves, beneath a tilted cover of yellow oil-cloth, which sheltered us from the rain. A handsome young man, one of the people of the Phalanstery, drove the pair of fat horses which drew us, and after we had plowed the sand for a couple of hours, we arrived at the Phalanstery, a couple of large houses, with several lesser ones standing around them, without any thing remarkable in their style of architecture. The landscape around had a pleasant, park-like appearance; the fields and the trees were yet quite green. New Jersey is celebrated for its mild climate and its fine fruits. We were conducted into a hall and regaled with a dinner which could not have been better if it had been in Arcadia; it would have been impossible to have produced better milk, bread, or cheese. They had also meat here.

I here met with the family which had first invited me to the Phalanstery, and found them to be the sister and brother-in-law of Marcus, two earnest, spiritual-minded people, who have a profound faith in and love for the principle of association. He is the president of the institution at this place. Mr. A., who has not alone enthusiasm, but who is evidently a clever and straight-forward man of business, gifted with the power of organization, was originally a minister, and devoted himself for a long time most beneficially as a missionary of the poor; "a minster at large," as they are called in this country; after which he lived for ten years as a farmer in one of the Western States, in the valley of the Mississippi, cultivating maize and fruit, and finding himself well off amid the affluent solitudes of nature. As his children, however, grew up, it appeared to him too solitary for

Fredrika Bremer, *The Homes of the New World: Impressions of America* (New York, 1853), I, pp. 76-81.

them; the house became too small, and, for the sake of their education, and their moral and intellectual development, he removed again, and came nearer to the great world of man. But in so doing he resolved to unite himself with that portion of it which, as it appeared to him, came the nearest to his idea of a Christian community. He, and his wife and children, therefore, joined this association, which was established eight years before by a few married couples, all enthusiasts for this idea, and which now calls itself "the North American Phalanstery." Each member advanced the sum of one thousand dollars; land was purchased, and they began to labor together, according to laws which the society had laid down beforehand. Great difficulties met them in the commencement, in particular from their want of means to build, for the purchase of implements, and so on. It was beautiful and affecting to hear what fatigue and labor the women subjected themselves to—women who had been but little accustomed to any thing of this kind; how steadfastly and with what noble courage they endured it; and how the men, in the spirit of brotherhood, did their part in any kind of work as well as the women, merely looking at the honor and the necessity of the work, and never asking whether it was the fit employment for man or for woman. They had suffered much from calumny, but through it all they had become a stronger and more numerous body.

They had now overcome the worst, and the institution was evidently improving. It was in contemplation at this time to build a new house, in particular a large eating-hall and place for social meeting, together with a cooking and wash house, provided with such machinery as should dispense with the most onerous hand-labor. The number of members was at this time somewhat above seventy. The establishment has its own peculiar income from mills and from tillage, as well as from its orchards. They cultivate peaches, melons, and tomatoes. In the mills they prepare hominy (ground maize), which is boiled into a sort of pudding, and eaten universally, especially for breakfast.

One evening a great portion of the members of the Phalanstery assembled in one of the sitting-rooms. Various individuals were introduced to me, and I saw a great number of very handsome young people; in particular, I remarked the niece and nephew of Marcus, Abby and her brother, as being beautiful according to one's ideal standard. Many among the men wore coarse clothes; but all were neat, and had a something of great earnestness and kindness in their whole demeanor.

Needle-work was brought in and laid upon a table. This was the making of small linen bags for containing hominy, and which, filled and stamped with the name of the Phalanstery, are sent for sale to New York. I sewed one bag; (William Ellery) Channing, also, made another, and maintained that he sewed quicker than I did; my opinion, however, is that my sewing was the best. After this I played Swedish dances and ballads for the young people, which excited them in a remarkable manner, especially the Nec's polka. I related also to them the legend of the Neck and the Priest, and the Wand which became verdant, a legend which shows that even the spirits of nature might be saved. This struck them very much, and the tears came into many eyes.

I had a little room to myself for the night, which some of the young girls had vacated for me. It was as small as a prison cell; had four bare, white walls, but was neat and clean, and had a large window with a fine and beautiful prospect; and I was exceedingly comfortable in that little chamber, and slept well upon a good sofa-bed to the sound of the plashing rain, and in the mild atmosphere which entered through the half opened window. The bed-making sisters, two handsome, kind young girls, were the last which I saw in my room. I was awoke in the morning by the sound of labor throughout the house; people were going and coming, all full of business; it sounded earnest and industrious. I thought the "Essenes and the Pythagoreans began the day with a song, a consecration of the day's work to the service of the holy powers," and I sighed to think that the associations of the West were so far behind those of the East. I dressed myself and went down.

As there is always an impulse within me to enter body and soul into the life which at that time exists around me, so would I now live here as a true and earnest member of the Phalanstery, and therefore I entered as a worker into one of the bands of workers. I selected that in which cooking was going forward, because I consider that my genius has a bent in that direction. I was soon standing, therefore, by the fire with the excellent Mrs. A., who had the management of this department; and I baked a whole pile of buckwheat cakes, just as we bake cakes in Sweden, but upon a large iron plate, until breakfast, and had then the pleasure of serving Marcus and Channing with some of them quite hot for breakfast. I myself thought that I had been remarkably fortunate with my cakes. In my fervor of association, I labored also with hands and arms up to my very elbows in a great kneading-trough, but had very nearly stuck fast in the dough. It was quite too heavy for me, though I would not confess it; but they were kind enough to release me from the operation in the politest manner, and place it in abler hands.

The rain had ceased, and the sun began to find his way through the clouds. I now, therefore, went out to look about me, accompanied by Mrs. A. and the lady of the president, the latter of whom wore a short and pantaloons, which were very becoming to her fine and picturesque figure, and besides which, were well calculated for walking through the wet fields and woods. We first paid a visit to the mills. Two handsome young girls, also in short dresses and blouses, girt with leathern bands, and with jaunty little caps on their heads, which were remarkably becoming, went, or rather danced along the foot-path before us, over hill and dale, as light and merrily as birds. They were going to assist at the hominy mills. I went through the mills, where every thing seemed excellent and well arranged, and where the little millers were already at their work.

Thence we went across the meadows to the potato-fields, where I shook hands with the chief, who, in his shirt-sleeves, was digging up potatoes among his senators. Both the chief and the other members looked clever and excellent people; and the potato crop promised this year to be remarkably rich. The land in New Jersey appears to be very good and fruitful. The sun shone pleasantly over the potato-field, the chief, and his laborers, among whom were many men of education and intelligence.

In my conversation with the two sensible women, my conductresses, I learned various particulars regarding the laws and life of the Phalanstery; among others, that they are wise enough not to allow the public to absorb private property. Each individual may invest as much as he likes in the association, and retain as much of his own property as he wishes. For that which he so invests he receives interest. The time required for labor is ten hours a day. All who work over hours are paid for such overwork. The women participate in all rights equally with the men; vote, and share in the administration of law and justice. "But," said Mrs. A., "we have had so much to do with our domestic affairs, that we have hitherto troubled ourselves very little about these things."

Anyone who makes known his desire to become a member may be received as such after a probation of one year in the Phalanstery, during which time he must have shown himself to be unwearied in labor, and steadfast in brotherly love and good-will. As regards his religion, rank, or his former mode of life, no questions are asked. The association makes a new experiment in social and economic life; it regards the active principle of love as the ruling power of life, and wishes to place every thing within the sphere of its influence; it will, so to say, begin life anew, and makes experimental researches into its laws; like those plants called exogens, it grows from the exterior inward, but has, it appears to me, its principle much less determinate than the vegetable.

Being asked in the evening my opinion of this community, I candidly confessed in what it appeared to be deficient; in particular, as regarded a profession of religion and public divine service— its being based merely upon a moral principle, the validity of which might be easily called in question, as they did not recognize a connection with a life existing eternally beyond earth and time with any eternally binding law, nor even with a divine Lawgiver.

Thoreau

Ralph Waldo Emerson

Henry David Thoreau was the last male descendent of a French ancestor who came to this country from the Isle of Guernsey. His character exhibited occasional traits drawn from this blood, in singular combination with a very strong Saxon genius.

He was born in Concord, Massachusetts, on the 12th of July, 1817. He was graduated at Harvard College in 1837, but without any literary distinction. An iconoclast in literature, he seldom thanked colleges for their service to him, holding them in small esteem, whilst yet his debt to them was important. After leaving the University, he joined his brother in teaching a private school, which he soon renounced. His father was a manufacturer of lead-pencils, and Henry applied himself for a time to this craft, believing he could make a better pencil than was then in use. After completing his experiments, he exhibited his work to chemists and artists in Boston, and having obtained their certificates to its excellence and to its equality with the best London manufacture, he returned home contented. His friends congratulated him that he had now opened his way to fortune. But he replied that he should never make another pencil. "Why should I? I would not do again what I have done once." He resumed his endless walks and miscellaneous studies, making every day some new acquaintance with Nature, though as yet never speaking of zoology or botany, since, though very studious of natural facts, he was incurious of technical and textual science.

At this time, a strong, healthy youth, fresh from college, whilst all his companions were choosing their profession, or eager to begin some lucrative employment, it was inevitable that his thoughts should be exercised on the same question, and it required rare decision to refuse all the accustomed paths and keep his solitary freedom at the cost of disappointing the natural expectations of his family and friends: all the more

Ralph Waldo Emerson, *Lectures and Biographical Sketches* (Boston, 1889), pp. 421-452.

difficult that he had a perfect probity, was exact in securing his own independence, and in holding every man to the like duty. But Thoreau never faltered. He was a born protestant. He declined to give up his large ambition of knowledge and action for any narrow craft or profession, aiming at a much more comprehensive calling, the art of living well. If he slighted and defied the opinions of others, it was only that he was more intent to reconcile his practice with his own belief. Never idle or self-indulgent, he preferred, when he wanted money, earning it by some piece of manual labor agreeable to him, as building a boat or a fence, planting, grafting, surveying, or other short work, to any long engagements. With his hardy habits and few wants, his skill in woodcraft, and his powerful arithmetic, he was very competent to live in any part of the world. It would cost him less time to supply his wants than another. He was therefore secure of his leisure.

A natural skill for mensuration, growing out of his mathematical knowledge and his habit of ascertaining the measures and distances of objects which interested him, the size of trees, the depth and extent of ponds and rivers, the height of mountains, and the air-line distance of his favorite summits,—this, and his intimate knowledge of the territory about Concord, made him drift into the profession of land surveyor. It had the advantage for him that it led him continually into new and secluded grounds, and helped his studies of Nature. His accuracy and skill in this work were readily appreciated, and he found all the employment he wanted.

He could easily solve the problems of the surveyor, but he was daily beset with graver questions, which he manfully confronted. He interrogated every custom, and wished to settle all his practice on an ideal foundation. He was a protestant à outrance, and few lives contain so many renunciations. He was bred to no profession; he never married; he lived alone; he never went to church; he never voted; he refused to pay a tax to the State; he ate no flesh, he drank no wine, he never knew the use of tobacco; and, though a naturalist, he used neither trap nor gun. He chose, wisely no doubt for himself, to be the bachelor of thought and Nature. He had no talent for wealth, and knew how to be poor without the least hint of squalor or inelegance. Perhaps he fell into his way of living without forecasting it much, but approved it with later wisdom. "I am often reminded," he wrote in his journal, "that if I had bestowed on me the wealth of Croesus, my aims must be still the same, and my means essentially the same." He had no temptations to fight against,—no appetites, no passions, no taste for elegant trifles. A fine house, dress, the manners and talk of highly cultivated people, were all thrown away on him. He much preferred a good Indian, and considered these refinements as impediments to conversation, wishing to meet his companion on the simplest terms. He declined invitations to dinner-parties, because there each was in every one's way, and he could not meet the individuals to any purpose. "They make their pride," he said, "in making their dinner cost much; I make my pride in making my dinner cost little." When asked at table what dish he preferred, he answered, "The nearest." He did not like the taste of wine, and never had a vice in his life. He said, "I have a faint recollection of pleasure derived from smoking dried lily-stems, before I was a man. I had commonly a supply of these. I have never smoked anything more noxious."

He chose to be rich by making his wants few, and supplying them himself. In his travels, he used the railroad only to get over so much country as was unimportant to the present purpose, walking hundreds of miles, avoiding taverns, buying a lodging in farmers' and fishermen's houses, as cheaper, and more agreeable to him, and because there he could better find the men and the information he wanted.

There was somewhat military in his nature, not to be subdued, always manly and able, but rarely tender, as if he did not feel himself except in opposition. He wanted a fallacy to oppose, a blunder to pillory, I may say required a little sense of victory, a roll of the drum, to call his powers into full exercise. It cost him nothing to say No; indeed he found it much easier than to say Yes. It seemed as if his first instinct on hearing a proposition was to controvert it, so impatient was he of the limitations of our daily thought. This habit, of course, is a little chilling to the social affections; and though the companion would in the end acquit him of any malice or untruth, yet it mars conversation. Hence, no equal companion stood in affectionate relations with one so pure and guileless. "I love Henry," said one of his friends, "but I cannot like him; and as for taking his arm, I should as soon think of taking the arm of an elm tree."

Yet, hermit and stoic as he was, he was really fond of sympathy, and threw himself heartily and childlike into the company of young people whom he loved, and whom he delighted to entertain, as he only could, with the varied and endless anecdotes of his experiences by field and river; and he was always ready to lead a huckleberry-party or a search for chestnuts or grapes. Talking, one day, of a public discourse, Henry remarked that whatever succeeded with the audience was bad. I said, "Who would not like to write something which all can read, like Robinson Crusoe? and who does not see with regret that his page is not solid with a right materialistic treatment, which delights everybody?" Henry objected, of course, and vaunted the better lectures which reached only a few persons. But, at supper, a young girl, understanding that he was to lecture at the Lyceum, sharply asked him "whether his lecture would be a nice, interesting story, such as she wished to hear, or whether it was one of those old philosophical things that she did not care about." Henry turned to her, and bethought himself, and, I saw, was trying to believe that he had matter that might fit her and her brother, who were to sit up and go to the lecture, if it was a good one for them.

He was a speaker and actor of the truth, born such, and was ever running into dramatic situations from this cause. In any circumstance it interested all bystanders to know what part Henry would take, and what he would say; and he did not disappoint expectation, but used an original judgment on each emergency. In 1845 he built himself a small framed house on the shores of Walden Pond, and lived there two years alone, a life of labor and study. This action was quite native and fit for him. No one who knew him would tax him with affectation. He was more unlike his neighbors in his thought than in his action. As soon as he had exhausted the advantages of that solitude, he abandoned it. In 1847, not approving some uses to which the public expenditure was applied, he refused to pay his town tax, and was put in jail. A friend paid the tax for him, and he was released. The like annoyance was threatened the next year. But as his friends paid the tax, notwithstanding his protest, I believe he ceased to resist. No opposition or ridicule had any weight with him. He coldly and fully stated his opinion without affecting to believe that it was the opinion of the company. It was of no consequence if every one present held the opposite opinion. On one occasion he went to the University Library to procure some books. The librarian refused to lend them. Mr. Thoreau repaired to the President, who stated to him the rules and usages, which permitted the loan of books to resident graduates, to clergymen who were alumni, and to some others resident within a circle of ten miles' radius from the College. Mr. Thoreau explained to the President that the railroad had destroyed the old scale of distances,—that the library was useless, yes, and President and College useless, on the terms of his rules,—that the one benefit he owed to the College was its library,—that, at this moment, not only his want of books was imperative but he wanted a large number of books, and assured him that he, Thoreau, and not the librarian, was the proper custodian of these. In short, the President found the petitioner so formidable, and the rules getting to look so ridiculous, that he ended by giving him a privilege which in his hands proved unlimited thereafter.

No truer American existed than Thoreau. His preference of his country and condition was genuine, and his aversation from English and European manners and tastes almost reached contempt. He listened impatiently to news or *bon-mots* gleaned from London circles; and though he tried to be civil, these anecodotes fatigued him. The men were all imitating each other, and on a small mould. Why can they not live as far apart as possible, and each be a man by himself? What he sought was the most energetic nature; and he wished to go to Oregon, not to London. "In every part of Great Britain," he wrote in his dairy, "are discovered traces of the Romans, their funereal urns, their camps, their dwellings. But New England, at least, is not based on any Roman ruins. We have not to lay the foundations of our houses on the ashes of a former civilization."

But idealist as he was, standing for abolition of slavery, abolition of tariffs, almost for abolition of government, it is needless to say he found himself not only unrepresented in actual politics, but almost equally opposed to every class of reformers. Yet he paid the tribute of his uniform respect to the Anti-slavery party. One man, whose personal acquaintance he had formed, he honored with exceptional regard. Before the first friendly word had been spoken for Captain John Brown, he sent notices to most houses in Concord that he would speak in a public hall on the condition and character of John Brown, on Sunday evening, and invited all people to come. The Republican Committee, the Abolitionist Committee, sent him word that it was premature and not advisable. He replied,— "I did not send to you for advice, but to announce that I am to speak." The hall was filled at an early hour by people of all parties, and his earnest eulogy of the hero was heard by all respectfully, by many with a sympathy that surprised themselves.

It was said of Plotinus that he was ashamed of his body, and 'tis very likely he had good reason for it,—that his body was a bad servant, and he had not skill in dealing with the material world, as happens often to men of abstract intellect. But Mr. Thoreau was equipped with a most adapted and serviceable body. He was of short stature, firmly built, of light complexion, with staring, serious blue eyes, and a grave aspect,—his face covered in the late years with becoming beard. His senses were acute, his frame well-knit and hardy, his hands strong and skillful in the use of tools. And there was a wonderful fitness of body and mind. He could pace sixteen rods more accurately than another man could measure them with rod and chain. He could find his path in the woods at night, he said, better by his feet than his eyes. He could estimate the measure of a tree very well by his eye; he could estimate the weight of a calf or a pig, like a dealer. From a box containing a bushel or more of loose pencils, he could take up with his hands fast enough just a dozen pencils at every grasp. He was a good swimmer, runner, skater, boatman, and would probably outwalk most countrymen in a day's journey. And the relation of body to mind was still finer than we have indicated. He said he wanted every stride his legs made. The length of his walk uniformly made the length of his writing. If shut up in the house he did not write at all.

He had a strong common sense, like that which Rose Flammock, the weaver's daughter in Scott's romance, commends in her father, as resembling a yardstick, which, whilst it measures dowlas and diaper, can equally well measure tapestry and cloth of gold. He had always a new resource. When I was planting forest trees, and had procured half a peck of acorns, he said that only a small portion of them would be sound, and proceeded to examine them and select the sound ones. But finding this took time, he said, "I think if you put them all into water the good ones will sink"; which experiment we tried with success. He could plan a garden or a house or a barn; would have been competent to lead a "Pacific Exploring Expedition"; could give judicious counsel in the gravest private or public affairs.

He lived for the day, not cumbered and mortified by his memory. If he brought you yesterday a new proposition, he would bring you today another not less revolutionary. A very industrious man, and setting, like all highly organized men, a high value on his time, he seemed the only man of leisure in town, always ready for any excursion that promised well, or for conversation prolonged into late hours. His trenchant sense was never stopped by his rules of daily prudence, but was always up to the new occasion. He liked and used the simplest food, yet when some one urged a vegetable diet, Thoreau thought all diets a very small matter, saying that "the man who shoots the buffalo lives better than the man who boards at the Graham House." He said, "You can sleep near the railroad, and never be disturbed: Nature knows very well what sounds are worth attending to, and has made up her mind not to hear the railroad-whistle. But things respect the devout mind, and a mental ecstasy was never interrupted." He noted what repeatedly befell him, that, after receiving from a distance a rare plant, he would presently find the same in his own haunts. And those pieces of luck which happen only to good players happened to him. One day, walking with a stranger, who inquired where Indian arrowheads could be found, he replied, "Everywhere," and, stooping forward, picked one on the instant from the ground. At Mount Washington, in Tuckerman's Ravine, Thoreau had a bad fall, and sprained his foot. As he was in the act of getting up from his fall, he saw for the first time the leaves of the *Arnica mollis*. . . .

The other weapon with which he conquered all obstacles in science was patience. He knew how to sit immovable, a part of the rock he rested on, until the bird, the reptile, the fish, which had retired from him, should come back and resume its habits, nay, moved by curiosity, should come to him and watch him.

It was a pleasure and a privilege to walk with him. He knew the country like a fox or a bird, and passed through it as freely by paths of his own. He knew every track in the snow or on the ground, and what creature had taken this path before him. One must submit abjectly to such a guide, and the reward was great. Under his arm he carried an old music-book to press plants; in his pocket, his diary and pencil, a spy-glass for birds, microscope, jack-knife, and twine. He wore a straw hat, stout shoes, strong gray trousers, to brave scrub-oaks and smilax, and to climb a tree for a hawk's or a squirrel's nest. He waded into the pool for the water-plants, and his strong legs were no insignificant part of his armor. On the day I speak of he looked for the Menyanthes, detected it across the wide pool, and, on examination of the florets, decided that it had been in flower five days. He drew out of his breast-pocket his diary, and read the names of all the plants that should bloom on this day, whereof he kept account as a banker when his notes fall due. The Cypripedium not due till tomorrow. He thought that, if waked up from a trance, in this swamp, he could tell by the plants what time of the year it was within two days. The redstart was flying about, and presently the fine grosbeaks, whose brilliant scarlet "makes the rash gazer wipe his eye," and whose fine clear note Thoreau compared to that of a tanager which has got rid of its hoarseness. Presently he heard a note which he called that of the night-warbler, a bird he had never identified, had been in search of twelve years, which always, when he saw it, was in the act of diving down into a tree or bush, and which it was in vain to seek; the only bird which sings indifferently by night and by day. I told him he must beware of finding and booking it, lest life should have nothing more to show him. He said, "What you seek in vain for, half your life, one day you come full upon, all the family at dinner. You seek it like a dream, and as soon as you find it you become its prey."

His interest in the flower or the bird lay very deep in his mind, was connected with Nature,—and the meaning of Nature was never attempted to be defined by him. He would not offer a memoir of his observations to the Natural History Society. "Why should I? To detach the description from its connections in my mind would make it no longer true or valuable to me: and they do not wish what belongs to it." His power of observation seemed to indicate additional senses. He saw as with microscope, heard as with ear-trumpet, and his memory was a photographic register of all he saw and heard. And yet none knew better than he that it is not the fact that imports, but the impression or effect of the fact on your mind. Every fact lay in glory in his mind, a type of the order and beauty of the whole.

His determination on Natural History was organic. He confessed that he sometimes felt like a hound or a panther, and, if born among Indians, would have been a fell hunter. But, restrained by his Massachusetts culture, he played out the game in this mild form of botany and ichthyology. His intimacy with animals suggested what Thomas Fuller records of Butler the apiologist, that "either he had told the bees things or the bees had told him." Snakes coiled round his legs; the fishes swam into his hand, and he took them out of the water; he pulled the woodchuck out of its hole by the tail, and took the foxes under his protection from the hunters.

Our naturalist had perfect magnanimity; he had no secrets: he would carry you to the heron's haunt, or even to his most prized botanical swamp,—possibly knowing that you could never find it again, yet willing to take his risks.

No college ever offered him a diploma, or a professor's chair; no academy made him its corresponding secretary, its discoverer or even its member. Perhaps these learned bodies feared the satire of his presence. Yet so much knowledge of Nature's secret and genius few others possessed; none in a more large and religious synthesis. For not a particle of respect had he to the opinions of any man or body of men, but homage solely to the truth itself; and as he discovered everywhere among doctors some lacking of courtesy, it discredited them. He grew to be revered and admired by his townsmen, who had at first known him only as an oddity. The farmers who employed him as a surveyor soon discovered his rare accuracy and skill, his knowledge of their lands, of trees, of birds, of Indian remains and the like, which enabled him to tell every farmer more than he knew before of his own farm; so that he began to feel a little as if Mr. Thoreau had better rights in his land than he. They felt, too, the superiority of character which addressed all men with a native authority.

Indian relics abound in Concord—arrowheads, stone chisels, pestles and fragments of pottery; and on the riverbank, large heaps of clam-shells and ashes mark spots which the savages frequented. These, and every circumstance touching the Indian, were important in his eyes. His visits to Maine were chiefly for love of the Indian. He had the satisfaction of seeing the manufacture of the bark canoe, as well as of trying his hand in its management on the rapids. He was inquisitive about the making of the stone arrowhead, and in his last days charged a youth setting out for the Rocky Mountains to find an Indian who could tell him that: "It was well worth a visit to California to learn it." Occasionally, a small party of Penobscot Indians would visit Concord, and pitch their tents for a few weeks in summer on the river-bank. He failed not to make acquaintance with the best of them; though he well knew that asking questions of Indians is like catechizing beavers and rabbits. In his last visit to Maine he had great satisfaction from Joseph Polis, an intelligent Indian of Oldtown, who was his guide for some weeks.

He was equally interested in every natural fact. The depth of his perception found likeness of law throughout Nature, and I know not any genius who so swiftly inferred universal law from the single fact. He was no pedant of a department. His eye was open to beauty, and his ear to music. He found these, not in rare conditions, but wheresoever he went. He thought the best of music was in single strains; and he found poetic suggestion in the humming of the telegraph-wire.

His poetry might be bad or good; he no doubt wanted a lyric facility and technical skill, but he had the source of poetry in his spiritual perception. He was a good reader and critic, and his judgment on poetry was to the ground of it. He could not be deceived as to the presence or absence of the poetic element in any composition, and his thirst for this made him negligent and perhaps scornful of superficial graces. He would pass by many delicate rhythms, but he would have detected every live stanza or line in a volume and knew very well where to find an equal poetic charm in prose. He was so enamoured of the spiritual beauty that he held all actual written poems in very light esteem in the comparison. He admired Æschylus and Pindar; but when some one was commending them, he said that Æschylus and the Greeks, in describing Apollo and Orpheus, had given no song, or no good one. "They ought not to have moved trees, but to have chanted to the gods such a hymn as would have sung all their old ideas out of their heads, and new ones in." His own verses are often rude and defective. The gold does not yet run pure, is drossy and crude. The thyme and marjoram are not yet honey. But if he want lyric fineness and technical merits, if he have not the poetic temperament, he never lacks the casual thought, showing that his genius was better than his talent. He knew the worth of the Imagination for the uplifting and consolation of human life, and liked to throw every thought into a symbol. The fact you tell is of no value, but only the impression. For this reason his presence was poetic, always piqued the curiosity to know more deply the secrets of his mind. He had many reserves, an unwillingness to exhibit to profane eyes what was still sacred in his own, and knew well how to throw a poetic veil over his experience. All readers of Walden will remember his mythical record of his disappointments:

"I long ago lost a hound, a bay horse, and a turtle-dove, and am still on their trail. Many are the travellers I have spoken concerning them, describing their tracks, and what calls they answered to. I have met one or two who have heard the hound, and the tramp of the horse, and even seen the dove disappear behind a cloud; and they seemed as anxious to recover them as if they had lost them themselves." . . .

The tendency to magnify the moment, to read all the laws of Nature in the one object or one combination under your eye, is of course comic to those who do not share the philosopher's perception of identity. To him there was no such thing as size. The pond was a small ocean; the Atlantic, a large Walden Pond. He referred every minute fact to cosmical laws. Though he meant to be just, he seemed haunted by a certain chronic assumption that the science of the day pretended completeness, and he had just found out that the *savans* had neglected to discriminate a particular botanical variety, had failed to describe the seeds or count the sepals. "That is to say," we replied, "the blockheads were not born in Concord; but who said they were? It was their unspeakable misfortune to be born in London, or Paris, or Rome; but poor fellows, they did what they could, considering that they never saw Bateman's Pond, or Nine-Acre Corner, or Becky Stow's Swamp; besides, what were you sent into the world for, but to add this observation?"

Had his genius been only contemplative, he had been fitted to his life, but with his energy and practical ability he seemed born for great enterprise and for command; and I so much regret the loss of his rare powers of action, that I cannot help counting it a fault in him that he had no ambition. Wanting this, instead of engineering for all America, he was the captain of a huckleberry-party. Pounding beans is good to the end of pounding empires one of these days; but, if at the end of years, it is still only beans!

But these foibles, real or apparent, were fast vanishing in the incessant growth of a spirit so robust and wise, and which effaced its defeats with new triumphs. His study of Nature was a perpetual ornament to him, and inspired his friends with curiosity to see the world through his eyes, and to hear his adventures. They possessed every kind of interest.

He had many elegancies of his own, whilst he scoffed at conventional elegance. Thus, he could not bear to hear the sound of his own steps, the grit of gravel; and therefore never willingly walked in the road, but in the grass, on mountains and in woods. His senses were acute, and he remarked that by night every dwelling-house gives out bad air, like a slaughter-house. He liked the pure fragrance of melilot. He honored certain plants with special regard, and, overall, the pond-lily,—then, the gentian, and the *Mikania scandens,* and "life-everlasting," and a bass-tree which he visited every year when it bloomed, in the middle of July. He thought the scent a more oracular inquisition than the sight,—more oracular and trustworthy. The scent, of course, reveals what is concealed from the other senses. By it he detached earthliness. He delighted in echoes, and said they were almost the only kind of kindred voices that he heard. He loved Nature so well, was so happy in her solitude, that he became very jealous of cities and the sad work which their refinements and artifices made with man and his dwelling. The axe was always destroying his forest. "Thank God," he said, "they cannot cut down the clouds! All kinds of figures are drawn on the blue ground with this fibrous white paint." . . .

The Great American Entertainment
Frances Trollope

I never saw any people who appeared to live so much without amusement as the Cincinnatians. Billiards are forbidden by law, so are cards.
To sell a pack of cards in Ohio subjects the seller to a penalty of fifty
dollars. They have no public balls, excepting, I think, six during the
Christmas holydays. They have no concerts. They have no dinner-parties.

They have a theatre, which is, in fact, the only public amusement of
this triste little town; but they seem to care little about it, and either from
economy or distaste, it is very poorly attended. Ladies are rarely seen
there, and by far the larger proportion of females deem it an offence
against religion to witness the representation of a play. It is in the churches
and chapels of the town that the ladies are to be seen in full costume; and
I am tempted to believe that a stranger from the Continent of Europe
would be inclined, on first reconnoitring the city, to suppose that the
places of worship were the theatres and cafes of the place. No evening in
the week but brings throngs of the young and beautiful to the chapels
and meeting-houses, all dressed with care, and sometimes with great
pretension; it is there that all display is made, and all fashionable distinction sought. The proportion of gentlemen attending these evening meetings is very small, but often, as might be expected, a sprinkling of smart
young clerks makes this sedulous display of ribands and ringlets intelligible and natural. Were it not for the churches, indeed, I think there might
be a general bonfire of best bonnets, for I never could discover any other
use for them.

The ladies are too actively employed in the interior of their houses to
permit much parading in full dress for morning visits. There are no public
gardens or lounging shops of fashionable resort, and were it not for
public worship, and private tea-drinkings, all the ladies in Cincinnati
would be in danger of becoming perfect recluses.

The influence which the ministers of all the innumerable religious sects
throughout America have on the females of their respective congregations

Frances Trollope, *Domestic Manners of the Americans* (London, 1832), pp. 74-80.

approaches very nearly to what we read of in Spain, or in other strictly Roman Catholic countries. There are many causes for this particular influence. Where equality of rank is affectedly acknowledged by the rich, and clamorously claimed by the poor, distinction and pre-eminence are allowed to the clergy only. This gives them high importance in the eyes of the ladies. I think, also, that it is from the clergy only that the women of America receive that sort of attention which is so dearly valued by every female heart throughout the world. With the priests of America, the women hold that degree of influential importance which, in the countries of Europe, is allowed them throughout all orders and ranks of society, except, perhaps, the very lowest; and in return for this they seem to give their hearts and souls into their keeping. I never saw, or read of any country where religion had so strong a hold upon the women, or a slighter hold upon the men.

I mean not to assert that I met with no men of sincerely religious feelings, or with no women of no religious feelings at all; but I feel perfectly secure of being correct as to the great majority in the statement I have made.

We had not been many months in Cincinnati when our curiosity was excited by hearing the 'revival' talked of by every one we met throughout the town. 'The revival will be very full'—'We shall be constantly engaged during the revival'—were the phrases we constantly heard repeated, and for a long time without in the least comprehending what was meant; but at length I learned that the un-national church of America required to be roused, at regular intervals, to greater energy and exertion. At these seasons the most enthusiastic of the clergy travel the country, and enter the cities and towns by scores, or by hundreds, as the accommodation of the place may admit, and for a week or fortnight, or, if the population be large, for a month; they preach all day, and often for a considerable portion of the night, in the various churches and chapels of the place. This is called a revival.

I took considerable pains to obtain information on this subject; but in detailing what I learned I fear that it is probable I shall be accused of exaggeration; all I can do is cautiously to avoid deserving it. The subject is highly interesting, and it would be a fault of no trifling nature to treat it with levity.

These itinerant clergymen are of all persuasions, I believe, except the Episcopalian, Catholic, Unitarian, and Quaker. I heard of Presbyterians of all varieties; of Baptists of I know not how many divisions; and of Methodists of more denominations than I can remember; whose innumerable shades of varying belief it would require much time to explain, and more to comprehend. They enter all the cities, towns, and villages of the Union in succession; I could not learn with sufficient certainty to repeat, what the interval generally is between their visits. These itinerants are, for the most part, lodged in the houses of their respective followers, and every evening that is not spent in the churches and meeting-houses, is devoted to what would be called parties by others, but which they designate as prayer-meetings. Here they eat, drink, pray, sing, hear confessions, and make converts. To these meetings I never got invited, and therefore I have nothing but hearsay evidence to offer, but my information comes from an eyewitness, and one on whom I believe I may depend. If one-half of what I heard may be believed, these social prayer-meetings are by no means the most curious, or the least important part of the business.

It is impossible not to smile at the close resemblance to be traced between the feelings of a first-rate Presbyterian or Methodist lady, fortunate enough to have secured a favourite itinerant for her meeting, and those of a first rate London blue, equally blest in the presence of a fashionable poet. There is a strong family likeness among us all the world over.

The best rooms, the best dresses, the choicest refreshments solemnize the meeting. While the party is assembling, the load-star of the hour is occupied in whispering conversations with the guests as they arrive. They are called brothers and sisters, and the greetings are very affectionate. When the room is full, the company, of whom a vast majority is always women, are invited, entreated, and coaxed to confess before their brothers and sisters all their thoughts, faults, and follies.

These confessions are strange scenes; the more they confess, the more invariably are they encouraged and caressed. When this is over, they all kneel, and the itinerant prays extempore. They then eat and drink; and then they sing hymns, pray, exhort, sing, and pray again, till the excitement reaches a very high pitch indeed. These scenes are going on at some house or other every evening during the revival, nay, at many at the same time, for the churches and meeting-houses cannot give occupation to half the itinerants, though they are all open throughout the day, and till a late hour in the night, and the officiating ministers succeed each other in the occupation of them.

It was at the principal of the Presbyterian churches that I was twice witness to scenes that made me shudder; in describing one I describe both, and every one; the same thing is constantly repeated.

It was in the middle of summer, but the service we were recommended to attend did not begin till it was dark. The church was well lighted, and crowded almost to suffocation. On entering we found three priests standing side by side, in a sort of tribune, placed where the altar usually is, handsomely fitted up with crimson curtains, and elevated about as high as our pulpits. We took our places in a pew close to the rail which surrounded it.

The priest who stood in the middle was praying; the prayer was extravagantly vehement, and offensively familiar in expression; when this ended, a hymn was sung, and then another priest took the centre place, and preached. The sermon had considerable eloquence, but of a frightful kind. The preacher described, with ghastly minuteness, the last feeble fainting moments of human life, and then the gradual progress of decay after death, which he followed through every process up to the last loathsome stage of decomposition. Suddenly changing his tone, which had been that of sober accurate description, into the shrill voice of horror, he bent forward his head, as if to gaze on some object beneath the pulpit. And as Rebecca made known to Ivanhoe what she saw through the window, so the preacher made known to us what he saw in the pit that seemed to open before him. The device was certainly a happy one for giving effect to his description of hell. No image that fire, flame, brimstone, molten lead, or red-hot pincers could supply; with flesh, nerves, and sinews quivering under them, was omitted. The perspiration ran in streams from the face of the preacher; his eyes rolled, his lips were covered with foam, and every feature had the deep expression of horror it would have borne had he in truth been gazing at the scene he described. The acting was excellent. At length he gave a languishing look to his supporters on each side, as if to express his feeble state, and then sat down, and wiped the drops of agony from his brow.

The other two priests arose, and began to sing a hymn. It was some seconds before the congregation could join as usual; every up-turned face looked pale and horror-struck. When the singing ended, another took the centre place, and began in a sort of coaxing affectionate tone, to ask the congregation if what their dear brother had spoken had reached their hearts? Whether they would avoid the hell he had made them see? 'Come, then!' he continued, stretching out his arms toward them, 'come to us, and tell us so, and we will make you see Jesus, the dear gentle Jesus, who shall save you from it. But you must come to him! You must not be ashamed to come to him! This night you shall tell him that you are not ashamed of him; we will make way for you; we will clear the bench for anxious sinners to sit upon. Come, then! come to the anxious bench, and we will show you Jesus! Come! Come! Come!'

Again a hymn was sung, and while it continued, one of the three was employed in clearing one or two long benches that went across the rail, sending the people back to the lower part of the church. The singing ceased, and again the people were invited, and exhorted not to be ashamed of Jesus, but to put themselves upon 'the anxious benches,' and lay their heads on his bosom. 'Once more we will sing,' he concluded, 'that we may give you time.' And again they sung a hymn.

And now in every part of the church a movement was perceptible, slight at first, but by degrees becoming more decided. Young girls arose, and sat down, and rose again; and then the pews opened, and several came tottering out, their hands clasped, their heads hanging on their bosoms, and every limb trembling, and still the hymn went on; but as the poor creatures approached the rail their sobs and groans became audible. They seated themselves on the 'anxious benches;' the hymn ceased, and two of the three priests walked down from the tribune, and going, one to the right, and the other to the left, began whispering to the poor tremblers seated there. These whispers were inaudible to us, but the sobs and groans increased to a frightful excess. Young creatures, with features pale and distorted, fell on their knees on the pavement, and soon sunk forward on their faces; the most violent cries and shrieks followed, while from time to time a voice was heard in convulsive accents, exclaiming, 'Oh Lord!' 'Oh Lord Jesus!' 'Help me, Jesus!' and the like.

Meanwhile the two priests continued to walk among them; they repeatedly mounted on the benches, and trumpet-mouthed proclaimed to the whole congregation 'the tidings of salvation,' and then from every corner of the building arose in reply, short, sharp cries of 'Amen!' 'Glory!' 'Amen!' while the prostrate penitents continued to receive whispered confrontings, and from time to time a mystic caress. More than once I saw a young neck encircled by a reverend arm. Violent hysterics and convulsions seized many of them, and when the tumult was at the highest, the priest who remained above again gave out a hymn, as if to drown it.

It was a frightful sight to behold innocent young creatures, in the gay morning of existence, thus seized upon, horror-struck, and rendered feeble and enervated for ever. One young girl, apparently not more than fourteen was supported in the arms of another, some years older; her face was pale as death; her eyes wide open, and perfectly devoid of meaning; her chin and bosom wet with slaver; she had every appearance of idiotism. I saw a priest approach her; he took her delicate hands, 'Jesus is with her! Bless the Lord!' he said, and passed on.

Did the men of America value their women as men ought to value their wives and daughters, would such scenes be permitted among them?

It is hardly necessary to say that all who obeyed the call to place themselves on the 'anxious benches' were women, and by far the greater number, very young women. The congregation was, in general, extremely well dressed, and the smartest and most fashionable ladies of the town were there; during the whole revival the churches and meeting-houses were every day crowded with well-dressed people.

It is thus the ladies of Cincinnati amuse themselves; to attend the theatre is forbidden; to play cards is unlawful; but they work hard in their families, and must have some relaxation. For myself, I confess that I think the coarsest comedy ever written would be a less detestable exhibition for the eyes of youth and innocence than such a scene.

A Plain-Speaking Evangelist

Peter Cartwright

From the general Methodist Conference in Baltimore I journeyed on toward my home in Christian County, Kentucky. Saturday night came on, and found me in a strange region of country, and in the hills, knobs, and spurs of the Cumberland Mountains. I greatly desired to stop on the approaching Sabbath and spend it with a Christian people; but I was now in a region of country where there was no Gospel minister for many miles around, and where, as I learned, many of the scattered population had never heard a Gospel sermon in all their lives, and where the inhabitants knew no Sabbath only to hunt and visit, drink and dance. Thus lonesome and pensive, late in the evening, I hailed at a tolerably decent house, and the landlord kept entertainment. I rode up and asked for quarters. The gentleman said I could stay, but he was afraid I would not enjoy myself very much as a traveler, inasmuch as they had a party meeting there that night to have a little dance. I inquired how far it was to a decent house of entertainment on the road; he said seven miles. I told him if he would treat me civilly and feed my horse well, by his leave I would stay. He assured me I should be treated civilly. I dismounted and went in. The people collected, a large company. I saw there was not much drinking going on.

I quietly took my seat in one corner of the house, and the dance commenced. I sat quietly musing, a total stranger, and greatly desired to preach to this people. Finally, I concluded to spend the next day (Sabbath) there, and ask the privilege to preach to them. I had hardly settled this point in my mind, when a beautiful ruddy young lady walked very gracefully up to me, dropped a handsome courtesy, and pleasantly, with winning smiles, invited me out to take a dance with her. I can hardly describe my thoughts or feelings on that occasion. However, in a moment I resolved on a desperate experiment. I rose as gracefully as I could; I

William P. Strickland (ed.), *Autobiography of Peter Cartwright, the Backwoods Preacher* (New York, 1856), pp. 206-208, 222-228, 236-237, 242-243.

will not say with some emotion, but with many emotions. The young lady moved to my right side; I grasped her right hand with my right hand, while she leaned her left arm on mine. In this position we walked on the floor. The whole company seemed pleased at this act of politeness in the young lady, shown to a stranger. The colored man, who was the fiddler, began to put his fiddle in the best order. I then spoke to the fiddler to hold a moment, and added that for several years I had not undertaken any matter of importance without first asking the blessing of God upon it, and I desired now to ask the blessing of God upon this beautiful young lady and the whole company, that had shown such an act of politeness to a total stranger.

Here I grasped the young lady's hand tightly and said, "Let us all kneel down and pray," and then instantly dropped on my knees, and commenced praying with all the power of soul and body that I could command. The young lady tried to get loose from me, but I held her tight. Presently she fell on her knees. Some of the company kneeled, some stood, some fled, some sat still, all looked curious. The fiddler ran off into the kitchen saying, "Lord a marcy, what de matter? what is dat mean?"

While I prayed some wept, and wept out aloud, and some cried for mercy. I rose from my knees and commenced an exhortation, after which I sang a hymn. The young lady who invited me on the floor lay prostrate, crying earnestly for mercy. I exhorted again, I sang and prayed nearly all night. About fifteen of that company professed religion, and our meeting lasted next day and next night, and as many more were powerfully converted. I organized a society, took thirty-two into the Church, and sent them a preacher. My landlord was appointed leader, which post he held for many years. This was the commencement of a great and glorious revival of religion in that region of country, and several of the young men converted at this Methodist preacher dance became useful ministers of Jesus Christ. . . .

There was, in the bounds of the Goose Creek Circuit, a Baptist minister, who was a tolerably smart man, and a great proselyter from other Churches, and who almost always was harping on immersion as the only mode of Christian baptism, and ridiculing what he called "baby sprinkling." We had an appointment for a camp-meeting in this circuit, in what was called Poplar Grove. There was a fine little widow woman, a member of the Methodist Episcopal Church, lived here; and this Baptist preacher tried his best to proselyte her, and make a Baptist of her. She at length got tired of his water talk, and told him if he would come to the camp-meeting, and patiently hear the presiding elder, Peter Cartwright, preach one sermon on baptism, on Sunday, she would give him a new suit of clothes, out and out. He agreed to it; but he was to sit patiently, and hear the sermon through; if he did not, then he was not to have the suit of clothes.

When I got to the camp-ground, my little spunky Methodist widow was tented on the ground. She came and invited me to her tent, and then told me the proposition she had made to Mr. W., the Baptist preacher. "And now," said she, "do your best; if he runs, the suit of clothes is yours; and if he stands his ground, and you do your very best, you shall have as good a suit, any how."

This is a very large encampment, well arranged; and there were about twenty strong, talented Methodist preachers, from the traveling and local ranks, present. The meeting commenced and progressed with great interest, and there were many melting Gospel sermons preached. Many sinners were awakened and converted, both among the whites and colored people. Sunday morning came, and my Baptist preacher arrived; and we were soon made acquainted. He proposed that he, if he felt like it, should have the privilege of replying to me. "Certainly," said I, "with all my heart."

Eleven o'clock arrived, the hour appointed me to commence my sermon on baptism. It was supposed that there were ten thousand people on the ground. My heart rather quailed within me, but I prayed for light, a ready mind, and success. I took no text in particular, but submitted the four following propositions for discussion:

First. The design and intent of water baptism.

Second. Who were the Divinely-appointed administrators of water baptism.

Third. The proper mode of water baptism.

Fourth. Who were the qualified subjects of baptism.

My Baptist minister took his seat in the altar, in front of me. He listened with tolerable attention while I was on the first and second propositions. As I approached the third point, the galled jade winced a little; but when I came to the fourth point, and took my position that all infants had the first and only indisputable title to baptism, and that all adults must become converted, and be like little children, before they could claim any valid title to water baptism, my preacher became very restive. Finally, I propounded this question: "Is not that Church which has no children in it more like hell than heaven?" I then added, "if all hell was searched, there would not be a single child found in it; but all children are in heaven; therefore, there being no children in the Baptist Church, it was more like hell than heaven."

The Baptist preacher here rose to his feet, and started. I called out to him to stop and hear me out; but he replied he could not stand it, and kept on and cleared the ground; so he lost his suit of clothes and I gained one. But what was much better than all this, I was listened to for three hours; and the attention of the multitude seemed not to falter, but they heard with profound interest, and it was the opinion of hundreds that this discussion did a vast amount of good.

At a camp-meeting held in the edge of Tennessee, a considerable revival took place, and some tall sons and daughters of Belial were brought down to cry for mercy. Religion made its mark in several wealthy families. Persecution was pretty fierce; the rowdies sent off and got whisky, drank freely, and disturbed us considerably. We arrested some of them, and they were fined. Finally, they collected their forces in the woods, a short distance from the camp-ground, and resolved to break up our camp-meeting; they then elected their captain and all other subordinate officers. Their plan was to arm themselves with clubs, to mount their horses, and ride bravely through the camp-ground, and break down officers, preachers, and anybody else that would oppose them.

Saturday afternoon was the time appointed for them to drive us from the ground, but in the meantime we found out their plans, and many of their names. Their captain called his name Cartwright; all their officers assumed the name of some preacher. We made our preparations accordingly, and were perfectly ready for them. They drank their whisky, mounted their horses, armed with sticks and clubs, and then came, almost full speed, into our camp. As I was captain of the interior, I met the captain of the Philistines, and planted myself near the opening between the two tents, where they were to enter the inclosure. As the mounted captain drew near the entering place I sprang into the breach; he raised his club, bidding me to stand by, or he would knock me down.

I cried, "Crack away."

He spurred his horse and made a pass at me, sure enough; but, fortunately, I dodged his stroke. The next lick was mine, and I gave it to him, and laid him flat on his back, his foot being in the stirrup. His horse got my next stroke, which wheeled him *"right about;"* he dragged his rider a few steps and dropped him, and then gave this redoubtable captain leg bail at a mighty rate. The balance of the mounted rowdies, seeing their leader down and kicking, wheeled and ingloriously fled. We took care of the captain, of course, and fined him fifty dollars. This gave us entire control of the encampment, and peace in all our borders during our meeting.

And on the other hand, in reference to the Methodist Episcopal Church, when we consider that her ministers were illiterate, and not only opposed and denounced by the Catholics, but by all Protestant Churches; that we were everywhere spoken against, caricatured, and misrepresented; without colleges and seminaries, without religious books or periodicals, without missionary funds, and almost all other religious means; and our ministers did not for many years, on an average, receive over fifty dollars for a support annually, and a Methodist preacher's library almost entirely consisted of a Bible, Hymn Book, and a Discipline, may we not, without boasting, say with one of old, "What hath God wrought?"

A Methodist preacher in those days, when he felt that God had called him to preach, instead of hunting up a college or Biblical institute, hunted up a hardy pony of a horse, and some traveling apparatus, and with his library always at hand, namely, Bible, Hymn Book, and Discipline, he started, and with a text that never wore out nor grew stale, he cried, "Behold the Lamb of God, that taketh away the sin of the world." In this way he went through storms of wind, hail, snow, and rain; climbed hills and mountains, traversed valleys, plunged through swamps, swam swollen streams, lay out all night, wet, weary, and hungry, held his horse by the bridle all night, or tied him to a limb, slept with his saddle blanket for a bed, his saddle or saddle-bags for his pillow, and his old big coat or blanket, if he had any, for a covering. Often he slept in dirty cabins, on earthen floors, before the fire; ate roasting ears for bread, drank buttermilk for coffee, or sage tea for imperial; took, with a hearty zest, deer or bear meat, or wild turkey, for breakfast, dinner, and supper, if he could get it. His text was always ready, "Behold the Lamb of God," &c. This was old-fashioned Methodist preacher fare and fortune. Under such circumstances, who among us would now say, "Here am I, Lord, send me?"

American Religion
Alexis de Tocqueville

The philosophers of the eighteenth century explained the gradual decay of religious faith in a very simple manner. Religious zeal, said they, must necessarily fail, the more generally liberty is established and knowledge diffused. Unfortunately, facts are by no means in accordance with their theory. There are certain populations in Europe whose unbelief is only equalled by their ignorance and their debasement, whilst in America one of the freest and most enlightened nations in the world fulfills all the outward duties of religious fervor.

Upon my arrival in the United States, the religious aspect of the country was the first thing that struck my attention; and the longer I stayed there the more did I perceive the great political consequences resulting from this state of things, to which I was unaccustomed. In France I had almost always seen the spirit of religion and the spirit of freedom pursuing courses diametrically opposed to each other; but in America I found that they were intimately united, and that they reigned in common over the same country. My desire to discover the causes of this phenomenon increased from day to day. In order to satisfy it I questioned the members of all the different sects; and I more especially sought the society of the clergy, who are the depositaries of the different persuasions, and who are more especially interested in their duration. As a member of the Roman Catholic Church I was more particularly brought into contact with several of its priests, with whom I became intimately acquainted. To each of these men I expressed my astonishment and I explained my doubts; I found that they differed upon matters of detail alone; and that they mainly attributed the peaceful dominion of religion in their country to the separation of Church and State. I do not hesitate to affirm that during my stay in America I did not meet with a single individual, of the clergy or of the laity, who was not of the same opinion upon this point.

Alexis de Tocqueville, *Democracy in America*, trans. Henry Reeve (New York, 1900), I, pp. 313-320.

This led me to examine more attentively than I had hitherto done, the station which the American clergy occupy in political society. I learned with surprise that they filled no public appointments; not one of them is to be met with in the administration, and they are not ever represented in the legislative assemblies. In several States the law excludes them from political life, public opinion in all. And when I came to inquire into the prevailing spirit of the clergy I found that most of its members seemed to retire of their own accord from the exercise of power, and that they made it the pride of their profession to abstain from politics.

I heard them inveigh against ambition and deceit, under whatever political opinions these vices might chance to lurk; but I learned from their discourses that men are not guilty in the eye of God for any opinions concerning political government which they may profess with sincerity, any more than they are for their mistakes in building a house or in driving a furrow. I perceived that these ministers of the gospel eschewed all parties with the anxiety attendant upon personal interest. These facts convinced me that what I had been told was true; and it then became my object to investigate their causes, and to inquire how it happened that the real authority of religion was increased by a state of things which diminished its apparent force: these causes did not long escape my researches.

The short space of threescore years can never content the imagination of man; nor can the imperfect joys of this world satisfy his heart. Man alone, of all created beings, displays a natural contempt of existence, and yet a boundless desire to exist; he scorns life, but he dreads annihilation. These different feelings incessantly urge his soul to the contemplation of a future state, and religion directs his musings thither. Religion, then, is simply another form of hope; and it is no less natural to the human heart than hope itself. Men cannot abandon their religious faith without a kind of aberration of intellect, and a sort of violent distortion of their true natures; but they are invincibly brought back to more pious sentiments; for unbelief is an accident, and faith is the only permanent state of mankind. If we only consider religious institutions in a purely human point of view, they may be said to derive an inexhaustible element of strength from man himself, since they belong to one of the constituent principles of human nature.

I am aware that at certain times religion may strengthen this influence, which originates in itself, by the artificial power of the laws, and by the support of those temporal institutions which direct society. Religions, intimately united to the governments of the earth, have been known to exercise a sovereign authority derived from the twofold source of terror and of faith; but when a religion contracts an alliance of this nature, I do not hesitate to affirm that it commits the same error as a man who should sacrifice his future to his present welfare; and in obtaining a power to which it has no claim, it risks that authority which is rightfully its own. When a religion founds its empire upon the desire of immortality which lives in every human heart, it may aspire to universal dominion; but when it connects itself with a government, it must necessarily adopt maxims which are only applicable to certain nations. Thus, in forming an alliance with a political power, religion augments its authority over a few, and forfeits the hope of reigning over all.

As long as a religion rests upon those sentiments which are the consolation of all affliction, it may attract the affections of mankind. But if it be mixed up with the bitter passions of the world, it may be constrained to defend allies whom its interests, and not the principle of love, have given to it; or to repel as antagonists men who are still attached to its own spirit, however opposed they may be to the powers to which it is allied. The Church cannot share the temporal power of the State without being the object of a portion of that animosity which the latter excites.

The political powers which seem to be most firmly established have frequently no better guarantee for their duration than the opinions of a generation, the interests of the time, or the life of an individual. A law may modify the social condition which seems to be most fixed and determinate; and with the social condition everything else must change. The powers of society are more or less fugitive, like the years which we spend upon the earth; they succeed each other with rapidity, like the fleeting cares of life; and no government has ever yet been founded upon invariable disposition of the human heart, or upon an imperishable interest.

As long as a religion is sustained by those feelings, propensities, and passions which are found to occur under the same forms, at all the different periods of history, it may defy the efforts of time; or at least it can only be destroyed by another religion. But when religion clings to the interests of the world, it becomes almost as fragile a thing as the powers of earth. It is the only one of them all which can hope for immortality; but if it be connected with their ephemeral authority, it shares their fortunes, and may fall with those transient passions which supported them for a day. The alliance which religion contracts with political powers must needs be onerous to itself; since it does not require their assistance to live, and by giving them its assistance it may be exposed to decay.

The danger which I have just pointed out always exists, but it is not always equally visible. In some ages governments seem to be imperishable; in others, the existence of society appears to be more precarious than the life of man. Some constitutions plunge the citizens into lethargic somnolence, and others rouse them to feverish excitement. When governments appear to be so strong, and laws so stable, men do not perceive the dangers which may accrue from a union of Church and State. When governments display so much weakness, and laws so much inconstancy, the danger is self-evident, but it is no longer possible to avoid it; to be effectual, measures must be taken to discover its approach.

In proportion as a nation assumes a democratic condition of society, and as communities display democratic propensities, it becomes more and more dangerous to connect religion with political institutions; for the time is coming when political theories will be bandied from hand to hand, when political theories will succeed each other, and when men, laws, and constitutions will disappear, or be modified from day to day, and this, not for a season only, but unceasingly. Agitation and mutability are inherent in the nature of democratic republics, just as stagnation and inertness are the law of absolute monarchies.

If the Americans, who change the head of the Government once in four years, who elect new legislators every two years, and renew the provincial officers every twelvemonth; if the Americans who have abandoned the political world to the attempts of innovators, had not placed religion beyond their reach, where could it abide in the ebb and flow of human opinions? Where would that respect which belongs to it be paid, amidst the struggles of faction? and what would become of its immortality, in the midst of perpetual decay? The American clergy were the first to perceive this truth, and to act in conformity with it. They saw that they must renounce their religious influence, if they were to strive for political power; and they chose to give up the support of the State, rather than to share its vicissitudes.

In America, religion is perhaps less powerful than it has been at certain periods in the history of certain peoples; but its influence is more lasting. It restricts itself to its own, and under its undisputed control.

On every side in Europe we hear voices complaining of the absence of religious faith, and inquiring the means of restoring to religion some remnant of its pristine authority. It seems to me that we must first attentively consider what ought to be the natural state of men with regard to religion at the present time; and when we know what we have to hope and to fear, we may discern the end to which our efforts ought to be directed.

PART VIII

THE PLAIN PEOPLE

*In the Jacksonian era the common people rose not only in political power
but also into a better economic position. In the North they formed labor
unions, and in 1842 Chief Justice Lemuel Shaw of Massachusetts rendered
an epochal decision that strikes were not unlawful conspiracies but were
a legal right of the laboring men. Philip Hone of New York City, who held
the conservative point of view of the employer class, expressed strong
disapproval of strikes in his diary, an excerpt from which is quoted in the
following pages. One of the most interesting documents of labor in America is the speech of Ely Moore, the first labor congressmen, whose career
is sketched by Ben Perley Poore, editor of the Congressional Directory
and veteran journalist of Washington.*

*The conditions of living of the working class in the northern states are
described in two extracts from William Thomson's* A Tradesman's Travels
*and from Michel Chevalier's description of the factory girls in the Lowell,
Massachusetts, mills in his* Society, Manners and Politics in the United
States. *The handicaps under which the free Negro worked and lived above
the Mason and Dixon line and the bitter prejudice against the Negro in
northern cities, especially on the part of the lower-class whites, are portrayed in Sir Charles Lyell's travel account and poignantly in the letter
of Sarah Forten, below. Sarah was a Negro abolitionist, the daughter of
a successful sailmaker of Philadelphia, who corresponded with Angelina
Grimké. William Thomson's description of a mob that attacked Negroes
in Cincinnati shows that race prejudice was far from being confined to the
southern states.*

*In the southern states the plain people consisted chiefly of the large
class of small farmers, or the southern yeomen, the tradesmen, mechanics,
and overseers. The yeoman farmers were a respectable group, very much
like northern farmers, who owned their lands and in some cases a few
slaves (the researches of Professor Owsley and his graduate students at
Vanderbilt University, previously mentioned, have established from evidence in the manuscript census reports of 1850 and 1860 that approximately 80 percent of the southern farmers in 1860 owned the farms they
cultivated). A portion of Daniel R. Hundley's chapter on "The Southern
Yeoman" is here included to show how the yeomen lived. Hundley makes*

a distinction between "the middle classes" and the southern yeoman, yet in his description of these two groups there is so much overlapping that he presents a confused picture of class structure, a confusion that probably existed in reality.

His greatest contribution was to combat the idea that the mass of southern whites were "poor whites"; in fact they were a small and special class, probably not more than 10 percent in most states, who lived in the infertile and isolated regions of the South and were victims of endemic diseases, poor nutrition, isolation, and an inferiority complex. Though some poor whites lived in the mountains, probably the majority lived in the "piny woods," which the Virginia artist David Hunter Strother ("Porte Crayon") described in his book of sketches written in 1856.

Another depressed class, both in the South and the North, was that of the Irish immigrants. They worked in gangs for cheap wages building railroads and in the South engaging in dangerous and unhealthy occupations such as digging drainage canals on the sugar plantations, where masters did not wish to risk the lives of their valuable slaves. The Irish actor, Tyrone Power, in traveling through the South on a theatrical tour, noted the miserable condition of the Irish and set it down in his journal. A more hopeful side of Irish life in America was the opportunity of rising in the world offered to enterprising and sober Irish youth, which is illustrated by two letters in the Southern Collection of the University of North Carolina written by Maunsel White, the sugar planter and great merchant of New Orleans whose life in America was a great success story.

Ely Moore: The First Labor Congressman

Ben Perley Poore

The first man elected to Congress as a representative of the rights of the laboring classes was Eli (Ely) Moore, a New York journeyman printer, who had organized trades unions and successfully engineered several strikes by mechanics against their employers. He was a thin, nervous man, with keen, dark hazel eyes, long black hair brushed back behind his ears, and a strong, clear voice which rang through the hall like the sound of a trumpet. He especially distinguished himself in a reply to General Waddy Thompson, of South Carolina, who had denounced the mechanics of the North as willing tools of the Abolitionists. With impetuous force and in tones tremulous with emotion, he denounced aristocracy and advocated the equality of all men. The House listened with attention, and a Southern politician exclaimed to one of his colleagues, "Why, this is the high-priest of revolution singing his war song." What added to the effect of this remarkable speech was its dramatic termination. Just as he had entered upon his peroration he grew deathly pale, his eyes closed, his outstretched hands clutched at vacancy, he reeled forward, and fell insensible. His friends rushed to his support, and his wife, who was in the gallery, screamed with terror. His physician positively prohibited his speaking again, and in subsequent years, when the Democratic party was in power, he enjoyed the positions of Indian Agent under Polk, and of Land Agent under Pierce.

Ben Perley Poore, *Perleys' Reminiscences of Sixty Years in the National Metropolis* (Philadelphia, 1886), I, pp. 150-151.

The Laboring Classes
Ely Moore

Mr. Chairman: Previous to entering upon the subject properly before the committee, I shall avail myself of this opportunity—the first that has been afforded me—of replying to certain misrepresentations that have been made, both here and elsewhere, concerning the laboring classes. The committee, I trust, will the more readily excuse this digression, when the relation in which I stand to the workingmen is considered. Having been long and intimately connected with their cause, and approving, as I do, of their principles and measures, I cannot consent to hear them assailed, without making an effort to vindicate them. They have been denounced as agrarians, levelers, and anarchists, and their *unions* as unlawful and mischievous. I shall endeavor to show, sir, that in all this great injustice has been done them. It is not my intention at this time to notice all the slanders that have been cast upon them, whether in or out of the Halls of Congress; my more immediate object is to reply to the honorable gentleman from South Carolina, whom I see before me [Mr. Thompson,] or at least to so much of his speech on the Navy appropriation bill as relates to the laboring classes. The honorable gentleman, in the course of his remarks, holds the following language:

"I entreat gentlemen to look well to the consequences of the experiment of sending the Government there (to the North) as a competitor in the labor market, and under the constraint of positive orders to expend this vast sum, let labor rise ever so high. It is already one dollar a day, when in the South and West it is less than fifty cents. These appropriations are not for this year alone. They are the beginning of a system of lavish expenditure, which will last until 1842; no longer—no, sir, no longer, my word for it. Are the judicious men of the North, the property holders of the North, disposed to organize in their bosom, this army of day-laborers—men who, all over the world, spend, between Saturday and Monday, the wages of the week; and who, at the period of their disbandment in 1842, will be penniless, and who must go supperless to bed,

Appendix to the Congressional Globe (24th Cong., 1st Sess. May 5, 1836), pp. 444-447.

unless they rob by lawless insurrection, or by the equally terrible process of the *ballot-box.* Let gentlemen look to it; they are in quite as much danger of insurrection as we are."

The laboring classes, the backbone of the Democracy of the country, rob through the ballot-boxes! What are we to understand by this? Sir, it admits but of this construction—that government ought to be founded on property; that none but the wealthy ought to be allowed to vote; and that the minority should govern. It recognizes a doctrine which strikes at the very root of free government. It is, in fact, the doctrine of despotism itself. No measure, sir, can be carried through the medium of the ballot-box but by the majority. Consult the annals of the past, and you will find that whenever despotism resolved to strengthen itself, or the aristocracy of a country had determined to trench upon the rights and liberties of the people, that the people were first charged with rapacious and seditious designs. The cry of agrarianism, of sedition and revolution, was raised, in order that their calumniators might have an excuse for plundering and oppressing them. Can it be that the new fledged aristocracy of this country have similar designs upon the people at the present time? I confess there are strong indications of it, not only in that spirit of monopoly and of mercenary ambition which is spreading with such fearful and reckless rapidity, but especially in the calumnies which are constantly propagated against the working men, against democratic principles, and against the advocates of liberal sentiments generally. Nay, to those who have paid any attention for the last few years to the movements of the aristocratic or anti-democratic party of this country, it must be evident that a clandestine but vigorous war is waging against popular freedom. Let the people look to it while yet they may. Let them not be deceived neither by *names* nor by *professions.* Let them not suppose that all who pretend to be their friends, politically, are so in reality. It is not all who cry "Lord, Lord, that are worthy of the kingdom."

Mr. Chairman, I regret the attack has been made. It may lead to a controversy from which it will be most difficult to exclude jealousies, heart-burnings, and recriminations. I am not quite certain, however, that it will not, in the main, be productive of good. It may serve to establish more distinctly, and more permanently, the landmarks which distinguish the two great political parties of this country—the *democracy* and the *aristocracy.* And, sir, it is idle to attempt to disguise the fact, that "the time is coming, and now is," when the political gulf between these two parties must be widened and deepened. The people begin to distinguish between mere *methodical* and *practical* Democrats—between those who but have the doctrine of equal rights on their lips and those who wear it in their hearts; and here the days of political amalgamations and political jugglery, are numbered. Henceforth, I trust, the battle will be fought on the ground of principle alone.

Mr. Chairman, it has been more than insinuated that danger is to be apprehended from the turbulent spirit of democracy; that the signs of the times are portentous of evil; that the foundations of the moral and political deep are in danger of being broken up, that the waves of anarchies, rapacity and misrule, threaten to burst their barriers, and deluge the land. It was with great regret that I heard the integrity of the laboring classes, and the principles of democracy, so unjustly impugned; and if it shall be the last act of my life, I will attempt to hurl back the impositions. Sir, I fear that those attacks upon the people—the democracy—which would circumscribe and destroy. Let this doctrine be carried out, and the principles upon which the Government is founded are utterly subverted.

The line which separates the friends and enemies of equal rights is broad and distinct, and need not, must not, be mistaken. The political principles by which these two parties are governed, are utterly and eternally incompatible and antagonistical. It behooves the people therefore, to *discriminate*, and to bear constantly in mind that the friends of pure and unadulterated democracy (as contradistinguished from the friends of aristocracy) are in favor of a government founded on *persons*, and *not on property;* on equal rights, and *not* on exclusive privileges. The friends of freedom hold that legislation, to be just, must be equal; that all chartered monopolies are incompatible with the spirit of free governments, and prejudicial to the interests and liberties of the people. They contend for equality of political franchise. They maintain that the only righteous system of government is that which is based on the will of the majority, and administered by persons freely chosen by the people; and that the people are the only rightful sovereigns. Such, then, are the leading principles of the working men; such the principles of democracy; and if these principles are dangerous and mischievous in their nature, and calculated to produce anarchy and sedition, as has been alleged, then is liberty a bitter *curse*, instead of a *blessing;* and the founders of our free institutions were the authors of a most pernicious political heresy! But who will assert such to be the fact? Who will affirm, openly and unqualifiedly, that the doctrine of political equality is the doctrine of anarchy and outrage; or that the democracy is the party of sedition, of pillage, and of violence? But few can be found bold enough to make the charge openly and distinctly. No. The sign is not quite right yet. The calumny must be insinuated for the present. The charge must be indirect, the war must be conducted with great caution and circumlocution. The assailants must assume as many shapes as fabled Proteus, and wear as many disguises as Harlequin; they must use secret weapons, deal foul blows, and deal them in the dark. Nothing like daylight and fair play must be tolerated; no outward and evident demonstration must yet be made; the people, the laboring classes, the *democracy*, are first to be slandered and traduced, *vaguely*. Something must be hinted about agrarianism, and about the insecurity of the rights of property. But ask these calumniators what they mean by agrarianism, and they are puzzled to explain. Some think that it is a species of political monster which was created by two celebrated brothers of the olden time; but whether it was by Moses and Aaron, or by Tiberius and Cornelius, they are not quite certain. Others suppose that agrarianism means an equal distribuition of property, but are not quite confident of that even. Well, ask them if they ever saw or conversed with an individual holding such sentiments; and they will tell you no, if they tell you the truth. Ask them if they believe that there is any such party in this country; and they will tell you no, if they tell you what they think and believe. Sir, those who circulate such slanders do so either ignorantly or maliciously; and the greater part because they are slanders. The people, the laboring classes, are neither so unwise nor so unreasonable as to either expect or desire a perfect equality of wealth. They know and feel that it would not only be unjust, but that it is impracticable. So long as some are more industrious, more provident, and more frugal than others, an inequality of wealth *must*, and *ought* to exist. The people, the democracy, contend for no measure that does not hold out to individual enterprise proper motives for exertion. All they ask is, that the great principle upon which the Government is founded, the principle of equal rights, should be faithfully observed, and carried out to the *exclusion* of all *exclusive privileges*. This they do ask, and no more; they will be satisfied with no less.

Sir, can it be seriously and honestly believed by any man in the possession of his wits, that the principles of democracy or of equal rights, endanger the rights of property; or that the interest and safety of the State will be plotted against by three fourths of the people composing the State? The notion is too absurd and ridiculous to be entertained for a moment. There is no danger, sir, that three fourths of the people will turn political suicides at this time of day. No one believes that the rights of property and the institutions of the country are in danger from the influence of democratic principles, or from the political ascendency of the people. No, sir, these insinuations against the virtue and intelligence of the people are made for sinister purposes and are the offspring of political depravity; and, as I have before intimated, are the sure and unerring indications of a vigorous attack upon popular liberty. Again, I repeat, let the people look to it.

Public violence and disorders generally, if not universally, have their origin in a violation of the principles of equality and justice; and when these principles are outraged, it is generally by the *few* and *not* by the *many*, it being the manifest interest of the majority to preserve them pure and unimpaired. All the horrors, enormities, and abominations, consequent upon the French revolution, be it remembered, had their origin in the oppressions practiced by the aristocratic few.

In Europe the aristocracy are the *Conservative party.* The English House of Lords was originally composed of men who had associated for the purpose of protecting the property which they had plundered from the people. The property thus unjustly obtained, and the onerous laws designed for its protection, have been the means by which the people of that country have been so long and so sorely oppressed. It is the consciousness of the injustice which has been done the people, that causes the aristocracy of Europe so much dread of sedition and revolution, and so much apprehension about the security of property. In a Government where the people are well informed, property can never be respected where it has been obtained in violation of just and equal rights, and used as an instrument of oppression. But, on the other hand, no danger need to be apprehended for the security of property where obtained by fair and honest means. The right of property in free and intelligent communities, is safe in proportion to the number it has to protect it. Hence in this country, where the people are the *conservative* party, there can be no danger of a violation of this right. It has a protector in every friend of equality and justice. The people, the true source of all political power, are its defenders; it is their interest to be so. If, then, there be a set of men among us who would violate the rights of property, they cannot belong to the real democracy of the country; they can form no portion of, can have no alliance with, the friends of equal rights. No, they must be sought elsewhere. They must be sought among the friends of exclusive privileges, of monopolies and of aristocracy; but not in the ranks of the democracy.

Again, our system of government being based on the principle of equal rights, claims the friends of equal rights as its supporters. They are in fact the party whose interest and welfare are identified with the preservation of the Union, and with the stability and integrity of the Government. They are the *conservative party.* Who, then, are the malcontents, if any there be? Which is the party of sedition, if such there be? Not the people, not the democracy. No; but the opponents of democracy, the enemies of equal rights, the champions of exclusive privileges and of monopolies; they are the aristocracy. What can be more unjust and preposterous, then, than the insinuation of the aristocracy, that there is danger of their being despoiled of their property by the people, the democracy? But what say facts? Why, sir, they tell us, what everybody knows to be true, that where there is one instance where the rights of property have been violated by the people, or popular institutions, there are five thousand instances where the people have been plundered and beggared by the heartless cupidity of the privileged few. Sir, there is much greater danger that capital will unjustly appropriate to itself the avails of labor, than that labor will unlawfully seize on capital. I defy gentlemen to point to a solitary instance where the people possessing legislative powers have prostituted those powers to the purpose of plunder. But, on the other hand, where political power has been concentrated in the hands of the few, you will find that the rights of the multitude, whether pecuniary, natural, or political, have been violated, disregarded, and trampled in the dust. And, for the proof, I appeal to the page of history. History, sir, will bear me out in the declaration, that the aristocracy, of whatever age or country, have, at all times and under all circumstances, invariably and eternally robbed the people, sacrificed their rights, and warred against liberty, virtue, and humanity. I am aware that it is quite fashionable to impute the domestic feuds and civil dissensions which have convulsed nations to the inconstancy and profligacy of the people. The imputation is both false and insolent. In despotic and arbitrary Governments the agitation of the people is but the restiveness of a sick man, who incessantly changes his position, because none of them which he assumes will afford him relief. The people generally complain, but at the last extremity; for their regard and reverence for the law acts ever as a restraint upon their just complaints while they have a hope of redress. They more readily forgive than avenge their wrongs, and are never fickle nor seditious when in the enjoyment of their equal and natural sum of happiness. The true causes of sedition and tumult are too well known to be mistaken. The oppressions of the aristocracy; the insolence of caste; the power of concentrated wealth; the blight of avarice, such are the causes which ever tend to destroy the equipoise of a State, and sow dissensions amongst its members. Run over the history of nations, and point out a single one which, becoming rich as Carthage, for instance, maintained, like Sparta and Rome in their days of glory, the talents and virtues which are the groundwork of republican security. Name a single State, a single kingdom, where the concentration of power and wealth did not generate a spirit of tyranny. Where has concentrated wealth failed to breathe division, injustice, and the consequent contempt of laws natural and political? In what country has it not invited the march of the invader and the yoke of the tyrant? Why did Sparta, enriched by the advice and policy of Lysander, lose the virtue and the power which she had retained during six hundred years of frugal independence? Why did the Roman Republic fall to decay as soon as her nobility were cumbered with the accumulated wealth and fatal spoils of conquered nations?

Many of the republics of the middle ages, in the south of Europe, withstood the shock of foreign invasion, and fought with success against the stranger, but to see their liberties cloven down by the blows of domestic

tyranny. Why instance the example of Florence—until the thirteenth century the freest republic of the modern era? Why show the people, wronged
in their most sacred rights, tortured in their dearest feelings, trodden
under foot by the contending aristocratic parties of the day, pouring out
their life blood for Guelf and for Gibeline, till, exhausted by the fruitless
contest, they sat down in quiet submission, no longer able to resist the
yoke of titled despotism?

Genoa, too, once free, happy, and powerful, paid the forfeit of inequality. The curse of all republics lighted upon her head; and tossed
by passions, begotten of clashing privileges and contending interests,
which seemed to grow out of the lust of ambition rather than out of
the love of freedom, settled down, after various vicissitudes, into a rigid
oligarchy.

The once free and happy Venitians trusted to the hollow promises of
the aristocracy, and mark the consequences of their credulity. They continued to sleep over the imminence of danger until awakened from their
lethargy by the shriek of expiring freedom and the clank of patrician
chains. An unsparing and iron-handed aristocracy gave the charter of
their liberties to the winds of the Adriatic; and beneath the ruins of their
free institutions sat the dark conclave of a gloomy inquisition, and the
titled murderers of the Secret Tribunal.

All States, in their infancy, have laws favorable to equality; all, however, have been condemned to see distinctions and preferences grow up
among their citizens; and although wealth and dignities were at first but
little regarded, so influential were their gradual sway, that they proved
all-sufficient to undermine the stability of the laws, and subjugate the
spirit of the multitude. Consider the length of time which elapsed before
the plebeians of Rome could come to the resolve of sharing the magis-
tracy with the patricians. Yet the people were not unconscious of their
influence and their power. The exile of Tarquin had inspired them with
an extreme love of freedom. The banishment of the lewd tyrant had
induced the hope among the people of yielding to the omnipotence of the
laws alone. They had sustained a long and obstinate war of principles,
which must have elevated their sentiments. And yet we all know how
many indignities, how many exactions, how many tortures; we all know
how often the lash of the patrician's taskmaster resounded in the *ergas-
tula;* how often the hard earnings of the laborer were wrung from his
toil-worn palms, to dower the patrician wife, or furnish the extravagan-
cies of a patrician bridal; how often the plebeian debtor was limbed,
joint by joint, to answer the claims of his patrician creditor; how often
the Roman gemonia echoed with the agony of a tortured people, before
they thought, I will not say to hurl their claims at their oppressors, but
to stand on the imprescriptible law of self-protection. Goaded at last

beyond endurance by the tyranny of the aristocracy, they secede, and intrench their rights on the sacred mount. They were sufficiently powerful to have crushed their enemies, or, at least, to have vindicated the equality of the laws; yet I know not what lurking sense of dependence, what lingering habits of deference to the wealthy, arrests, the thought of vengeance; all that they ask, all they desire, is not to be tortured—not to be oppressed. We have eaten the bread of panda, the bread of communion, with you, they say to the patricians; let not its promise be a lie to ourselves, our wives, and our children! The magistrates whom they appoint to watch over their safety bear no badge of authority, and are content to sit at the outer door of the patrician Senate. The tribunes, who knew their power, and exerted every faculty to uphold the dignity of their order, how long it was before they could bring the plebeians properly to value the principle of equality? If the multitude swell around the forum; if it reecho with their angry murmurs; if they show a disposition to wrest the authority from lawless hands, fear not, it is all a show; a sort of blind and confused instinct, the fruit of habit, holds back the plebeians; and unconscious of the fact, that very instinct militates against their best and most sacred interest, and clams every burst of indignation into order and peace. They must gradually become familiar with the extent of their rights, and if, in a moment of violence and strife, they assert the privilege of sharing the fasces with the patricians, a whole century will have passed away before they dare fully to enjoy that privilege. So much for the disposition to insurgency against the rich, attributed to the poor or laboring classes. And yet, in the teeth of all these facts, in contradiction to all experience, and in defiance of the concurrent testimony of history, our modern aristocracy have the presumption, nay, the bald-faced impudence, to allege that the people have ever a propension to sedition and plunder.

Sir, is it not strange, is it not marvelous, that the aristocracy of any country should have the hardihood to make pretensions to a higher sense of political justice, and claim to possess a greater share of morality and virtue, than the people, the democracy? What is the history of the aristocracy, whether of ancient or of modern times, but a history of aggression, of perfidy, sedition, debauchery, and of moral and political prostitution? What is it but a history of bands of political marauders, whose bonds of union was sordid ambition, and whose watch word and rallying cry was *rapine;* in a word, what is it but a history whose every page bears the indelible impress of omnipotent depravity? Sir, wherever the power of an aristocracy, especially of a *moneyed aristocracy, is fearlessly exercised,* the whole moral and political atmosphere becomes so contaminated, that the heart and its passions, life and its purposes, are alike prostituted to lust and infamy, to avarice and ambition. Within the circle of its influence no generous aspiration can spring, no moral verdure can flourish, no virtue can live; honor, gratitude, beneficence, patriotism—all, all perish. The maxim of the Athenian orator, that action, action, action, was the soul of oratory, appears to have been translated by all aristocracies construing the essence of political power into corruption, corruption, corruption!

Sir, when man becomes so far regardless of the rights and welfare of his fellow man as first deliberately to despoil him of the fruits of his labor, and of those inalienable rights which God and nature vouchsafed to him, and then deride his misfortunes and exult over his degradation, as is the wont of the aristocrat, he is and must be fitted for any and every enormity, and would, nay does, in very deed, spurn the breast that feeds him—"crams, and blasphemes the feeder."

Do I speak in terms too strong of the corrupting influence and of the abominations of aristocracy? By no means. Turn to the page of history, and point me to the people whose virtue or whose patriotism was proof against such influence, *after such influence had once been felt.* In the footsteps of aristocracies, especially of moneyed aristocracies, ever follows venal and enervating luxury; that common bane of all prosperous Governments; that fell destroyer of all manly and patriotic virtue; that seductive syren who sings of glory while she scatters pestilence and withering mildews round the land. Sir, the history of the past is before us; let us be admonished by the lessons it inculcates. Classic Greece, and stern republican Rome, those former lights and wonders of the world, in an evil hour took to their bosoms the serpent luxury, and, ere they were aware, became entangled in its folds; they struggled, and struggled, but in vain—its subtle, sickly poison had reached their vitals, unstrung their sturdy nerves, palsied their giant arms, and stretched them helpless and hopeless in the dust!

The dialects of Aristotle, the philosophy of Plato, and the eloquence of Cicero, were opposed in vain to the moral and political pestilence which swept the land. The influence of wealth and luxury not only banished virtue and patriotism from the Grecian and Roman States, but carried vice and corruption into the very heart of Christendom! It not only debased the principles of Socrates and Seneca, but the vicars of Christ and the defenders of the faith. It triumphed alike over heathen philosophy and Christian divinity; and for the proof, I would refer you to both profane and ecclesiastical history. During the three first centuries, the professors of Christianity kept themselves comparatively "pure and unspotted from the world," and their consciences innocent from secret conspiracy or open rebellion. When persecuted by their enemies, they retaliated not, but, in imitation of their Heavenly Teacher, meekly bowed their necks to the blow. But after Christianity had become the ally of wealth and power, mark the change! behold how soon its whole garb and character are altered! No sooner had it become the favorite of royalty, and the associate of aristocracy, than its professors (the once humble followers of the meek and lowly Jesus) rushed from the cloister and the cell, like lions from their lairs, or rather, like wolves from their dens, thirsting for blood, and howling for revenge. The symbols of peace and purity, the chalice and the cross, were exchanged for the spear and javelin; the robes of sanctity, the gown and surplice for the mail of steel, the cuirass, and the casque. The clang of arms and the war shout were preferred to the morning hymn and the evening orison; and, instead of singing hallelujahs to the Prince of Peace, those sanguinary heroes shouted hosannas to the Demon of War! The cross was raised in the battle, and glittered on their shields; and *corrupted* Christianity was spread, by dint of arms, from the Thracian Bosphorus to the banks of the Wolga. But, alas! as it advanced, virtue receded! No sooner were the pagans repulsed than the spurious Christians turned their swords, still reeking with the blood of the infidel, against each other. The heretics were massacred, and their estates confiscated, and some of the penal regulations were copied from the edicts of that very Dioclesian who had dealt destruction among the Christians. "And this method of conversion was applauded by the same bishops who had felt the hand of oppression, and pleaded for the rights of humanity."

But I will pursue this subject no further. My object was merely to show that neither the teachings of philosophy nor the inspiration of religion, were capable of counteracting or resisting the corrupt and unhallowed influence of associated power and wealth—of aristocracy. And yet, with a knowledge of these facts, with a full and *practical* knowledge of the immoral and corrupting tendency and character of aristocratic principles, our venal, flippant, upstart aristocrats, with heads thrown back, and arms akimbo, presume to prate of virtue and morality, and *dare* to impugn the integrity and patriotism of their betters, the democracy. Their arrogance and folly can only be paralleled by their depravity.

But, sir, much has been said against associations—not of bankers, nor of brokers, but of *mechanics and laborers.* Why, it has been asked with alarm and indignation, why this commotion among the laboring classes? Why this banding together and forming of unions throughout the country? Sir, these associations are intended as counterpoises against capital, whenever it shall attempt to exert an unlawful or undue influence. They are a measure of *self-defense* and of *self-preservation,* and therefore are *not illegal!* Both the laws of God and man *justify resistance* to the robber and the homicide, *even unto death!* They are considered necessary guards against the encroachments of mercenary ambition and tyranny, and the friends of exclusive privileges, therefore, may, with propriety, dread their power and their influence. The union of the working men is not only a shield of defense against hostile combinations, but also a weapon of attack that will be successfully wielded against the oppressive measures of a corrupt and despotic aristocracy. It is the brand of IOLAUS searing and annihilating the Lernaean monster.

The present indications of disquietude in the public mind excite no alarm among the friends of equal rights. It is proof that liberty is abroad, and that the "bone and muscle of the country" are imbued with its spirit. It is an evidence that the Republic retains a goodly share of its original purity and freshness, and that the blood flows fast and the pulse beats strongly in the body-politic, denoting *youthful health and vigor*. The friends of equal rights, therefore, I say, are not alarmed at these signs of concert and energy in the ranks of the people. They perceive, in the gathering cloud, the lightning that is to purify the political atmosphere. It flashes, but terrifies the foes of freedom!

And who are they that clamor against the efforts of the laboring classes to protect their rights and elevate their condition? Who that approve of indictments and prosecutions against them for seeking refuge in unions and association from combination and oppression, and hold guiltless at the same time the confederates of all conspiracies against them? Sir, I will tell you who they are: they are the sordid champions of exclusive privileges, and of chartered monopolies; those cunningly-devised substitutes of feudal tenures, and the "insolent prerogative of primogeniture." They are the common enemies of equal rights, and of that just and benign policy which would secure the greatest good to the greatest number. They are the aristocracy, and therefore, *traitors* to the principles of the Government which affords them protection.

But it is denied that there are any such party in this country as an aristocracy. The Constitution, it is said, recognizes no such *order*. True, sir, neither does the Constitution recognize a paper currency; but does it follow, therefore, that no such currency exists? The Constitution of the United States positively *prohibits* the emission of bills of credit, by the State governments; and yet it is notorious, that such issues, in the shape of bank bills, are made daily, by and with the consent of every State government in the Union. It is absurd, therefore, to argue that there is no aristocracy in this country, *because* the Constitution recognizes no such party or order. But as names do not alter the nature of things, it makes but very little difference by what name that political party is called, which advocates *exclusive privileges*, or an *inequality of rights*. Their principles are equally adverse to the spirit of democracy, by whatever name they may be designated.

A purely democratic Government must necessarily be opposed, in its very character and nature, to all monopolies and unequal legislation; and no party, therefore, in favor of charters and exclusive privileges, can, with any propriety, claim to be the party of democracy: it would be equally proper for a disciple of Mahomet to call himself a Christian. Sir, is it not base and horrible mockery, nay, downright perfidy, for any party or individual to profess the principles of democracy, or political equality, and pursue monopoly or aristocratic measures at the same time? Whoever professes to be a Democrat and acts upon federal or monopoly principles, deserves to be stigmatized as a political dissembler and traitor.

Sir, shall I be told that the *Democratic party* numbers amongst its nominal supporters monopolists, or aristocrats? I am aware of the fact, sir, without being advised of it at this time. Nevertheless, I do contend that the Democratic party, as a *party*, have, from the organization of the Government to the present time, ever been *distinguished* from their political adversaries, whether known as federalists, aristocrats, monopolists, nationals, or modern Whigs, by their advocacy of liberal or popular principles. The history of the two parties shows this. The first prominent anti-democratic measure proposed in this country, was that of the funding or banking system. Alexander Hamilton, the avowed advocate of an aristocracy, was the fit champion of this unequal and onerous measure, and from which has emanated that whole system of monopoly which now overshadows the land, and threatens to subvert the liberties of the people. . . .

Such, then, sir, is the character and tendency of the paper or banking system. And, with this system is identified the aristocracy; they are, in fact, inseparable. The banking system of this country, be it ever remembered, originated with, and has been uniformly cherished and advocated by, the anti-democratic or aristocratic party. The struggle of the United States Bank (one of the first fruits of aristocratic policy) was emphatically a struggle for power and privilege, nay, for dominion. Its friends, emboldened by the hope and prospect of success, threw by the mask, and not only avowed, but carried out into practice, the principles which govern all moneyed aristocracies; and arrogance, corruption, oppression, and proscription, were openly practiced in the face of day.

The aristocracy are not only distinguished by their corrupt and despotic measures, and their penchant for monopolies and exclusive privileges, but also, by the virulency and constancy of their animosity towards the advocates of the rights and happiness of the multitude; and hence Jefferson and Jackson, those devoted and efficient champions of *equal rights*, have each in their turn, been the objects of their peculiar hatred and unmitigated slanders. In fact, those who most deserve the confidence and support of the people, are ever the most obnoxious to the assaults and denunciations of the aristocracy. Who, for example, have been more grossly slandered and abused by them than Martin Van Buren and Richard M. Johnson? And who have stronger claims upon the regard and confidence of the democracy of the country than those gentlemen? Have they not, both in Congress and the Legislatures of their respective States, uniformly opposed chartered monopolies, and all other aristocratic encroachments upon the equal rights and liberties of the people? Have they not, at all times, and under all circumstances, openly and unreservedly avowed their hostility to all *exclusive legislation,* and to all measures calculated to prejudice the cause of political equality? Have they not ever reposed the utmost confidence in the intelligence and integrity of the people, and uniformly exerted their best energies in behalf of the people's rights and welfare? Let the history of their lives furnish the answer.

The aristocracy are also known by yet another characteristic—their *contempt* of the *common people.* I do not recollect that I have ever met with any production in which this feeling was so strongly and *heartily* expressed as it is in the late address of Mr. Biddle before the Alumni Association of Nassau Hall. Permit me, sir, to call your attention for a moment to the following extract, as a specimen:

"From your own quiet elevation, watch calmly this servile rout, [the people,] as it triumphantly sweeps before you. The avenging hour will at last come. It cannot be that our free nation will long endure the vulgar dominion of ignorance and profligacy. You will live to see the laws reestablished. These banditti [the people] will be scourged back to their caverns; the penitentiary will reclaim its fugitives in office, and the only remembrance which history will preserve of them is the energy with which you resisted and defeated them."

It is difficult, sir, to determine whether *audacity* or hypocrisy is most preeminent in the extract which I have just read. Sir, must it not strike every one, possessing the least sense of propriety, as very remarkable that an individual in Mr. Biddle's *peculiar situation,* being at the time president of an institution notoriously corrupt and unconstitutional, should presume to make pretensions to patriotism or to political integrity? Why sir, with about as much propriety might the wanton prate of virtue, or the father of lies of truth and righteousness, as *this man* of love of country or of political honesty. In his abuse of the people is exhibited the profanity of Alcibiades, defacing the images of the gods! In his professions of patriotism is manifested the hypocrisy of Clodius dedicating a temple to liberty! And let it be remembered, sir, that this enemy of equal rights, this contemner and libeler of the people, is the chief priest, nay, the very Moloch, of the Bank-Whig aristocracy. No prince better reserves the homage of his subjects; none so well qualified to direct the councils of that political Tartarus, which he has obtained the empire of, and delights to reign over!

[NOTE.—In consequence of indisposition, Mr. MOORE was unable to proceed in his remarks.]

Suppression of a Strike in New York

Philip Hone

Monday, June 6, 1836.—[Rise of Labor Unions]. In corroboration of the remarks which I have occasionally made of late, on the spirit of faction and contempt of the laws which pervades the community at this time, is the conduct of the journeymen tailors instigated by a set of vile foreigners (principally English), who unable to endure the restraint of wholesome laws, well administered in their own country, take refuge here, establish trade unions, and villify Yankee judges and juries. Twenty odd of these "knights of the thimble" were convicted at the oyer and terminer of a conspiracy to raise their wages and to prevent any of the craft from working at prices less than those for which they "struck." Judge Edwards gave notice that he would proceed to sentence them this day, but in consequence of the continuance of Robinson's trial the court postponed the sentence until Friday.

This, however, being the day on which it was expected, crowds of people have been collected in the park, ready for any mischief to which they may have been instigated, and a most diabolical and inflammatory handbill was circulated yesterday, headed by a coffin. The board of Aldermen held an informal meeting this evening, at which a resolution was adopted authorizing the mayor to offer a reward for the discovery of the author, printer, publisher, or distributor of this incendiary publication. The following was the handbill.—

"The Rich Against the Poor!

"Judge Edwards, the tool of the aristocracy, against the people! Mechanics and Workingmen! A deadly blow has been struck at your liberty! The prize for which your fathers fought has been robbed from you! The freemen of the North are now on a level with the slaves of the South! With no other privilege

The Diary of Philip Hone, I, pp. 210-211.

than laboring, that drones may fatten on your life-blood! Twenty of your brethren have been found guilty for presuming to resist a reduction of their wages! And Judge Edwards has charged an American jury, and agreeably to that charge, they have established the precedent that workingmen have no right to regulate the price of labor, or, in other words, the rich are the only judges of the wants of the poor man. On Monday, June 6, 1836, at ten o'clock, these freemen are to receive their sentence, to gratify the hellish appetites of the aristocrats!

"On Monday, the liberty of the workingmen will be interred! Judge Edwards is to chant the requiem! Go! Go! Every freeman and workingman and hear the hollow and the melancholy sound of the earth on the coffin of equality! Let the courtroom, the City Hall, yea! the whole park be filled with *mourners*. But remember, offer no violence to Judge Edwards. Bend meekly, and receive the chain wherewith you are to be bound! Keep the peace! Above all things, keep the peace!"

The Factory Girls of Lowell

Michel Chevalier

Boston, June 22, 1834

The introduction of the manufacturing system into a new country, under the empire of very different circumstances, is an event worthy of the closest attention. No sooner was I recovered from the sort of giddiness with which I was seized at the sight of this extemporaneous town [of Lowell], hardly had I taken time to touch it, to make sure that it was not a pasteboard town, like those which Potëmkin erected for Catherine along the road to Byzantium, when I set out to find out how far the creation of manufactures in this country had given rise to the same dangers in regard to the welfare and morals of the working class and in regard to the security of the rich and public order, as in Europe. Through the polite attention of the agents of the two principal companies (the Merrimack and the Lawrence), I was able to satisfy my curiosity. The cotton factories alone employ six thousand persons in Lowell. Of this number nearly five thousand are young women from seventeen to twenty-four years of age, the daughters of farmers from the different New England States, particularly Massachusetts, New Hampshire, and Vermont; they are here far from their families and on their own. Seeing them pass through the streets, morning and evening and at mealtimes, neatly dressed; finding their scarfs, and shawls, and the green silk hoods which they wear as a shelter from the sun and dust (for Lowell is not yet paved) hanging in the factories between vases of flowers and shrubs which they cultivate, I said to myself, this, then, is not Manchester. When I was informed of the rate of their wages, I understood that it was not at all like Manchester. The following are the average weekly (that is, six days of work) wages paid by the Merrimack corporation last May.

Michel Chevalier, *Society, Manners, and Politics in the United States* (Boston, 1839), pp. 136-143.

For picking and carding	$\begin{cases} 3.00 \text{ Dolls.} \\ 3.10 \\ 2.78 \end{cases}$
For spinning	3.00
For weaving	$\begin{cases} 3.10 \\ 3.12 \end{cases}$
For warping and sizing	$\begin{cases} 3.45 \\ 4.00 \end{cases}$
In the Cloth-room	3.12

These numbers are, I repeat, averages. The wages of skilled hands amount to $5.00 and sometimes nearly $6.00. Note that last March, in consequence of the crisis occasioned by the President's quarrel with the Bank, there was a general reduction of from $.30 to $.40 a week. You know how much smaller are the wages of women than of men; there are few women in Europe, outside of some of the great cities, who can earn more than $.20 a day or $1.00 a week. It must be remembered also that in the United States the necessaries of life are not only much cheaper than in England, but even than in France, so that a great many of these girls can save $1.00 or $1.50 a week. After spending four years in the factories, they may have a little fortune of $250 or $300, when they often quit work and marry. Out of one thousand females in the Lawrence mills, only eleven are married women, and nineteen widows.

In France, it would be difficult to conceive of a state of things in which young girls, generally pretty, should be separated from their families, fifty or a hundred miles from home, in a town in which their parents could have no one to advise and watch over them. It is a fact, however, with the exception of a small number of cases which only prove the rule, that this state of things has yet had no bad effects in Lowell. The manners of the English race are totally different from those of us French; all their habits and all their notions wholly unlike ours. The Protestant education, much more than our Catholic discipline, draws round each individual a line over which it is difficult to step. The consequence is more coldness in domestic relations, the more or less complete absence of a full and free expression of the stronger feelings of the soul, but, in turn, everyone is obliged and accustomed to show more respect for the feelings of others. What among us would pass for a youthful imprudence, a pretty trick, is severely frowned upon by the English and Americans, and particularly by the Americans of New England, who are, as has been said, double-distilled English. Nobody in this country, then, is surprised to see the daughters of rural proprietors, after having received a tolerable education, quit their native village and their parents, take up their residence fifty or a hundred miles off, in a town where they know no one, and pass three or four years in this state of isolation and independence. They are under the safeguard of the public faith. All this presupposes an extreme reserve of manners, a vigilant, inexorable, and rigid public opinion. It must be acknowledged that under this rigorous system there is a somber hue, an air of listlessness, thrown over society; but, when one reflects on the dangers to which the opposite system exposes the daughter of the poor who has no one to look out for her, when one counts the victims, however slight may be his sympathies for humanity, it is difficult to deny that Anglo-American prudery, all things considered, is fully worth our ease and freedom of manners, whatever may be their attractions.

The manufacturing companies exercise the most careful supervision over these girls. I have already said that twelve years ago Lowell did not exist. When, therefore, the factories were set up, it also became necessary to provide lodgings for the workers. Each company has built for this purpose a number of houses within its own limits, to be used exclusively as boarding houses for them. These are under the care of a matron who is paid by the company at the rate of one dollar and a quarter a week for each boarder, that sum being taken out of the weekly wages of the girls. These housekeepers, who are generally widows, are each responsible for the conduct of her boarders, and they are themselves subject to the control and supervision of the company in the management of their little communities. Each company has its rules and regulations, which are not merely paper-laws but are carried into execution with all that spirit of vigilant perseverance that characterizes the Yankee. I will give you a short summary of one of these codes, for they seem to me to throw great light on some of the most striking peculiarities of this country. I will take those of the Lawrence company which is the most recently formed; they are a revised and corrected edition of the rules and regulations of the other companies. They bear the date May 21, 1833.

The first Article of the general rules is as follows:

All persons employed by the Company must devote themselves assiduously to their duty during working-hours. They must be capable of doing the work which they undertake, or use all their efforts to this effect. They must on all occasions, both in their words and in their actions, show that they are penetrated by a laudable love of temperance and virtue, and animated by a sense of their moral and social obligations. The Agent of the Company shall endeavor to set to all a good example in this respect. Every individual who shall be notoriously dissolute, idle, dishonest, or intemperate, who shall be in the practice of absenting himself from divine service, or shall violate the Sabbath, or shall be addicted to gaming, shall be dismissed from the service of the Company.

Article 2: All ardent spirits are banished from the Company's grounds, except when prescribed by a physician. All games of hazard and cards are prohibited within their limits and in the boarding-houses.

The articles following from 3 to 13 determine the duties of the agent, assistant agent, foremen, watch, and firemen. Article 13 directs that every female employed by the company shall live in one of the company's boarding houses, attend divine service regularly at one of the churches in the city, and rigidly observe the rules of the Sabbath. Article 14, the last, contains an appeal to the operatives on the necessity of subordination and on the compatibility of obedience with civil and religious liberty.

There is, besides, a special rule relative to boarding houses. It recounts that the company has built those houses and lets them at a low price, wholly for the good of the hands, and that the company, therefore, imposes certain duties on the persons who hire them. It makes them responsible for the neatness and comfortable condition of the houses, the punctuality and good quality of the meals, good order and harmony among the boarders. It requires that the matrons shall receive no persons as boarders who are not employed in the company's works and obliges them to keep an account of the behavior of the girls. It also prescribes that the doors shall be shut at ten and repeats the injunction of attendance at divine worship.

These regulations, which among us would excite a thousand objections and would be in fact impracticable, are here regarded as the most simple and natural thing in the world. They are enforced without opposition or difficulty. Thus in regard to Sunday, for instance, which with us is a holiday, a day of amusement and gaiety, it is here a day of retirement, meditation, silence, and prayer. In the United States, the theaters are generally closed on Sunday, out of respect for the rules of the Sabbath; the only exception to this custom is among the French population of Louisiana. In New England, religious scruples on this point are carried further than elsewhere; thus in Boston a city ordinance prescribes the shutting up of the theaters on Saturday evening because, according to some precisionists, the Sabbath begins at sunset on that day. This is one of the features in which the French type most strongly contrasts with the Anglo-American. In a moral and religious point of view, there prevail among us a laxity and a toleration which offer a counterpart to the American *let-alone* principle in political matters; while the principle of political authority which has always been established in great vigor among us under all forms of government, monarchy, empire, or republic, corresponds to the austere reserve of American manners, to their rigid habits of life, and to the religious severity which exists here by the side of the great multiplicity of sects. So true is it, that both order and liberty are essential to human nature and that it is impossible to establish a society on one of these principles alone! If you abandon a portion of the social institutions exclusively to the spirit of liberty, be assured that the principle of order will take no less exclusive possession of some other

portion. Yield up to liberty the whole field of politics and you are compelled to give religion and manners wholly up to order. Leave manners
and religion to liberty, and you find yourself obliged to strengthen the
principle of order in politics, under pain of suffering society itself to fall
into ruins. Such are the general laws of equilibrium which govern nations
and the universe of worlds.

Up to this time, then, the rules of the companies have been observed.
Lowell, with its steeple-crowned factories, resembles a Spanish town
with its convents; but with this difference, that in Lowell, you meet no
rags nor Madonnas, and that the nuns of Lowell, instead of working
sacred hearts, spin and weave cotton. Lowell is not amusing, but it is
neat and decent, peaceable and sage. Will it always be so? Will it be so
long? It would be rash to affirm it. Up to now the life of manufacturing
has elsewhere proved little favorable to the preservation of severe morals.
So it has been in France, as well as in England; in Germany and Switzerland, as well as in France.

The Plain People's Style of Living

William Thomson

The style of living amongst tradesmen in the "Queen City of the West" (Cincinnati), is superior to anything I had hitherto seen. The usual rate of boarding is two dollars per week. In the house where I boarded (J. G. Jones's, Seventh Street), we paid two and a half dollars per week. In this house we had, as lodgers, two single ladies—seamstresses, or, as they are called here, tailoresses. I believe they paid rather less; perhaps one and three-quarters or two dollars. They managed to pay this by working at the needle, and to dress genteelly. There were also one housepainter, whose wages, in winter, was one and a quarter dollar a day, in summer one and a half; a man that wrought in a pork-house, whose wages varied from one to two dollars per day; three cabinet-makers, whose general wages, at piece-work, varied from seven to ten dollars per week (one of them sometimes as high as fourteen dollars); a *loafer* (that is, an idle fellow), whose wife managed, at dress-making, to keep them both; and myself, a wool-spinner, making from seven to eight dollars per week. This was our family; whose wages are a fair sample of what tradesmen can make here. Our bed-rooms were large and airy, but crowded. In my room there were three beds, two sleeping in each; but the mistress would not venture to put two together without the consent of both parties. I observed they were cleanly in their habits—using nightshirts, washing as regularly as they rose, and rising regularly as day-light began to glimmer. An hand-bell was rung about a quarter of an hour before breakfast, and again when it was on the table where all, as they came from their rooms, took their regular seats, without *grace,* or waiting for their neighbours; and, having swallowed their breakfast hurriedly, got up and went off to work. The morning salutations were such as are not very common amongst tradesmen in this country. 'Good morning, Miss Stone;' 'Good morning, sir;'—'Morning,'—'Morning,' 'Morning,' all round. Coffee and tea; ham and eggs (which they eat out of tumblers, breaking

Thomson, *A Tradesman's Travels*, pp. 133-135.

in three or four, stirring in a little salt, supping it all up in the time one would be of scraping out the shell of an egg after the fashion of the Old Country); roasted chickens, sallads, pickles, vinegar, pepper (black and red), hot biscuits, Jonney cake, and buck-wheat cakes and butter, were the constant fare at breakfast. But the dinner was glorious:—roast pig, a turkey (the very ruins of which would have dined a small family), and rounds of splendid beef. Capt. Barclay of Ury may say what he chooses about the breed of cattle; I only wish, amidst all his improvements, he could introduce a breed that the working people of this country could get half as good a share of as the labourers in America get of theirs.

Race Prejudice in the North

Sarah Forten

Philadelphia [Pa.] April 15 th, 1837

To Angelina Grimké

Esteemed Friend,

I have to thank you for the interest which has led you to address a letter to me on a subject which claims so large a share of your attention. In making a reply to the question proposed by you, I might truly advance the excuse of inability; but you well know how to compassionate the weakness of one who has written but little on the subject, and who has until very lately lived and acted more for herself than for the good of others. I confess that I am wholly indebted to the Abolition cause for arousing me from apathy and indifference, shedding light into a mind which has been too long wrapt in selfish darkness.

In reply to your question—of the "effect of Prejudice" on myself, I must acknowledge that it has often embittered my feelings, particularly when I recollect that we are the innocent victims of it; for you are well aware that it originates from dislike to the color of the skin, as much as from the degradation of Slavery. I am peculiarly sensitive on this point, and consequently seek to avoid as much as possible mingling with those who exist under its influence. I must also own that *it* has often engendered feelings of discontent and mortification in my breast when I saw that many were preferred before me, who by education, birth, or worldly circumstances were no better than myself, THEIR sole claim to notice depending on the superior advantage of being White; but I am striving to live above such heart burnings, and will learn to "bear and forbear" believing that a spirit of forebearance under such evils is all that we as a people can well exert.

Colonization is, as you well know, the offspring of Predjudice. It has doubtless had a baneful influence on our People. I despise the aim of that Institution most heartily, and have never yet met one man or

Weld-Grimké Letters, I, pp. 379-382.

woman of Color who thought better of it than I do. I believe, with all just and good persons, that it originated more immediately from prejudice than from philanthropy. The longing desire of a separation induces this belief, and the spirit of "This is not your Country" is made manifest by the many obstacles it throws in the way of their advancement mentally and morally. No doubt but there has always existed the same amount of predjudice in the minds of Americans towards the descendants of Africa; it wanted only the spirit of colonization to call it into action. It can be seen in the exclusion of the colored people from their churches, or placing them in obscure corners. We see it in their being barred from a participation with others in acquiring any useful knowledge; public lectures are not usually free to the colored people; they may not avail themselves of the right to drink at the fountain of learning, or gain an insight into the arts and science of our favored land. All this and more do they feel accutely. I only marvel that they are in possession of any knowledge at all, circumscribed as they have been by an all pervading, all-powerful predjudice. Even our professed friends have not yet rid themselves of it—to some of them it clings like a dark mantle obscuring their many virtues and choking up the avenues to higher and nobler sentiments. I recollect the words of one of the best and least predjudiced men in the Abolition ranks. Ah said he, "I can recall the time when in walking with a colored brother, the darker the night, the better Abolitionist was I." He does not say so now, but my friend, how much of this leaven still lingers in the hearts of our white brethren and sisters is oftentimes made manifest to us; but when we recollect what great sacrifices to public sentiment they are called upon to make, we cannot wholly blame them. Many, very many are anxious to take up the cross, but how few are strong enough to bear it. For our own family, we have to thank a kind Providence for placing us in a situation that has hitherto prevented us from falling under the weight of this evil; we feel it but in a slight degree compared with many others. We are not much dependant upon the tender mercies of our enemies, always having resources within ourselves to which we can apply. We are not disturbed in our social relations; we never travel far from home and seldom go to public places unless quite sure that admission is free to all; therefore, we meet with none of these mortifications which might otherwise ensue. I would recommend to my colored friends to follow our example and they would be spared some very painful realities.

My Father bids me tell you that white and colored men have worked with him from his first commencement in business. One man (a white) has been with him nearly thirty seven years; very few of his hired men have been foreigners; nearly all are natives of this country; the greatest harmony and good feeling exists between them; he has usually 10 or twenty journeymen, one half of whom are white; but I am not aware of any white sailmaker who employs colored men; I think it should be reciprocal—do not you?

Do you know w[h]ether the Ladies have fixed on the day for holding their Convention? Do you not think it would be best to hold it the day before the mens meeting, for most of us would be desirous to be present at both meetings. Could you not suggest this plan? There will probably be a large delegation from our society. My sisters purpose going but not as Delegates. I presume there will be a sale of fancy articles there, as we were requested to send some of our work. We are all quite busy preparing something pretty and useful. Several of our schools will have specimens of work and penmanship to be sent. My Brother James will mark those Handkerchiefs with pleasure but we hope you do not think there will be anything to pay for them—by no means—he generally marks those we sell for the society when he has leisure, and it is gratifying to him to do so.

Our noble Friend Burleigh is spending his strength daily in the good cause. He should be more careful of his health for it is yielding fast by reason of his much speaking. Shall I apologize for taking up such a large share of your valuable time as will be requisite to peruse this long letter? but in writing to you I forget that I address you for the first time. We *all* feel deeply sensible of your labors of love for our people, and we trust that you may continue to receive strength from above to sustain you in your trials. My Parents and Sisters unite with me in affection to you and your excellent sister.

The Negro in the North

Sir Charles Lyell

A rare event, the death of a wealthy man of colour [probably Sarah For-ten's father], took place during my stay here [Philadelphia], and his funeral was attended not only by a crowd of persons of his own race, but also by many highly respectable white merchants, by whom he was held in high esteem. He had made his fortune as a sail-maker, and is said to have been worth, at one time, sixty thousand pounds, but to have lost a great part of his riches by lending money with more generosity than prudence. I was rejoicing that his colour had proved no impedi-ment to his rising in the world, and that he had been allowed so much fair play as to succeed in over-topping the majority of his white com-petitors, when I learnt, on further inquiry, that, after giving an excellent education to his children, he had been made unhappy, by finding they must continue, in spite of all their advantages, to belong to an inferior caste. It appeared that, not long before his death, he had been especially mortified, because two of his sons had been refused a hearing at a public meeting, where they wished to speak on some subject connected with trade which concerned them.

In many states, the free blacks have votes, and exert their privileges at elections, yet there is not an instance of a single man of colour, al-though eligible by law, having been chosen a member of any state legis-lature. The schools for the coloured population at Boston are well managed, and the black children are said to show as much quickness in learning as the whites. To what extent their faculties might be developed as adults we have as yet no means of judging; for if their first efforts are coldly received, or treated with worse than indifference, as in the case of the young Philadelphians before alluded to, it is impossible that the higher kinds of excellence can be reached in literature, the learned profes-sions, or in a political career. If any individual be gifted with finer genius than the rest, his mind will be the more sensitive to discouragement, espe-

Sir Charles Lyell, *Travels in North America*, I, pp. 164-170.

cially when it proceeds from a race whose real superiority over his coloured fellow-citizens, in their present condition, he of all others would be the first to appreciate. It is after many trials attended with success, and followed by willing praise and applause, that self-confidence and intellectual power are slowly acquired; and no well educated black has ever yet had an opportunity of ripening or displaying superior talents in this or any other civilised country. Canada and Ireland teach us how much time and how many generations are required for the blending together, on terms of perfect equality, both social and political, of two nations, the conquerors and the conquered, even where both are of the same race, and decidedly equal in their natural capacities, though differing in religion, manners, and language. But when, in the same community, we have two races so distinct in their physical peculiarities as to cause many naturalists, who have no desire to disparage the negro, to doubt whether both are of the same species, and started originally from the same stock; when one of these, found in Africa in a savage and unprogressive state, has been degraded, by those who first colonized North America, to the lowest place in the social scale—to expect, under such a combination of depressing circumstances, that, in half a century, and in a country where more than six-sevenths of the race are still held in bondage, the newly-emancipated citizens should, under any form of government, attain at once a position of real equality, is a dream of the visionary philanthropist, whose impracticable schemes are more likely to injure than to forward a great cause.

In the West Indies, where circumstances are far more favourable to a fair experiment, we have found how much easier it is to put an end to slavery than to elevate the blacks to an equal standing with the whites in society, and in the management of public affairs. They are however advancing slowly; and although we hear complaints of commercial losses, consequent on emancipation, and of exports of sugar and coffee falling off, there seems little doubt that the negro population, comprising the great bulk of the inhabitants, are better informed, better clothed, and happier, in their own way, than during the period when all were slaves. A gradual transfer of land is going on in Barbadoes, Jamaica, and other large islands, from the original proprietors to the negroes, who are abandoning the cultivation of sugar, and raising such crops and fruits of the earth as they can obtain with moderate labour. There has not been time to ascertain whether the freed men will ever have aspirations after that higher civilization, which distinguishes a few of the more advanced among the nations of western Europe; but this problem has still to be solved with regard to the Chinese and many other large sections of the human family.

The near approach to universal suffrage in the United States appears to me one of the most serious obstacles, both to the disfranchisement of the slaves in the South, and to their obtaining, when freed, a proper station relatively to the whites. Whereas property confers the right of voting, the men of colour can at once be admitted without danger to an absolute equality of political rights, the more industrious alone becoming invested with privileges which are withheld from the indigent and most worthless of the dominant race. Such a recognition of rights not only raised the negroes in their opinion of themselves, but, what is of far more consequence, accustoms a portion of the other race to respect them. In the free states, we were often painfully reminded of the wide chasm which now separates the whites from the emancipated man of colour.

If there be any place where distinctions of birth, wealth, station, and race should be forgotten, it is the temple where the Christian precept is inculcated that all men are equal before God. On one occasion in New England, when we were attending the administration of the sacrament in an Episcopal church, we saw all the white communicants first come forward, and again retire to their pews, before any of the coloured people advanced, most of whom were as well dressed as ourselves, and some only a shade darker in complexion. In another Episcopal church in New York, the order and sanctity of the service was, for a moment, in danger of being disturbed because some of the whites had been accidentally omitted, so that they came to the altar after the coloured communicants. After a slight confusion, however, our feelings were relieved by the officiating minister proceeding and showing his resolution not to allow any interruption from this accident. I had no opportunity of witnessing the good example said to be set by the Roman Catholic clergy in prohibiting all invidious distinctions in their churches; but we know in Europe how much more the poor and the rich are mingled together indifferently in the performance of their devotions in Romanist churches than in most of the Anglo-protestant congregations.

The extent to which the Americans carry their repugnance to all association with the coloured race on equal terms remained to the last an enigma to me. They feel, for example, an insurmountable objection to sit down to the same table with a well-dressed, well-informed, and well-educated man of colour, while the same persons would freely welcome one of their own race of meaner capacity and ruder manners to boon companionship. I have no doubt that if I remained here for some years I should imbibe the same feelings, and sympathise with what now appears to me an almost incomprehensible prejudice. If the repugnance arose from any physical causes, any natural antipathy of race, we should not see the rich Southerners employing black slaves to wait on their persons, prepare their food, nurse and suckle their white children, and live with them as mistresses. We should never see the black lady's maid sitting in the same carriage with her mistress, and supporting her when fatigued, and last, though not least, we should not meet with a numerous mixed breed springing up every where from the union of the two races.

We must seek then for other causes of so general and powerful a nature as to be capable of influencing almost equally the opinions of thirteen millions of men. We well know that the abolition of villeinage and serfdom has never enabled the immediate descendants of freed-men, however rich, talented, and individually meritorious, to intermarry and be received on a footing of perfect equality with the best families of their country, or with that class on which their fathers were recently dependent. If in Europe there had been some indelible mark of ancestral degradation, some livery, handed down indefinitely from one generation to another, like the colour of the African, there is no saying how long the most galling disabilities of the villein would have survived the total abolition by law of personal servitude. But, fortunately, in Western Europe, the slaves belonged to the same race as their masters, whereas, in the United States, the negro cannot throw off the livery which betrays to the remotest posterity the low condition of his forefathers.

Lynch Law—North and South

William Thomson

There was an abolition mob in Cincinnati a fortnight before my arrival, and the excitement had hardly subsided then. Let it be remembered, Ohio is a non-slave state. Two boys were playing near the canal, and bothering a negro man, who got into a passion, and stabbed one of them with a knife. The negro was apprehended; but the citizens were so indignant at the outrage that they determined to hunt the negroes out of the town altogether. For this purpose, they met at Fifth Street Market, some thousands strong, with rifles and two fieldpieces, and marched in regular order to the district of the city where the negroes principally resided. The blacks were numerous, and rumour said they were to show fight. Many of them had arms. Some said they fired on the citizens, and others not. There *was* some firing; but I could not ascertain if any of the blacks were killed, the accounts were so various. Some of them, I believe, did not want to tell the truth. The end of the matter was, that they hounded them out of the town, and not a negro durst show his black face in the town for a week. Many of them fled to the authorities of the town for protection; and the jail-yard was crowded with the poor creatures who had fled for their lives.

An arrangement was immediately come to, between the authorities and the citizens; to the effect that no negro should be allowed to live in the city who could not find a white man to become his security, and be answerable for his conduct.

There were two days of mobbing. The second day they gutted an abolition printing establishment, and sunk the press in the middle of the Ohio River, where it now lies—while perhaps the outlandish-looking fishes, in happy ignorance of the strife and contention of the world above, are snuffing about it, and making as sage conjectures about its use, as some of our philosophers do when they attempt to enlighten

William Thomson, *A Tradesman's Travels in the United States and Canada in the Years 1840, 41 & 42* (Edinburgh, 1842), pp. 160-170.

an ignorant world, by explaining things they know nothing about themselves.

While I was in Cincinnati a very serious bank mob took place. In order that this case may be understood, I may mention that there were a number of small banking establishments which, although not strictly legal, managed, by 'hook or by crook' to get a large quantity of their notes into circulation, and as the times grew worse they fell in value. Such a thing as getting cash for them at *par* was never heard of in the best of times; and now, as there was some prospect of the state passing an act, compelling all to resume specie payments, these establishments got embarrassed, and some of them began to fail in being able to redeem their issues with notes of other banks. Several throughout the state and in the city became bankrupt in the most fraudulent manner. The people were roused, and made a run upon them. One morning the run upon the Miami Exporting Company's Bank was so great that their funds also run short. Now, although their notes bore to be payable in specie, the people only demanded the notes of other banks in which they had a little more confidence. However, they stopped about ten o'clock in the morning, and a shout ran through the crowd to mob them. Immediately the window-frames were smashed, the doors broken, and the establishment completely gutted;—counters, desks, books, papers, money, &c., being promiscuously hurled to the street, amidst the shouts and execrations of the mob.

When I got to the scene of action, which was at the corners of Main and Third Street, a party of sixteen or eighteen soldiers had taken possession of the ransacked building. The mayor and the marshal of the city attempted to address the mob, but in vain, for they could not be heard. The marshal, a bold, active man, was on horseback, riding through the streets, calling upon all good citizens to disperse, but few such were to be found. They then tried a *ruse;*—they rung the city bells to the startling and well-known tune of 'Fire,' but this also failed. The firemen and many of the citizens, with the involuntary movement of well-trained soldiers, started at the word of command, and began to run to their stations.

At this time I was standing on the steps in front of the Old United States' Bank, which was crowded with spectators looking down upon the scene, when I observed one of those little incidents that have turned the fate of greater field days than this. As the firemen and others were running past, just opposite to where we stood, a fellow got up on a cask or box, at one of the shop doors, where he stood conspicuous, with his thumb at his nose, and his fingers stretched out, thereby intimating, in his way, that a deceit was about to be practised on them. The people 'smelled a rat,' and immediately returned to the work of demolition in greatly-increased numbers, and apparently more exasperated, both at the cheat practised on them, and at the sight of the soldiers. They stood at bay for some minutes, moving a little backwards and forwards, evidently preparing for a struggle. The troops had their bayonets fixed and their muskets levelled. There was not more than ten yards between them. The crowd began to throw brick-bats. Two or three of the company fired. The crowd then came forward like a wave of the sea; the company fired a volley, and several of the rioters fell wounded. Such a shout was then raised, all along the crowded streets, and from the spectators on the tops of the houses, as I never heard before; for I had never seen the 'sovereign people' in a rage till now.

By the time the smoke and dust cleared away, and the astonishment of the moment past, there was not a feather of the soldiers' caps to be seen. The authorities ordered them to fall back to the mayor's office, which was immediately in the rear. This was a wise movement; for, I think, if they had remained another five minutes it would have been doubtful if any of them would have 'chewed their cud' over their pork that night. I believe the mayor had strong doubts whether he had any legal right to shoot the citizens on such an occasion; and no more soldiers appeared that day. It is true, all the *companies* were ordered out, but they paid no attention to this order; in fact, the greater part of them had not time, for they were busy, in the mob, helping to wind up the affairs of the banks; and this they did, effectually, before night.

After this, the mob had complete possession of the city, and the *run* upon the banks continued; but they gave them fair-play. As long as they were able to redeem their notes they allowed them to go on, but the moment the funds run short, smash went the windows and doors; and the work of destruction commenced. The bankers fled for their lives. In this way they demolished the inside of five of these "shinplaster manufactories," as they called them, before night.

There were a great number of special constables sworn in, and they came out about two o'clock, each with a handkerchief tied round his hat to distinguish them. They threw themselves in lines across the streets leading to the mobbed parts of the city, allowing every body to pass away from, but none towards, the disturbed districts; but it would not do. The people broke through; and I do not think the constables cared much. The sympathies of the most respectable citizens were with the people; and I observed many of them, in the streets, rubbing their hands with glee, and laughing, as one after another of these swindling establishments were turned inside out. The mayor was even suspected of not doing all he could, and was tried for it afterwards, but acquitted.

The mob went to work very deliberately, and, after they had everything their own way, with good humour. I was pleased with the spirit of 'fair-play' shown to the Planters' and Mechanics' Banks, which were thought to be weak. The cry to pull them down was frequently raised, but a number of the active rioters defended the premises stoutly, and they continued, through the day, to redeem their notes. The run upon them was tremendous, but they stood out the storm; and, at night, posted bills, stating that they would open next morning an hour before the usual time.

There were several of those engaged in the riot apprehended through-out the day; some of them with considerable sums of money on them. Everybody had plenty of money that day, such as it was. The very child-ren were running about with handfuls of dollar bills; several of which fell to my share; and I have them yet as trophies, and an evidence of the mode of regulating the currency in the 'Queen City of the West.' There were several other banks in the city, respectable establishments, in which there was plenty of good money and specie, but the mob never made the slightest move towards them.

These are examples enough, to give some idea of how the Americans execute judgment when they take the law into their own hands. There was one case more in which I nearly got into the hands of Judge Lynch.

In my passage out from Liverpool to Charleston, in the barque 'Harriet and Jessie,' of Charleston, Captain M'Kown, the captain and I had many arguments about slavery. He held that the negroes did not belong to the same species of human beings as white men. I combatted this argument; and held out against the assumed right of any class of men holding other in bondage. Although we differed in opinion on this and some other things, we got along very pleasantly; but the morning after our arrival in Charleston, when he went ashore to the custom-house, he reported me as a *rank Scottish abolitionist,* and as such I was entered in their books. There was an excitement immediately. The authorities and mob were after me, but, fortunately, I had left early that morning in the steamer 'Beaufort District,' for Beaufort, in happy ignorance of the risk I ran; for if they had caught me there, I would have been tarred and feathered, at the very least; and any very rough treatment, or exposure, in my then delicate state of health would, in all probability, have ended my days. Some of my brothers' friends, who were aware of the circum-stances under which I came to the country, endeavoured to allay the excitement. The captain disappeared, and could not be found for two days. After diligent search by the owners of the vessel, he was found, and, on further examination, retracted his report, and my name, as an abolitionist, was deleted from the custom-house books. I have not the vanity to suppose they thought me the celebrated George Thompson [the English abolitionist, who came to the United States in the 1830's]; but still I do not think Thomson is a favourite name there.

The principal owner of the vessel, a highly-respectable gentleman in Charleston, did everything in his power to place the circumstance in its proper light; and to him I am under great obligations. I do not know whether to call the captain a fool or a rascal: he was probably both. However, he left the vessel, and Captain O'Conner now commands her.

I was afterwards in Charleston, and lived at the Planters' Hotel, where I entered my name in the books of arrival, as is usual, and the country to which I belonged, but received no molestation whatever.

I probably would not have taken notice of this circumstance, if it had not been to warn others, travelling in slave states, to be extremely guarded in their expressions upon the subject of slavery. There is an officer in every town, whose duty it is to look after all strangers; and the summary mode of treating suspected persons is a very cogent reason for carefulness.

The Sad Lot of Irish Laborers

Tyrone Power

One of the greatest works now in progress here, is the canal planned to connect Lac Pontchartrain with the city [New Orleans]. In the month of February it was completed to within three miles of the lake; and as it was a pleasant ride to the point where the digging was in progress, I two or three times visited the scene, after its bearings had been explained by the two intelligent persons under whose guidance I first penetrated the swamp.

I only wish that the wise men at home who coolly charge the present condition of Ireland upon the inherent laziness of her population, could be transported to this spot, to look upon the hundreds of fine fellows labouring here beneath a sun that at this winter season was at times insufferably fierce, and amidst a pestilential swamp whose exhalations were fœtid to a degree scarcely endurable even for a few moments; wading amongst stumps of trees, mid-deep in black mud, clearing the spaces pumped out by powerful steam-engines; wheeling, digging, hewing, or bearing burdens it made one's shoulders ache to look upon; exposed meantime to every change of temperature, in log-huts, laid down in the very swamp, on a foundation of newly-felled trees, having the water lying stagnant between the floor-logs, whose interstices, together with those of the side-walls, are open, pervious alike to sun or wind, or snow. Here they subsist on the coarsest fare, holding life on a tenure as uncertain as does the leader of a forlorn hope; excluded from all the advantages of civilization; often at the mercy of a hard contractor, who wrings his profits from their blood; and all this for a pittance that merely enables them to exist, with little power to save, or a hope beyond the continuance of the like exertion.

Such are the labourers I have seen here, and have still found them civil and courteous, with a ready greeting for the stranger inquiring into

Tyrone Power, Impressions of America during the Years 1833, 1834 and 1835 (London, 1836), II, pp. 238-245.

their condition, and a quick jest on their own equipment, which is frequently, it must be admitted, of a whimsical kind.

Here too were many poor women with their husbands; and when I
contemplated their wasted forms and haggard sickly looks, together with
the close swamp whose stagnant air they were doomed to breathe, whose
aspect changeless and deathlike alone met their eyes, and fancied them,
in some hour of leisure, calling to memory the green valley and the pure
river, or the rocky glen and sparkling brook of their distant home, with
all the warmth of colouring the imaginative spirit of the Irish peasant
can so well supply, my heart has swelled and my eyes have filled with
tears.

I cannot hope to inspire the reader with my feelings upon a mere
sketch like this; but if I could set the scene of these poor labourers' exile
fairly forth, with all the sad accompaniments detailed; could I show the
course of the hardy, healthy pair, just landed, to seek fortune on these
long-sighed-for shores, with spirits newly lifted by hope and brighter
prospects from the apathy into which compulsory idleness and consequent recklessness had reduced them at home; and then paint the spirit-
sinking felt on a first view of the scene of their future labour,—paint the
wild revel designed to drown remembrance, and give heart to the new-
comers; describe the nature of the toil where exertion is taxed to the
uttermost, and the weary frame stimulated by the worst alcohol, supplied
by the contractor, at a cheap rate for the purpose of exciting a rivalry
of exertion amongst these simple men.

Next comes disease, either a sweeping pestilence that deals, wholesale
on its victims, or else a gradual sinking of mind and body; finally, the
abode in the hospital, if any comrade is interested enough for the sufferer
to bear him to it; else, the solitary log-hut and quicker death. Could
these things with their true colours be set forth in detail before the veriest
grinder of the poor that ever drove the peasant to curse and quit the
soil of his birth, he would cover his eyes from the light of heaven, and
feel that he yet possessed a heart and human sympathy.

At such works all over this continent the Irish are the labourers chiefly
employed, and the mortality amongst them is enormous,—a mortality I
feel certain might be vastly lessened by a little consideration being given
to their condition by those who employ them. At present they are, where
I have seen them working here, worse lodged than the cattle of the field;
in fact, the only thought bestowed upon them appears to be, by what
expedient the greatest quantity of labour may be extracted from them
at the cheapest rate to the contractor. I think, however, that a better
spirit is in progress amongst the companies requiring this class of labourers; in fact it becomes necessary this should be so, since, prolific as is
the country from whence they are drawn, the supply would in a little

time cease to keep pace with the demand, and slave labour cannot be substituted to any extent, being much too expensive; a good slave costs at this time two hundred pounds sterling, and to have a thousand such swept off a line of canal in one season, would call for prompt consideration.

Independent of interest, Christian charity and justice should alike suggest that the labourers ought to be provided with decent quarters, that sufficient medical aid should always be at hand, and above all, that the brutalizing, accursed practice of extorting extra labour by the stimulus of corn spirit should be wholly forbidden.

Let it be remembered that, although rude and ignorant, these men are not insensible to good impressions, or incapable of distinguishing between a kindly and paternal care of their well-doing, and the mercenary cold-blooded bargain which exacts the last scruple of flesh it has paid for.

I have inquired much, and have heard many worthy, well-informed men comment upon this subject, and feelingly regret the existing system; but it is only by the close supervision of the Directors of Public Works that this crying evil can be effectively checked, and the condition and character of the labourer improved.

At present the priest is the only stay and comfort of these men; the occasional presence of the minister of God alone reminds them that they are not forgotten of their kind: and but for this interference, they would grow in a short time wholly abandoned and become uncontrollable; unfortunately of these men, who conscientiously fulfill their holy functions, there are but too few,—the climate, and fatigue soon incapacitates all but the very robust. Those who follow the ministry of God in the swamp and in the forest must have cast the pride of flesh indeed out from them, since they brave the martyr's fate without a martyr's triumph.

If a few of our goodly Cheltenham Parsons, the non-resident gentlemen, who so laudably desire to uphold their church, were to come here, they would find ample employment for their leisure, and might make hosts of converts; for courage and kindliness of heart are irresistible in appeal; and it is on these foundations, whether amongst the bogs and mountains of Ireland, or in the wilderness of America, that the Catholic priest of our days has built the unimpeachable influence he exercises over his people.

The gloomy picture of the labourer's condition, which my mention of this canal has drawn from me, may by some be considered overcharged; but I protest I have, on the contrary, withheld details of suffering from heat, and cold, and sickness, which my heart at this moment aches when I recall.

To return to the canal. It in all probability will never be used for the purpose designed, even when completed; it was, in fact, the bonus proffered to the legislature by a bank which required a certain charter; it will, at least, answer the purpose of a great drain, and so far must prove of infinite local importance, the more especially since it is in contemplation to redeem the whole of the surrounding swamp,—a measure that, if effectually carried out, will probably render New Orleans as healthy as any city south of the Potomac.

America as a Land of Opportunity for Irishmen

Maunsel White

New Orleans, Feb. 17, 1848

To Captain Wm. V. Graves
Shannon Vale, Clanakilty
County Cork

My dear Captain,

I have this day written too your cousin S. K. Graves, Liverpool send-ing him thirty Bales Cotton to sell & to send the proceeds of to Robert Shaw to pay off all incumbrance of Jockey Hall. I have in order to interest him in this matter (which I believe was unnecessary) mentioned all the circumstances which [I] hope you will pardon me doing, which I would not have done to a stranger but as I believe him a good hearted & gen-erous man he would not diminish by charges the proceeds of the Cotton which I trust will be enough to meet the payment of all your patrimony ows [sic]—I hope ere this the amount will be ascertained & I have written to Shaw if it was not enough to draw upon me for the balance.

I wrote to you previous to my leaving the plantation [*Deer Range*] some six weeks since. I am now here attending the session of the legis-lature in capacity of senator which I find an irksome business & for which I have very little taste. Yet I am compelled to enter pretty deeply into politics from the sincere desire I have to see my Friend General Taylor Elected president of the U. S. Some how or other my destiny has thrown me among the greatest men which we have had in this country for nearly half a Century. Gen. Jackson until the day of his death was my most intimate Friend I hold the last letter he ever wrote but one before his death and another written a little before, which was evidently written for my children & posterity. I refer to them with some pride, merely to

Maunsel White Letters, Southern Collection, University of North Carolina.

shew [*sic*] that no one no matter how humble by good conduct and the aid of an almighty providence may raise himself to consideration and respect from the highest, those things teach your children—with a good Business Education, good conduct & sterling Integrity no one need fear for the Future. Excuse I pray you this digression from the business I set down to write you about. & I promise you I shall not again intrude myself on your consideration in this way—do let me hear from you when you get all these matters settled to your liking.

June 23, 1849
Deer Range

To J Edwards Esq.

It gives me great pleasure to introduce to your acquaintance the bearer my very particular Friend. the Honorable, John K Elgee of [undecipherable] late Judge of the U. States District Court for the Western District of La & who after resigning that high & honorable office conferred upon him by the President of the U. States for real merit & brilliant Talents, now after twenty years of service Visits his native Country [Ireland], proving what I have frequently maintained to you, that it is in this free country men of high mental attainments, correct principles, [   ] Industry & perseverance arrive at & obtain the highest Honors in the gift of the people who know how to reward merit & discover where it lies, but the Honble Judge is not a solitary instance, it has occurred to hundreds of our countrymen, who nobly wear their Honors—May I claim for him at your hands a kind reception & Introduction to our relatives, he can tell you all about me & give you the best advice what to do with your youngest son, who you intend for the Legal profession

The Piny Woods: Home of the Poor Whites

David Hunter Strother

Nearly the whole of the eastern part of North Carolina is covered with pine forests, extending from the swampy country bordering the sea-board as far back as Raleigh, the capital of the State. This section is sparsely populated, but little improved, and although it furnishes the greater portion of all the resinous matter used in ship-building in the United States, it has hitherto been little known. It is called by the Carolinians "The Piny Woods," and we must prepare to follow our persevering traveler, Porte Crayon, in his wanderings through this primitive and lonely region.

At Plymouth we find him seated on the porch, at Enoch Jones's Hotel, looking as lazy and listless as if he were a citizen of the place. Plymouth, we believe, is the county town of Washington, situated on the opposite side of the Sound from Edenton, a short distance up the Roanoke, and contains a thousand or twelve hundred inhabitants.

It is the successful commercial rival of Edenton, and plumes itself on its business activity, not without reason, for Crayon reports that its wharves were crowded with six or seven sloops; and during the day he staid there, no less than three vessels loaded with lumber hauled up to take in grog and then passed on their way. The shores of the Roanoke in the vicinity are low and swampy, and although the village is not unpleasing to the eye, it contains nothing of sufficient interest to detain the traveler long. How Porte Crayon came to remain here for thirty-six hours, happened in this wise. . . .

Hurrying on his clothes, and slinging his knapsack, our hero hastened to the place of rendezvous on the banks of the river [to go to Roanoke Island]. He arrived a little before the appointed hour, and finding no one to meet him, shouted, called, and signaled in vain, until the time

Harper's Monthly Magazine, XIV (May, 1857), pp. 741-746.

was past. He then visited the half dozen tenantless sloops lying at the wharves, thinking it possible that the *Empire* might have changed her position during the night; and, finally, wearied with the fruitless search, he lay down upon a bale of cotton and slept. About sunrise the wharf-master came down, and informed him that the faithless skipper had weighed anchor about midnight, and by this time was probably far out on the Sound. Sloth and philosophy are said to be near akin, but it required the assistance of both to enable Crayon to keep cool on the reception of this intelligence. To his honor be it said, that he succeeded in his efforts. He only shrugged his shoulders, and mildly expressed a hope that the sloop with her commander might sink to the bottom of the sea, then, feeling amiable as Uncle Toby, returned to the hotel.

The attempt to get off by this line having proved a failure, Crayon ascertained that the stage-coach for Washington started early on the following morning. Here was a chance, but what was he to do in the mean time. The loungers on the tavern porch spent the morning in discussing the merits of a dispute between Williamston, a little place up the Roanoke, and the proprietors of the steamboat line. The Williamston-ians desired the extension of the line to their city. The boats thought it wouldn't pay; hence the controversy. As there was not much in the subject, it died out about the heat of the day, and then followed a dead calm. This was disturbed at intervals by a dogfight; a negro brat tumbling down the steps; and, finally, about twelve o'clock, by a drunken fellow who called for "licker." The request was negatived. Boosey obstreperously insisted. The landlord stood firm, and there was great hope of a row. But just at the crisis of the dispute, Boosey basely yielded and retired—so completely does drunkenness undermine a man's high moral nature.

After dinner, Crayon repaired to the wharf and sat upon the cotton bales again, from whence he watched two boys fishing. They caught nothing, and our hero sunk to sleep.

Toward evening the tavern porch got more lively. Some one had set a negro boy to trying the speed of a trotter up and down the level street, and this entertainment collected all the available idlers and horse-fanciers in the vicinity.

"That hoss," said the stage-driver, addressing himself to Mr. Crayon, "that hoss reminds me of a hoss that old Major Bulbonus used to drive in that old stick gig of his'n. I see him once," continued the narrator, "atwixt G—— and E——, where I druv a coach for a while, a-coming up through the Piny Woods, in sich a pickle as I never see a man before or sence. At first I thought it was one of these steam engines tearing along the road by itself, but as he come alongside I see it was the Major in his gig. His skin was pretty full, he was driving like thunder, and his gig all afire. 'Halloo, Major,' says I, 'stop!' But he only cussed me black and blue. Then one of the passengers cried out, 'Halloo, old fellow, whar did you come from?' 'From hell,' says he, giving his hoss the whip. 'Well, I should have thought so from appearances,' said the passenger. By this time the Major was out of sight, leaving a streak of smoke behind him, perhaps a quarter of a mile long. No doubt the gig caught fire from a cigar, for he was much in the habit of smoking as he traveled."

"And what became of him?"

"Why, they say, in passing through the swamp near his house, the wheel struck a cypress-knee and flung him out into the water. The horse run home with the gig in a blaze and made straight for the barn-yard. By good luck the gate was shut, or he might have set the whole premises on fire. They say the Major didn't get drunk for well-nigh a month arterward."

From Plymouth to Washington the road is generally good, and the coaches make very fair speed. Nevertheless, the leisurely habits of the people during the necessary stoppages for watering and changing teams, give ample time to note the peculiarities of the country. Its features are monotonous in the extreme, varied only by alternate swamp and piny woods; the former bordering the water-courses, the latter covering the sandy ridges between.

These forests are of the long-leafed pine, the *Pinus palustris* of the Southern States. From them is gathered one of the great staples of North Carolina—the turpentine. And although this product and its derivatives are, in our country, almost in as common use as bread and meat, very little is known of the manner of procuring them. We will therefore endeavor to describe it accurately, relying upon such sketches and observations as Crayon was enabled to make during his tour.

These trees at maturity are seventy or eighty feet high, and their trunks eighteen or twenty inches in diameter near the base. They grow close together, very straight, and without branches to two-thirds of their height. Overhead, their interlocking crowns form a continuous shady canopy; while beneath, the ground is covered with a thick, yellow matting of pinestraw, clean, dry, level, and unbroken by undergrowth. The privilege of tapping the trees is generally farmed out by the landowner, at a stated price per thousand, say from twenty to thirty dollars. Under this privilege the laborer commences his operations. During the winter he chops deep notches in the base of the tree, a few inches from the ground, and slanting inward. Above, to the height of two or three feet, the surface is scarified by chipping off the bark and outer wood. From this surface the resinous sap begins to flow about the middle of March, at first very slowly, but more rapidly during the heat of summer, and slowly again as winter approaches. The liquid turpentine runs into the notches, or boxes, as they are technically called, each holding from a quart to half a gallon. This, as it gathers, is dipped out with a wooden spoon, barreled, and carried to market, where it commands the highest price. That which oozes out and hardens upon the scarified surface of the tree is scraped down with an iron instrument into a sort of hod, and is sold at an inferior price. Every year the process of scarifying is carried two or three feet higher up the trunk, until it reaches the height of twelve or fifteen feet—as high as a man can conveniently reach with his long-handled cutter. When this ceases to yield, the same process is commenced on the opposite side of the trunk. An average yield is about twenty-five barrels of turpentine from a thousand trees, and it is estimated that one man will dip ten thousand boxes.

The produce is carried to market on a sort of dray or cart which holds but two barrels, consequently the barrels are always seen setting about in the woods in couples. The trees at length die under these repeated operations. They are then felled, split into small sticks, and burned for tar. The dead trees are preferred for this purpose, because when life ceases the resinous matter concentrates in the interior layers of the wood. In building a tar-kiln a small circular mound of earth is first raised, declining from the circumference to the centre, where a cavity is formed, communication by a conduit with a shallow ditch surrounding the mound. Upon this foundation the split sticks are stacked to the height of ten to twelve feet.

The stack is then covered with earth as in making charcoal, and the fire applied through an opening in the top. As this continues to burn with a smouldering heat, the wood is charred, and the tar flows into the cavity in the centre, and thence by the conduit into the ditch, or into vessels sunk to receive it.

In a country endowed by nature with such unlimited plantations, yielding their valuable products for so small an amount of labor, one might expect to see some signs of wealth and prosperity; yet here all appearances seem to indicate the reverse. Human habitations are few and far between; and when found, are but little better in appearance than the huts of our Western borders. An accurate observer, however, may see about the dwellings in the Piny Woods many little peculiarities indicative of an older civilization. They almost always have fruit trees about them, and a trellis supporting an extensive scuppernong grapevine. There are besides four characteristic indispensables to every cottage: a well-sweep with a cypress-knee bucket, in shape and size like a slouched hat; a group of slim fodder-stacks, made of corn blades tied to high stakes; three sweet potato hills, carefully protected, and a tall pole hung with empty gourds to entertain the martins. This unfailing care to provide for the comfort of these social chattering little sojourners impresses the stranger favorably in regard to the inhabitants of this region, and if circumstances should throw him upon their simple hospitality he will not be disappointed.

After traveling some twelve miles by the coach Crayon resolved to see more of the country than could conveniently be viewed from his seat beside the driver; consequently he shouldered his knapsack and thenceforth pursued his journey on foot. Turning from the main road into the first bypath that presented itself, he was soon wandering ad libitum among the turpentine-trees. It is impossible to resist the feeling of loneliness that creeps over one on entering these silent forests, or to repress a sentiment of superstitious dread as you glance through the somber many-columned aisles, stretching away on every side in interminable perspective. When the trees have been recently blazed, the square-cut markings, white on the black trunks, strikingly resemble marble grave-stones, and the traveler may imagine himself in a vast cemetery. In the older workings, if he should pass near the hour of twilight, he may see misty white, horned ghosts, starting and staring from every tree—silence and monotony, like two evil spirits following every where, suggesting uncouth and dreary fancies.

The Crackers

Henry Benjamin Whipple

December 1, 1843, Today we returned to St. Marys (Georgia) and right glad was I to get back, altho' such trips are very conducive to health. Mr. Du B has invited me to accompany him on a bear hunt in a few days and I think I shall go. Today we have another yellow day. I am very much amused with the southern peculiarities of expression. A southerner says for "I think" "I reckon," for "sun rise" "sun up," for "sun set" "sun down," for "carry" "tote," "right smart chance" for "a good opportunity," for "a great many," "a heap." "Ugly" is used entirely to express homeliness & there are thousands of these peculiar expressions which we notice each day. But the negro race have many more than any race I have ever seen. They abound in queer phrases and comical blunders—but of all the men I have ever seen a plantation hand beats all for clipping his words & using odd sayings. For a long time it was impossible for me to understand a word of what they said—and their singing was as unintelligible. It is a peculiar kind of idiom peculiar to themselves. Their fondness for high flown comparisons and large sounding words lead them into the most egregious and laughable blunders. The cracker population have a drawling way of speaking and use a great many words much like the backwoods population of North Carolina. It is a crackerism, not a specimen of the English language.

There is no court of appeals in Georgia & of course there is but little certainty of right & justice being properly meted out to those who engage in law. The judge has great power & can exercise a great influence over such men as are found on petit juries. Mrs. Reid told me of an amusing revenge the "crackers" had on her husband by sending him to Congress to get rid of him as judge. Judge Reid was once taken all aback, as the sailors say, after performing the ceremony of marrying two of these crackers, the man ugly enough but the woman beyond all comparison

Lester B. Shippee (ed.,), *Bishop Whipple's Southern Diary* (courtesy of University of Minnesota Press, Minneapolis, 1937), pp. 38-39, 45-46.

for hideousness. Says Judge R "now kiss her, you are one." "After your honor is manners," said the cracker, causing members of the bar present to shout with laughter. The Rev. Mr. Baird related to me a very humorous story of one of these backwoods crackers who received a love letter from his inamorata & the question was how he could learn its contents and not have any one else know it, as he could not read, so he went to one of his neighbors who could read and made an arrangement that he should read it aloud & the cracker should stand behind him and stop his ears so that the reader could not hear it. Mr. Bacon of this place, speaking of some members of the legislature of Georgia, said that they only needed long ears and a tail to have their classification among beasts distinctly marked out. . . .

The Southern Yeoman

Daniel R. Hundley

But you have no Yeomen in the South, my dear Sir? Beg your pardon, our dear Sir, but we have—hosts of them. *I thought you had only poor White Trash?* Yes, we dare say as much—and that the moon is made of green cheese! You have fully as much right or reason to think the one thing as the other. *Do tell, now; want to know?* Is that so, our good friend? do you really desire to learn the truth about this matter? If so, to the extent of our poor ability, we shall endeavor to enlighten you upon a subject, which not one Yankee in ten thousand in the least understands.

Know, then, that the Poor Whites of the South constitute a separate class to themselves; the Southern Yeomen are as distinct from them as the Southern Gentleman is from the Cotton Snob. Certainly the Southern Yeomen are nearly always poor, at least so far as this world's goods are to be taken into the account. As a general thing they own no slaves; and even in case they do, the wealthiest of them rarely possess more than from ten to fifteen. But even when they are slaveholders, they seem to exercise but few of the rights of ownership over their human chattels, making so little distinction between master and man, that their negroes invariably become spoiled, like so many rude children who have been unwisely spared the rod by their foolish guardians. Such negroes are lazy as the day is long, saucy and impertinent, and besides are nearly as useless members of society as the free blacks of the North, or Jamaica, or the Central American States. Indulged from their infancy, never receiving a stripe unless some one of their young masters is stout enough to give them a *lamming* in a regular fisticuffs fight, and in all things treated more like equals than slaves, it is certainly no cause of wonder that they impudently call their masters by their proper names, and, when permitted, address all other white persons in the same ill-bred and familiar manner. Indeed, Senator Seward himself could not demand any greater show of equality, than what

Daniel R. Hundley, *Social Relations in Our Southern States* (New York, 1860), pp. 193-220.

is often exhibited by the Yeomen of the South in the treatment of their negroes; ...

Now it is chiefly owing, as we conceive, to this universal prejudice
against color in the North, that the citizens of the Free States will insist
free labor is degraded by the existence of African slavery, and that the
Poor Whites of the South because thereof prefer to starve rather than to
labor side by side with slaves. Because they themselves will not consent
to work on a level with the free negroes in their own midst, of course (such
is their reasoning) any poor Southerner would feel degraded to labor in
company with enslaved persons possessing the same objectionable color.
Capital logicians! Now, Sirs, what are the facts? Would you believe the
declaration, that honest Southern Yeomen (these are the industrious poor
whites of the South) always work side by side with their own human
chattels in the fields, in the forests, and every where else? Nothing, we
assure you, is more common. No man can travel a day through any thickly-
settled portion of the South, but he will come up with some sturdy yeoman
and his sons working in company of their negroes; sometimes their own
property, at other times hirelings whom they have employed by the month
or year. In portions of Western Virginia, particularly in the districts settled
by the Pennsylvania Dutch, such spectacles are to be witnessed on almost
every other farm. Passing by their fields of rich clover, nearly waist-high,
and blushing as red in a rich profusion of purple blooms as the cheeks of
the plump country maiden who sits singing and knitting under the big
apple-tree in front of the neat farmhouse, you can not fail of being amused
to observe the lazy deliberation with which the broad-shouldered farm-
boys, and their equally broad-shouldered sooty companions, lay down
their hoes or scythes to gaze at a stranger—gazing long and steadfastly,
with hanging lip and open mouth, until you are hidden from their sight by
a turn in the green lane, when they all simultaneously burst out a laughing,
(at what, Heaven knows!) but in so hearty and boisterous a manner as to
wake up the dozing cattle, whose sleek fat sides are scarcely visible about
in spots among the clover-leaves, refulgent and glistening in the shimmer-
ing rays of the glorious summer sun. So, too, if you leave Virginia and pass
down into the Old North State—the State so famous for its tar, pitch, and
turpentine—you will hear the axe of master and man falling with alternate
strokes in the depth of the whispering forests of dark evergreens, as with
redoubled blows they attack the lofty pines, felling them to the ground for
lumber, or simply barking them for their resinous sap. Here you will frequently see black and white, slave and freeman, camping out together, living sometimes in the same tent or temporary pine-pole cabin; drinking, the
darkies always after mas'r, out of the same tin dipper or long-handled
gourd their home-distilled apple-brandy; dining on the same homely but
substantial fare, and sharing one bed in common, *videlicet,* the *cabin floor.*

Again, should you go among the hardy yeomanry of Tennessee, Kentucky, or Missouri, whenever or wherever they own slaves (which in these States is not often the case) you will invariably see the negroes and their masters ploughing side by side in the fields; or bared to the waist, and with old-fashioned scythe vieing with one another who can cut down the broadest swath of yellow wheat, or of the waving timothy; or bearing the tall stalks of maize and packing them into the stout-built barn, with ear and fodder on, ready for the winter's husking. And when the long winter evenings have come, you will see blacks and whites sing, and shout, and husk in company, to the music of Ole Virginny reels played on a greasy fiddle by some aged Uncle Edward, whose frosty pow proclaims that he is no longer fit for any more active duty, and whose long skinny fingers are only useful now to put life and mettle into the fingers of the younger huskers, by the help of de fiddle and de bow.

And yet, notwithstanding the Southern Yeoman allows his slaves so much freedom of speech and action, is not offended when they call him familiarly by his Christian name, and hardly makes them work enough to earn their salt, still he is very proud of being a slaveholder; and when he is not such, his greatest ambition is to make money enough to buy a negro. We recall a very amusing anecdote illustrative of this ambition of the Southern Yeoman.

A man named Horne, who was a bachelor, had entered some land at government price, or at all events at a very small sum. In a few years his land increased so in value that he sold out at an enormous profit, taking as part payment one negro man, whom we will call Jeff. The next morning after the bargain had been closed, the negro was awakened quite early by hearing his new master bawling at the top of his voice:

"Jeff! you, Jeff! Come here, you big black nigger, you!"

"Bres God, Mas'r, what's de marter?" said Jeff, rushing *sans culotte* into his master's room, and nearly out of breath with alarm.

"O nuthin," replied Horne dryly, "*I only wanted to see how 'twould sound jist—that's all!*"

In his origin, aside from the German settlers in Western Virginia, the Southern Yeoman is almost purely English. He nearly always bears some good old Anglo-Saxon name, and will tell you, if interrogated about his ancestors, that "grandfather so and so came over from the Old Country"— by which familiar and endearing phrase he always designates Great Britain. He is thorough English in fact, in both physical heartiness and dogged perseverance. Very seldom is he troubled with dyspepsia, or melancholy, or discontent with his humble lot—evils which in most cases have their origin in a disordered stomach. Just so rarely, too, will you ever meet a Southern Yeoman who has learned to fear mortal man, or who would under any circumstances humiliate himself to curry favor with the rich or those in authority. He always possesses a manly independence of character, and though not so impetuous as the gentry of the South usually are, still, in the midst of the dangers and carnage of the battlefield, and in the thickest of the fray, his eye never quails; but with steady tramp and unflinching nerve he marches right on to where duty and honor call, and with unblanched cheek meets death face to face. His wounds, like the scars of the old Roman, themselves bespeak his praise, for they are ever received from the front and never from behind.

The usual weapon of the Southern Yeoman is the deadly rifle—even in his sports—and this he handles with such skill as few possess, even in America. He likes the quick sharp report which announces in a clear tongue when the leaden messenger is *sent home;* and affects to despise the rattling fowling piece, the peculiar sporting gun of the Southern Gentleman. With his rifle the Yeoman shoots squirrels, ducks, turkeys, deer, bear, buffalo, and whatever else he pleases. The best riflemen are found in Georgia, Mississippi, Tennessee, and Kentucky—*the* best, perhaps, in the last-named brave and chivalrous Commonwealth. Herein turkey-shooting is practised by all classes, but chiefly by the yeomen. A live turkey is securely fastened to a stake at the distance of one hundred paces, and you pay five or ten cents for the privilege of each shot; if you hit the fowl in the head the carcass is yours, but any other *hit* is considered *foul,* and so passes for nothing. This is the kind of school in which were trained the hunting-shirt heroes of King's Mountain, and those unerring riflemen who, at the memorable battle of New-Orleans, made such havoc in the ranks of Packenham's veterans. So also were trained those brave defenders of Texan independence—Crockett, Travis, and their compeers, who buried themselves beneath the countless heaps of Mexicans slain at the heroic defense of the Alamo. And it was because of a similar schooling that Col. Jeff. Davis was enabled to say to the retreating Indianians at the battle of Buena Vista, pointing proudly to the gallant yeomanry of Mississippi: "Stay, and re-form behind that wall!" For well the brave Colonel knew the rifles in the hands of his favorite regiment would soon with their iron hail beat down the advancing foe, and cause them to rush back in disorderly rout to their tents and entrenchments. Indeed, take them all in all, and we doubt if the world can produce a more reliable citizen soldiery than the yeomanry of our Southern States. They only require the right sort of leaders—officers under whom they are willing to fight, and in whose mettle and abilities they have perfect confidence. General Taylor was such a man, and in this regard no American General of late years has been his peer. Southern born himself, and Southern bred, plain and unostentatious in his manners, and at all times cool and determined in the hour of danger; his soldiers loved the *man,* while they respected and trusted the *general.* Noble old Soldier! no true heart can fail to regret, that the exigencies of politics forced you to lay aside the sword for our republican sceptre, and thus with the weighty cares and perplexities of a station which you never were fitted to adorn, too soon consigned you to the grave and deprived the Union of one of her most able and patriotic defenders. Green be the turf above you, honest Roman, and may your successors in office learn to emulate your virtues!

The Southern Yeoman much resembles in his speech, religious opinions, household arrangements, indoor sports, and family traditions, the middle class farmers of the Northern States. He is fully as intelligent as the latter, and is on the whole much better versed in the lore of politics and the provisions of our Federal and State Constitutions. This is chiefly owing to the public barbecues, court-house-day gatherings, and other holiday occasions, which are more numerous in the South than in the North, and in the former are nearly always devoted in part to political discussions of one kind or another. Heard from the lips of their neighbors and friends, and having the matter impressed upon their minds by the presentation of both sides of every disputed question at the same time, it is not strange that poor men in the South should possess a more comprehensive knowledge of the fundamental principles of our artificial and complex system of government, or should retain a clearer perception of the respective merits of every leading political issue, than if they derived their information solely from books or newspapers; which always furnish but one view of the matter in dispute, and which they must painfully peruse after a long day of toil, being more exercised meanwhile (aside from the drawback of physical weariness) in laboring to interpret the meaning of the "dictionary words," than in attempting to follow the facts or the argument of the writer, be he never so lucid and perspicuous.

We know a pretty general belief prevails throughout the entire North, and in Europe as well, (owing to the misrepresentations of our patriotic book-makers of the Free States,) that the great mass of the Southern people are more ignorant than the mass of Northern laborers; and, although this opinion is no sounder than the baseless fabric of a vision, there is yet a plausible excuse at least to be urged on behalf of those citizens of the North who entertain it. For the North, taken as a whole, is an inventive and manufacturing community, and her citizens, in consequence, love to agglomerate in towns, villages, etc. etc. Hence, they entertain a very foolish prejudice against the country, and every thing almost that pertains to country life; while such a personage as a country gentleman proper, is unknown from Maine to Oregon, and to speak of "our country cousins" as very annoying and troublesome, is a standing witticism in every Free State. But the South is almost exclusively agricultural, and, of course, the great mass of her citizens fall under the bann of the cockney prejudices of the trades-people of the North, equally with their own country cousins from Down East, or the sun-embrowned Hoosiers from the West. Now, we do not pretend to claim that the yeomen of the South are as intelligent or well-instructed about a great many things, as the mechanics, artisans, small shopkeepers, and others, who in a great measure constitute the population of the Northern towns; but we do insist, from a pretty extensive acquaintance with the peculiarities and characteristics of both, that the Southern Yeoman is the peer in every respect of the small farmers in the Free States, as well as their superior in a great many. For, as has already been shown, he is certainly better informed than the latter about the political history of the country; is more accustomed to the use of fire-arms, particularly the rifle; and (which is no small recommendation) he has a better appreciation of good liquors, for, instead of swallowing the vile stuff sent forth from Cincinnati and other places in the shape of mean whisky, the Southern yeoman usually confines himself to home-brewed ale, or native apple-jack, or home-distilled peach brandy, all of which drinks are said to be both wholesome and harmless, if taken in moderation.

From the yeomanry usually springs the overseer class—a very useful and important class of persons in the South; very much-abused and slandered though they always have been, owing to the drunken habits, libertinism, coarse brutalities, and general bad conduct of many of their number. But there are to be found among them men of sterling worth and incorruptible integrity—good citizens, intelligent managers, kind disciplinarians, and even sometimes they evince gentlemanly instincts, though but little polished in speech or manners.

We think the reading public, Southern as well as Northern, in forming its judgment of overseers, has never sufficiently considered the responsibilities and temptations of their peculiar position. They constitute the Southern police, or patrol, just as every Northern city has its squads of police to protect the property and lives of its citizens from the hands of thieves, burglars, incendiaries, garroters, midnight assassins, and street bullies. The "beat" of each Southern overseer, is the plantation on which he resides; and the collective body of overseers in every neighborhood, constitutes a regularly organized patrol called by the negroes "Paterollers," and upon set times these "paterollers" form a troop and gallop from plantation to plantation during the whole night, arresting and punishing all slaves found off their proper premises without a permit from their master or mistress. But on the whole, the Southern overseer has a much more laborious duty to perform than his brother policeman of any Northern city. The latter has only to look after freemen—in most cases intelligent white men, who entertain some respect for the officers of the law; whereas the Southern overseer has confided to his care the kinky-headed descendants of those pagans who, only a century ago, made no bones of eating one another, and whose kindred yet remaining in Africa still look upon a white missionary stewed with onions and cayenne pepper, or even better perhaps eaten raw and without salt, as the greatest "delicacy of the season." . . .

He must be a very bold man who will deny that the overseers on many Southern plantations, are cruel and unmercifully severe, when permitted to be so by the carelessness or connivance of their employers. Despite all which, however, we are yet prepared to contend, that, compared with the police of all other places, the world over, and taken *en masse,* there is not any where a more respectable and well-behaved patrol than the Southern overseers.

So far as hospitality goes, the Yeomen of the South are not a whit behind the Southern Gentleman, or any other class of gentlemen the world over. And we make this declaration boldly, despite the assertions to the contrary of a certain literary Peripatetic of New-York, who has been in the habit of taking a jaunt through some portions of the South every few years, and afterwards publishing in book-form an account of what he saw and heard. Affecting the utmost candor and impartiality, as well as the very essence and spirit of Truth, this peripatetical maker of books scarcely succeeds in spreading his poppies broad and thick enough, to conceal even from simple eyes the malice which underlies his plausible style . . . [probably Frederick Law Olmsted].

But to return once more to the subject of this chapter. Besides being given to hospitality, although in a very primitive way, as has been shown, the Yeomen of the South are also quite social and gregarious in their instincts, and delight much in having all kinds of frolics and family gatherings during the long winter evenings. On all such occasions, nearly, something serviceable is the ostensible cause of their assembling, though the time is devoted almost wholly to social pleasures: sometimes, 'tis true, there is a wedding, or a birth-day party, or a candy-pulling; but much more frequently it is a corn-husking, or the everlasting quilting—this last being the most frequent and most in favor of all the merrymakings which call the young people together. There is, indeed, nothing to compare to a country quilting for the simple and unaffected happiness which it affords all parties. The old women and old men sit demurely beside the blazing kitchen fire, and frighten one another with long-winded ghost stories; thus leaving the young folks all to themselves in the "big room," wherein is also the quilt-frame, which is either suspended at the corners by ropes attached to the ceiling, or else rests on the tops of four chairs. Around this assemble the young men and the young maidens, robust with honest toil and honestly ruby-cheeked with genuine good health. The former know nothing of your *dolce far niente* or dyspepsia, and the latter are not troubled with crinoline or consumption, but all are merry as larks and happy as it is possible for men and women to be in this lower world. No debts, nor duns, nor panics, nor poverty, nor wealth disturbs their thoughts or mars the joyousness of the hour. Serene as a summer's day, and cloudless as the skies in June, the moments hurry by, as they ply their nimble needles and sing their simple songs, or whisper their tales of love, heedless of the great world and all the thoughtless worldlings who live only to win the smiles of "our best society." Meanwhile the children play hide and seek, in-doors and out, whooping, laughing, and chatting like so many magpies; and, in the snug chimney-corner, Old Bose, the faithful watch-dog, stretches himself out to his full length and doses comfortably in the genial warmth of the fire, in his dreams chasing after imaginary hares, or baying the moon; . . .

In their religious convictions and practices, the Southern Yeomen very much resemble the Middle Classes; are prone to shout at camp-meetings, and to see visions and dream dreams. Although generally moral in their conduct and punctilious in all religious observances, they do yet often entertain many very absurd ideas in regard to Christianity, ideas wholly at variance with any rational interpretation of the Sacred Scriptures; and hence they are led not infrequently, to mistake animal excitement for holy ecstasy, and seem to think, indeed, with the old-time priests of Baal, that God is not to be entreated save with *loud* prayers, and much beating of the breasts, and clapping of the hands, accompanied with audible groans and sighs. For all which, however, their officiating clergy are more to blame than themselves; for they are often ignorant men of the Whang Doodle description, illiterate and dogmatic, and blessed with a nasal twang which would do no discredit to New-England. They very seldom know any thing about their Bibles, but, like the star political priests of the North, seem to exert themselves to ignore all the facts and precepts of the Gospel of Jesus Christ as revealed in the Sacred Scriptures, preferring to teach "for doctrines the commandments of men;" just as did the Levites and Pharisees with their talmudistic theologies in the days of our Saviour. And truly, it has always been to us a singular circumstance why religious people are so easily gulled. . . .

As to the Vital Question of the Day, to make use of the cant phrase so greatly in vogue at the present writing, although not as a class pecuniarily interested in slave property, the Southern Yeomanry are almost unanimously pro-slavery in sentiment. Nor do we see how any honest, thoughtful person can reasonably find fault with them on this account. Only consider their circumstances, negrophilist of the North, and answer truthfully; were you so situated would you dare to advocate emancipation? Were you situated as the Southern Yeomen are—humble in worldly position, patient delvers in the soil, daily earning your bread by the toilsome sweat of your own brows—would you be pleased to see four millions of inferior blacks suddenly raised from a position of vassalage, and placed upon an equality with yourselves? made the sharers of your toil, the equals and associates of your wives and children? You know you would not. Despite your maudlin affectation of sympathy in behalf of the Negro, you are yet inwardly conscious that you heartily despise the sooty African, and that you deny to even the few living in your own midst an equality of rights and immunities with yourselves. You well know that you entertain a natural repugnance to coming in contact with Sambo—a repugnance so great that you slam your church doors in his face, shut him out of the theatres, refuse him a seat in your public conveyances, and, so fearful are you of the contamination of a black man's presence any where, in nine tenths of your States drive him away from the ballot-box, thus making your statute-books even belie your professions of philanthropy. And yet you seek to turn loose upon your white brethren of the South *four millions of these same despised Africans,* congratulating yourselves meanwhile that you would be doing a most disinterested act of benevolence! Shame on your consistency, gentlemen. Judged by your own acts, were you situated as the Southern people are to-day, stronger pro-slavery men than yourselves would not be found in the world. Hence we ask you again, did you occupy the position of the Southern Yeomanry in particular, is there a man in your midst who would favor emancipation?

PART IX

THE AMERICAN CHARACTER AND REGIONAL DIFFERENCES

Travelers from abroad often wrote of Americans as if they had a general character that distinguished them from Europeans. The Cambridge University tutor, Edward S. Abdy, who traveled in the United States in 1833-34, for example, wrote: "The Americans are too anxious to make money and too apt to spoil their children." In the Jacksonian era the Americans were a remarkably mobile people as compared with Europeans, but perhaps not more mobile than they are today. Although only a fraction of the people lived on the cutting edge of the frontier, semifrontier conditions prevailed in many areas remote from the western edge of settlement—the southerners, for example, retained many frontier characteristics and the yeoman farmers of the Northwest and Southwest often lived a rather primitive existence. Moreover, the existence of the frontier affected the mind of the American people even though most of them had never lived on the frontier. Europeans were impressed with the vertical fluidity of American society that was quite different from the rigid class molds of Europe. The Americans, they found, boasted of the superiority of their institutions and their democratic government, the unlimited opportunities of the nation with its vast extent of undeveloped land, and the naturalness and youthful vigor of its people.

Since the society of the United States included both a democracy and an aristocracy there was a great variance in the manners of the upper and lower classes as well as in different regions of America. Mrs. Frances Trollope in her lively but prejudiced book, Domestic Manners of the Americans, *created a stereotype of the crudity of American manners which was bitterly resented in the United States. Most of her observations of Americans were derived from a steamboat trip up the Mississippi in 1827, when she came from England to this country, and her life in Cincinnati where she operated a bazaar until it failed disastrously and she returned in 1831 to England. British visitors in general were critical of American manners, although some Englishmen (such as Sir Charles Lyell) who visited the homes of southern planters were favorably impressed with the naturalness, refinement, and hospitality of the southern upper class.*

The United States was such a large and sprawling country with different belts of climate that a pronounced regionalism was bound to develop.

453

Gradually this regionalism was converted into a virulent sectionalism, beginning with the debates over the Missouri Compromise in 1820 and greatly accentuated by the controversy over nullification, the rise of the abolition movement, and the expansion of slavery into the federal territory acquired as a result of the Mexican War. The differences between the southern and northern states, though real, were exaggerated by political agitators, abolitionists, and fire-eaters until the concept of two different societies in mutual antagonism arose.

The keenest foreign observer of the working of American democracy was the Frenchman Alexis de Tocqueville, who crossed the Atlantic with Gustave de Beaumont in 1831 to study American penitentiaries. De Tocqueville was only twenty-five years old when he visited the United States but he had a philosophical and trenchant mind and a remarkable power of detachment and observation, so that his book Democracy in America *(1835-1840, two volumes) is one of the most important commentaries on American government and society of the Jacksonian period. He made some errors in his analysis of the American government, notably his prediction that the state governments would in the future grow stronger and the national government weaker, and he failed properly to appreciate regional differences in his broad generalizations on American society. At the same time he was remarkably prescient in his predictions that Russia and the United States would become the great world powers of the future and that the Yankee type would eventually dominate American characteristics. His description of New England town government presents one of the success stories of American politics; even Thomas Jefferson at an earlier day had praised the New England town meeting as superior to the southern county system. Perhaps the gravest defect that De Tocqueville found in American politics was the resistless power of the majority, riding roughshod at times over the rights of the minority, and crushing the spirit of free inquiry in religion.*

Jacksonian Innocence

Edward Livingston

Another species of offence is also omitted, [from the penal code of Louisiana] though it figures in every code, from the Mosaic downward, to those of our days, and generally with capital punishments denounced against its commission; yet I have not polluted the pages of the law which I am preparing for you by mentioning it; for several reasons:

First. Because, although it certainly prevailed among most of the ancient nations, and is said to be frequently committed in some of the modern, yet, I think, in all these cases it may be traced to causes and institutions peculiar to the people where it has been known, but which cannot operate here; and that the repugnance, disgust, and even horror, which the very idea inspires, will be a sufficient security that it can never become a prevalent one in our country.

Secondly. Because, as every crime must be defined, the details of such a definition would inflict a lasting wound on the morals of the people. Your criminal code is no longer to be the study of a select few: it is not the design of the framers that it should be exclusively the study even of our own sex; and it is particularly desirable, that it should become a branch of early education for our youth. The shock which such a chapter must give to their pudicity, the familiarity their minds must acquire with the most disgusting images, would, it is firmly believed, be most injurious in its effects: and if there was no other objection, ought to make us pause before we submitted such details to public inspection.

Thirdly. It is an offence necessarily difficult of proof, and must generally be established by the evidence of those who are sufficiently base and corrupt to have participated in the offence. Hence, persons shameless and depraved enough to incur this disgrace, have made it the engine of extortion against the innocent, by threatening them with a denunciation for this crime, and they were generally successful: because, against such an

Edward Livingston, *A System of Penal Law for the State of Louisiana* (courtesy of Vergil Bedsole, Louisiana State University Archivist; Pittsburg, 1833), p. 17.

accusation, it was known that the infamy of the accuser furnished no sure defence.

My last reason for the omission was, that as all our criminal proceedings must be public, a single trial of this nature would do more injury to the morals of the people than the secret, and therefore always uncertain, commission of the offence. I was not a little influenced, also, by reflecting on the probability, that the innocent might suffer, either by malicious combinations of perjured witnesses, in a case so difficult of defence, or by the ready credit that would be given to circumstantial evidence, where direct proof is not easily procured, and where, from the nature of the crime, a prejudice is created by the very accusation.

Social Mores of the Americans

William Thomson

It is generally known that marriages are contracted earlier in life in America than in perhaps any other country—fifteen to eighteen years is a very common age. Many ladies are married even before they arrive at that early age. The girls are good-looking, and free from affectation; in general slight and delicate in their form. They wear bustles and stays, and light thin shoes, following all the absurdities in dress of older and more foolish nations. Some of the worst practices may be abolished in the course of time. There are several 'anti-corset societies,' besides tee-total societies opposed to the use of tobacco and tea. These have not made much progress, nor attracted much notice. I have heard many public speakers on moral reform declare that, as soon as they can conquer the great master-evil, *intemperance*, they will set their face against every absurd custom; for they have no love for anything merely because *it is old*.

I have said the girls are good-looking: but they have not the stamina to stand the tear and wear of every-day life. After having three or four children, they fade and wither away. It is rare to see a hale *old wife* stepping about for a quarter of a century after rearing a large family, enjoying the sight and prattle of her children's children. They have made great progress in developing the mental faculties of youth, but very little in cultivating the physical powers.

Very little children have their place at table, their tea and coffee, and a little bit of chicken. 'Will you have a little bit of ham, Anne, my dear?' says an affectionate mother to her little daughter, that can hardly lisp 'Yes, ma'am.' I used to tell them how they reared the buirdly chiels and strapping lasses in Scotland; and they could scarcely believe that the strong and healthy emigrants they are accustomed to see arriving from the 'Old Country' did not get their sairin of beef, except perhaps once a year, such as at Christmas, or some other set time.

I think if the men of America and those of Britain were to have a fight,

William Thomson, *A Tradesman's Travels*, pp. 30-36.

it might be an even bet who would win; but if the ladies were to take up the quarrel, 'my conscience!' what a whipping the Transatlantic ladies would get. There are *wives* in Stonehaven that I would back against a dozen of them.

Amongst the working classes it is common, when about the same age, to call each other 'brother;' or if one is older than the other, he will call him 'uncle,' or if very old, 'grandfather.' Little boys and girls call each other 'bub' and 'sis,' contractions for brother and sister. A mother calling to her little girl will say, 'Come here, my daughter;' or it may be 'Come here, my son,' or 'Go away, sonne.' The dress of children is much the same as in this country. The girls wear breeches, or what they call pantanets, very commonly. The roundabout jacket is not much worn by boys. The most common dress is a very neat coat of the surtout species, made of material to suit the season. In the different houses where I lived, when opportunity offered, I frequently introduced some stories about ghosts. Some I told so frequently that I almost began to believe them myself, although my only object was to learn whether the people had any tinge of superstition in them; and I found that, although generally professing to disbelieve in anything supernatural, and although not well versed in the poetry of fairies and bogles, they have their superstitions and their ghost stories as well as people in the same degree of intelligence in this country.

The abominable custom of swearing is universal—not indeed in the more polished circles, or before ladies—but on the whole it is more common than in Scotland. The most fashionable oath is 'By Jesus Christ;' and this sacred name is used as an exclamation either of surprise, of joy, or anger. Many are so fond of swearing that they will put in an oath in the most nonsensical way. For instance, if one is determined to take his own way, he will tell you 'I guess I can do as I damned please.' This is nearly equal to the Scotch gentleman, who managed to put an oath in the middle of a word; when his clerk, in making a circumflex, turned it the wrong way, he exclaimed 'How now, Charles; what the devil kind of a *circum* hell of a *flex* is that?' They have introduced a number of new words. These I omit taking notice of, as they are pretty well known. In their houses they have rocking arm-chairs, that are a real luxury. Their fire-places, when they use wood, are without grates; instead of which they have 'fire-dogs' —two angular pieces of iron, sometimes handsomely mounted with brass, on which they pile the fire-wood. These irons answer the purpose remarkably well; and I liked the wood fires better than coal. I was once asked what kind of fire-wood there was in Scotland. When I told them there was nothing but coal and turf, they were surprised, and said it must be a poor country in which there was no fire-wood.

I never saw a woman going without shoes. And as for the process of tramping clothes in a tub, it is doubtful if ever such a sight was exhibited on any burn-side or washing green in all that wide country. If it were to take place, I suppose the authorities would interfere, in the same way as they do to prevent boys bathing within sight of any public thoroughfare.

Neither young nor married ladies wear caps or mutches, except when they get very old and grey. They follow the English fashion of putting on a bonnet whenever they go out, the same as a man puts on his hat. There are few illegitimate children see the light. I have seen in one quarter of an hour, in the Saltmarket of Glasgow, more vagabond-looking women then I have seen in all my travels through the United States.

There are many honest respectable people all over the country, who do not believe in Christianity, nor make any pretensions to it; yet this does not appear to hurt their standing in society. On Sunday they will sing songs, sew or amuse themselves; but seldom work out of doors, except sometimes in the harvest season; and then I have seen a lot of young men meet together and go and cut down a field of wheat for a farmer who was behind with his work.

The men are most inveterate chewers of tobacco; but it is rare to meet with a snuffer, unless it be an old Scotsman. Some of the ladies use snuff; but, instead of snuffing it, they eat it. Gold watches, chains, and breast-pins are very common; and they frequently descend in the scale of wealth as low as mechanics. Most families bake their own bread, and make their own yeast: and, instead of the meal cask that has its appropriate corner in the Scotch mechanic's house, they send to the store for a barrel of flour; when it is empty they break it up, burn it, and send for another. In the south, Indian corn is the principal bread stuff, in Canada and the northern states, flour-bread is the principal. In the different states there are different modes of cooking and baking, with great variety of roots, vegetables, and fruit. One thing I found common to all the different sections of the country I visited—that there was always *plenty*.

American Manners
Frances Trollope

In relating all I know of America, I surely must not omit so important a feature as the cooking. There are sundry anomalies in the mode of serving even a first-rate table; but as these are altogether matters of custom, they by no means indicate either indifference or neglect in this important business; and whether castors are placed on the table or on the sideboard; whether soup, fish, patties, and salad be eaten in orthodox order or not, signifies but little. I am hardly capable, I fear, of giving a very erudite critique on the subject; general observations therefore must suffice. The ordinary mode of living is abundant, but not delicate. They consume an extraordinary quantity of bacon. Ham and beefsteaks appear morning, noon, and night. In eating, they mix things together with the strangest incongruity imaginable. I have seen eggs and oysters eaten together; the sempiternal ham with apple-sauce; beefsteak with stewed peaches; and salt fish with onions. The bread is everywhere excellent, but they rarely enjoy it themselves, as they insist upon eating horrible half-baked hot rolls both morning and evening. The butter is tolerable; but they have seldom such cream as every little dairy produces in England; in fact, the cows are very roughly kept, compared with ours. Common vegetables are abundant and very fine. I never saw sea-cale, or cauliflowers, and either from the want of summer rain, or the want of care, the harvest of green vegetables is much sooner over than with us. They eat the Indian corn in a great variety of forms; sometimes it is dressed green, and eaten like peas, sometimes it is broken to pieces when dry, boiled plain, and brought to table like rice; this dish is called hominy. The flour of it is made into at least a dozen different sorts of cakes; but in my opinion all bad. This flour, mixed in the proportion of one-third, with fine wheat, makes by far the best bread I ever tasted.

I never saw turbot, salmon, or fresh cod; but the rock and shad are excellent. There is a great want of skill in the composition of sauces; not

Frances Trollope, *Domestic Manners of the Americans*, (London, 1832), pp. 238-245.

only with fish, but with every thing. They use very few made dishes, and I never saw any that would be approved by our savants. They have an excellent wild duck, called the canvass back, which, if delicately served, would surpass the black cock; but the game is very inferior to ours; they have no hares, and I never saw a pheasant. They seldom indulge in second courses, with all their ingenious temptations to the eating a second dinner; but almost every table has its dessert (invariably pronounced desart), which is placed on the table before the cloth is removed, and consists of pastry, preserved fruits, and creams. They are 'extravagantly fond,' to use their own phrase, of puddings, pies, and all kinds of 'sweets,' particularly the ladies; but are by no means such connoisseurs in soups and ragouts as the gastronomes of Europe. Almost every one drinks water at table, and by a strange contradiction, in a country where hard drinking is more prevalent than in any other, there is less wine taken at dinner; ladies rarely exceed one glass, and the great majority of females never take any. In fact, the hard drinking, so universally acknowledged, does not take place at jovial dinners, but to speak plain English, in solitary dram-drinking. Coffee is not served immediately after dinner, but makes part of the serious matter of tea-drinking, which comes some hours later. Mixed dinner parties of ladies and gentlemen are very rare, and unless several foreigners are present, but little conversation passes at the table. It certainly does not, in my opinion, add to the well ordering of a dinner-table, to set the gentlemen at one end of it, and the ladies at the other; but it is very rarely that you find it otherwise.

Their large evening parties are supremely dull; the men sometimes play cards by themselves; but if a lady plays, it must not be for money; no ecarte, no chess, very little music, and that little lamentably bad. Among the blacks, I heard some good voices, singing in tune; but I scarcely ever heard a white American, male or female, go through an air without being out of tune before the end of it; nor did I ever meet any trace of science in the singing I heard in society. To eat inconceivable quantities of cake, ice, and pickled oysters—and to show half their revenue in silks and satins, seems to be the chief object they have in these parties.

The most agreeable meetings, I was assured by all the young people, were those to which no married women are admitted; of the truth of this statement I have not the least doubt. These exclusive meetings occur frequently, and often last to a late hour; on these occasions, I believe, they generally dance. At regular balls, married ladies are admitted, but seldom take much part in the amusement. The refreshments are always profuse and costly, but taken in a most uncomfortable manner. I have known many private balls, where every thing was on the most liberal scale of expense, where the gentlemen sat down to supper in one room, while the ladies took theirs standing, in another.

What we call pic-nics are very rare, and when attempted, do not often succeed well. The two sexes can hardly mix for the greater part of a day without great restraint and ennui; it is quite contrary to their general habits; the favourite indulgences of the gentlemen (smoking cigars and drinking spirits), can neither be indulged in with decency, nor resigned with complacency.

The ladies have strange ways of adding to their charms. They powder themselves immoderately, face, neck, and arms, with pulverized starch; the effect is indescribably disagreeable by daylight, and not very favourable at any time. They are also most unhappily partial to false hair, which they wear in surprising quantities; this is the more to be lamented, as they generally have very fine hair of their own. I suspect this fashion to arise from an indolent mode of making their toilet, and from accomplished ladies' maids not being very abundant: it is less trouble to append a bunch of waving curls here, there, and everywhere, than to keep their native tresses in perfect order.

Though the expense of the ladies' dress greatly exceeds, in proportion to their general style of living, that of the ladies of Europe, it is very far (excepting in Philadelphia) from being in good taste. They do not consult the seasons in the colours or in the style of their costume; I have often shivered at seeing a young beauty picking her way through the snow with a pale rose-coloured bonnet, set on the very top of her head: I knew one young lady whose pretty little ear was actually frostbitten from being thus exposed. They never wear muffs or boots, and appear extremely shocked at the sight of comfortable walking shoes and cotton stockings, even when they have to step to their sleighs over ice and snow. They walk in the middle of winter with their poor little toes pinched into a miniature slipper, incapable of excluding as much moisture as might bedew a primrose. I must say in their excuse, however, that they have almost universally extremely pretty feet. They do not walk well, nor, in fact, do they ever appear to advantage when in movement. I know not why this should be, for they have abundance of French dancing-masters among them, but somehow or other it is the fact. I fancied I could often trace a mixture of affectation and of shyness in their little mincing unsteady step, and the ever-changing position of the hands. They do not dance well; perhaps I should rather say they do not look well when dancing; lovely as their faces are, they cannot, in a position that exhibits the whole person, atone for the want of *tournure*, and for the universal defect in the formation of the bust, which is rarely full, or gracefully formed.

I never saw an American man walk or stand well: notwithstanding their frequent militia drillings, they are nearly all hollow-chested and round-shouldered: perhaps this is occasioned by no officer daring to say to a brother free-born 'hold up your head;' whatever the cause, the effect is very remarkable to a stranger. In stature and in physiognomy, a great majority of the population, both male and female, are strikingly handsome, but they know not how to do their own honours; half as much comeliness elsewhere would produce ten times as much effect.

Nothing can exceed their activity and perseverance in all kinds of speculation, handicraft, and enterprise, which promises a profitable pecuniary result. I heard an Englishman, who had been long resident in America, declare that in following, in meeting, or in overtaking, in the street, on the road, or in the field, at the theatre, the coffee-house, or at home, he had never overheard Americans conversing without the word DOLLAR being pronounced between them. Such unity of purpose, such sympathy of feeling, can, I believe, be found nowhere else, except, perhaps, in an ants' nest. The result is exactly what might be anticipated. This sordid object, for ever before their eyes, must inevitably produce a sordid tone of mind, and, worse still, it produces a seared and blunted conscience on all questions of probity. I know not a more striking evidence of the low tone of morality which is generated by this universal pursuit of money, than the manner in which the New-England states are described by Americans. All agree in saying that they present a spectacle of industry and prosperity delightful to behold, and this is the district and the population most constantly quoted as the finest specimen of their admirable country; yet I never met a single individual in any part of the Union who did not paint these New-Englanders as sly, grinding, selfish, and tricking. The Yankees (as the New-Englanders are called) will avow these qualities themselves with a complacent smile, and boast that no people on the earth can match them at overreaching in a bargain. I have heard them unblushingly relate stories of their cronies and friends, which, if believed among us, would banish the heroes from the fellowship of honest men for ever; and all this is uttered with a simplicity which sometimes led me to doubt if the speakers knew what honour and honesty meant. Yet the Americans declare that 'they are the most moral people upon earth.' Again and again I have heard this asserted, not only in conversation, and by their writings, but even from the pulpit. Such broad assumption of superior virtue demands examination, and after four years of attentive and earnest observation and inquiry, my honest conviction is, that the standard of moral character in the United States is very greatly lower than in Europe. Of their religion, as it appears outwardly, I have had occasion to speak frequently; I pretend not to judge the heart, but, without any uncharitable presumption, I must take permission to say, that both Protestant England and Catholic France show an infinitely superior religious and moral aspect to mortal observation, both as to reverend decency of external observance, and as to the inward fruit of honest dealing between man and man.

In other respects I think no one will be disappointed who visits the country, expecting to find no more than common sense might teach him to look for, namely, a vast continent, by far the greater part of which is still in the state in which nature left it, and a busy, bustling, industrious population, hacking and hewing their way through it. What greatly increases the interest of this spectacle is the wonderful facility for internal commerce, furnished by the rivers, lakes, and canals, which thread the country in every direction, producing a rapidity of progress in all commercial and agricultural speculation altogether unequalled. This remarkable feature is perceptible in every part of the Union into which the fast-spreading population has hitherto found its way, and forms, I think, the most remarkable and interesting peculiarity of the country. I hardly remember a single town where vessels of some description or other may not constantly be seen in full activity.

Their carriages of every kind are very unlike ours; those belonging to private individuals seem all constructed with a view to summer use, for which they are extremely well calculated, but they are by no means comfortable in winter. The wagons and carts are built with great strength, which is indeed necessary, from the roads they often have to encounter. The stage-coaches are heavier and much less comfortable than those of France; to those of England they can bear no comparison. I never saw any harness that I could call handsome, nor any equipage which, as to horses, carriage, harness, and servants, could be considered as complete. The sleighs are delightful, and constructed at so little expense that I wonder we have not all got them in England, lying by, in waiting for the snow, which often remains with us long enough to permit their use. Sleighing is much more generally enjoyed by night than by day, for what reason I could never discover, unless it be, that no gentlemen are to be found disengaged from business in the mornings. Nothing, certainly, can be more agreeable than the gliding smoothly and rapidly along, deep sunk in soft furs, the moon shining with almost midday splendour, the air of crystal brightness, and the snow sparkling on every side, as if it were sprinkled with diamonds. And then the noiseless movement of the horses, so mysterious and unwonted, and the gentle tinkling of the bells you meet and carry, all help at once to sooth and excite the spirits: in short, I had not the least objection to sleighing by night; I only wished to sleigh by day also.

Almost every resident in the country has a carriage they call a carryall, which name I suspect to be a corruption of the cariole so often mentioned in the pretty Canadian story of Emily Montague. It is clumsy enough, certainly, but extremely convenient, and admirably calculated, with its thick roof and moveable draperies, for every kind of summer excursion.

Their steamboats, were the social arrangements somewhat improved, would be delightful as a mode of travelling; but they are very seldom employed for excursions of mere amusement; nor do I remember seeing pleasure-boats, properly so called, at any of the numerous places where they might be used with so much safety and enjoyment.

How often did our homely adage recur to me, "All work and no play would make Jack a dull boy;" Jonathan is a very dull boy. We are by no means so gay as our lively neighbours on the other side of the channel: but, compared with Americans, we are whirligigs and tetotums; every day is a holyday, and every night a festival.

Perhaps if the ladies had quite their own way, a little more relaxation would be permitted; but there is one remarkable peculiarity in their manners which precludes the possibility of any dangerous outbreaking of the kind; few ladies have any command of ready money intrusted to them. I have been a hundred times present when bills for a few dollars, perhaps for one, have been brought for payment to ladies living in perfectly easy circumstances, who have declared themselves without money, and referred the claimant to their husbands for payment. On every occasion where immediate disbursement is required, it is the same: even in shopping for ready cash they say, "send the bill home with the things, and my husband will give you a draft."

The New England Character

Tyrone Power

In the same street, and immediately opposite the great hotel, is the Tremont Theatre, certainly the most elegant exterior in the country, and with
a very well-proportioned, but not well-arranged *salle,* or audience part.

I commenced here on Monday the 30th of September, three days after
closing at Philadelphia, to a well-filled house, composed, however, chiefly
of men, as on my *début* at New York. My welcome was cordial and kind
in the extreme; but the audience, although attentive, appeared exceedingly cold. On a first night I did not heed this much, especially as report
assured me they were very well pleased; but throughout the week this
coldness appeared to me to increase rather than diminish, and so much
was I affected by it, that, notwithstanding the houses were very good, I,
on the last day of my first engagement of six nights, declined positively to
renew it, as was the custom in such cases, and as, in fact, the manager
and myself had contemplated: on this night, however, the aspect of affairs brightened up amazingly; the house was crowded; a brilliant show
of ladies graced the boxes; the performances were a repetition of two
pieces which had been previously acted, and from first to last the mirth
was electric; the good people appeared, by common consent, to abandon
themselves to the fun of the scene, and laughed *à gorge deployée.* At the
fall of the curtain, after, in obedience to the call of the house, I had made
my bow, the manager announced my re-engagement; and from this night
forth I never met a merrier or a pleasanter audience.

It was quite in accordance with the character ascribed to the New-
Englanders that they should coolly and thoroughly examine and understand the novelty presented for their judgment, and that, being satisfied
and pleased, they should no longer set limits to the demonstration of their
feelings.

In matters of graver import they have always evinced the like deliberate judgment and apparent coldness of bearing; but beneath this pru-

dential outward veil they have feelings capable of the highest degree of excitement and the most enduring enthusiasm.

I do not agree with those who describe the Yankee as a naturally cold-blooded, selfish being. From both the creed and the sumptuary regulations of the rigid moral censors from whom they sprung, they have inherited the practice of a close self-observance and a strict attention to conventional form, which gives a frigid restraint to their air that nevertheless does not sink far beneath the surface.

A densely-populated and ungrateful soil has kept alive and quickened their natural gifts of intelligence and enterprise, whilst the shifts poverty imposes upon young adventure may possibly at times have impelled prudence to degenerate into cunning. But look at their history as a community; they have been found ever ready to make the most generous sacrifices for the commonwealth. In their domestic relations they are proverbial as the kindest husbands and most indulgent fathers; whilst as friends they are found to be, if reasonably wary, at least steadfast, and to be relied on to the uttermost of their professions.

I can readily understand a stranger, having any share of sensibility, not liking a people whose observances are so peculiar and so decidedly marked; but I do think it impossible for an impartial person to spend any time in the country, or have any close intercourse with the community, without learning to respect and admire them, *malgré* their calculating prudence, and the many prejudices inseparable from a system of education even to this day sufficiently narrow and sectarian.

As far as my personal experience is worthy of consideration, I must declare that some of the kindest, gentlest, and most hospitable friends I had, and, I trust I may add, have, in the Union, were natives of New-England, or, as they say here, "real Yankee, born and raised within sight of the State-house of Bosting."

Town Government in New England

Alexis de Tocqueville

Town meetings are to liberty what primary schools are to science; they bring it within the people's reach, they teach men how to use and how to enjoy it. A nation may establish a system of free government, but without the spirit of municipal institutions it cannot have the spirit of liberty. The transient passions and the interests of an hour, or the chance of circumstances, may have created the external forms of independence; but the despotic tendency which has been repelled will, sooner or later, inevitably reappear on the surface. . . .

The township of New England is a division which stands between the commune and the canton of France, and which corresponds in general to the English tithing, or town. Its average population is from two to three thousand; so that, on the one hand, the interests of its inhabitants are not likely to conflict, and, on the other, men capable of conducting its affairs are always to be found among its citizens. . . .

In New England the majority acts by representatives in the conduct of the public business of the State; but if such an arrangement be necessary in general affairs, in the township, where the legislative and administrative action of the government is in more immediate contact with the subject, the system of representation is not adopted. There is no corporation; but the body of electors, after having designated its magistrates, directs them in everything that exceeds the simple and ordinary executive business of the State.

In order to explain to the reader the general principles on which the political organization of the counties and townships of the United States rests, I have thought it expedient to choose one of the States of New England as an example, to examine the mechanism of its constitution, and then to cast a general glance over the country. The township and the county are not organized in the same manner in every part of the Union; it is, however, easy to perceive that the same principles have guided the

Alexis de Tocqueville, *Democracy in America*, I, pp. 59-68.

formation of both of them throughout the Union. I am inclined to believe that these principles have been carried further in New England than elsewhere, and consequently that they offer greater facilities to the observations of a stranger. The institutions of New England form a complete and regular whole; they have received the sanction of time, they have the support of the laws, and the still stronger support of the manners of the community, over which they exercise the most prodigious influence; they consequently deserve our attention on every account. . . .

The public duties in the township are extremely numerous and minutely divided, as we shall see further on; but the larger proportion of administrative power is vested in the hands of a small number of individuals, called "the Selectmen." The general laws of the State impose a certain number of obligations on the selectmen, which they may fulfil without the authorization of the body they represent, but which they can only neglect on their own responsibility. The law of the State obliges them for instance, to draw up the list of electors in their townships; and if they omit this part of their functions, they are guilty of a misdemeanor. In all the affairs, however, which are determined by the town-meeting, the selectmen are the organs of the popular mandate, as in France the Maire executes the decree of the municipal council. They usually act upon their own responsibility, and merely put in practice principles which have been previously recognized by the majority. But if any change is to be introduced in the existing state of things, or if they wish to undertake any new enterprise, they are obliged to refer to the source of their power. If, for instance, a school is to be established, the selectmen convoke the whole body of the electors on a certain day at an appointed place; they explain the urgency of the case; they give their opinion on the means of satisfying it, on the probable expense, and the site which seems to be most favorable. The meeting is consulted on these several points; it adopts the principle, marks out the site, votes the rate, and confides the execution of its resolution to the selectmen.

The selectmen have alone the right of calling a town-meeting, but they may be requested to do so: if ten citizens are desirous of submitting a new project to the assent of the township, they may demand a general convocation of the inhabitants; the selectmen are obliged to comply, but they have only the right of presiding at the meeting.

The selectmen are elected every year in the month of April or of May. The town-meeting chooses at the same time a number of other municipal magistrates, who are entrusted with important administrative functions. The assessors rate the township; the collectors receive the rate. A constable is appointed to keep the peace, to watch the streets, and to forward the execution of the laws; the town-clerk records all the town votes, orders, grants, births, deaths, and marriages; the treasurer keeps the funds; the overseer of the poor performs the difficult task of superintending the action of the poor laws; committeemen are appointed to attend to the schools and to public instructions; and the road-surveyors, who take care of the greater and lesser thoroughfares of the township, complete the list of the principal functionaries. They are, however, still further subdivided; and amongst the municipal officers are to be found parish commissioners, who audit the expenses of public worship; different classes of inspectors, some of whom are to direct the citizens in case of fire; tithing-men, listers, haywards, chimney-viewers, fence-viewers to maintain the bounds of property, timber-measurers, and sealers of weights and measures.

There are nineteen principal officers in a township. Every inhabitant is constrained, on the pain of being fined, to undertake these different functions; which, however, are almost all paid, in order that the poorer citizens may be able to give up their time without loss. In general the American system is not to grant a fixed salary to its functionaries. Every service has its price, and they are remunerated in proportion to what they have done. . . .

In this part of the Union the impulsion of political activity was given in the townships; and it may almost be said that each of them originally formed an independent nation. When the Kings of England asserted their supremacy, they were contented to assume the central power of the State. The townships of New England remained as they were before; and although they are now subject to the State, they were at first scarcely dependent upon it. It is important to remember that they have not been invested with privileges, but that they have, on the contrary, forfeited a portion of their independence to the State. The townships are only subordinate to the State in those interests which I shall term social, as they are common to all the citizens. They are independent in all that concerns themselves; and amongst the inhabitants of New England I believe that not a man is to be found who would acknowledge that the State has any right to interfere in their local interests. The towns of New England buy and sell, sue or are sued, augment or diminish their rates, without the slightest opposition on the part of the administrative authority of the State.

They are bound, however, to comply with the demands of the community. If the State is in need of money, a town can neither give nor withhold the supplies. If the State projects a road, the township cannot refuse to let it cross its territory; if a police regulation is made by the State, it must be enforced by the town. A uniform system of instruction is organized all over the country, and every town is bound to establish the schools which the law ordains. In speaking of the administration of the United States I shall have occasion to point out the means by which the townships are compelled to obey in these different cases: I here merely show the existence of the obligation. Strict as this obligation is, the government of the State imposes it in principle only, and in its performance the township resumes all its independent rights. Thus, taxes are voted by the State, but they are levied and collected by the township; the existence of a school is obligatory, but the township builds, pays, and superintends it. In France the State-collector receives the local imposts; in America the town-collector receives the taxes of the State. Thus the French Government lends its agents to the commune; in America the township is the agent of the Government. This fact alone shows the extent of the differences which exist between the two nations.

PUBLIC SPIRIT OF THE TOWNSHIP OF NEW ENGLAND

In America, not only do municipal bodies exist, but they are kept alive and supported by public spirit. The township of New England possesses two advantages which infallibly secure the attentive interest of mankind, namely, independence and authority. Its sphere is indeed small and limited, but within that sphere its action is unrestrained; and its independence gives to it a real importance which its extent and population may not always ensure.

It is to be remembered that the affections of men generally lie on the side of authority. Patriotism is not durable in a conquered nation. The New Englander is attached to his township, not only because he was born in it, but because it constitutes a social body of which he is a member, and whose government claims and deserves the exercise of his sagacity. In Europe the absence of local public spirit is a frequent subject of regret to those who are in power; everyone agrees that there is no surer guarantee of order and tranquillity, and yet nothing is more difficult to create. If the municipal bodies were made powerful and independent, the authorities of the nation might be disunited and the peace of the country endangered. Yet, without power and independence, a town may contain good subjects, but it can have no active citizens. Another important fact is that the township of New England is so constituted as to excite the warmest of human affections, without arousing the ambitious passions of the heart of man. The officers of the county are not elected, and their authority is very limited. Even the State is only a second-rate community, whose tranquil and obscure administration offers no inducement sufficient to draw men away from the circle of their interests into the turmoil of public affairs. The federal government confers power and honor on the men who conduct it; but these individuals can never be very numerous. The high station of the Presidency can only be reached at an advanced period of life, and the other federal functionaries are generally men who have been favored by fortune, or distinguished in some other career. Such cannot be the permanent aim of the ambitious. But the township serves as a centre for the desire of public esteem, the want of exciting interests, and the taste for authority and popularity, in the midst of the ordinary relations of life; and the passions which commonly embroil society change their character when they find a vent so near the domestic hearth and the family circle.

In the American States power has been disseminated with admirable skill for the purpose of interesting the greatest possible number of persons in the common weal. Independently of the electors who are from time to time called into action, the body politic is divided into innumerable functionaries and officers, who all, in their several spheres, represent the same powerful whole in whose name they act. The local administration thus affords an unfailing source of profit and interest to a vast number of individuals.

The American system, which divides the local authority among so many citizens, does not scruple to multiply the functions of the town officers. For in the United States it is believed, and with truth, that patriotism is a kind of devotion which is strengthened by ritual observance. In this manner the activity of the township is continually perceptible; it is daily manifested in the fulfillment of a duty or the exercise of a right, and a constant though gentle motion is thus kept up in society which animates without disturbing it.

The American attaches himself to his home as the mountaineer clings to his hills, because the characteristic features of his country are there more distinctly marked than elsewhere. The existence of the townships of New England is in general a happy one. Their government is suited to their tastes, and chosen by themselves. In the midst of the profound peace and general comfort which reign in America the commotions of municipal discord are unfrequent. The conduct of local business is easy. The political education of the people has long been complete; say rather that it was complete when the people first set foot upon the soil. In New England no tradition exists of a distinction of ranks; no portion of the community is tempted to oppress the remainder; and the abuses which may injure isolated individuals are forgotten in the general contentment which prevails. If the government is defective (and it would no doubt be easy to point out its deficiencies), the fact that it really emanates from those it governs, and that it acts, either ill or well, casts the protecting spell of parental pride over its faults. No term of comparison disturbs the satisfaction of the citizen: England formerly governed the mass of the colonies, but the people was always sovereign in the township where its rule is not only an ancient but a primitive state.

The native of New England is attached to his township because it is independent and free: his co-operation in its affairs ensures his attachment to its interest; the well-being it affords him secures his affection; and its welfare is the aim of his ambition and of his future exertions: he takes a part in every occurrence in the place; he practises the art of government in the small sphere within his reach; he accustoms himself to those forms which can alone ensure the steady progress of liberty; he imbibes their spirit; he acquires a taste for order, comprehends the union or the balance of powers, and collects clear practical notions on the nature of his duties and the extent of his rights.

The Virginian and the Yankee

Michel Chevalier

The Virginian and the Yankee have planted themselves in the wilderness, each in a manner conformable to his nature and condition. The part they have taken in founding the new States of the West explains the fact so often mentioned of fifty or sixty members of Congress being natives of Virginia or Connecticut. In this conquest over nature, Europe has not remained an idle spectator; she has sent forth vigorous laborers who have co-operated with the sons of New England, for slavery fills them with horror and drives them from the men of the South. Many Irish and Scotch, a number of Germans, Swiss, and some French are now settled in Michigan, Ohio, Indiana, and Illinois. The traveler who descends the Ohio, passes on the way Gallipolis, a French settlement, Vevay, a Swiss village, and Marietta, so called in honor of Marie Antoinette. The terminations in *burg* are scattered among Indian names, Jacksonvilles, Washingtons, and Columbias. But the co-operation of Europeans does not deprive the Yankees of the principal share in the honor of the work; they began it, they have borne and still bear the burden and heat of the day. In comparison with them, the European has been only the eleventh-hour-man, the apprentice, the hireling. The fusion of the European with the Yankee takes place but slowly, even on the new soil of the West; for the Yankee is not a man of promiscuous society; he believes that Adam's oldest son was a Yankee. Enough, however, of foreign blood has been mingled with Yankee blood to modify the primitive character of the New England race and to form a third American type, that of the West, whose features are not yet sharply defined but are daily assuming more distinctness; this type is characterized by its athletic forms and ambitious pretensions and seems destined ultimately to become superior to the others.

The Yankee and the Virginian are very unlike each other; they have no great love for each other and are often at variance. . . .

Michel Chevalier, *Society, Manners, and Politics in the United States* (Boston, 1839), pp. 113-120.

The Virginian of pure race is frank, hearty, open, cordial in his manners, noble in his sentiments, elevated in his ideas; he is a worthy descendant of the English gentleman. Surrounded from infancy by his slaves who relieve him from all personal exertion, he is rather indisposed to activity, even indolent. He is generous and profuse; around him, but more in the new States than in impoverished Virginia, abundance reigns. When the cotton crop has been good and the price is high, he invites everybody, excepting only the slaves that cultivate his fields, to partake in his wealth without much thought of next year's produce. To him the practice of hospitality is at once a duty, a pleasure, and a happiness. Like the patriarchs of the East or the heroes of Homer, he spits an ox to regale the guest whom Providence sends him and an old friend recommends to his attention, and to moisten this solid repast he offers Madeira—of which he is as proud as of his horses—which has been twice to the East Indies and has been ripening full twenty years. He loves the institutions of his country, yet he shows with pride his family plate, the arms on which, half effaced by time, attest his descent from the first colonists and prove that his ancestors were of a good family in England. When his mind has been cultivated by study and a tour in Europe has polished his manners and refined his imagination, there is no place in the world in which he would not appear to advantage, no destiny too high for him to reach; he is one of those whom a man is glad to have as a companion and desires as a friend. Ardent and warm-hearted, he is of the stuff from which great orators are made. He is better able to command men than to conquer nature and subdue the soil. When he has a certain degree of the spirit of method, and I will not say of will (for he has enough of that), but of that active perseverance so common among his brethren of the North, he has all the qualities needful to form a great statesman.

The Yankee, on the contrary, is reserved, cautious, distrustful; he is thoughtful and pensive, but equable; his manners are without grace, modest but dignified, cold, and often unprepossessing; he is narrow in his ideas but practical; and, possessing the idea of the proper, he never rises to the grand. He has nothing chivalric about him, and yet he is adventurous and he loves a roving life. His imagination is active and original, producing, however, not poetry, but drollery, what is called here "Yankee notions." The Yankee is the laborious ant; he is industrious and sober, frugal, and, on the sterile soil of New England, niggardly; transplanted to the promised land in the West, he continues moderate in his habits, but is less inclined to count the cents.

In New England he has a large share of prudence, but once thrown into the midst of the treasures of the West he becomes a speculator, a gambler even, although he has a great horror of cards, dice, and all games of hazard and even of skill, except the innocent game at bowls. He is crafty, sly, always calculating, boasting even of the tricks which he plays upon them as marks of his superior sagacity; he is, moreover, well provided with rationalizations to lull his conscience. With all his nice subtleties, he is, nevertheless, expeditious in business because he knows the value of time. His house is a sanctuary which he does not open to the profane; he is little given to hospitality, or rather he displays it only on rare occasions and then he does so on a great scale. He is a ready speaker and a close reasoner, but not a brilliant orator. For a statesman, he wants that greatness of mind and soul which enables a man to enter into and love another's nature and leads him naturally to consult his neighbor's good in consulting his own. He is individualism incarnate; in him the spirit of locality and division is carried to the utmost. But if he is not a great statesman, he is an able administrator, an unrivaled man of business. If he is not suited to command men, he has no equal in acting upon things, in combining, arranging, and giving them a value. There are nowhere merchants of more consummate ability than those of Boston.

But it is particularly as the colonist of the wilderness that the Yankee is admirable. Fatigue has no hold on him. He has not, like the Spaniard, the capacity to bear hunger and thirst, but he has the much superior faculty of finding at all times and in all places something to eat and to drink, and of being always able to contrive a shelter from the cold, first for his wife and children and afterward for himself. He grapples with nature in close fight and, more unyielding than she, subdues her at last, obliging her to surrender at discretion, to yield whatever he wills, and to take the shape he chooses. Like Hercules, he conquers the hydra of the pestilential morass and chains the rivers; more daring than Hercules, he extends his dominion not only over the land, but over the sea; he is the best sailor in the world. The ocean is his tributary and enriches him with the oil of her whales and with all her lesser fry. Wiser than the hero of the twelve labors, he knows no Omphale who can seduce him, no Dejanira whose poisoned gifts can balk his searching glance. In this respect he is rather a Ulysses who has his Penelope, counts upon her faith, and remains steadfastly true to her. He does not even need to stop his ears when he passes near the Sirens, for in him the tenderest passions are deadened by religious austerity and devotion to his business. Like Ulysses in another point, he has a bag full of tricks. Overtaken at night by a storm in the woods, in a half hour, with no other resource than his knife, he will have made a shelter for himself and his horse. In winter, caught in one of those snowstorms which are unknown among us, he will construct a sled in the twinkling of an eye and keep on his way, like an Indian, by watching the bark of the trees. This to the genius of business, by means of which he turns to profit whatever the earth yields him, he joins the genius of industry which makes her prolific, and that of mechanical skill which fashions her produce to his wants. He is incomparable as a pioneer, unequaled as a settler of the wilderness.

The Yankee has set his mark on the United States during the last half century. He has been eclipsed by Virginia in the councils of the nation, but he has in turn had the upper hand throughout the country and eclipsed her on her own soil; for in order to arouse the Virginian from his Southern indolence, it has been necessary that the Yankee should come to set him an example of activity and enterprise at his own door. But for the Yankee, the vast cotton plantations of the South would still be an uncultivated waste. It was a Yankee, Eli Whitney, who toward the end of the last century invented the cotton gin which has made the fortune of the South. To give an enterprise success in the South, some Yankee must come a thousand miles to suggest the idea to the natives and carry off the profit before their eyes. New England has given only two Presidents to the Union, both popular on the eve of their election, both unpopular on the morrow, both rejected at the end of their first term, while all the others have been natives of Virginia or South Carolina and have been re-chosen for a second term. But then what a revenge has she taken in business matters, at the North and the South, in the East as well as the West! Here the Yankee is a true Marquis of Carabas. At Baltimore as well as at Boston, in New Orleans as well as at Salem, in New York as well as at Portland, if a merchant is mentioned who has made and kept a large fortune by sagacity and forecast, you will find that he is a Yankee. If you pass a plantation in the South in better order than the others, with finer avenues, with the Negroes' cabins better arranged and more comfortable, you will be told, "Oh! that is a Yankee's; he is a *smart man!*" In a village in Missouri, by the side of a house with broken windows, dirty in its outward appearance, around the door of which a parcel of ragged children are quarreling and fighting, you may see another, freshly painted, surrounded by a simple, but neat and nicely whitewashed fence, with a dozen of carefully trimmed trees about it, and through the windows in a small room shining with cleanliness you may espy some nicely combed little boys and some young girls dressed in almost the last Paris fashion. Both houses belong to farmers, but one of them is from North Carolina and the other from New England. On the western rivers, you will hear a boat mentioned which never meets with an accident and in which all travelers and merchants are eager to take their passage; the master is a Yankee. At New Orleans, alongside the levee, you may be struck with the fine appearance of a ship which all the passers-by stop to admire; the master is also a Yankee.

The pre-eminence of the Yankee in the colonization of the country has made him the arbiter of manners and customs. It is from him that the country has taken a general tone of austere severity that is religious and even bigoted; because of him all sorts of amusements, which among us are considered innocent relaxations, are here proscribed as immoral pleasures. It is he that has introduced Prison Reform, multiplied schools, founded Temperance Societies. It is through his agency, with his money, that the missionaries endeavor silently to found colonies in the South Seas for the benefit of the Union. If one wished to form a single type, representing the American character of the present moment as a single whole, it would be necessary to take at least three fourths of the Yankee and to mix with it hardly one fourth of the Virginian.

The physical labour of colonisation is now brought to an end; the physical basis of society is laid. On this base it is necessary now to raise a social structure of a form yet unknown but which, I am fully convinced, will be on a new plan, for all the materials are new; besides, neither humanity nor Providence ever repeats itself. Which of the two, Yankee or Virginian, is best suited to execute this new task? I cannot tell; but it seems to me that the Virginian is now about to take his turn and that, in the phase which the United States are now on the point of entering, the social qualities of the Virginian will win the advantage which naturally belonged to the laborious Yankee in the period of settling the forest. In a word, I believe that, if the Union lasts and the West continues to form a united mass from the falls of Niagara to New Orleans, this third type of the West, which is growing and aspires to rule over the others, will take a great deal from the Virginian and very little from the Yankee.

A Northerner's Assessment of
Southern Characteristics

The wealthy and educated, and especially the fashionable people of all civilized countries, are now so nearly alike in their ordinary manners and customs, that the observations of a passing traveler upon them, must commonly be of much too superficial a character to warrant him in deducing from them, with confidence, any important conclusions. I have spent an evening at the plantation residence of a gentleman in Louisiana, in which there was very little in the conversation or customs and manners of the family to distinguish them from others whom I have visited in Massachusetts, England and Germany. I shall, therefore, undertake with diffidence to describe certain apparently general and fundamental peculiarities of character in the people, which it is a part of my duty to notice, from their importance with reference to the condition and prospects of the Slave States and their institution.

Slavery exerts an immense quiet influence upon the character of the master, and the condition of the slave is greatly affected by the modifications of character thus effected. I do not believe there are any other people in the world with whom the negro would be as contented, and, if contentment is happiness, so happy, as with those who are now his masters. The hopeless perpetuation of such an intolerable nuisance as this labor-system, it is, however, also apparent, depends mainly upon the careless, temporizing, *shiftless* disposition, to which the negro is indebted for this mitigation of the natural wretchedness of slavery.

The calculating, indefatigable New-Englander, the go-ahead Western man, the exact and stern Englishman, the active Frenchman, the studious, observing, economical German would all and each lose patience with the frequent disobedience and the constant indolence, forgetfulness and carelessness, and the blundering, awkward, brute-like manner of work of the

"The South: Slavery in its Effects on Character, and the Social Relations of the Master Class," *New York Daily Times* (Jan. 12, 1854), p. 2. This essay is reprinted in Arthur M. Schlesinger (ed.), *The Cotton Kingdom* . . . by Frederick Law Olmsted (New York, 1953).

plantation-slave. The Southerner, if he sees anything of it, generally disregards it and neglects to punish it. Although he is naturally excitable and passionate, he is less subject to impatience and passionate anger with the slave, than is, I believe, generally supposed, because he is habituated to regard him so completely as his inferior, dependent and subject. For the same reason, his anger, when aroused, is usually easily and quickly appeased, and he forgives him readily and entirely, as we do a child or a dog who has annoyed us. And, in general, the relation of master and slave on small farms, and the relations of the family and its household servants everywhere, may be considered a happy one, developing, at the expense of decision, energy, self-reliance and self-control, some of the most beautiful traits of human nature. But it is a great error,—although one nearly universal with Southerners themselves—to judge of Slavery by the light alone of the master's fireside.

The direct influence of Slavery is, I think, to make the Southerner indifferent to small things; in some relations, we should say rightly, *superior* to small things; prodigal, improvident, and ostentatiously generous. His ordinarily uncontrolled authority, (and from infancy the Southerner is more free from control, in all respects, I should judge, than any other person in the world,) leads him to be habitually impulsive, impetuous, and enthusiastic: gives him self-respect and dignity of character, and makes him bold, confident, and true. Yet it has not appeared to me that the Southerner was frank as he is, I believe, commonly thought to be. He seems to me to be very secretive, or at least reserved, on topics which most nearly concern himself. He minds his own business, and lets alone that of others; not in the English way, but in a way peculiarly his own; resulting partly, perhaps, from want of curiosity, in part from habits formed by such constant intercourse as he has with his inferiors, (negroes,) and partly from the caution in conversation which the "rules of honor" are calculated to give. Not, I said, in the English way, because he meets a stranger easily, and without timidity, or thought of how he is himself appearing, and is ready and usually accomplished in conversation. He is much given to vague and careless generalization, and greatly disinclined to exact and careful reasoning. He follows his natural impulses nobly, has nothing to be ashamed of, and is, therefore, habitually truthful; but his carelessness, impulsiveness, vagueness, and want of exactness in everything, make him speak from his mouth that which is in point of fact untrue, rather oftener than any one else.

From early intimacy with the negro, (an association fruitful in other respects of evil,) he has acquired much of his ready, artless and superficial benevolence, good nature and geniality. The comparatively solitary nature and somewhat monotonous duties of plantation life, make guests usually exceedingly welcome, while the abundance of servants at command, and other circumstances, make the ordinary duties of hospitality very light. The Southerner, however, is greatly wanting in hospitality of mind, closing his doors to all opinions and schemes to which he has been bred a stranger, with a contempt and bigotry which sometimes seems incompatible with his character as a gentleman. He has a large but unexpansive mind.

The Southerner has no pleasure in labor except with reference to a result. He enjoys life itself. He is content with being. Here is the grand distinction between him and the Northerner; for the Northerner enjoys progress in itself. He finds his happiness in doing. Rest, in itself, is irksome and offensive to him, and however graceful or beatific that rest may be, he values it only with reference to the power of future progress it will bring him. Heaven itself will be dull and stupid to him, if there is no work to be done in it—nothing to struggle for—if he reaches perfection at a jump, and has no chance to make an improvement.

The Southerner cares for the end only; he is impatient of the means. He is passionate, and labors passionately, fitfully, with the energy and strength of anger, rather than of resolute will. He fights rather than works to carry his purpose. He has the intensity of character which belongs to Americans in general, and therefore enjoys excitement and is fond of novelty. But he has much less curiosity than the Northerner; less originating genius, less inventive talent, less patient and persevering energy. And I think this all comes from his want of aptitude for close observation and his dislike for application to small details. And this, I think, may be reasonably supposed to be mainly the result of habitually leaving all matters not either of grand and exciting importance, or of immediate consequence to his comfort, to his slaves, and of being accustomed to see them slighted or neglected as much as he will, in his indolence, allow them to be by them.

Of course, I have been speaking of the general tendencies only of character in the North and the South. There are individuals in both in whom these extreme characteristics are reversed, as there are graceful Englishmen and awkward Frenchmen. There are, also, in each, those in whom they are more or less harmoniously blended. Those in whom they are the most enviably so—the happiest and the most useful in the social sphere— are equally common, so far as I know, in both; and the grand distinction remains in the mass-manifesting itself, by strikingly contrasting symptoms, in our religion, politics and social life.

In no way more than this: The South endeavors to close its eyes to every evil the removal of which will require self-denial, labor and skill. If, however, an evil is too glaring to be passed by unnoticed, it is immediately declared to be constitutional, or providential, and its removal is declared to be either treasonable or impious—usually both; and, what is worse, it is improper, impolite, ungentlemanly, unmanlike. And so it is ended at the

South. But, at the North this sort of opposition only serves to develop the reform, by ridding it of useless weight and drapery.

Northern social life usually leaves a rather melancholy and disagreeable feeling upon the minds of our Southern friends, as many have confessed to me. I think the different tendency of life at the North from that of existence at the South, which I have asserted, will give a key to this unfavorable impression which the Southerner obtains of our social character.

The people of the North are generally well aware of their social deficiencies, and of the unfitness of many of the customs and mannerisms, required by conventional politeness, to their character and duties. A man comes to our house, and custom requires that our countenance should brighten, and that we should say we are glad to see him. This custom makes it unkind in us towards him not to do so. We have no unkindness in our hearts, to the man, but entirely the contrary; yet it happens that we are *not* glad to see him, and such is our constitution that we have no impulsive and natural brightening up under hardly any circumstances. Now we have to choose between a forced, artificial, formal and false expression of a true kindness, and truth and simplicity. Amiable people take sides with kindness—the silent and reliable sort—with truth. Each are constantly aware, to a greater or less degree, of the difficulty they are engaged with. Some attach an absurd importance to the value of expression, and become "affected"; others rebel against the falseness of the conventional forms of expression, and become supercilious or sour and forbidding. Both classes are constantly led to make awkward attempts to compromise their quarrel with themselves.

The Southerner can understand nothing of all this. He naturally accepts the institutions, manners and customs in which he is educated, as necessities imposed upon him by Providence. He is loyal to "Society," and it is opposed to his fundamental idea of a gentleman to essentially deduct from them or add to them. This "clothes philosophy" of the North, he does not in the least comprehend, or if he does he sees nothing in it but impudent and vulgar quackery. And yet I think there is, perhaps, good to come out of it. We believe not, in our day, in good William of Wickham's maxim. This new Democratic man is not "made of manners"; it may be best he should make manners to suit himself. Between this slavish conformity and anarchical non-conformity—it is to be hoped that the good sense of our society is drifting towards both a nobler and a happier social life.

But, at the present, the social intercourse of the wealthy people of the South is certainly more agreeable, rational, and to be respected, than that of the nearest corresponding class at the North. I should be sorry to think this the highest compliment it deserved.

The wealthy class is the commanding class in most districts of the South, and gives character to all the slaveholding class. Wealth is less distributed, and is more retained in families at the South than the North. With the slaveholding class there is a pride of birth and social position, much more than in any class at the North. This affects the character and conduct of individuals, and reacts on their associates, and on the whole community— in some respects perniciously, but in many respects favorably.

The "high-toned gentleman" (a Southern expression) of the South is rare at the North. He is not an article of city manufacture, as the most cultivated people of the North are. He has a peculiar character, and peculiar habits—more like those of the "old English gentleman" than any class to be found now, perhaps, even in England itself. He rides much, and hunts, and is given to field sports, and never knows the want of oxygen; for, even in Winter, his windows and doors are always forgotten to be closed. Accordingly, though his diet is detestable, he is generally well physically developed—lighter and more delicate of frame than the English squires, but tall and sinewy. His face would commonly be handsome but that his mouth is made gross, lifeless, and inexpressive, by his habit of using tobacco excessively. He has a peculiar pride and romance, and, though he often appears laughably Quixotic, he is, in the best sense of the word, also chivalrous. He is brave and magnanimous, courteous and polite, to all white people. If he often values his comfort, or the success of his designs, or the gratification of his passions, more than he does a strict adherence to the received rules of Christian morality, he never values life or aught else more than he does his honor. This "honor"—though if you analyze it, it comes to be little else than a conventional standard of feelings and actions, which must be habitual to entitle a man to consider himself a gentleman —is often really far nobler, and makes a nobler man than what *often* passes for religion at the North—at least in this world.

There is, however, a quality, or perhaps it is a faculty of the soul, which is distinct, though seldom separate, from love to the person of God and love to man, or in our time from the Christian faith, which is most nearly defined by the term, an enlightened conscience,—a spontaneous requisite perception and loyal love of the fundamental laws of Right—the laws that God himself is subject to. This quality or faculty is the noblest endowment of man, and is essential to the noblest character. I think it is strongly developed in more individuals at the North than at the South, and I think there are obvious causes for its absence at the South. The habitual reference of the Southerner in his judgment of conduct, whether of himself or another, whether past or contemplated, to the conventional standard of honor, prevents the ascendancy of a higher standard. This habitual contemplation of a relation so essentially wrong as that of slavery, as a permanent and necessary one not reformable, not in progress of removal and abolition, destroys or prevents the development of his sense of any standard of right and wrong above a mere code of laws, or conventional rules.

But to the Southern gentleman, (by distinction,) as I have often met him, I wish to pay great respect. The honest and unstudied dignity of character, the generosity and the real nobleness of habitual impulses, and the well-bred, manly courtesy which distinguish him in all the relations and occupations of life, equally in his business, in his family, and in general society, are sadly rare at the North—much more rare at the North than at the South. I acknowledge it freely but with deep regret and melancholy. There are qualities of character, (not of deportment, merely,) which are common among the planters of many parts of the South, as they are among the aristocratic classes of Europe, which are incompatible with the possession of nothing else than a man should glory in, which the mass of the people of the North have nearly lost, or have failed to gain.

This has been often observed by intelligent travelers visiting us, and is sometimes thought sufficient to condemn our democratic form of government, and our approximately democratic state of society. This is the judgment of many Southerners, (for the government and society of the South is the most essentially aristocratic in the world,) and I have reason to believe that there are many whose confidence in the democracy of the North is so small that they anticipate, and are acting politically with reference to, a division of the present Union and the formation of another great Southern republic—that is, a republic of white capitalists, in which the slavery of the working classes shall be provided for, and every means taken to make it complete and permanent.

But acknowledging the rarity of the thoroughbred gentleman at the North; is an inference to be drawn from it unfavorable to Democratic Institutions? I think not. Without regard to the future, and to what we may yet become under Democracy, the condition and character of our people *as a whole,* to the best of my judgment, is better, more gentlemanly even, far more entitled to respect than that of the people, *including all classes,* of any other nation. Very much more so than of those of the South. I do not say more happy. The people of the Northern States, as a whole, probably enjoy life less than any other uncivilized people. . . .

But the only conclusion which the fact seems to me to suggest, with regard to our Democratic Government, is perhaps this: that simple protection to capital and letting-alone to native genius and talent is not the whole duty of Government; possibly that patent laws, and the common schools, with their common teachers, and common instruction, (not education) such as our institutions as yet give to the people, are not enough. That the aesthetic faculties need to be educated—drawn out; that taste and refinement need to be encouraged as well as the useful arts. That there need to be places and time for *re-unions,* which shall be so attractive to the nature of all but the most depraved men, that the rich and the poor, the cultivated

and *well-bred,* and the sturdy and self-made people shall be attracted together and encouraged to assimilate.

I think there is no sufficient reason why the aid of the State should not
be given to assist corporations and voluntary associations for such purposes, on the same principle, and with the same restrictions, that it is in
New-York to schools, to colleges, and to agricultural societies. Thus, I
think, with a necessity for scarcely any additional governmental offices, or
increase of the friction of governmental machinery, might be encouraged
and sustained, at points so frequent and convenient that they would exert
an elevating influence upon all the people, public parks and gardens, galleries of art and instruction in art, music, athletic sports and healthful
recreations, and other means of cultivating taste and lessening the excessive materialism of purpose in which we are, as a people, so cursedly
absorbed, that even the natural capacity for domestic happiness, and, more
obviously, for the enjoyment of simple and sensible social life in our community, seems likely to be entirely destroyed. The enemies of Democracy
could bring no charge more severe against it, than that such is its tendency,
and that it has no means of counteracting it.

Slavery is claimed at the South to be the remedy for this evil. In some respects it is a remedy. But (disregarding the slaves and the poor whites)
where there is one true gentleman, and to be respected, at the South, there
are two whose whole life seems to be absorbed in sensualism and sickly
excitements. Everywhere you meet them, well dressed and spending
money freely, constantly drinking, smoking and chewing; card-playing and
betting; and unable to converse upon anything that is not either grossly
sensual or exciting, such as street rencounters, filibustering schemes, or
projects of disunion or war. These persons are, however, gentlemen, in the
sense that they are familiar with the forms and usages of the best society,
that they are deferential to women, and that (except in money matters)
their word is to be implicitly relied upon. They far exceed in numbers any
class of at all similar habits that we yet have at the North.

They are invariably politicians, and they generally rule in all political
conventions and caucuses. They are brave, in the sense that they are reckless of life, and they are exceedingly fond of the excitement of the hazard
of life. They are as careless of the life of others as of themselves. They are
especially ambitious of military renown, and in the Mexican war they vol-
unteered almost to a man, many of those who went as privates taking with
them several negro servants. If they were not dependent on the price of
cotton for the means of their idleness, they would keep the country incessantly at war. Being so, however, they are as conservative in the policy
they favor towards any powerful nation as the cotton lords of England or
the land lords of Austria. They hate and despise the Democrats of Europe

as much as Francis Joseph himself. They glorify Napoleon, and they boast of the contempt with which they were able to treat the humbug Kossuth.

They call themselves Democrats, and sometimes Democratic Whigs. Call them what you will, they are a mischievous class,—the dangerous class at present of the United States. They are not the legitimate offspring of Democracy, thanks to God, but of slavery under a Democracy.

YEOMAN

The Tyranny of the Majority

Alexis de Tocqueville

It is in the examination of the display of public opinion in the United States that we clearly perceive how far the power of the majority surpasses all the powers with which we are acquainted in Europe. Intellectual principles exercise an influence which is so invisible, and often so inappreciable, that they baffle the toils of oppression. At the present time the most absolute monarchs in Europe are unable to prevent certain notions, which are opposed to their authority, from circulating in secret throughout their dominions, and even in their courts. Such is not the case in America; as long as the majority is still undecided, discussion is carried on; but as soon as its decision is irrevocably pronounced, a submissive silence is observed, and the friends, as well as the opponents, of the measure unite in assenting to its propriety. The reason of this is perfectly clear: no monarch is so absolute as to combine all the powers of society in his own hands, and to conquer all opposition with the energy of a majority which is invested with the right of making and of executing the laws. . . .

I know no country in which there is so little true independence of mind and freedom of discussion as in America. In any constitutional state in Europe every sort of religious and political theory may be advocated and propagated abroad; for there is no country in Europe so subdued by any single authority as not to contain citizens who are ready to protect the man who raises his voice in the cause of truth from the consequences of his hardihood. If he is unfortunate enough to live under an absolute government, the people is upon his side; if he inhabits a free country, he may find a shelter behind the authority of the throne, if he require one. The aristocratic part of society supports him in some countries, and the democracy in others. But in a nation where democratic institutions exist, organized like those of the United States, there is but one sole authority, one single element of strength and of success, with nothing beyond it.

In America the majority raises very formidable barriers to the liberty of

Alexis de Tocqueville, *Democracy in America*, I, pp. 267-274.

opinion: within these barriers an author may write whatever he pleases, but he will repent it if he ever step beyond them. Not that he is exposed to the terrors of an auto-da-fé, but he is tormented by the slights and persecutions of daily obloquy. His political career is closed forever, since he has offended the only authority which is able to promote his success. Every sort of compensation, even that of celebrity, is refused to him. Before he published his opinions he imagined that he held them in common with many others; but no sooner has he declared them openly than he is loudly censured by his overbearing opponents, whilst those who think without having the courage to speak like him, abandon him in silence. He yields at length, oppressed by the daily efforts he has been making, and he subsides into silence, as if he was tormented by remorse for having spoken the truth.

Fetters and headsmen were the coarse instruments which tyranny formerly employed; but the civilization of our age has refined the arts of despotism which seemed, however, to have been sufficiently perfected before. The excesses of monarchical power had devised a variety of physical means of oppression: the democratic republics of the present day have rendered it as entirely an affair of the mind as that will which it is intended to coerce. Under the absolute sway of an individual despot the body was attacked in order to subdue the soul, and the soul escaped the blows which were directed against it and rose superior to the attempt; but such is not the course adopted by tyranny in democratic republics; there the body is left free, and the soul is enslaved. The sovereign can no longer say, "You shall think as I do on pain of death;" but he says, "You are free to think differently from me, and to retain your life, your property, and all that you possess; but if such be your determination, you are henceforth an alien among your people. You may retain your civil rights, but they will be useless to you, for you will never be chosen by your fellow-citizens if you solicit their suffrages, and they will affect to scorn you if you solicit their esteem. You will remain among men, but you will be deprived of the rights of mankind. Your fellow-creatures will shun you like an impure being, and those who are most persuaded of your innocence will abandon you too, lest they should be shunned in their turn. Go in peace! I have given you your life, but it is an existence incomparably worse than death." . . .

Works have been published in the proudest nations of the Old World expressly intended to censure the vices and deride the follies of the times: Labruyère inhabited the palace of Louis XIV when he composed his chapter upon the Great, and Molière criticised the courtiers in the very pieces which were acted before the Court. But the ruling power in the United States is not to be made game of; the smallest reproach irritates its sensibility, and the slightest joke which has any foundation in truth renders it indignant; from the style of its language to the more solid virtues of its character, everything must be made the subject of encomium. No writer, whatever be his eminence, can escape from this tribute of adulation to his fellow-citizens. The majority lives in the perpetual practice of self-applause, and there are certain truths which the Americans can only learn from strangers or from experience.

If great writers have not at present existed in America, the reason is very simply given in these facts; there can be no literary genius without freedom of opinion, and freedom of opinion does not exist in America. The Inquisition has never been able to prevent a vast number of anti-religious books from circulating in Spain. The empire of the majority succeeds much better in the United States, since it actually removes the wish of publishing them. Unbelievers are to be met with in America, but, to say the truth, there is no public organ of infidelity. Attempts have been made by some governments to protect the morality of nations by prohibiting licentious books. In the United States no one is punished for this sort of works, but no one is induced to write them; not because all the citizens are immaculate in their manners, but because the majority of the community is decent and orderly. . . .

The tendencies which I have just alluded to are as yet very slightly perceptible in political society, but they already begin to exercise an unfavorable influence upon the national character of the Americans. I am inclined to attribute the singular paucity of distinguished political characters to the ever-increasing activity of the despotism of the majority in the United States. When the American Revolution broke out they arose in great numbers, for public opinion then served, not to tyrannize over, but to direct the exertions of individuals. Those celebrated men took a full part in the general agitation of mind common at that period, and they attained a high degree of personal fame, which was reflected back upon the nation, but which was by no means borrowed from it. . . .

In that immense crowd which throngs the avenues to power in the United States I found very few men who displayed any of that manly candor and that masculine independence of opinion which frequently distinguished the Americans in former times, and which constitutes the leading feature in distinguished characters, wheresoever they may be found. It seems, at first sight, as if all the minds of the Americans were formed upon one model, so accurately do they correspond in their manner of judging. A stranger does, indeed, sometimes meet with Americans who dissent from these rigorous formularies; with men who deplore the defects of the laws, the mutability and the ignorance of democracy; who even go so far as to observe the evil tendencies which impair the national character, and to point out such remedies as it might be possible to apply; but no one is there to hear these things besides yourself, and you, to whom these secret reflections are confided, are a stranger and a bird of passage. They are very ready to communicate truths which are useless to you, but they continue to hold a different language in public.

If ever these lines are read in America, I am well assured of two things: in the first place, that all who peruse them will raise their voices to condemn me; and in the second place, that very many of them will acquit me at the bottom of their conscience.

I have heard of patriotism in the United States, and it is a virtue which may be found among the people, but never among the leaders of the people. This may be explained by analogy; despotism debases the oppressed much more than the oppressor: in absolute monarchies the king has often great virtues, but the courtiers are invariably servile. It is true that the American courtiers do not say "Sire," or "Your Majesty"—a distinction without a difference. They are forever talking of the natural intelligence of the populace they serve; they do not debate the question as to which of the virtues of their master is preeminently worthy of admiration, for they assure him that he possesses all the virtues under heaven without having acquired them, or without caring to acquire them; they do not give him their daughters and their wives to be raised at his pleasure to the rank of his concubines, but, by sacrificing their opinions, they prostitute themselves.